An Introduction to Professional Responsibility

An Introduction to Professional Responsibility

Nathan M. Crystal

Roy Webster Professor of Law
University of South Carolina

Aspen Law & Business
A Division of Aspen Publishers, Inc.

Permissions
Aspen Law & Business
1185 Avenue of the Americas
New York, NY 10036

Printed in the United States of America

Library of Congress Cataloging-in-Publication Data

Crystal, Nathan M.
An introduction to professional responsibility / Nathan M. Crystal.
p. cm.
Includes index.
ISBN 1-56706-698-4 (alk. paper)
1. Legal ethics—United States. I. Title.
KF306.C787 1998
174′.3′0973—DC21 97-51282
CIP

About Aspen Law & Business, Law School Division

In 1996, Aspen Law & Business welcomed the Law School Division of Little, Brown and Company into its growing business — already established as a leading provider of practical information to legal practitioners.

Acquiring much more than a prestigious collection of educational publications by the country's foremost authors, Aspen Law & Business inherited the long-standing Little, Brown tradition of excellence — born over 150 years ago. As one of America's oldest and most venerable publishing houses, Little, Brown and Company commenced in a world of change and challenge, innovation and growth. Sharing that same spirit, Aspen Law & Business has dedicated itself to continuing and strengthening the integrity begun so many years ago.

ASPEN LAW & BUSINESS
A Division of Aspen Publishers, Inc.
A Wolters Kluwer Company

For Abe and Miriam

Summary of Contents

Contents

Chapter 4
Confidentiality 173

Chapter 5
Zealousness and its Limits 229

Acknowledgments

I would like to thank the following authors and copyright holders for permission to reprint portions of their work:

American Bar Association, Canons of Ethics (as amended), Code of Judicial Conduct (1972 and 1990), Code of Professional Responsibility, various Formal and Informal Ethics Advisory Opinions, Model Rules of Professional Conduct (as amended), Standards for Criminal Justice. Reprinted by permission of the American Bar Association. Copies of these publications are available from Service Center, American Bar Association, 750 North Lake Shore Drive, Chicago, IL 60611.

American Law Institute, Copyright 1997 by the American Law Institute. Material reproduced with the permission of the American Law Institute from the Restatement of the Law Third, The Law Governing Lawyers, Tentative Draft No. 8 (March 21, 1997) and Proposed Final Draft No. 1 (March 29, 1996). All rights are reserved. Tentative Draft No. 8 was prepared for submission to the Members of the American Law Institute for discussion at the 74th Annual Meeting in May in Washington, D.C. A Tentative Draft does not represent the position of the Institute on any issue with which it deals. The bylaws of the American Law Institute provide that "No restatement, model code, or recommended revision of the law shall be published as representing the position of the Institute unless authorized by the membership of the Institute and approved by the Council." Any approval of a Tentative Draft by the membership is tentative until the project is completed and final publication has been authorized. Thus, the material reproduced here is subject to further revision, and should be cited only as a Tentative Draft. Tentative Draft No. 8 and Proposed Final Draft No. 1 (1996) contain all current sections of the proposed Restatement. They are available for sale by contacting the Institute's Customer Service Department at 1-800-CLE-News.

Cramton, Roger C., The Lawyer as Whistleblower: Confidentiality and the Government Lawyer, 5 Geo. J. Legal Ethics 291, 294-295, 313 (1991). Reprinted with permission of the publisher, Georgetown University and the Georgetown Journal of Legal Ethics. Copyright 1991.

Developments in the Law — Conflicts of Interest in the Legal

Profession, 94 Harv. L. Rev. 1244, 1428-1433 (1981). Copyright 1981 by the Harvard Law Review Association. Reprinted with permission.

Fortune, William H., Richard H. Underwood & Edward J. Imwinkelried, Modern Litigation and Professional Responsibility Handbook 169-170, 461-462, (1996). Copyright 1996. Aspen Law & Business/Panel Publishers, a division of Aspen Publishers, Inc. Reprinted with permission.

Frankel, Marvin E., The Search for Truth: An Umpireal View, 123 U. Pa. L. Rev. 1031, 1035-1036, 1039, 1057-1058 (1975). Reprinted with permission of the author.

Freedman, Monroe H., Judge Frankel's Search for Truth, 123 U. Pa. L. Rev. 1060, 1063-1064 (1975). Reprinted with permission of the author. Professor Freedman has updated and expanded his analysis and related it to the Model Code and the Model Rules in his book, Understanding Lawyers' Ethics (Mathew Bender, 1990).

Freedman, Monroe H., Understanding Lawyer's Ethics 208-209 (1990). Copyright 1990. Reprinted with permission of Mathew Bender & Co.

Hazard, Geoffrey C., Jr. & W. William Hodes, 1 The Law of Lawyering 588 (2d ed. 1994). Copyright 1994 Aspen Law & Business/Panel Publishers, a division of Aspen Publishers, Inc. Reprinted with permission.

Horowitz, Michael, Making Ethics Real, Making Ethics Work: A Proposal for Contingency Fee Reform, 44 Emory L.J. 173, 175-176 (1995). Reprinted with permission of the Emory Law Journal.

Lanctot, Catherine J., The Duty of Zealous Advocacy and the Ethics of the Federal Government Lawyer: The Three Hardest Questions, 64 S. Cal. L. Rev. 951, 955-957 (1991). Reprinted with permission of the Southern California Law Review.

Louis Harris & Associates, Judges' Opinions on Procedural Issues: A Survey of State and Federal Trial Judges Who Spend at Least Half Their Time on General Civil Cases, 69 B.U. L. Rev. 731, 737 (1989) (Table 2.1). Copyright 1989 Trustees of Boston University. Boston University bears no responsibility for any errors which have occurred in reprinting or editing. Reprinted with permission of the Boston University Law Review and the Program in Civil Liability, Yale Law School.

Mallen, Ronald E., & Jeffrey M. Smith, Legal Malpractice vol. 4 at 20 (4th ed. 1996). Reprinted with permission of the publisher, the West Group.

Mathias, Sara, Electing Justice: A Handbook of Judicial Election Reforms 5 (1990). Reprinted with permission of the American Judicature Society.

Miller, Geoffrey P., Government Lawyers' Ethics in a System of Checks and Balances, 54 U. Chi. L. Rev. 1293, 1294-1295 (1987). Reprinted with permission of the University of Chicago Law Review.

Minkus, Leslie A., The Sale of a Law Practice: Toward a Professionally Responsible Approach, 12 Golden Gate L. Rev. 353, 356-357 (1982). Reprinted with permission of the Golden Gate University Law Review.

National Association of Criminal Defense Lawyers, Opinion 92-2, page 26, The Champion (March, 1993). Reproduced by permission.

Powell, Arthur G., I Can Go Home Again 291 (1943). Reprinted with permission of the University of North Carolina Press, 116 South Boundary Street, Chapel Hill, NC 27514.

Warrick, Lyle, Judicial Selection in the United States: A Compendium of Provisions (2d ed. 1993). Reprinted with permission of the American Judicature Society.

White, James J., Machiavelli and the Bar: Ethical Limitations on Lying in Negotiation, 1980 Am. B. Found. Res. J. 926, 927-928. Reprinted with permission of the University of Chicago Press. Copyright 1980 by the American Bar Foundation.

Wigmore on Evidence at 554 (McNaughton ed. 1961). Copyright 1961 Aspen Law & Business/Panel Publishers, a division of Aspen Publishers, Inc. Reprinted with permission.

Wolfram, Charles W., Modern Legal Ethics 724, copyright 1986. Reprinted with permission of the West Publishing Corporation.

My wife, Nancy McCormick, made substantial contributions to this book, critically reading the manuscript, copyreading, and assisting in preparation of tables.

Nathan M. Crystal

University of South Carolina
School of Law
Main & Greene Streets
Columbia, SC 29208

Voice Mail: 1 (803) 777-2851
Fax: 1 (803) 777-8613
nathan@law.sc.edu

CHAPTER 1
Introduction

A. THE LEO FRANK CASE: AN EXAMPLE OF THE DIMENSIONS OF LAWYERS' OBLIGATIONS

In 1914 Leo Frank, the Jewish manager of an Atlanta pencil factory, awaited execution after his conviction for the rape and murder of a 14-year-old factory employee, Mary Phagan.[1] Frank was innocent. His conviction occurred in an atmosphere of rampant anti-Semitism, inflamed by the press. The actual murderer was James Conley, a factory employee.[2] After both the Georgia and U.S. Supreme Courts denied relief, a prominent Georgia lawyer (and later a judge), Arthur Gray Powell, learned in the context of an attorney-client relationship the identity of the actual murderer. Powell

1. State v. Frank, 80 S.E. 1016 (Ga. 1914), *aff'd*, 237 U.S. 309 (1915). See generally Richard H. Underwood, Perjury: An Anthology, 13 Ariz. J. Int'l & Comp. L. 307, 336-344 (1996).

2. In 1982, Alonzo Mann, a young office boy when the crime was committed, came forward to admit that he had seen Conley carrying Phagan's body; Mann had remained silent because Conley threatened to kill him. Wendall Rawls, Jr., After 69 Years of Silence, Lynching Victim is Cleared, N.Y. Times, Mar. 8, 1982, at A12.

kept his client's confidence and remained silent about Frank's innocence. In his memoirs published in 1943, Powell stated:

> I am one of the few people who know that Leo Frank was innocent of the crime for which he was convicted and lynched. Subsequent to the trial, and after his conviction had been affirmed by the Supreme Court, I learned who killed Mary Phagan, but the information came to me in such a way that, though I wish I could do so, I can never reveal it so long as certain persons are alive. We lawyers, when we are admitted to the bar, take an oath never to reveal the communications made to us by our clients; and this includes facts revealed in an attempt to employ the lawyer, though he refuse the employment. . . . The law on this subject may or may not be a wise law — there are some who think that it is not — but naturally since it is the law, we lawyers and the judges cannot honorably disobey it.[3]

A short time after the Supreme Court denied Frank's appeal, Georgia's Governor John Stanton commuted Frank's sentence to life in prison. In response to Stanton's decision a mob attacked the Governor's mansion. The mob then turned on Frank, kidnaping him from prison and lynching him.[4]

The Frank case is a horrible story of injustice the pain of which still reverberates in the Atlanta Jewish community. Our focus, however, is on Powell. If such a case were to arise today, what would Powell's obligations be?[5]

Since Powell is a lawyer, he should turn to the Rules of Professional Conduct governing lawyers. Rule 1.6 of the American Bar Association's Model Rules of Professional Conduct provides as follows:[6]

3. Arthur G. Powell, I Can Go Home Again 291 (1943).

4. Id. at 287-292.

5. The obligations of lawyers, psychiatrists, and clergy when they learn in confidence that an innocent person is about to be executed are explored in Symposium, Executing the Wrong Person: The Professionals' Ethical Dilemmas, 29 Loy. L.A. L. Rev. 4 (1996).

6. For discussion of the influence of the American Bar Association on regulation of professional conduct, see text at Chapter 1.B.1 infra. The vast majority of state courts have adopted rules of professional conduct modeled on the ABA's Model Rules of Professional Conduct. On the controversial issue of the scope of the duty of confidentiality, however, many state courts have adopted rules that vary from ABA Model Rule 1.6. See Chapter 4.D.1. See generally Kathryn W. Tate, The Hypothetical as a Tool for Teaching the Lawyer's Duty of Confidentiality, 29 Loy. L.A. L. Rev. 1659, 1667-1673 (1996).

RULE 1.6 CONFIDENTIALITY OF INFORMATION

(a) A lawyer shall not reveal information relating to representation of a client unless the client consents after consultation, except for disclosures that are impliedly authorized in order to carry out the representation, and except as stated in paragraph (b).

(b) A lawyer may reveal such information to the extent the lawyer reasonably believes necessary:

(1) to prevent the client from committing a criminal act that the lawyer believes is likely to result in imminent death or substantial bodily harm; or

(2) to establish a claim or defense on behalf of the lawyer in a controversy between the lawyer and the client, to establish a defense to a criminal change or civil claim against the lawyer based upon conduct in which the client was involved, or to respond to allegations in any proceeding concerning the lawyer's representation of the client.

Rule 1.6 establishes a general duty of confidentiality: A "lawyer shall not reveal information relating to representation of a client." Section (a) offers two exceptions — client consent and "disclosures that are impliedly authorized to carry out the representation." Powell could counsel Conley[7] about the horrible injustice of allowing an innocent man to remain in prison. The Rules of Professional Conduct authorize Powell to refer to justice, morality, and other nonlegal factors when counseling a client. Model Rule 2.1 states that lawyers shall render candid advice to their clients: "In rendering advice, a lawyer may refer not only to law but to other considerations such as moral, economic, social and political factors, that may be relevant to the client's situation." Powell could urge Conley to consent to disclosure to the authorities of Frank's innocence and of Conley's guilt. He might succeed.[8]

Suppose, however, Conley refuses to consent to disclosure of his guilt.[9] Powell could then turn to the two exceptions found in Model Rule 1.6(b). The exception in (b)(2), sometimes referred to as the "self defense" exception, is inapplicable. That exception applies when the lawyer's conduct is the subject of a claim or

7. Powell did not state in his memoirs who his client was, but for the purpose of this analysis I am treating Conley as Powell's client.

8. See Gerald F. Uelmen, An Ethical Fairy Tale, 29 Loy. L.A. L. Rev. 1685 (1996).

9. Since Conley has expressly refused to authorize disclosure, Powell could not rely on the other exception in Rule 1.6(a), the one dealing with implied authorization. Because Conley has refused to give express consent, consent to disclosure could not reasonably be implied.

defense, and disclosure is necessary to protect the lawyer's interests.[10] Powell is not the subject of any claim or defense.

The exception in (b)(1) seems to be most closely applicable to the situation facing Powell. Frank may be facing imminent death. Remember that at the time Powell learned that Frank was innocent, Frank was still subject to a death sentence. Even after Governor Stanton commuted Frank's sentence to life in prison, he still faced "bodily harm," loss of freedom for a crime he did not commit. But Rule 1.6(b)(1) states that a lawyer may reveal confidential information when necessary "to prevent the client from committing a criminal act." The difficulty facing Powell is that Conley is not planning to commit any criminal act. He has already committed the murder. If Conley and Powell remain silent, an injustice will occur, but not a crime. Uncomfortable with this analysis, Powell might review the literature and case law on professional responsibility or might consult with experts on the subject. These sources are likely to confirm Powell's analysis. The Rules of Professional Conduct require Powell to remain silent.

Lawyers are subject to statutes, administrative rules and regulations, and to common law principles in addition to the Rules of Professional Conduct. Do these sources of law authorize or require Powell to reveal the information that he received from Conley about Frank's innocence? Some statutes require individuals with knowledge of criminal conduct to report the conduct to appropriate authorities. For example, medical providers and social workers generally have a statutory duty to report child abuse to the authorities. Powell's research does not reveal any statute that requires or authorizes him to disclose Conley's confidences. Turning to tort law, Powell finds that at least one court has stated in dictum that a lawyer has a duty to warn intended victims when the lawyer's client "intends to commit a crime or inflict injury upon unknowing third persons."[11] This tort duty, however, seems very similar to the exception to confidentiality found in Model Rule 1.6(b)(1). Conley's silence will result in a terrible injustice, but that injustice is not the same as Conley's planning to commit a crime or to inflict injury on an unknowing person.

Powell might turn to the law of evidence for guidance. Here he would find a vast body of law involving the attorney-client privi-

10. See Meyerhofer v. Empire Fire & Marine Ins. Co., 497 F.2d 1190 (2d Cir.), *cert. denied,* 419 U.S. 998 (1974), and text at Chapter 4.G.

11. Hawkins v. King County, 602 P.2d 361, 366 (Wash. Ct. App. 1979).

lege.[12] The attorney-client privilege, however, deals with the question of whether a lawyer may be compelled to give testimony regarding communications received in confidence from his client. The privilege does not authorize or require Powell to reveal any information when he is not acting under compulsion of law. In fact, consideration of the attorney-client privilege may reinforce Powell's analysis of his professional obligations. If Powell decides to reveal what Conley told him to authorities, he may be called on to give testimony in a proceeding to set aside Frank's conviction. If Conley objects, Powell's testimony is likely to be inadmissible because of the attorney-client privilege.[13] Powell would, however, find at least one legal standard that authorizes him to reveal Conley's confidences to prevent Frank's execution or continued incarceration. Section 117A of the American Law Institute's proposed Restatement of the Law Governing Lawyers, entitled "Using or Disclosing Information to Prevent Death or Serious Bodily Injury," provides that a lawyer may disclose confidential information to the extent that the lawyer reasonably believes is necessary "to prevent death or serious bodily injury to a person."[14]

12. 8 John H. Wigmore, Evidence in Trials at Common Law §§2290 et seq. (McNaughton ed. 1961). See also Restatement of the Law Governing Lawyers §§118-135 (Prop. Final Draft #1, Mar. 29, 1996); Unif. Rules Evid., Rule 502, 13A U.L.A. 518 (1994). Comment 5 to Model Rule 1.6 summarizes the distinction between the evidentiary privilege and the ethical duty of confidentiality. On the history of the privilege, see Geoffrey C. Hazard, Jr., An Historical Perspective on the Attorney-Client Privilege, 66 Cal. L. Rev. 1061 (1978).

13. In an article written a year after his memoirs, Powell argued that his decision to remain silent was correct, not only because of his professional duty to his client, but because disclosure would be ineffective. A court could not legally receive his testimony because of the attorney-client privilege. Arthur G. Powell, Privilege of Counsel and Confidential Communications, 6 Ga. B.J. 333 (1944). See also State v. Macumber, 544 P.2d 1084 (Ariz. 1976) (en banc) (holding that attorney-client privilege bars testimony from lawyers that their client, who was not deceased, had admitted committing crime for which Macumber was charged), *cert. denied,* 439 U.S. 1006 (1978). For a discussion of the *Macumber* case and of the options available to lawyers when they learn in confidence that their client has committed a crime for which another person has been convicted, see W. William Hodes, What Ought to be Done—What Can be Done—When the Wrong Person is in Jail or About to be Executed? An Invitation to a Multi-Disciplined Inquiry, and a Detour About Law School Pedagogy, 29 Loy. L.A. L. Rev. 1547 (1996).

14. See Monroe H. Freedman, The Life-Saving Exception to Confidentiality: Restating Law Without the *Was,* The *Will Be,* or the *Ought to Be,* 29 Loy. L.A. L. Rev. 1631, 1639 (1996). The exact language of §117A remains to be approved by the Institute. See Restatement of the Law Governing Lawyers §117A (Council Draft #13, Oct. 8, 1997).

With the one exception of the Restatement, however, analysis of legal principles leads to the same conclusion that Powell reached under the Rules of Professional Conduct: Powell is not required or authorized to reveal Conley's confidences even to prevent an innocent man from being executed or wrongfully incarcerated.

Powell might turn from rules of professional conduct and law in general to another source of guidance: ethical and moral principles. Powell might reason that professional and legal obligations are not absolutely clear and that such standards must be interpreted to include an implied exception to the duty of confidentiality when disclosure is necessary to avoid violation of a universal moral principle — that a person should not be punished for a crime he did not commit. In the alternative, Powell might reason that even if his professional and legal obligations are clear, it is ethically and morally wrong to allow an innocent person to die, and that he could not sit by while this injustice occurred. In making this decision, Powell would be engaging in a form of civil disobedience, violating his professional and legal obligations because of his commitment to what he considers to be a higher ethical or moral value.[15]

B. SOURCES OF LAWYERS' OBLIGATIONS

Few lawyers will face the dilemma that Arthur Powell encountered in the Leo Frank case, but analysis of Powell's obligations illustrates a more general point. Lawyers' obligations flow from three sources: professional standards, law in general, and principles of ethics and morality. Indeed, the titles given to law school courses in this field — Professional Responsibility, The Law of Lawyering, Legal Ethics — often reflect emphasis on these different perspectives. While adopting the conventional title of Professional Responsibility, this book is not limited to professional standards. Instead, this book focuses more broadly on lawyers' obligations, whether based on professional standards, law in general, or ethical principles.

15. See Mary C. Daly, To Betray Once? To Betray Twice?: Reflections on Confidentiality, A Guilty Client, An Innocent Condemned Man, and An Ethics-Seeking Defense Counsel, 29 Loy. L.A. L. Rev. 1611 (1996).

1. *Professional Standards: ABA Codes of Ethics, Ethics Advisory Opinions, Specialized Codes, and Practice Norms*

In almost all states, authority to regulate the practice of law in the state courts rests with the highest court in the state. New York is a notable exception. In New York under §90 of the Judiciary Law the four appellate divisions of the New York Supreme Court have the authority to issue rules of conduct for lawyers in the state. Each federal court has its own rules of admission and practice, but these rules often follow those of the state in which the federal court sits.[16]

Pursuant to their authority to regulate the practice of law, courts issue a number of rules. The set of rules that is the primary focus of this book is the rules of professional conduct. Rather than writing their own rules of professional conduct, most state and federal courts have based their rules of professional conduct on the American Bar Association's Model Rules of Professional Conduct, adopted by the ABA in 1983.

While the ABA has no legal authority over the practice of law, it does wield considerable influence in the area of professional responsibility. The Model Rules of Professional Conduct is the third in a series of ABA standards of lawyers' ethics. The immediate predecessor to the Model Rules was the ABA's Model Code of Professional Responsibility, which the ABA adopted in 1969. The 1969 Code succeeded the ABA's Canons of Ethics, issued by the ABA in 1908 and amended on a number of occasions until replaced by the Code.

Even though the Code of Professional Responsibility is no longer in effect in most jurisdictions, some familiarity with the Code is useful because many provisions of the Model Rules are based on provisions of the Code and because a number of important court decisions under the Code of Professional Responsibility continue to be relevant under the Model Rules. This book refers to significant provisions of the Code when relevant.

The format of the Code differs significantly from that of the Model Rules. The Code has a three-part structure: canons, ethical

16. See Bruce A. Green, Whose Rules of Professional Conduct Should Govern Lawyers in Federal Court and How Should The Rules be Created?, 64 Geo. Wash. L. Rev. 460 (1996).

considerations (ECs), and disciplinary rules (DRs). The canons consist of nine axioms of lawyers' obligations:

Canon 1	A lawyer should assist in maintaining the integrity and competence of the legal profession.
Canon 2	A lawyer should assist the legal profession in fulfilling its duty to make legal counsel available.
Canon 3	A lawyer should assist in preventing the unauthorized practice of law.
Canon 4	A lawyer should preserve the confidences and secrets of a client.
Canon 5	A lawyer should exercise independent professional judgment on behalf of a client.
Canon 6	A lawyer should represent a client competently.
Canon 7	A lawyer should represent a client zealously within the bounds of the law.
Canon 8	A lawyer should assist in improving the legal system.
Canon 9	A lawyer should avoid even the appearance of professional impropriety.

Each of the canons is followed by extensive ethical considerations and disciplinary rules. The drafters intended the ethical considerations to serve as aspirational norms that lawyers should strive to achieve, but which were not to be the basis of discipline. By contrast, the disciplinary rules were minimum standards of conduct the violation of which would be the basis of a disciplinary action.[17]

Soon after its adoption, the Code of Professional Responsibility was criticized on two grounds: First, the division into canons, ethical considerations, and disciplinary rules was complex and confusing.[18] Second, the Code concentrated on the role of lawyers as advocates, largely ignoring representation as counselors or transactional attorneys. In 1977, only eight years after adopting the Code, the ABA appointed a Commission on Evaluation of Professional Standards (the Kutak Commission) to recommend revisions to the Code. The Kutak Commission instead proposed replacement

17. See ABA, Model Code of Professional Responsibility, Preliminary Statement.
18. Geoffrey C. Hazard, Jr., Address, Legal Ethics: Legal Rules and Professional Aspirations, 30 Clev. St. L. Rev. 571 (1981).

of the Code, and in 1983 the ABA adopted the Model Rules of Professional Conduct.

The Model Rules abandoned the structure of the Code and adopted a simpler framework of black-letter rules followed by comments, much like the Restatements. The Model Rules are grouped under eight articles:

1. Client-lawyer relationship
2. Counselor
3. Advocate
4. Transactions with persons other than clients
5. Law firms and associations
6. Public service
7. Information about legal services
8. Maintaining the integrity of the profession

Some of the rules, such as Rule 1.8 dealing with prohibited transactions, are quite specific; others, such as Rule 1.7 dealing with conflicts of interest, set forth general standards. Some provisions of the Model Rules are not rules at all because they give lawyers discretion as to how to act. For example, Rule 1.6(b), quoted above, and comments 13 and 14 state that lawyers have professional discretion to reveal confidential information in some situations. Other provisions are aspirational, as illustrated by Model Rule 6.1, which states that lawyers "should aspire" to render at least 50 hours of pro bono service per year. As to the authority of the comments, the Scope states: "The Comments are intended as guides to interpretation, but the text of each Rule is authoritative."

At this writing, more than 40 states have adopted the Model Rules, although most states have approved some variations from the ABA's Model Rules.[19] New York has a Code of Professional Responsibility that in form is based on the ABA's 1969 Code but actually is a medley of the Code, the Model Rules, and provisions unique to New York.[20] California has adopted its own Rules of Professional Conduct that vary considerably from the ABA's Model

19. For a listing of the states that have adopted the Model Rules, the dates of their adoption, and a summary of variations from the ABA's Model Rules, see Lawyers' Manual on Prof. Conduct (ABA/BNA), 1:3 et seq. For an argument in support of federalization of legal ethics, see Fred C. Zacharias, Federalizing Legal Ethics, 73 Tex. L. Rev. 335 (1994).

20. See N.Y. Sup. Ct. App. Div. Rules 1200 et seq.

Rules. Other jurisdictions with significant deviations from the Model Rules include the District of Columbia, Illinois, North Carolina, Oregon, and Virginia. In 1997, the President of the ABA appointed an "Ethics 2000" Committee to consider changes in the Model Rules.[21]

The ABA has also been influential in the area of judicial ethics. In 1972, the ABA adopted a Model Code of Judicial Conduct that has since been adopted in most states. In 1990, the ABA revised the Code of Judicial Conduct. While the 1990 Code carries forward many of the provisions of the 1972 Code, it includes important changes, particularly with regard to racial bias and sexual discrimination. Chapter 7 examines ethical issues facing judges.

Any set of rules raises issues of interpretation. National, state, and local bar associations have established committees to offer interpretations of the Code of Professional Responsibility and the Model Rules, one of the most influential of which is the American Bar Association Standing Committee on Ethics and Professional Responsibility.[22] Bar association ethics advisory opinions are not binding on courts, but good faith reliance on an opinion could be used in defense of a disciplinary or perhaps even a malpractice case. Professors Finman and Schneyer have evaluated the ethics opinions issued by the American Bar Association Standing Committee on Ethics and Professional Responsibility. While finding the Committee's work to be of substantial influence, they also conclude that "these opinions are seriously flawed, so much so that their overall influence may well be unfortunate."[23]

While the rules of professional conduct set forth general standards of behavior, the practice of law is highly specialized. Because of this gap between general professional standards and specific problems that lawyers encounter in practice, various bodies, including associations of lawyers and bar-appointed study commissions, have prepared standards or codes of conduct focusing on ethical problems in particular areas of practice. Although these standards or codes are of no legal effect unless adopted by a court

21. See Lawyers' Manual on Prof. Conduct (ABA/BNA), 13 Curr. Rpts. 140, 168 (1997).

22. ABA Committee opinions are published in the ABA Journal, the ABA/BNA Lawyers' Manual on Professional Conduct, and in computerized research services. Opinions from state and local bar associations are available in the ABA/BNA Lawyers' Manual and computerized research services.

23. Ted Finman & Theodore Schneyer, The Role of Bar Association Ethics Opinions in Regulating Lawyer Conduct: A Critique of the Work of the ABA Committee on Ethics and Professional Responsibility, 29 UCLA L. Rev. 67, 72 (1981).

or legislature, they may provide guidance to practitioners in those fields, may be evidence of the appropriate standard of conduct in a malpractice case, and may help support a good faith defense if a lawyer faces disciplinary charges. Some of the more important of these standards are the following:

- *Arbitration and Mediation:* Code of Ethics of the American Arbitration Association for Arbitrators in Commercial Disputes and Standards of Conduct for Mediators.[24]
- *Criminal Defense and Prosecution:* American Bar Association, Standards for Criminal Justice, the Prosecution Function and the Defense Function.
- *Matrimonial Practice:* American Academy of Matrimonial Lawyers, The Bounds of Advocacy.[25]
- *Professionalism in General:* American Bar Association "Lawyer's Creed of Professionalism."[26] Many state bar associations have also adopted standards of professionalism.
- *Trust and Estate Practice:* American College of Trust and Estate Counsel, Commentaries on the Model Rules of Professional Conduct.[27]

Norms of conduct or mores of the legal institutions in which lawyers practice are also an important source of lawyers' obligations. For example, issues of professional responsibility arise in a wide range of day-to-day settings in which lawyers practice: small firms in rural communities, mega law firms practicing throughout the world, boutique law firms with highly specialized practices, offices of prosecutors or public defenders, legal services programs, private corporations, federal or state agencies, to name just a few. Every practice context will have its own norms of behavior — ways in which the lawyers in that organization handle professional problems that they encounter.[28] These norms of behavior will, of course,

24. Howard M. Holtzmann, The First Code of Ethics for Arbitrators in Commercial Disputes, 33 Bus. Law. 309 (1977); 50 Disp. Resol. J. #1 at 78 (Jan. 1995) (Text of agreement on Standards of Conduct for Mediators between American Arbitration Association, American Bar Association, and Society of Professionals in Dispute Resolution).

25. 9 J. Am. Acad. Matrimonial Law. #9 (Fall 1992).

26. Lawyers' Manual on Prof. Conduct (ABA/BNA) 01:401.

27. 28 Real Prop. Prob. & Tr. J. 865 (1994).

28. Compare John P. Heinz & Edward O. Laumann, Chicago Lawyers: The Social Structure of the Bar (rev. ed. 1994), with Donald D. Landon, Country Lawyers: The Impact of Context on Professional Practice (1990).

be heavily influenced by formal professional standards, but some institutions may develop norms that conflict with established professional standards.

2. *Law Governing Lawyers*

When adopted by a court with authority to regulate the practice of law, rules of professional conduct become law, and lawyers who violate these rules are subject to professional discipline. The rules of professional conduct are not, however, the only source of law applicable to lawyers. Court decisions, statutory law, administrative rules and regulations, and procedural rules all apply to lawyers.[29]

As in most fields of law, *court decisions* are an important source of standards of professional conduct. In the field of lawyers' obligations, courts have rendered decisions in four major categories of cases: discipline, malpractice, disqualification, and sanctions. Disciplinary cases are proceedings brought against lawyers charging them with violation of the rules of professional conduct. The ultimate punishment for misconduct is disbarment from the practice of law; lesser sanctions include suspensions and reprimands. The structure and efficacy of the disciplinary process has been controversial for a number of years. The principal charge made by critics of the disciplinary process is that the system has been run by lawyers for their own benefit rather than the public interest.[30]

The term *legal malpractice* is often used to refer to lawyers' civil liability, but the term is a misnomer because the law does not recognize a single cause of action for legal malpractice. Legal malpractice is a catch-all that refers to a group of causes of action by which clients, and in some cases third parties, can recover damages from lawyers (or their malpractice insurers) for some form of misconduct by lawyers.[31] When a client claims that a lawyer mishandled a legal matter, the client's cause of action will

29. See generally Geoffrey C. Hazard, Jr. & W. William Hodes, The Law of Lawyering (2d ed. 1990) (hereinafter cited as "Hazard & Hodes, The Law of Lawyering").

30. For a discussion of changes in the disciplinary process during the last 25 years, see the Conclusion at page 426.

31. See Ronald E. Mallen & Jeffrey M. Smith, Legal Malpractice (4th ed. 1996) (hereinafter cited as "Mallen & Smith, Legal Malpractice"). See also Restatement of the Law Governing Lawyers, ch. 4, "Lawyer Civil Liability" (Tent. Draft #8, March 21, 1997).

typically be for negligence. The duty of care that lawyers owe to their clients requires them to "exercise the competence and diligence normally exercised by lawyers in similar circumstances, unless the lawyer represents that the lawyer will exercise greater competence or diligence."[32] Lawyers who practice in a specialized field, such as securities or tax, are held to the standard of care normally exercised by specialists.[33] If a lawyer in the course of representation intentionally violates a fiduciary obligation to the client — for example, a violation of the duty of loyalty by representing conflicting interests — then the client may have a cause of action for breach of fiduciary duty.[34] In some cases, clients have alleged that their lawyers misrepresented facts to them or failed to disclose material information giving rise to causes of action for fraud, misrepresentation, or nondisclosure.[35]

Causes of action by nonclients against lawyers have traditionally been much more difficult to sustain than causes of action by clients because of the "privity" rule. Under this rule, lawyers generally have not been liable to persons other than their clients. The privity rule has been justified for two reasons: First, liability to nonclients would create conflicts of interest between lawyers' duties to their clients and their duties to third persons. Second, liability to nonclients would expose lawyers to potentially vast damages of uncertain amount and scope. Despite these policies, the privity rule has been eroded in recent years, and lawyers are increasingly being held liable to third parties.[36]

What is the relationship between the rules of professional responsibility and malpractice liability?[37] The Code of Professional Responsibility and the Model Rules impose an obligation of competence on lawyers. See DR 6-101 and Model Rule 1.1. See also

32. Restatement of the Law Governing Lawyers §74(1) (Tent. Draft #8, March 21, 1997).

33. See Horne v. Peckham, 158 Cal. Rptr. 714 (Cal. Ct. App. 1979); Restatement of the Law Governing Lawyers §74, comm. *d* (Tent. Draft #8, March 21, 1997).

34. Restatements of the Law Governing Lawyers §76A (Tent. Draft #8, March 21, 1997).

35. Id. §77.

36. See Mallen & Smith, Legal Malpractice ch. 7; Restatement of the Law Governing Lawyers §§73 (duty of care to certain nonclients), 77 (liability to client or nonclient under general law) (Tent. Draft #8, March 21, 1997). See generally Symposium, The Lawyer's Duties and Liabilities to Third Parties, 37 S. Tex. L. Rev. 957 (1996).

37. See generally John Leubsdorf, Legal Malpractice and Professional Responsibility, 48 Rutgers L. Rev. 101 (1995).

Model Rule 1.3 (diligence). Both the Code of Professional Responsibility and now the Model Rules, however, state in their preambles that violation of the rules is not a basis for malpractice liability. Thus, merely because a lawyer has violated the rules of professional conduct does not per se produce malpractice liability. To establish malpractice liability for negligence, it is necessary to show that the attorney's conduct fell below generally accepted standards of conduct in the profession. This typically requires expert testimony. Most courts will allow experts to consider rules of ethics in deciding whether the attorney's conduct did not meet generally accepted standards of the profession.[38] In addition, to establish malpractice liability a plaintiff must also prove that the attorney's breach of duty caused damages to the plaintiff.[39] Potential malpractice liability can be a powerful force affecting the conduct of lawyers, just as it has been for doctors.

Modern litigation has seen an explosive growth of disqualification motions — motions filed by one party seeking a court order that the other party's lawyer may not continue to represent that party because of some violation of the rules of professional responsibility, typically a conflict of interest.[40] Disqualification motions are not separate proceedings but are filed as part of civil or criminal actions. Originally, disqualification motions were used in cases in which the party filing the motion was a former client and was seeking disqualification to prevent that former lawyer from now using confidential information on behalf of a new client against the former client. This situation (discussed in Chapter 4) continues to be a major area in which disqualification motions have come before the courts. Disqualification motions, however, are now being filed in many other situations, for example if the opposing lawyer might be called as a witness in the case or if the lawyer had used some improper investigative technique, such as contacting the employees of the moving party. Courts have begun to register some

38. See, e.g., Allen v. Lefkoff, Duncan, Grimers & Dermer, P.C., 453 S.E.2d 719 (Ga. 1995) (ethics rules relevant on standard of care in legal malpractice case). See generally Note, The Evidentiary Use of the Ethics Codes in Legal Malpractice: Erasing a Double Standard, 109 Harv. L. Rev. 1102 (1996).

39. See Restatement of the Law Governing Lawyers §75 (Tent. Draft #8, March 21, 1997).

40. See generally Kenneth L. Penegar, The Loss of Innocence: A Brief History of Law Firm Disqualification in the Courts, 8 Geo. J. Legal Ethics 831 (1995).

skepticism about disqualification motions because they deprive clients of the right to counsel of their choice, because they can interfere with the efficient processing of cases, and because they can be used for strategic purposes.

Monetary sanction for litigation abuse is another form of civil liability that in recent years has come to have an increasingly important impact on lawyer conduct. The principal source of this body of law is Rule 11 of the Federal Rules of Civil Procedure. Under this rule, if a lawyer files a motion or other paper in court, the lawyer certifies that the document is not "frivolous" either in law or in fact. During the last 20 years, courts have rendered a vast body of decisional law establishing obligations of lawyers regarding frivolous lawsuits and motions under Rule 11.[41] Courts have ordered lawyers who have violated this rule to pay monetary sanctions, such as attorney fees of the opposing party. Rule 11 only applies to actions in federal court, but many states have rules of civil procedure modeled on federal Rule 11.

Statutory law is somewhat less significant in the area of lawyers' obligations than in many other fields of law because the regulation of lawyers and judges is largely the constitutional province of courts. Indeed, courts have declared some legislation dealing with the practice of law unconstitutional as a violation of the doctrine of separation of powers.[42] A number of federal and state statutes, however, may be applicable to lawyers. At the federal level, statutes govern the conduct of lawyers (and nonlawyers) entering or leaving government service.[43] Federal statutes also govern the disqualification and discipline (short of removal) of federal judges.[44] Various statutes and rules also apply to lawyers acting in other capacities, such as members of Congress or lobbyists.

41. See Chapter 5.B.3 for an analysis of Rule 11.

42. Charles W. Wolfram, Modern Legal Ethics §2.2.3, at 27-31 (1986) (hereinafter cited as "Wolfram, Modern Legal Ethics").

43. E.g., Restrictions on Former Officers, Employees, and Elected Officials of the Executive and Legislative Branches, 18 U.S.C. §207 (1994); Acts Affecting a Personal Financial Interest, 18 U.S.C. §208 (1994); Disclosure of Confidential Information Generally, 18 U.S.C. §1905 (1994).

44. Disqualification of Justice, Judge, or Magistrate, 28 U.S.C. §455 (1994); Retirement for Disability; Substitute Judge on Failure to Retire; Judicial Discipline, 28 U.S.C. §372(c) (1994). Note, however, that federal judges may only be removed from office through impeachment under the U.S. Constitution.

Statutory regulation of lawyers varies widely from state to state. Both California and New York have fairly extensive schemes of statutory regulation; most other states do not.[45] For example, a California statute provides that sexual relations between a lawyer and a client may subject the attorney to discipline under some circumstances.[46] California also has a statutory provision limiting the percentage of fees that attorneys may charge in contingent fee cases against health care providers.[47] Most states will also have ethics-in-government statutes regulating the activities of governmental officials, governmental employees, and lobbyists, a number of whom will be lawyers.

Many lawyers practice before federal and state agencies, such as the Internal Revenue Service (IRS), the Securities and Exchange Commission (SEC), the Patent and Trademark Office (PTO), workers' compensation boards, zoning commissions, and so on. These agencies, particularly federal agencies, may have *administrative rules and regulations* governing admission of practitioners and rules of conduct for practitioners before such agencies.[48] (It should be noted that many administrative agencies like the IRS allow nonlawyers as well as lawyers to practice before the agency.) Agency rules often provide standards similar to the Rules of Professional Conduct, but they may specify different or additional obligations. For example, the IRS has adopted standards of conduct with respect to matters such as preparing tax returns and issuing tax shelter opinions.[49] Administrative agencies can also render decisions that determine standards of conduct for lawyers. For example, In re Carter & Johnson[50] (discussed in Chapter 4) was a disciplinary proceeding brought against two lawyers claiming that they violated SEC Rule of Practice (2)(e)(1)(ii), which prohibits a practitioner from engaging in "unethical or improper professional conduct." The case established duties for attorneys admitted to

45. Cal. Bus. & Prof. Code, Attorneys, §§6000 et seq. (1990); N.Y. Jud. Law, Attorneys and Counselors, §§460 et seq. (1983).

46. Cal. Bus. & Prof. Code §6106.9 (Supp. 1997).

47. Id. §6146.

48. E.g., SEC, 17 C.F.R. pt. 201; IRS, 31 C.F.R. pt. 10 (1997).

49. 31 C.F.R. §§10.33, 10.34 (1997).

50. Fed. Sec. L. Rep. (CCH) ¶82,847 (SEC 1981). See generally Simon M. Lorne & W. Hardy Callcott, Administrative Actions Against Lawyers Before the SEC, 50 Bus. Law. 1293 (1995).

practice before the SEC who learn their clients are engaged in fraud.

In court proceedings lawyers have a duty to comply with applicable *court rules.* Indeed, the Rules of Professional Conduct incorporate by reference procedural rules as standards of conduct. Model Rule 3.4(c) states that a lawyer shall not "knowingly disobey an obligation under the rules of a tribunal except for an open refusal based on an assertion that no valid obligation exists." As mentioned previously, lawyers who violate court rules, such as Rule 11 of the Federal Rules of Civil Procedure, may be subject to monetary sanctions.

In an effort to bring some order to the body of law dealing with lawyers obligations, the American Law Institute has undertaken the preparation of a Restatement of the Law Governing Lawyers.[51] The current list of chapters for the Restatement is as follows:

Chapter 1	Regulation of the Legal Profession
Chapter 2	The Client-Lawyer Relationship
Chapter 3	Client and Lawyer: The Financial and Property Relationship
Chapter 4	Lawyer Civil Liability
Chapter 5	Confidential Client Information
Chapter 6	Representing Clients—In General
Chapter 7	Representing Clients in Litigation
Chapter 8	Conflict of Interest
Chapter 9	Delivery of Legal Services

3. *Ethical Standards*

The terms *ethical* or *moral* refer to conduct that is right or good based on some religious tradition or philosophy to which the actor adheres. Ethical or moral principles can influence lawyers' obligations at two levels: individual decisionmaking and institutional structure. At the level of individual decisionmaking, lawyers fre-

51. The bulk of the current work on the Restatement can be found in Proposed Final Draft #1 (March 29, 1996) and Tentative Draft #8 (March 21, 1997). See Lawyers' Manual Prof. Conduct (ABA/BNA), 12 Curr. Rpts. 170 (1996) and 13 Curr. Rpts. 141 (1997). Drafts of the Restatement are available on Westlaw.

quently encounter perplexing questions of professional obligation. In some extreme cases, like the Leo Frank case, a lawyer's professional and legal duties may conflict with deeply held moral values. In such situations lawyers face a difficult choice: either to subordinate their moral values to professional role and legal obligation, or to violate their professional and legal obligations based on what they consider to be a higher value.

More often, professional standards and legal rules require lawyers to use judgment or to exercise discretion in deciding how to act. Many rules of conduct are formulated in such general language that lawyers must utilize judgment in deciding how to apply the rules. For example, Model Rule 1.7, which deals with conflicts of interest, provides that a lawyer may undertake representation of actually or potentially conflicting interests if the lawyer "reasonably believes" the representation will not be adversely affected and if each client consents after full disclosure of relevant information. Other rules, like Model Rules 1.6 and 2.1, discussed above in connection with the Frank case, expressly grant lawyers discretion whether to reveal confidential information in some circumstances and whether to counsel clients about nonlegal factors. In deciding how to use judgment or exercise discretion in the application of rules, ethical and moral principles can provide guidance to lawyers.

The term *philosophy of lawyering* can be used to refer to the way in which lawyers incorporate ethical or moral values into their decisionmaking. For a number of years, two general philosophies of lawyering have been debated in the profession. Under one theory (call it the "adversarial theory"), lawyers should act as neutral partisans who are required to advocate their clients' interests as zealously as possible without regard to the moral implications of their representation.[52] Under a second approach (call it the "morality theory"), lawyers can and must incorporate ethical and moral principles into all aspects of their representation.[53] These

52. See Murray L. Schwartz, The Zeal of the Civil Advocate, 1983 Am. B. Found. Res. J. 543; Murray L. Schwartz, The Professionalism and Accountability of Lawyers, 66 Cal. L. Rev. 669 (1978). See generally Monroe H. Freedman, Understanding Lawyers' Ethics (1990).

53. Daniel R. Coquillette, Lawyers and Fundamental Moral Responsibility (1995); Alan H. Goldman, The Moral Foundations of Professional Ethics (1980); David Luban, Lawyers and Justice: An Ethical Study (1988); Thomas L. Shaffer & Robert F. Cochran, Jr., Lawyers, Clients, and Moral Responsibility (1994); Gerald

broad descriptions do not do justice, however, to the subtleties of the approaches that scholars have suggested. For example, Professor Monroe Freedman has often been characterized as the leading proponent of the adversarial theory of lawyering. In fact, Freedman has repeatedly stated that he believes that lawyers should consider issues of morality when they decide to take cases and in connection with counseling of their clients.[54] Similarly, proponents of morality theories of lawyering disagree as to the source and method by which lawyers incorporate moral values into their representation.[55]

Moral and ethical values can also have an influence on lawyers' obligations at the level of institutional structure.[56] The policy question of what a rule should be requires analysis of ethical and moral principles. Some rules of professional conduct, like the confidentiality rule involved in the Leo Frank case, clearly implicate principles of morality. Other rules of professional conduct appear to have little to do with conventional morality. Consider, for example, the rules dealing with unauthorized practice of law (Model Rule 5.5) and advertising of legal services (Model Rules 7.1 and 7.2). But even these rules have an ethical dimension. Economic analysis, which is founded on utilitarian principles, has a great deal to say about restrictions on delivery of professional services, the topic of Chapter 6.

J. Postema, Moral Responsibility in Professional Ethics, 55 N.Y.U. L. Rev. 63 (1980); William H. Simon, Ethical Discretion in Lawyering, 101 Harv. L. Rev. 1083 (1988); William H. Simon, The Ideology of Advocacy: Procedural Justice and Professional Ethics, 1978 Wis. L. Rev. 30; Serena Stier, Legal Ethics: The Integrity Thesis, 52 Ohio St. L.J. 551 (1991); and Richard Wasserstrom, Lawyers as Professionals: Some Moral Issues, 5 Human Rights 1 (1975). For criticisms of the morality theory of representation, see Stephen Ellmann, Lawyering for Justice in a Flawed Democracy, 90 Colum. L. Rev. 116 (1990) (reviewing David Luban, Lawyers and Justice: An Ethical Study (1988)); Stephen L. Pepper, The Lawyer's Amoral Ethical Role: A Defense, A Problem, and Some Possibilities, 1986 Am. B. Found. Res. J. 613 (1986); Ted Schneyer, Moral Philosophy's Standard Misconception of Legal Ethics, 1984 Wis. L. Rev. 1529.

54. Monroe H. Freedman, Understanding Lawyers' Ethics 50-52 (counseling) and 66-70 (decision to take case) (1990).

55. See generally Thomas L. Shaffer & Robert F. Cochran, Jr., Lawyers, Clients, and Moral Responsibility (1994).

56. See David B. Wilkins, Who Should Regulate Lawyers?, 105 Harv. L. Rev. 799 (1992); Special Issue, Institutional Choices in the Regulation of Lawyers, 65 Fordham L. Rev. #1 (1996).

C. AN OVERVIEW OF THIS BOOK

Drawing on professional, legal, and ethical standards, this book seeks to describe and to critically examine significant principles and rules dealing with lawyers' obligations to clients, to the legal system and third parties, and to the public. The book is organized into three parts. The first part focuses on lawyers' obligations to clients. Chapter 2 deals with various aspects of the client-attorney relationship, including formation of the relationship, legal fees and expenses, client property, authority between lawyer and client, and termination of the relationship. Chapter 3 continues the examination of lawyers' obligations to clients, focusing on conflicts of interest in litigation and in nonlitigation matters. In one sense the second part of the book continues the examination of lawyers' duties to clients. Chapter 4 deals with the duty of confidentiality, while Chapter 5 addresses the duty of zealous representation. In both chapters, however, the focus shifts from the client to limitations on duties to clients flowing from responsibilities that lawyers have to others. The third part examines public obligations of lawyers. Chapter 6 deals with delivery of legal services. Chapter 7 examines obligations of lawyers in two public roles: judges and government attorneys. The book's conclusion offers my reflections on the status of the legal profession at the end of the twentieth century. There are two appendixes with review questions and analysis. Appendix A contains multiple choice questions based on the format used on the Multistate Professional Responsibility examination. Appendix B consists of essay questions.

CHAPTER 2
The Client-Lawyer Relationship

A. LAWYERS AS FIDUCIARIES

Courts, disciplinary bodies, and scholars often state that lawyers have a fiduciary relationship with their clients.[1] A fiduciary relationship is distinguished from an arm's-length business relationship. In an arm's-length transaction the parties do not have obligations to protect the interests of the other party, although they do owe each other certain obligations, such as the duty not to engage in fraud. Instead, parties to an ordinary business transaction have the responsibility to protect their own interests. By contrast, fiduciaries have special obligations to care for and to protect the interests of their beneficiaries or clients.[2] What is it about the client-lawyer relationship that justifies imposing these special fiduciary duties on lawyers? The answer lies in the nature of the relationship between attorney and client. While ordinary business contracts are transactions between people who generally stand on equal footing, the relationship between lawyer and client is one of

1. Wolfram, Modern Legal Ethics 145 (referring to lawyers as "fiduciary agents"). See also Restatement of the Law Governing Lawyers Intro. Note to Ch. 2 (Prop. Final Draft #1, March 29, 1996).
2. See Restatement (Second) of Agency §13, comm. *a* (1958).

dependence. Clients have a need for representation that normally only lawyers can provide, and lawyers possess expertise that clients lack.

The ABA Model Rules of Professional Conduct outline the following fiduciary duties that lawyers owe to their clients:

- Competence and diligence (Model Rules 1.1 (competence) and 1.3 (diligence))
- Communication (Model Rules 1.4 (communication) and 2.1 (advisor))
- Confidentiality (Model Rule 1.6)
- Loyalty (Model Rules 1.7-1.9)
- Safekeeping of property (Model Rule 1.15)

Section 28 of the Restatement of the Law Governing Lawyers defines lawyers duties to their clients as follows:

> (1) proceed in a manner reasonably calculated to advance a client's lawful objectives, as defined by the client after consultation;
> (2) act with reasonable competence and diligence;
> (3) comply with obligations concerning the client's confidences and property, avoid impermissible conflicting interests, deal honestly with the client, and not employ advantages arising from the client-lawyer relationship in a manner adverse to the client; and
> (4) fulfill valid contractual obligations to the client.[3]

Most lawyers practice in law firms or other organizations, and many legal matters require the services of several lawyers and of paralegals and other nonlawyer assistants. Partners in a law firm (or the equivalent of a partner, such as a shareholder in a professional corporation or the general counsel of a corporate legal department) have a professional obligation to have their organizations develop measures designed to give reasonable assurances that all lawyers and nonlawyer assistants in the firm comply with

3. Various provisions of the Restatement of Agency set forth duties similar to those found in the proposed Restatement of the Law Governing Lawyers. See Restatement (Second) of Agency §379(1) (1958) (agent subject to duty to principal to act with standard care and with the skill that is standard in locality for kind of work the agent is employed to perform and, in addition, to exercise any special skill that agent has); §387 (1958) (loyalty) §395 (1958) (confidentiality).

the rules of professional conduct.[4] Lawyers who are not partners (senior associates, for example) have a similar duty over lawyers and nonlawyers who are subject to their supervision.[5] Partners or supervisory lawyers who learn of misconduct by a subordinate have a duty to take reasonable remedial action.[6] Even though subordinate lawyers are subject to the direction and control of their superiors, they nonetheless continue to have personal responsibility to comply with their professional and legal obligations.[7] A subordinate lawyer may, however, rely on a senior lawyer's "reasonable resolution of an arguable question of professional duty."[8]

Law firms have vicarious civil liability for the actions of their lawyers and employees acting within the scope of their employment.[9] Lawyers who practice in partnerships are jointly and severally liable for the conduct of other lawyers and employees of the firm.[10] Depending on state law, lawyers who practice in other forms of organizations, such as professional corporations, limited liability partnerships, or limited liability companies, may not have vicarious liability for malpractice by others lawyers in the firm.[11]

B. FORMATION OF THE CLIENT-LAWYER RELATIONSHIP

1. *Formation by Mutual Consent*

While lawyers owe fiduciary obligations to their clients, they have only limited duties to nonclients. Thus, whether a client-lawyer

4. Model Rules 5.1(a) (responsibility of partners as to other lawyers) and 5.3(a) (responsibility of partner as to nonlawyer assistants).
5. Model Rules 5.1(b) and 5.3(b).
6. Model Rules 5.1(c) and 5.3(c).
7. Model Rule 5.2(a).
8. Model Rule 5.2(b).
9. Restatement of the Law Governing Lawyers §79(1) (Tent. Draft #8, March 21, 1997).
10. Id. §79(2).
11. Id. §79(3). See Henderson v. HSI Fin. Servs., Inc., 471 S.E.2d 885 (Ga. 1996) (lawyers allowed to practice under professional corporation statute that eliminates vicarious liability of shareholders).

relationship exists is crucial in determining the scope of a lawyer's obligations.

A client-lawyer relationship is normally formed by mutual consent of the lawyer and the client. Often the relationship is reflected in a writing, customarily referred to as an *engagement agreement* or *engagement letter,* although a writing is generally not necessary to form the relationship. Nor is it necessary for the client to pay the lawyer; pro bono representation still involves a client-lawyer relationship. The Rules of Professional Conduct do require lawyers to have written contingent fee agreements.[12] A lawyer who entered into an oral contingent fee agreement with a client, however, would still have a client-lawyer relationship, although the lawyer would be subject to disciplinary action, and a court might refuse to allow the lawyer to recover any compensation for services rendered, even on a quantum meruit basis.[13]

2. *Client-Lawyer Relationships Formed by Court Appointment or Implied from the Conduct of the Parties*

Not all client-lawyer relationships are formed by mutual consent. In some cases, courts appoint lawyers to represent indigent clients. (See Chapter 6 and Model Rule 6.2.) In the absence of a court appointment, however, it is still possible for a client-lawyer relationship to come into existence even though the lawyer does not intend to represent the client. One of the leading cases dealing with creation of a client-lawyer relationship in the absence of a mutual consent is Westinghouse Elec. Corp. v. Kerr-McGee Corp.[14] In *Westinghouse,* an association of petroleum producers retained the Washington office of Kirkland & Ellis as independent special counsel to prepare a report on competition in the industry. The firm planned to use the report to lobby against legislation meant to break up the oil companies. To collect information for the report, the firm sent a questionnaire to 59 oil companies that were members of the association; the firm also interviewed representatives of some of these companies. The firm told the companies that all information

12. Model Rule 1.5(c).
13. See Estate of Pinter v. McGee, 679 A.2d 728 (N.J. Sup. Ct. App. Div. 1996).
14. 580 F.2d 1311 (7th Cir.), *cert. denied,* 439 U.S. 955 (1978).

divulged to the law firm would be confidential. The final report released by the firm presented facts and arguments to show that legislation to break up the oil companies was unnecessary in light of overall competitive conditions in the energy industry. On the same day that the Washington office of Kirkland & Ellis issued the report, the firm's Chicago office filed a complaint on behalf of Westinghouse against a number of defendants, several of whom were members of the petroleum association, charging violations of the federal antitrust laws. The complaint presented theories diametrically opposed to those set forth in the report that the firm had prepared for the association.

Three members of the association moved to disqualify Kirkland & Ellis from representing Westinghouse in the antitrust case because the firm had prepared the report for the petroleum association. The district court denied the disqualification motion, finding that no client-lawyer relationship existed between the firm and the members of the association. Relying on agency principles, the court reasoned that the members of the association had not given the law firm express or implied authority to act on their behalf. The Court of Appeals for the Seventh Circuit rejected the district court's agency approach and reversed. Focusing on the fact that the law firm had been retained as "independent counsel" and on the fact that the firm had assured confidentiality to members of the association, the Court of Appeals ruled that a client-lawyer relationship existed between the law firm and the members of the association.

In *Westinghouse,* Kirkland & Ellis had an express client-lawyer relationship with an entity, the association of petroleum producers. The issue before the court was whether a client-lawyer relationship with the members of the association should be implied based on the facts and circumstances. The normal rule in entity representation cases is that an attorney who represents an entity has a client-attorney client relationship with the entity and not with any of the officers, directors, shareholders, or members of the entity. Model Rule 1.(a) expresses the entity representation principle.[15] Thus, if Kirkland & Ellis had done nothing more than represent the association, it would not have had a client-lawyer relationship with the members of the association. In *Westinghouse,* however, Kirkland & Ellis had more than simply a vicarious relationship

15. See also Restatement of the Law Governing Lawyers §201, comm. *d* (Prop. Final Draft #1, March 29, 1996).

with the members of the association. It held itself out as independent counsel, communicated directly with members of the association, and assured them of confidentiality, one of the hallmarks of a client-lawyer relationship.

Westinghouse has come to stand for a "reasonable expectation" principle, under which a client-lawyer relationship will be implied if the purported client reasonably relies on the lawyer to provide legal services and the lawyer reasonably should know of the purported client's reliance. The Restatement of the Law Governing Lawyers adopts the reasonable expectation test as part of its §26 on formation of the client-lawyer relationship:

> §26 FORMATION OF CLIENT-LAWYER RELATIONSHIP
>
> A relationship of client and lawyer arises when:
>
> (1) a person manifests to a lawyer the person's intent that the lawyer provide legal services for the person; and either
>
> (a) the lawyer manifests to the person consent to do so; or
>
> (b) the lawyer fails to manifest lack of consent to do so, and the lawyer knows or reasonably should know that the person reasonably relies on the lawyer to provide the services; or
>
> (2) a tribunal with power to do so appoints the lawyer to provide the services.

How does one decide if a reasonable expectation of a client-lawyer relationship exists? All the facts and circumstance must be evaluated to determine whether the purported client reasonably relied on the lawyer and whether the lawyer reasonably should have known of the reliance. Of course, if the lawyer opens a file in the client's name for a particular matter or bills the client for legal services, a court is likely to find that an express attorney-client relationship exists. If the attorney has not opened a file or billed for services, the following factors should be particularly significant:

- Has the attorney dealt directly with the purported client, as in *Westinghouse*?
- Did the client convey information to the attorney in confidence as in *Westinghouse*?
- Has the purported client sought legal advice from the attorney?
- Has the attorney given legal advice to the purported client?

- Has the attorney made clear in writing or otherwise to the purported client that the attorney is not agreeing to represent that person?

In addition, when the existence of the relationship is uncertain, especially in cases that involve closely held entities, it seems reasonable to resolve doubt in favor of creating a client-lawyer relationship because the attorney is in the best position to inform the purported client that the attorney is not representing that person. By contrast, if a lawyer answers general questions about the law (rather than providing advice about a client's particular situation) in an informal setting, a client-lawyer relationship should not be formed,[16] although a prudent lawyer would be careful to warn the inquirer that the lawyer is only providing general legal information, not specific advice to the person.

Westinghouse dealt with formation of a client-lawyer relationship between a law firm that represented an association and members of the association. The same reasonable expectation principle has also been applied in other cases of entity representation. Thus, a lawyer who represents a corporation does not by virtue of that fact alone also represent an officer of the corporation with whom the lawyer deals. See Model Rule 1.13(a). However, a client-lawyer relationship between a lawyer for a corporation and an officer of the corporation can be formed based on the facts and circumstances. See Model Rule 1.13(e). For example, when a lawyer deals directly with the CEO of a corporation on business matters, absent other facts, the lawyer has a client-attorney relationship with the corporation and not with the CEO. If the lawyer or his firm also does estate planning work for the CEO, however, then the lawyer has a client-lawyer relationship with both the corporation and the president.

Similarly, a law firm that represents a partnership does not automatically have a client-lawyer relationship with the partners, but such a relationship can be formed if the facts and circumstances show that the client and the lawyer have a reasonable expectation of such a relationship.[17] Likewise, a law firm representing a closely

16. Id. §26, comm. *c*.

17. See Hopper v. Frank, 16 F.3d 92 (5th Cir. 1994) (summary judgment for law firm affirmed in legal malpractice action claiming that law firm that represented limited partnership in securities offering had client-attorney relationship with general partners of partnership); ABA Comm. on Ethics and Prof. Resp., Formal Opinion 91-361.

held corporation does not per se have a client-lawyer relationship with the shareholders, but one can be formed based on the facts and circumstances.[18]

In contrast to these cases, some courts have held that when a lawyer represents a member of a corporate group, the lawyer will be treated as having a client-lawyer relationship with subsidiaries, affiliates, or other members of the corporate group. In McCourt Co., Inc. v. FPC Properties, Inc.,[19] the Massachusetts Supreme Court stated the principle as follows:

> A law firm that represents client A in the defense of an action may not, at the same time, be counsel for a plaintiff in an action brought against client A, at least without the consent of both parties. . . . Nor does it matter that client A is a corporation or that client A consists, collectively, of a parent corporation and various wholly owned subsidiaries.[20]

The corporate group cases seem inconsistent with the general principles governing formation of client-lawyer relationships. Indeed, the corporate group cases are probably weaker ones for creation of client-lawyer relationships because the connection between the attorney and the purported corporate client is likely to be more remote than in partnerships or in closely held corporations. A few recent decisions have indicated a willingness to apply a facts-and-circumstances test to determine whether a law firm that represents a member of a corporate group has a client-lawyer relationship with other members of the group.[21] Further, in Formal Opinion 95-390, the ABA Committee on Ethics and Professional Responsibility supported use of a facts-and-circumstances test rather than a per se rule to determine formation of client-lawyer relationships in corporate groups.

Westinghouse shows that a client-lawyer relationship can be created either by mutual consent or by implication. Moreover, even

18. See Meyer v. Mulligan, 889 P.2d 509 (Wyo. 1995) (summary judgment for lawyer reversed because unclear whom lawyer represented).

19. 434 N.E.2d 1234 (Mass. 1982).

20. Id. at 1235.

21. See In re Wingspread Corp., 152 B.R. 861 (S.D.N.Y. Bank. 1993); Vanderveer Group, Inc. v. Petruny, 1993 WL 308720 (E.D. Pa. 1993) (disqualification motion of parent corporation denied in action brought by law firm against one subsidiary when law firm simultaneously represented another subsidiary in unrelated matter; in-house counsel was aware of but failed to object to representation).

when a client-lawyer relationship is not formed, lawyers still owe duties to prospective clients with whom they have dealt.[22] The case of Togstad v. Vesely, Otto, Miller & Keefe[23] is instructive. Ms. Togstad consulted with attorney Miller about a possible medical malpractice action involving her husband. She testified that after an interview lasting about 45 minutes, Miller told her "he did not think we had a legal case, however, he was going to discuss this with his partner." When she did not hear anything further from the attorney, Togstad assumed that the attorney and his partner had concluded that they did not have a cause of action. Ms. Togstad did not consult with another attorney until a year later, when the statute of limitations had run.

Miller testified that he told Togstad at the conclusion of the interview that "there was nothing related in her factual circumstances that told me that she had a case that our firm would be interested in undertaking." He also testified that because of the serious injuries that her husband had suffered, that she should obtain an opinion from another attorney and should do so promptly. Miller further testified that he told Ms. Togstad that his firm did not have expertise in medical malpractice actions and that it associated counsel in cases of that nature. Finally, Miller said that he would talk with associate counsel about Togstad's case and would inform her if the opinion of that counsel differed from Miller's. Miller's "impression" was that he did discuss the matter with associate counsel and that associate counsel thought that there was no liability for medical malpractice. Accordingly, Miller did not communicate further with Togstad.

The jury returned a verdict of $610,500 for Mr. Togstad and $39,000 for his wife. The Minnesota Supreme Court affirmed. It found that the Togstads presented sufficient evidence on which the jury could conclude that Miller was negligent in two ways: first, in giving advice that the Togstads did not have a cause of action without adequate factual investigation; second, in failing to inform Togstad of the upcoming expiration of the statute of limitations.

Westinghouse and *Togstad* show that lawyers face substantial risks even when they do not formally undertake representation of a client. As *Westinghouse* shows, informal contacts can lead to the

22. On duties to prospective clients, see Restatement of the Law Governing Lawyers §27 (Prop. Final Draft #1, March 29, 1996); Chapter 3.D.

23. 291 N.W.2d 686 (Minn. 1980).

formation of a client-lawyer relationship. *Togstad* warns attorneys that they owe duties even to prospective clients to use due care in evaluating cases and in declining representation. Note also the consequences of counsels' failures in these cases: disqualification (and resulting loss of fees) in *Westinghouse* and malpractice liability in *Togstad.*

What can lawyers do to minimize the risks presented by these cases? Use of written agreements that clarify the lawyers' role is an important step. In *Westinghouse* the firm's engagement agreement should have been with the association and should have stated that the firm represented only the association and not any of its members unless the firm entered into a written engagement agreement with a member. In communications with members of the association the firm should have informed the members in writing that it was acting in its capacity as counsel for the association, that it was not undertaking representation of a member, and that members were advised to consult with counsel. With these steps it would be difficult for a member to claim that it had a reasonable expectation of a client-lawyer relationship with the firm. In *Togstad,* counsel should have used a written *nonengagement agreement.* A well-drafted nonengagement agreement will address three major points. First, the firm is not undertaking representation of the client in the matter. Second, the client should consider obtaining a second opinion from other counsel about the merits of the client's case. Third, the client should act promptly because a statute of limitations applicable to her claim might expire.

3. *Declining Representation*

Because the client-attorney relationship is normally based on mutual consent, lawyers may generally refuse to undertake representation for any reason. The Rules of Professional Conduct, however, qualify the lawyer's right to decline representation in two respects. First, lawyers should assist in providing pro bono legal services. See Model Rule 6.1 and Chapter 6.B.3 infra. Second, lawyers should not seek to decline court appointments except for good cause. See Model Rule 6.2. Among the circumstances that show good cause are the lawyer's lack of competence to handle the appointed case,[24] the existence of a conflict of interest,[25] or unreasonable financial hardship resulting from the appointment.[26]

Suppose a lawyer refuses to represent a client for a discriminatory reason: race, national origin, sex, sexual orientation, religion, age, disability? Some states have amended their rules of conduct to prohibit lawyers from engaging in discriminatory practices. These amendments often prohibit lawyers from discriminating in accepting or terminating representation of a client. For example, Rule 2-400 of the California Rules of Professional Conduct provides that in managing or operating a law practice, a California lawyer

> shall not unlawfully discriminate or knowingly permit unlawful discrimination on the basis of race, national origin, sex, sexual orientation, religion, age or disability in
>
> (1) hiring, promoting, discharging or otherwise determining the conditions of employment of any person; or
>
> (2) *accepting or terminating representation of any client.* (Emphasis added.)

DR 1-102(A)(6) of the New York Code of Professional Responsibility is similar.[27] Note that the California and New York rules also prohibit discrimination in employment practices as well as discrimination in accepting or terminating representation of clients. Thus, lawyers in a firm that terminated the employment of an

24. See Zarabia v. Bradshaw, 912 P.2d 5 (Ariz. 1996) (en banc) (invalidating trial court's rotation plan for providing representation to criminal defendants on the ground that it did not provide adequate assistance of counsel or adequate compensation for representation).

25. State of Lynch, 796 P.2d 1150 (Okla. 1990) (conflict of interest constitutes good cause to seek to avoid appointment).

26. See Ex parte Dibble, 310 S.E.2d 440 (S.C. Ct. App. 1983) (not unconstitutional to appoint counsel without compensation in civil cases, but trial courts should exercise appointment power to prevent undue hardship to lawyers).

27. For discussions of the issue of discrimination in the profession, see Susan D. Gilbert & Michael P. Allen, Commentary, Overcoming Discrimination in the Legal Profession: Should the *Model Rules* be Changed?, 6 Geo. J. Legal Ethics 933 (1993) (proposing rule that would prohibit discrimination by lawyers in the practice of law and in operation of a law office); Ronald D. Rotunda, Racist Speech and Lawyer Discipline, 6 Prof. Lawyer 1 (Feb. 1995) (arguing against disciplinary rules prohibiting racist speech on First Amendment grounds).

associate for discriminatory reasons would be acting unethically and might face civil liability as well.[28] The movie *Philadelphia* dramatizes just such a case.[29]

C. LEGAL FEES AND EXPENSES

1. *Fees Established by Contract or by Court Order*

Payment of fees for legal services is largely a matter of contract between lawyer and client. Indeed, Model Rule 1.5(b) imposes obligations on lawyers to reach clear agreement with clients about the manner in which lawyers charge for their services: "When the lawyer has not regularly represented the client, the basis or rate of the fee shall be communicated to the client, preferably in writing, before or within a reasonable time after commencing the representation."[30]

Normally, the client is responsible for paying the lawyer's fees, but in some cases a third party will pay them. For example, in a divorce case, the parents of one of the spouses may agree to pay the lawyer's fees. Corporations often pay legal fees when their officials are accused of wrongdoing. By contract, insurance companies pay legal fees of defense counsel for the insured. The Model Rules allow lawyers to receive payment of fees from third persons provided the client consents to the arrangement, there is no interference with the lawyer's independent professional judgment on behalf of the client, and the lawyer maintains confidentiality of client communications. Model Rule 1.8(f).

Lawyers charge fees for their services in a wide variety of ways. The fee can be determined strictly on an *hourly basis;* under this method, the fee is computed by multiplying the number of hours worked on the matter by each lawyer (or paralegal) times the

28. See Hishon v. King & Spalding, 467 U.S. 69 (1984) (female associate who had been passed over for partnership stated cause of action for sex discrimination against her firm under Title VII of the Civil Rights Act of 1964).

29. See Doe v. Kohn Nast & Graf, P.C., 862 F. Supp. 1310 (E.D. Pa. 1994) (facts similar to movie *Philadelphia*).

30. See also Restatement of the Law Governing Lawyers §50(1) (Prop. Final Draft #1, March 29, 1996).

hourly rate for that provider. Hourly rates for lawyers and paralegals are set based on their experience and type of practice in comparison with the fees commonly charged by other lawyers and paralegals providing similar services. Hourly fees are quite common in business and tax matters; lawyers engaged in civil defense litigation also typically bill on a hourly basis.

Contingent fees are normally used by plaintiffs' lawyers in personal injury matters. The essence of the contingent fee is that the lawyer's right to receive compensation is contingent on the client receiving an award, either by settlement or judgment. Typically, contingent fees are set based on a percentage of the amount recovered, and normally the fee varies depending on the stage at which the matter is concluded. Thus, a common contingent fee in a personal injury action is 25 percent if the matter is settled before trial, 33 percent if the matter is settled after a jury is selected, and 50 percent if the matter is concluded after appeal.

Fixed fees are often employed in routine estate planning and real estate matters. Thus, a lawyer might charge a fee of $1,000 to examine title and prepare documents to close a residential real estate transaction. A fixed fee could also be based on a percentage of the value of the transaction. Thus, for many years lawyers customarily charged fees for estate administration based on a percentage of the estate. In a number of jurisdictions, however, fees based on a percentage of the estate have been declared improper either by legislation or court decision on the ground that a fee based on a percentage of the estate, regardless of the difficulty of the work, is unreasonable.[31]

Some lawyers charge fees based on the *value of the services*. Under this approach the fee is not set in advance, but rather is determined by the lawyer at the conclusion of the matter, taking

31. See, e.g., In re Estate of Painter, 567 P.2d 820 (Colo. Ct. App. 1977) (Colorado legislature has repealed authorization for percentage fees and adopted reasonable fee standard); Estate of Davis, 509 A.2d 1175 (Me. 1986) (abuse of discretion for probate court to rely on local custom of using percentage method in setting attorney fee); In re Estate of Rolfe, 615 A.2d 625 (N.H. 1992) (disapproval of fee guidelines based on size of estate); In re Estate of Preston, 560 A.2d 160 (Pa. Super. Ct. 1989) (rejecting use of attorney general's percentage fee schedule). But see Fla. St. Ann. §733.6171 (West Supp. 1998) (attorneys are entitled to compensation at a flat rate for estates under $100,000 and on a percentage basis for larger estates for ordinary services; attorneys may seek additional compensation for extraordinary services).

into account a variety of factors. One way in which a lawyer could employ this "value billing" approach would be to use the fee computed on an hourly basis as a lodestar, and then to adjust this figure either upward or downward depending on various factors, such as the result obtained and the time pressures imposed by the case.

Various combinations of fees are also possible. For example, in a personal injury matter, a lawyer might charge a client a fixed fee of a certain amount coupled with a percentage of the recovery. Presumably the percentage in this case would be less than in a pure contingency matter because the lawyer would face less risk due to receiving a fixed fee. Some lawyers have begun charging fees based on a *blended rate*, a single rate that applies to both lawyers and paralegals. This method of billing may be attractive to clients because the hourly rate for services rendered is less than that charged for lawyers, while also being desirable for lawyers because it allows lawyers to increase their profit margins by having the work done by employees who charge the least. Some firms have also experimented with fees computed on an hourly basis, coupled with a bonus for a successful outcome.[32]

For a number of years in many jurisdictions bar associations established minimum *fee schedules* that lawyers were required to use in setting their fees. In 1975, the Supreme Court declared fee schedules to be invalid in violation of the antitrust laws.[33]

While legal fees are generally determined by contract between lawyer and client, in some cases courts must determine a reasonable fee because one party has the right to recover a reasonable fee pursuant to statute, court rule, or contract.[34] For example, many federal and state statutes provide that the prevailing party is entitled to recover reasonable attorney fees from the opposing party. By agreement the lawyer and client may specify that any court-awarded fees are paid to the lawyer. In the absence of an agreement, court-awarded fees belong to the client and are credited against any amount that the client is required to pay to the lawyer.[35]

32. For a discussion of innovative billing techniques, see Bradford W. Hildebrandt, chair, Alternative Pricing Practices (PLI 1995); Richard C. Reed, Billing Innovations (ABA 1996).

33. Goldfarb v. Virginia State Bar, 421 U.S. 773 (1975).

34. See generally Mary Frances Derfner & Arthur D. Wolf, Court Awarded Attorney Fees (1997).

35. See Evans v. Jeff D., 475 U.S. 717 (1986) (recovery of attorney fees under federal fee shifting statutes); Restatement of the Law Governing Lawyers §50, comm. *f* (Prop. Final Draft #1, March 29, 1996).

Court rules generally allow recovery of attorney fees as sanctions for litigation abuse. Commercial contracts typically state that a prevailing party is entitled to recover its reasonable attorney fees.

When a client has been involved in some form of illegal activity, payment of legal fees, particularly cash payments, can expose a lawyer to legal and professional risks. If the lawyer knows that the client's payment of fees is derived from illegal activity, the lawyer may be guilty of a crime. For example, the federal "money laundering" statute provides that it is illegal if any person "knowingly engages or attempts to engage in a monetary transaction in criminally derived property of a value greater than $10,000 and is derived from specified unlawful activity [such as drug dealing]."[36] Fees received from illegal activity can also be subject to forfeiture in an action brought by the government.[37] It is not per se illegal or unethical for a lawyer to receive a cash payment of legal fees, but lawyers must report[38] to the Internal Revenue Service the receipt of cash[39] in excess of $10,000 in a single transaction or a group of related transactions.

2. *The Reasonableness Principle*

Fiduciaries have an obligation to deal fairly with their clients in any business transaction between them. Model Rule 1.5(a) reflects this principle, providing that a lawyers' fees shall be reasonable. Courts regulate the reasonableness of lawyers' fees in three important ways.[40] First, courts can discipline lawyers for charging exces-

36. 18 U.S.C. §1957 (1994).

37. See 18 U.S.C. §1963(c) (1994) (forfeiture of property used in or derived from criminal activity in violation of RICO, Racketeer Influenced and Corrupt Organizations) and 21 U.S.C. §853(c) (1994) (forfeiture of property used in or derived from violation of drug felony statutes). The Supreme Court upheld the constitutionality of forfeiture statutes when applied to attorney fees in Caplin & Drysdale, Chartered v. United States, 491 U.S. 617 (1989).

38. 26 U.S.C. §6050I (1994).

39. While the statute uses the word "cash," it defines the term more broadly than the common understanding of the term. Cash includes foreign currency and "any monetary instrument (whether or not in bearer form) with a face amount of not more than $10,000." 26 U.S.C. §6050I(d) (1994); Treas. Reg. §1.6050I-1(c).

40. See generally Wolfram, Modern Legal Ethics §9.1 (discussing supervisory power that courts exercise over fee agreements).

sive fees.[41] Unfortunately, some studies have provided distressing documentation of lawyers' improper billing practices, such as double billing (for example, billing two clients for the time spent in preparing a research memo involving an issue applicable to both clients) and undisclosed markups on costs.[42] In response to these abuses, the ABA Committee on Ethics and Professional Responsibility issued Formal Opinion 93-379 in which it addressed a number of issues regarding fees and expenses. The ABA Committee advised lawyers who bill strictly on an hourly basis that it is improper for lawyers to charge more than the actual time expended. Thus, lawyers who have agreed to charge their clients on an hourly basis could not ethically double bill for court appearances, travel time, or for work product used in more than one case. The ABA's opinion indicated, however, that lawyers could agree to alternative methods of billing that were not strictly time based, provided the method was fully disclosed to the client. Similarly, the Committee reasoned that lawyers could not charge more than the actual cost of expenses, absent full disclosure to the client. Other professional organizations have also taken steps to control improper billing practices.[43]

Second, courts have the power to reduce the amount of fees charged by attorneys if the court finds the fee to be unreasonable. The issue could arise in a variety of ways: in an action by the client to recover from the attorney an excessive fee retained by the attorney, in an action by the attorney to collect a fee, or in a collateral proceeding or motion incident to a matter already in court.[44] Third, in some cases the court must determine a reasonable

41. E.g., Bushman v. State Bar, 522 P.2d 312 (Cal. 1974) (en banc) (exorbitant fee in divorce case); In re Teichner, 470 N.E.2d 972 (Ill. 1984) (improper to charge 25 percent contingent fee for collection of life insurance proceeds when no dispute with company), *cert. denied,* 470 U.S. 1053 (1985); see Dale R. Agthe, Annotation, Attorney's Charging Excessive Fee as Ground for Disciplinary Action, 11 A.L.R.4th 133 (1982).

42. The seminal study is Lisa G. Lerman, Lying to Clients, 138 U. Pa. L. Rev. 659 (1990). See also Sonia S. Chan, ABA Formal Opinion 93-379: Double Billing, Padding and Other Forms of Overbilling, 9 Geo. J. Legal Ethics 611 (1996); William G. Ross, The Ethics of Hourly Billing by Attorneys, 44 Rutgers L. Rev. 1 (1991).

43. See ABA, Task Force on Lawyer Business Ethics, Statements of Principles, 51 Bus. Law. 745 (1996) (statements on billing for legal services, billing disbursements and other charges, and marketing legal services).

44. E.g., In re A.H. Robins Co. (Bergstrom v. Dalkon Shield Claimants Trust), 86 F.3d 364 (4th Cir. 1996) (courts have inherent power to determine reasonable-

fee because the fee will be paid by the defendant pursuant to statute, court rule, or contract.[45]

3. *Limitations on Contingent Fees*

Contingent fees are widely used in the United States, particularly in personal injury cases. The major justification for contingent fees is that they allow people who could not afford an attorney to obtain access to the legal system for vindication of their rights. It is interesting to note that contingent fees are considered improper in many other countries. The difference in attitude toward contingency fees between the United States and other nations reflects deeper cultural factors and institutional arrangements. In many other countries, litigation is viewed as an evil, while in the United States litigation is often a mechanism for vindication of important rights. In addition, many other countries provide access to the legal system by regulating legal fees and by providing for shifting of fees to the losing party.[46] Although the United States is experiencing trends in those directions, legal fees in this country continue to be largely a matter of contract between the client and the lawyer.

While the use of contingent fees in the United States is well established, contingent fees have been criticized on the ground that in some cases they are unreasonable when compared to the risk of nonrecovery.[47] To take an extreme example, suppose a widow retained an attorney to represent her regarding administration of her husband's estate. If the attorney charged the client a contin-

---

ness of contingent fees; 10 percent limit for supplementary distribution in Dalkon Shield case); McKenzie Constr., Inc. v. Maynard, 758 F.2d 97 (3d Cir. 1985) (in action by client to recover portion of contingent fee retained by lawyer, court should determine reasonableness of fee based on circumstances surrounding negotiation and performance, but "courts should be reluctant to disturb contingent fee arrangements freely entered into by knowledgeable and competent parties"); Kirby v. Liska, 351 N.W.2d 421 (Neb. 1984) (in action by attorney to collect fee in quiet title action, court reduced fee from $65,340 to $6,500 based on time and difficulty of matter).

45. See, e.g., Evans v. Jeff D., 475 U.S. 717 (1986) (recovery of attorney fees under federal fee shifting statutes).

46. Restatement of the Law Governing Lawyers §47, comm. *b* (Prop. Final Draft #1, March 29, 1996).

47. See Frederick B. MacKinnon, Contingent Fees for Legal Services 157-211 (1964). See also Restatement of the Law Governing Lawyers §47, comm. *b* (Prop. Final Draft #1, March 29, 1996).

gency fee for collecting life insurance proceeds on the husband's estate when no bona fide dispute with the insurance company existed, the attorney fee would clearly be excessive.[48]

Some scholars have argued that this same principle applies to many personal injury cases when liability is clear and only the amount of damages is uncertain.[49] An important difference exists, however, between the life insurance example and typical personal injury cases. In the life insurance situation both liability and amount of recovery are clear. In the personal injury case, however, while liability is largely (although probably not completely) uncontested, the amount of recovery is uncertain.

The proposed Restatement of the Law Governing Lawyers indicates that contingent fees can be unreasonable in two situations: "those in which there was a high likelihood of substantial recovery by trial or settlement, so that the lawyer bore little risk of nonpayment; and those in which the client's recovery was likely to be so large that the lawyer's fee would clearly exceed the sum appropriate to pay for services performed and risks assumed."[50]

One recent proposal has attempted to resolve the problem of determining the risk-free amount of damages involved in personal injury litigation by imposing a duty on plaintiff's counsel to seek early settlement offers from the defendant.[51] The amount of the early settlement offer would then become the riskless amount against which plaintiffs' counsel could not ethically charge a contingency fee. The principal features of the proposal are as follows:

(1) Contingency fees cannot not be charged against settlement offers made prior to the retention of counsel by personal injury claimants.
(2) Defendants in personal injury cases receive the opportunity to make early settlement offers in personal injury cases, but only if made within sixty days from receipt from plaintiffs'

48. See White v. McBride, 937 S.W.2d 796 (Tenn. 1996) (one-third contingent fee in contested probate proceeding was clearly excessive).

49. See Michael Horowitz, Essay, Making Ethics Real, Making Ethics Work: A Proposal for Contingency Fee Reform, 44 Emory L.J. 173 (1995) (proposal made by Mr. Horowitz, Professor Jeffrey O'Connell of the University of Virginia Law School, and Professor Lester Brickman of Cardozo Law School).

50. Section 47, comm. *c* (Prop. Final Draft #1, March 29, 1996).

51. For a description of one insurance company's effort to eliminate lawyers by making early, settlement offers to accident victims, see Richard C. Reuben, Insurer Out to Eliminate Middleman, 82 A.B.A. J. 20 (Sept. 1996) (Allstate's early settlement offer program).

counsel of a demand for compensation. If the offer is accepted, plaintiffs' counsel fees are limited to hourly rate charges and are capped at 10 percent of the first $100,000 of the offer and 5 percent of any greater amounts.

(3) Demands for settlement submitted by plaintiffs' counsel must include basic, routinely discoverable information in order to assist defendants in evaluating plaintiffs' claims. To assist plaintiffs in evaluating defendants' offers, discoverable material "in the . . . [defendant's] possession concerning the alleged injury upon which [the defendant] relied in making his offer of settlement" must be made available to plaintiffs for a settlement offer to be effective.

(4) If early offers are rejected, contingency fees may only be charged against net recoveries in excess of those offers.

(5) If no offer is made within the sixty day period, contingency fee contracts are unaffected by the proposal.[52]

In Formal Opinion 94-389, the ABA Committee on Ethics and Professional Responsibility rejected the proposal. The Committee decided that contingent fees were generally proper even in cases in which liability was clear and some recovery certain, provided the client was fully informed of and consented to the contingency fee:

> [T]he Committee is of the view that the argument may rest on a faulty notion as to the number of cases regarding which at the onset of the engagement the lawyer can say with certainty that the client will recover. Defendants often vigorously defend and even win cases where liability seems certain. Additionally, a previously undiscovered fact or an unexpected change in the law can suddenly transform a case that seemed a sure winner at the outset of representation into a certain loser. . . .
>
> Moreover, even in cases where there is no risk of non-recovery, and the lawyer and client are certain that liability is clear and will be conceded, a fee arrangement contingent on the amount recovered may nonetheless be reasonable. As the increasing popularity of reverse contingent fees demonstrates, for almost all cases there is a range of possible recoveries. Since the amount of recovery will be largely determined by the lawyer's knowledge, skill, experience and time expended, both the defendant and the plaintiff may best be

52. 44 Emory L.J. at 175-176. For a more detailed presentation of the proposal in the form of a proposed court rule or statute, see id. at 194-211.

> served by a contingency fee arrangement that ties the lawyer's fee to the amount recovered.
>
> Also, an early settlement offer is often prompted by the defendant's recognition of the ability of the plaintiff's lawyer fairly and accurately to value the case and to proceed effectively through trial and appeals if necessary. There is no ethical reason why the lawyer is not entitled to an appropriate consideration for this value that his engagement has brought to the case, even though it results in an early resolution.[53]

The Committee also found no support in the Model Rules or the Model Code for imposing an obligation on plaintiff's counsel to solicit early settlement offers.[54] The Committee did note in its opinion that rules of ethics impose some limitations on contingency fees, including the requirement of reasonableness. See Model Rule 1.5(a). Professor Lester Brickman, one of the authors of the proposal submitted to the ABA Committee, has criticized the ABA opinion for ignoring the fundamental issue: whether it is proper for lawyers to charge a *standard* contingency fee in cases in which liability is certain. Brickman contends that the ABA Committee acts in the financial and political interests of lawyers rather than the public.[55]

Model Rule 1.5(c) imposes special requirements with regard to contingent fees. Agreements for contingent fees must

- Be in writing
- State the method by which the fee is computed, including the percentages if the matter is concluded by settlement, trial, or appeal
- Identify litigation or other expenses that the client is responsible to pay
- State whether expenses are deducted before or after the contingent fee percentage is computed

The Rule also requires lawyers to provide clients with a written settlement statement at the conclusion of the matter stating the outcome and showing how the client's remittance is computed.

53. ABA Comm. on Ethics and Prof. Resp., Formal Opinion 94-389, at 8-9.
54. Id. at 8.
55. Lester Brickman, ABA Regulation of Contingency Fees: Money Talks, Ethics Walks, 65 Fordham L. Rev. 247 (1996).

Violation of these requirements will not necessarily result in forfeiture of the lawyer's fee. For example, if the lawyer fails to obtain a written contingency fee agreement, but the client does not contest the amount of the fee, the lawyer will probably be able to recover at least for the reasonable value of the lawyer's services.[56] Some states, either by statute or court rule, have imposed limitations on contingent fee percentages. For example, the following limits apply in New Jersey:

> (1) 33⅓% on the first $500,000 recovered;
> (2) 30% on the next $500,000 recovered;
> (3) 25% on the next $500,000 recovered;
> (4) 20% on the next $500,000 recovered; and
> (5) on all amounts recovered in excess of the above by application for reasonable fee in accordance with the provisions of paragraph (f) hereof; and
> (6) where the amount recovered is for the benefit of a client who was a minor or incompetent when the contingent fee arrangement was made, the foregoing limits shall apply, except that the fee on any amount recovered by settlement without trial shall not exceed 25%.[57]

When a client receives a lump-sum settlement, the lawyer's contingent fee, like other expenses, is paid at the time of the settlement. Suppose the client agrees to a structured settlement. In the typical structured settlement, the client receives a lump-sum payment coupled with periodic payments either directly from the defendant or perhaps through an annuity issued by an insurance company. When is the attorney's contingent fee paid under a structured settlement? Courts have generally upheld fee agreements in which the client agrees to pay the lawyer's contingent fee out of any lump-sum payment, even if the lawyer would be receiving the bulk of the lump sum. If the fee agreement provides for payment of the lawyer's contingent fee out of the lump-sum settlement, the

56. Restatement of the Law Governing Lawyers §46, comm. *g* (Prop. Final Draft #1, March 29, 1996). But see Estate of Pinter v. McGee, 679 A.2d 728 (N.J. Sup. Ct. App. Div. 1996) (failure to put contingency fee agreement in writing bars claim for quantum meruit).

57. N.J. Sup. Ct. R. 1:21-7. See also Fla. R. of Prof. Conduct 4-1.5(f)(4) and Cal. Bus. & Prof. Code §6146 (West 1990) (limitations on contingent fees in claims against health care providers).

amount of fee would be based on the present value of the settlement or the cost of the annuity if the settlement was being funded through an annuity, whichever is lower.[58] In the absence of an agreement allowing the lawyer to be paid out of the lump-sum payment, the lawyer's contingent fee would be paid pro rata out of each payment received by the client.[59]

In certain cases contingent fee agreements are professionally improper. Model Rule 1.5(d)(2) prohibits contingent fees in criminal cases, although it is difficult to offer a sound rationale for the rule. Indeed, the comments to Rule 1.5 offer no justification.[60] It has been argued that the purpose of the rule is to prevent corruption of justice by criminal defense counsel who would have a financial interest in the outcome through a contingent fee, but the same argument could be made against contingent fees in civil cases.[61] Some commentators have suggested that the prohibition of contingent fees in criminal cases exists to avoid a conflict of interest: If the contingent fee were earned only by an acquittal, defense counsel would have a conflict of interest because counsel would have a financial disincentive against plea bargaining.[62] This problem could be avoided, however, by requiring a sliding scale of contingent fees depending on the outcome, much like the sliding scale typically used in personal injury cases.[63] The rule prohibiting contingent fees in criminal defense cases may have little practical importance, however, because the custom among criminal defense attorneys is to require payment of all or a substantial portion of their fees in advance.[64] Further, even if a lawyer charges a criminal

58. See Nguyen v. Los Angeles County Harbor/UCLA Medical Ctr., 48 Cal. Rptr. 2d 301 (Cal. Ct. App. 1996). See also Restatement of the Law Governing Lawyers §47, comm. *e* (Prop. Final Draft #1, March 29, 1996).

59. In re Myers, 663 N.E.2d 771 (Ind. 1996) (in absence of agreement lawyer cannot take total fee in structured settlement out of initial payments to client). See Restatement of the Law Governing Lawyers §47, comm. *e* (Prop. Final Draft #1, March 29, 1996).

60. For a criticism of the traditional justifications of the rule and an argument that contingent fees should be allowed in criminal cases in some limited circumstances, see Pamela S. Karlan, Contingent Fees and Criminal Cases, 93 Colum. L. Rev. 595 (1993).

61. See Wolfram, Modern Legal Ethics §9.4.3, at 535-536.

62. See 1 Hazard & Hodes, The Law of Lawyering §1.5:501.

63. Restatement of the Law Governing Lawyers §47, comm. *f(i)* (Prop. Final Draft #1, March 29, 1996).

64. See Thomas D. Morgan, The Evolving Concept of Professional Responsibility, 90 Harv. L. Rev. 702, 734 (1977) (arguing that the prohibition of contingent fees in criminal cases protects the defense bar's practice of charging up-front fixed fees by suppressing competition through contingent fees).

defendant an unethical contingent fee, it will not necessarily invalidate the defendant's conviction. In Winkler v. Keane,[65] the Second Circuit held that a fee agreement in which defense counsel was to receive an additional $25,000 if defendant was found not guilty constituted an unethical contingent fee. The court found that such an agreement created an actual conflict of interest between defense counsel and his client, but the court still refused to set aside the defendant's conviction because it found that the defendant had failed to prove that trial counsel's representation was adversely affected by the conflict of interest.[66]

Rule 1.5(d)(1) states that contingent fees are improper in domestic relations matters when the amount of the fee is "contingent upon the securing of a divorce or upon the amount of alimony or support, or property settlement in lieu thereof." Two rationales support the rule: First, public policy favors reconciliation in domestic cases. If contingent fees were permitted in divorce cases, the lawyer's financial interest would be inconsistent with that public policy. Second, contingent fees are unnecessary to secure counsel in divorce cases. A spouse with assets can afford counsel, and in most jurisdictions courts will require the spouse with assets to pay a reasonable attorney fee if the other spouse is unable to afford counsel.[67] Since the rule only applies when the fee is contingent upon divorce or settlement in lieu of divorce, it should not prohibit contingent fees to collect past due alimony and child support because the policy in favor of reconciliation is not involved in these cases.

Divorce statutes usually allow the court to award either of the parties attorney fees or "suit money." Under such statutes, courts must determine the amount of a reasonable attorney fee. Some courts have held that a judicial enhancement of the lodestar amount to take into account the results obtained in the case amounts to an improper contingent fee in a domestic case.[68] These cases seem wrongly decided. The possibility that a fee can be adjusted to reflect a variety of factors, including results obtained, does not make the fee contingent on the outcome of the case.

65. 7 F.3d 304 (2d Cir. 1993), *cert. denied*, 511 U.S. 1022 (1994).

66. Id. at 310.

67. Restatement of the Law Governing Lawyers §47, comm. *g* (Prop. Final Draft #1, March 29, 1996).

68. State ex rel. Oklahoma Bar Assn. v. Fagin, 848 P.2d 11 (Okla. 1992); Glasscock v. Glasscock, 403 S.E.2d 133 (S.C. 1991). *Contra* Eckell v. Wilson, 597 A.2d 696 (Pa. Super. Ct. 1991), *app. denied*, 607 A.2d 253 (1992).

Further, the fact that an enhancement is subject to judicial approval safeguards the public policy against giving lawyers financial incentives to promote divorce.

Contingent fees are typically charged by plaintiff's counsel. May a defense attorney charge a contingent fee? In Wunschel Law Firm, P.C. v. Clabaugh,[69] the Iowa Supreme Court held that a defense contingent fee based on a percentage of the difference between the amount demanded by the plaintiff in the complaint and the amount the defendant was required to pay was void as against public policy. The court reasoned that a defense percentage contingent fee in unliquidated tort cases was likely to produce unreasonable fees because the amount demanded in the complaint does not bear a logical relationship to the amount of any recovery. The Model Rules do not address the issue, but in Formal Opinion 93-373, the ABA's Committee on Ethics and Professional Responsibility ruled that defense contingent fee contracts were not unethical per se under the Model Rules. The Committee stated that "the *Wunschel* court quite properly condemned the use of the prayer for relief as the sole basis for calculating a reverse contingent fee," but the Committee went on to assert that in other cases defense contingent fees could be reasonable and in the best interest of the client.

Comment 3 to Rule 1.5 states: "When there is doubt whether a contingent fee is consistent with the client's best interest, the lawyer should offer the client alternative bases for the fee and explain their implications." In Informal Opinion 86-1521, the ABA Committee on Ethics and Professional Responsibility ruled that an attorney should not unilaterally set a contingent fee but should give a client who is in a position to pay a fixed fee the option of either a reasonable fixed fee or a contingent fee.

4. *Retainers*

In some cases, lawyers ask their clients to pay a retainer. The term *retainer* is often used loosely in the practice of law to refer to any advanced payment. It is important to distinguish, however, between general retainers, engagement retainers, special retainers, and expense deposits. A *general retainer* is a payment to a lawyer

69. 291 N.W.2d 331 (Iowa 1980).

(or the lawyer's firm) to ensure the lawyer's availability to handle the client's legal work. For example, suppose a large corporation that participates in a substantial number of mergers and acquisitions wants to make sure that a law firm with special expertise in this area will be available to handle its work. The corporation and the firm could agree to a general retainer. Under the terms of the general retainer, the firm would typically agree to avoid conflicts of interest and to stand ready to handle the corporation's legal work.[70] The general retainer is not based on work actually done; the client will be billed for such services as rendered. Thus, the general retainer is earned by the firm when received and should not be deposited in the firm's trust account. See Model Rule 1.15 on lawyers' obligations regarding trust accounts.

Since the general retainer is earned when received, it is nonrefundable, although circumstances could arise in which the firm would be required to refund the retainer in whole or in part. Suppose, for example, the firm was unable to represent the client in a matter due to a conflict of interest that developed unexpectedly. Presumably the client would be entitled to a refund of at least a portion of the general retainer because the firm was unable to comply with its contractual obligation to be available to handle the corporation's legal work. In addition, a court might declare a general retainer invalid if the retainer were unreasonable in amount. In cases involving sophisticated corporate clients, such circumstances are likely to be rare.[71]

An *engagement retainer* is a payment to a lawyer or law firm for undertaking representation in a particular matter, as opposed to general availability to do the client's legal work. Like the general retainer, the engagement retainer is earned when received and must not be deposited in trust.

A *special retainer* is an advanced payment for legal work in a particular case (as opposed to a payment to obtain the lawyer's general availability or to take a particular case). Thus, if a client retains a law firm to handle a matter in litigation, the firm and the client might agree that the client would pay the firm a retainer of

70. The law firm of Skadden, Arps, Slate, Meagher & Flom made extensive use of this type of general retainer. See Lincoln Caplan, Skadden: Power, Money, and the Rise of a Legal Empire 81-86 (1993).

71. Restatement of the Law Governing Lawyers §46, comm. *e* (Prop. Final Draft #1, March 29, 1996). The Restatement uses the term "engagement retainer" to refer to what the text calls a general retainer.

$25,000. In the typical case, the special retainer is not earned when received by the firm. Instead, the special retainer represents an advance against fees to be billed by the firm. Thus, the special retainer should be deposited in the firm's trust account. Payments to the firm from the trust account would be made as services are rendered.[72] If the amount of the firm's services are less than the amount of the special retainer, the firm must refund to the client the balance of the retainer.[73]

An *expense deposit* is an amount paid to the firm to be applied to future expenses in the client's case. Like the special retainer, the expense deposit is not earned when received, but must be deposited in the firm's trust account and deducted as the firm incurs expenses. Advances or deposits received by a lawyer from a client without clear designation should ordinarily be presumed to be special retainers because clients reasonably assume that they are paying for services rendered.[74]

In criminal defense and marital practice, some lawyers have charged their clients nonrefundable special retainers. Under this fee arrangement, the client agrees that the lawyer may keep the entire retainer regardless of whether the client discharges the lawyer and regardless of how the matter is concluded. Thus, under a nonrefundable retainer, if a divorce client decides to reconcile with her spouse, the lawyer still is entitled to keep the entire fee payment. Similarly, in a criminal case, if the defendant agrees to a plea, the lawyer is entitled to keep the entire retainer. Some scholars have criticized nonrefundable retainers on the ground that they can result in excessive fees and can compromise clients' rights to discharge their lawyers,[75] and a few courts, most notably the New York Court of Appeals in In re Cooperman,[76] have held nonrefundable special retainers to be invalid.[77] The court in *Cooperman* stated:

72. On the distinction between general and special retainers, see Wong v. Michael Kennedy, P.C., 853 F. Supp. 73 (E.D.N.Y. 1994).

73. See Wolfram, Modern Legal Ethics §9.2.2, at 505-506.

74. See Restatement of the Law Governing Lawyers §50, comm. *g* (Prop. Final Draft #1, March 29, 1996).

75. See generally Lester Brickman & Lawrence A. Cunningham, Nonrefundable Retainers Revisited, 72 N.C. L. Rev. 1 (1993); Lester Brickman & Lawrence A. Cunningham, Nonrefundable Retainers: A Response to Critics of the Absolute Ban, 64 U. Cin. L. Rev. 11 (1995).

76. 633 N.E.2d 1069 (N.Y. 1994).

77. See also In re Thonert, 682 N.E.2d 522 (Ind. 1997) (nonrefundable retainer unethical in criminal case); In re Gastineau, 857 P.2d 136 (Or. 1993) (en banc) (use of numerous engagement agreements with nonrefundable retainers improper).

"Special nonrefundable retainer fee agreements diminish the core of the fiduciary relationship by substantially altering and economically chilling the client's unbridled prerogative to walk away from the lawyer."[78] If a nonrefundable special retainer is invalid, the attorney would be compensated for the reasonable value of the services rendered and would be required to refund to the client the balance of the retainer.

5. *Fee Splitting and Referral Fees*

The term *fee splitting* can refer to transactions both with nonlawyers and with lawyers. Fee splitting with nonlawyers has traditionally been improper because the practice can undermine the independence of lawyers and promote the unauthorized practice of law. See Model Rule 5.4(a). We will examine the wisdom of the rules prohibiting fee splitting with nonlawyers in Chapter 6.

Fee splitting between lawyers occurs when lawyers who are not members of a firm divide a fee in a matter. Fee splitting can arise in a variety of ways, for example, referral of a matter from one lawyer to another, association of attorneys in a case to handle different aspects of the matter, completion of a case by a second lawyer after the first lawyer withdrew from representation or after the client discharged the lawyer, and continuation of compensation to a retired member by the lawyer's former firm.

The most controversial aspect of fee splitting arises when a lawyer receives a pure referral or forwarding fee without performing any services. For example, suppose a lawyer who practices business and commercial law has a client with a personal injury claim. The lawyer might refer the case to a litigation specialist and seek a referral fee, typically one-third of the personal injury lawyer's one-third contingent fee.

The argument against allowing lawyers to pay and to receive referral fees rests on two concerns: First, referral fees result in clients paying excessive legal fees. If the lawyer performing services can afford to pay the referring lawyer a fee when the referring lawyer has performed no service, then the client is being overcharged. Second, the restriction prevents unethical practices, such as solicitation of business.

Critics of the prohibition on referral fees respond, however, that

78. 633 N.E.2d at 1072.

these concerns do not justify the prohibition. First, if rules permitted referral fees, clients would not be overcharged because referral fees would give lawyers a financial incentive to turn matters over to specialists, who presumably can handle matters more efficiently and with a higher degree of competence than generalists. Second, any concern about unethical practices should be dealt with by regulating those practices directly. Critics of the prohibition on pure referral fees also point out that it creates an arbitrary discrimination against sole practitioners and small firms because it only applies to lawyers who are not members of a firm. Lawyers in large firms are free to divide fees based on their partnership or shareholder agreements.

Under the Code of Professional Responsibility a pure referral fee —one in which the referring lawyer did nothing more than make the referral and did not perform any substantial services in the matter—was unethical. The Code provided that lawyers not in the same firm could divide fees only if the "division is made in proportion to the services performed and responsibility assumed by each." DR 2-107(A)(2). (The Code also required that the client consent to the division and that the total fee be reasonable.) Despite this prohibition, the practice of referral fees was apparently fairly widespread in the profession.[79]

The Model Rules have loosened the restriction on referral fees from that found in the Code of Professional Responsibility. Under Rule 1.5(e) a referral fee is permitted if:

> (1) The division is in proportion to the services performed by each lawyer *or,* by written agreement with the client, each lawyer assumes joint responsibility for the representation;
>
> (2) The client is advised of and does not object to the participation of all the lawyers involved; and
>
> (3) The total fee is reasonable. (Emphasis added.)

The key change from the Code is that the Model Rules allow a referral fee even in the absence of services performed by the referring lawyer if by written agreement with the client, each lawyer assumes joint responsibility for the matter. When does a referring lawyer assume joint responsibility for the matter? The comment

79. Wolfram, Modern Legal Ethics §9.2.4, at 510 (practice "both rife and virtually respectable in many communities").

provides: "Joint responsibility for the representation entails the obligations stated in Rule 5.1 for purposes of the matter involved." Rule 5.1, which deals with the obligations of partners and supervisory lawyers, states that a partner must take reasonable steps to ensure compliance by members of the firm with the Rules of Professional Conduct. Thus, a referring lawyer would assume joint responsibility if the lawyer undertook reasonable steps to make sure the lawyer handling the matter complied with the Rules of Professional Conduct. Periodic consultations on the strategy and progress of the matter should meet this requirement.

Professors Hazard and Hodes argue that the prohibition on pure referral fees should be repealed and lawyers allowed to act as "talent scouts."[80] Professor Wolfram argues that the Model Rule does not adequately address the issue of client consent because it only requires the clients to be advised of the referral arrangement and "not object." He argues in favor of rules, like those adopted in California and Illinois, that require client consent after the client is fully informed about the terms and reasons for the fee sharing arrangement.[81] It should be noted that many states in addition to California and Illinois have modified the ABA's version of Rule 1.5(e).[82]

Suppose lawyers enter into a fee splitting agreement that violates Rule 1.5(e) (for example, suppose the lawyers fail to obtain a written agreement with the client regarding their joint responsibilities). Is the agreement between the lawyers unenforceable? The courts are divided on the issue of the contractual effect of a fee splitting agreement that violates the Rules of Professional Conduct. Some courts refuse to enforce such an agreement because it violates public policy, while others will enforce the agreement under principles of estoppel to prevent unjust enrichment.[83]

80. 1 Hazard & Hodes, The Law of Lawyering §1.5:601.

81. Wolfram, Modern Legal Ethics §9.2.4, at 512.

82. See Lawyers' Manual on Prof. Conduct (ABA/BNA) 41:702-704.

83. Compare Lemond v. Jamail, 763 S.W.2d 910 (Tex. Ct. App. 1989, writ ref'd n.r.e.) (fee splitting agreement void because it violates public policy), with King v. Housel, 556 N.E.2d 501 (Ohio 1990) (attorney estopped to claim that fee splitting agreement was invalid). Panels of the Seventh Circuit have reached opposite conclusions on this issue. Compare Kaplan v. Pavalon & Gifford, 12 F.3d 87 (7th Cir. 1993) (under Illinois law oral fee splitting agreement that had not been approved by client was unenforceable), with Freeman v. Mayer, 95 F.3d 569 (7th Cir. 1996) (under Indiana law lawyer may not rely on technical failure of fee splitting agreement to comply with rules of ethics to justify refusal to honor agreement with another lawyer because the rule was for the protection of clients).

6. *Lawyer Interests in Literary or Media Rights*

Another provision restricting legal fees is Model Rule 1.8(d), which provides as follows:

> Prior to the conclusion of representation of a client, a lawyer shall not make or negotiate an agreement giving the lawyer literary or media rights to a portrayal or account based in substantial part on information relating to the representation.[84]

While the rule applies to both civil and criminal cases, it comes up more frequently in criminal cases because they are more likely to be sensational than civil cases.

The rule prohibits lawyers in highly publicized criminal cases from entering into fee agreements with their clients in which the lawyers' fees would consist of an interest in literary or movie rights resulting from the cases. The rationale for the rule is to prevent lawyers from having a financial interest that would interfere with their independent professional judgment. For example, with such a fee agreement a lawyer might be inclined to forgo plea bargaining to sensationalize the case and thereby increase the value of the lawyer's interest in media or literary rights.[85] The scope of the rule, however, is such that its restrictions may not be important. The rule only applies to agreements made "[p]rior to the conclusion of representation of a client." Presumably this means that after the conclusion of the criminal matter, a lawyer could agree to represent the client in connection with literary or media rights growing out of the case, with the lawyer receiving an interest in such rights as payment for the lawyer's services. Even before the conclusion of representation, the rule does not prohibit a lawyer from representing a client with regard to the client's literary or media rights, so long as the lawyer did not have an interest in the client's literary or media rights, even if the client might use the income that resulted to pay the lawyer's fees.[86]

The California Supreme Court has held that, in order to be able to retain counsel, a criminal defendant may consent to a fee agree-

84. See also Restatement of the Law Governing Lawyers §48(3) (Prop. Final Draft #1, March 29, 1996).

85. See id. §48, comm. *d*.

86. Id.

ment in which the lawyer has an interest in literary or media rights.[87] The California Rules of Professional Conduct, however, do not have a provision like Model Rule 1.8(d). It appears that the drafters of the Model Rules intended to prohibit such fee agreements even with client consent because the drafters concluded that such fee agreements inherently involved a conflict of interest.[88]

It is also interesting to note that a number of states have enacted statutes to prevent criminal defendants from profiting from commercial exploitation of their crimes. (Such statutes are often referred to as "Son of Sam" laws, after the New York serial killer David Berkowitz, who used that signature.) These statutes typically require convicted criminals to pay any funds received from commercial portrayals of their crimes to a fund for victims of their crimes. In Simon & Schuster, Inc. v. Members of the New York State Crime Victims Board,[89] the Supreme Court held the New York statute invalid under the First Amendment. In 1992, the New York legislature passed a revised law.[90]

7. *Expenses*

Deposition costs, expert witness fees, copying charges, and travel expenses all make litigation costly. Who is responsible for these expenses? Lawyers act as agents for their clients; since the client is the principal, the client is legally responsible for the expenses of litigation. If the lawyer has advanced the expense on behalf of the client, the client is legally obligated to indemnify the lawyer.[91] Although the client is ultimately responsible for these expenses, the lawyer may also be liable to the provider of the service. For example, in Cahn v. Fisher,[92] the Arizona Court of Appeals held that while a client is responsible for litigation costs, based on "custom and usage," an attorney was also legally responsible for

87. Maxwell v. Superior Court, 639 P.2d 248 (Cal. 1982) (en banc).

88. See 1 Hazard & Hodes, The Law of Lawyering §1.8:501, at 271 n.1.

89. 502 U.S. 105 (1991).

90. See N.Y. Exec. Law §632-a (McKinney 1996). For an analysis of the Supreme Court's decision in *Simon & Schuster* and of the revised law, see Amr F. Amer, Comment, Play it Again Sam: New York's Renewed Effort to Enact a "Son of Sam" Law that Passes Constitutional Muster, 14 Loy. L.A. Ent. L.J. 115 (1993).

91. Restatement of the Law Governing Lawyers §29(2) (Prop. Final Draft #1, March 29, 1996).

92. 805 P.2d 1040 (Ariz. Ct. App. 1991, rev. den.).

paying a court reporter's charges when the attorney orders a transcript.[93]

While the client is legally responsible for expenses of litigation, many clients may not be able to afford these costs. May lawyers loan or advance litigation expenses on behalf of their clients? At common law the crime of *maintenance* prohibited advances of money to pay expenses or otherwise support litigation. A related offense, *champerty,* involved the purchase of a portion of the lawsuit. The evil to be prevented in both cases was "stirring up" litigation.[94] A more modern rationale for the prohibition against lawyers' advancing expenses other than expenses of litigation to their clients is that the lawyer becomes a creditor, with interests adverse to those of the client, and this interest may cause the lawyer to conduct the litigation to protect the lawyer's rather than the client's interest. This justification is weak, however, because contingent fee agreements also give lawyers an interest in litigation that may cause them to conduct the litigation to protect their interest over those of their clients. These prohibitions have been gradually relaxed so that lawyers can now advance "court costs and expenses of litigation," with repayment contingent on the outcome of the case. See Model Rule 1.8(e)(1).[95] The Model Rules go even further in the case of indigent clients, allowing lawyers to agree to pay litigation expenses with no responsibility for repayment. Model Rule 1.8(e)(2). While the rules of professional conduct allow lawyers to advance litigation expenses, lawyers are not required to do so. Lawyers may demand that clients make expense deposits and may bill them periodically for expenses incurred in their cases.

Although the rules of ethics permit lawyers to advance litigation

93. See Restatement of the Law Governing Lawyers §42(2)(b) (Prop. Final Draft #1, March 29, 1996):

> A lawyer is subject to liability to a third person on contracts the lawyer entered into on behalf of a client, unless the lawyer or third person disclaimed such liability, if: . . .
>
> (b) the contract is between the lawyer and a third person who provides goods or services used by lawyers and who, as the lawyer knows or reasonably should know, relies on the lawyer's credit.

94. Wolfram, Modern Legal Ethics §8.13, at 489-490.

95. See also Restatement of the Law Governing Lawyers §48(2)(a) (Prop. Final Draft #1, March 29, 1996).

expenses on behalf of clients, the rules still prohibit attorneys from making general advances or loans. Thus, in Formal Opinion 288, the ABA Committee on Ethics and Professional Responsibility stated:

> For a lawyer to make advances to an injured client to cover subsistence for him and for the members of his family while the case is pending, does not constitute the advancement of expenses, the latter term referring to court costs, witness fees and expenses resulting from the conduct of the litigation itself, and not expenses unconnected with the litigation, although resulting from the accident.

The prohibition against advancing living expenses to clients apparently also extends to guarantees by lawyers of loans to clients made by third parties. Disciplinary Rule 5-103(B) states that a lawyer must not "advance or guarantee financial assistance." Model Rule 1.8(e) states that a lawyer may not "provide financial assistance," without mentioning guarantees, but Professor Wolfram argues that the change in wording is not significant and that the Model Rules as well as the Code were intended to prohibit a lawyer from helping the client to obtain a loan on the lawyer's credit.[96] Presumably a lawyer could, however, assist a client in obtaining a loan for living expenses, so long as the lawyer did not make any guarantees to the lender.

Early drafts of the Model Rules would have allowed lawyers to advance living expenses to clients, but this proposal was rejected in Model Rule 1.8(e).[97] The drafters of the Restatement of the Law Governing Lawyers proposed to change the rule. Proposed §48(2) would have allowed a lawyer to

> [m]ake or guarantee a loan on fair terms, the repayment of which to the lawyer may be contingent on the outcome of the matter, if: (i) the loan is needed to enable the client to withstand delay in litigation that otherwise might unjustly induce the client to settle or dismiss a case because of financial hardship rather than on the merits; and (ii) if the lawyer does not promise or offer the loan before being retained.

96. Wolfram, Modern Legal Ethics §9.2.3, at 509 n.87.

97. ABA Comm. on Evaluation of Prof. Standards, Model Rules of Prof. Conduct Rule 1.8(e)(1) (Prop. Final Draft, May 30, 1991).

The ALI, however, ultimately decided to reject this proposal in favor of the traditional prohibition against advancement of living expenses. The Restatement proposal seems correct. In some cases clients may be desperately in need of funds for living expenses, but unable to obtain those funds from any source. These circumstances could force clients to agree to settle their cases on unfavorable terms. Most lawyers already have substantial financial interests in their clients' cases under contingent fee and expense advancement agreements. Giving lawyers the additional interest resulting from making loans for living expenses is unlikely to reduce their independence. Some courts have agreed and allow lawyers to advance living expenses to their clients for humanitarian reasons, while others continue to apply the traditional prohibition.[98]

What litigation expenses may lawyers properly charge to their clients? Expenses involved in litigation commonly include the following: filing fees, costs of transcribing depositions, fees of expert witnesses, travel expenses, photocopying, long-distance telephone or fax charges, and computer research charges. In Formal Opinion 93-379, the ABA Committee on Ethics and Professional Responsibility considered various billing practices by lawyers. The Committee ruled that general office overhead (library, insurance, rent, utilities, and similar items) was not properly chargeable as an expense to clients absent disclosure to the client in advance of the engagement.[99] The Committee decided that lawyers could not ethically charge clients for expenses in excess of actual disbursements, absent disclosure to the contrary.[100] In other words, markups or surcharges on expenses are improper unless the client consents after clear disclosure from the lawyer. The Committee also considered in-house provision of services, such as photocopying, in-house meals, and similar items. As to these expenses, absent agreement to the contrary, lawyers may not ethically charge more than "the direct cost associated with the service (i.e., the actual cost

98. See Florida Bar v. Taylor, 648 So. 2d 1190 (Fla. 1994) (lawyer not subject to discipline for providing needy client with used clothing and $200 loan when lawyer acted for humanitarian reasons). But see Mississippi Bar v. Attorney HH, 671 So. 2d 1293 (Miss. 1995) (advancement of living expenses even for humanitarian purposes is improper).

99. ABA Comm. on Ethics and Prof. Resp., Formal Opinion 93-379, at 8. See also Restatement of the Law Governing Lawyers §50(3)(a) (Prop. Final Draft #1, March 29, 1996).

100. Opinion 93-379, at 9.

of making a copy on the photocopy machine) plus a reasonable allocation of overhead expenses directly associated with the provision of the service (e.g., the salary of a photocopy machine operator)," as determined by standard accounting methods.[101] In its opinion, the Committee emphasized the lawyer's duty to disclose to clients at the beginning of the representation the basis of the fee and other charges to the client.[102]

8. *Lawyers' Liens*

Model Rule 1.8(j) prohibits lawyers from acquiring a proprietary interest in the cause of action or subject of litigation except for reasonable contingent fees in civil cases and "a lien granted by law to secure the lawyer's fee or expenses."[103] Courts have generally recognized two types of lawyers' liens. The *retaining lien* is the attorney's right to retain client papers or other valuable client property in the lawyer's possession as security for any unpaid amount the client owes the lawyer.[104] The lien arises as a matter of law rather than pursuant to contract and is based on equitable principles: The attorney has rendered substantial services or advanced expenses on the client's behalf and should be entitled to compensation. The lien is purely possessory; the lawyer may not sell the client's property to satisfy the client's debt to the lawyer. Because of the coercive aspects of the lien, some jurisdictions no longer recognize the lien, and others have cautioned lawyers against exercising the lien when the client would be prejudiced. For example, in Informal Opinion 1461 (1980), the ABA Committee on Ethics and Professional Responsibility suggested that attorneys should forgo exercising a retaining lien if the client would be seriously prejudiced by the lawyer's actions. The Committee stated

101. Id.
102. Id. at 3.
103. See Restatement of the Law Governing Lawyers §48(1) (Prop. Final Draft #1, March 29, 1996). Lawyers may acquire an interest in a client's venture that is not subject to litigation. Thus, a lawyer may obtain an ownership interest in a client's business while representing the client provided the lawyer complies with the stringent requirements for business transactions between lawyer and client. See Model Rule 1.8(a); Chapter 3.N infra.
104. On the retaining lien, see generally Wolfram, Modern Legal Ethics §9.6.3, at 559-560.

that a lawyer could properly exercise the lien when the client was engaging in fraud or "gross imposition."

The Restatement of the Law Governing Lawyers rejects the general concept of a retaining lien unless established by statute because of its coercive aspects,[105] although the drafters recognize that their position represents a minority view.[106] Under the Restatement, however, a lawyer may retain a document prepared by the lawyer for which the client has not paid the lawyer, but even in this situation the lawyer cannot do so if retention of the document will unreasonably harm the client.[107] Thus, a lawyer may not refuse to record a deed because the client has not paid the lawyer's fee.[108]

The second form of lien is the *charging lien,* which is applied against the proceeds of any settlement or judgment for the amount of any unpaid fees or expenses due the attorney. Where recognized, the charging lien is generally based on statute.[109] When created by statute, lawyers must obviously comply with statutory requirements for perfection and enforcement of a charging lien.[110]

May a lawyer ethically enter into a fee agreement that provides for a contractual charging lien? Professor Wolfram argues that contractual charging liens are of doubtful validity because Model Rule 1.8(j) prohibits a lawyer from acquiring an interest in the client's cause of action, except for liens recognized by law.[111] In a few jurisdictions, however, courts recognize contractually created liens,[112] and the proposed Restatement of the Law Governing Lawyers would allow lawyers to contract with clients for charging liens, unless prohibited by statute or court rule.[113] For a lien to be

105. Restatement of the Law Governing Lawyers §55(1) and comms. *a, b* (Prop. Final Draft #1, March 29, 1996).

106. Id. §55, comm. *b.*

107. Id. §55, comm. *c.*

108. Id.

109. Wolfram, Modern Legal Ethics §9.6.3, at 561-562.

110. See In re Marriage of Etcheverry, 921 P.2d 82 (Colo. Ct. App. 1996) (against public policy to allow statutorily created charging lien to attach to child support payments).

111. Wolfram, Modern Legal Ethics §9.6.3, at 562.

112. See Eleazer v. Hardaway Concrete Co., 315 S.E.2d 174 (S.C. Ct. App. 1984) (recognizing common law charging lien on settlement or judgment for expenses, but not for legal fees; attorney and client may agree that attorney has lien on settlement or judgment).

113. Restatement of the Law Governing Lawyers §55(2) and comms. *d, e* (Prop. Final Draft #1, March 29, 1996).

effective against third parties (for example, an insurance company or successor counsel), lawyers must give notice of a charging lien to such party.[114]

Lawyers may also enter into contracts with their clients in which they obtain a security interest or mortgage in the clients' property to secure payment of their fees. Because security agreements between clients and lawyers are somewhat unusual, courts are likely to scrutinize such a security arrangement under fiduciary principles of fairness and full disclosure.[115] Some states may prohibit or limit lawyers from obtaining security interests or mortgages to secure payment of their fees. For example, in domestic cases in New York, lawyers may obtain a mortgage or security interest to secure their fees only when the retainer agreement provides for such an interest, notice of an application for a security interest has been given to the other spouse, and the court grants approval for the application of a security interest after submission of an application for counsel fees. In addition, a lawyer in New York may not foreclose a mortgage on a primary residence while the consenting spouse remains in the residence.[116]

D. TRUST ACCOUNTS AND CLIENT PROPERTY

Lawyers often come into possession of client money or property, or money or property belonging to a third person. In personal injury matters, lawyers receive and disburse settlement proceeds. In real estate matters, lawyers receive and disburse payments for property. In business transactions, lawyers can receive and disburse funds in a corporate acquisition. Model Rule 1.15,[117] dealing with lawyers' obligations regarding money and property belonging to clients and third parties, imposes several obligations:

114. Id. §55, comm. *e*.
115. See id. §55(4) and comm. *i*.
116. Procedure for Attorneys in Domestic Relations Matters, N.Y. Sup. Ct. Rules §1400.5.
117. Restatement of the Law Governing Lawyers §§56 and 57 (Prop. Final Draft #1, March 29, 1996) impose similar duties.

- *The duty not to commingle.* Lawyers must keep money and property belonging to clients and third persons separate from their personal and firm funds.

The rule against commingling acts as a prophylactic against lawyer misuse of client funds and protects such funds from being subject to the claims of lawyers' creditors.[118] Lawyers have been disciplined for commingling even when clients have not suffered any financial harm and even when the lawyer acted innocently.[119] The standard method used to prevent commingling is establishment of escrow or trust accounts, separate from lawyers' general accounts, into which money belonging to a client or third party is deposited. It is unnecessary for lawyers to have a separate account for each client or third party. Client and third party funds may be combined with the funds of other clients and third parties in one account, so long as lawyers' records identify the share of each client or third party and so long as the account is separate from the lawyer's funds.[120] Since funds in trust accounts belong to the clients, lawyers may not receive interest on the account. If the account is interest-bearing, the interest must be allocated to the clients. In many states, court rules allow lawyers to participate in IOLTA (interest on lawyer trust account) programs, in which interest in trust accounts is paid to a special fund to be used for a public purpose, typically delivery of legal services to indigents.[121] As noted previously, lawyers must deposit special retainers and expense advances in their trust accounts. When fees are earned or expenses incurred, lawyers must withdraw these funds from their trust accounts, so long as there is no dispute about the lawyer's right to receive these funds.[122]

- *The duty to maintain records.* Lawyers must keep careful records of client money and property that comes into their possession. Model Rule 1.15(a) provides that records shall be kept for a

118. Id. §56, comm. *b*.

119. See State ex rel. Oklahoma Bar Assn. v. Watson, 897 P.2d 246 (Okla. 1994).

120. Restatement of the Law Governing Lawyers §56, comm. *d* (Prop. Final Draft #1, March 29, 1996).

121. In Washington Legal Found. v. Texas Equal Access to Justice Found., 94 F.3d 996 (5th Cir. 1996), *cert. granted*, 117 S. Ct. 2535 (1997), the Fifth Circuit held that Texas's IOLTA program was unconstitutional because it deprived clients of property rights without their consent.

122. Restatement of the Law Governing Lawyers §56, comm. *f* (Prop. Final Draft #1, March 29, 1996).

period of five years after termination of representation, but prudent lawyers will keep important records indefinitely.

- *The duty to notify promptly* clients or third parties when lawyers receive money or property in which clients or third parties have an interest.
- *The duty to deliver promptly* to clients or third parties any funds or other property in which such person has an interest.
- On request, *the duty to render a full accounting* regarding such money and property.

An issue that comes up quite frequently in personal injury matters deals with a lawyer's obligation to make payments to third parties out of the proceeds of personal injury settlements. Clients often make assignments of the proceeds of their personal injury claims to providers of medical services or to businesses (for example, the client might assign the proceeds to purchase a vehicle or to pay a debt). When the case is settled, however, the client may object to the lawyer honoring the assignment. Model Rule 1.15(b) provides that "a lawyer shall promptly deliver to the client or third person any funds or other property that the client or third person is entitled to receive." The rule recognizes that parties other than the client may have an interest in money that comes into the lawyer's possession. Comment 3 to Rule 1.15 provides that "under applicable law" a lawyer may have a duty to a third party that precludes the lawyer from surrendering property to the client. When does applicable law provide such a duty? In some cases, statutes may provide for subrogation or lien rights of third party providers. The courts that have considered the issue have held that lawyers have a contractual and ethical duty to honor any valid assignment or lien of which the lawyer has received notice.[123] In the event of a dispute between the client and a third party, a lawyer should hold the funds in trust until the dispute is resolved. See Model Rule 1.15(c).

Real estate practice has also generated issues regarding trust accounts. A major issue that has troubled real estate attorneys deals

123. E.g., Kaiser Found. Health Plan, Inc. v. Aguiluz, 54 Cal. Rptr. 2d 665 (Cal. Ct. App. 1996) (lawyer who disbursed entire settlement to client was liable to health care provider when lawyer had received notice of client's assignment to provider); Herzog v. Irace, 594 A.2d 1106 (Me. 1991) (lawyer liable to doctor for failure to honor assignment); Leon v. Martinez, 638 N.E.2d 511 (N.Y. 1994) (lawyer required to honor assignment of portion of personal injury proceeds made by client).

with disbursement of funds at closing. The parties who receive money from the transaction, usually the seller and any real estate brokers, want to take their checks with them from the closing. The closing attorney typically receives funds at closing from the lender and the buyer. But even if the lawyer deposits these funds immediately, the lawyer's bank has not yet collected these funds. If the lawyer issues checks to the seller and broker at closing and later either the buyer's or the lender's check is not honored for some reason, then the lawyer has an escrow account problem. If the escrow account contains the funds of other clients, which is normally the case, the lawyer will have disbursed funds belonging to other clients. The lawyer could try to stop payment on checks issued to the seller or brokers, but it may be too late to do so.[124]

Various ways exist for lawyers to avoid the problem of disbursement against uncollected funds: In Advisory Opinion 454 (1980),[125] the New Jersey Supreme Court Advisory Committee on Professional Ethics suggested three possibilities:

> (1) escrow closings in which no funds are disbursed and no closing completed until all funds have cleared;
> (2) pre-arrangement by the attorneys involved so that the necessary closing figures are known far enough in advance for the parties to provide funds in such a manner as to obviate the necessity of using the trust account (undoubtedly this would require cooperation of the bank-mortgagee which may be asked to provide mortgage funds in several checks);
> (3) establishment of an account by the attorney of his own funds which can be used to accommodate a client when there is no other solution.

The Committee understood, however, that these solutions might not be practical. It then addressed the question of whether it was ever proper for an attorney to disburse funds at a real estate closing from uncollected funds. Recognizing the practical reasons and customary practice of doing so among many attorneys, the Committee ruled that an attorney could properly disburse at closing from uncollected funds if the funds consisted of a certified or cashier's check issued by a bank. The Committee concluded that such disbursements involved almost nonexistent risk because the

124. See Legacy Homes, Inc. v. Cole, 421 S.E.2d 127 (Ga. Ct. App. 1992).
125. 1980 WL 78467, at 2-3.

checks were the obligations of the bank rather than a private party. Later the Committee extended this rule to cashier's and certified checks issued by savings and loan institutions. The Committee went on to make clear that disbursement against the personal check of the buyer was improper.[126]

While receptive to the practicalities of real estate practice, the approach authorized by the New Jersey Committee does expose attorneys and clients who have funds in escrow accounts to some degree of risk. Indeed, given the debacle in the savings and loan industry, the Committee's assumption that checks issued by financial institutions bear almost no risk can be questioned. Most states do not follow the New Jersey approach and prohibit lawyers from making disbursements against uncollected funds.

Regardless of the area of practice, every client matter involves one form of client property—the client's file. Model Rule 1.15 does not speak directly to lawyer's obligations regarding the client's file, but §58 of the proposed Restatement of the Law Governing Lawyers does provide some specific standards. Lawyers have a duty to take reasonable steps to safeguard documents in the lawyer's possession relating to representation of a client.[127] Clients ordinarily have the right to inspect and copy documents in their files, but a lawyer may refuse to allow the client to do so when a substantial reason exists, for example if the file contains documents subject to a protective order.[128] Clients do not have a right, however, to inspect or copy internal firm memoranda (as distinguished from research memoranda) that may be in the file.[129] On termination of representation, the client is entitled to receive all documents in the file, except internal firm memoranda.[130] The firm may not charge the client for making copies of documents that the client is entitled to receive; if the firm wishes to retain copies, it may do so at its own expense.[131] As noted above, some jurisdictions recognize a retaining lien that allows lawyers to retain possession of the file

126. See In re Moras, 619 A.2d 1007, 1010 (N.J. 1993).

127. Restatement of the Law Governing Lawyers §58(1) (Prop. Final Draft #1, March 29, 1996).

128. Id. §58(2) and comm. *c*.

129. Id.

130. Id. §58(3).

131. Id. comm. *e*. See In re Admonition Issued to X.Y., 529 N.W.2d 688 (Minn. 1995) (absent specific provision in engagement agreement lawyer may not charge client for copying file on withdrawal because file belongs to client).

until outstanding fees and expenses are paid.[132] The Restatement rejects the general concept of a retaining lien, but the Restatement allows lawyers to retain specific documents that they have prepared when the client has not paid the fee or expenses associated with preparation of the document, provided that nondelivery would not substantially harm the client.[133]

E. POWER IN THE CLIENT-LAWYER RELATIONSHIP

1. *Scope of Representation*

Client-lawyer agreements are contracts, subject to the rules of contract law, but are also governed by a number of special rules that apply because of the fiduciary relationship between attorney and client.[134] The agreement between the client and the lawyer determines the matters in which the lawyer represents the client. Courts are likely, however, to resolve any ambiguities and uncertainties in the agreement against the lawyer;[135] thus, lawyers must define clearly the matters for which they are agreeing to represent their clients. For example, if a lawyer agrees to represent a client in "your suit," a court is likely to conclude that the lawyer has agreed to represent the client in any appeal arising from the action.[136] Even if the agreement between the client and the lawyer provided that the lawyer agreed only to represent the client at trial, the lawyer would still be required to move to withdraw from the case after trial and to take reasonable steps to protect the client's right to appeal if the lawyer did not plan to handle the appeal.[137]

When lawyers undertake representation on behalf of a client in one matter arising from an occurrence in which the client may have

132. See Chapter 2.C.8 supra.

133. Restatement of the Law Governing Lawyers §55(1) (Prop. Final Draft #1, March 29, 1996).

134. Id. §29A, comm. *c*.

135. Id. §29A(2) (agreement should be construed from the standpoint of a reasonable person in the client's circumstances).

136. Id. §29A, comm. *h* & illus. 4.

137. See id. §45.

multiple claims, lawyers must exercise due care to inform their clients of their other rights. In Nichols v. Keller,[138] the California Court of Appeals held that a lawyer who was retained to handle a worker's compensation case had a duty either to investigate claims against third parties arising from the occurrence or to advise the client to seek other representation with regard to such claims.

While it is clearly permissible for the client and lawyer to define the matters in which the attorney is undertaking representation, may they agree to limit the extent of the lawyer's duties in handling a matter? A lawyer may not enter into an agreement with the client prospectively limiting the lawyer's liability for malpractice.[139] Such an agreement undermines the lawyer's duty to represent the client competently and diligently; moreover, clients may not have sufficient information to evaluate the reasonableness of such a disclaimer.[140] Thus, it would be unethical and contractually unenforceable for an engagement agreement to disclaim liability for malpractice. An agreement to submit fees disputes or malpractice claims to arbitration may, however, be enforceable, depending on the jurisdiction.[141]

Suppose, however, that the agreement does not go this far. For example, may the lawyer and client agree that the lawyer will "spend no more than five hours on this matter"? Agreements that limit the scope of a lawyer's duties can be beneficial to clients because they allow clients to obtain the degree of representation that they desire. Clients, like buyers of other goods and services, should be entitled to purchase different degrees of quality. On the other hand, some clients, particularly unsophisticated ones, may not understand the level of service that they are purchasing. The

138. 19 Cal. Rptr. 2d 601 (Cal. Ct. App. 1993).

139. Model Rule 1.8(h). The Model Rule qualifies the prohibition by stating "unless permitted by law and the client is independently represented in making the agreement." The Restatement of the Law Governing Lawyers, however, contains an absolute prohibition because no such law exists. Section 76, Reporter's Notes to comm. *b* (Tent. Draft #8, March 21, 1997).

140. Id. comm. *b*.

141. Compare Ohio Sup. Ct. Bd. of Commn. on Grievances & Disc. Op. #96-9 (1996), 1996 WL 734408 (engagement agreement should not contain arbitration provision) with Powers v. Dickson, Carlson & Campillo, 63 Cal. Rptr. 2d 261 (Cal. Ct. App. 1997) (under California law agreements to submit fee disputes and malpractice claims to arbitration are enforceable).

Model Rules are unclear on whether agreements that limit the scope of a lawyers' duties are valid. Model Rule 1.2(c) states that a "lawyer may limit the objectives of the representation if the client consents after consultation." The comments, however, state that an agreement that limits the scope of representation so as to violate the duty of competency is unenforceable under Model Rule 1.1. See Comments 4 and 5.

The Restatement of the Law Governing Lawyers is more tolerant of agreements limiting the scope of representation. Section 30 of the proposed Restatement allows such agreements if (1) the client is adequately informed and consents and (2) the terms of the limitation are reasonable in the circumstances. The comments elaborate on the reasonableness requirement:

> When the client is sophisticated in such waivers, informed consent ordinarily permits the inference that the waiver is reasonable. For other clients, the requirement is met if, in addition to informed consent, the benefits supposedly obtained by the waiver—typically, a reduced legal fee or the ability to retain a particularly able lawyer—could reasonably be considered to outweigh the potential risk posed by the limitation.[142]

2. *Allocation of Authority Between Lawyer and Client*

Issues of authority between attorney and client can arise in two ways. First, as between lawyer and client, has the attorney acted with authority? Second, is the client bound to a third party by virtue of an agreement or action taken by the lawyer, even if the lawyer acted without authority?[143]

As to the allocation of authority between client and lawyer, traditionally many attorneys viewed themselves as experts entrusted to handle their clients' matters as they thought to be in the best interest of the client.[144] The Rules of Professional Conduct and Restatement of the Law Governing Lawyers reject this paternalistic

142. Restatement of the Law Governing Lawyers §30, comm. *c* (Prop. Final Draft #1, March 29, 1996).

143. Compare id. Ch. 2, Topic 3 (Authority to Make Decisions) and Topic 4 (Lawyer's Authority to Act for Client).

144. See Douglas E. Rosenthal, Lawyer and Client, Who's in Charge? 7 (1974).

view of the client-lawyer relationship because it suffers from fundamental defects. The expert model subordinates the actual client to the lawyer's view of the client's interests. In addition, this approach ignores the fact that the full participation of clients can improve the quality of the lawyer's representation because clients have information and perspectives that lawyers lack.[145]

Under the Model Rules and principles of agency law, a distinction is drawn been objectives of representation and means to achieve those objectives. Thus, Model Rule 1.2(a) provides: "A lawyer shall abide by a client's decisions concerning the objectives of representation [subject to certain limitations] and shall consult with the client as to the means by which they are to be pursued."[146] Model Rule 1.2(a) identifies the following matters as decisions for the client to make: whether to accept an offer of settlement in a civil case, and in criminal cases, the plea to be entered, whether to waive jury trial, and whether the client will testify.[147] While the Model Rules do not mention the determination whether to appeal as a decision for the client to make, most other authorities do so.[148]

Although clients are entitled to make decisions regarding the objectives of representation, lawyers have a duty to counsel their clients regarding these matters. See Model Rule 2.1.[149] The role of counselor gives lawyers broad authority to advise their clients on both legal and nonlegal considerations involved in a proposed course of action. Model Rule 2.1 states that in providing advice, "a lawyer may refer not only to law but to other considerations such as moral, economic, social and political factors, that may be relevant to the client's situation."[150] The client's right to make decisions regarding the objectives of representation does not mean, however, that lawyers must follow every decision that clients make. In rep-

145. See Restatement of the Law Governing Lawyers, Ch. 2, Topic 3, Introductory Note (Prop. Final Draft #1, March 29, 1996).

146. See ABA Standards for Criminal Justice, Defense Function Standard 4-5.2 (3d ed. 1992) (hereinafter cited as "ABA Defense Function Standard") (distinguishing fundamental decisions that clients are entitled to make based on advice of lawyers from strategic and tactical decisions that lawyers are authorized to make after consultation with clients where feasible).

147. See also Restatement of the Law Governing Lawyers §33 (Prop. Final Draft #1, March 29, 1996).

148. See id. §33(1); ABA Defense Function Standard 4-5.2.

149. See Restatement of the Law Governing Lawyers §31(3) (Prop. Final Draft #1, March 29, 1996).

150. See also Restatement of the Law Governing Lawyers §151(3) (Tent. Draft #8, March 21, 1997).

resenting clients lawyers may not counsel or assist them to engage in conduct that the lawyer knows to be criminal, fraudulent, or in violation of a court order; lawyers who do so face the possibility of professional discipline[151] and civil liability either to the client or to third persons.[152] For example, a lawyer may not advise a client to destroy documents to hide criminal activity,[153] may not draft documents to transfer a client's assets when the lawyer knows that the transfer would be a fraud on creditors,[154] and may not prepare fraudulent tax returns for a client.[155] Chapter 4.F considers the application of this principle to situations in which lawyers obtain possession of tangible criminal material, including physical evidence of a crime, stolen property, and contraband. The prohibition on counseling or assisting a client in conduct that the lawyer knows to be criminal, fraudulent, or in violation of a court order is, however, a narrow one. The Restatement proposes the following test:

> [T]he lawyer may counsel or assist a client to take or fail to take action for which the lawyer reasonably believes the client can assert a nonfrivolous argument that the client's action will not constitute a crime or fraud or violate a court order, such as when the action constitutes a good faith effort to determine the validity, scope, meaning, or application of a law or court order.[156]

Further, a lawyer must "know" that a client's conduct is illegal or fraudulent; mere suspicion is not sufficient, although a lawyer's knowledge can be inferred from the circumstances.[157]

A vast number of decisions in a case are strategic or tactical rather than relating to the objectives of representation. What causes of action should be included in the complaint? How many expert witnesses should the client retain? What discovery should be done? What witnesses will be called to testify at trial? Should counsel object to a question at trial? Lawyers have broad authority

151. See Model Rule 1.2(d); Restatement of the Law Governing Lawyers §151(2) (Tent. Draft #8, March 21, 1997).

152. See id. §151(1).

153. United States v. Perlstein, 126 F.2d 789 (3d Cir. 1942), *cert. denied*, 316 U.S. 679 (1942).

154. Townsend v. State Bar of California, 197 P.2d 326 (Cal. 1948) (en banc).

155. Committee on Legal Ethics v. Hart, 410 S.E.2d 714 (W. Va. 1991).

156. See Restatement of the Law Governing Lawyers §151(2) (Tent. Draft #8, March 21, 1997) and Model Rule 1.2(d).

157. See Restatement of the Law Governing Lawyers §151, comm. *g* (Tent. Draft #8, March 21, 1997).

to make strategic and tactical decisions in connection with the representation to advance the client's interest.[158] The lawyer's authority to make these decisions can be limited in several ways. Clients and lawyers are generally free to allocate the authority to make strategic and tactical decisions by contract.[159] The lawyer's engagement could, for example, specify that the lawyer may not employ an expert witness without the client's approval, or it could authorize the lawyer to engage in such discovery as the lawyer believes necessary, subject to a budget. Further, lawyers are required to keep their clients reasonably informed about the client's matter.[160] Clients may give lawyers instructions during the course of representation regarding strategic and tactical decisions, and lawyers are generally bound to follow these instructions, unless the client directs the lawyer to act unethically or illegally.[161] Thus, a client could instruct the lawyer that the client does not want to go to the expense of taking the deposition of an expert witness. Some tactical matters require immediate action—for example, the decision whether to object to a question at trial—so that consultation with the client is impractical. In these situations, lawyers have the authority to make the decision without client consultation.[162]

Suppose a lawyer believes that the client's instructions are "tying my hands" so that the lawyer cannot effectively carry out the representation? The lawyer may counsel the client about the wisdom of the client's decision. See Model Rule 2.1. If the issue involves a litigation expense that the client is unwilling to incur, with client consent the lawyer could advance the expense. See Model Rule 1.8(e). Finally, the lawyer could move to withdraw from the matter if the client's instructions make it unreasonably difficult for the lawyer to carry out the representation.[163]

158. See Model Rule 1.2(a); Restatement of the Law Governing Lawyers §32(3) and comm. *e* (Prop. Final Draft #1, March 29, 1996).

159. Restatement of the Law Governing Lawyers §32(1) and comm. *c* (Prop. Final Draft #1, March 29, 1996).

160. See Model Rule 1.4; Restatement of the Law Governing Lawyers §31(1) (Prop. Final Draft #1, March 29, 1996).

161. Restatement of the Law Governing Lawyers §32(2), comm. *d* and §34 (Prop. Final Draft #1, March 29, 1996).

162. See id. §32, comm. *e* and §34, comm. *d*.

163. See Model Rule 1.16(b), which allows a lawyer to withdraw if the client decides on a course of action that the lawyer believes is "imprudent" or if "good cause" exists for withdrawal. See also Restatement of the Law Governing Lawyers §44(3) (Prop. Final Draft #1, March 29, 1996).

The principles discussed above govern the allocation of authority between lawyer and client. Under what circumstances is a client legally bound to a third person as a result of the lawyer's actions on behalf of the client? When a lawyer proceeds with express authority, the lawyer's action binds the client.[164] In addition, agency law provides that the actions of an agent bind the principal when the agent acts with implied or apparent authority, when the principal ratifies the agent's conduct, or when the principal is estopped to deny the agent's authority. For example, normally an attorney would have implied authority to agree to a trial date.[165]

Settlement of a lawsuit is a common situation involving the impact of the lawyer's authority on third persons. Suppose the plaintiff authorizes a lawyer to settle a case for any amount in excess of $200,000. The client is bound if the lawyer agrees to such a settlement. If the client then refuses to proceed with the settlement, the opposing party could take legal steps to enforce the settlement (for example, a motion to the tribunal before which the case is pending to compel settlement). On the other hand, suppose a lawyer agrees to a settlement that the client has not authorized. Normally, an attorney does not have apparent authority to settle a case on behalf of a client.[166] Thus, the client is not bound by the settlement. A lawyer who acts without authority is subject to disciplinary action, legal liability to the client, and legal liability to third persons harmed by the lawyer's unauthorized action.[167]

3. *Disabled Clients*

The rules of professional conduct generally assume that lawyers represent clients who are able to communicate with their lawyers and to make decisions about their cases based on the advice of counsel. See Model Rule 1.2(a). Suppose this assumption fails: A

164. Restatement of the Law Governing Lawyers §38 and comm. *d* (Prop. Final Draft #1, March 29, 1996).

165. See id. §§38, 39 & illus. 1.

166. Id. §39, comm. *d*. But see Clark v. Burden, 917 S.W.2d 574 (Ky. 1996) (normally client is only bound to settlement when lawyer acts with express authority, but client is bound by unauthorized settlement if other party is "substantially and adversely" affected).

167. See Restatement of the Law Governing Lawyers §42 (Prop. Final Draft #1, March 29, 1996).

lawyer represents a client who is not fully competent and who is making decisions that the lawyer believes to be harmful to the client, such as refusing to raise certain defenses or refusing to accept a favorable plea bargain. A client's incompetency could be caused by mental retardation, physical disability, or addiction to drugs. In addition, lawyers who represent children also face the issue of dealing with clients who may have less than full capacity. How should lawyers proceed when they represent impaired clients?

In civil cases it is helpful to distinguish three roles that lawyers perform. First, in some cases a court may appoint a lawyer to serve as guardian ad litem for an incompetent client. When appointed as a guardian, the lawyer is no longer acting in a legal capacity. The guardian's role is to determine what is in the best interest of the ward and to report those findings to the court.[168] Second, in some cases a court may appoint both a guardian ad litem and an attorney to represent the guardian in court. The appointment of a separate guardian and lawyer clarifies the lawyer's responsibilities. In this situation the lawyer is acting in a legal capacity as attorney for the guardian. Generally, the lawyer should look to the guardian for decisions that affect the client. The guardian, after all, has been appointed by the court to make those decisions. See Model Rule 1.14, Comment 3.[169] Occasions will arise, however, when lawyers may need to take action to protect the interests of the ward against misconduct by the guardian. The clearest case occurs when the guardian is improperly using the ward's money or property. See Model Rule 1.14, Comment 4.

The most difficult role for an attorney occurs when the attorney represents a client suffering from some degree of disability but the court has not appointed a guardian ad litem to make decisions on the client's behalf. Such cases are troublesome because the lawyer has not been appointed as guardian for the client and is therefore not authorized to make decisions on the client's behalf, yet at the same time the client is not fully competent to make decisions. Typical situations in which lawyers can face this problem are

168. Roy T. Stuckey, Guardians Ad Litem as Surrogate Parents: Implications for Role Definition and Confidentiality, 64 Fordham L. Rev. 1785 (1996).

169. See also 1 Hazard & Hodes, The Law of Lawyering §1.14:302; Restatement of the Law Governing Lawyers §35(3) (Prop. Final Draft #1, March 29, 1996).

domestic cases involving custody of minor children, cases involving developmentally disabled clients, and civil commitment proceedings.

As a general proposition lawyers should maintain a normal client-attorney relationship with an impaired client to the maximum extent possible. Model Rule 1.14(a).[170] Thus, the lawyer is required to communicate information to the client and to assist the client in making decisions regarding the representation. This view is based on two propositions, one empirical, the other moral. Empirically, clients suffer from different degrees of impairment, from the relatively mild to the incapacitating. Many clients with some degree of impairment can participate in decisions affecting their lives. Morally, even when a client suffers from an impairment, the client is still entitled to exercise personal liberty to the maximum extent possible.[171] In In re M.R.,[172] the New Jersey Supreme Court described the role of an attorney appointed to represent the interests of a developmentally disabled client:

> [A] declaration of incompetency does not deprive a developmentally-disabled person of the right to make all decisions. The primary duty of the attorney for such a person is to protect that person's rights, including the right to make decisions on specific matters. Generally, the attorney should advocate any decision made by the developmentally-disabled person. On perceiving a conflict between that person's preferences and best interests, the attorney may inform the court of the possible need for a guardian ad litem. . . . Our endeavor is to respect everyone's right of self-determination, including the right of the developmentally disabled. . . .[173]

Suppose a lawyer is unsure whether a client is competent to participate in making decisions. How should the lawyer proceed? As an initial step, the lawyer may want to consult with a psychiatrist or psychologist to obtain medical advice about the client's condition. May the lawyer do so if the client refuses to consent to such a consultation? In Informal Opinion 89-1530, the ABA Committee on Ethics and Professional Responsibility advised that law-

170. See also Restatement of the Law Governing Lawyers §35(1) (Prop. Final Draft #1, March 29, 1996).

171. See Model Rule 1.14, comm. 2; Restatement of the Law Governing Lawyers §35, comm. *c* (Prop. Final Draft #1, March 29, 1996).

172. 638 A.2d 1274 (N.J. 1994).

173. Id. at 1285.

yers may do so and that any disclosures they made would not violate their duty of confidentiality:

> [D]isclosures necessary for the lawyer to seek expert advice when there is reason to suspect impairment threatening serious harm to the client are impliedly authorized in order to carry out the representation within the meaning of Model Rule 1.6. Otherwise, Rule 1.14 could not work effectively and the Model Rules would be internally inconsistent. Disclosures necessary under Rule 1.14 would be prohibited by the provisions of Model Rule 1.6.[174]

If a lawyer concludes that the client is incompetent and is unable to make decisions regarding the representation, the lawyer has several choices on how to proceed. The lawyer could seek the appointment of a general guardian for the clients' property (referred to as a conservator in many jurisdictions) or a guardian ad litem to determine the client's interest in litigation. See Model Rule 1.14(b).[175] When a guardian has been appointed, the guardian is then legally authorized to make decisions on behalf of the client. The lawyer should generally follow the decisions of the guardian unless the guardian is engaged in conduct that amounts to a breach of fiduciary duty.[176]

Appointment of a guardian is a serious step that deprives the client of a substantial degree of personal liberty. Comment 3 to Model Rule 1.14 notes that appointment of a guardian may be "expensive or traumatic for the client." Thus, lawyers must exercise professional discretion in deciding whether to seek the appointment of a guardian, considering the costs and benefits to the client, along with the other possible options for dealing with the client's incompetency.[177]

What options other than appointment of a guardian ad litem should a lawyer consider? Some clients may be willing to execute general or limited powers of attorney giving another person the

174. ABA Comm. on Ethics and Prof. Resp., Informal Opinion 89-1530, at 3. In Formal Opinion 96-404, the ABA Committee reaffirmed Informal Opinion 89-1530 and discussed other issues facing lawyers who represent disabled clients. See also Model Rule 1.14, comm. 5; Restatement of the Law Governing Lawyers §35, comm. *d* (Prop. Final Draft #1, March 29, 1996).

175. See also Restatement of the Law Governing Lawyers §35(4) (Prop. Final Draft #1, March 29, 1996).

176. See id. §35(3) and comm. *f*.

177. See Model Rule 1.14(b) and comm. 2.

power to make decisions on their behalf.[178] The attorney may enlist the participation of family members to assist the client in making decisions. Finally, the attorney may assume greater decisionmaking authority, deciding what a reasonable person in the client's position would do, even if that decision conflicts with the view expressed by the client.[179] Acting as a "de facto" guardian is obviously an extreme step that lawyers should take only under unusual circumstances. In Formal Opinion 96-404, the ABA Committee on Ethics and Professional Responsibility advised lawyers that the "action taken should be the least restrictive of the client's autonomy that will yet adequately protect the client in connection with the representation."[180]

Criminal cases pose special problems for lawyers representing incapacitated clients because due process requires that criminal defendants be competent to stand trial.[181] If a lawyer in a criminal case believes that the client is incompetent, one option to deal with the problem is for the lawyer to inform the court so that the court can hold a hearing on the defendant's competency to stand trial. In some cases, however, defense counsel may conclude that it is more advantageous for an incompetent defendant to proceed to trial than to raise an incompetency issue. The American Bar Association's Criminal Justice Mental Health Standards summarize the reasons why defense counsel could reach this conclusion:

> An involuntary commitment for treatment to restore competence may extend well beyond the maximum sentence imposable for a relatively minor offense. A defendant could view the stigma flowing from a finding of mental illness as more opprobrious than that

178. Restatement of the Law Governing Lawyers §35, comm. *e* (Prop. Final Draft #1, March 29, 1996).

179. See Model Rule 1.14 comm. 2 (lawyer must sometimes act as de facto guardian). See also Restatement of the Law Governing Lawyers §35(2) and comm. *d* (Prop. Final Draft #1, March 29, 1996).

180. ABA Comm. on Ethics and Prof. Resp., Formal Opinion 96-404, at 9. See also Paul R. Tremblay, On Persuasion and Paternalism: Lawyer Decisionmaking and the Questionably Competent Client, 1987 Utah L. Rev. 515. Working from a premise of informed consent by clients, Tremblay argues that all of the choices available to lawyers who represent questionably competent clients are troublesome, but that some of the choices are ethically more defensible than others. He would prohibit lawyers from acting as de facto guardians except in emergencies and would only allow lawyers to seek the appointment of guardians in extreme cases. He favors enlisting the support of family members and persuasion for dealing with clients who have diminished capacity.

181. Drope v. Missouri, 420 U.S. 162 (1975); Pate v. Robinson, 383 U.S. 375 (1966).

> generated by a criminal conviction. An evaluation may force a defendant to reveal to a court-appointed expert information the defendant would prefer to keep secret. . . . A defendant might even prefer to be punished through imprisonment than to experience commitment to a mental hospital for treatment, given the marginal conditions in many public mental institutions. If the prosecution case against a defendant is weak, or if a defendant's assistance is not actually required during trial, defense counsel may believe that an acquittal is likely even though defendant is incompetent.[182]

One federal study has shown that confinement for mental illness typically exceeds that for the underlying offense. In the study, the median length of commitment of felony not-guilty-by-reason-of-insanity patients was 49.2 months, while that for convicted felons was 33.4 months.[183]

May defense counsel decide as a matter of strategy not to inform the court when counsel has substantial doubts about a criminal defendant's competence to stand trial? (Of course, even if defense counsel does not raise the issue, either the prosecutor or the court on its own motion may do so.)[184] Despite the considerations noted above, the ABA's Criminal Justice Mental Health Standards require defense counsel to move the court for a competency determination when "defense counsel has a good faith doubt as to the defendant's competence."[185] While recognizing that in some cases it may not be to the advantage of a defendant to raise the issue of competency, the commentary to the Standards justifies imposing a duty on defense counsel to inform the court of the defendant's incompetency because of counsel's duty to the system: "Because the trial of an incompetent defendant necessarily is invalid as a violation of due process, a defense lawyer's duty to maintain the integrity of judicial proceedings requires that a trial court be advised of the defendant's possible incompetence."[186]

The Model Rules, in contrast to the Mental Health Standards, do not in Rule 1.14 impose on the lawyer a duty of disclosure. Com-

182. ABA, Criminal Justice Mental Health Standard 7-4.2, at 179-180 (1989).

183. Paul A. Chernoff & William G. Schaffer, Defending the Mentally Ill: Ethical Quicksand, 10 Am. Crim. L. Rev. 505, 523-524 n.65 (1972).

184. See ABA, Criminal Justice Mental Health Standard 7-4.2 (1989).

185. Id. Standard 7-4.2(c).

186. Id. at 180. See Norma Schrock, Note, Defense Counsel's Role in Determining Competency to Stand Trial, 9 Geo. J. Legal Ethics 639 (1996) (arguing that lawyers should have duty to bring to attention of court issue of defendant's competency to stand trial).

ment 5 to Rule 1.14 simply states that the "lawyer's position in such cases is an unavoidably difficult one." Similarly, the Restatement of the Law Governing Lawyers states that lawyers do not have a duty to inform a tribunal of a defendant's possible incompetency when the lawyer concludes that such disclosure would not be in the client's interest, unless law imposes such an obligation.[187] In some jurisdictions, however, court decisions may impose a duty on defense counsel to bring the client's possible incompetency to the attention of a tribunal. In State v. Johnson,[188] the Wisconsin Supreme Court held that a defendant had been denied effective assistance of counsel in a murder case when his lawyer did not inform the court that the defendant might not be competent to stand trial. The court rejected arguments that defense counsel had acted properly because he had concluded that the defendant was competent and because he decided that it was not strategically wise to raise the incompetency issue. The court held that when defense counsel has "a reason to doubt the competency of his client to stand trial, he must raise the issue with the trial court."[189]

Suppose counsel represents a defendant that the lawyer concludes is competent to stand trial, or that the court has found to be competent to stand trial. The lawyer may still have doubts about the defendant's decisionmaking capacities. What if anything should the lawyer do if the defendant insists on entering a plea or demands that the lawyer conduct the case in a fashion that the lawyer concludes is clearly not in the client's best interest? Competent clients generally have the authority to make the ultimate decisions about their cases.[190] Federal and state courts have recognized that competent defendants cannot be compelled to raise insanity defenses against their wishes.[191] The view that a competent defendant cannot be compelled to raise an insanity defense finds support in the Supreme Court's decision in Faretta v. California,[192] where the Court held that the Sixth Amendment guarantees

187. Restatement of the Law Governing Lawyers §35, comm. *d* (Prop. Final Draft #1, March 29, 1996).

188. 395 N.W.2d 176 (Wis. 1986).

189. Id. at 182.

190. See ABA Model Rule 1.2(a); ABA Defense Function Standard 4-5.2(a).

191. See United States v. Marble, 940 F.2d 1543 (D.C. Cir. 1991); People v. Gauze, 542 P.2d 1365 (Cal. 1975) (en banc).

192. 422 U.S. 806 (1975).

criminal defendants the right to proceed without counsel when they voluntarily and intelligently elect to do so.

If a competent defendant has the right to decide whether to plead guilty or to raise an insanity defense, defense counsel who strongly disagrees with the decision has a limited number of choices: attempt to persuade the defendant, bring the matter to the attention of the court so that the court can determine the defendant's competency to make the decision, move to withdraw on the ground that the client "insists upon pursuing an objective that the lawyer considers repugnant or imprudent" under Model Rule 1.16(b)(3), or follow the client's directions.[193]

4. *Sexual Relations Between Lawyers and Clients*

In 1992 the ABA Committee on Ethics and Professional Responsibility made the following observation:

> Although no detailed statistics are presently available to document the incidence of sexual relations between clients and their lawyers, there is information enough to substantiate both the existence and the seriousness of problems in this area.[194]

The Committee went on to conclude that although no specific Model Rule prohibited sexual relations between lawyers and clients, such relationships could lead to abuse of fiduciary obligations, impairment of independent judgment, involvement in conflicts of interest, and exposure of confidential information. Because of these risks the Committee warned that the "lawyer would be well advised to refrain from such a relationship." If such a relationship occurs and the client-lawyer relationship has been impaired, the lawyer will have violated the rules of professional conduct.[195]

193. See Red Dog v. State, 625 A.2d 245 (Del. 1993) (defendant has right to decide to forgo appeals and accept death penalty; defense counsel who finds client's decision repugnant should move to withdraw; defense counsel who has "reasonable and objective basis" to doubt client's competency must in a timely fashion inform trial court and request competency determination).

194. ABA Comm. on Ethics and Prof. Resp., Formal Opinion 92-364, at 1-2.

195. Id. at 9.

Some states have gone further to deal with the problem of sexual relations between lawyers and clients. A California statute provides that an attorney engages in misconduct if the attorney (1) expressly or impliedly conditions performance of legal services on the client's willingness to engage in sexual relations, (2) employs coercion or undue influence in entering into sexual relations, or (3) continues representation of the client if the sexual relationship would cause the lawyer to act incompetently or to otherwise prejudice the client's case.[196] The statute provides several exceptions, one of which is for sexual relationships that predate the formation of the client-lawyer relationship.[197]

A number of state supreme courts have adopted rules defining when sexual relationships between lawyers and their clients are improper. These rules typically provide that such relationships are improper unless the relationship was in existence before the attorney began representing the client.[198]

These rules do not seem sufficiently responsive to the problem. Given human nature, sexual relationships between lawyers and clients will occur, but there is no justification for a lawyer continuing to represent a client in an adversarial proceeding when such a relationship develops.[199] Any lawyer who has a sexual relationship with a client should immediately withdraw from the representation and assist the client in obtaining other counsel. In In re DiPippo,[200] the Rhode Island Supreme Court held that it was impermissible for a lawyer to continue representation of a client in a divorce case that involved issues of child custody, support, and distribution of marital assets when the lawyer had an intimate, consensual relationship with the client. Even that case, however, did not go far enough because the court's per se rule only applies to representation in divorce cases.

196. Cal. Bus. & Prof. Code §6106.9(a) (Supp. 1997).

197. Id. §6106.9(b).

198. See Minn. R. Prof. Conduct 1.8(k); Or. Code Prof. Resp. DR 5-110; Wis. R. Prof. Conduct 1.8(k).

199. On representation in transactional matters, see Model Rule 1.8(c) which provides that a lawyer "shall not prepare an instrument giving the lawyer or a person related to the lawyer as parent, child, sibling, or spouse any substantial gift from a client, including a testamentary gift, except where the client is related to the donee."

200. 678 A.2d 454 (R.I. 1996).

F. TERMINATION OF THE CLIENT-LAWYER RELATIONSHIP

1. *Discharge of Lawyer by Client*

Almost all jurisdictions follow the rule that a client has the absolute right to discharge an attorney, regardless of cause. Courts reason that the relationship of client and attorney is highly personal, and that clients should not be limited in their right to select counsel of their choice.[201] Recognition that the client has the right to discharge an attorney at any time for any reason, however, creates a potential problem of unfairness to the attorney. How should an attorney be compensated when the client has exercised the right to discharge the attorney?

In the typical case, it seems equitable to compensate discharged attorneys for the reasonable value of their services, i.e., on a quantum meruit basis.[202] This method of compensation protects the client's right to discharge an attorney and protects the attorney's right to compensation for services rendered. Extreme cases could justify deviation from the quantum meruit rule. For example, if the client discharged the attorney because of the attorney's serious misconduct, a court might find that fee forfeiture was appropriate.[203] At the other extreme, if the client discharged an attorney shortly before concluding a settlement, to deprive the attorney of a contingent fee that was all but earned, a court might allow the attorney to receive the full contractual amount rather than quan-

201. See Wolfram, Modern Legal Ethics §9.5.2, at 545; Restatement of the Law Governing Lawyers §44(1) and comm. *b* (Prop. Final Draft #1, March 29, 1996). See also Cohen v. Radio-Electronics Officers Union, Dist. 3, NMEBA, 679 A.2d 1188 (N.J. 1996) (retainer agreement may not limit client's right to discharge lawyer but agreement may provide for compensation to attorney when client exercises right; six month's notice of termination held to be unreasonable, but court finds one month's notice reasonable).

202. See Wolfram, Modern Legal Ethics §9.5.2, at 546-547. See, e.g., Searcy, Denney, Scarola, Barnhart & Shipley, P.A. v. Poletz, 652 So. 2d 366 (Fla. 1995) (quantum meruit compensation to discharged contingent fee attorney measured by variety of factors rather than simply "lodestar," i.e., hourly rate amount).

203. See White v. McBride, 937 S.W.2d 796 (Tenn. 1996) (charging of excessive contingent fee in probate case was improper and justifies forfeiture of all compensation, including quantum meruit) and Restatement of the Law Governing Lawyers §49 (Prop. Final Draft #1, March 29, 1996).

tum meruit.[204] In this case, the client typically has acted in bad faith to deprive the lawyer of her fee. Moreover, allowing recovery at the full contractual rate does not burden the client's right to select counsel because the matter has been completed.[205]

In deciding the amount of quantum meruit recovery, courts should not determine the amount of recovery mechanically based simply on the number of hours that the attorney worked on the case. Instead, courts should examine a variety of factors, including the number of hours worked, the lawyer's hourly rate, the difficulty of the case, the stage of the case at which the lawyer was discharged, and the benefits received by the client. A number of courts limit the amount of quantum meruit recovery to the ratable portion of the contract that has been performed (not always an easy task) on the theory that a discharged attorney should not receive a benefit in excess of the contract amount. In addition, allowing recovery in excess of the contract amount would burden the client's right to select new counsel. The Restatement of the Law Governing Lawyers adopts the view that a discharged attorney is entitled to recover quantum meruit, limited by the ratable portion of the contract that has been performed.[206] When awarding quantum meruit compensation under a contingent fee contract, it seems appropriate to defer the lawyer's right to recover in quantum meruit until the client receives an award, otherwise the client's right to discharge the attorney would be burdened by the obligation to pay the attorney immediate quantum meruit compensation.[207]

When an attorney is also an employee of an organization, rather than private counsel, the client's right of discharge has come into conflict with the attorney/employee's rights to be protected against wrongful discharge as reflected in various federal and state statutes. Because these statutes typically embody strong public policies, most courts have held that an attorney/employee who is

204. See Taylor v. Shigaki, 930 P.2d 340 (Wash. Ct. App. 1997) (lawyer entitled to full contingent fee when client discharged lawyer nine days before trial date, after substantial offer of settlement had been made, and six hours before client met with claims adjuster to negotiate final settlement); Restatement of the Law Governing Lawyers §52(2) (Prop. Final Draft #1, March 29, 1996).

205. See id. §52(2) and comm. *c*.

206. Id. §52(1).

207. See Rosenberg v. Levin, 409 So. 2d 1016 (Fla. 1982).

wrongfully discharged retains the same rights as other employees under such statutes.[208]

A lawyer who has been discharged may have a retaining lien on the client's file for unpaid fees and expenses, but as discussed previously lawyers must be cautious in asserting such a lien to avoid prejudice to the clients.[209] As a condition for releasing the file, some lawyers have demanded that clients' sign a release of liability. Such releases are generally unethical and unenforceable, unless the client is independently represented by counsel.[210]

2. *Withdrawal by Lawyer*

The rules on withdrawal by attorneys are divided into two categories: mandatory and permissive withdrawal. Under Model Rule 1.16(a), a lawyer must withdraw from representation if the representation will result in a violation of the Rules of Conduct (for example, if the lawyer faces a conflict of interest or if the client demands that the lawyer engage in illegal conduct). In addition, a lawyer must withdraw if the client discharges the lawyer or if the lawyer's physical or mental condition impairs the lawyer's ability to represent the client.[211] When a matter is pending before a tribunal, a lawyer who is ethically required to withdraw must still file a motion with the tribunal to obtain permission to withdraw.

Model Rule 1.16(b) deals with permissive withdrawal. The rule gives lawyers broad power to withdraw if "withdrawal can be accomplished without material adverse effect on the interests of the client." In addition to withdrawal without material adverse effect, Rule 1.16(b) specifies six situations in which withdrawal is permissive:

208. See General Dynamics Corp. v. Superior Court, 876 P.2d 487 (Cal. 1994) (en banc); GTE Prods. Corp. v. Stewart, 653 N.E.2d 161 (Mass. 1995); see also Restatement of the Law Governing Lawyers §44, comm. *b* (Prop. Final Draft #1, March 29, 1996).

209. See Chapter 2.C.8 supra.

210. See Model Rule 1.8(h); Restatement of the Law Governing Lawyers §76 (Tent. Draft #8, March 21, 1997). The Restatement makes some distinctions between the enforceability of such releases and standards for professional discipline. Compare §§76(2) and 76(3)(b).

211. See also Restatement of the Law Governing Lawyers §44(2) (Prop. Final Draft #1, March 29, 1996).

(1) the client persists in a course of action involving the lawyer's services that the lawyer reasonably believes is criminal or fraudulent;
(2) the client has used the lawyer's services to perpetrate a crime or fraud;
(3) a client insists upon pursuing an objective that the lawyer considers repugnant or imprudent;
(4) the client fails substantially to fulfill an obligation to the lawyer regarding the lawyer's services and has been given reasonable warning that the lawyer will withdraw unless the obligation is fulfilled;
(5) the representation will result in an unreasonable financial burden on the lawyer or has been rendered unreasonably difficult by the client; or
(6) other good cause for withdrawal exists.[212]

The proper scope of the withdrawal rules has engendered a good deal of discussion and debate. When the client is abusing the professional relationship, by demanding that the lawyer engage in illegal or unethical conduct, the lawyer's duty or right to withdraw is clear. May a lawyer withdraw if the client's conduct does not rise to this level? In extreme cases a lawyer may withdraw if the client insists on conduct that the lawyer considers to be "repugnant or imprudent."[213] Is this ground for withdrawal determined subjectively by the lawyer or is it subject to an objective standard? Given the fiduciary nature of the client-attorney relationship and the disruption that withdrawal can engender, it seems appropriate to require lawyers to have a reasonable basis for withdrawal. The Restatement takes the view that right to withdraw on this ground is limited to cases in which the client is demanding that the lawyer engage in conduct that no reasonable lawyer should be required to do.[214] Thus, in a death penalty case, if a client demanded that the lawyer put up no defense and dismiss all appeals, the lawyer would be justified in moving to withdraw because the client is in essence asking the lawyer to assist the client in committing suicide.

212. Restatement of the Law Governing Lawyers §44(3) (Prop. Final Draft #1, March 29, 1996), is substantially similar to Model Rule 1.16(b).

213. See Model Rule 1.16(b)(3); Restatement of the Law Governing Lawyers §44(3)(f) (Prop. Final Draft #1, March 29, 1996).

214. See Restatement of the Law Governing Lawyers §44, comm. *j* (Prop. Final Draft #1, March 29, 1996).

Some lawyers, however, in good conscience could proceed with this representation.

On the other hand, if the lawyer simply disagrees with the client's decision, even if the disagreement is strongly held, ground for withdrawal does not exist. For example, suppose a lawyer who represents a client in a personal injury action receives an offer to settle the case that the lawyer believes is reasonable, but which the client is unwilling to accept. Since the client retains the right to accept or reject settlement offers, a lawyer would not be justified in withdrawing when the client refused to accept the lawyer's recommendation regarding the settlement offer. Some courts have held that lawyers who withdraw under such circumstances forfeit their right to receive any fee.[215]

By agreeing to accept representation, attorneys make commitments to their clients to provide personal services. In addition, as discussed previously, in many cases attorneys agree to advance expenses on behalf of their clients. Sometimes cases turn out to be less valuable or more expensive than the attorney anticipated when the litigation began. May an attorney withdraw due to extreme financial hardship? The Model Rules allow an attorney to withdraw in such a situation provided court approval is obtained, Rule 1.16(b)(5); but the Restatement of the Law Governing Lawyers takes the position that financial hardship alone is not sufficient to justify withdrawal, although financial hardship is a factor that along with other factors can establish good cause for withdrawal.[216] The position of the Model Rules on this issue seems correct. Under general contract law a party may be excused from performance of the contract due to extreme expense when performance would be impracticable.[217] Attorneys should have the same right to seek contractual relief due to impracticability as other contracting parties, although the circumstances under which such relief is granted are likely to be rare. Some courts have agreed that lawyers should

215. See Augustson v. Linea Aerea Nacional-Chile, S.A., 76 F.3d 658 (5th Cir. 1996) (when law firm withdraws from case in dispute with client over settlement, firm is not entitled to any fee). But see Kannewurf v. Johns, 632 N.E.2d 711 (Ill. Ct. App. 1994) (lawyer who withdrew when fundamental disagreement about settlement of case entitled to quantum meruit compensation).

216. Restatement of the Law Governing Lawyers §44, comm. *m* (Prop. Final Draft #1, March 29, 1996).

217. See Restatement (Second) of Contracts §261 (1981).

be allowed to withdraw if continued representation would constitute an extreme financial hardship to the lawyer.[218] If the attorney voluntarily withdraws without cause, however, the lawyer may forfeit all right to compensation.[219]

Both the Model Rules and the Restatement of the Law Governing Lawyers allow a lawyer to withdraw if withdrawal can be accomplished without material adverse effect on the client.[220] For example, suppose a law firm represents corporate client *A* in a minor litigation matter that is in its early stages. Corporation *B* approaches the law firm to seek representation against client *A* in a major matter that is unrelated to the matter the firm is handling for client *A*. The firm seeks client *A*'s consent to undertake the representation, but client *A* refuses to consent. May the firm withdraw from representation of client *A* in order to take on the more lucrative representation of Corporation *B*, provided substitute counsel can be retained to represent *A* without material adverse effect on *A*? Professors Hazard and Hodes argue that the rules allow a lawyer to drop a client like a "hot potato" if withdrawal can be accomplished without material harm to the client, even if the lawyer is motivated solely by economic considerations.[221] Both the Model Rules and the Restatement of the Law Governing Lawyers seem to support this view by allowing a lawyer to withdraw for any reason, provided withdrawal can be accomplished without material adverse effect on the interests of the client.[222] Indeed, the Restatement recognizes that withdrawal in this case constitutes a breach of contract, but refers to the breach as "nominal." This approach seems wrong. First, the rule almost certainly violates reasonable client expectations. Most clients believe that when a lawyer has agreed to represent them, the lawyer cannot withdraw from representation for the lawyer's own financial interest, even if

218. Compare Haines v. Liggett Group, Inc., 814 F. Supp. 414 (D.N.J. 1993) (withdrawal denied; court notes absence of provision in contingent fee agreement allowing for withdrawal in event of financial hardship), with Smith v. R.J. Reynolds Tobacco Co., 630 A.2d 820 (N.J. Super. Ct. App. Div. 1993) (withdrawal for financial hardship permissible but case remanded for determination of probable recovery and anticipated litigation costs).

219. See Faro v. Romani, 641 So. 2d 69 (Fla. 1994).

220. See Model Rule 1.16(b); Restatement of the Law Governing Lawyers §44(3)(a) (Prop. Final Draft #1, March 29, 1996).

221. See 1 Hazard & Hodes, The Law of Lawyering §1.16:302 (authors recognize, however, that many courts and commentators disagree with this view).

222. See Model Rule 1.16(b); Restatement of the Law Governing Lawyers §44(3)(a) and comm. *h(ii)* (Prop. Final Draft #1, March 29, 1996).

the client would not be harmed. Second, it is unlikely that many cases would arise in which a lawyer could withdraw because of lack of material adverse effect. In almost any case that has gone beyond its earliest stages, withdrawal would result in material harm to the client. Finally, the rule does not serve any substantial lawyer interest. Lawyers can avoid the problem of undertaking representation during early stages by using *investigation agreements,* in which the lawyer agrees to investigate the matter before undertaking representation.

In terminating representation an attorney must take reasonable steps to protect the client's interest from prejudice.[223] Thus, if the time for filing an appeal is about to run out, an attorney whose representation has terminated should nonetheless file notice of the appeal to protect the client's interest.[224] The lawyer could then file a motion with the appellate court to withdraw from representation.

223. Restatement of the Law Governing Lawyers §45 (Prop. Final Draft #1, March 29, 1996).

224. Id. §45, comm. *b.*

CHAPTER 3
Loyalty

A. INTRODUCTION

One of the touchstones of a fiduciary relationship is loyalty to clients. The various rules dealing with conflicts of interest embody the scope and limitations of the principle of loyalty. What is a conflict of interest? The Restatement of the Law Governing Lawyers offers the following definition:

> A conflict of interest is involved if there is a substantial risk that the lawyer's representation of the client would be materially and adversely affected by the lawyer's own interests or by the lawyer's duties to another current client, a former client, or a third person.[1]

Two points about the concept of a conflict of interest are particularly worth noting. First, a conflict of interest exists not only when an interest has an actual impact on the lawyer's representation, but also when a substantial risk for an adverse impact occurs. As we will see, it is analytically useful to categorize conflicts as either

1. Restatement of the Law Governing Lawyers §201 (Prop. Final Draft #1, March 21, 1996).

"actual" or "potential." Second, conflicts of interest can arise from a variety of sources: current clients, former clients, lawyer's own interests, and interests of third parties. The various ways in which conflicts of interest occur make this area of lawyers' obligations particularly difficult.

Since a conflict of interest by definition poses a substantial risk of material harm to a client, it is plausible to suggest a simple rule governing conflicts of interest: "A lawyer may not represent a client if the representation involves a conflict of interest." Indeed, the rule could be simplified even further to the biblical injunction: "No man can serve two masters." This direct and simple approach to conflicts of interest, however, would be undesirable when applied to lawyers. The effect of this rule would be that lawyers could represent only one client at a time. Other clients who wanted to retain the services of the lawyer would be unable to do so. Further, a client who benefitted from the conflict of interest rule now would be barred from obtaining the lawyer's services in the future, if the lawyer was then representing another client. The only way in which a client could avoid this result would be to place the lawyer under contract where the lawyer agreed to represent only one client. Thus, a prohibition on conflicts of interest would likely result in the elimination of the private practice of law, with lawyers only being allowed to practice as employees of their clients. Since only large, corporate clients could afford to have lawyer/employees, representation of individuals would practically disappear. Our society already faces substantial problems in delivery of legal services; a prohibition on conflicts of interest would cause this problem to mushroom.

This analysis of the consequences of an absolute prohibition on conflicts of interest points toward a solution to this problem. If the clients who are affected by a conflict of interest are willing to consent to the lawyer's representation despite the existence of the conflict, the lawyer should be allowed to proceed. The Model Rules and the Restatement of the Law Governing Lawyers adopt this consent solution.[2] The principle that a lawyer may represent a client despite the presence of a conflict of interest if all affected parties consent to the representation poses a number of questions

2. See generally Model Rule 1.7; Restatement of the Law Governing Lawyers §202 (Prop. Final Draft #1, March 29, 1996). See also Task Force on Conflicts of Interest, Conflict of Interest Issues, 30 Bus. Law. 1381 (1995).

that are discussed in the sections that follow: Is a lawyer ever prohibited from representing clients with conflicting interests even when they are willing to consent to the representation? May a lawyer ever represent conflicting interests without the consent of all affected parties? When consent is required, what must a lawyer do to obtain effective consent?

As we will see in the material that follows, the conflict of interest rules are designed to protect both loyalty and confidentiality interests of clients. When lawyers practice together in a law firm or similar organization, the lawyers in the organization typically are linked financially so that the economic interest of one becomes the economic interest of all. In addition, in firms and other legal organizations, lawyers usually have access to all client files. Thus, the rules of professional conduct and court decisions have recognized the principle that conflict of interest rules apply vicariously or are imputed from one member of a firm to all members. In other words, if a lawyer in a firm cannot handle a matter because of a conflict of interest, the problem cannot be solved by having another lawyer in the firm handle the matter because that lawyer will be treated as having a conflict of interest by imputation.[3] The imputation rules obviously expand the scope of the conflict of interest rules, quite far in the case of multinational law firms. We will consider some of the issues involved in the imputation rule after examining the variety of conflicts of interests that lawyers face.

Part I
Actual Conflicts of Interest Between Clients

B. CURRENT CLIENTS IN A SINGLE, CONTESTED LITIGATION MATTER

Suppose a lawyer is asked to represent both sides in a contested litigation matter. May a lawyer do so with the consent of both parties? An initial reaction to this question is that such a case will never arise. Why would clients even consent to representation by

3. See Model Rule 1.10(a); Restatement of the Law Governing Lawyers §203 (Prop. Final Draft #1, March 29, 1996).

one lawyer in a contested litigation matter? Although such cases are rare, it is not difficult to imagine situations in which clients might believe that representation by a single lawyer in a contested matter was in their interest. Take, for example, a divorce case in which the parties have agreed on many major issues but have disagreed on one or two points, such as the amount of child support to be paid by one spouse. The clients might be willing to have one lawyer present their case to the court, outlining the areas in which they have reached agreement and presenting arguments on behalf of each as to the contested issue of child support. A desire to minimize legal fees coupled with trust in the lawyer are reasons why the clients might consent to such an arrangement.

Notwithstanding client consent, representation of clients with interests that are actually adverse in a single litigation matter is improper. As the California Court of Appeals stated in Klemm v. Superior Court[4]:

> As a matter of law a purported consent to dual representation of litigants with adverse interests at a contested hearing would be neither intelligent nor informed. Such representation would be per se inconsistent with the adversary position of an attorney in litigation, and common sense dictates that it would be unthinkable to permit an attorney to assume a position at a trial or hearing where he could not advocate the interests of one client without adversely injuring those of the other.[5]

While the court in *Klemm* based its prohibition on the clients' inability to give informed consent, a systemic justification can also be offered for the rule prohibiting a lawyer from representing clients with adverse interests in a single litigation matter. Our legal system produces decisions that serve as guidance for future conduct by third parties and as means for vindication of public interests. The adversarial nature of the system is based on the assumption of zealous representation by lawyers of the interests of their clients. If a lawyer's representation of a client is infected by a conflict of interest, the adversarial nature of the representation is undermined, and the public benefits flowing from the adversar-

4. 142 Cal. Rptr. 509 (Cal. Ct. App. 1977).

5. Id. at 512. See also Developments in the Law, Conflicts of Interest in the Legal Profession, 94 Harv. L. Rev. 1244, 1295-1296 (1981).

ial system may be reduced.[6] As the Restatement of the Law Governing Lawyers puts it, "the institutional interest in vigorous development of each client's position renders the conflict nonconsentable."[7]

Both the Model Rules and the Restatement of the Law Governing Lawyers adopt the view that representation of interests that are directly adverse in a contested litigation matter is improper, even with consent of all of the affected clients. The Restatement states:

> Notwithstanding the informed consent of each affected client or former client, a lawyer may not represent a client if: . . .
>
> (b) one client will assert a claim against the other in the same litigation;[8]

The Model Rules express the same prohibition against representation of adverse parties in a single contested litigation more obliquely than the Restatement. Rule 1.7(a) states that a lawyer may not represent a client whose interest is "directly adverse" to another client unless (1) "the lawyer reasonably believes the representation will not adversely affect the relationship with the other client; and (2) each client consents after consultation." While the text of the rule seems to allow such representation with client consent, comment 5 makes it clear that situations exist in which adverse representation is improper even with client consent. Comment 5 states that "when a disinterested lawyer would conclude that the client should not agree to the representation under the circumstances, the lawyer involved cannot properly ask for such agreement or provide representation on the basis of the client's consent." Given the nature of the adversarial system, a disinterested lawyer would not approve of representation of clients with directly adverse interests in a single contested litigation matter.

6. Professor Nancy Moore, however, has criticized the "public interest" justification for limiting client consent to multiple representation. She argues that the focus should be on the client's capacity for informed and voluntary consent. Nancy J. Moore, Conflicts of Interest in the Simultaneous Representation of Multiple Clients: A Proposed Solution to the Current Confusion and Controversy, 61 Tex. L. Rev. 211, 229-230 (1982).

7. Restatement of the Law Governing Lawyers §202, comm. *g(iii)* (Prop. Final Draft #1, March 29, 1996).

8. Id. §202(2)(b).

It is important to note the limitations of the principle prohibiting lawyers from representation of clients with such directly adverse interests. The prohibition does not apply when the adversity is potential rather than actual. In such cases, representation is often possible with the consent of the clients. Nor does the prohibition apply when the conflict arises in unrelated matters rather than in a single contested matter. Here also representation with client consent is permitted. Finally, lawyers may serve as intermediaries to attempt to resolve disputes between clients with their consent outside of litigation. These situations are discussed more fully in the sections that follow.

The rule prohibiting a lawyer from representing clients with directly adverse interests in a contested litigation matter applies even if the clients are nominally aligned on the same side of the case. A common situation involves representation of a driver and a passenger in litigation against the driver of another vehicle. A lawyer may not represent the driver and the passenger if the passenger will also be asserting a claim against her driver for negligence. The passenger's cross claim against her driver creates an actual conflict of interest in a single matter that cannot be cured by consent.[9] Once again careful analysis of the facts is important. If the passenger's claim against her driver is a potential rather than an actual one (for example, if it appears unlikely that the driver of the passenger's vehicle was negligent), then the lawyer may proceed with multiple representation provided the clients give appropriate consent.[10]

Sometimes what appears to be an actual conflict of interest between co-parties in litigation disappears because of a contractual relationship between the parties. Suppose a driver of a vehicle and the driver's employer are sued for negligence arising from a motor vehicle accident. If the driver were negligent, the employer would have a claim against the driver for indemnification. If the employer agreed to indemnify the driver against any negligence, however, then the actual conflict disappears and the lawyer may proceed

9. E.g., In re Shaw, 443 A.2d 670 (N.J. 1982); Fugnitto v. Fugnitto, 452 N.Y.S.2d 976 (App. Div. 1982); Jedwabny v. Philadelphia Trans. Co., 135 A.2d 252 (Pa. 1957), *cert. denied*, 355 U.S. 966 (1958).

10. Restatement of the Law Governing Lawyers §209, comm. *d(i), Clients aligned as co-plaintiffs* (Prop. Final Draft #1, March 29, 1996).

with multiple representation with the informed consent of the employee and employer.[11]

C. CURRENT CLIENTS IN UNRELATED MATTERS

Suppose a lawyer is asked to undertake representation of one person against another client of the lawyer, not in the same matter, but in an unrelated matter. Grievance Committee of the Bar of Hartford County v. Rottner illustrates this type of conflict.[12] In *Rottner,* Twible retained a law firm to represent him in a minor collection matter. While this case was pending, O'Brien asked the same firm to represent him in an action for assault and battery against Twible. Although the firm informed O'Brien that it had represented Twible in prior matters and was currently representing him in the collection case, the firm did not discuss O'Brien's case with Twible, nor did the firm obtain Twible's consent to representation. The firm then filed suit on O'Brien's behalf against Twible. The complaint sought both actual and punitive damages, claiming that Twible's conduct was "wilful, wanton, malicious, premeditated, and vindictive."[13] Despite protests from Twible, the firm continued representing O'Brien and even proceeded to attach Twible's home in connection with the case.

In finding that the lawyers involved in the matter were guilty of misconduct, the Connecticut Supreme Court discussed how a lawyer's representation against a client in an unrelated matter violates the principle of loyalty:

> When a client engages the services of a lawyer in a given piece of business he is entitled to feel that, until that business is finally disposed of in some manner, he has the undivided loyalty of the one upon whom he looks as his advocate and his champion. If, as in this case, he is sued and his home attached by his own attorney,

11. Restatement of the Law Governing Lawyers §209, comm. *d(ii), Clients aligned as co-defendants in civil case* (Prop. Final Draft #1, March 29, 1996).
12. 203 A.2d 82 (Conn. 1964).
13. Id. at 83.

> who is representing him in another matter, all feeling of loyalty is necessarily destroyed, and the profession is exposed to the charge that it is interested only in money.[14]

Rottner involved an individual client, but the courts have applied the same principle of loyalty to corporate clients. International Business Machines Corp. v. Levin[15] was an action under the federal antitrust laws by the plaintiffs, Levin and Levin Computer Corporation (LCC). The plaintiffs were represented by a law firm that had represented Levin since 1965. Beginning in 1971, the firm represented Levin and LCC in negotiations with IBM to purchase certain computer equipment on credit. IBM refused to grant purchasers of equipment financing terms as favorable as those offered to lessees. As a result Levin and LCC filed suit in June 1972, claiming that IBM had committed antitrust violations. Beginning in April 1970, other lawyers in the same firm had been representing IBM in unrelated labor matters. On the date when the firm filed the antitrust action, the firm was not handling a specific matter for IBM, but it did undertake labor work for IBM after commencing the litigation.

IBM representatives were originally unaware of the firm's dual representation. When they learned of the conflict, almost five years after the antitrust action was filed, IBM moved to disqualify the firm in the antitrust action. The firm argued that the dual representation would not have an adverse effect on its independent professional judgment on behalf of IBM. The Court of Appeals for the Third Circuit disagreed: "[A] possible effect on the quality of the attorney's services on behalf of the client being sued may be a diminution in the vigor of his representation of the client in the other matter."[16]

The court also held that there was a client-attorney relationship between the law firm and IBM even though the firm was not currently handling a matter for IBM at the time the firm filed suit on behalf of Levin and Levin Computer Corporation against IBM. The court stated:

14. Id. at 84. See also Committee on Legal Ethics v. Frame, 433 S.E.2d 579 (W. Va. 1993) (improper for lawyer to represent controlling shareholder of corporation in her divorce action while another lawyer in firm represented plaintiff in personal injury action against her corporation).

15. 579 F.2d 271 (3d Cir. 1978).

16. Id. at 280.

> Although [the law firm] had no specific assignment from IBM on hand on the day the antitrust complaint was filed and even though [it] performed services for IBM on a fee for service basis rather than pursuant to a retainer arrangement, the pattern of repeated retainers, both before and after the filing of the complaint, supports the finding of a continuous relationship.[17]

As these cases show, a lawyer's duty of loyalty precludes the lawyer from undertaking representation of one client against another client even if the matters are unrelated to one another.[18] Conflicts involving unrelated matters differ, however, from cases of adverse representation against a client in a single matter in two respects. First, because the matters are unrelated, the impact on the duty of loyalty is decreased. Second, the adverse representation in unrelated matters does not undermine the integrity of an adversarial presentation. Because of these differences, with informed client consent a lawyer may undertake representation of clients in unrelated matters.[19]

A good example of informed consent by a client to representation against it in unrelated matters is Unified Sewerage Agency v. Jelco, Inc.[20] In *Unified Sewerage*, a law firm was representing Teeples & Thatcher, a client that the firm had represented

17. Id. at 281.

18. Professor Thomas Morgan has criticized the per se rule prohibiting representation against a current client in an unrelated matter absent consent of both clients. He argues that *Rottner*, the foundation case for the rule, was correctly decided because of the personal nature of the case, but he claims that the decisions went awry when they began using a per se rule of disqualification regardless of the context. Morgan contends that the appearance of the per se rule in Model Rule 1.7(a) was a surprise that occurred late in the development of the Model Rules without adequate analysis of the cases or policy basis for the rule. Morgan argues that a materiality standard should be used. Lawyers should be prohibited from undertaking representation against current clients in unrelated matters without their consent only when the representation of either client may be materially limited. Thomas D. Morgan, Suing a Current Client, 1 J. Inst. Study Leg. Ethics 87 (1996). There are problems, however, with Morgan's approach. The per se rule found in Model Rule 1.7(a) has the advantage of clarity. Further, if the lawyer's representation would truly not have a material effect on the representation of either client, then the lawyer should be able to obtain client consent. If a client is unwilling to consent, the client is expressing a belief that the representation may be materially limited, and that should be enough to disqualify a lawyer from acting against a current client.

19. Model Rule 1.7(a) and comment 8; Restatement of the Law Governing Lawyers §209(2) (Prop. Final Draft #1, March 29, 1996).

20. 646 F.2d 1339 (9th Cir. 1981).

for over ten years, in an embryonic dispute with its general contractor, Jelco, when Jelco asked the same firm to represent it in a dispute with an electrical subcontractor. The firm advised Jelco of its representation of Teeples & Thatcher and informed Jelco that it could not undertake representation unless Jelco consented to the firm's continued representation of Teeples & Thatcher. Jelco's management, with full knowledge of the firm's representation of Teeples & Thatcher and with the advice of its general counsel, consented to the law firm's representation of Teeples & Thatcher. Subsequently, the firm filed suit in the name of Unified Sewerage for the benefit of Teeples & Thatcher against Jelco. The firm again asked Jelco whether it consented to the firm's continued representation of Teeples & Thatcher and Jelco once again gave its consent. A few months later, however, Jelco discharged the firm from handling the matter with the electrical subcontractor and also moved to disqualify the firm in the pending action brought by Unified.

The Court of Appeals for the Ninth Circuit affirmed the trial court's decision denying the motion for disqualification. While recognizing the general rule precluding representation against a present client, the court held that such representation was proper because Jelco had given informed consent. The court noted that the attorney must do more than simply inform the client of the conflict and obtain approval of the representation. The lawyer must explain the implications of the conflict to the client. On the facts of the case the court found that this requirement was satisfied. The court placed particular emphasis on the fact that Jelco's consent had been obtained after Jelco had consulted with its general counsel about the matter.

By contrast to *Unified Sewerage*, the court in International Business Machines Corp. v. Levin, above, held that the firm had not effectively obtained IBM's consent. Two partners in the law firm testified that they had independently obtained IBM's consent to the firm's representation of Levin, but representatives of IBM denied that they had given their consent. The Court of Appeals for the Third Circuit rejected the consent argument because it concluded that the law firm had not carried its burden of proving a "full disclosure" to IBM as required by DR 5-105(C) (the predecessor to Model Rule 1.7). The court noted that the alleged consent occurred during a telephone call that took at most three minutes.

D. FORMER CLIENTS AND FORMER PROSPECTIVE CLIENTS

In the first conflict of interest situation discussed in this chapter—representation of two clients with adverse interests in a contested matter — client consent is not sufficient to allow the lawyer to undertake the representation. In the second situation considered in this chapter—representation of one client against a second client in an unrelated matter—client consent is sufficient to allow the lawyer to proceed on behalf of both clients. Both of these types of conflicts of interest contrast with the form of conflict of interest discussed in this section: representation against a former client or a former prospective client.

Consider this example: A lawyer represented a manufacturing company (MANCO) in both litigation and nonlitigation matters for a number of years until the company decided to retain other counsel. A prospective client, a technology corporation (TECHIE), approaches the lawyer seeking representation in a patent litigation matter against MANCO. May the lawyer take the case? Is consent required? If so, who must consent?

An initial point to note is that before undertaking representation of TECHIE, the lawyer must fully disclose the lawyer's former representation of MANCO and must obtain TECHIE'S consent to the representation. The lawyer's prior representation of MANCO could have an impact on the lawyer's representation of TECHIE in several ways. First, the prior representation may reduce the lawyer's zealousness on behalf of TECHIE against MANCO. The lawyer may be inclined to "pull his punches," because he is dealing with a client with whom he had a prior professional relationship. Second, as discussed more fully below, it is often difficult to determine whether a lawyer may undertake representation against a former client without that client's consent. If the lawyer agrees to represent TECHIE against MANCO, MANCO might object to the representation and might take legal steps to prevent the representation from continuing, for example, by filing a motion to disqualify the lawyer from representing TECHIE. These collateral proceedings could delay TECHIE'S lawsuit and could increase its cost of litigation if new counsel must be retained to undertake the representation. In short, TECHIE has a right to a conflict-free counsel if it so desires. The lawyer must fully disclose its relationship with MANCO to enable TECHIE to make this decision.

In making disclosure to a prospective client of a lawyer's prior representation of a potential adversary, the lawyer must respect the confidentiality of the former client. Normally, the identity of a client and the fact of representation are not confidential. Thus, a lawyer could properly disclose the name of the former client and the general nature of the prior representation to the prospective client. For example, a disclosure of the following form would be proper:

> This firm previously represented MANCO from 1985 through 1995 in a variety of litigation and nonlitigation matters. In the firm's opinion, its prior representation of MANCO does not create a conflict of interest or preclude the firm from representing TECHIE in the patent litigation against MANCO for which TECHIE has sought the firm's services. Nonetheless, TECHIE should be aware that MANCO may object to the firm's representation of TECHIE and may take legal action to prevent this representation, such as filing a motion to disqualify this firm. If TECHIE wishes to retain this firm to represent it in the patent litigation against MANCO described above, TECHIE should indicate its understanding of and consent to the law firm's representation by signing this consent. By signing this consent, TECHIE represents to law firm that it has consulted with and obtained the advice of its in-house counsel regarding this potential conflict of interest to the extent it considers necessary. Should MANCO file a motion to disqualify this firm from representing TECHIE, this firm will defend such a motion without expense to TECHIE.

In some cases, however, the fact or nature of the prior representation may be confidential. Suppose, for example, that the prior representation involved a highly secret matter, perhaps a corporate acquisition that the former client decided to forgo. The lawyer's duty of confidentiality would preclude the lawyer from being able to make the disclosures necessary to obtain the consent of the prospective client to the representation. In such a situation, the lawyer must decline the representation of the prospective client.

Suppose the prospective client is willing to consent to the lawyer's representation against the firm's former client after the lawyer fully discloses the prior relationship to the prospective client. May the lawyer undertake the representation against the former client without that client's consent? To answer this question requires an analysis of the scope of the duty of loyalty and of the duty of confidentiality owed to former clients.

To what extent should a lawyer owe a duty of loyalty to a former client? A plausible answer is that a lawyer should have an absolute duty loyalty to a former client and may not do anything that will harm a former client. While plausible, this answer is unsound for a number of reasons. First, a duty of absolute loyalty to a former client would mean that a lawyer could never undertake representation against a former client without that client's consent. This rule would substantially limit the ability of other clients to select counsel of their choice. Second, a per se prohibition on representation against former clients might deter lawyers from taking on representation in relatively small matters because of concern that the representation would disqualify the lawyer from handling all unknown future matters against that client. Third, a duty of lifetime loyalty would almost certainly increase legal fees because lawyers would be forced to take into account the preclusive effect of representation of a client in deciding how much to charge the client for the lawyer's services. Finally, lawyers serve as agents for their clients. Under agency law, an agent after termination of employment may not use confidential information against the principal, but the agent is not prevented from competing with the principal.[21]

These considerations support rejection of the view that lawyers should have a general duty of loyalty to former clients. This is not to say, however, that lawyers have no duty of loyalty to former clients. If the prospective representation involves side switching, where the lawyer will be acting adversely to the former client in the very matter in which the lawyer previously represented the client, or if its involves an attack on the lawyer's own work product (for example, a challenge to a will drafted by the lawyer), then the duty of loyalty should preclude the lawyer from undertaking representation against a former client. Cases of side switching and attack on work product are quite different from a general duty of loyalty to a former client. Unlike a general duty of loyalty, the duty of loyalty in these two cases applies to specific matters in which the lawyer previously represented a client. In these cases, the lawyer has been compensated by the first client for performing

21. Restatement (Second) of Agency §396 (1958).

certain services and now purports to seek compensation from a second client for undoing the work that was done for the first client.[22]

While lawyers should owe former clients a limited but not a general duty of loyalty—a duty not to switch sides or to attack work product prepared for a former client—lawyers should have a general duty of confidentiality to former clients. Clients reasonably expect lawyers to keep their affairs confidential, not just for the duration of the representation but after the representation terminates as well. Further, a general duty of confidentiality does not have any of the adverse consequences associated with a general duty of loyalty because it does not result in a total prohibition on representation of other clients. Thus, both the Model Rules and the Restatement of the Law Governing Lawyering recognize the principle that lawyers owe a general duty of confidentiality to former clients.[23]

When a lawyer undertakes representation of a new client against a former client, a risk exists that the lawyer will intentionally or inadvertently disclose or use confidential information against the former client for the benefit of the new client. How can former clients be assured that their confidences will be protected against such misuse? One possible answer is absolute prohibition of representation against former clients, but as we saw previously the adverse consequences of this draconian solution warrant its rejection. Another possibility is to eschew the need for any special protection of the confidentiality of former clients. The machinery of the disciplinary system coupled with potential civil liability for breach of fiduciary obligations by disclosing confidential information already operate to protect the confidentiality interest of former clients. By way of comparison, lawyers owe a duty of confidentiality to current clients, yet no special protections or safeguards have been erected to protect the confidentiality interest of current clients. Why should such safeguards be necessary for former clients?

Although the argument against special safeguards to protect the confidentiality of former clients is a plausible one, the rules of professional conduct have developed to provide former clients

22. For a discussion of the prohibition on side switching and on attacking the lawyer's own work product, see Restatement of the Law Governing Lawyers §213, comms. *d(i), d(ii)* (Prop. Final Draft #1, March 29, 1996).

23. Model Rule 1.9(c); Restatement of the Law Governing Lawyers §§112, 213, comm. *f* (Prop. Final Draft #1, March 29, 1996).

with additional protection of their interest in confidentiality. Originally, neither the Code of Professional Responsibility nor the Canons of Ethics had a specific rule dealing with representation against a former client. In T.C. Theatre Corp. v. Warner Bros. Pictures, Inc.,[24] however, Judge Weinfeld articulated a principle for deciding when a lawyer could properly undertake representation against a former client:

> I hold that the former client need show no more than that the matters embraced within the pending suit wherein his former attorney appears on behalf of his adversary are substantially related to the matters or cause of action wherein the attorney previously represented him, the former client. The court will assume that during the course of the former representation confidences were disclosed to the attorney bearing on the subject matter of the representation. It will not inquire into their nature and extent. Only in this manner can the lawyer's duty of absolute fidelity be enforced and the spirit of the rule relating to privileged communications be maintained.
>
> . . . In cases of this sort the court must ask whether it can reasonably be said that in the course of the former representation the attorney might have acquired information related to the subject of his subsequent representation. If so, then the relationship between the two matters is sufficiently close to bring the later representation within the prohibition of Canon 6 [which prohibited lawyers from representing clients with conflicting interest and from revealing confidential information]. . . .[25]

Judge Weinfeld developed what is now widely referred to as the "substantial relationship" test for deciding when representation against a former client is permissible. Several aspects of the substantial relationship test developed by Judge Weinfeld are worth noting. First, implicit in this test is recognition of the principle that if the matters are not substantially related, representation against a former client is permissible, even without the consent of that former client. Second, Judge Weinfeld stated that if the current and former matters were substantially related, a court should make no further inquiry to determine whether confidential information is actually being used. To engage in such an inquiry would defeat the

24. 113 F. Supp. 265 (S.D.N.Y. 1953).
25. Id. at 268-269.

very confidentiality that the rule is designed to protect. Thus, the substantial relationship test in its original form amounted to an "irrebuttable presumption" that confidential information was likely to be used if the matters were substantially related. As noted below, however, some courts have moved away from this view and will allow the attorney to offer evidence to rebut the presumption that confidential information will be used in the subsequent representation. Finally, the remedy most frequently used for violation of the substantial relationship test has been disqualification of the lawyer and the lawyer's firm from continuing the representation of the current client in the substantially related matter against the former client.

Model Rule 1.9(a) codifies the substantial relationship test first developed by Judge Weinfeld. While the test itself is widely accepted, the courts have adopted differing interpretations of its meaning.[26] Some courts focus on the *facts* involved in the two matters to determine if they are substantially related. For example, in Kaminski Brothers, Inc. v. Detroit Diesel Allison,[27] the law firm representing the plaintiff in a products liability case involving design and installation of a fuel line in heavy equipment had previously represented the defendant in 15 cases that involved passenger vehicles or light weight trucks. In denying the motion for disqualification, the court focused on the factual difference between passenger vehicles and heavy equipment. The court also rejected the defendant's argument that the firm should be disqualified because it may have been privy to negotiation techniques or defense theories.[28] In Trone v. Smith,[29] the Ninth Circuit stated the following fact-based application of the substantial relationship test:

> The substantial relationship test does not require that the issues in the two representations be identical.
>
> The relationship is measured by the allegations in the complaint and by the nature of the evidence that would be helpful in establishing those allegations.[30]

26. See generally Chrispens v. Coastal Ref. & Mktg., Inc., 897 P.2d 104 (Kan. 1995) (discussing various approaches to meaning of the substantial relationship test and adopting facts-and-circumstances test).

27. 638 F. Supp. 414 (M.D. Pa. 1985).

28. Id. at 417. See also Ciba-Geigy Corp. v. Alza Corp., 795 F. Supp. 711 (D.N.J. 1992).

29. 621 F.2d 994 (9th Cir. 1980).

30. Id. at 1000.

By contrast, other courts focus on the *legal issues* involved in the two matters. For example, the Second Circuit has ruled that disqualification is justified only when the relationship between the issues involved in the two matters is "patently clear."[31]

The Seventh Circuit has developed a three-pronged test that combines both factual and legal analysis:

> Initially, the trial judge must make a factual reconstruction of the scope of the prior legal representation. Second, it must be determined whether it is reasonable to infer that the confidential information allegedly given would have been given to a lawyer representing a client in those matters. Finally, it must be determined whether that information is relevant to the issues raised in the litigation pending against the former client.[32]

The courts are divided on whether the attorney's representation of a former client over an extended period of time in matters that are similar to the current representation is sufficient to amount to a substantial relationship. In Duncan v. Merrill Lynch, Pierce, Fenner & Smith, Inc.,[33] the Fifth Circuit held that a law firm was not disqualified from representing the plaintiff in a securities fraud action arising from the sale of municipal bonds even though the firm had previously represented Merrill Lynch in ten different securities matters over a ten-year period. The court stated that the firm's representation of "Merrill Lynch, even on a variety of matters and over a relatively long period of time, is alone insufficient to establish the required nexus with the present case." The court decided that Merrill Lynch had done nothing more than offer a "catalogue of such generalities," when disqualification required a "painstaking analysis of the facts."[34] Other courts, however, have held that representation over an extended period of time in similar matters is sufficient to warrant disqualification because the prior representation gives insight and understanding of the client's business practices and legal strategy and can create what one court

31. Government of India v. Cook Indus., Inc., 569 F.2d 737, 740 (2d Cir. 1978).

32. Novo Terapeutisk Laboratorium A/S v. Baxter Travenol Lab., Inc., 607 F.2d 186, 190 (7th Cir. 1979). See also State ex rel. Wal-Mart Stores, Inc. v. Kortum, 559 N.W.2d 496 (Neb. 1997) (matters are substantially related if combination of factual and legal issues creates genuine threat that confidential information may be used against former client).

33. 646 F.2d 1020 (5th Cir. 1981), *cert. denied*, 454 U.S. 895 (1981).

34. Id. at 1029.

called a "climate for disclosure of relevant confidential information."[35]

The Restatement of the Law Governing Lawyers adopts a functional approach to the definition of a substantial relationship. Under the Restatement approach, a substantial relationship between the current and former representation exists if "there is a substantial risk that representation of the present client will involve the use of information acquired in the course of representing the former client, unless that information has become generally known."[36] The Restatement approach seems correct. The court decisions that have adopted elaborate and apparently conflicting definitions of what amounts to a substantial relationship have obscured the underlying interest—protection of the former client's right to confidentiality. The Restatement formulation properly focuses on confidentiality.

The Restatement also rejects the view that general insight or understanding of the client gained during the prior representation are sufficient to amount to a substantial relationship:

> A lawyer might also have learned a former client's preferred approach to bargaining in settlement discussions or negotiating business points in a transaction, willingness or unwillingness to be deposed by an adversary, and financial ability to withstand extended litigation or contract negotiations. Only when such information will be directly in issue or of unusual value in the subsequent matter will it be independently relevant in assessing a substantial relationship.[37]

Here also the Restatement approach seems correct. If insight and understanding of the former client's activities or personnel is enough to amount to a substantial relationship, then the test has come very close to establishing a continuing duty of loyalty to the

35. Kaselaan & D'Angelo Assocs., Inc. v. D'Angelo, 144 F.R.D. 235, 240 (D.N.J. 1992). *Accord* Cardona v. General Motors Corp., 942 F. Supp. 968 (D.N.J. 1996) (plaintiff's law firm disqualified in lemon law suit against GM when lawyer hired by firm had previously represented GM in similar litigation even though the lawyer was screened from participation; counsel was aware of defendant's claims and litigation philosophy, as well as its methods and procedures for defending claims).

36. Restatement of the Law Governing Lawyers §213(2) and comm. *d(iii)* (Prop. Final Draft #1, March 29, 1996).

37. Id. §213, comm. *d(iii)*.

former client, a duty that is unsound for reasons discussed previously. Further, as time passes, any insight or understanding gained in the prior representation diminishes in value.

Does the existence of a substantial relationship operate as a per se bar or can a lawyer rebut the application of the test by showing that confidential information was not in fact received? Most courts, following Judge Weinfeld's original formulation, appear to hold that the presumption is conclusive. For example, in Allegaert v. Perot,[38] the Court of Appeals for the Second Circuit stated:

> Our rule . . . is that an attorney may be disqualified pursuant to Canon 4 if he has accepted employment adverse to the interests of a former client on a matter substantially related to the prior litigation. Once the substantial relationship is established, the court need not inquire whether the attorney in fact received confidential information, because the receipt of such information will be presumed.[39]

Other courts, however, will allow former counsel to rebut the presumption of use of confidential information.[40]

The Restatement warns that extensive inquiry into the confidences of the former client would undermine the very interest the substantial relationship test is designed to protect.[41] Thus, "[w]hen the prior matter involved litigation, it will be conclusively presumed that the lawyer obtained confidential information about the issues involved in the litigation."[42] In other cases, the inquiry should be on "the work that the lawyer undertook and the array of information that a lawyer ordinarily would have obtained to carry out that work."[43] To the extent that inquiry into specific confidential information is necessary, the Restatement suggests the use of in camera proceedings to protect the former client's right to confidentiality.[44]

38. 565 F.2d 246 (2d Cir. 1977).

39. Id. at 250. See also In re American Airlines, Inc., 972 F.2d 605, 614 (5th Cir. 1992), *cert. denied,* 507 U.S. 912 (1993); Kevlik v. Goldstein, 724 F.2d 844, 851 (1st Cir. 1984).

40. See LaSalle Natl. Bank v. County of Lake, 703 F.2d 252, 265 (7th Cir. 1983).

41. Restatement of the Law Governing Lawyers §213, comm. *d(iii)* (Prop. Final Draft #1, March 29, 1996).

42. Id.

43. Id.

44. Id.

Canon 9 of the Code of Professional Responsibility provided that a lawyer should avoid "even the appearance of professional impropriety." Some courts relied on this concept to disqualify lawyers from undertaking representation against former clients, even without an inquiry into whether the current and former representations were substantially related.[45]

Many commentators and courts criticized the use of the appearance of impropriety as a basis for disqualification principally because of its vagueness: From whose perspective—the public, the bar, reasonable people, the former client—is the appearance to be judged?[46] The Model Rules do not include the concept of the appearance of impropriety, and comment 5 to Rule 1.9 specifically rejects this principle as a basis for analysis. Similarly, the Restatement also rejects the appearance of impropriety as a basis for prohibiting representation against former clients.[47]

Despite this widespread rejection, occasional decisions still rely on the appearance of impropriety as a basis of disqualification. For example, in Crawford W. Long Memorial Hospital of Emory University v. Yerby,[48] the hospital moved to disqualify plaintiff's attorney, who had previously represented the hospital in 18 medical malpractice actions. In 1984, when the attorney was representing the hospital on other medical malpractice claims, Yerby entered the hospital for back surgery and died the same day. The court found that it was unnecessary to decide if the matters were substantially related:

> In this case, we need not determine whether the medical-malpractice claim that Bennett has brought *against* the hospital is "substantially related" to any of the eighteen medical-malpractice claims that he had defended *on behalf* of the hospital. The circumstance of representing a client against a former client in an action that is of the same general subject matter, and grows out of an event that occurred *during the time* of such representation, creates an impermissible appearance of impropriety.[49]

45. E.g., Renshaw v. Ravert, 460 F. Supp. 1089 (E.D. Pa. 1978) (in civil rights case substantial relationship test does not require disqualification of plaintiff's attorney, but disqualification is warranted under Canon 9 because attorney represented one of defendant police officers ten years previously).

46. Wolfram, Modern Legal Ethics §7.1.4, at 320-323.

47. Restatement of the Law Governing Lawyers §201, comm. *c(iv)* (Prop. Final Draft #1, March 29, 1996).

48. 373 S.E.2d 749 (Ga. 1988).

49. Id. at 751.

The *Yerby* decision is unusual because it involves both similar subject matter and the fact that the claim arose during the time of the former representation. Nonetheless, to the extent that the case stands for the proposition that the appearance of impropriety is an independent basis for disqualification of a lawyer from undertaking representation against a former client, it should be rejected. Representation against a former client should only be prohibited if the representation involves violation of the lawyer's limited duty of loyalty to a former client — attacking the attorney's work product or side switching — or if it involves a substantial risk that the lawyer will use information gained in the prior representation on behalf of the current client against the former client.

Suppose a lawyer is not engaged after preliminary discussions with a prospective client. The lawyer may be unable to undertake the representation because of a conflict of interest between the prospective client and another client of the lawyer's firm. Sometimes the client may decide to retain other counsel; in an increasingly competitive market for legal services, many corporate clients shop around through a series of "beauty contests" before retaining counsel. The Model Rules do not address the issue of duties owed to a former prospective client. The Restatement takes the position that a lawyer owes a former prospective client a duty of confidentiality but that the broader protection of the substantial relationship test does not apply unless the lawyer acquired from the prospective client confidential information that could be "significantly harmful" in the matter.[50] The Restatement approach giving former prospective clients somewhat less protection than former clients seems sound. Beauty contests in which prospective clients interview a number of firms before retaining counsel are common. A broad disqualification rule in such situations would interfere with the ability of other clients to retain counsel and with the legitimate financial interests of law firms. Further, some prospective clients have used beauty contests tactically to attempt to disqualify counsel that they fear might represent the other side. The prospective client's interests are also weaker in these situations because the relationship has not risen to the level of attorney-client, and in the typical case the prospective client has not paid any fees to the firm.[51]

50. Restatement of the Law Governing Lawyers §27 and comm. *c* (Prop. Final Draft #1, March 29, 1996).

51. See Chapter 3.H infra on screening to avoid disqualification of a firm when a member of the firm obtained confidential information from a former prospective client.

E. KNOWN DISPUTES OUTSIDE OF LITIGATION

1. *General Principles for Intermediation under Model Rule 2.2*

As with litigation, nonlitigation matters can involve either actual or potential conflicts of interests. Suppose two or more individuals who are involved in a dispute ask a lawyer to represent them for the purpose of resolving their dispute without litigation. As we have seen, a lawyer cannot represent clients with directly adverse interests in a litigation matter even with client consent, because of the systemic interest in an adversarial presentation. (See Chapter 3.B supra.) May a lawyer represent clients with directly adverse interests outside of litigation for the purpose of resolving their dispute in a nonadversarial fashion? Clients may have a number of reasons for seeking representation by a single lawyer to resolve their dispute. First, clients may prefer a nonadversarial resolution of their dispute to the adversarial process, particularly when the clients will continue to have a personal or business relationship with each other. Second, the clients may hope that use of one lawyer to resolve their dispute will reduce overall legal fees. Finally, clients may be fearful of publicity if their dispute goes to court and may instead prefer to try to resolve their dispute privately. Moreover, the systemic interest in having an adversarial presentation is not involved when the parties seek a nonadversarial resolution of their dispute.

An objection can be made, however, to this analysis. Assuming that clients do have legitimate interests in nonadversarial dispute resolution, it does not follow that lawyers should be allowed to *represent* both parties in resolving their dispute. Instead, lawyers (or nonlawyers for that matter) could act as "neutrals," either mediators or arbitrators, rather than as attorneys. In other words, attorneys should either act as neutrals or as lawyers, but not as both. The argument in favor of this approach is that if a lawyer serves both as counsel for the parties and as a neutral, the lawyer then faces a multitude of conflicts. Moreover, the lawyer's multifaceted role is bound to confuse the parties. This argument, however, ignores an important difference between neutrals and lawyers. The principal function of a neutral is to resolve the dispute. Neutrals generally do not give legal advice to the parties to the proceeding. Indeed, neutrals typically warn participants in alternative dispute resolution to retain counsel for legal advice. Thus, if lawyers are prohibited from serving as counsel for parties in an effort to resolve their dispute, the parties are deprived of the ability to have one person who can serve both as a neutral and as a legal counsel. Fully informed clients should have this option.

The Rules of Professional Conduct accept this analysis and allow lawyers to serve either as neutrals or as attorneys representing clients in an effort to resolve a dispute. Model Rule 2.2, dealing with a lawyer as an *intermediary*, authorizes representation of conflicting interests in nonlitigation matters when the lawyer is attempting to resolve a dispute between the clients. While the rule uses the term "intermediary," this role differs from that of an arbitrator or a mediator. Arbitrators and mediators do not represent parties in a legal capacity. By contrast, a lawyer serving as an intermediary under Rule 2.2 represents all of the parties. See comment 2 to Model Rule 2.2.[52] The drafters of Rule 2.2 considered it to be a specific application of general principles of loyalty and confidentiality found in Model Rules 1.6 and 1.7. They decided, however, to create a separate rule to emphasize and perhaps to validate the distinctive role of lawyers as counselors for clients who, "though adverse in their respective positions, share a more compelling interest in reaching agreement as a group."[53]

The rule imposes obligations on lawyers at three stages of the representation. Rule 2.2(a) deals with lawyers' obligations before undertaking representation. The rule parallels Rule 1.7; it requires lawyers to reasonably believe that they can undertake representation and to obtain the consent of their clients to such representation after consultation regarding the implications of common representation. Rule 2.2(a), however, is more specific than Rule 1.7 in several respects. It sets three requirements before the lawyer may serve as an intermediary:

- consultation and consent (Model Rule 2.2(a)(1))
- reasonableness of representation (Model Rule 2.2(a)(2))
- impartiality (Model Rule 2.2(a)(3))

52. See 1 Hazard & Hodes, The Law of Lawyering §2.2:101, at 511.
53. 1 id. §2.2:101, at 512.

While the rule lists consultation and consent first, a lawyer must first address the other two requirements to decide if multiple representation is permissible. If these requirements are met, then the lawyer must consult with the potential clients and seek their consent under 2.2(a)(1).

Under Rule 2.2(a)(2) the lawyer must reasonably believe that "each client will be able to make adequately informed decisions in the matter and that there is little risk of material prejudice to the interest of any of the clients if the contemplated resolution is unsuccessful." When a prospective client is unsophisticated, a lawyer's service as an intermediary is particularly likely to be dangerous. Under Rule 2.2(a)(3), the lawyer must reasonably believe that the representation can be undertaken impartially. When a lawyer has a long-standing relationship with one of the prospective clients, the risk of partiality is great.

Assuming a lawyer concludes that he can meet the requirements of Rule 2.2(a)(2) and (3), Model Rule 2.2(a)(1) requires the lawyer to consult with "each client concerning the implications of the common representation, including the advantages and risks involved, and the effect on the attorney-client privileges." Among the points to be addressed are the following:

- *Advantages of intermediation.* If one lawyer represents all of the parties, the lawyer has duties to all of them. The lawyer cannot favor one party at the expense of any other. The lawyer has a duty to raise any issue that may be material to any of the parties. Intermediation can save legal fees because the parties are only hiring one lawyer rather than multiple lawyers. In addition, the use of a single lawyer may increase the likelihood that the dispute will be resolved because one lawyer can focus on common interests and agreement rather than on possible points of disagreement.
- *Disadvantages of intermediation.* If the dispute cannot be resolved, the lawyer will be forced to withdraw from representation of all of the parties. Model Rule 2.2(c). The lawyer's withdrawal would force the parties to hire new counsel, unfamiliar with the matter, at added expense. The rule followed in most jurisdictions is that the attorney-client privilege does not apply to any dispute between jointly represented clients. See Comment 6 to Model Rule 2.2.[54] Thus, the lawyer may be

54. See also 1 id. §2.2:202, at 515.

> required to testify as to any communications received from any other party. The lawyer's files would also be available to any party to the dispute. While a lawyer who represents multiple parties has a duty to treat all of the parties evenhandedly, the lawyer may intentionally or unconsciously favor one of the parties over the others. This risk exists particularly when the lawyer has a long-standing relationship with one of the parties.

Rule 2.2(b) deals with a lawyer's obligations once the lawyer assumes the role of intermediary. The rule requires full consultation with each of the clients so that each client can make informed decisions. During mediation it is common practice to meet with each of the parties privately and to maintain confidentiality of information received in these private sessions. May a lawyer serving as an intermediary also receive confidential information during private sessions? Comment 6 to Rule 2.2 points out a tension between the duty of confidentiality owed to each of the clients and the obligation to keep each client informed, but it does not offer lawyers specific guidance on this issue. Since a lawyer who acts as an intermediary is in essence serving in the dual capacity of lawyer and neutral, it makes sense for the lawyer to have the same flexibility as a mediator. With client consent, lawyers serving as intermediaries should be able to have private sessions with the clients at which the lawyer receives confidential information. The clients should understand, however, that if the intermediation fails, the lawyer might be called on to testify regarding information received in these sessions because the attorney-client privilege would not apply.

Rule 2.2(c) deals with termination of intermediation. The lawyer must withdraw from representation at the request of any client or if the lawyer is no longer able to serve in the role of intermediary. On withdrawal, the lawyer may not represent any of the parties without the consent of all. This rule is a specific application of the former client rule, Model Rule 1.9.[55]

55. 1 id. §2.2:401, at 519-520. Professor John Dzienkowski has authored a comprehensive study of the role of the lawyer as intermediary under Model Rule 2.2. While approving of the concept in principle, he argues that Rule 2.2 requires a fundamental reworking because it fails to answer a number of basic questions regarding the role of the lawyer as intermediary. Among his criticisms, Professor Dzienkowski faults the rule for failing to provide sufficient guidance to lawyers on how they should function as intermediaries and on the scope of the duty of

2. *Intermediation in Business and Domestic Cases*

The Restatement of the Law Governing Lawyers also approves of the concept of lawyers representing clients to a known dispute in an effort to resolve the dispute, provided the clients give informed consent. The Restatement gives two illustrations of situations in which lawyers could properly undertake representation of clients to resolve known disputes. In one situation, partners face the possibility that the business will fail unless the partnership obtains additional funding. Only one partner has the financial ability to make increased capital contributions. The partner is willing to do so, provided the partner's interest in the partnership increases, but the other partners believe that the capital partner is demanding too great a share. A lawyer may undertake multiple representation in this situation in an effort to resolve this dispute, with the informed consent of the clients. In doing so, the lawyer may not favor the interests of any client over the others.[56]

The second illustration offered by the Restatement involves a domestic matter. A lawyer may represent a husband and wife who wish to obtain an uncontested divorce in helping them to reach an agreement on disposition of their property, but the lawyer may represent only one of the parties in the actual dissolution proceeding. Presumably the other party would be unrepresented since all matters will have been resolved by agreement.[57]

Courts have been divided on the question of whether a lawyer could represent spouses in an uncontested divorce. In some jurisdictions such representation is improper. Courts in these jurisdictions reason that divorces are inherently adversarial, and a lawyer cannot represent opposing parties in litigation. Further, many of these courts question whether divorces are ever so simple or uncontested as to warrant the use of a single lawyer.[58] In other

confidentiality during intermediation. John S. Dzienkowski, Lawyers as Intermediaries: The Representation of Multiple Clients in the Modern Legal Profession, 1992 U. Ill. L. Rev. 741, 768-771.

56. Restatement of the Law Governing Lawyers §211, illus. 5 (Prop. Final Draft #1, March 29, 1996).

57. Id. illus. 6.

58. See, e.g., Hale v. Hale, 539 A.2d 247 (Md. Ct. Sp. App. 1988), *cert. denied,* 542 A.2d 857 (1988). The Bounds of Advocacy, Standards of Conduct, adopted by the American Academy of Matrimonial Lawyers in 1991, also condemns multiple representation. Standard 2.20 provides: "An attorney should not represent both

jurisdictions courts have allowed multiple representation. These courts reason that societal attitudes toward divorce have changed to remove many divorces from the adversarial arena. In addition, the issues involved in many divorces do not warrant the use of more than one lawyer.[59] The Restatement approach is a creative compromise. Under the Restatement view, a lawyer could act as an intermediary between a husband and wife who seek an uncontested divorce in negotiating an agreement to resolve differences between them, but the lawyer avoids representing opposite sides in litigation.

Assuming that a lawyer is not prohibited from acting as an intermediary between spouses in an effort to reach agreement, when is it proper for a lawyer to do so? Under Rule 2.2(a)(2) a lawyer may not act as an intermediary unless the lawyer "reasonably believes that the matter can be resolved on terms compatible with the clients' best interests, that each client will be able to make adequately informed decisions in the matter and that there is little risk of material prejudice to the interest of any of the clients if the contemplated resolution is unsuccessful." Cases will arise in which a lawyer could not have the reasonable belief required by the rule:

> [An] attorney should decline dual representation because of her inability to represent adequately the interests of both spouses if it is likely that (1) advocacy will be needed, (2) independent counseling will be necessary, or (3) the lawyer will not be able to function as a neutral intermediary.
>
> *1. The Need for Advocacy.* If a contested issue develops in a divorce case, advocacy will be required. In deciding whether it is likely that a contested issue will develop, the attorney should consider the following:
>
> (a) The degree to which the parties have discussed significant issues and reached agreement on them, at least in principle. . . .
>
> (b) The presence of minor children, substantial debts, or substantial assets. As the divorce becomes more complex, the potential for a contest increases. While mere complexity of the case

---

husband and wife even if they do not wish to obtain independent representation." The comment offers the following rationale: "[I]t is impossible for the attorney to provide impartial advice to both parties, and even a seemingly amicable separation or divorce may result in bitter litigation over financial matters or custody."

59. Klemm v. Superior Court, 142 Cal. Rptr. 509 (Cal. Ct. App. 1977); Levine v. Levine, 436 N.E.2d 476 (N.Y. 1982).

> should not preclude dual representation, if complexity is coupled with lack of agreement or consideration of basic issues, dual representation should be declined because a contested issue is likely.
>
> 2. *The Need for Independent Counsel.* If either spouse is in a dependent condition, the spouse needs the services of an independent advisor. Whether a spouse is in this condition depends on the following:
>
> (a) The emotional condition of the parties. If either person is severely emotionally disturbed because of the crisis of the divorce or otherwise, the lawyer should not undertake dual representation.
> (b) The relationship between the spouses. It is not uncommon for one spouse to dominate the other. If the lawyer perceives that one spouse dominates the decision making of the other, dual representation should not be accepted.
>
> 3. *The Lawyer's Ability to Act Neutrally.* As the representative of the spouses, the lawyer has obligations of loyalty and care to both. The lawyer should not undertake dual representation if his personal relationship with either spouse is such that he cannot fulfill this role. A dangerous situation exists if the lawyer has had a close relationship with one of the parties, for example, as business counselor to the husband, and is asked to handle the divorce on behalf of both. The prior relationship, coupled with the prospects for future legal work from the husband, may undermine the lawyer's neutrality.[60]

Assuming the lawyer reasonably believes that she can act as an intermediary between divorce clients under Rule 2.2, the lawyer must obtain the clients' consent to intermediation after consultation. Consultation should include a full explanation of "the implications of the common representation, including the advantages and risks involved, and the effect on the attorney-client privileges."[61]

Even if intermediation in divorce or separation cases is ethically permissible, many lawyers may not be willing to face the risks that such representation entails. Indeed, even courts that have permitted simultaneous representation have warned lawyers of the po-

60. Nathan M. Crystal, Ethical Problems in Marital Practice, 30 U. S.C. L. Rev. 321, 329-330 (1979).

61. For a detailed discussion of matters that lawyers should discuss in a consultation prior to undertaking intermediation, see id. at 330-332.

tential risks of this course of action, including malpractice liability, disciplinary proceedings, and invalidation of any agreement entered into between the jointly represented parties.[62]

F. LAW REFORM ACTIVITIES AND POSITIONAL CONFLICTS

1. *Law Reform*

Lawyers frequently become active members of charitable, religious, civic, community, governmental, and educational organizations. Often lawyers provide such organizations pro bono legal services. Indeed, the profession has debated extensively the question whether lawyers should have an obligation to provide a specified amount of pro bono representation per year, an issue discussed in Chapter 6.

When lawyers render pro bono service, sometimes the activities of organizations to which they render such services may conflict with the economic or other interests of one of the lawyer's clients. For example, suppose a lawyer is member of the board of a legal services program. The program is considering litigation priorities, one of which is landlord/tenant. The lawyer has several major real estate clients who could be the target of actions brought by the program if it adopts landlord/tenant as a priority.

Representation of a client imposes obligations on a lawyer with regard to the particular matter the lawyer is handling. The fundamental issue involved in this example is whether representation of a client imposes obligations on a lawyer that go beyond the particular matter into the more general public life of the lawyer. Both for libertarian and public policy reasons, the answer should be a negative one. If representation of clients limits the ability of lawyers to participate in public activities that adversely affect their

62. See Klemm v. Superior Court, 142 Cal. Rptr. 509, 514 (Cal. Ct. App. 1977). See also Ishmael v. Millington, 50 Cal. Rptr. 592 (Cal. Ct. App. 1966) (summary judgment for attorney reversed in malpractice action brought by wife claiming that attorney favored interests of husband in preparation of agreement); Columbus Bar Assn. v. Grelle, 237 N.E.2d 298 (Ohio 1968) (attorney reprimanded because of misunderstandings resulting from multiple representation).

clients, then the public side of a lawyer's career becomes largely the sum of the interests of the lawyer's clients. A lawyer could not have a public life independent of that of his clients. Further, the training and experience of lawyers enables them to offer important insights into public issues. The public would lose these benefits if lawyers could not participate in public matters that affected the interests of their clients.

Model Rule 6.4, which deals with law reform activities that affect a client's interests, seems to adopt the general approach recommended here:

> A lawyer may serve as a director, officer or member of an organization involved in reform of the law or its administration notwithstanding that the reform may affect the interests of a client of the lawyer. When the lawyer knows that the interests of a client may be materially benefitted by a decision in which the lawyer participates, the lawyer shall disclose that fact but need not identify the client.

The comment goes on to state: "In determining the nature and scope of participation in such activities, a lawyer should be mindful of obligations to clients under other Rules, particularly Rule 1.7."

The Restatement adopts a similar matter-specific approach to law reform and other public activities by lawyers:

> In general, a lawyer may publicly take personal positions on controversial issues without regard to whether the positions are consistent with those of some or all of the lawyer's clients. Consent of the lawyer's clients is not required. Lawyers usually represent many clients, and professional detachment is one of the qualities a lawyer brings to each client. Moreover, it is a tradition that a lawyer's advocacy for a client should not be construed as an expression of the lawyer's personal views. Resolution of many public questions is benefitted when independent legal minds are brought to bear on them. For example, if tax lawyers advocating positions about tax reform were obliged to advocate only positions that would serve the positions of their present clients, the public would lose the objective contributions of policy making of some persons most able to help.[63]

If, however, a lawyer's public position on an issue would materially and substantially affect a client *in a particular matter,* the lawyer may not take the position absent client consent. "Thus, a lawyer

63. Restatement of the Law Governing Lawyers §206, comm. *e* (Prop. Final Draft #1, March 29, 1996).

may not publicly take a policy position that is adverse to the position of a client that the lawyer is currently representing if doing so would materially and adversely affect the lawyer's representation of the client in the matter."[64]

2. *Positional Conflicts*

Sometimes a conflict of interest can arise when a lawyer takes a legal position on behalf of one client that is adverse to the interests of another client. The term *positional conflict of interest* has been coined to refer to such conflicts. Positional conflicts can arise in a variety of ways: The purest form involves a firm taking opposing legal positions on behalf of different clients in different courts. A subtler form of positional conflict occurs when a firm represents one client in a matter that can harm the economic interests of another client.

Positional conflicts differ from the conflicts arising from law reform and other public activities because positional conflicts do not involve either the lawyer's interest in individual liberty or the public interest in obtaining valuable contributions to public issues. Like the issue of representation of former clients, however, positional conflicts do involve the interest of other clients in being able to obtain representation by counsel of their choice. Thus, a matter-specific approach to positional conflicts seems appropriate. Under this approach, a lawyer may advocate opposing legal positions so long as the advocacy does not pose a substantial risk of harm to a client in a particular matter. Thus, a lawyer could not advocate opposing legal positions before a state supreme court because success on behalf of one client would irreparably harm the interests of the other. A lawyer could, however, advocate opposing legal positions in lower courts and could advocate opposing legal positions in appellate courts in different jurisdictions or in different federal circuits.

The Model Rules do not have a specific provision dealing with positional conflicts, but comment 9 to Model Rule 1.7 states:

> A lawyer may represent parties having antagonistic positions on a legal question that has arisen in different cases, unless representation of either client would be adversely affected. Thus, it is

64. Id.

> ordinarily not improper to assert such positions in cases pending in different trial courts, but it may be improper to do so in cases pending at the same time in an appellate court.

The Restatement elaborates on when representation of adverse legal positions would be improper:

> [A] conflict is presented when there is a substantial risk that a lawyer's action in Case A will materially and adversely affect another of the lawyer's clients in Case B. Factors relevant in determining the risk of such an effect include whether the issue is before a trial court or an appellate court; whether the issue is substantive or procedural; the temporal relationship between the matters; the practical significance of the issue to the immediate and long-run interests of the clients involved; and the clients' reasonable expectations in retaining the lawyer.[65]

If advocacy of one client's legal position would materially and adversely affect another client, the lawyer may proceed only with the informed consent of both clients.[66]

Sometime a positional conflict of interest arises not because of adverse legal positions but because the lawyer represents competing economic interests. Comment 3 to Model Rule 1.7 states that representation of competing economic interests is generally proper without the need for client consent: "On the other hand, simultaneous representation in unrelated matters of clients whose interests are only generally adverse, such as competing economic enterprises, does not require consent of the respective clients."

In Maritrans GP Inc. v. Pepper, Hamilton & Scheetz,[67] the Pennsylvania Supreme Court stirred a good deal of concern in the profession when it held that under some circumstances it was a conflict of interest and breach of fiduciary duty for a law firm to represent competitors. In *Maritrans,* the defendant law firm had been Maritrans's labor counsel for a number of years, and then began representing some of Maritrans's competitors. The firm and Maritrans initially reached an understanding in which Pepper, Hamilton agreed not to represent Maritrans's chief competitor, while Maritrans consented to the firm's representation of lesser

65. Id. §209, comm. *f.*

66. See id.; ABA, Comm. on Legal Ethics and Prof. Resp., Formal Opinion 93-377.

67. 602 A.2d 1277 (Pa. 1992).

competitors, provided the firm put in place screening mechanisms to prevent confidential information from passing between the lawyers representing Maritrans and those representing the competitors. Pepper, Hamilton, however, reneged on the agreement by "parking" the chief competitor with a labor lawyer in another firm who soon joined the firm. Maritrans sought an injunction to prevent Pepper, Hamilton from representing its competitors. The firm argued that the case involved a "business conflict" between competitors rather than an ethical violation. The Pennsylvania Supreme Court, however, enjoined Pepper, Hamilton from representing Maritrans's competitors because the firm was using confidential information gained during its prior representation against a former client. The court stated that it was not adopting a per se rule prohibiting a lawyer from undertaking representation of competitors, but it noted that each case must be judged on its facts. While *Maritrans* has generated a good deal of discussion, the case should not be read as prohibiting representation of clients with competing economic interests. The facts of *Maritrans* were extreme, involving abuse of a fiduciary relationship, misrepresentation to a client, and misuse of confidential information. Such conduct is far more egregious than simply representing clients with competing economic interests.

G. PROSPECTIVE CLIENT CONSENT TO REPRESENTATION OF CONFLICTING INTERESTS

In the previous sections we have seen that a lawyer may usually undertake representation of conflicting interests with consent of all clients who may be affected. (Representation of adverse parties in a single contested matter is the notable exception. See Chapter 3.B supra.) The consent contemplated in those cases was consent after the conflict had been identified and explained to the clients. May a client give effective consent to a conflict of interest prospectively?

In Formal Opinion 93-371, the ABA Ethics Committee noted that the impetus for prospective waivers has arisen from the dramatic change in the practice of law that has occurred in the last few decades:

> In an era when law firms operated in just one location, when there were few mega-conglomerate clients and when clients typically hired only a single firm to undertake all of their legal business, the thought of seeking prospective waivers rarely arose.[68]

Recognizing these changes, the Committee gave limited endorsement to prospective waivers. The Committee ruled that it was "not ordinarily impermissible to seek such prospective waivers," but "that the mere existence of a prospective waiver will not necessarily be dispositive of the question whether the waiver is effective." The waiver will not be effective as to matters not reasonably contemplated at the time the waiver was executed. In addition, the waiver will not be effective to allow use of confidential information.

Consider the following analysis of the enforceability of prospective waivers:

> A blanket waiver . . . should not be enforced. Central to the effectiveness of client consent is communication of information sufficient to enable the client to make an informed decision. It is difficult to believe that a client can receive sufficient information to make an informed decision when the client, at the time of the consent, knows neither the nature of the conflict or the person or entity with whom the conflict exists.
>
> Moreover, the argument in support of judicial recognition of a blanket waiver is weak. The argument is based on the policy in favor of selection of counsel; it posits that if such waivers are not valid, a law firm may be unwilling to undertake representation of a new client in a matter because it fears that the new representation may require the firm's disqualification in a matter on behalf of a more substantial client who has or may have an interest adverse to that of the new client. Thus, clients may be deprived of the opportunity of obtaining the services of law firms with particular expertise.
>
> This argument in favor of the validity of a blanket waiver ignores the economic forces that drive law firms. . . . To say that the firm would refuse to undertake representation in that matter because of some unknown, future conflict is to say that firms will refuse to take on new business because a new client might some day have a conflict with an existing client. While such a conflict might develop, the client also represents new business to the firm. Therefore, the

68. ABA Comm. on Ethics and Prof. Resp., Formal Opinion 93-371, at 2.

> economic drive of firms will give them a powerful incentive to take on such new business. . . .
>
> While courts should refuse to enforce blanket prospective waivers, it would be appropriate for courts to accept more limited prospective consents. A good example of such a situation is City of Cleveland v. Cleveland Elec. Illuminating Co. [440 F. Supp. 193 (N.D. Ohio 1976), *aff'd*, 573 F.2d 1310 (6th Cir. 1977), *cert. denied*, 435 U.S. 996 (1978).] In that case the law firm of Squire, Sanders & Dempsey had represented Cleveland Electric Company for over 65 years when the City asked the firm to handle a bond matter involving the City's competing utility company. The City was well aware of the law firm's long-time representation of Cleveland Electric because of numerous prior dealings with the Electric Company; it wished to retain the firm's services, however, because it was one of the few firms in Ohio that handled sophisticated bond work. Squire, Sanders was willing to take on the bond work only if the City waived any objection to future conflicts. The City had independent advice from its law department and waived its objections to any conflict of interest. Subsequently, the City moved to disqualify the firm in an antitrust action brought by the City against Cleveland Electric. The United States District Court for the Northern District of Ohio denied the motion for disqualification. In a lengthy opinion the court held that the City had waived any conflict of interest. The court also ruled that the City failed to show that the firm was using confidential information against its interests.
>
> In cases like *City of Cleveland* a prospective consent should be enforced. The client was a sophisticated corporate entity with independent legal advice about the waiver. The waiver itself was limited to the firm's representation of an identified long-term client rather than a blanket prospective consent. When such factors are present, it seems reasonable to conclude that the client has sufficient information to consent to the dual representation. Moreover, unless the City had agreed to the waiver it would have been unable to obtain representation in specialized bond work. Thus, the policy argument in favor of recognizing a waiver in such a case, which rests on the ability of a client to retain counsel of its choice, seems strong. Finally, the case did not involve the use of confidential information against the client.[69]

The Restatement of the Law Governing Lawyering generally adopts this approach. The Restatement provides that a consent to

69. Nathan M. Crystal, Disqualification of Counsel for Unrelated Matter Conflicts of Interest, 4 Geo. J. Legal Ethics 273, 307-309 (1990).

future conflicts is ineffective unless the client "possesses sophistication in the matter in question and has had the opportunity to receive independent legal advice about the consent." The Restatement also recognizes the possibility that in a continuing client-attorney relationship, the client might consent in advance to types of conflicts with which it is familiar.[70]

H. IMPUTATION OF CONFLICTS, MOVEMENT BETWEEN FIRMS, AND SCREENING TO AVOID CONFLICTS

Both the Code of Professional Responsibility in DR 5-105(D) and the Model Rules in Rule 1.10(a) recognize a principle of "imputed" or "vicarious" disqualification. Under this principle, when lawyers are currently associated in a firm, and one of the lawyers is disqualified from handling a matter, that disqualification is imputed to disqualify all members of the firm. The rationale for the rule of imputed disqualification is based on the fact that lawyers practicing in a firm have access to firm files and have mutual financial interests. As a result, it is assumed that any confidential information that one member of the firm has is accessible to other members of the firm, and that any conflict of interest that affects a member of the firm will also affect other members. One can question the validity of these assumptions, especially in large firms, but the principle of imputed disqualification seems to be firmly established in the law of professional ethics. There are, however, qualifications and limitations to the principle.

One of the most important limitations on the rule of imputed disqualification deals with movement of a lawyer from one firm to another. Strictly applied, the rule of imputed disqualification could lead to extreme instances of disqualification, even when no realistic risk of use of confidential information exists. Consider this example: Lawyer works for Old Firm. Lawyer leaves Old Firm to join New Firm. Arguably, all lawyers in New Firm are precluded from

70. Restatement of the Law Governing Lawyers §202, comm. *d* (Prop. Final Draft #1, March 29, 1996).

undertaking representation against any client of Old Firm on a matter that is substantially related to any matter that Old Firm was handling while Lawyer was a member of the firm, *even if Lawyer was not involved in the matter.* This result could flow from a "double imputation" of disqualification: Lawyer would be disqualified vicariously because of her membership in Old Firm. Lawyer's vicarious disqualification would then be imputed to all members of New Firm when Lawyer joins the firm.

This "double imputation" (from Old Firm members to Lawyer and from Lawyer to New Firm members) was questionable as a matter of policy. First, the risk of misuse of confidential information in this situation is small because Lawyer was not directly privy to any confidential information. Second, the use of imputed disqualification could unfairly restrict the mobility of lawyers between firms and unnecessarily limit the ability of clients to select counsel.

The leading case dealing with application of the rule of imputed disqualification when lawyers move between firms is Silver Chrysler Plymouth, Inc. v. Chrysler Motors Corp.[71] Silver Chrysler Plymouth sued Chrysler Motors for breach of contract. The Kelley Drye law firm represented its long-time client, Chrysler Motors, in the action. The firm of Hammond & Schreiber, P.C. represented the plaintiff. Dale Schreiber, a member of that firm, had worked as an associate at Kelley Drye. The defendant moved to disqualify the plaintiff's firm because of Schreiber's prior employment with Kelley Drye. The Court of Appeals for the Second Circuit rejected the notion that Schreiber should be conclusively presumed to have received confidential information:

> It is . . . well known that the larger firms in the metropolitan areas have hundreds (collectively thousands) of clients. It is unquestionably true that in the course of their work at large law firms, associates are entrusted with the confidences of some of their clients. But it would be absurd to conclude that immediately upon their entry on duty they become the recipients of knowledge as to the names of all the firm's clients, the contents of all files relating to such clients, and all confidential disclosures by client officers or employees to any lawyer in the firm. Obviously such legal osmosis does not occur. The mere recital of such a proposition should be self-

71. 518 F.2d 751 (2d Cir. 1975).

> refuting. And a rational interpretation of the Code of Professional Responsibility does not call for disqualification on the basis of such an unrealistic perception of the practice of law in large firms.[72]

The court ruled that Schreiber should only be disqualified if he had actually acquired confidential information. While Schreiber had worked on some Chrysler matters, his involvement was relatively minor, consisting principally of research.[73] Accordingly, the court found that Schreiber had rebutted any inference that he had received confidential information and would not be disqualified.

The *Silver Chrysler Plymouth* decision has been codified in Model Rules 1.9(a) and (b). Under these rules a lawyer who moves from one firm to another is only disqualified from handling a matter against a former client of the lawyer's old firm if the lawyer is personally disqualified, either because she would be handling a matter that is substantially related to a matter that she personally handled for the former client (Rule 1.9(a)), or because she received confidential information (Rule 1.9(b)). The lawyer will not be disqualified simply by imputation from her membership in the old firm. If the lawyer is not personally disqualified under either Rule 1.9(a) or (b), then her new firm is also not disqualified under Rule 1.10(a).[74]

Imputation of disqualification issues can also arise as to the former firm when a lawyer leaves the firm and takes cases with her. Is the former firm precluded from handling a matter against the former client if the matter is substantially related to work done by the former lawyer for the client during the course of the firm's representation? Considering the approach of the Model Rules to imputation when a lawyer joins a firm, the answer should not be surprising. The old firm is not disqualified from handling a matter against a former client when the matter was handled by a departed lawyer unless the current matter is substantially related to the prior representation *and* some lawyer still remaining with the firm actually received confidential information regarding the former client. Model Rule 1.10(b).[75]

72. Id. at 753-754.
73. Id. at 756.
74. But see State ex rel. FirsTier Bank, N.A. v. Buckley, 503 N.W.2d 838 (Neb. 1993) (adopting "bright line" test disqualifying new firm when lawyer who worked for old firm that represents opposing party joins new firm, regardless of disclosure of confidential information).
75. See Novo Terapeutisk Laboratorium A/S v. Baxter Travenol Labs., Inc., 607 F.2d 186 (7th Cir. 1979) (en banc) (law firm not disqualified from representing

The *Silver Chrysler Plymouth* case dealt with a situation in which the lawyer moving to the new firm was not personally disqualified. Suppose, however, that the lawyer is personally disqualified, either because he acquired confidential information or because the matter that he is being asked to handle is substantially related to a matter that he handled while a member of his old firm. While the lawyer cannot personally handle the matter, can another member of his new firm do so, or is the lawyer's disqualification imputed to the new firm? Strict application of the rule of imputed disqualification would disqualify all members of the new firm. It has been suggested, however, that this is an overly broad application of the rule of imputed disqualification and that the new firm should not be disqualified from handling a matter if the personally disqualified lawyer is "screened" from any involvement in the matter (the term *Chinese Wall* is also used).

The drafters of the Model Rules debated whether screening should be allowed when a disqualified lawyer moved from one firm to another. Strong arguments were made in favor of this approach. First, the argument for absolute disqualification of the new firm was based on the assumption that the lawyer joining the new firm would violate his ethical obligation to maintain confidences of the former client. Advocates of screening argued that it was not reasonable to base rules of ethics on the assumption that lawyers would generally violate such a fundamental duty. Second, a rule of absolute disqualification unfairly penalizes clients of the new firm, who are deprived of the counsel of their choice. Third, the rule is unfair to lawyers seeking a change in employment since firms may be unwilling to hire them because of the risk of disqualification of the entire firm. Such lawyers would be viewed as "typhoid Marys."[76] In addition, it was pointed out that the Model Rules did allow screening in another context, when a lawyer moved from government service to private practice. Model Rule 1.11(a).[77] Despite these arguments, the drafters of the Model

plaintiff when former partner of firm, while member of firm, had conference with defendant, but had not shared confidential information with other members of the firm); Solow v. W.R. Grace & Co., 610 N.Y.S.2d 128 (N.Y. 1994) (no disqualification of law firm from representing plaintiff in asbestos case against manufacturer when member of firm who previously represented manufacturer has departed firm and no evidence that confidential information was shared with other members of firm).

76. 1 Hazard & Hodes, The Law of Lawyering §1.10:207, at 336.

77. Imputation of disqualification when a lawyer was a former government attorney or judge raises somewhat different issues. See Chapter 7.J.

Rules chose to reject the possibility of screening when a disqualified lawyer joined a firm. Apparently, the drafters concluded that clients were entitled to assurances of confidentiality, and that this was only possible by a rule that disqualified the entire firm that hired a personally disqualified lawyer.[78]

Although the Model Rules reject screening as a way for dealing with conflicts of interest when a lawyer moves from one firm to another, the issue continues to be debated and litigated. A number of courts follow the Model Rules approach and reject screening.[79] Some courts, however, have held that despite the Model Rules, screening should be permitted.[80] In Cromley v. Board of Educ. of Lockport Township High Sch. Dist. 205,[81] the Seventh Circuit elaborated on what would be required to effectively screen the attorney and thereby avoid disqualification:

> The types of institutional mechanisms that have been determined to protect successfully the confidentiality of the attorney-client relationship include: (1) instructions, given to all members of the new firm, of the attorney's recusal and of the ban on exchange of information; (2) prohibited access to the files and other information on the case; (3) locked case files with keys distributed to a select few; (4) secret codes necessary to access pertinent information on electronic hardware; and (5) prohibited sharing in the fees derived from such litigation. . . . Moreover, the screening devices must be employed "as soon as the 'disqualifying event occurred.'" . . . Other factors have been considered helpful in determining whether adequate protection of the former client's confidences has been achieved: the size of the law firm, its structural divisions, the "screened" attorney's position in the firm, the likelihood of contact between the "screened" attorney and one representing another party, and the fact that a law firm's and lawyer's most valuable asset is "their reputations for honesty and integrity, along with competence." . . . In addition, the attorneys in question must have affirmed these screening devices under oath.[82]

78. 1 Hazard & Hodes, The Law of Lawyering §1.10:207, at 336.
79. E.g., Roberts v. Hutchins, 572 So. 2d 1231, 1234 n.3 (Ala. 1990).
80. E.g., Manning v. Waring, Cox, James, Sklar & Allen, 849 F.2d 222 (6th Cir. 1988).
81. 17 F.3d 1059 (7th Cir. 1994).
82. Id. at 1065.

The Restatement of the Law Governing Lawyers has also approved of the use of screening to avoid disqualification of a firm when a lawyer is disqualified from representing a new client against a former client.[83] Under the Restatement approach, however, screening may be used only when the confidential information held by the personally disqualified lawyer is "unlikely to be significant in the subsequent matter."[84]

The Restatement authorizes an even broader use of screening when a lawyer obtained confidential information from a former *prospective client.* In that case, the lawyer's firm may undertake representation against the former prospective client even if the lawyer obtained confidential information that could be significantly harmful to the former prospective client, provided the lawyer who received the information is screened from any participation in the matter.[85] If the information would not be significantly harmful, the lawyer could personally undertake representation against the former prospective client.[86]

Disqualification of a law firm can result from hiring paralegals or other nonlawyer employees who previously worked for an adverse party in substantially related matters. Here the courts are likely to allow screening to avoid disqualification. A law firm that hires a nonlawyer previously employed by the opposing firm may rebut the presumption that confidential information has been disclosed to the firm by showing that adequate screening measures were adopted.[87] If the firm does not adopt adequate screening procedures, disqualification is likely to result.[88]

83. Restatement of the Law Governing Lawyers §204(2) (Prop. Final Draft #1, March 29, 1996).

84. Id. §204(2)(a). Comment *d* outlines certain factors that can be used to determine whether the information is significant.

85. Id. §27(1)(b)(i).

86. Id. §27(1)(b).

87. See Phoenix Founders, Inc. v. Marshall, 887 S.W.2d 831 (Tex. 1994); ABA Comm. on Ethics and Prof. Resp., Informal Opinion 1526 (1988).

88. Grant v. Thirteenth Court of Appeals, 888 S.W.2d 466 (Tex. 1994). See also In re Complex Asbestos Litig. (Widger v. Owens-Corning Fiberglas Corp.), 283 Cal. Rptr. 732 (Cal. Ct. App. 1991) (allowing screening for nonlegal personnel).

Part II
Potential Conflicts of Interest Between Clients

I. CO-PLAINTIFFS OR CO-DEFENDANTS IN CIVIL LITIGATION

As we saw previously, if co-plaintiffs or co-defendants have actual claims against each other, the systemic interest in an adversarial presentation precludes multiple representation, even with the consent of both parties.[89] Suppose, however, co-parties have a potential rather than an actual claim against each other. For example, in an automobile accident the passenger in one vehicle might have only a potential claim against the driver of that vehicle if the facts indicate that the other driver was at fault. In such cases of potential conflict, the systemic interest in an adversarial presentation can be protected by a rule that would require the lawyer to withdraw should the potential conflict ripen into an actual conflict. A lawyer should be allowed to represent co-parties with potential claims provided the clients give informed consent to the representation. Both the Model Rules and the Restatement follow this approach and authorize representation of clients with potentially conflicting interests in litigation provided the clients give informed consent. Model Rule 1.7(b), which governs cases of potential conflicts, provides as follows:

> A lawyer shall not represent a client if the representation of that client may be materially limited by the lawyer's responsibilities to another client or to a third person, or by the lawyer's own interests, unless:
>
> (1) the lawyer reasonably believes the representation will not be adversely affected; and
>
> (2) the client consents after consultation. When representation of multiple clients in a single matter is undertaken, the consultation shall include explanation of the implications of the common representation and the advantages and risks involved.

While the structure and language of the rule is quite similar to Model Rule 1.7(a), which deals with directly adverse representation, important differences exist. First, when the interests of

89. See Chapter 3.B supra.

the clients are not directly adverse, representation is prohibited only if the lawyers' representation of one client would be "materially limited" by the representation of the other. Second, the rule specifies the disclosures that the attorney should make to obtain informed consent.

Figueroa-Olmo v. Westinghouse Electric Corp.[90] illustrates the application of the conflict of interest rules in tort litigation involving multiple plaintiffs with potential claims against each other. In *Figueroa-Olmo*, four individuals were killed when the truck in which they were riding collided with one of Westinghouse's trailers at an intersection near San Juan. Consolidated actions were brought by 40 relatives of the decedents; all of the plaintiffs were represented by one law firm. Westinghouse filed counterclaims claiming that the driver and passengers of the truck were contributorily negligent. Some of the plaintiffs were heirs of the decedents, while others were not. Under Puerto Rico law an heir who accepted an interest in an estate (filing of a lawsuit on behalf of the estate amounted to acceptance of an interest in the estate) also become legally responsible for any claims against the estate. Westinghouse filed a motion to disqualify the law firm from representing all of the plaintiffs because of a conflict of interest, claiming that the plaintiffs who were not heirs had potential cross claims against the plaintiffs who were heirs and who had accepted an interest in the estate.

The law firm filed written statements with the court in which each plaintiff consented to representation by the firm. Westinghouse objected to the statements on the ground that they did not show that the firm had made the full disclosure required by the rules of professional conduct. The district court ruled that the potential for a conflict of interest between the plaintiffs did not automatically prevent multiple representation and result in disqualification. The court discussed the circumstances under which multiple representation of potentially conflicting interests would be permitted:

> According to Model Rule 1.7(b), disqualification of counsel on grounds of potential conflicting interests in multiple client representation in the same lawsuit is not automatic but may depend on whether the clients agree to being so represented after having been informed of all the risks and disadvantages involved. . . . The prem-

90. 616 F. Supp. 1445 (D.P.R. 1985).

> ise behind this pragmatic approach is to safeguard a person's right to hire a particular attorney of certain expertise who may not be affordable except by the joint resources of various litigants who team up as plaintiffs or as defendants. . . . Parties also have a right to control their litigation in light of whatever interests they consider more important and worthy of litigating. . . . However, the right to be represented by a particular attorney is not an unfettered one. Even informed consent may be insufficient to prevent disqualification, if it is not obvious to the court that the attorney will be able to represent all clients adequately, . . . or if the court believes no waiver may cure the damage to the integrity of the judicial process that such joint representation will cause, . . . The court may also examine the circumstances surrounding the consent to determine if it was truly voluntary and informed. . . . It has also been held that if the conflicts of interest involve abuse of confidential information from the client rather than the mere possibility of disloyalty in advocacy during a litigation, the client's consent might be insufficient. . . . If the simultaneously represented clients' interests are or become actually opposed or directly adverse, then disqualification should be ordered. . . . Our circuit has cautioned that it is "more important that unethical conduct be prevented than that defendant have an unfettered right to counsel of its choice."[91]

The court ruled, however, that the plaintiffs' lawyers had failed to comply with the obligation of consultation required by Rule 1.7(b); it ordered plaintiffs' counsel to conduct meetings with the plaintiffs to explain their legal rights, and to file with the court written consents in a format specified by the court.[92]

Rule 1.7(b)(2) states that "the consultation shall include explanation of the implications of the common representation and the advantages and risks involved." What are the implications, advantages, and risks that should be disclosed?[93] One advantage that is often mentioned in connection with simultaneous representation is the reduction of legal fees by having one lawyer involved instead of two. While this may well be an advantage in a matter in which

91. Id. at 1451-1452.

92. See Gustafson v. City of Seattle, 941 P.2d 701 (Wash. Ct. App. 1997) (attorney must obtain informed consent before representing driver and passenger unless it reasonably appears that other parties are solely liable).

93. See Zador Corp. v. Kwan, 37 Cal. Rptr. 2d 754 (Cal. Ct. App. 1995) (quoting well-drafted consent form with detailed explanations of advantages and disadvantages of multiple representation of co-defendants in real estate litigation).

the client pays for the lawyer's services on an hourly basis, it is questionable whether it is an advantage in tort matters, which are usually handled on a contingency basis. For example, if one lawyer represents both the driver and passenger, recovers $5,000 for the driver and $10,000 for the passenger, and charges a one-third fee, the legal fees will be the same as when two lawyers independently represent the driver and the passenger, obtain the same recoveries, and charge their clients the same one-third fee. Another possible advantage of simultaneous representation deals with the costs involved in the case. Lawyers normally charge their clients for expenses incurred in a matter, such as filing fees, deposition costs, and costs of expert witnesses. If one lawyer rather than several handles the case, the clients could share the expenses, rather than each being required to pay her own expenses.

In addition to expense sharing, there are other possible advantages to the clients of simultaneous representation. Dealings between opposing sides in the case and particularly with the insurance carrier for the defendant may be simplified and thereby expedited if one lawyer is involved for the plaintiffs rather than two. Further, both the driver and passenger may have trust and confidence in the particular lawyer. Permitting simultaneous representation allows both to have the lawyer of their choice.

On the other hand, disadvantages to multiple representation exist. While the matter may not seem initially to involve an actual conflict between the clients, during the progress of the case, a conflict may arise. For example, discovery may produce evidence showing that the driver of the vehicle in which the passenger was riding may have been at fault and that the passenger therefore has a claim against the driver. Comment 7 to Model Rule 1.7 identifies other possible conflicts when a lawyer represents multiple parties in litigation:

> An impermissible conflict may exist by reason of substantial discrepancy in the parties' testimony, incompatibility in positions in relation to an opposing party or the fact that there are substantially different possibilities of settlement of the claims or liabilities in question.

Representation of multiple parties can produce "aggregate settlement" conflicts. Suppose the defendant offers a lump sum to settle the entire case. A lawyer representing multiple plaintiffs cannot ethically agree to an aggregate settlement unless each client consents after consultation. Model Rule 1.8(g). The settlement desires of one client may therefore lead to rejection of a settlement that the other client considers advantageous.

If an actual conflict develops between co-plaintiffs or co-defendants, the lawyer will be required to withdraw from representation. On withdrawal the lawyer could not represent either party unless both consented to the representation. After withdrawal both the clients would then be former clients. As discussed previously, a lawyer may not undertake representation against a former client in the same or substantially related matter without the consent of that client. Model Rule 1.9(a).[94] Both would be forced to hire new lawyers. At a minimum this would cause delay in their case and might well result in additional expenses. The lawyer must disclose to potential co-clients the possible conflicts that may arise and inform them that he would be required to withdraw from representation of both of them if an actual conflict arose.

The lawyer should also advise co-plaintiffs or co-defendants of another aspect of joint representation—the impact on the attorney-client privilege. It is well established as a matter of evidence law that no attorney-client privilege exists between joint clients as to communications made by either of the clients to the lawyer should a dispute develop between the joint clients.[95] For example, if a driver provides a lawyer with information showing that the driver was negligent, this information would not be privileged should the passenger later file a cross claim against the driver. The parties should be advised about this limitation on the attorney-client privilege before they agree to simultaneous representation. A lawyer who fails to obtain informed consent is exposed to the risk of malpractice liability.[96]

94. See 1 Hazard & Hodes, The Law of Lawyering §1.7:307. But see Zador Corp. v. Kwan, 37 Cal. Rptr. 2d 754 (Cal. Ct. App. 1995) (law firm represented multiple defendants in real estate litigation; firm was allowed to represent one defendant after withdrawing from representation of other defendant due to conflict of interest because written consent to multiple representation specified which defendant law firm could continue to represent if conflict developed).

95. 1 McCormick on Evidence §91 (John W. Strong ed., 4th ed. 1992); cf. Model Rule 2.2, Comment 6.

96. See Woodruff v. Tomlin, 616 F.2d 924 (6th Cir. 1980), *cert. denied*, 449 U.S. 888 (1980) (cause of action for legal malpractice stated against attorney who represented two sisters—one the driver and the other a passenger—in collision case without disclosure of possible claim that passenger had against driver).

What form should consent to simultaneous representation take? Rule 1.7(b) does not require the consent of the clients to be in writing. (Compare Rule 1.5(c), which requires contingent fee agreements to be in writing.) Thus, oral consent by the clients after consultation with the lawyer about the advantages, risks, and implications of multiple representation is sufficient. Prudent lawyers, however, do not rely on oral consent. Should a client later charge the lawyer with misconduct or sue for malpractice, the lawyer would not have any documentation of the client's consent. Instead, lawyers should obtain their clients' consent in writing. A letter to the clients in which the lawyer outlines the advantages and disadvantages of multiple representation and asks the clients to sign the letter if they consent to multiple representation is ideal.

J. CLASS ACTIONS

The contemporary legal scene has witnessed an explosive growth of mass tort litigation involving products such as asbestos, tobacco, and contraceptive devices. Procedurally, some of these cases have been brought as class actions under Rule 23 of the Federal Rules of Civil Procedure and corresponding state rules, but others involve mass consolidations of thousands of individual claims. Regardless of the procedural device used, however, mass torts present a host of unique ethical problems, including conflicts of interest.[97] Federal district judge Jack B. Weinstein, who has presided over a number of significant mass tort cases, has identified three major types of conflicts of interest in mass torts: between lawyer and client, among present clients, and between present and future claimants.[98]

In the ordinary tort case in which the plaintiff's lawyer is handling the matter on a contingency fee basis and is advancing expenses on behalf of the client, a conflict of interest can exist between lawyer and client with regard to settlement. When the

97. The leading article is Jack B. Weinstein, Ethical Dilemmas in Mass Tort Litigation, 88 Nw. U. L. Rev. 469 (1994). The literature on class actions in mass torts is voluminous. See Symposium, Mass Tortes: Serving Up Just Desserts, 80 Cornell L. Rev. 811 (1995); Symposium, The Institute of Judicial Administration Research Conference on Class Actions, 71 N.Y.U. L. Rev. 1 (1996).

98. Weinstein, note 97 supra, at 502-510.

defendant makes a settlement offer, both the lawyer and the client face the risk of loss of this amount if the client decides to reject the offer and proceed to trial. Because the positions of the lawyer and the client differ, however, there is a likelihood that they may attach unequal values to a settlement offer. The differences between lawyer and client flow from disparities in investment, prospective cost, value of money, and nonfinancial values. In a contingency fee case, the lawyer has both time and money invested in the case. If the client rejects the settlement offer, the lawyer's investment is put at risk. It is true that the client will also have an investment of time and perhaps some money, but often not as much as the lawyer. Thus, the investment risk of the client is usually less than that of the lawyer.

If the case proceeds to trial, the lawyer must devote substantial additional time and expense to preparing the case for trial, to trying the case, and in handling any appeal that may result. The client will also be required to expend time at trial, but in the typical tort case the client's time is less valuable than the lawyer's. Thus, the prospective financial cost of a trial is usually less to the client than to the lawyer. On the other hand, most clients will attach higher monetary value to a settlement because the marginal value of money to most clients is greater than for most lawyers.

Finally, some cases may have nonfinancial considerations that affect the value of settlement. If the case involves a matter of principle and not simply money, clients are likely to attach greater value than their lawyers to this principle. On the other hand, in some cases nonfinancial factors may lead clients to assign greater value than their lawyers to a settlement. For example, some clients may be fearful of going to trial and may award a higher value to a settlement to avoid the trauma of trial.

In ordinary tort cases we tolerate this conflict of interest between lawyer and client because we believe that the overall benefit of the contingency fee system in ensuring access to the courts outweighs the potential cost flowing from this conflict of interest. In addition, in normal tort cases, a client's direct stake in the matter operates as a control on the incentive of lawyers to act in their self interest. In class actions and mass torts, however, this client control model tends to break down. The sheer number of plaintiffs, any one of whose claim is dwarfed by the aggregate of all claims, means that lawyers exercise largely unfettered control over the handling of the case and the negotiation of a settlement.

The obvious answer to the problem of lack of client oversight of lawyers in class actions and mass torts is to create some institutional mechanism to substitute for client control. Judicial approval of any settlement, which is required in class actions under Rule 23, is one mechanism for controlling lawyer self interest, but this may not always be a satisfactory solution because the adequacy of any judicial oversight depends on the quality of the information presented to the judge. When all of the parties to the settlement have an interest in supporting the settlement, the judge may lack adequate information to evaluate the settlement. Judicial appointment of a guardian ad litem for the class who is authorized to investigate the fairness of a settlement and to make recommendations to the court is a possibility, although this approach does increase the cost and create possible delays in settlement. Another alternative is for the attorneys general of states who have a significant number of residents affected by a class action to monitor the action and to make recommendations to the court regarding any proposed settlement. Indeed, attorneys general in a number of states have now brought suit against tobacco companies seeking damages incurred by their states in treating residents who have been harmed by tobacco products.

Conflicts of interest among current clients and between current and future claimants are also significant problems in class actions and mass torts.[99] Most class actions and mass torts involve groups of clients with differences in their claims. In addition, because of the long latency period involved in discovery of injuries caused by some products, most such cases involve future claimants as well as those with current injuries. Even among future claimants, conflicts can develop. Some future claimants may be identifiable as having been exposed to the product causing the illness but may not exhibit disease, while other claimants may be unidentified or even unidentifiable (the unborn, for example). One solution to these conflicts is to create subclasses, each of which would be represented by separate lawyers. The creation of subclasses, however, increases the cost and reduces the efficiency of class action or mass consolidation devices. In addition, most lawyers who have significant experience in mass product cases will have many clients

99. See Amchem Prods., Inc. v. Windsor, 117 S. Ct. 2231 (1997) (holding that requirements of Rule 23 must be satisfied in "settlement class actions" and discussing conflicts of interest when lawyers represent both present and future claimants).

that overlap the various subclasses. May a lawyer continue to represent these multiple clients, or must these clients be reassigned to new lawyers who represent their class?

Given the number and complexity of conflicts of interest in class actions and mass torts, Judge Weinstein's observation of the role of the court seems particularly apt: "This exercise of court oversight and discretion is, I submit, the only available adequate substitute for traditional ethical rules."[100]

K. INSURANCE DEFENSE

The standard liability policy is a contract between the insurance company and the insured. For a specified premium, the insurance company agrees (a) to defend any suit against the insured within the coverage of the policy regardless of the merit of the suit (commonly called the "duty to defend") and (b) to pay any judgment against the insured up to the applicable policy limit. Under the typical policy, the insurance company reserves the right to control the defense, including the right to accept or reject any offer of settlement, and to select counsel to defend the insured. In addition to paying the premium, the insured promises to give the insurer prompt notice of any claim or occurence within the coverage of the policy, to cooperate fully in the defense, and to subrogate the insurance company for any amount paid on behalf of the insured.[101]

Traditionally courts and commentators have viewed defense counsel as representing *both* the insured and the insurance company (sometimes referred to as the "two-client" model or "tripartite relationship").[102] Dual representation has been justified on the ground that the insurance company and insured generally have a

100. Weinstein, note 97 supra, at 507.

101. See generally ABA Comm. on Ethics and Prof. Resp., Formal Opinion 282 (1950).

102. ABA Formal Opinion 96-403 states that by express agreement insurer, insured, and defense counsel could agree that counsel represents (1) only the insured, (2) both insured and the insurer for all purposes, (3) both insured and insurer for all purposes except settlement, in which case counsel represents the insurer. As discussed below, the one-client model in which defense counsel represents only the insured offers a number of advantages over the current two-client model.

"community of interest" with respect to any claim brought by a third party within the policy coverage: Both the insurance company and the insured have an interest in defeating the claim or in minimizing the amount of the recovery.[103]

While normally a harmony of interests exists between insurer and insured, a number of situations can develop in which the harmony of interests disintegrates.[104] The most common such situations are the following:

- *Coverage Disputes.* The insurer's contractual obligation is limited to amounts that the insured is legally liable to pay and that fall within the scope of the policy's coverage. Intentional torts and punitive damages typically are excluded from coverage under liability policies. Sometimes the existence of a coverage issue is apparent to the insurer at the outset of the case (for example, if the policy excludes coverage for intentional torts and punitive damages and the complaint alleges a cause of action for both). In other cases, however, facts that could establish lack of coverage may come to the attorney in confidence and may not be known by the insurer.
- *Excess Claims.* In an "excess" situation, the plaintiff is seeking damages that exceed the policy limits, but has made a settlement offer that is within the policy limits. The insured has an interest in having the insurer accept this settlement since the insured will not suffer any financial loss. The insurer may have an interest in rejecting the offer, however, if the insurer believes the offer is excessive, even though within the policy limits.
- *Uninsured or Underinsured Motorist Claims.* Many automobile policies have uninsured or underinsured coverage. Under such a provision, if the other driver does not have insurance (or is underinsured), the insured's own company provides

103. See Home Indem. Co. v. Lane Powell Moss & Miller, 43 F.3d 1322, 1330-1331 (9th Cir. 1995) (insurer may bring malpractice claim against law firm retained to defend tort action because law firm has client-attorney relationship both with insured and insurer); see also ABA Comm. on Ethics and Prof. Resp., Formal Opinion 282 (1950); William H. Fortune et al., Modern Litigation and Professional Responsibility Handbook §15.3.1, at 502-505 (1996); 3 Mallen & Smith, Legal Malpractice §28.14, at 553-554.

104. See generally Brooke Wunnicke, The Eternal Triangle: Standards of Ethical Representation by the Insurance Defense Lawyer, 31 For the Defense 7 (February, 1989).

coverage subject to the limits in the policy. As a result the same insurance company may be defending the insured and the opposing party.

- *Counterclaims.* As noted above, the typical liability policy provides that the insurance company has a "duty to defend" the insured. Suppose the insured has a counterclaim against the opposing party. The insured has an interest in pursuing this claim, but the insurance company has no financial interest in paying for an attorney to obtain recovery on behalf of the insured.
- *Fraud or Collusion by the Insured.* In some cases (if the plaintiff is a friend or relative, for example), the insured may have an interest in conceding liability or in colluding with the plaintiff.
- *Multiple Insureds.* In some cases, the insurance company may have multiple insureds in a single matter. For example, an insurance company may issue medical malpractice policies that cover several doctors involved in a malpractice case. The insureds may have conflicting interests if their degrees of fault or amount of coverage are different.
- *Subrogation.* Insurance policies typically provide that the insurance company is "subrogated" to the rights of the insured. This means that if the insurance company makes a payment to the insured (for example, for property damage), the insurance company takes over any rights that insured may have against a third party. A conflict of interest may develop between the insured and the insurer if the insured also has claims against the third party that are not covered by the policy.

Each of these situations represents a potential conflict of interest between insurance company and insured. Under standard conflict of interest principles, a lawyer may represent multiple clients with potential conflicts of interest in a single matter provided the lawyer fully explains to the clients the advantages, disadvantages, and risks of multiple representation, and provided both clients consent to the representation. See Model Rule 1.7(b). Surprisingly, insurance defense counsel have largely ignored these obligations of full disclosure and consent. Instead, when suit is filed against the insured, the insurance company typically forwards the case to defense counsel selected by it. Defense counsel then contacts the insured and proceeds to defend the case with little if any explanation of the relationship between defense counsel, insured, and insurance company. Failure by defense counsel to make full disclosure of their role and to obtain consent by the insured to multiple representation has been justified on the ground that the insured has given "consent" to the representation by forwarding court process to the insurance company,[105] but this consent is implied rather than expressed and in any event does not include a full disclosure of defense counsel's role.

Insurance defense counsel should take seriously their ethical obligations under Rule 1.7(b).[106] One approach would be for defense counsel to provide the insured with a brochure ("The Role and Ethical Obligations of Defense Counsel" would be an appropriate title) that describes the relationship between insured, insurance company, and defense counsel, and that highlights any limitations imposed by the insurance contract on defense counsel's representation. After outlining the general harmony of interest between insured and insurer, the brochure could then describe the standard conflicts of interests that could arise and the procedure that would be followed in dealing with them. The insured could be asked to consent to the terms of the engagement as set forth in the brochure and could also be advised of the insured's right to retain counsel at its own expense should it so desire.

Assuming defense counsel has undertaken representation, what action should counsel take if one of the potential conflicts of interest outlined above ripens into an actual conflict? Under standard principles of lawyer's obligations, when a lawyer faces an actual conflict of interest between two clients, the lawyer must withdraw from representation of both. Applied to insurance defense counsel, however, this approach is unsatisfactory. If defense counsel is required to withdraw, new defense counsel must be appointed at additional expense to the company and ultimately to its insureds. Thus, insurance defense practice has developed a different approach. In almost all of the conflict situations outlined above, the conflict between insured and insurance company does not involve confidential information that defense counsel has received from the insured. For example, excess claims, uninsured or underin-

105. See ABA Comm. on Ethics and Prof. Resp., Formal Opinion 282, at 3 (1950).

106. See ABA Comm. on Ethics and Prof. Resp., Formal Opinion 96-403, at 3-5 (defense counsel should communicate to insured nature and limits on representation at earliest possible opportunity; insured consents by accepting defense).

sured motorist claims, counterclaims, multiple insureds, and subrogation situations rarely involve any confidential information. In these nonconfidential information situations, the standard practice for dealing with the conflict is for the insurance company to notify the insured in writing and to inform the insured that it should consider retaining independent counsel at its own expense to protect its interests. For example, when the plaintiff makes a settlement demand within the policy limits, the insurer will send the insured an "excess letter," informing the insured of its potential liability in the event the case is not settled and the plaintiff obtains a recovery in excess of the policy limits. Similarly, when coverage is in doubt, the insurance company will send the insured a "reservation of rights letter," informing the insured that the company is defending the claim but is reserving its rights to contest coverage, typically in an independent declaratory judgment action. Defense counsel will continue to handle the case on behalf of both the insurer and the insured. The insured, with its own counsel, can participate in the proceedings to the extent appropriate to protect the insured's interest that is in conflict with the insurer's. Independent counsel can, for example, advocate on behalf of the insured that the insurer accept a settlement offer within the policy limits; similarly, independent counsel may represent the insured in any declaratory judgment action to determine coverage.[107]

Should the insurer be required to pay for the insured's independent counsel when the insured is notified of a conflict of interest? A growing number of courts have so held, but the wisdom of these decisions is questionable.[108] If the insurance company must pay for independent defense counsel every time one of the standard insurance defense conflicts arises, insureds have no incentive not to retain counsel. As a result, total defense fees and insurance

107. Guidance for defense counsel in dealing with standard conflict of interest situations can be found in the Guiding Principles of the National Conference of Lawyers and Liability Insurers. Reprinted in 20 Fedn. of Ins. Couns. Q. 93 (#4, Spring, 1970). The ABA approved the principles in 1972. The ABA rescinded its approval of the principles in 1980 under pressure from the Justice Department because of concern about the anticompetitive effect of intraprofessional agreements, not because of substantive problems with the principles. Wolfram, Modern Legal Ethics §8.4.2, at 429 n.97. Nonetheless, the Guiding Principles do provide a set of standards for the most common problems that defense counsel face.

108. San Diego Navy Fed. Credit Union v. Cumis Ins. Socy., 208 Cal. Rptr. 494 (Cal. Ct. App. 1984). *Accord* CHI of Alaska, Inc. v. Employers Reins. Corp., 844 P.2d 1113 (Alaska 1993).

premiums are likely to increase. A better approach is to place the cost of hiring independent counsel on insureds, who can then determine whether hiring counsel to deal with the particular conflict is truly cost effective. In addition, if a sufficient market for insurance for conflicts counsel exists, insurance companies will respond to the demand by offering riders providing for such coverage on payment of an additional premium.

What should defense counsel do when counsel learns of a conflict between insured and insurance company in confidence? Suppose, for example, the insured tells defense counsel of facts unknown to the insurer that would constitute a defense of lack of coverage. If the facts show that the insured is engaged in fraud or collusion, defense counsel should at a minimum withdraw from representation. Further, depending on the confidentiality rule that applies in the jurisdiction where the lawyer practices, the lawyer may be authorized to reveal the insured's confidences to prevent a crime or fraud. (See Chapter 4.D infra on the scope of the duty of confidentiality.) If the facts revealed to defense counsel simply establish a possible coverage defense, but do not involve fraud by the insured, defense counsel faces a fundamental conflict between two clients. The traditional answer to such a conflict is for the lawyer to withdraw, but in insurance defense practice this solution would do nothing but increase the cost of handling the case. In this difficult situation, the best solution is probably for defense counsel to continue the representation without revealing the insured's confidences to the insurer.[109]

The most common failing of defense counsel in dealing with these conflicts between insurer and insured is to protect the interest of the insurer over the insured. Defense counsel typically has an ongoing financial relationship with the insurance company. The company will be referring matters to defense counsel on a regular basis and paying its fees. On the other hand, defense counsel's relationship with the insured is typically transitory, lasting only for the one case, and the insured does not pay any fees. As a result, it is not surprising that some defense counsel have fallen into the ethical trap of protecting the interests of the insurance company at the expense of the insured.

For example, in Parsons v. Continental National American

109. See Guiding Principle VI of the Guiding Principles of the National Conference of Lawyers and Liability Insurers, note 107 supra.

Group,[110] the insured was a 14-year-old charged with assault and battery of his neighbors. The liability policy issued by CNA had a $25,000 limit and excluded intentional torts. The attorney retained by the insurance company obtained the child's confidential file from a boys' school were he was being kept. The attorney wrote the insurer advising it that the file showed that the boy was "fully aware of his acts" and that "the assault he committed on claimants can only be a deliberate act on his part." In preparing for trial, the attorney interviewed the child and received a narrative statement from him. In a letter to CNA, he wrote as follows: "His own story makes it obvious that his acts were willful and criminal."[111] At trial the attorney offered no evidence on the child's behalf, and a judgment was entered against the child in the amount of $50,000. The plaintiffs then brought a garnishment action against CNA seeking the amount of the policy.[112] CNA defended on the ground that the policy excluded intentional torts. The Arizona Supreme Court ruled that the company was estopped to deny liability because the attorney retained by the insurance company to defend the insured had violated his duty of confidentiality by revealing information obtained from the insured to the insurer in an effort to help the insurer establish a defense of lack of coverage:

> The attorney in the present case continued to act as Michael's attorney while he was actively working against Michael's interests. When an attorney who is an insurance company's agent uses the confidential relationship between an attorney and a client to gather information so as to deny the insured coverage under the policy in the garnishment proceeding we hold that such conduct constitutes a waiver of any policy defense, and is so contrary to public policy that the insurance company is estopped as a matter of law from disclaiming liability under an exclusionary clause in the policy.[113]

The court warned that an attorney confronted with such a conflict —confidential information received from the insured showing lack

110. 550 P.2d 94 (Ariz. 1976) (en banc).

111. Id. at 96.

112. In many jurisdictions, issues of coverage are resolved by declaratory judgment action. E.g., Employers Casualty Co. v. Tilley, 496 S.W.2d 552 (Tex. 1973) (declaratory judgment action brought by insurer against insured seeking determination of whether insured's failure to give timely notice as required by policy relieved insurer of obligations under policy).

113. 550 P.2d at 99.

of coverage — should withdraw from representation of the insurer.[114] The insurance company was held liable for the full $50,000, an amount in excess of the policy limit, because the company had rejected an opportunity to settle the case for $25,000.[115]

One way of eliminating the conflicts of interest facing defense counsel in representation of both the insured and the insurer is to change from a two-client to a one-client model of representation.[116] Under a one-client model, defense counsel would represent only the insured and would be required to take into account only the insured's interests, not those of the insurer. The insurance company would pay the fees of defense counsel pursuant to its duty to defend under the policy. The one-client model would be fully consistent with the rules of ethics. Model Rule 1.8(f) provides that a lawyer may represent a client while receiving payment from a third party so long as the client consents after consultation, the payor does not interfere with the lawyer's independent professional judgment on behalf of the client, and the lawyer adheres to the duty of confidentiality.

Insurance companies are likely to object to proposals for a one-client model on several grounds. First, companies might contend that under the one-client model they would lose the ability to select competent counsel. If the choice were left to the insured, companies would have no guarantee that the insured would select capable counsel. The result might well be less capable representation, harming both the insured and the insurer. Selection of counsel and

114. Id. at 98.

115. *Accord* Montanez v. Irizarry-Rodriguez, 641 A.2d 1079 (N.J. Super. App. Div. 1994) (improper for defense counsel to attempt to impeach testimony of insured to benefit insurer's interest; when conflict between insured and insurer, insurer can intervene in action or bring separate declaratory judgment action); Employers Casualty Co. v. Tilley, 496 S.W.2d 552 (Tex. 1973) (insurer estopped to deny coverage when attorney hired by insurer to defend insured worked on behalf of company to obtain statements from insured's employees establishing lack of coverage due to failure to file timely notice of claim). For an excess case in which the lawyer favored the interests of the insurer over the insured, see Lysick v. Walcom, 65 Cal. Rptr. 406 (Cal. Ct. App. 1968).

116. Robert E. O'Malley, Ethics Principles for the Insurer, the Insured, and Defense Counsel: The Eternal Triangle Reformed, 66 Tul. L. Rev. 511 (1991) (proposing set of Guiding Principles II based on one-client model); see also Douglas R. Richmond, Lost in the Eternal Triangle of Insurance Defense Ethics, 9 Geo. J. Legal Ethics 475 (1996) (surveying problem areas, but arguing that primary duty must be to insured). Compare Charles Silver & Kent Syverud, The Professional Responsibilities of Insurance Defense Lawyers, 45 Duke L.J. 255 (1995) (insurance contract should control responsibilities of defense counsel).

identification of the client, however, are different issues. Insurers could protect their legitimate interest in competent counsel by reserving in their policies the right either to select counsel or to approve counsel selected by the insured.

Second, companies might argue that the one-client model would deprive them of their contractual right to control the defense because counsel of record would owe its allegiance only to the insured. The one-client model does not, however, limit the insurer's contractual right to control the defense. For example, under the policy the insurer could reserve the right to establish a reasonable budget for the defense of the case. Further, as is the case now, insurance policies could provide that any settlement offer is subject to the insurer's acceptance.

Third, insurers might argue that a change to the one-client model would mean that they would lose the ability to receive objective advice from defense counsel on whether to accept a settlement offer. This argument is correct, but the benefits of the change may well outweigh the costs. Under the current two-client model, defense counsel has a difficult task when the insurer asks for advice about acceptance of a settlement offer. Defense counsel represents both the insured and the insurer. As attorney for the insured, defense counsel should advocate acceptance of any settlement that the insured finds favorable. As attorney for the insurer, however, defense counsel should give objective advice about the advantages and disadvantages of the settlement. Under the one-client model defense counsel would become an advocate for the insured rather than an objective advisor to the insurer. How significant would be the loss of advice from defense counsel? Insurers could still rely on advice from adjusters and in-house counsel, but their analysis of the case is unlikely to be as deep as that of defense counsel who is more familiar with the facts and context of the case. On the other hand, the one-client model might reduce the amount of bad faith litigation growing out of insurance defense.

Some courts may be moving toward a one-client model. In Atlanta International Insurance Co. v. Bell,[117] the Michigan Supreme Court held that an insurer could not bring a malpractice

117. 475 N.W.2d 294 (Mich. 1991). See also San Diego Navy Fed. Credit Union v. Cumis Ins. Socy., 208 Cal. Rptr. 494 (Cal. Ct. App. 1984) (when insurer defends under reservation of rights because of a coverage issue, insured is entitled to retain counsel at insurer's expense).

action against a lawyer that it had retained to defend the insured because the attorney represented only the insured and not the insurer. Over a strong dissent, however, the court recognized the right of the insurer to equitable subrogation from the lawyer. The movement toward a one-client model, however, may not be cause for applause. One commentator has stated: "The insurance industry will continue to bear the adverse economic consequences of high legal costs as they deal with lawyers typically less experienced than those usually selected by the insurer."[118]

L. MULTIPLE DEFENDANTS IN CRIMINAL CASES

Representation of multiple defendants in criminal cases poses both ethical and constitutional issues. Some scholars have argued that conflicts of interest are so pervasive in the representation of multiple criminal defendants that such representation should be prohibited either as a matter of constitutional law or rules of ethics.[119] Despite these arguments, neither the rules of ethics nor constitutional decisions create a per se prohibition against multiple representation, although multiple representation is discouraged. Model Rule 1.7(b) deals with multiple representation of clients in a single matter. While the text of Rule 1.7 makes no distinction between civil and criminal cases, Comment 7 states: "The potential for conflict of interest in representing multiple defendants in a criminal case is so grave that ordinarily a lawyer should decline to represent more than one codefendant." Both the ABA Defense Function Standards[120] and the proposed Restatement of the Law Governing Lawyers express similar views.[121]

Under what circumstances is the likelihood of an actual conflict

118. See Ronald E. Mallen, A New Definition of Insurance Defense Counsel, 53 Ins. Couns. J. 108, 123 (1986).

119. See John S. Geer, Representation of Multiple Criminal Defendants: Conflicts of Interest and the Professional Responsibilities of the Defense Attorney, 62 Minn. L. Rev. 119 (1978); Gary T. Lowenthal, Joint Representation in Criminal Cases: A Critical Appraisal, 64 Va. L. Rev. 939 (1978).

120. See also ABA Defense Function Standard 4-3.5(c).

121. Restatement of the Law Governing Lawyers §210 (Prop. Final Draft #1, March 29, 1996).

so great that the lawyer should decline multiple representation even if the clients are willing to consent? Professors Fortune, Underwood, and Imwinkelried offer the following checklist of questions to consider in deciding whether multiple representation of criminal defendants is permissible:

1. Does one defendant have evidence to offer that inculpates the codefendant?
2. Is one defendant more culpable than the other? If so, conflict is almost inevitable, either because the prosecution will offer a deal to the one less culpable or because distinctions will need to be drawn during the case.
3. Are the defenses inconsistent in any way?
4. Will one testify and the other not? A defendant who testifies inevitably calls attention to the failure of the other defendant to take the stand. This problem is exacerbated by joint representation.
5. Will the prosecution's evidence strike the defendants unequally? If a prosecution witness implicates *A*, but not *B*, the attorney is put in the position of attacking the witness on behalf of *A*, but implying that he is telling the truth about *B*.
6. Should distinctions be drawn in closing argument? The attorney representing codefendants cannot do so.
7. Should distinctions be drawn at sentencing because of either the defendants' relative culpability or their different backgrounds?[122]

Burger v. Kemp[123] illustrates the dangers of multiple representation. Two law partners represented defendants in a murder case. Both defendants confessed to the crime. Each defendant was tried separately, and the strategy of each defendant was to emphasize the culpability of the other to avoid the death penalty. Burger's attorney assisted in the trial of the other defendant; he also wrote briefs on appeal for both defendants. On appeal, the lawyer did not make a "lesser culpability" argument, even though this was Burger's defense at trial. Burger claimed that his lawyer's conduct amounted to ineffective assistance of counsel. The Supreme Court, however, rejected his argument, finding that it was a reasonable strategic decision to abandon this argument, given that Burger was

122. William H. Fortune et al., Modern Litigation and Professional Responsibility Handbook §14.3.1, at 461-462 (1996).
123. 483 U.S. 776 (1987).

the actual killer and that the Georgia Supreme Court had characterized his conduct as "outrageously and wantonly vile and inhuman under any reasonable standard of human conduct."[124]

Suppose the lawyer, after considering the facts and potential conflicts, concludes that multiple representation would be proper. For lawyers in private defense practice, an initial personal decision must be made: Am I willing to undertake multiple representation even if it is ethically and constitutionally permitted? Some lawyers may believe that representing multiple defendants will so frequently involve a conflict that such representation should always be avoided. In addition, if a lawyer undertakes multiple representation, a conviction will often produce a claim of ineffective assistance of counsel, requiring the lawyer to withdraw from further representation in the matter and involving the lawyer in time consuming post-conviction relief proceedings. On the other hand, the potential clients may be financially unable to afford separate counsel, and joint representation may be strategically desirable because it facilitates a common defense.

Lawyers who decide to proceed with multiple representation may do so provided the clients consent after consultation with the lawyer. The Model Rules state that "consultation shall include explanation of the implications of the common representation and the advantages and risks involved." Model Rule 1.7(b). Advantages of multiple representation that should be discussed typically include pooling of resources, obtaining the benefit of counsel with particular expertise or with knowledge of the case, and presenting a united defense front. Laywers should be careful to point out the disadvantages of multiple representation. In broad terms, multiple representation precludes defense counsel from advocating a position on behalf of one defendant that casts the blame on another represented defendant, whether in plea bargaining, witness selection, witness examination, argument, sentencing, or appeal. The defendants should recognize and understand that the lawyer will zealously act on their behalf but will not do anything to benefit one defendant at the expense of another. The defendants should be advised that they should not consent to multiple representation if they foresee such a situation developing because the lawyer would be required to withdraw should an actual conflict of interest emerge. If the defendants conclude that the advantages of mul-

124. Id. at 784.

tiple representation outweigh any disadvantages, and if they are willing to consent to multiple representation, the lawyer may proceed. Ideally, the clients should consent to multiple representation in writing. The consent should acknowledge a full consultation with the lawyer about the advantages and disadvantages of multiple representation, and should provide that the defendants have been advised of their right to retain independent counsel.

Under what circumstances does multiple representation of criminal defendants result in a violation of a defendant's constitutional right to effective assistance of counsel? The Supreme Court first considered cases in which trial courts appointed one lawyer to represent multiple defendants over the objection of one of the defendants or defense counsel. The Court held that such an appointment violates a defendant's constitutional right to effective assistance of counsel,[125] even if the defendant is unable to show prejudice resulting from the multiple representation.[126] In later cases, the Court ruled on situations in which the defendant consented or waived objections to multiple representation. In these cases the Court held that the defendant must show that "an actual conflict of interest adversely affected his lawyer's performance."[127] More recently, the Court decided that to ensure protection of defendants' constitutional rights, trial courts must inquire into the adequacy of multiple representation and may refuse to allow such representation, in spite of the consent of the defendants, when a serious potential conflict of interest exists.[128]

The Federal Rules of Criminal Procedure require courts to inquire into the adequacy of multiple representation.[129] In making this inquiry, however, courts should take steps to prevent disclosure of confidential information.[130] In state court lawyers must, of

125. Glasser v. United States, 315 U.S. 60 (1942); Holloway v. Arkansas, 435 U.S. 475 (1978).

126. 315 U.S. at 76; 435 U.S. at 487-490.

127. Cuyler v. Sullivan, 446 U.S. 335, 348 (1980). Although *Cuyler* failed to find a Sixth Amendment violation, lower courts have done so on appropriate facts. E.g. Griffin v. McVicar, 84 F.3d 880 (7th Cir. 1996), *cert. denied,* 117 S. Ct. 1288 (1997) (ineffective assistance of counsel shown when lawyer adopted common defense strategy for defendants with different degrees of culpability); Hoffman v. Leeke, 903 F.2d 280 (4th Cir. 1990) (ineffective assistance of counsel when lawyer represented codefendants in murder case and negotiated plea bargain in which one defendant implicated other).

128. Wheat v. United States, 486 U.S. 153 (1988).

129. See Fed. R. Crim. P. 44(c).

130. Id. (Advisory Committee Notes).

course, follow state rules of criminal procedure.[131] In the absence of a court rule, a lawyer who has accepted multiple representation should make the clients' consent a matter of judicial record as recommended by ABA Defense Function Standard 4-3.5(c).[132]

M. TRANSACTIONAL MATTERS WITH COMMON OBJECTIVES

Earlier we considered situations in which lawyers are asked to represent parties in an effort to resolve a known dispute informally outside of litigation. Even though the dispute exists, the clients share a common desire to resolve the matter without litigation, and they may have other common interests as well.

Lawyers are also often asked to undertake representation of multiple clients outside of litigation with regard to a common venture rather than a known dispute. Business formations, estate planning, and real estate sales are common examples. In each of these situations, the parties have a common purpose, but some differences may exist between their interests.

1. *Business Formations*

Business formations raise a number of issues about which the owners of the business may have differing interests. Typically, some owners will provide capital while others will contribute technical, management, or marketing services. Some of the questions and issues that can arise include the following: Will the capital contribution be in the form of a loan or equity capital? Will the owner who contributes capital be entitled to a preference in repayment of capital before distributions of income are made to the other owners? During the start-up phase, new businesses typi-

131. See, e.g., People v. Mroczko, 672 P.2d 835 (Cal. 1983) (en banc) (trial court must initially appoint separate counsel with an instruction to inform the court if counsel, after investigation and consultation with their clients, conclude that the interests of justice and of their clients will best be served by multiple representation; court will then make such on-the-record disposition as is appropriate).

132. See Shongutsie v. State, 827 P.2d 361 (Wyo. 1992) (consent should preferably be in writing and should be included in the record).

cally generate little income. Will the owners who provide services receive a salary during this period? If so, how much? If any owners decide to leave the business, will their interests be subject to purchase? If so, at what price? How will control of the business be determined? Will supramajority or veto rights be included? These issues illustrate a few of the many topics on which the owners may have differing interests. By agreeing to handle the legal work involved in the formation of the business, an attorney is agreeing to represent all of the owners and the entity that will be formed. Is the attorney ethically permitted to undertake this representation?

Under the Code of Professional Responsibility it was unclear whether a lawyer could represent multiple clients in the formation of a business. DR 5-105(C) provided that "a lawyer may represent multiple clients if it is obvious that he can adequately represent the interest of each and if each consents to the representation after full disclosure of the possible effect of such representation on the exercise of his independent professional judgment on behalf of each." The use of the word *obvious* made it questionable whether a lawyer should represent multiple parties in a business transaction with potentially conflicting interests.[133]

The drafters of the Model Rules decided that lawyers should have greater freedom to undertake multiple representation in business matters than the language of the Code seemed to permit. They changed the basic conflict of interest rule, Rule 1.7, to eliminate the requirement that it be obvious that the lawyer could adequately represent the clients. In addition, they added Model Rule 2.2, which allows lawyers to act as intermediaries between clients to resolve disputes or to assist them in reaching a common objective even when they have significant differences. Comment 3 to Model Rule 2.2 specifically refers to the rule's application to business formations. The requirements for representation under Model Rule 2.2 were discussed earlier in this chapter.[134]

2. *Estate Planning and Administration*

Estate planning for a husband and wife is another transactional matter in which a lawyer may be asked to undertake multiple

133. For a debate on the issue see Legal Ethics Forum, Representation of Multiple Clients, 62 A.B.A. J. 648 (1976).

134. See Chapter 3.E.1 supra.

representation.[135] While spouses who are planning their estates may have differences on issues such as distributions to heirs and appointment of personal representatives or trustees, they usually share overriding common objectives to coordinate their estates and to minimize taxes. Thus, lawyers may properly represent both spouses in estate planning with their informed consent.[136]

The Restatement of the Law Governing Lawyers takes the position that in situations where the lawyer knows the spouses and no apparent differences exist, he may proceed to represent the spouses in estate planning without disclosure and consent.[137] This approach seems unwise. All estate planning involves the potential for a conflict of interest. Given this potential, disclosure and client consent seem both appropriate and necessary. The Restaters may have felt that in routine estate planning, lawyers would find it ritualistic and perhaps offensive to their clients to make disclosures about far-fetched conflicts of interest. Nonetheless, lawyers can devise courteous methods for making the appropriate disclosures and obtaining client consent to multiple representation that avoid these problems. For example, disclosure and consent could be obtained through a simple letter to the clients, which also thanks them for seeking the lawyer's services and explains the terms of the lawyer's engagement.

Some practitioners take the view that when a lawyer represents both a husband and a wife in estate planning, the lawyer may structure the representation in either of two ways: as separate representation or as joint representation. In separate representation, the lawyer represents each spouse separately as to that spouse's rights and interests.[138] Further, in separate representation, the lawyer must maintain the confidentiality of information received from either spouse, even if the information might affect the estate plan of the other spouse.[139] The lawyer, however, may have a duty to withdraw if the receipt of confidential information means

135. For a comprehensive treatment of ethical issues in estate planning and administration, see Jeffrey N. Pennell, Ethics, Professionalism, and Malpractice Issues in Estate Planning and Administration, ALI-ABA Course of Study: Estate Planning in Depth, SB90 ALI-ABA 51, June 15, 1997 (on Westlaw).

136. Restatement of the Law Governing Lawyers §211, comm. *c* (Prop. Final Draft #1, March 29, 1996).

137. Id. §211, comment *c* and illus. 1.

138. ABA Real Property, Probate and Trust Section, Comments and Recommendations on the Lawyer's Duties in Representing Husband and Wife, 28 Real Prop. Prob. & Trust J. 765, 772 (1994).

139. Id. at 796.

that an actual conflict of interest exists between the spouses.[140] By contrast, in joint representation the lawyer represents both spouses "joined to accomplish a mutual goal."[141] If a lawyer who is engaged in joint representation receives confidential information from one spouse that has an impact on the estate plan of the other spouse, the lawyer must act as a fiduciary to both spouses and must choose to disclose, to maintain confidentiality, or to withdraw based on the lawyer's determination of which action does the least harm.[142]

The concept of separate representation is unsound. Nothing in the rules of professional conduct authorizes lawyers to represent multiple clients while keeping information obtained from one secret from the other. Indeed, the essence of multiple representation is full disclosure in an effort to reach common objectives or to resolve differences between the parties. Professor Geoffrey Hazard has criticized probate and estate lawyers for claiming that their practice should be subject to special rules. He argues that while joint representation is consistent with the Model Rules, separate representation is "incorrect as a matter of law and therefore a legally dangerous mode of practice."[143] The Restatement of the Law Governing Lawyers, while not rejecting the concept of separate representation outright, refers to it as "novel" and cautions lawyers about the substantial risks involved in undertaking this form of representation.[144]

Conflicts of interest can also arise in connection with estate administration. In most jurisdictions, a lawyer retained to handle the administration of the estate represents the personal representative or other fiduciary appointed to handle the estate, rather than the beneficiaries.[145] Treating the fiduciary rather than the

140. Id. at 794-795.

141. Id. at 771.

142. Id. at 787.

143. Geoffrey C. Hazard, Jr., Conflict of Interest in Estate Planning for Husband and Wife, 20 Prob. Law. 1, 6 (1994) (published by the Am. Coll. of Trust & Estate Counsel).

144. Restatement of the Law Governing Lawyers §211, Reporter's Note to comm. *c* (Prop. Final Draft #1, March 29, 1996).

145. See, e.g., Goldberg v. Frye, 266 Cal. Rptr. 483 (Cal. Ct. App. 1990) (no cause of action by beneficiaries against lawyer for administrator of estate because attorney does not owe duty to beneficiaries); In re Estate of Gory, 570 So. 2d 1381 (Fla. Dist. Ct. App. 1990) (personal representative rather than estate or beneficiaries as client); Succession of Wallace, 574 So. 2d 348 (La. 1991) (citing cases from nine jurisdictions); Trask v. Butler, 872 P.2d 1080 (Wash. 1994) (en banc) (attorney for personal representative does not owe duty of care to estate beneficiaries). See also S.C. Code Ann. §62-1-109 (West Supp. 1997) (lawyer retained by fiduciary represents fiduciary rather than beneficiaries).

beneficiaries as the lawyer's client makes sense. The fiduciary, not the beneficiaries, has the legal authority to make a number of decisions regarding the estate. It would be odd to place the lawyer in the position of representing a group of individuals who do not have authority to act, while not representing the one person who does. Further, although it is true that the estate is being administered in the interest of the beneficiaries, it does not follow that the beneficiaries' desires or decisions should control. The testator appointed the fiduciary for the purpose of making decisions, in some cases because the testator did not fully trust the beneficiaries to make such decisions. The fiduciary should be entitled to retain independent counsel to receive advice about these matters.

While it seems sound to treat the personal representative as the estate lawyer's client, it is unsound to conclude that the lawyer has no duties whatsoever to the beneficiaries. Lawyers for fiduciaries must take into account a number of duties to beneficiaries. First, beneficiaries may well misunderstand the role of the lawyer and may view the lawyer as protecting or representing their interests. Such misunderstanding is especially likely to occur when the lawyer has represented the beneficiary in the past or is currently handling an unrelated matter on behalf of the beneficiary. Under Model Rule 4.3, when a lawyer "knows or reasonably should know that the unrepresented person misunderstands the lawyer's role in the matter, the lawyer shall make reasonable efforts to correct the misunderstanding."[146] Prudent lawyers should clarify to beneficiaries in writing that they represent the fiduciary and that the beneficiaries may want to retain independent counsel for advice.

Second, a lawyer for a fiduciary may not counsel or assist the fiduciary in illegal or fraudulent conduct. See Model Rule 1.2(d). See also Model Rules 3.3(a)(1) and 4.1, prohibiting lawyers from making false statements of law or fact to a tribunal or third person. This prohibition would include participation in the preparation or filing of fraudulent tax returns or assisting the fiduciary in self-dealing.[147]

146. See also ABA Real Property, Probate and Trust Section, Counseling the Fiduciary, 28 Real Prop. Prob. & Trust J. 825, 837-840 (1994); American College of Trust and Estate Counsel, Commentaries on the Model Rules of Professional Conduct, 28 Real Prop. Prob. & Trust J. 865, 980 (1994) (commentary to Rule 4.3).

147. ABA Real Property, Probate and Trust Section, Counseling the Fiduciary, 28 Real Prop. Prob. & Trust J. 825, 836-837 (1994); see Pierce v. Lyman, 3 Cal. Rptr. 2d 236 (Ct. App. 1991) (beneficiaries state cause of action against trustee's lawyer for participation in trustee's breach of fiduciary duty).

Third, under some circumstances a lawyer may have a duty to inform either the beneficiaries or the court of wrongdoing by a fiduciary. We will consider this issue in the next chapter, which focuses on the duty of confidentiality.

Although estate lawyers normally represent only the personal representative or other fiduciary who is appointed to administer the estate, sometimes a lawyer may be asked to undertake multiple representation—representation of a beneficiary and a fiduciary, or multiple beneficiaries, or multiple fiduciaries. While potential conflicts of interest exist in such situations, a harmony of interests normally occurs between the beneficiaries and the fiduciary.[148] The lawyer may proceed with multiple representation provided the lawyer makes full disclosure to the clients of potential conflicts of interest and obtains their informed consent, as required by Model Rule 1.7(b).[149] If an actual conflict develops between clients, the lawyer should not continue to represent the parties.[150] The lawyer will be required to withdraw from representation of both clients unless one of the clients is willing to consent under Model Rule 1.9.[151]

3. *Real Estate*

Real estate transactions vary considerably in their form and complexity, from large commercial transactions, in which all or almost all of the interested parties will be independently represented by counsel, to relatively routine residential sales where in many jurisdictions one attorney handles the closing on behalf of all of the parties. Indeed, in some jurisdictions, nonlawyers may handle all aspects of residential real estate transactions.

How can lawyers avoid confusion about whom they represent in real estate transactions? In large commercial transactions, the possibility of confusion is reduced because each of the parties is

148. American College of Trust and Estate Counsel, Commentaries on the Model Rules of Professional Conduct, 28 Real Prop. Prob. & Trust J. 865, 934 (1994) (commentary to Model Rule 1.7, example 1.7-3) (permissible for lawyer to represent both bank and wife with full disclosure and consent). On multiple representation of fiduciaries, see also ABA Real Property, Probate and Trust Section, Counseling the Fiduciary, 28 Real Prop. Prob. & Trust J. 825, 855-860 (1994) (multiple representation of cofiduciaries).

149. ABA Real Property, Probate and Trust Section, Counseling the Fiduciary, 28 Real Prop. Prob. & Trust J. 825, 842-846 (1994).

150. Id. at 847.

151. Id. at 848.

typically represented by counsel. Even in commercial transactions, however, if a lawyer is preparing documents that will be executed by other parties, it would be prudent for the lawyer to have the other parties sign statements acknowledging that the attorney does not represent them and that they will look to their own counsel for advice in the transaction. In fairly routine residential real estate transactions, the expense of separate counsel renders this option infeasible.

If the parties to a real estate transaction are not separately represented, real estate attorneys have two models available to clarify their roles: the multiple-representation model and the single-client model. In the multiple-representation model, the lawyer has multiple clients: buyer and seller; buyer and lender; buyer, seller, and lender; or perhaps even, buyer, seller, lender, and title company. As discussed earlier, Model Rules 1.7 and 2.2 authorize lawyers to represent multiple clients in business transactions under some circumstances. To do so, lawyers must conclude that they can reasonably undertake the representation without adverse impact on either of the clients, and each client must consent after consultation with the lawyer about the advantages and risks of multiple representation.

Is a real estate transaction the type of matter in which a lawyer can reasonably undertake multiple representation without adverse impact on the representation of either of the clients? In some cases, courts have found that lawyers have acted improperly by representing multiple clients in real estate transactions. These cases, however, typically involved attorneys who failed to obtain the informed consent of their clients or who neglected to carry out their duties to one of the clients.[152] While such cases highlight the dangers of multiple representation, they do not go so far as to establish a per se bar to multiple representation in real estate transactions.[153] On the other hand, attorneys should recognize that multiple representation, even in fairly routine residential real estate

152. E.g., Florida Bar v. Teitelman, 261 So. 2d 140 (Fla. 1972) (failure to obtain informed consent to multiple representation); Attorney Grievance Comm. v. Lockhart, 403 A.2d 1241 (Md. 1979) (improper certifications of title and release of funds). See generally Annotation, Attorney and Client: Conflict of Interest in Real Estate Closing Situations, 68 A.L.R.3d 967 (1976).

153. See Westport Bank & Trust Co. v. Corcoran, Mallin & Aresco, 605 A.2d 862 (Conn. 1992) (potential for conflict of interest does not preclude such representation). But see Baldasarre v. Butler, 625 A.2d 458 (N.J. 1993) (because of high likelihood of actual conflict of interest in complex commercial real estate transactions, multiple representation is improper even with consent of parties).

transactions, has risks. Further, the climate of professional opinion may be shifting against the practice. For example, the leading treatise on legal malpractice states:

> Historically, the practice of an attorney representing both parties to a transaction in the transfer of a property interest was common and, seemingly, approved. Today such representation is doubtful, at best, and usually is improper.[154]

If a lawyer concludes that she can adequately represent both of the parties, the lawyer must also obtain the informed consent of both parties. Informed consent requires more than a statement that the lawyer does not have a conflict of interest.[155] Given the possibility for confusion regarding the lawyer's role, written disclosure of the advantages and disadvantages of the lawyer's role, and written consent if the attorney will be representing multiple parties, is highly desirable.

If an attorney decides to undertake multiple representation, the fundamental problem facing the attorney is how to advise and counsel the clients on solutions to issues that may benefit one party at the expense of the other. The problem is especially acute if the attorney is employed before the parties have executed a binding contract. Real estate contracts like other agreements can be drafted to favor either of the parties. Even if the attorney is not employed until after the parties sign a contract, as is usually the case in residential transactions, issues may still arise. For example, suppose the contract fails to specify which party bears the cost of a certain item, such as repairs resulting from a termite inspection. Or, suppose at closing a question arises as to whether certain fixtures are included with the sale to the purchaser or may be taken by the seller. One way in which an attorney could respond to such issues is to act in essence as an arbitrator. The attorney informs the parties how the issue should be resolved, either based on the lawyer's opinion or based on what the lawyer believes is customarily done. While it is possible for the clients to agree for the lawyer to act as arbitrator of any disputes they may have, absent such an

154. 4 Mallen & Smith, Legal Malpractice §30.6, at 20.

155. See In re Lanza, 322 A.2d 445 (N.J. 1974) (lawyer disciplined for representing buyer and seller without informed consent and for continuing representation of both once actual conflict developed over payment of portion of purchase price).

agreement the arbitration approach seems inconsistent with the lawyer's obligations as a representative of both parties.

How can lawyers act consistently with their obligations as representatives of both of the parties? Consider the possibility of acting as a "neutral information source." In this role, the lawyer identifies any issue that is likely to be of concern to either of the parties, whether raised by the parties or not. The lawyer provides information to the clients about how they could resolve the issue. This information includes the lawyer's understanding of how such matters are customarily resolved in the locality, but the method of presenting this information differs from the approach when the lawyer assumes the role of arbitrator. In the capacity of "neutral information source," the lawyer supplies this information but also advises the parties that the custom is not necessarily binding on them and that they can agree to a different resolution of the issue. The lawyer should also inform the parties that if the issue is significant to them, and if they are unable to reach agreement, the lawyer cannot proceed with the closing. See Model Rule 2.2(c).

Instead of undertaking multiple representation, lawyers handling real estate transactions could decide to adopt a single-client representation model. Under this approach, the lawyer represents only one party to the transaction. Whom does the lawyer represent? The natural answer is either the buyer or the lender, since they are the principal parties in the transaction. As between the buyer and the lender, the buyer is obviously more in need of legal advice and protection than a sophisticated lender. Further, statutes in some jurisdictions grant borrowers in residential real estate financing transactions the right to select counsel.[156] On the other hand, some lenders may insist that lawyers represent their interests at closing. Lawyers who want to do business with such lenders must accept an client-attorney relationship with the lender as well as with the buyer. A lawyer who represents only the lender, however, may still be held liable in malpractice to a purchaser.[157] The following discussion assumes that single-client representation is a feasible alternative for the lawyer.

The fact that the lawyer represents only the buyer does not

156. E.g., S.C. Code Ann. §37-10-102(a) (West Supp. 1997).

157. See Seigle v. Jasper, 867 S.W.2d 476 (Ky. Ct. App. 1993) (attorney for lender could be liable to purchasers for negligent title examination under Restatement (Second) of Torts §552).

prevent the lawyer from preparing documents to be signed by other parties to the transaction, nor does the fact that the lawyer is preparing documents for the other parties necessarily result in the formation of an client-attorney relationship with those parties.[158] The lawyer would be acting as agent for the buyer, preparing documents that must be signed by other parties for the buyer's benefit.

How are the lender's legal interests protected if the lawyer represents only the buyer? Lenders' commitment letters will attach various conditions to the closing of the loan to protect the lender. These conditions typically include use of the lenders' closing documents and issuance of a title insurance policy to protect the lender. Many lenders have their own general or in-house counsel who review the lenders' standard form closing package and advise them should any problems arise. The use of the lenders' closing package generally precludes the possibility of the lawyer negotiating changes in the forms on behalf of the buyer. Since the forms are fairly standard in most jurisdictions, rarely would there be much to negotiate in any event. The attorney would, of course, have an obligation to advise the buyer generally as to the nature of the documents the buyer is signing and to point out any unusual provisions of which the buyer should be aware. Although the lender requires the buyer's attorney to use its forms, this should not be considered to be improper third-party interference with the lawyer's relationship with the buyer. See Model Rule 5.4(c). The use of the lender's forms is simply a condition to the loan, similar to other conditions, such as the buyer's creditworthiness. Even though the lender may be a sophisticated commercial party, a prudent closing attorney will clarify in writing that the attorney is handling the closing as the attorney for the buyer, not the lender. It should be noted, however, that while a lawyer who makes it clear that he represents only the buyer does not have a client-attorney relationship with the lender, the lawyer may still be liable for malpractice to the lender, depending on the approach of the jurisdiction to the requirement of privity of contract. Traditionally, lawyers have only been liable to their clients for negligence. Nonclients could not recover against attorneys for negligence because of lack of privity of contract. In many jurisdictions, however, lack

158. E.g., Dolan v. Hickey, 431 N.E.2d 229 (Mass. 1982) (drafting and presentation of documents does not amount to legal advice).

of privity of contract will not prevent recovery against an attorney for negligence in a real estate transaction because the attorney's work was intended to benefit the other parties to the transaction.[159]

Similarly, the fact that the attorney is representing the buyer should not preclude the attorney from preparing documents for the seller's signature that are necessary to close the transaction, such as the deed from the seller, affidavits from the seller regarding liens on the property, and the closing statement. The attorney should advise the seller that the attorney represents the buyer, that such documents are being prepared for the benefit of the buyer, and that the seller may wish to hire separate counsel for advice about these documents. Notification of the lawyer's role should be given to the seller in writing in advance of the closing so that the seller has sufficient time to retain counsel. This may not be easy given the time pressures under which many real estate closings occur. Even though the attorney does not represent the seller, the attorney may still be liable to the seller for malpractice in connection with any documents prepared for the seller.[160]

4. *Evaluation on Behalf of Client for Third Person*

Clients often ask their lawyers to provide opinions or evaluations to a third person. Common examples of such situations are responses to auditors' requests for opinions on the clients' legal affairs that auditors then rely on in preparing clients' financial statements,[161] legal opinions prepared by counsel for issuers in securities transactions on tax and other matters that are relied on by investors, and opinions about mortgages and security interests issued by borrowers' counsel to lenders.[162] As discussed in the previous section, in real estate matters lawyers sometimes prepare

159. See 4 Mallen & Smith, Legal Malpractice §30.4.

160. Cf. Petrillo v. Bachenberg, 655 A.2d 1354 (N.J. 1995) (purchaser has cause of action against seller's attorney for supplying misleading information regarding condition of property); Collins v. Binkley, 750 S.W.2d 737 (Tenn. 1988) (lawyer who represented seller in closing was liable to purchaser for negligent preparation of deed).

161. See ABA Statement of Policy Regarding Lawyers' Responses to Auditors' Requests for Information, 31 Bus. Law. 1709 (1976).

162. See ABA Committee on Legal Opinions, Third-Party Legal Opinion Report, 47 Bus. Law. 167 (1991).

documents or opinions for third parties. Ethically, lawyers may prepare such opinions if the lawyer reasonably believes that issuance of the opinion is compatible with the client's interest and the client consents after consultation. Model Rule 2.3. The Model Rules provide the following example: "[I]f the lawyer is acting as advocate in defending the client against charges of fraud, it would normally be incompatible with that responsibility for the lawyer to perform an evaluation for others concerning the same or a related transaction." Model Rule 2.3, comm. 4. Lawyers who issue third-party opinions do not normally have a client-attorney relationship with the recipient of the opinion, but do have duties to recipients, including a duty to exercise due care in preparing the opinion and a duty not to engage in misrepresentation of material facts.[163]

Part III
Other Conflicts of Interest

N. FINANCIAL INTEREST CONFLICTS BETWEEN LAWYER AND CLIENT

1. *General Principles*

The first two parts of this chapter have focused on actual and potential conflicts between clients. Another form of conflict arises when a lawyer has a financial interest in a transaction with a client while representing the client in the transaction. Probably the most common situation of this sort is when the lawyer represents the client on a contingency fee basis (see Chapter 2.C supra), but financial interest conflicts also arise frequently in transactional matters. This section discusses four such situations: real estate matters in which lawyers have a financial interest in title insurance; business formations in which lawyers are also investors; service on the board of directors of a client's business; and estate planning in

163. See Greycas, Inc. v. Proud, 826 F.2d 1560 (7th Cir. 1987), *cert. denied,* 484 U.S. 1043 (1988) (lawyer liable to recipient of opinion for failure to verify security interest in equipment). See generally Restatement of the Law Governing Lawyers §151 (Tent. Draft #8, March 21, 1997).

which lawyers may serve as personal representatives of their clients' estates.

An initial question to ask about these financial interest conflicts is whether a per se rule prohibiting lawyers from representing clients in transactions in which lawyers have a financial interest is appropriate. As we have seen several times in this chapter, the general approach followed by the rules of ethics for conflicts of interest is that a lawyer may represent a client despite the existence of an actual or potential conflict, provided the client consents to the matter after full disclosure. Only in the limited situation involving adverse representation in a single litigation matter, when the social interest in an adversarial presentation is involved, does a per se prohibition apply. (See Chapter 3.B supra.) Thus, it seems consistent to allow lawyers in transactional matters to represent clients even if they have a financial interest in the matter, provided the client consents after full disclosure. Further, since lawyers may enter into contingency fee agreements with their clients, even though the agreement gives the lawyer an interest in the case and may affect the lawyer's judgment, it seems inconsistent to prohibit absolutely other forms of business transactions between lawyers and their clients. Moreover, general contract law provides that agreements between fiduciaries and their principals are not per se invalid but are instead subject to special restrictions in addition to normal contract defenses (fraud, duress, mistake, and so forth). Principals may rescind contracts with their fiduciaries if the contract is unfair to the principal or if the fiduciary fails to disclose all material facts to the principal regarding the transaction.[164] These special rules are justified because of the high degree of trust and confidence that principals repose in fiduciaries.[165] Model Rule 1.8(a), which reflects these principles, provides that business agreements between lawyers and their clients are not per se invalid, but are subject to special requirements:

> (a) A lawyer shall not enter into a business transaction with a client or knowingly acquire an ownership, possessory, security or other pecuniary interest adverse to a client unless:
>
> (1) the transaction and terms on which the lawyer acquires the interest are fair and reasonable to the client and are fully

164. Restatement (Second) of Contracts §173 (1981).

165. See generally Charles L. Knapp & Nathan M. Crystal, Problems in Contract Law 646-660 (3d ed. 1993).

> disclosed and transmitted in writing to the client in a manner which can be reasonably understood by the client;
>
> (2) the client is given a reasonable opportunity to seek the advice of independent counsel in the transaction; and
>
> (3) the client consents in writing thereto.

Notice that the section requires disclosure in writing and mandates that clients have a reasonable opportunity to seek advice of independent counsel. Section 207 of the Proposed Restatement of the Law Governing Lawyers is similar to Model Rule 1.8(a).

Ordinary fee contracts between lawyers and clients are, of course, a type of business transaction. It appears, however, that the drafters of the Model Rules did not intend the restrictions of Rule 1.8(a) to apply to standard fee agreements in which lawyers receive only money and not any form of ownership interest in their clients' property, probably because of the impracticality of clients' obtaining independent advice regarding standard fee agreements.[166] Fee contracts are, however, subject to a "fairness" requirement by virtue of Rule 1.5(a), which provides that legal fees must be "reasonable." Comment 1 to Rule 1.8 also states that Rule 1.8(a) does not apply to "standard commercial transactions between the lawyer and the client for products or services that the client generally markets to others."

2. *Real Estate Transactions*

In residential real estate transactions, lawyers often have a financial interest in the transaction arising from their relationship with title insurance companies. Lawyers frequently act as agents for title insurance companies, receiving a commission from the sale of title insurance to owners and lenders. Further, some lawyers have an ownership interest in title insurance companies. In Formal Opinions 304 (1962) and 331 (1972), the ABA Committee on Ethics and Professional Responsibility decided that lawyers could properly advise their clients about the availability of title insurance even though they received a commission or had a financial interest in a title insurance company, but such financial relationships should be

166. See Restatement of the Law Governing Lawyers §207, comm. *a* (Prop. Final Draft #1, March 29, 1996).

fully disclosed and consented to by the client. These opinions seem consistent with Model Rule 1.8(a), which involves business transactions between lawyer and client. In addition, the Real Estate Settlement Procedures Act (RESPA),[167] requires lawyers to disclose to buyers commissions received from selling title insurance.

In some commercial real estate transactions, lawyers may have a financial interest in the transaction or in one of the parties to the transaction. A lawyer who has a financial interest has a duty to comply with Model Rule 1.8(a) regarding the transaction. Note that the rule requires the client's written consent and an opportunity to seek the advice of independent counsel. Lawyers have been disciplined and held liable for damages to their clients for failing to disclose their financial interest in real estate transactions.[168] If the lawyer's financial interest in the transaction is substantial, prudence dictates that the lawyer decline representation in the matter.

3. *Investment in a Client's Business*

Clients sometimes offer their lawyers an opportunity to invest in their businesses. Such situations can arise in connection with the formation of a new business with the investment being in lieu of a fee, or it can occur in an established business because of the relationship between the lawyer and client.

Such investments are proper so long as the lawyer meets the requirements of Model Rule 1.8(a), but prudent lawyers should be aware of the risks they face in making such an investment. To comply with the rule, the transaction must be fair to the client, the lawyer must fully disclose all material information, and must give the client an opportunity to seek independent advice. Fairness and full disclosure are vague concepts and a lawyer can rarely be confident that these standards have been met. As a result, a lawyer who invests in a client's business faces substantially increased malpractice risk and even the possibility of disciplinary charges. A leading illustration of this risk is Committee on Professional Ethics & Conduct v. Mershon.[169]

167. 12 U.S.C. §2607(c) (1994).

168. E.g., Attorney Grievance Comm. v. Collins, 457 A.2d 1134 (Md. 1983) (lawyer failed to disclose ownership interest in seller partnership).

169. 316 N.W.2d 895 (Iowa 1982).

In *Mershon*, an attorney formed a corporation to develop farm land owned by his client. The owners of the corporation were the attorney, an engineer who prepared the development plans, and the client. The attorney and the engineer each contributed their services to the corporation, while the client contributed the land. The engineer and the client each received 40 percent interests in the corporation, while the attorney obtained a 20 percent share. According to the attorney, the parties had an oral agreement that the attorney and the engineer would release their shares if the development did not take place. The corporation never obtained financing and the attorney reconveyed his shares, but the engineer refused to do so. After the client's death, the attorney was appointed as executor of the client's estate, but he resigned when the client's two daughters expressed unhappiness with the conveyance of the farm land to the corporation. The engineer continued to claim that he was entitled to his interest in the corporation.

Disciplinary proceedings were instituted against the lawyer resulting in a public reprimand. The court found that the lawyer had failed to comply with the full disclosure obligation required by DR 5-104(A) of the Code of Professional Responsibility, the predecessor to Model Rule 1.8(a). The court stated that the lawyer had an obligation either to advise the client to seek independent legal advice or to provide the client with the kind of advice that an independent lawyer would give; the court found that Mershon did neither. Because of the stringent requirements of fairness and full disclosure articulated by the *Mershon* court, the only safe course for a lawyer who is entering into a business transaction with a client is to make sure the client receives independent legal advice about the transaction.[170]

4. *Service on the Board of Directors of a Client*

The issue of whether lawyers should serve as members of the boards of directors of their clients has been controversial in the

170. A number of other courts have also found that lawyers acted improperly in business transactions with their clients. See, e.g., Miller v. Sears, 636 P.2d 1183 (Alaska 1981) (clients able to rescind contract for sale of property by lawyer to them because of lawyer's failure to disclose personal liability of clients on note); In re James, 452 A.2d 163 (D.C. 1982), *cert. denied*, 460 U.S. 1038 (1983) (lawyer disciplined for failure to make full disclosure to client of risks and advantages of sale of building from clients to lawyer).

profession for a number of years.[171] The Model Rules do not prohibit lawyers from serving on the boards of directors of their clients, but comment 14 to Rule 1.7 cautions lawyers about the possible conflicts of interest that can arise and advises lawyers that if "there is material risk that the dual role will compromise the lawyer's independence of professional judgment, the lawyer should not serve as a director."[172]

Why would a lawyer agree to serve on the board of directors of a client? Prestige is one reason; service on the board of a major corporate client brings a measure of prominence to the lawyer. Service on the board can also strengthen the business relationship between the lawyer's firm and the client. In addition, service on the board can facilitate the lawyer's role as counselor because the lawyer is more familiar with the activities of the client. On the other hand, any lawyer who contemplates serving on the board of directors of a client should be aware of the substantial risks involved, including the following:[173]

- *Risk of Loss of the Attorney-Client Privilege.* The privilege only applies to communications between lawyer and client for the purpose of seeking legal advice. To the extent that communications were with the lawyer in the lawyer's capacity as director or to the extent they involved business rather than legal matters, the privilege is lost. In addition, the privilege only applies if the communications were made in confidence, a condition that may not be met when the communications occur in board meetings.
- *Disqualification of the Lawyer's Firm.* If the corporation is a party to litigation, the lawyer's firm may be disqualified from handling the matter because the lawyer may be a witness in the matter. Similarly, if the lawyer is a party to the litigation,

171. Compare David S. Ruder, The Case Against the Lawyer-Director, 30 Bus. Law. 51 (Spec. Issue, Mar. 1975), with Sam Harris, The Case for the Lawyer-Director, 30 Bus. Law. 58 (Spec. Issue, Mar. 1975).

172. See Syscon Corp. v. United States, 10 Cl. Ct. 200 (1986) (law firm not disqualified from representing corporation under Rule 1.7(b), even though one of its partners was general counsel, founder, and member of the board of corporation).

173. See Craig C. Albert, The Lawyer-Director: An Oxymoron?, 9 Geo. J. Legal Ethics 413 (1996) (examining the benefits and risks of dual role and arguing against rule prohibiting lawyers from serving as directors). See also James H. Cheek, III & Howard H. Lamar, III, Lawyers as Directors of Clients: Conflicts of Interest, Potential Liability and Other Pitfalls, 712 PLI/Corp. 461 (1990) (on Westlaw).

the firm may be disqualified because of a conflict of interest between it and the client. If the corporation is forced into bankruptcy, the firm may be disqualified from representing the corporation in bankruptcy because of the lawyer's service on the board.

- *Increased Exposure to Liability.* Service on the board exposes the lawyer to increased liability. Not only is the lawyer subject to liability for malpractice, but the lawyer also becomes subject to liability as a director on various theories, including violation of federal and state securities laws. Law firms may also face increased liability when one of their members serves on the board of a client. The law firm could be held vicariously liable for the lawyer's conduct.
- *Inadequate Insurance.* Many malpractice policies exclude from coverage service on a board of directors or other nonlegal activities.

5. *Gifts by Clients to Lawyers and Service as Personal Representative of a Client's Estate*

It is important to distinguish situations in which a client wishes to make a gift to a lawyer, either inter vivos or by will, from situations in which a client asks the lawyer to serve as personal representative of the client's estate (or as a trustee or other similar fiduciary). Although the Code of Professional Responsibility did not contain a disciplinary rule making it improper for a lawyer to draft an instrument in which the lawyer was also a beneficiary, some courts disciplined lawyers who did so.[174]

Model Rule 1.8(c) now deals with this problem:

> A lawyer shall not prepare an instrument giving the lawyer or a person related to the lawyer as parent, child, sibling, or spouse any substantial gift from a client, including a testamentary gift, except where the client is related to the donee.

Note that the rule does not preclude a lawyer from preparing a will for the lawyer's spouse or other relative when the lawyer will

174. E.g., Committee on Prof. Ethics & Conduct v. Behnke, 276 N.W.2d 838 (Iowa), *appeal dismissed,* 444 U.S. 805 (1979); Office of Disciplinary Counsel v. Galinas, 666 N.E.2d 1083 (Ohio 1996) (indefinite suspension for drafting will in which lawyer named as beneficiary).

be receiving a bequest under the will. If a client wishes to leave a bequest to a lawyer to whom the client is not related, the lawyer must advise the client that the lawyer cannot prepare the will and that the will must be drafted by independent counsel. Another lawyer in the lawyer-beneficiary's firm could not prepare the will because disqualification would be imputed to the other lawyer under Model Rule 1.10(a).[175] Some states such as California have statutory provisions invaliding gifts and bequests to the person who drafted the instrument.[176]

The Restatement goes somewhat beyond the Model Rules with regard to client gifts. Under the Restatement, a lawyer may not draft an instrument making a gift or bequest to the lawyer even when the lawyer is related to the donor if the amount of the transfer is significantly disproportionate to those made to other similarly situated donees.[177] This prohibition would not prevent a lawyer from preparing a will in which the lawyer's spouse left the spouse's entire estate to the lawyer because it would not run afoul of the disproportionality rule, but it could apply if a lawyer drafted an instrument for a parent that gave the lawyer a greater share of the estate than other children.[178] The Restatement also prohibits lawyers from receiving substantial gifts from clients to whom they are not related, even if the lawyer does not prepare a document effectuating the gift, when the client has not had the opportunity to receive independent advice before making the gift.[179]

A more common situation in which a lawyer has a financial interest in the will occurs when a client asks if the lawyer would be willing to serve as a fiduciary under the will. Clients may make this request because of reasons such as trust in the lawyer, distrust of corporate fiduciaries, and a desire to save fees that would otherwise be payable to a corporate fiduciary. May a lawyer draft a will in which the lawyer will be named as a fiduciary? Lawyers are not prohibited from serving as fiduciaries on behalf of their clients and of drafting instruments in which they are so named. Model Rule 1.8(c) does not apply to this situation because the

175. Cf. People v. Berge, 620 P.2d 23 (Colo. 1980) (en banc) (lawyer-beneficiary who received bequest from client under will drafted by attorney who shared office space with lawyer-beneficiary was suspended for 90 days).

176. Cal. Prob. Code §21350, 21351 (West Supp. 1997).

177. Restatement of the Law Governing Lawyers §208(1) (Prop. Final Draft #1, March 29, 1996).

178. Id. illus. 1.

179. Id. §208(2).

lawyer is not receiving a gift from the client. Lawyers must exercise care in undertaking such responsibility, however, because a variety of ethical duties are implicated by the client's request to name the lawyer as fiduciary, including: (1) the duty to provide a client with competent, estate planning advice (Model Rules 1.1 and 2.1); (2) the duty to exercise independent judgment on behalf of a client (Model Rule 2.1); (3) the duty to provide competent fiduciary services (Model Rule 1.1); (4) the prohibition on limitation of malpractice liability (Model Rule 1.8(h)); (5) the avoidance of conflicts of interest with other clients (Model Rule 1.7(b)); and (6) the duty not to charge unreasonable fees (Model Rule 1.5).[180]

O. ADVOCATE-WITNESS CONFLICTS

Situations arise in which a lawyer or a member of a lawyer's firm may be a witness in a client's case. Suppose, for example, that a lawyer has negotiated a contract on behalf of a client, but litigation subsequently develops about the interpretation of the contract. Three forms of appearance in such a case can be distinguished. First, the lawyer may wish to serve both as counsel for the client at trial and also appear as a witness on the client's behalf. Call this an "advocate-witness appearance." Second, another attorney in the lawyer's firm may handle the litigation on the client's behalf, with the lawyer's only involvement in the matter being as witness. Call this a "witness appearance." Finally, rather than appearing as a voluntary witness on behalf of the client, it is possible that the opposing side may call the lawyer as its own witness. Call this an "adverse witness appearance."

Why would a lawyer ever want to appear as both an advocate and a witness on behalf of a client? Typically, such a situation arises when the client has confidence in the skills of the particular lawyer and wants that lawyer to represent the client at trial, even if the lawyer may need to be a witness in the matter. May a lawyer properly appear as both an advocate and a witness? Such an

180. See ABA Real Property, Probate and Trust Section, Preparation of Wills and Trusts that Name Drafting Lawyer as Fiduciary, 28 Real Prop. Prob. & Trust J. 803 (1994).

appearance creates several risks. The lawyer may have difficulty arguing his own credibility to the trier of fact. The trier of fact may be confused about whether statements made by the lawyer amount to testimony or advocacy. Further, in some cases a conflict of interest may exist between the testimony of the lawyer and the client's interests.[181]

The Code of Professional Responsibility took a very restrictive view of when it was proper for a lawyer to appear both as advocate and witness. The Code provided that it was unethical for a lawyer to accept or to continue representation of a client if the lawyer or a member of the lawyer's firm "ought to be called as a witness" on behalf of a client. DR 5-101(B), 5-102(A). DR 5-101(B) listed four exceptions to the prohibition against a lawyer serving as both advocate and witness: (1) uncontested matters; (2) matters of formality when the lawyer had no reason to believe that substantial evidence would be offered in opposition; (3) nature and value of legal services; and (4) substantial hardship to the client. The exceptions dealing with uncontested matters, matters of formality, and legal fees have generated little litigation and should provide few problems in application. Thus, if a lawyer must testify to identify a document so that it can be offered into evidence, when there is no dispute about the authenticity of the document, the lawyer is not disqualified from continuing as an advocate in the matter because of this testimony. Similarly, in a suit for breach of contract or for collection of a note, where the contract or note provides for recovery of legal fees, testimony by the trial attorney to establish these fees is permissible and does not require disqualification of the attorney as advocate in the case.

Under the Code, however, even the substantial hardship was very limited. The Code required the substantial hardship to result from the "distinctive value of the lawyer or his firm as counsel in the particular case." DR 5-101(B)(4). This exception was narrowly construed by the courts and the ABA to apply only in unusual circumstances. In Formal Opinion 339, the ABA Committee on Ethics and Professional Responsibility stated:

> [E]xceptional situations may arise when . . . disadvantages to the client would clearly be outweighed by the real hardship to the client

181. Model Rule 3.7, comms. 1, 2, 5; Code of Prof. Resp. EC 5-9; Restatement of the Law Governing Lawyers §168, comms. *a*, *b* (Tent. Draft #8, March 21, 1997).

> of being compelled to retain other counsel in the particular case. For example, where a complex suit has been in preparation over a long period of time and a development which could not be anticipated makes the lawyer's testimony essential, it would be manifestly unfair to the client to be compelled to seek new trial counsel at substantial additional expense and perhaps to have to seek a delay of the trial. Similarly, a long or extensive professional relationship with a client may have afforded a lawyer, or a firm, such an extraordinary familiarity with the client's affairs that the value to the client of representation by that lawyer or firm in a trial involving those matters would clearly outweigh the disadvantages of having the lawyer, or a lawyer in the firm, testify to some disputed and significant issue.[182]

Both the Model Rules and the proposed Restatement of the Law Governing Lawyers continue the position of the Code that a lawyer's simultaneous appearance as an advocate and as a witness is generally improper absent an exception.[183] Both the Model Rules and the Restatement, however, broaden somewhat the substantial hardship exception by deleting the requirement of "distinctive value" and focusing instead on balancing of various factors.[184]

If an attorney is disqualified from serving as an advocate in the case because the attorney is likely to be a necessary witness, may the attorney continue to provide legal services during discovery and after trial on appeal? In Culebras Enterprises Corp. v. Rivera-Rios,[185] the First Circuit ruled that disqualification only applied at trial, not to pretrial matters, because representation at pretrial did not involve any of the purposes generally served by the rule, and the Restatement adopts this view.[186] Other courts, however, dis-

182. ABA Comm. on Ethics and Prof. Resp., Formal Opinion 339, at 3 (1975).

183. Model Rule 3.7(a); Restatement of the Law Governing Lawyers §168(1)(a) and (2) (Tent. Draft #8, March 21, 1997).

184. See Model Rule 3.7, comm. 4; Restatement of the Law Governing Lawyers §168, comm. *h* (Tent. Draft #8, March 21, 1997). See also McElroy v. Gaffney, 529 A.2d 889 (N.H. 1987) (disqualification of plaintiff's lawyer in shareholders' derivative action denied; attorney's knowledge of transactions, complexity of litigation, and expense to plaintiff to hire new counsel are factors supporting denial of motion).

185. 846 F.2d 94 (1st Cir. 1988).

186. Restatement of the Law Governing Lawyers §168, comm. *c* (Tent. Draft #8, March 21, 1997). See also ABA Comm. on Ethics and Prof. Resp., Informal Op. 83-1503 (lawyer who has withdrawn as trial counsel because of advocate-witness rule may prepare brief and argue case on appeal so long as lawyer's testimony is not in issue and no conflict of interest is present); Informal Op. 89-1529 (lawyer who anticipates testifying at trial may represent party in discovery and other pretrial matters if client consents after consultation).

agree and have disqualified counsel from participation in pretrial matters.[187]

Suppose the lawyer's appearance will be limited to serving as witness on behalf of the client, rather than simultaneously acting as advocate. Another attorney in the lawyer's firm will act as advocate for the client. Disciplinary Rule 5-102(A) of the Code of Professional Responsibility provided that the disqualification of a lawyer from handling a case because of the advocate-witness rule was imputed to the entire firm, preventing any lawyer in the firm from handling the case. Even under the Code, however, some courts had refused to disqualify a firm simply because it was claimed that a member of the firm ought to be a witness.[188]

Both the Model Rules and the Restatement reject the principle of imputation of disqualification when one lawyer will be appearing as a witness while another attorney in the lawyer's firm will serve as the client's advocate, unless a conflict of interest exists. Rule 3.7(b) provides that "[a] lawyer may act as advocate in a trial in which another lawyer in the lawyer's firm is likely to be called as a witness unless precluded from doing so by Rule 1.7 or Rule 1.9." As Comment 4 to Rule 3.7 states: "The principle of imputed disqualification stated in Rule 1.10 has no application to this aspect of the problem." The Restatement agrees.[189]

The most obvious situation in which a conflict of interest exists is when the lawyer's testimony would be adverse to the client's interests. Even in this case, however, the firm would not necessarily be disqualified if the lawyer's testimony, although adverse, plays a relatively minor role in the case and the client consents after being informed of the conflict.[190] On the other hand, if the lawyer's testimony would have a substantial effect on the case, the lawyer's firm should be disqualified even if the client were willing to consent. Under Rule 1.7(b) a client may consent to a conflict of

187. World Youth Day, Inc. v. Famous Artists Merchandising Exch., Inc., 866 F. Supp. 1297 (D. Colo. 1994) (lawyer disqualified from handling depositions because of likelihood that depositions would be used at trial); Freeman v. Vicchiarelli, 827 F. Supp. 300 (D.N.J. 1993) (early application of rule is necessary for smooth operation of adversarial system).

188. E.g., S & S Hotel Ventures Ltd. Partnership v. 777 S.H. Corp., 508 N.E.2d 647 (N.Y. 1987).

189. Restatement of the Law Governing Lawyers §168(3) and comms. *f*, *i* (Tent. Draft #8, March 21, 1997).

190. See Model Rule 3.7, comm. 5 (representation is improper when there is likely to be a substantial conflict between the testimony of the client and the lawyer); 1 Hazard & Hodes, The Law of Lawyering §3.7:301, at 685 (consent permissible if the client is adequately counseled).

interest, but only if the "lawyer reasonably believes the representation will not be adversely affected." It is hard to imagine that this condition could ever be met if the lawyer would be testifying adversely to the interests of the client on a significant issue in the case.

While rejection of the rule of imputed disqualification in the Model Rules and the Restatement has substantially reduced the impact of the advocate-witness rule, the rule still applies to a lawyer who personally will be a witness. As a result, attorneys who engage in trial practice need to be aware of the possible disqualifying effect of the rule and to guard against this eventuality when participating in matters that may lead to litigation or when interviewing witnesses in matters that are in litigation. Consider the following advice from Professors Fortune, Underwood, and Imwinkelried for dealing with this problem:

> In interviewing witnesses, however, it is prudent to assume that the witness will give a different version of the facts at a later time, and that the attorney may become a necessary witness to challenge the turncoat. . . .
>
> What precautions can be taken to guard against being considered a necessary impeachment witness? First, consider having someone else conduct witness interviews, either an employee or an independent investigator. Second, have someone else present when interviewing a witness who may deny or vary a statement. Third, reduce the interview to a signed statement.[191]

Even if a party does not intend to call its lawyer as a witness, the other side may attempt to invoke the advocate-witness rule. The other side could move to disqualify the lawyer because it claims that the lawyer should appear as a witness or it could attempt to invoke the advocate-witness rule by giving notice of its intention to call the other party's lawyer as a witness. To guard against the possible tactical use of the advocate-witness rule, the

191. William H. Fortune et al., Modern Litigation and Professional Responsibility Handbook §4.5, at 169-170 (1996). See also Restatement of the Law Governing Lawyers §168, comm. *j* (Tent. Draft #8, March 21, 1997) (advocate-witness rule does not apply to testimony by nonlawyer employee who does not sit at counsel table or act in advocacy support role).

Model Rules and the Restatement apply only if the lawyer is "likely to be a necessary witness."[192]

One important application of the "necessary witness" requirement is that the lawyer is not disqualified from serving as an advocate if the lawyer's testimony would be cumulative with that of other witnesses. For example, Cannon Airways, Inc. v. Franklin Holdings Corp.,[193] was a suit for breach of an aircraft lease agreement. The agreement provided for recovery of "reasonable attorneys' fees." Defendant moved to disqualify plaintiff's counsel because a dispute existed regarding the scope of the clause, and defendant contended that plaintiff's counsel would be required to testify about the negotiations that resulted in the clause. The court denied this motion because the attorney was not the only witness available to testify about the negotiations on behalf of the plaintiff, and the defendant had failed to show that the attorney's testimony was "necessary to supplement or to corroborate" testimony of plaintiff's other witness about the negotiations.[194]

192. Model Rule 3.7(a); Restatement of the Law Governing Lawyers §168(1)(b) and comm. *e* (Tent. Draft #8, March 21, 1997). This represents a change in language from the Code of Professional Responsibility, which provided that the lawyer must withdraw if "it is obvious that he or a lawyer in his firm ought to be called as a witness." DR 5-101(B). Under the Code, some courts had ruled that the lawyer was disqualified if the lawyer's testimony could possibly be used at trial. See Comden v. Superior Court, 576 P.2d 971 (Cal.) (en banc), *cert. denied*, 439 U.S. 981 (1978).

193. 669 F. Supp. 96 (D. Del. 1987).

194. Id. at 102. See also Chappell v. Cosgrove, 916 P.2d 836 (N.M. 1996) (lawyer who accompanied client to meeting not disqualified; because four other witnesses could testify about what took place at meeting, lawyer's testimony was cumulative).

CHAPTER 4

Confidentiality

A. COMPARISON OF THE EVIDENTIARY ATTORNEY-CLIENT PRIVILEGE, THE WORK PRODUCT DOCTRINE, AND THE PROFESSIONAL DUTY OF CONFIDENTIALITY

Confidentiality of communications between clients and lawyers is one of the pillars of the client-attorney relationship. Yet, the scope and even the foundations of the principle of confidentiality are controversial. Initially, it is important to distinguish three doctrines all of which relate to the principle of confidentiality: the attorney-client evidentiary privilege, the work product doctrine, and the professional duty of confidentiality.

The attorney-client evidentiary privilege applies when a person or entity seeks to compel by legal process disclosure of confidential communications between lawyer and client for the purpose of rendering legal services. The scope of the attorney-client privilege depends on the rules of evidence of the jurisdiction in which the matter arises. Professor Wigmore's treatise contains a traditional formulation of the privilege:

> (1) Where legal advice of any kind is sought (2) from a professional legal adviser in his capacity as such, (3) the communications relating

> to that purpose, (4) made in confidence (5) by the client, (6) are at his instance permanently protected (7) from disclosure by himself or by the legal adviser, (8) except the protection be waived.[1]

The Restatement of the Law Governing Lawyers offers the following statement of the attorney-client privilege:

> [The] attorney-client privilege may be invoked . . . with respect to:
> (1) a communication
> (2) made between privileged persons
> (3) in confidence
> (4) for the purpose of obtaining or providing legal assistance for the client.[2]

The attorney work product doctrine has its genesis in the Supreme Court's decision in Hickman v. Taylor.[3] *Hickman* was an action for wrongful death of a seaman against the owners of a tug that sank. Plaintiffs sought to obtain by discovery copies of all written statements from members of the crew taken by defendants. The Court first held that the statements were not protected by the attorney-client evidentiary privilege since they did not involve confidential communications from the client.[4] The Court went on to hold, however, that the material sought by the plaintiff was still not subject to discovery:

> Historically, a lawyer is an officer of the court and is bound to work for the advancement of justice while faithfully protecting the rightful interests of his clients. In performing his various duties, however, it is essential that a lawyer work with a certain degree of privacy, free from unnecessary intrusion by opposing parties and their counsel. Proper preparation of a client's case demands that he assemble information, sift what he considers to be the relevant from the irrelevant facts, prepare his legal theories and plan his strategy without undue and needless interference. That is the historical and

1. John H. Wigmore, Evidence in Trials at Common Law §2292, at 554 (McNaughton ed. 1961). See also Unif. Rules Evid., Rule 502, 13A U.L.A. 518 (1994). Comment 5 to Model Rule 1.6 summarizes the distinction between the evidentiary privilege and the professional duty of confidentiality. See generally Geoffrey C. Hazard, Jr., An Historical Perspective on the Attorney-Client Privilege, 66 Cal. L. Rev. 1061 (1978).
2. Restatement of the Law Governing Lawyers §118 (Proposed Final Draft #1, March 29, 1996).
3. 329 U.S. 495 (1947).
4. Id. at 508.

> the necessary way in which lawyers act within the framework of our system of jurisprudence to promote justice and to protect their clients' interests. This work is reflected, of course, in interviews, statements, memoranda, correspondence, briefs, mental impressions, personal beliefs, and countless other tangible and intangible ways — aptly though roughly termed by the Circuit Court of Appeals in this case . . . as the "Work product of the lawyer." Were such materials open to opposing counsel on mere demand, much of what is now put down in writing would remain unwritten. An attorney's thoughts, heretofore inviolate, would not be his own. Inefficiency, unfairness and sharp practices would inevitably develop in the giving of legal advice and in the preparation of cases for trial. The effect on the legal profession would be demoralizing. And the interests of the clients and the cause of justice would be poorly served.[5]

The Court concluded that work product material was not absolutely immune from discovery: "Where relevant and non-privileged facts remain hidden in an attorney's file and where production of these facts is essential to the preparation of one's case, discovery may properly be had."[6]

The work product doctrine is embodied in Rule 26(b)(3) of the Federal Rules of Civil Procedure:

> **Trial Preparation: Materials.** Subject to the provisions of subdivision (b)(4) of this rule, a party may obtain discovery of documents and tangible things otherwise discoverable under subdivision (b)(1) of this rule and prepared in anticipation of litigation or for trial by or for another party or by or for that other party's representative (including the other party's attorney, consultant, surety, indemnitor, insurer, or agent) only upon a showing that the party seeking discovery has substantial need of the materials in the preparation of the party's case and that the party is unable without undue hardship to obtain the substantial equivalent of the materials by other means. In ordering discovery of such materials when the required showing has been made, the court shall protect against disclosure of the mental impressions, conclusions, opinions, or legal theories of an attorney or other representative of a party concerning the litigation.

Two aspects of the work product doctrine should be noted. First, for the doctrine to apply, the material must be prepared "in antici-

5. Id. at 510-511.
6. Id. at 511.

pation of litigation." Second, a party may obtain discovery of work product material by showing "substantial need" coupled with "undue hardship."[7]

The professional duty of confidentiality finds expression in Model Rule 1.6, which provides as follows:

> (a) A lawyer shall not reveal information relating to representation of a client unless the client consents after consultation, except for disclosures that are impliedly authorized in order to carry out the representation, and except as stated in paragraph (b).
>
> (b) A lawyer may reveal such information to the extent the lawyer reasonably believes necessary:
>
> (1) to prevent the client from committing a criminal act that the lawyer believes is likely to result in imminent death or substantial bodily harm; or
>
> (2) to establish a claim or defense on behalf of the lawyer in a controversy between the lawyer and the client, to establish a defense to a criminal change or civil claim against the lawyer based upon conduct in which the client was involved, or to respond to allegations in any proceeding concerning the lawyer's representation of the client.

Three examples may help clarify the distinction among these three concepts:

Example 1: State prosecutors are investigating an individual for tax fraud. During the course of investigation, the prosecutors subpoena the files of the law firm that has represented the target in real estate transactions. Whether the prosecutors are legally entitled to access to the files raises a question of the scope of the evidentiary attorney-client privilege. One of the most important exceptions to the attorney-client privilege is the "crime-fraud" exception. Under this exception, the privilege does not apply if the client sought legal services for the purpose of commiting a crime or fraud.[8] This example does not raise an issue involving the work product doctrine, because work product immunity only applies to information gathered in anticipation of litigation. Since this matter involves an investigation of tax fraud and since the legal work

7. The Restatement of the Law Governing Lawyers contains an extensive discussion of the elements of the work product doctrine. See Restatement of the Law Governing Lawyers §§136-142 (Prop. Final Draft #1, March 29, 1996).

8. See In re Sealed Case, 107 F.3d 46 (D.C. Cir. 1997); Purcell v. District Attorney for Suffolk Dist., 676 N.E.2d 436 (Mass. 1997) (crime-fraud exception

involved real estate, the information in the client's files was not gathered in anticipation of litigation. The prosecutors' subpoena of the client's files also raises a professional issue for the lawyer of how to respond to the subpoena. In response to the prosecutors' demand for the files, the lawyer has a professional duty to invoke the client's evidentiary privilege. See Model Rule 1.6, comm. 19.

Example 2: A law firm is retained to defend a manufacturer in a products liability action. The firm interviews various witnesses to the accident. Interviewers make notes of their interviews. These notes are not subject to the evidentiary attorney-client privilege because the information was not conveyed by the client to the lawyer in confidence. The notes are, however, subject to the work product doctrine because they are materials prepared by a party's agent in anticipation of litigation.

Example 3: A lawyer learns sensitive financial information from a client that is a publicly traded corporation. If the lawyer uses this information for his benefit, the lawyer violates the professional duty of confidentiality (and perhaps state and federal securities laws as well) because the professional duty requires lawyers to maintain confidentiality of all information "relating to representation," subject to certain exceptions that we will be discussing. The attorney-client privilege and the work product doctrine do not apply in this situation because these doctrines are limited to adversarial matters, in which one party seeks to compel an attorney to reveal information.

The discussion that follows focuses on the professional duty of confidentiality rather than the attorney-client privilege or the work product doctrine. The Restatement of the Law Governing Lawyers is a useful source of information regarding these doctrines.

B. INTERESTS INVOLVED IN DETERMINING THE SCOPE OF THE DUTY OF CONFIDENTIALITY

A clash of competing interests makes resolution of the issue of the appropriate scope of the professional duty of confidentiality con-

---

does not apply unless client sought legal advice for purpose of commiting crime or fraud).

troversial. What are the interests at stake in this issue? First, clients have an interest in individual freedom and autonomy. Protection of personal liberty often involves the legal system. Criminal cases are obvious examples, but in civil cases important liberty, property, or personal interests are often at stake as well. Representation by counsel thus becomes an important aspect of individual liberty. Unless clients can feel secure that information conveyed to their lawyers will not be used against them, their ability to exercise and protect their autonomy is seriously compromised. Second, like clients, third parties have an interest in personal autonomy. Illegal or tortious actions by clients can infringe the autonomy of third persons. Finally, the scope of the duty of confidentiality involves social interests. Confidentiality may prevent tribunals from receiving information that they need for truthful or efficient resolution of disputes. Further, if confidentiality of information allows clients to engage in wrongful conduct, this increases social costs for dealing with the resulting harms.

The professional duty of confidentiality is broadly worded to include all information "relating to representation" of a client. The duty therefore also applies to information obtained from third parties and to information that the client may have given to other people. Thus, the policy issue of the scope of the duty of confidentiality focuses on exceptions to the doctrine. The following sections discuss the major exceptions to the obligation of confidentiality. The fundamental issue dealing with the scope of the duty of confidentiality as expressed in these exceptions is whether the current rules of professional ethics make the wisest resolution of the clash between these competing interests.

C. CLIENT CONSENT OR IMPLIED AUTHORIZATION TO DISCLOSE CONFIDENTIAL INFORMATION

Model Rule 1.6 states that a lawyer may disclose information when the "client consents after consultation" or when "impliedly authorized in order to carry out the representation." An interesting example of the application of the consent exception is People v.

Lopez.[9] *Lopez* was a disciplinary proceeding growing out of a criminal case. The defendant had retained Lopez to defend him against felony charges arising from a kidnapping and shooting. At Lopez's request, the defendant prepared an eight-page summary of his version of the events. The document contained various damaging admissions. During plea negotiations Lopez gave the document to the prosecutor without the defendant's knowledge or express consent. The prosecutor retained the document but did not use it at trial. The defendant was convicted, but later obtained a new trial. Lopez claimed that he had informed his client that he planned to deliver the document to the prosecutor in an effort to obtain a favorable plea bargain and that his client had not objected to this plan. In rejecting this argument the Colorado Supreme Court held that a lawyer may reveal confidential information only after full disclosure and express consent: "This provision [DR 4-101(C)(1), which is substantially identical to Model Rule 1.6(a)] does not encompass "implied" consent, even if the facts warranted a finding that Kingery [the original defendant] by his conduct impliedly consented to the respondent's conduct."[10]

The Model Rules also allow lawyers to reveal confidential information when they are "impliedly authorized" to do so to carry out the representation, but the rules provide little guidance about the scope of the implied authorization exception. Comment 7 states that "a lawyer may disclose information by admitting a fact that cannot properly be disputed, or in negotiation by making a disclosure that facilitates a satisfactory conclusion." In light of cases like *Lopez,* lawyers should be wary of disclosing sensitive information without express client consent, preferably in writing.

D. DISCLOSURE OF CONFIDENTIAL INFORMATION TO PREVENT CLIENTS FROM COMMITTING WRONGFUL ACTS THAT HARM OTHERS

One of the most hotly debated issues in the profession over the last 20 years has been the extent to which the duty of confidentiality

9. 845 P.2d 1153 (Colo. 1993) (en banc).
10. Id. at 1155.

should be limited when disclosure would either prevent the client from committing a wrongful act or would rectify the consequences of a wrongful act that the client has committed. The next section addresses the issue of disclosure of confidential information to rectify past wrongful client conduct. This section deals with disclosure to prevent future wrongful conduct by a client.

Two cases, one from criminal defense practice (Hawkins v. King County[11]) and one from securities practice (In re Carter & Johnson[12]) provide interesting fact patterns to illustrate the issues involved in disclosure of confidential information to prevent wrongful conduct. In *Hawkins,* the court appointed an attorney to represent the defendant, who was accused of possession of marijuana. The attorney learned from another lawyer employed by his client's mother that his client was mentally ill and dangerous. A psychiatrist advised the attorney that his client was dangerous to himself and to others and should not be released from custody. The attorney represented the client at a bail hearing and obtained his release on a personal surety bond. The attorney did not inform the court of the information that he had learned about his client's dangerousness. Neither the judge nor the prosecutor raised any questions about the client's dangerousness. Eight days after his release, Hawkins assaulted his mother and committed suicide.

In re Carter & Johnson was a disciplinary proceeding before the Securities and Exchange Commission (SEC). Carter and Johnson represented National Telephone Company (National), which leased telephone equipment to commercial customers. The company ultimately filed for bankruptcy. During the period when the company's financial problems were escalating, the company issued a misleading press release and filed overstated financial information with the SEC. Carter and Johnson gave repeated warnings to National's chairman that the company was violating the securities laws, but they took no further action. In discussing these cases it is useful to examine both the professional and the legal obligations of lawyers.

1. *Professional Obligations*

The legal profession has oscillated on the issue of whether the duty of confidentiality should apply in cases like *Hawkins* and *Carter &*

11. 602 P.2d 361 (Wash. Ct. App. 1979).
12. Fed. Sec. L. Rep. (CCH) ¶82,847 (SEC 1981).

Johnson. DR 4-101(C)(3) of the Code of Professional Responsibility provided that a lawyer "may reveal . . . [t]he intention of his client to commit a crime and the information necessary to prevent the crime." Under the Code, it was professionally proper for lawyers to reveal otherwise confidential information to prevent clients from committing both personal crimes (assault as in *Hawkins*) and financial crimes (securities fraud as in *Carter & Johnson*). The use of the word *may* was somewhat ambiguous. The natural reading was that lawyers had discretion but were not required to reveal confidential information to prevent a client from committing a crime. Another possible reading was that the rule authorized lawyers to reveal confidential information when they were required by law to do so to prevent a client from committing a crime.

When the ABA adopted the Model Rules in 1983, it substantially narrowed the exception to confidentiality from DR 4-101 of the Code. The ABA limited the rule allowing disclosure to prevent future harm to cases in which the client intends to engage in criminal conduct that is likely to result in imminent death or substantial bodily injury. This restriction eliminated discretion to reveal confidential information to prevent criminal or fraudulent conduct that would damage the property or financial interests of third parties. Rule 1.6 also made it clear that disclosure was within the professional discretion of the lawyer rather than mandatory. Comment 12 states that "the lawyer has professional discretion to reveal information in order to prevent such consequences." Thus, under ABA Model Rule 1.6, disclosure of National's fraud by Carter and Johnson to the SEC or to victims of the fraud would be professionally improper. Disclosure by the attorney in *Hawkins*, on the other hand, would be within the professional discretion of the lawyer, assuming the lawyer concluded that his client posed a threat of imminent harm to others.

Is the ABA's position in Model Rule 1.6 sound as a matter of policy? A reasonable justification for the ABA's position can be developed: Confidentiality is central to the client-attorney relationship. Any exceptions to the duty should be narrowly confined. Common decency demands an exception to confidentiality when a lawyer knows that a client is about to engage in criminal conduct that is likely to result in imminent death or substantial bodily harm, but such cases are so unlikely to occur that this exception is a very narrow one that does not significantly undermine the general duty of confidentiality. By contrast, an exception for financial fraud is more likely to occur and does not present as compelling a case for an exception to the duty of confidentiality. Most financial frauds are subsequently discovered and losses can be compensated in whole or in part.

On the other hand, some critics of the ABA's rules of professional ethics have argued that the rules actually reflect the economic interest of powerful groups in the ABA rather than disinterested policy. Major law firms are a significant force in ABA activities. Since the 1970s, many major law firms have been concerned about possible legal liability for failing to disclose confidential information to prevent or rectify financial frauds by their clients. If the rules of professional ethics allowed lawyers to disclose confidential information to prevent a financial fraud, the rules would support liability claims against firms that failed to disclose confidential information. Narrowing of authorized disclosure in Model Rule 1.6 thus fosters the financial interest of major law firms that have extensive business practices.[13]

The ABA's action in adopting Model Rule 1.6 has hardly ended the controversy on the scope of confidentiality. Most states that have generally adopted the Model Rules have nonetheless refused to follow the ABA's position on confidentiality. More than half of the states have simply returned to the formulation found in the Code of Professional Responsibility, giving lawyers discretion to reveal confidential information to prevent clients from committing crimes.[14]

While corporate lawyers like Carter and Johnson have neither the duty nor the discretion under Model Rule 1.6 to reveal confidential information to third parties to prevent a financial fraud from occurring, the Model Rules do require corporate lawyers to take steps within the corporation when they learn of fraud. Model Rule 1.13(a) adopts an "entity representation" principle, providing that a lawyer retained by an organization represents the entity rather than any of its "constituents." The term *constituents* includes directors, officers, employees, members, and shareholders. Model Rule 1.13(d). (The Code of Professional Responsibility

13. See John P. Freeman, Current Trends in Legal Opinion Liability, 1989 Colum. Bus. L. Rev. 235.

14. Restatement of the Law Governing Lawyers §117A, at 332-333 (Prop. Final Draft #1, March 29, 1996) (chart showing different approaches taken by states on scope of duty of confidentiality). A similar chart can be found in Thomas D. Morgan & Ronald E. Rotunda, Selected Standards on Professional Responsibility, Appendix A to Model Rules (1998).

also followed the entity representation principle in Ethical Consideration 5-18). The principle means that a lawyer does not have a client-lawyer relationship with any of the constituents of an entity merely because the lawyer represents the entity. Even though a lawyer does not represent a constituent of an entity, information received from any constituent of the entity may still be subject to the attorney-client evidentiary privilege, depending on how broadly a court interprets the privilege.[15]

The absence of a client-attorney relationship with the constituents of an entity has important implications if a lawyer learns about wrongdoing by a constituent. Suppose a lawyer for an entity learns about misconduct committed by one of the officers of the entity. How should the lawyer proceed? Because of the entity representation principle, the lawyer cannot simply follow instructions from the officer to keep the matter confidential. Further, the lawyer must advise the officer that the lawyer represents the entity not the officer. See Model Rule 1.13(d). Normally, the lawyer should discuss the matter with the officer before consideration of any further action to give the officer an opportunity to take corrective action. Model Rule 1.13(b) states: "Any measures taken shall be designed to minimize disruption of the organization and the risk of revealing information relating to the representation to persons outside the organization." Voluntary reporting by the officer to other officials in the organization is one possible option.

Suppose the officer refuses to take any action regarding the matter. The officer could offer various reasons for inaction: "it's common industry practice," or "it's too small to worry about," or "that would kill the company," or "you're fired." How should a lawyer proceed in that event? Model Rule 1.13(b) provides that a lawyer must take further action to protect the entity when a constituent is engaged in conduct that is a "violation of a legal obligation to the organization, or a violation of law which reasonably

15. Compare Upjohn Co. v. United States, 449 U.S. 383 (1981) (under federal law attorney-client privilege extends to communications between lawyers and lower-level employees and is not limited to corporate officials in "control group"), with Consolidation Coal Co. v. Bucyrus-Erie Co., 432 N.E.2d 250 (Ill. 1982) (control group test applies under Illinois law). For a criticism of the corporate attorney-client privilege, see Elizabeth G. Thornburg, Sanctifying Secrecy: The Mythology of the Corporate Attorney-Client Privilege, 69 Notre Dame L. Rev. 157 (1993). See also Garner v. Wolfinbarger, 430 F.2d 1093 (5th Cir. 1970), *cert. denied,* 401 U.S. 974 (1971) (in shareholder derivative litigation corporate attorney-client privilege does not apply if shareholders establish good cause).

might be imputed to the organization, and is likely to result in substantial injury to the organization." The section apparently envisions two types of cases. In the first, the official is engaged in some type of breach of fiduciary duty, such as misappropriation of the entity's funds. In the second, the official is involved in illegal conduct as to third parties, for example securities fraud.

Assuming the lawyer has a duty to act under Rule 1.13(b), what must the lawyer do? The rule provides that the lawyer "shall proceed as is reasonably necessary in the best interest of the organization." Note that the focus of the rule is on protecting the interests of the organization, not third parties. The rule goes on to identify factors that the lawyer should take into account in deciding how to proceed, along with possible ways in which the lawyer could proceed. The ultimate step allowed by Rule 1.13(b) is "referring the matter . . . to the highest authority that can act in behalf of the organization as determined by applicable law." In the case of a corporation, this will typically be the board of directors. See Comment 5 to Rule 1.13.

Suppose the lawyer informs the board of directors, but the board decides not to take any action in the matter. Rule 1.13(c) allows but does not requires the lawyer to withdraw; this provision, however, must be read in connection with other rules. See Comment 6, which provides as follows: "If the lawyer's services are being used by an organization to further a crime or fraud by the organization, Rule 1.2(d) can be applicable." As discussed more fully below, under Rule 1.2(d) a lawyer would be required to withdraw from the matter if the lawyer's services would be used to perpetuate a fraud. The comment states that lawyers could disclose confidential information if permitted under Rule 1.6, but as discussed previously, under the ABA's Model Rule 1.6, lawyers would rarely be able to do so.[16]

The preceding discussion assumes that the entity is fairly large. The lawyer's obligations are likely to be different if the entity is

16. For criticisms of Model Rule 1.13, see Monroe Freedman, Understanding Lawyers' Ethics 201-205 (1990) (arguing that it gives greater protection to corporations than to individuals); Stephen Gillers, Model Rule 1.13(c) Gives the Wrong Answer to the Question of Corporate Counsel Disclosure, 1 Geo. J. Legal Ethics 289 (1987) (arguing that lawyers should have discretion to reveal confidential information to prevent or rectify substantial injury resulting from conduct or inaction set forth in Rule 1.13(b)).

closely held. Unless the lawyer's engagement clearly specifies otherwise, in closely held entities it is likely that the lawyer has a client-attorney relationship with all of the principals.[17] If such a relationship with the principals does exist, two courses of action seem available to the attorney. The lawyer could make full disclosure to all clients; disclosure would be justified on the ground that there is no expectation of confidentiality nor does the attorney-client privilege apply to joint clients. Cf. Model Rule 2.2, comm. 6. On the other hand, the lawyer could withdraw from the matter, based on the principle that an irreconcilable conflict of interest exists between multiple clients. Cf. Model Rule 2.2(c).

2. *Legal Obligations*

The Model Rules state professional but not legal obligations. It is possible that a court or administrative body could hold that lawyers have a legal obligation to disclose information to prevent a client from committing a wrong even if disclosure was discretionary or prohibited under the Model Rules. Presumably lawyers would be required to obey these legal obligations since they are more authoritative than professional codes. In general, however, it appears that lawyers are not subject to legal liability for failure to disclose confidential information to prevent a client from committing a wrongful act. Once again, *Hawkins* and *In re Carter & Johnson* are instructive.

In *Hawkins,* the Hawkinses brought suit naming the attorney as one of the defendants. They alleged two theories. First, the attorney violated a duty imposed by rules of ethics and court rules to disclose to the court information about his client's dangerousness. Second, the attorney violated a common law duty to warn the Hawkinses of the client's dangerousness. The court rejected the first theory. It found no specific provision in either the rules of ethics or court rules that required a lawyer to reveal adverse information about a client:

17. E.g., Rosman v. Shapiro, 653 F. Supp. 1441 (S.D.N.Y. 1987) (in two-person corporation, it is reasonable for each shareholder to view corporate counsel as his individual attorney); Meyer v. Mulligan, 889 P.2d 509 (Wyo. 1995) (facts-and-circumstances test used to determine whether lawyer for closely-held corporation has client-attorney relationship with shareholders).

> We believe that the duty of counsel to be loyal to his client and to represent zealously his client's interest overrides the nebulous and unsupported theory that our rules and ethical code mandate disclosure of information which counsel considers detrimental to his client's stated interest. Because disclosure is not "required by law," appellants' theory of liability on the basis of ethical or court rule violations fails for lack of substance.[18]

The court also rejected the common law duty to warn theory on the facts of the case. In doing so, the court distinguished an earlier case, Tarasoff v. Regents of the University of California,[19] in which the California Supreme Court held that a psychotherapist had a duty to warn an intended victim of threats made by a patient who the therapist knew was dangerous. The court indicated, however, that given appropriate facts a lawyer could be held liable for failure to warn likely victims of a client's intention to commit harm:

> In the instant case Michael Hawkins' potential victims, his mother and sister, knew he might be dangerous and that he had been released from confinement, contrary to Tatiana Tarasoff's ignorance of any risk of harm. Thus, no duty befell Sanders to warn Frances Hawkins of a risk of which she was already fully cognizant. Further, it must not be overlooked that Sanders received no information that Hawkins planned to assault anyone, only that he was mentally ill and likely to be dangerous to himself and others. That Sanders received no information directly from Michael Hawkins is the final distinction between the two cases.
>
> The common law duty to volunteer information about a client to a court considering pretrial release must be limited to situations where information gained convinces counsel that his client intends to commit a crime or inflict injury upon unknowing third persons. Such a duty cannot be extended to the facts before us.[20]

In *Carter & Johnson*, the SEC focused on the issue of when lawyers have an obligation under the securities laws to go beyond simply giving warnings to corporate officials that their conduct is a violation of the law. Without defining precisely a lawyer's obli-

18. 602 P.2d at 365.
19. 551 P.2d 334 (Cal. 1976) (en banc).
20. 602 P.2d at 365-366. Cf. State v. Hansen, 862 P.2d 117 (Wash. 1993) (en banc) (attorney has duty to warn judge of client's intention to attack judge; *Hawkins* distinguished because mother and sister were aware of danger while judge was not).

gations, the SEC ruled that at some point a lawyer must do more than simply give warnings:

> When a lawyer with significant responsibilities in the effectuation of a company's compliance with the disclosure requirements of the federal securities laws becomes aware that his client is engaged in a substantial and continuing failure to satisfy those disclosure requirements, his continued participation violates professional standards unless he takes prompt steps to end the client's noncompliance.[21]

The SEC offered some suggestions on how lawyers should proceed in such cases:

> Initially, counseling accurate disclosure is sufficient, even if his advice is not accepted. But there comes a point at which a reasonable lawyer must conclude that his advice is not being followed, or even sought in good faith, and that his client is involved in a continuing course of violating the securities laws. At this critical juncture, the lawyer must take further, more affirmative steps in order to avoid the inference that he has been co-opted, willingly or unwillingly, into the scheme of non-disclosure.
>
> The lawyer is in the best position to choose his next step. Resignation is one option, although we recognize that other considerations, including the protection of the client against foreseeable prejudice, must be taken into account in the case of withdrawal. A direct approach to the board of directors or one or more individual directors or officers may be appropriate; or he may choose to try to enlist the aid of other members of the firm's management. . . .
>
> . . . [T]here may occur situations where the lawyer must conclude that the misconduct is so extreme or irretrievable, or the involvement of his client's management and board of directors in the misconduct is so thoroughgoing and pervasive that any action short of resignation would be futile. We would anticipate that cases where a lawyer has no choice but to resign would be rare and of an egregious nature.[22]

While the SEC decided that lawyers do have an obligation under the securities laws to do more than simply advise their clients to

21. Fed. Sec. L. Rep. (CCH) ¶82,847, at 84,172. See also In re Gutfreund, Sec. Ex. Act Rel. No. 31,554 [1992 Transfer Binder] Fed. Sec. L. Rep. (CCH) ¶85,067 (Dec. 3, 1992) (responsibilities of compliance counsel for brokerage firm regarding wrongdoing by firm's employees and management).

22. Fed. Sec. L. Rep. ¶82,847, at 84,172-84,173.

comply with the law, the SEC did not hold that lawyers had an obligation to disclose confidential information to prevent the client's wrongdoing. At most the lawyer's obligation was to withdraw from representation. It should be noted that the SEC's views of lawyers obligations in *Carter & Johnson* are very similar to the professional obligations under Model Rule 1.13.[23] By contrast, a different federal administrative agency, the Office of Thrift Supervision (OTS), created quite a stir in the legal profession when it brought an administrative complaint against Kaye, Scholer, Fierman, Hays & Handler,[24] a prominent New York firm, for its representation of Lincoln Savings & Loan. The complaint contained ten charges against Kaye Scholer, a number of which alleged that Kaye Scholer failed to disclose material facts to the Federal Home Loan Bank Board. The OTS claimed that in acting as Lincoln's agent under the governing statutory laws, Kaye Scholer had a duty not to omit material facts.

Two provisions of the proposed Restatement of the Law Governing Lawyers are particularly relevant to the issue of disclosure of confidential information to prevent wrongdoing. Section 155 of the Restatement largely follows Model Rule 1.13. The section adopts the principle of entity representation under which a lawyer for an entity has a client-attorney relationship with the entity rather than with any of its constituents.[25] A lawyer for an entity normally must follow the instructions of duly authorized representatives of the entity.[26] Under the Restatement, like Model Rule 1.13, a lawyer must take steps to protect the interest of the entity when either of two situations arise: (1) a representative is engaged in a violation of a legal obligation to the entity or (2) the representative is engaged in conduct or a failure to act that may be imputed to the entity.[27] Breach of fiduciary duty, such as misappropriation of entity property, is an example of the first situation. In the second situation, the representative may not actually intend to

23. Similarly, in Tew v. Arky, Freed, Stearns, Watson, Greer, Weaver & Harris, P.A., 655 F. Supp. 1571 (S.D. Fla. 1987), *aff'd*, 846 F.2d 753 (11th Cir.), *cert. denied*, 488 U.S. 854 (1988), the district court granted summary judgment for a law firm in a suit alleging that it had failed to disclose knowledge of its client's insolvency to its accountants.

24. Reported as In re Fishbein, OTS AP-92-19, 1992 WL 560939 (March 1, 1992).

25. Restatement of the Law Governing Lawyers §155, comm. *b* (Tent. Draft #8, March 21, 1997).

26. Id. comm. *d*.

27. Id. comm. *f*.

harm the entity, but the representative's conduct or inaction may be attributed to the entity. In both cases the threatened injury must be substantial, but if the lawyer has doubt whether the injury is substantial, the lawyer should take action so that corporate officials can exercise their business judgment regarding the matter.[28] Like Model Rule 1.13, the Restatement provides lawyers with discretion about the steps they can take when faced with wrongdoing by a constituent, including the ultimate step of reporting the matter to the highest authority on behalf of the entity, such as its board of directors.[29] When a lawyer learns of wrongdoing by a constituent, it is not sufficient for the lawyer to withdraw from representation because that action will not necessarily protect the interests of the entity, although it may be appropriate to withdraw after the lawyer takes steps to inform the entity of wrongdoing by a constituent and the entity fails to act on the matter.[30] Section 155 defines the duties of a lawyer for an entity to the entity, rather than to third parties. Thus, the section, like Model Rule 1.13, does not authorize disclosure of confidential information to protect third parties.[31]

Restatement §155 must be read in conjunction with §117A, which deals with disclosure of confidential information to protect third parties from harm. Section 117A provides that a lawyer may disclose confidential information to the extent that the lawyer reasonably believes is necessary "to prevent death or serious bodily injury to a person."[32] This provision was approved in principle after a vigorous debate, over the opposition of the chief reporter, who contended that it was inconsistent with prevailing doctrine.[33] The section gives lawyers discretion to reveal confidential information to prevent death or serious bodily harm as a result of any conduct (whether criminal or not) by anyone (whether a client or not). In addition, in proposed §117B the Restatement allows lawyers to reveal confidential information to prevent, rectify, or mitigate "substantial financial loss" resulting from a crime or fraud

28. Id.
29. Id. §155(3) and comm. *f.*
30. Id.
31. Id. comm. *a.*
32. See Monroe H. Freedman, The Life-Saving Exception to Confidentiality: Restating Law Without the *Was*, The *Will Be*, or the *Ought to Be*, 29 Loy. L.A. L. Rev. 1631, 1639 (1996).
33. For the history of the debate leading up to approval of §117A, see id. The exact language of §117A remains to be approved by the Institute. See Restatement of the Law Governing Lawyers §117A (Council Draft #13, Oct. 8, 1997).

threatened or committed by a client involving the lawyer's services. Thus, under the Restatement's approach, lawyers would have discretion to reveal confidential information on the facts of *Hawkins* and *Carter & Johnson*. This discretionary approach has interesting implications. Since disclosure is discretionary, lawyers would not have a duty to third parties to disclose confidential information and would not be subject to legal liability for nondisclosure. On the other hand, since disclosure is discretionary, lawyers would not be subject to legal liability to their clients if they decided to disclose confidential information. The result may be the best of all worlds for lawyers: liability to no one, with discretion to do what they think is best.

One final point needs to be made with regard to lawyers' professional and legal obligations regarding disclosure of confidential information to prevent wrongful client conduct. A distinction must be drawn between nondisclosure and participation in the client's wrong. As discussed more fully below, if the lawyer participates in the client's wrong, rather than simply deciding not to disclose confidential information, both professional violations and legal liability ensue.

E. DISCLOSURE OF CONFIDENTIAL INFORMATION TO RECTIFY PAST CRIMINAL OR TORTIOUS CONDUCT BY CLIENTS

As discussed above, Model Rule 1.6(b)(1) allows a lawyer to reveal confidential information "to prevent the client from committing a criminal act that the lawyer believes is likely to result in imminent death or substantial bodily harm." This exception to the duty of confidentiality only applies to contemplated or future client conduct. Because the Model Rules do not contain an exception for past wrongful conduct, by implication the rules prohibit lawyers from disclosing past wrongful conduct by their clients.

People v. Belge[34] — the "Lake Pleasant Bodies Case" — is a

34. 372 N.Y.S.2d 798 (County Ct. 1975), *aff'd*, 376 N.Y.S.2d 771 (App. Div. 1975), *aff'd*, 359 N.E.2d 377 (N.Y. 1976). For a personal account of the case co-authored by one of the lawyers, see Tom Alibrandi & Frank H. Armani, Privileged Information (1984).

famous illustration of the principle that lawyers do not have an obligation to reveal confidential information about a past crime. Two lawyers, Armani and Belge, were representing a defendant accused of murder when the defendant informed them that he had committed three unsolved murders. The defendant told his lawyers of the location of the body of one of the victims. Belge went to the location and inspected the body to verify the client's story. The lawyers did not reveal the information, but their knowledge later became public during the defendant's trial as part of their insanity defense. Because of public outrage against the lawyers' conduct, the district attorney presented the matter to a grand jury which returned an indictment against Belge, but not against Armani, for violation of two provisions of the New York Public Health Law, one requiring that the dead be given a decent burial, the other directing any person knowing of the death of a person without medical assistance to report the matter to the authorities. Neither statute expressly referred to attorneys. The trial court dismissed the indictment and the Appellate Division affirmed, but it expressed only lukewarm support for Belge's conduct:

> In view of the fact that the claim of absolute privilege was proffered, we note that the privilege is not all-encompassing and that in a given case there may be conflicting considerations. We believe that an attorney must protect his client's interests, but also must observe basic human standards of decency, having due regard to the need that the legal system accord justice to the interests of society and its individual members.
>
> We write to emphasize our serious concern regarding the consequences which emanate from a claim of an absolute attorney-client privilege. Because the only question presented, briefed and argued on this appeal was a legal one with respect to the sufficiency of the indictments, we limit our determination to that issue and do not reach the ethical questions underlying this case.[35]

Are Model Rule 1.6 and *Belge* based on sound policy? One argument in favor of the rule is that the client had already committed the murders. Disclosure by Belge and Armani could not, therefore, have prevented a crime from occurring. This argument is sound as far as it goes, but it ignores significant other harms that could have been prevented by disclosure. First, members of the victims' families continued to suffer the anguish of not knowing

35. 376 N.Y.S.2d at 772.

the fate of the victims and of not receiving the satisfaction of having the perpetrator of the crime brought to justice. Second, society was harmed because police resources continued to be spent to investigate an unsolved crime. Further, all members of society suffer an increase in general fear whenever a crime remains unsolved. A proponent of the rule of confidentiality could admit these harms but could claim that they are not of sufficient magnitude or immediacy to override the strong policy in favor of confidentiality. In the final analysis, the wisdom of the rule turns on how one appraises the seriousness of the harms and the extent of the benefits that result from confidentiality. Since people will evaluate these harms and benefits differently, it is not surprising that the scope of the duty of confidentiality remains controversial.

While the Model Rules prohibit lawyers from revealing confidential information about past wrongful client conduct, the comments to the rules authorize lawyers to engage in what is called a "noisy notice of withdrawal." The history of this concept provides interesting insight into the development of the Model Rules.

The Kutak Commission's 1982 Draft of the Model Rules contained a narrow exception to the duty of confidentiality with regard to rectification of past wrongful client conduct. Proposed Model Rule 1.6(b) provided as follows:

> A lawyer may reveal [confidential] information to the extent the lawyer reasonably believes necessary: . . .
>
> (2) to rectify the consequences of a client's criminal or fraudulent act in the furtherance of which the lawyer's services had been used . . .

The ABA's House of Delegates rejected this provision when it adopted the Model Rule in 1983. The House was apparently persuaded by the argument that the proper course of action when a lawyer learns that a client has committed a crime or fraud that involves the lawyer's services is to withdraw from the representation. Because the final version of Model Rule 1.6 adopted by the ABA differed substantially from the Kutak Commission's proposal, the original comments to Rule 1.6 needed revision as well. Representatives of the contending positions on confidentiality met to discuss modifications of the comments. During the negotiations over the comments, advocates of the Kutak Commission proposal pointed out that withdrawal was an ineffective solution when the client had already completed the fraud, or when the parties affected by the fraud were too unsophisticated to understand the significance of the lawyer's withdrawal.[36] As a result of these negotiations the ABA ultimately approved comments 14 and 15 to Rule 1.6, authorizing a "noisy notice of withdrawal":

> If the lawyer's services will be used by the client in materially furthering a course of criminal or fraudulent conduct, the lawyer must withdraw, as stated in Rule 1.16(a)(1).
>
> After withdrawal the lawyer is required to refrain from making disclosure of the clients' confidences, except as otherwise provided in Rule 1.6. *Neither this Rule nor Rule 1.8(b) nor Rule 1.16(d) prevents the lawyer from giving notice of the fact of withdrawal, and the lawyer may also withdraw or disaffirm any opinion, document, affirmation, or the like.* (Emphasis added.)

The comment thus allowed lawyers who were required to withdraw because of clients' criminal or fraudulent conduct to go beyond a simple withdrawal. It also authorized lawyers to withdraw or to disaffirm opinions or documents. While such a disaffirmance would constitute a clear signal that something was amiss, it would not amount to a direct revelation of confidential information.

Controversy over the past fraud issue continues to rage. Given the ABA's repeated rejections of exceptions to the duty of confidentiality, amendment of Rule 1.6 seems unlikely. Questions remain, however, about application of the present rules and particularly about the "noisy notice" comment. The Scope note to the Model Rules states: "The Comments are intended as guides to interpretation, but the text of each Rule is authoritative." Thus, arguably the noisy notice comment should be given no effect since it is not authorized by the text. In 1992, the ABA Committee on Ethics and Professional Responsibility issued Formal Opinion 92-366 dealing with the noisy notice of withdrawal. The Committee concluded that the comment was a proper interpretation of the text but only in the situation in which the client was continuing to use the lawyer's work product to commit a crime or fraud. In that situation, according to the Committee, the "representation" of the client continued and the noisy notice was required to effectuate a full withdrawal:

36. Geoffrey C. Hazard, Jr., Rectification of Client Fraud: Death and Revival of a Professional Norm, 33 Emory L.J. 271, 298-304 (1984).

> [W]here the client avowedly intends to continue to use the lawyer's work product, this amounts to a de facto continuation of the representation even if the lawyer has ceased to perform any additional work. The representation is not completed, any more than the fraud itself is completed. In order to fully effectuate the withdrawal mandated by Rule 1.16(a)(1), and to avoid assisting client fraud as mandated by Rule 1.2(d), the lawyer may have to repudiate her preexisting work product in addition to refusing to perform any further work for the client.[37]

In cases where the lawyer's work product was not being used, the Committee opined that use of the noisy notice was improper.[38]

As a result of the Committee's analysis, therefore, a lawyer could not use the noisy notice of withdrawal if the client had already completed the fraud, or if the fraud was ongoing but the lawyer's work product would not be used. Three members of the ABA Committee strongly dissented (historically dissents have been rare in ABA ethics opinions). The dissent argued that the proposition accepted by the majority—a noisy notice of withdrawal is mandatory to effectuate a complete withdrawal when the client continues the "representation" by using a lawyer's preexisting opinion to commit a crime or fraud—is not supported by the text of the rules, uses an artificial and strained conception of what constitutes "representation," and goes beyond even the comment by making a noisy notice mandatory.[39]

F. COUNSELING OR ASSISTING WRONGFUL CLIENT CONDUCT

The previous two sections discussed whether lawyers have an obligation to disclose confidential information that would prevent or rectify a client wrong. The general answer is that lawyers do not have either a professional or a legal obligation to disclose confiden-

37. ABA Comm. on Ethics and Prof. Resp., Formal Opinion 92-366, at 12.

38. Id. at 9 n.10.

39. Professor Hazard has also authored a stinging criticism of the Committee's reasoning and conclusions, and even of the realism of the hypothetical that the Committee considered. Geoffrey C. Hazard, Jr., Lawyers and Client Fraud: They Still Don't Get It, 6 Geo. J. Legal Ethics 701 (1993).

tial information to prevent or to rectify a wrong, but they have limited discretion to reveal confidential information to prevent a client from committing a crime (some states) or a criminal act involving an imminent threat of death or substantial bodily harm (Model Rules).

It is important to recognize, however, a distinction between confidentiality and conduct. Subject to narrow exceptions, lawyers must guard their clients' confidences; but lawyers simultaneously have a broad professional obligation not to counsel or assist their clients in transactions that they know are illegal or fraudulent. The Code of Professional Responsibility stated in DR 7-102(A)(7) that a lawyer shall not "[c]ounsel or assist his client in conduct that the lawyer knows to be illegal or fraudulent." Model Rule 1.2(d) carries forward this prohibition:

> A lawyer shall not counsel a client to engage, or assist a client, in conduct that the lawyer knows is criminal or fraudulent, but a lawyer may discuss the legal consequences of any proposed course of conduct with a client and may counsel or assist a client to make a good faith effort to determine the validity, scope, meaning or application of the law.

If a lawyer goes beyond mere knowledge of the client's crime to active participation in concealing the crime, the lawyer violates both professional and legal obligations.[40] The leading case illustrating this proposition is In re Ryder.[41] Ryder represented an individual who was accused of bank robbery using a sawed-off shotgun. The F.B.I. told Ryder that his client had possession of bills taken in the bank robbery when he was arrested. Ryder's client told him that a man whom he would not identify had paid him $500 to put a package in a safety deposit box. Ryder did not believe this story, and he had his client sign a power of attorney so that he could obtain possession of the client's safety deposit box. When Ryder opened his client's box, he found a sawed-off shotgun and a bag of money along with other items. Ryder transferred the contents of his client's box to a new box that he had opened in his name. The F.B.I. later discovered Ryder's box containing the money and gun. Ryder testified that he intended to return the money to the

40. See Restatement of the Law Governing Lawyers §151 (Tent. Draft #8, March 21, 1997).

41. 263 F. Supp. 360 (E.D. Va. 1967), *aff'd*, 381 F.2d 713 (4th Cir. 1967).

true owner in the future. His purpose in transferring the money and gun to his own box was to support an argument that the money and gun were inadmissible in a prosecution against his client because of the attorney-client privilege. The court removed Ryder from the case, and later the United States attorney instituted disciplinary proceedings against him. The district court suspended Ryder from practice for 18 months. The court ruled that Ryder had gone far beyond the receipt of confidential information to become an active participant in concealment of a crime. On appeal, the Fourth Circuit approved the district court's order:

> It is an abuse of a lawyer's professional responsibility knowingly to take possession of and secrete the fruits and instrumentalities of a crime. Ryder's acts bear no reasonable relation to the privilege and duty to refuse to divulge a client's confidential communication. Ryder made himself an active participant in a criminal act, ostensibly wearing the mantle of the loyal advocate, but in reality serving as accessory after the fact.[42]

A number of courts have gone beyond the decision in *Ryder* to hold that attorneys who come into possession of physical evidence of a crime have an obligation voluntarily on their own motion to turn the material over to the authorities. In State ex rel. Sowers v. Olwell,[43] Olwell, an attorney representing a suspect in a murder, came into possession of a knife. It was unclear from the case whether Olwell obtained the knife from his client or elsewhere. A few days before a coroner's inquest into the death, Olwell received a subpoena duces tecum, directing him to produce "all knives in your possession" that related to the victim's death. Olwell refused to comply with the subpoena claiming attorney-client privilege. The trial court held Olwell in contempt for his refusal to comply with the subpoena. On appeal the Washington Supreme Court reversed. The court's decision balanced the attorney's obligations as an officer of the court and the attorney-client privilege:

42. 381 F.2d at 714. *Accord* State ex rel. Oklahoma Bar Assn. v. Harlton, 669 P.2d 774, 777 (Okla. 1983) (attorney received five-year suspension after pleading guilty to charge of hindering prosecution by concealing shotgun; attorney "embraced the role of an accessory to a crime as a personal accommodation to its perpetrator").

43. 394 P.2d 681 (Wash. 1964).

> We are in agreement that the attorney-client privilege is applicable to the knife held by appellant, but do not agree that the privilege warrants that attorney, as an officer of the court, from withholding it after being properly requested to produce the same. The attorney should not be a depository for criminal evidence (such as a knife, other weapons, stolen property, etc.), which in itself has little, if any, material value for the purposes of aiding counsel in the preparation of the defense of his client's case. Such evidence given the attorney during legal consultation for information purposes and used by the attorney in preparing the defense of his client's case, whether or not the case ever goes to trial, could clearly be withheld for a reasonable period of time. It follows that the attorney, after a reasonable period, should, as an officer of the court, on his own motion turn the same over to the prosecution.
>
> We think the attorney-client privilege should and can be preserved even though the attorney surrenders the evidence he has in his possession. The prosecution, upon receipt of such evidence from an attorney, where charge against the attorney's client is contemplated (presently or in the future), should be well aware of the existence of the attorney-client privilege. Therefore, the state, when attempting to introduce such evidence at the trial, should take extreme precautions to make certain that the source of the evidence is not disclosed in the presence of the jury and prejudicial error is not committed. By thus allowing the prosecution to recover such evidence, the public interest is served, and by refusing the prosecution an opportunity to disclose the source of the evidence, the client's privilege is preserved and a balance is reached between these conflicting interests. The burden of introducing such evidence at a trial would continue to be upon the prosecution.[44]

Although Olwell was under subpoena, the court stated that he had an obligation "on his own motion" to turn the knife over to the authorities after a reasonable period of time for examination. A number of other courts[45] and the Restatement of the Law Governing Lawyers[46] agree with the voluntary disclosure approach used by the court in *Olwell.*

44. Id. at 684-685.

45. See Morrell v. State, 575 P.2d 1200 (Alaska 1978); State v. Carlin, 640 P.2d 324 (Kan. Ct. App. 1982); Commonwealth v. Stenhach, 514 A.2d 114 (Pa. Super. Ct. 1986), *appeal denied,* 534 A.2d 769 (1987).

46. Restatement of the Law Governing Lawyers §179 (Tent. Draft #8, March 21, 1997) (lawyer must either inform authorities or return evidence to its original location).

The duty to produce voluntarily applies not only to physical evidence of a crime, such as the knife in *Olwell,* but also to contraband (illegal drugs, for example) and to stolen property (such as money taken in a bank robbery as in *Ryder*).[47] Does the duty to produce apply to documentary evidence of a crime? The proposed Restatement takes the position that it does:

> It also includes such material as documents and material in electronically retrievable form used by the client to plan the offense, documents used in the course of a mail fraud violation, or transaction documents evidencing a crime.[48]

Whether the duty to produce should apply to documents is questionable, however. Unlike physical evidence of a crime, lawyers could come into possession of documentary evidence of a crime as part of their normal investigation of the matter. Moreover, whether a document is incriminating or not will frequently require an analysis of the significance of the document. Thus, a duty to produce documentary evidence could well infringe the work product privilege because production would reveal the attorney's analysis of the incriminating nature of the document. For these reasons, the Restatement's view that the duty to produce applies to documentary evidence should not be followed. The Restatement does recognize that material prepared by a lawyer, such as witness statements, trial exhibits, and the like, is subject to the work product privilege and is not subject to the duty to produce.[49]

Assuming lawyers have an obligation to turn over to the authorities physical evidence of a crime in their possession, rarely will it make sense for lawyers voluntarily to take possession of such material.[50] One reason for doing so would be if the material could prove to be exculpatory. In some cases, however, the attorney may not have a choice about obtaining or keeping possession. The material may be delivered anonymously to the lawyer or the party making the delivery may refuse to keep it.

47. Restatement of the Law Governing Lawyers §57, comm. *f* (Prop. Final Draft #1, March 29, 1996).

48. Restatement of the Law Governing Lawyers §179, comm. *a* (Tent. Draft #8, March 21, 1997).

49. Id.

50. See Barry S. Martin, Incriminating Criminal Evidence: Practical Solutions, 15 Pac. L.J. 807 (1984).

What should the lawyer do if the lawyer does have possession of physical evidence of a crime? One possibility would be to return the material to its original location rather than to the authorities. Some case law,[51] the ABA Standards for the Defense Function,[52] and the Restatement of the Law Governing Lawyers[53] support this approach, but this alternative may be questionable in other jurisdictions where decisions such as *Olwell* seem to impose a duty on lawyers to turn the evidence over to the authorities. In addition, if substantial risk exists that the material will be destroyed or will be used to harm someone if it is returned to its original location, it seems improper for the lawyer to take that step.[54] Another alternative would be to turn the material over to the authorities anonymously to protect client confidentiality to the maximum extent possible. The lawyer could hire another attorney for the purpose of delivering the materials to the authorities. Normally, the identity of a client is not subject to the attorney-client privilege, however, at least one court has held that the identity of a client who employed counsel to defend criminal charges and return stolen property was privileged.[55] On the other hand, an anonymous return may effectively deprive the prosecution of evidence of a crime: What is a prosecutor to do with a gun returned anonymously without any identification of the crime to which the gun is related?[56]

The principle of the *Ryder* case, which prohibits lawyers from counseling or assisting clients in criminal or fraudulent conduct, applies in business and other areas of practice as well as in criminal defense practice.[57] Lawyers who counsel or assist clients in fraud

51. See Hitch v. Pima County Superior Court, 708 P.2d 72 (Ariz. 1985) (en banc); People v. Meredith, 631 P.2d 46, 48 (Cal. 1981) (observation by lawyer or lawyer's agent loses its privileged character if "the defense by altering or removing physical evidence has precluded the prosecution from making that same observation").

52. ABA Defense Function Standard 4-4.6(b).

53. Restatement of the Law Governing Lawyers §179(2)(a) (Tent. Draft #8, March 21, 1997).

54. ABA Defense Function Standard 4-4.6(c); Restatement of the Law Governing Lawyers §179(2)(a) (Tent. Draft #8, March 21, 1997).

55. Anderson v. State, 297 So. 2d 871 (Fla. Dist. Ct. App. 1974).

56. See Norman Lefstein, Incriminating Physical Evidence, The Defense Attorney's Dilemma, and the Need for Rules, 64 N.C. L. Rev. 897, 936-937 (1986).

57. See Florida Bar v. Calvo, 630 So. 2d 548 (Fla. 1993), *cert. denied*, 115 S. Ct. 58 (1994) (lawyer disbarred for participation in fraudulent securities offering);

face not only the possibility of professional discipline but also civil liability for "aiding and abetting" the client's fraud. Common law liability as an aider or abettor exists when a person knowingly provides substantial assistance or encouragement to another person's primary wrong.[58] While the Supreme Court has decided that lawyers and other professionals may not be held liable as aiders and abettors under the federal securities laws,[59] securities lawyers could still be held liable for primary violations of the federal securities laws[60] or under a common law aider and abettor theory.

Although the principle that lawyers may not counsel or assist clients in illegal or fraudulent conduct is well established, the boundaries of this obligation are imprecise. First, it should be clear that a lawyer does not counsel or assist a client in committing a crime or fraud if the lawyer does nothing more than advise a client that the client's planned course of action would be illegal or fraudulent. Model Rule 1.2(d) states that a lawyer "may discuss the legal consequences of any proposed course of conduct with a client," and comment 6 states:

> A lawyer is required to give an honest opinion about the actual consequences that appear likely to result from a client's conduct. The fact that a client uses advice in a course of action that is criminal or fraudulent does not, of itself, make a lawyer a party to the course of action. However, a lawyer may not knowingly assist a client in criminal or fraudulent conduct. There is a critical distinction between presenting an analysis of legal aspects of questionable con-

---

ABA Comm. on Ethics and Prof. Resp., Formal Opinion 94-380 (in estate administration, lawyer represents fiduciary rather than beneficiaries; while lawyer must maintain fiduciary's confidences, lawyer may be required to withdraw if the lawyer's continued representation would involve assisting the fiduciary in fraud, or would involve misrepresentation by the attorney to a court or to third parties).

58. See Restatement (Second) of Torts §876(b) (1977) (actor liable for tort of another if actor knows that other's conduct is breach of duty to third person and provides substantial assistance or encouragement).

59. Central Bank of Denver, N.A. v. First Interstate Bank of Denver, N.A., 511 U.S. at 164 (1994). See Gareth T. Evans & Daniel S. Floyd, Secondary Liability Under Rule 10b-5: Still Alive and Well After *Central Bank*, 52 Bus. Law. 13 (Nov. 1996); Ann Maxey, Competing Duties? Securities Lawyers' Liability After *Central Bank*, 64 Fordham L. Rev. 2185 (1996).

60. *Central Bank*, 511 U.S. at 191. See In re American Continental Corp./Lincoln Sav. & Loan Sec. Litig., 794 F. Supp. 1424 (D. Ariz. 1992) (cause of action stated against law firm that represented Lincoln Savings and Loan for issuing misleading opinion in violation of §11 of Securities Act of 1933, which imposes liability on experts who make statements in connection with registration of securities).

duct and recommending the means by which a crime or fraud might be committed with impunity.[61]

Second, a lawyer may not counsel or assist a client in conduct that the lawyer *knows* is illegal or fraudulent, but when does the lawyer know of a crime or fraud? Later in this chapter we will examine the issue of when a lawyer knows that his client has committed perjury in a criminal case. Courts and commentators have suggested several possible standards for knowledge, including a "firm factual basis" or "beyond a reasonable doubt." Other commentators have suggested that "willful blindness" or "conscious ignorance" should be treated as the equivalent of knowledge.[62]

Third, as to the lawyer's ability to represent the client, what are the consequences of the duty not to counsel or assist a client in criminal or fraudulent conduct? The lawyer obviously cannot continue to handle legal aspects of illegal or fraudulent transactions (such as, preparing opinions or other documents, or participating in closings) since such conduct would amount to direct assistance of the client's wrongdoing. Must the lawyer formally resign from representation in connection with any wrongful transactions? For example, the client might retain other counsel who is unaware of the wrongdoing to handle the transaction, but might ask the first lawyer to refrain from formally resigning to avoid raising a "red flag." If the purpose of withholding the lawyer's resignation is to mislead new counsel into believing that the lawyer is still associated with the client and that the client is not engaged in misconduct, isn't the lawyer providing indirect assistance of fraud?

Is a lawyer who knows that a client is engaged in an illegal or fraudulent transaction prohibited from having any involvement whatsoever with the transaction? Suppose, for example, that a lawyer knows that a client is engaging in a fraudulent financial transaction, but the lawyer is not representing the client in the transaction. May the lawyer respond to a letter from the client's accountant asking the lawyer to state the amount of outstanding legal fees that the client owes to the lawyer, or does even providing

61. See also Geoffrey C. Hazard Jr., Rectification of Client Fraud: Death and Revival of a Professional Norm, 33 Emory L.J. 271, 281-282 (1984).

62. Cf. John P. Freeman & Nathan M. Crystal, Scienter in Professional Liability Cases, 42 S.C. L. Rev. 783, 833-838 (1991); Geoffrey C. Hazard, Jr., Rectification of Client Fraud: Death and Revival of a Professional Norm, 33 Emory L.J. 271, 282-283 (1984).

factual information constitute assistance of the fraud? In aider and abetter liability cases, the courts have held that lawyers were liable only if they provided "substantial" assistance to client fraud.[63]

A related aspect of the question of how far the prohibition on counseling or assisting a crime or fraud extends deals with representation in unrelated matters. Does the obligation mean that the lawyer can have no involvement in transactions that are unrelated to the crime or fraud? For example, suppose a law firm knows that a client is engaging in a fraudulent securities transaction. Must the firm refuse to represent the client in unrelated civil litigation? Must it refuse to represent the client in unrelated business matters? In essence, must the firm resign from all employment by the client?

In Formal Opinion 92-366, the ABA Committee on Legal Ethics and Professional Responsibility examined the ethical aspects of a lawyer's continued representation of a client who was engaged in fraud in matters that were both related and unrelated to the fraud. The Committee opined that a lawyer was ethically required to withdraw from representation in matters directly involving fraud. As to unrelated matters, the Committee concluded that withdrawal was more likely to be permissive under Model Rule 1.16. The Committee also advised, however, that "complete severance may be the preferred course in these circumstances, in order to avoid any possibility of the lawyer's continued association with the client's fraud."[64]

G. DISCLOSURE OF CONFIDENTIAL INFORMATION IN SELF DEFENSE

Model Rule 1.6(b)(2) allows a lawyer to reveal confidential information "to establish a claim or defense on behalf of the lawyer in a controversy between the lawyer and the client, to establish a defense to a criminal charge or civil claim against the lawyer based

63. See SEC v. National Student Marketing Corp., 457 F. Supp. 682, 713-715 (D.D.C. 1978); see also Restatement (Second) of Torts §876(b) (1977).

64. Formal Opinion 92-366, at 6. See also Geoffrey C. Hazard, Jr., Lawyers and Client Fraud: They Still Don't Get It, 6 Geo. J. Legal Ethics 701, 728-729 (1993) (arguing that duty not to counsel or assist in fraud does not preclude defense of litigation arising from fraud or representation in unrelated matters).

upon conduct in which the client was involved, or to respond to allegations in any proceeding concerning the lawyer's representation of the client." In broad terms, the rule allows lawyers to reveal confidential information to protect their interests in connection with matters in which the client is involved. The leading case dealing with the "self defense" exception to the duty of confidentiality is Meyerhofer v. Empire Fire & Marine Ins. Co.[65] The case involved a securities fraud action alleging that Empire had marketed securities using a registration statement and prospectus that were materially false and misleading. The complaint named Empire's law firm and several of its partners as defendants. In addition, the complaint included as a defendant Stuart Goldberg, an attorney who had worked on the Empire matter, but who had resigned from the firm in a dispute with the firm over the adequacy of disclosures being made in the Empire offering. On the same day that he resigned from the firm, Goldberg informed the SEC of his concerns about the offering; he subsequently filed an affidavit with the SEC about the matter. When Goldberg was named as a defendant in the securities fraud litigation, he contacted plaintiffs' counsel, informed them of his noninvolvement in the offering, and supplied them with a copy of the affidavit he filed with the SEC. As a result the plaintiffs dismissed Goldberg from the suit. Defendants then moved to disqualify plaintiffs' counsel from continuing in the case on the ground that they had received confidential information from Goldberg. The district court granted the disqualification motion but the Second Circuit Court of Appeals reversed:

> . . . DR 4-101(C) recognizes that a lawyer may reveal confidences or secrets necessary to defend himself against "an accusation of wrongful conduct." That is exactly what Goldberg had to face when, in their original complaint, plaintiffs named him as a defendant who wilfully violated the securities laws.
>
> The charge, of knowing participation in the filing of a false and misleading registration statement, was a serious one. The complaint alleged violation of criminal statutes and civil liability computable at over four million dollars. The cost in money of simply defending such an action might be very substantial. The damage to his professional reputation which might be occasioned by the mere pendency of such a charge was an even greater cause for concern.

65. 497 F.2d 1190, *cert. denied*, 419 U.S. 998 (1974).

> Under these circumstances Goldberg had the right to make an appropriate disclosure with respect to his role in the public offering. Concomitantly, he had the right to support his version of the facts with suitable evidence.[66]

Although the court expressed some concern with Goldberg's method of disclosure—turning over to plaintiffs' counsel a 30-page affidavit with 16 attached exhibits—the court concluded that his action was the "most effective way for him to substantiate his story."[67]

H. CANDOR TO THE TRIBUNAL: DISCLOSURE OF ADVERSE FACTS AND LAW

Previous sections have dealt with the issue of disclosure of confidential information to prevent harm either to third parties or to the attorney. When a lawyer is representing a client in a matter before a tribunal, the interests of the tribunal also affect the scope of the duty of confidentiality.

It is well-established doctrine that lawyers do not have an obligation to disclose voluntarily (as opposed to disclosure in compliance with discovery rules or court order) to the other side or to the tribunal evidence that is material to the case, even if nondisclosure would produce a result that is not consistent with the truth. The Model Rules reflect this principle by silence; because of the absence of a disclosure rule, a lawyer's general duty of confidentiality prevents the lawyer from disclosing adverse evidence.[68] Comment *b* to §180 of the proposed Restatement of the Law Governing Lawyers expresses the same principle:

> A lawyer might know of testimony or other evidence vital to the other party, but unknown to that party or their advocate. The advocate who knows of the evidence, and who has complied with applicable rules concerning pretrial discovery and other applicable

66. Id. at 1194-1195.
67. Id. at 1195.
68. Wolfram, Modern Legal Ethics §12.3.2, at 639.

disclosure requirements . . . , has no legal obligation to reveal the evidence, even though the proceeding thereby may fail to ascertain the facts as the lawyer knows them.

The absence of a duty of disclosure can be justified on several grounds. First, a duty to disclose would be inconsistent with our concept of an adversarial system of justice in which each side has the obligation to investigate and to present its case. Second, it is questionable whether a disclosure rule would increase the truthfulness of outcomes in civil and criminal cases. Liberal discovery under the Federal Rules of Civil Procedure and state systems modeled on those rules allows parties to obtain almost any nonprivileged evidence that could be material to the case. It seems problematic whether adding a disclosure obligation to the already-existing discovery system would increase truthful outcomes in civil cases.[69] In criminal cases, the prosecution already has a duty to disclose exculpatory evidence[70] and again it is doubtful that imposing a general disclosure obligation on the defense in criminal cases would increase truthful outcomes. More importantly, as discussed below, imposing such a duty on defense counsel might well violate fundamental rights.

Indeed, the incentive effects of a disclosure rule might be perverse. Attorneys would be wary about gathering adverse evidence for fear of triggering a disclosure obligation. As a result the quality of adversarial presentations, and ultimately the accuracy of legal proceedings, could suffer. Further, some lawyers would attempt to free-ride on the investigative efforts of the other side to obtain the fruits of that work without incurring the costs. Rules dealing with timing of disclosure could be created to minimize free rider effects, but the addition of such rules will increase the complexity of litigation and generate collateral disputes.

Finally, in many cases a disclosure rule would violate basic rights. Clients often communicate adverse evidence to their lawyers in confidence. A duty to disclose would, therefore, undermine the attorney-client privilege. Imposing a general disclosure obliga-

69. Lawyers may have difficulty obtaining information in response to discovery requests because of discovery abuse by the other side. It seems unlikely, however, that adding a disclosure obligation to the existing rules of discovery will be an effective way of controlling discovery abuse. On the issue of discovery abuse, see Chapter 5.D.3.

70. See Chapter 4.I infra.

tion on the defense in criminal cases might well violate the privilege against self-incrimination. The Supreme Court has held that when the government seeks to compel information from an attorney, the government violates the defendant's privilege against self incrimination if two elements are satisfied: (1) the defendant conveyed the information to the lawyer in a communication that was subject to the attorney-client privilege and (2) the information would have been subject to the privilege against self incrimination if the government had sought to compel the information directly from the defendant rather than indirectly from the lawyer.[71] Given these considerations, it seems clear that lawyers should not have a general obligation to disclose adverse evidence.

The general principle of nondisclosure is qualified, however, by several obligations. First, lawyers and their clients have an obligation to comply with various discovery rules requiring production of information in response to inquiries from the opposing side. Thus, Model Rule 3.4(d) states that a lawyer should not "fail to make reasonably diligent effort to comply with a legally proper discovery request by an opposing party." Second, the duty not to disclose adverse information cannot be used to justify personal involvement by the lawyer in fraud or criminal conduct. See Model Rule 8.4(b), (c).[72] Similarly, the duty not to disclose cannot be used to justify assisting clients in conduct that is criminal or fraudulent. See Model Rule 3.3(a)(2) (lawyer must disclose material fact when necessary to avoid assisting the client in a criminal or fraudulent act). Third, lawyers must disclose to a tribunal the commission of perjury by their clients when that is the only "reasonable remedial measure." See Model Rule 3.3(a)(4). The next section discusses this obligation in more detail. Fourth, in ex parte proceedings (for example, if a lawyer is seeking a temporary restraining order), lawyers must disclose all material facts. See Model Rule 3.3(d).[73] Because ex parte proceedings do not involve an adversarial proc-

71. See Fisher v. United States, 425 U.S. 391, 402-405 (1975), discussed in Chapter 4.J.2 infra, and United States v. Doe, 465 U.S. 605 (1984).

72. See also United States v. Thoreen, 653 F.2d 1332 (9th Cir. 1981), *cert. denied,* 455 U.S. 938 (1982) (improper for defense counsel to substitute individual for defendant at counsel table to test ability of witnesses to identify defendant).

73. See also Restatement of the Law Governing Lawyers §172 (Tent. Draft #8, March 21, 1997). See generally Jill M. Dennis, Note, The *Model Rules* and the Search for Truth: The Origins and Application of *Model Rule* 3.3(d), 8 Geo. J. Legal Ethics 157 (1994).

ess, the rationale for nondisclosure does not apply.[74] Finally, as discussed in more detail in the next section, prosecutors have a duty to disclose to defense counsel all evidence or information that tends to negate the guilt or mitigate the offense of the accused. See Model Rule 3.8(d). The Model Rules, however, apparently do not require lawyers to reveal knowledge of juror misconduct, although this position seems unsound.[75]

While the Model Rules do not generally require lawyers to disclose adverse factual information, the rules do impose a limited obligation to disclose adverse law. Model Rule 3.3(a)(3) states that a lawyer must disclose legal authority in the controlling jurisdiction that is directly adverse to the position of the client and not disclosed by the opposing lawyer. DR 7-106(B)(1) of the Code of Professional Responsibility is identical. Under the Model Rules, the duty to disclose continues until the conclusion of the proceeding.[76]

A duty to disclose adverse law can be distinguished from a duty to disclose adverse facts. If a court renders a decision without taking into account legal authority that is directly on point, the risk of an erroneous decision is substantial. Moreover, an erroneous legal decision has an adverse impact not only on the parties to the dispute, but on other lawyers and their clients who plan transactions based on decisions made by courts. While a duty to disclose adverse legal authority might produce adverse free rider effects, these are not likely to be great because legal research is not that costly. Even lawyers who do not have the time or temperament to do research can farm projects out to clerks or research services that will do competent work for a modest fee. Thus, on balance it appears that a duty to disclose adverse legal authority is likely to increase the truthfulness of judicial outcomes. Further, unlike a duty to disclose adverse facts, fundamental rights such as the attorney-client privilege are not implicated by a duty to disclose adverse law.

The Model Rules define the scope of the duty to disclose adverse legal authority quite narrowly. The duty to disclose is limited to authority in the "controlling jurisdiction" and to authority that is

74. Restatement of the Law Governing Lawyers §172, comm. *b* (Tent. Draft #8, March 21, 1997).

75. See Chapter 5.C.4.

76. See ABA Comm. on Ethics and Prof. Resp., Informal Opinion 84-1505 (lawyer must disclose appellate decision directly adverse to lawyer's position in motion to dismiss that had earlier been denied by trial court if the issue raised in the motion to dismiss can be revived because not final and appealable).

"directly adverse." Both of these limitations are questionable. Hazard and Hodes state:

> The "controlling jurisdiction" normally means the same state as the pending case for state law issues, and the same District or Circuit for federal law issues. In either event, of course, applicable decisions of the United States Supreme Court would be considered controlling.[77]

The "controlling jurisdiction" requirement means, therefore, that lawyers do not have an obligation to disclose adverse decisions from the highest courts of other states or from other federal circuits. This limitation seems unsound because decisions from sister jurisdictions on similar points are often the most important authorities.

The meaning of the term "directly adverse" in Rule 3.3(a)(3) is somewhat unclear. One interpretation, probably the one that lawyers seeking to avoid disclosure are likely to follow, is that an authority is not directly adverse if it can be distinguished in a nonfrivolous way. This interpretation effectively guts the disclosure rule, however, because lawyers can create a plausible distinction for any authority. Another possible interpretation is that an authority is directly adverse if a reasonable judge would attach importance to the authority. Hazard and Hodes argue for this interpretation:

> Formal Opinion 280 (1949) sounded the right note on this issue when it suggested that the standard should be whether the omitted authorities "would be considered important by the judge sitting on the case," or whether the judge might consider himself "misled" if he remained unaware of them.[78]

The difficulty with this interpretation is that it seems inconsistent with the legislative history of the Model Rules. The Discussion Draft of the Model Rules contained the following proposed rule:

> If a lawyer discovers that the tribunal has not been apprised of legal authority known to the lawyer that would probably have a

77. 1 Hazard & Hodes, The Law of Lawyering §3.3:206, at 588.
78. Id.

> substantial effect on the determination of a material issue, the lawyer shall advise the tribunal of that authority.[79]

This proposal, which seems sound as a matter of principle, was withdrawn, however, apparently because opponents believed that it imposed too broad a disclosure obligation on lawyers. Unfortunately, the proposed Restatement of the Law Governing Lawyers continues the limited disclosure rule found in the Model Rules.[80]

One special application of the duty to disclose adverse law in criminal cases involves the so-called *Anders* brief. In Anders v. California,[81] the Supreme Court held that appointed counsel who moves to withdraw from handling an appeal because counsel has concluded that the appeal is frivolous cannot simply file a "no-merit letter," but must instead accompany the motion with "a brief referring to anything in the record that might arguably support the appeal."[82] The Court made clear that the purpose of the *Anders* brief was not for counsel to act as advocate against the client, but rather to provide information so that the appellate court could more easily assess whether to appoint counsel to handle the appeal. Further, the brief requirement served as a mechanism to ensure that appointed counsel had thoroughly reviewed the record.[83]

In McCoy v. Court of Appeals,[84] the Supreme Court upheld the constitutionality of a Wisconsin rule that required appointed counsel to include in the *Anders* brief a discussion of why issues that might arguably support the appeal lacked merit. Three justices dissented on the ground that the decision in *McCoy* effectively turned appointed counsel into an advocate against the client.

While Model Rule 3.3(a)(3) requires lawyers to disclose adverse law in some situations, lawyers also have a duty not to engage in misleading argument. For example, partial quotations that are misleading or citation of cases that have been overruled or questioned

79. ABA Comm. on Evaluation of Prof. Standards, Rule 3.1(c) (Discussion Draft Jan. 30, 1980). See Geoffrey C. Hazard, Jr., Arguing the Law: The Advocate's Duty and Opportunity, 16 Ga. L. Rev. 821 (1982).

80. Restatement of the Law Governing Lawyers §171(2) (Tent. Draft #8, March 21, 1997).

81. 386 U.S. 738 (1967).

82. Id. at 744.

83. Id. at 745.

84. 486 U.S. 429 (1988).

would be improper because they amount to misleading argument. See Model Rule 3.3, comm. 3.

When a lawyer appears before a legislative, administrative, or other body in a nonadjudicative proceeding, the lawyer has a duty to inform the body that the lawyer is appearing in a representative capacity and to comply with applicable law governing such a body.[85]

I. SPECIAL DISCLOSURE OBLIGATIONS OF PROSECUTORS

The duty of prosecutors regarding adverse facts contrasts sharply with that of defense counsel. Prosecutors have both a constitutional and a professional obligation to disclose "exculpatory" material. The leading case dealing with the due process effect of a prosecutor's failure to disclose exculpatory material is Brady v. Maryland,[86] a prosecution for murder in which defense counsel asked the prosecution to be allowed to examine extrajudicial statements made by defendant's companion. The prosecution showed defense counsel several statements, but did not disclose one statement in which the companion admitted committing the homicide. The Supreme Court held that "suppression by the prosecution of evidence favorable to an accused upon request violates due process where the evidence is material either to guilt or to punishment, irrespective of the good faith or bad faith of the prosecution."[87]

In subsequent cases, the Court expanded the *Brady* rule to include situations in which the defendant has not made a specific request for exculpatory material[88] and to encompass impeachment as well as exculpatory evidence.[89] The Court has also refined the requirement that the prosecutorial duty to disclose only applies if the evidence is "material" either to guilt or punishment. In United

85. See Model Rule 3.9; Restatement of the Law Governing Lawyers §164 (Tent. Draft #8, March 21, 1997).
86. 373 U.S. 83 (1963).
87. Id. at 87.
88. United States v. Agurs, 427 U.S. 97, 106 (1976).
89. United States v. Bagley, 473 U.S. 667 (1985).

States v. Agurs,[90] the Court rejected the claim that the prosecution had a duty to turn over any evidence that might affect the jury. Such a standard would effectively require the prosecution to open its file to the defense.[91] Instead, the Court held that the failure to disclose violated the defendant's right to due process "if the omitted evidence creates a reasonable doubt that did not otherwise exist."[92] In United States v. Bagley,[93] the Court ruled that the prosecution's failure to disclose evidence would be treated as material only if there was a "reasonable probability" that the outcome would have been different if the evidence had been disclosed.[94] Justices Marshall and Brennan dissented, arguing that the prosecution should have a duty to reveal "*all* information known to the government that might reasonably be considered favorable to the defendant's case."[95] If the prosecutor failed to comply with this duty, they would uphold a conviction only if "the prosecution has shown beyond a reasonable doubt that the new evidence, if disclosed and developed by reasonably competent counsel, would not have affected the outcome of the trial."[96] While some commentators have criticized the standard for materiality used by the Court in *Bagley*,[97] the Court recently reaffirmed this test.[98] Given the uncertainty about whether the materiality test has been met, however, the Court has warned that the "prudent prosecutor will resolve doubtful questions in favor of disclosure."[99]

It should be noted that the constitutional duty of disclosure does not turn on the bad faith of the prosecutor. The prosecutor has "a duty to learn of any favorable evidence known to the others acting on the government's behalf in the case, including the police."[100] The

90. 427 U.S. 97 (1976).
91. Id. at 109.
92. Id. at 112.
93. 473 U.S. 667 (1985).
94. Id. at 682.
95. Id. at 696 (emphasis in original).
96. Id. at 707.
97. Terence J. Galligan, Comment, The Prosecutor's Duty to Disclose Exculpatory Evidence after *United States v. Bagley*, 1 Geo. J. Legal Ethics 213 (1987).
98. See Kyles v. Whitley, 514 U.S. 419 (1995).
99. Id. at 439 (quoting United States v. Agurs, 427 U.S. at 108).
100. Id. at 437. See also Giglio v. United States, 405 U.S. 150 (1972) (Assistant U.S. attorney who presented case to grand jury had promised witness that he would not be prosecuted if he testified before grand jury and at trial; conviction of defendant reversed because of failure to disclose this promise even though assistant who made promise did not have authority to do so and even though promise was not known by U.S. Attorney or trial counsel).

Brady rule only applies, however, if the evidence is in the possession of the government. If the government has failed to preserve the evidence, the defendant's constitutional rights have not been violated unless the defendant establishes that the prosecution acted in bad faith.[101]

The Model Rules of Professional Conduct and the ABA Standards for the Prosecution Function both include rules setting forth a prosecutorial obligation to disclose exculpatory material. Model Rule 3.8(d) provides that a prosecutor in a criminal case shall

> make timely disclosure to the defense of all evidence or information known to the prosecutor that tends to negate the guilt of the accused or mitigates the offense, and, in connection with sentencing, disclose to the defense and to the tribunal all unprivileged mitigating information known to the prosecutor, except when the prosecutor is relieved of this responsibility by a protective order of the tribunal.

ABA Standard for the Prosecution Function 3-3.11(a) is substantially the same. Rule 3.8(d) differs from the constitutional standard in at least two respects. First, the ethical duty only applies to evidence or information "known to the prosecutor," while the constitutional standard applies to any evidence in the hands of the government, even if not known by the prosecutor. Second, the "tends to" standard of the rule appears to require greater disclosure than the constitutional standard. A study of disciplinary sanctions against prosecutors for *Brady* violations, however, finds that cases are rarely brought and sanctions are light.[102]

101. Arizona v. Youngblood, 488 U.S. 51 (1988) (failure of prosecution to preserve semen samples and clothing of victim in child molestation case held not to be a violation of defendant's right to due process absent showing of prosecutorial bad faith even though expert testimony indicated that timely performance of tests could have exonerated defendant). On the application of the *Brady* rule to plea bargains, see Note, The Prosecutor's Duty to Disclose to Defendants Pleading Guilty, 99 Harv. L. Rev. 1004 (1986).

102. Richard A. Rosen, Disciplinary Sanctions Against Prosecutors for *Brady* Violations: A Paper Tiger, 65 N.C. L. Rev. 693 (1987) (recommending independent review of reported criminal cases by bar counsel for *Brady* violations and automatic reversal when prosecutors act in bad faith). For a recent case, however, in which a prosecutor had his license suspended for making false statements to a court and for failing to disclose material exculpatory evidence, see Committee on Prof. Ethics & Conduct v. Ramey, 512 N.W.2d 569 (Iowa 1994). See also Stanley Z. Fisher, "Just the Facts, Ma'am": Lying and the Omission of Exculpatory Evidence in Police Reports, 28 New Eng. L. Rev. 1 (1993).

J. CANDOR TO THE TRIBUNAL: DISCLOSURE OF CLIENT PERJURY IN CRIMINAL CASES

What should defense counsel do when the defendant insists on taking the stand and testifying perjuriously (contemplated perjury) or when defense counsel learns that the defendant has testified perjuriously (completed perjury)? The answer to this difficult question requires consideration of both professional obligations and constitutional requirements.

1. *Professional Obligations*

Five approaches have been suggested for dealing with the issue of how defense counsel should respond either to contemplated or to completed perjury. These approaches represent different views of the importance of three values that are involved in the issue of perjury by criminal defendants: the constitutional rights of defendants, the prohibition on lawyers' assisting in criminal conduct, and the integrity of the judicial process.

1. Full Representation. In a famous 1966 article, Professor Monroe Freedman argued that if a criminal defendant insists on taking the stand and testifying perjuriously, defense counsel should not move to withdraw from the case and should not inform the court of the perjury. Instead, defense counsel should allow the defendant to take the stand and to testify; defense counsel should not do anything that would either explicitly or implicitly disclose the attorney's knowledge to the judge or jury. More specifically, this meant that the attorney would examine the defendant in the normal fashion, even if the defendant's answers were perjurious, and that the attorney would make normal closing arguments to the finder of fact, including arguments based on perjured testimony.[103] In later works, Professor Freedman explained the basis for his position. At its deepest level, his view is founded on the value of the "dignity of the individual in a free society." Constitutional rights

103. Monroe H. Freedman, Professional Responsibility of the Criminal Defense Lawyer: The Three Hardest Questions, 64 Mich. L. Rev. 1469, 1475-1478 (1966).

such as due process of law, right to counsel, and the privilege against self incrimination express this basic value. Confidentiality of communications between lawyer and client is central to all of these rights, since without client trust and complete information, lawyers cannot adequately defend their clients' rights.[104] In addition, Professor Freedman has criticized the practicality and constitutionality of the alternatives that others have proposed for dealing with the issue of perjury by criminal defendants.[105]

2. *Disclosure.* Professor Freedman's position met with immediate criticism from then United States Circuit Judge (later Chief Justice of the Supreme Court) Warren Burger. Justice Burger claimed that a lawyer could never under any circumstances participate in a fraud on the court, and that for a lawyer to ask questions of a client that would elicit perjured testimony was clearly improper.[106] Logically, the opposite position to Freedman's position of full representation would be full disclosure by defense counsel to the court of the defendant's contemplated or completed perjury. Although Justice Burger did not go that far in his 1966 article, he later came to endorse that position in his opinion in Nix v. Whiteside,[107] discussed in detail below.

3. *Withdrawal Without Disclosure.* An attorney confronted with a client who plans to take the stand and commit perjury or who has already testified perjuriously could move to withdraw from the case while at the same time protecting the confidentiality of client communications. The lawyer could, for example, move to withdraw because of "ethical reasons" or because of a "conflict of interest" or because of "privileged reasons." Professor Freedman has criticized the withdrawal solution on a number of grounds, including the following: First, if the court grants the motion, the problem is simply passed on to successor counsel who will either face the

104. Monroe H. Freedman, Understanding Lawyers' Ethics 13-17 (1990). See also Jay S. Silver, Truth, Justice, and the American Way: The Case *Against* the Client Perjury Rules, 47 Vand. L. Rev. 339 (1994) (criticizing the disclosure obligations of the Model Rules because they impede the discovery of truth, subvert the rights of the accused, and undermine the adversarial process).

105. See Monroe H. Freedman, Lawyers' Ethics in an Adversary System 27-42 (1975); Monroe H. Freedman, Understanding Lawyers' Ethics 109-141 (1990).

106. Warren E. Burger, Standards of Conduct for Prosecution and Defense Personnel: A Judge's Viewpoint, 5 Am. Crim. L.Q. 11, 13 (1966). For a history of the Freedman/Burger dispute, see Lyle Denniston, When Your Client Lies, 6 Cal. Law. 55, 57 (July, 1986).

107. 475 U.S. 157 (1986).

same dilemma or who will not learn of the perjury because the client has now been educated about what can and cannot be told to a lawyer. If the latter occurs, the withdrawal solution is no solution at all since it allows perjury to take place, but adds cost to the operation of the judicial system. Second, if the matter occurs on the eve of or during the trial, the judge will almost certainly deny the motion. The "withdrawal approach" does not guide the attorney about how to act in that event. Third, if the attorney moves to withdraw, the court may order the lawyer to reveal the reason, so that it may be impossible to maintain confidentiality.[108] In addition, if the lawyer does reveal the reason for moving to withdraw, and the client takes the stand, the judge may take the client's perjury into account in sentencing.[109]

4. *Narrative Testimony.* In 1971 the American Bar Association adopted Defense Function Standard 7.7 to guide defense lawyers in dealing with perjury by the criminal defendant. In 1979 the ABA Committee on Standards for Criminal Justice proposed a revised version of 7.7, but then withdrew this proposal from consideration by the ABA on the understanding that the issue of perjury by the criminal defendant would be considered by the ABA Committee working on the Model Rules of Professional Conduct. Revised Defense Function Standard 7.7, however, did provide a detailed statement of the narrative approach to perjury by the criminal defendant.

Revised Standard 7.7 granted lawyers discretion to move to withdraw if the issue of client perjury arose before trial. If withdrawal was not feasible or was denied by the court, the standard provided as follows:

> (c) If withdrawal from the case is not feasible or is not permitted by the court, or if the situation arises immediately preceding trial or during the trial and the defendant insists upon testifying perjuriously in his or her own behalf, it is unprofessional conduct for the lawyer to lend aid to the perjury or use the perjured testimony. Before the defendant takes the stand in these circumstances, the lawyer should make a record of the fact that the defendant is taking

108. Monroe H. Freedman, Understanding Lawyers' Ethics 115-116 (1990).

109. See United States v. Grayson, 438 U.S. 41 (1978) (upholding sentencing increase because of defendant's perjury); United States v. Dunnigan, 507 U.S. 87 (1993) (upholding trial judge's enhancement of defendant's sentence under federal sentencing guidelines because of perjury committed at trial).

> the stand against the advice of counsel in some appropriate manner without revealing the fact to the court. The lawyer may identify the witness as the defendant and may ask appropriate questions of the defendant when it is believed that the defendant's answers will not be perjurious. As to matters for which it is believed the defendant will offer perjurious testimony, the lawyer should seek to avoid direct examination of the defendant in the conventional manner; instead, the lawyer should ask the defendant if he or she wishes to make any additional statement concerning the case to the trier or triers of the facts. A lawyer may not later argue the defendant's known false version of the facts to the jury as worthy of belief, and may not recite or rely upon the false testimony in his or her closing argument.

Section 7.7 represents an effort to walk a tightrope between the full representation and the disclosure approaches to perjury by the criminal defendant. Under the narrative approach defense counsel should not reveal client perjury, but at the same time defense counsel must strictly avoid any involvement in the perjury.

The principal objection to the narrative testimony approach is that it in fact sacrifices both of the principles that it seeks to protect: The solution does not prevent perjury from taking place, and it infringes confidentiality because both the judge and jury are almost certain to know that defendant's lawyer does not trust his own client's testimony.[110] Moreover, the narrative solution does not address the question of what the lawyer should do when the lawyer learns that the client has already testified perjuriously. Nevertheless, a few courts have adopted the narrative solution as an ethically proper way for defense counsel to deal with the problem[111] and it has been incorporated in the District of Columbia Rules of Professional Conduct.[112] Some commentators also support the narrative approach.[113]

110. Monroe H. Freedman, Understanding Lawyers' Ethics 117-119 (1990).

111. People v. Guzman, 755 P.2d 917 (Cal. 1988) (en banc), *cert. denied*, 488 U.S. 1050 (1989); Shockley v. State, 565 A.2d 1373 (Del. 1989); Commonwealth v. Jermyn, 620 A.2d 1128 (Pa. 1993), *cert. denied*, 510 U.S. 1049 (1994); In re Goodwin, 305 S.E.2d 578 (S.C. 1983).

112. D.C. Rules of Prof. Conduct 3.3(b).

113. The most extensive defense of the narrative approach can be found in Norman Lefstein, Client Perjury in Criminal Cases: Still in Search of an Answer, 1 Geo. J. Legal Ethics 521 (1988). See also Nathan M. Crystal, Confidentiality under the Model Rules of Professional Conduct, 30 Kan. L. Rev. 215, 236-244 (1982).

5. *Avoidance of Knowledge.* Some commentators have suggested that the most practical way for a lawyer to deal with the problem of perjury by a criminal defendant is to make sure that the lawyer avoids having knowledge that the client intends to commit perjury. For example, if defense lawyers ask their clients to inform them about "what the prosecution is likely to say" and "tell me your memory of what occurred," rather than "what happened," then defense counsel can get all the facts without committing their clients to a particular version of what occurred. Professor Freedman characterizes this as "sophistry" and a "disingenuous evasion" designed to achieve the same result that he advocates openly and defends on the basis of fundamental values.[114] Further, this solution does not address the issue of the lawyer's obligations if the lawyer learns of perjury despite efforts to avoid knowledge.

Prior to the Model Rules, the position of the ABA on the problem of client perjury reflected an oscillation between protection of client confidentiality and avoidance of lawyer involvement in perjury.[115] Model Rule 3.3(a)(4) and the accompanying comments adopt Justice Burger's position, requiring a lawyer to disclose perjury by a criminal defendant when necessary to rectify the consequences of the perjury:

> A lawyer shall not knowingly . . . offer evidence that the lawyer knows to be false. If a lawyer has offered material evidence and comes to know of its falsity, the lawyer shall take reasonable remedial measures.

Under Model Rule 3.3 when the lawyer knows of contemplated perjury, the lawyer's course of action is to attempt to dissuade the client from testifying, and, if this fails, to move to withdraw if that step is feasible.[116] Criminal defendants have a constitutional right

114. Monroe H. Freedman, Understanding Lawyers' Ethics 119, 141 (1990).

115. For a history of these developments, see Jeffrey L. Dunetz, Surprise Client Perjury: Some Questions and Proposed Solutions to an Old Problem, 29 N.Y.L. Sch. L. Rev. 407, 410-420 (1984).

116. Model Rule 3.3, comm. 7. In Formal Opinion 87-353, the ABA Committee on Ethics and Professional Responsibility ruled that a lawyer normally need not move to withdraw after a defendant initially states an intention to testify falsely because the lawyer can ordinarily conclude that a warning about the consequences of perjury, including the lawyer's duty to reveal the perjury to the court, would be sufficient to dissuade the client from committing perjury. If the client continues to insist on testifying falsely, however, the lawyer should move to withdraw.

to testify in their own behalf, so neither defense counsel nor the court has the right to stop a defendant from testifying, even if the defendant intends to testify perjuriously.[117] If the client insists on taking the stand and testifying perjuriously, under Model Rule 3.3 the lawyer must take "reasonable remedial measures." While the language of the rule is less than clear in its use of the term *reasonable remedial measures,* the comments are clear that the rule is intended to adopt the full disclosure position if necessary to correct the perjury. See Comments 8-11. In particular, note that comment 11 states: "If withdrawal will not remedy the situation or is impossible, the advocate should make disclosure to the court." Comments 9 and 10 express reasons for the ABA's adoption of the disclosure approach.

The Restatement of the Law Governing Lawyers also adopts the view that lawyers have a duty to disclose client perjury if other remedial measures are insufficient to remove the false impression caused by the client's testimony.[118] The Restatement explains that the preservation of the integrity of the tribunal is superior to any interest the client might have in the loyalty of and confidentiality of communication with counsel regarding false testimony.[119] Once false evidence has been introduced, withdrawal is not a reasonable remedial measure.[120] The lawyer could attempt to persuade the client to take the stand and correct the testimony. In some instances the lawyer may be able to move to have evidence withdrawn or stricken.[121]

Model Rule 3.3 requires lawyers to take action to deal with client perjury only if the lawyer "knows" that the client intends to or has committed perjury. When does a lawyer have knowledge of perjury? The terminology section of the Model Rules states:

> "Knowingly," "Known," or "Knows," denotes actual knowledge of the fact in question. A person's knowledge may be inferred from circumstances.

117. Rock v. Arkansas, 483 U.S. 44 (1987).

118. Restatement of the Law Governing Lawyers §180(2) (Tent. Draft #8, March 21, 1997). On remedial measures available to an attorney prior to disclosing confidential information, see id. §180, comm. *h.*

119. Id. comm. *b.*

120. Id. comm. *h.*

121. Id.

What does "actual knowledge" mean in the context of the issue of perjury by a criminal defendant? It would be absurd to suggest that actual knowledge requires the lawyer to have been a witness to the underlying crime so as to have personal knowledge of the falsity of the client's statements. A personal knowledge standard would negate the obligations of Rule 3.3 since the rule would only apply when an attorney could not represent a defendant because the lawyer would be a witness in the case. In Formal Opinion 87-353, the ABA stated that a lawyer should take action only when the client had a "clearly stated intention" to testify falsely at trial. The courts have not been quite that stringent. Several courts have said that the attorney must have a "firm factual basis" before taking any action to prevent or rectify perjury by the defendant[122] and this is the view adopted by the Restatement of the Law Governing Lawyers.[123] Other courts have adopted a requirement that the lawyer have evidence establishing "beyond a reasonable doubt" that the defendant has or will commit perjury.[124]

Disclosure of client perjury by defense counsel can result in serious prejudice to the defendant. It seems reasonable that the standard of disclosure should be at least as demanding as that required to convict the defendant, i.e., beyond a reasonable doubt. Under this standard, the mere fact that a client has given the attorney inconsistent statements should not in and of itself be sufficient to amount to knowledge of perjury.[125]

If a lawyer informs the court that a defendant either intends to or has testified falsely, what should the court do about the matter? Comment 11 to Model Rule 3.3 provides only a small degree of guidance: "It is for the court then to determine what should be done — making a statement about the matter to the trier of fact, ordering a mistrial or perhaps nothing." In United States v. Scott,[126] defendant's attorney moved to withdraw for unspecified ethical reasons. The trial judge informed the defendant that he had the choice of either proceeding pro se or with the assistance of counsel who would make the decision about whether to allow the defen-

122. United States v. Long, 857 F.2d 436, 445 (8th Cir. 1988); United States ex rel. Wilcox v. Johnson, 555 F.2d 115, 122 (3d Cir. 1977).

123. Restatement of the Law Governing Lawyers §180, comm. *c* (Tent. Draft #8, March 21, 1997).

124. E.g., Shockley v. State, 565 A.2d 1373, 1379 (Del. 1989).

125. See People v. Schultheis, 638 P.2d 8, 11 (Colo. 1981) (en banc).

126. 909 F.2d 488 (11th Cir. 1990).

dant to testify. The defendant chose to continue the case pro se. The Eleventh Circuit reversed the defendant's conviction holding that the trial judge improperly had forced the defendant to choose between the constitutional rights to testify and to effective assistance of counsel. The court stated that the trial judge should have simply decided the issue of whether to grant counsel's motion to withdraw. The court also held that without more information, the trial court should have denied the motion to withdraw.[127] The court conceded, however, that "a much more difficult case would have resulted had it been established on the record that defendant intended to commit perjury."[128]

2. *Constitutional Requirements*

Comment 12 to Model Rule 3.3 states that the lawyer's ethical obligation to disclose perjury to the court is limited by constitutional requirements:

> However, the definition of the lawyer's ethical duty in such a situation may be qualified by constitutional provisions for due process and the right to counsel in criminal cases. . . . The obligation of the advocate under these Rules is subordinate to such a constitutional requirement.

In Nix v. Whiteside,[129] the Supreme Court considered the relationship between client perjury and the Sixth Amendment right to effective assistance of counsel. Defendant Whiteside was accused of stabbing Love to death while Love was in bed. Whiteside originally told his lawyer, Robinson, that he was acting in self defense because he thought that Love was pulling a gun from under his pillow. Whiteside admitted to Robinson, however, that he had not seen a gun, and the police had not found a gun on the premises. Robinson advised Whiteside it was not necessary to establish self defense that Love had actually had a gun, only that Whiteside had a reasonable belief that Love had a weapon.

About a week before trial Whiteside told Robinson that he had seen something "metallic" in Love's hand. When Robinson ques-

127. Id. at 493.
128. Id. at 493-494.
129. 475 U.S. 157 (1986).

tioned Whiteside about the change in his story, Whiteside said: "If I don't say I saw a gun, I'm dead." Robinson told Whiteside that this testimony would amount to perjury, that it was unnecessary for Whiteside to lie to establish self defense, that as a lawyer he would be involved in suborning perjury, that he would inform the court if Whiteside testified in this fashion, and that Robinson would probably be allowed to testify to impeach Whiteside's testimony. Robinson also indicated that he would attempt to withdraw if Whiteside persisted in this testimony.[130]

At trial Whiteside testified that he "knew" Love had a gun and that he believed Love was reaching for a gun under his pillow, but he admitted on cross-examination that he had not actually seen a gun. Robinson presented evidence to substantiate Whiteside's belief that Robinson had a weapon. Nonetheless, Whiteside was convicted of second degree murder. Both on direct appeal and in subsequent habeas corpus proceedings, he contended that Robinson's conduct had denied him effective assistance of counsel.[131]

The Supreme Court found that Robinson's conduct did not amount to ineffective assistance of counsel. The Court's majority opinion, authored by Chief Justice Burger, judged Robinson's actions under the test for ineffective assistance of counsel set forth in Strickland v. Washington.[132] In *Strickland*, the Court established a two-part test for determining when ineffective representation required reversal of a conviction. First, the defendant must show that counsel's performance fell below an objective standard of "reasonably effective assistance."[133] In making this judgment, a court should consider all facts and circumstances, including prevailing norms of the profession. The Court warned that judicial scrutiny should be "highly deferential" and should engage in a "strong presumption" that counsel's conduct was reasonable.[134] Second, "any deficiencies in counsel's performance must be prejudicial to the defense in order to constitute ineffective assistance under the Constitution."[135] In defining prejudice, the Court rejected a test that would have required the defendant to show that the attorney's ineffective assistance was "outcome determinative." Instead, the

130. Id. at 161.
131. Id. at 161-162.
132. 466 U.S. 668 (1984).
133. Id. at 687.
134. Id. at 689.
135. Id. at 692.

Court stated: "The defendant must show that there is a reasonable probability that, but for counsel's unprofessional errors, the result of the proceeding would have been different. A reasonable probability is a probability sufficient to undermine confidence in the outcome."[136]

After reviewing the standard for ineffective assistance of counsel established by *Strickland,* the Court analyzed whether Robinson's conduct violated that standard. The majority first concluded that Robinson's actions amounted to a reasonable professional response to Whiteside's indication that he planned to give false testimony. The opinion noted that the Court's role was not to constitutionalize particular standards of professional conduct.[137] After making this concession, however, the opinion proceeded to consider various professional norms and to cite with approval Model Rule 3.3, requiring disclosure to the court to rectify client perjury.[138] Based on this review, the Court found that Robinson had acted reasonably:

> Whether Robinson's conduct is seen as a successful attempt to dissuade his client from committing the crime of perjury, or whether seen as a "threat" to withdraw from representation and disclose the illegal scheme, Robinson's representation of Whiteside falls well within accepted standards of professional conduct and the range of reasonable professional conduct acceptable under *Strickland.*[139]

The Court also found that Whiteside had not suffered prejudice, the second prong of the *Strickland* test, because of Robinson's conduct.[140] It is noteworthy that Whiteside did testify and presented the substance of his self-defense argument to the jury.

While *Nix* found no constitutional violation on the facts of the case, it is possible to imagine cases in which a defendant could establish a constitutional violation. Suppose Robinson had acted based on his belief that his client was committing perjury rather than his client's admission, and suppose the substance of the client's claim of self defense had not been submitted to the jury. In

136. Id. at 694.
137. 475 U.S. at 165.
138. Id. at 168.
139. Id. at 171.
140. Id. at 175-176.

such a case, the defendant might be able to establish both prongs of the *Strickland* test for ineffective assistance of counsel.[141]

Nix was a Sixth Amendment case. The Supreme Court has yet to address the question of the relationship between the Fifth Amendment privilege against self incrimination and client perjury.[142] The leading Supreme Court case on the privilege against self incrimination is Fisher v. United States.[143] In *Fisher*, the Supreme Court held that information conveyed to an attorney by a client is subject to the privilege against self incrimination if two requirements are met. First, the conveyance of the information from the client to the attorney must be protected by the attorney-client evidentiary privilege. Second, the information sought from the attorney must be subject to the privilege against self incrimination if the government had attempted to obtain the information directly from the client. Information obtained directly from the client is subject to the privilege against self incrimination if the production of the information compels the client to give incriminating testimony.[144]

It seems unlikely that an attorney's disclosure to the court of a defendant's *contemplated* perjury would violate the defendant's privilege against self incrimination. Under *Fisher*, the privilege against self incrimination does not apply if the information conveyed to the lawyer does not qualify as a communication subject to the attorney-client privilege. Because the defendant would be conveying information about a proposed crime, the information is probably not privileged because of the crime/fraud exception to the attorney-client privilege.[145] In addition, since the defendant's perjury is contemplated rather than completed, the attorney's disclosure to the court would not incriminate the client. Indeed, it would prevent the client from committing a crime.

On the other hand, if the defendant informs the lawyer of com-

141. See State v. Jones, 923 P.2d 560 (Mont. 1996) (defendant's Sixth Amendment right violated when lawyer moved to withdraw on unsubstantiated belief that defendant intended to commit perjury).

142. See Monroe H. Freedman, Client Confidences and Client Perjury: Some Unanswered Questions, 136 U. Pa. L. Rev. 1939 (1988).

143. 425 U.S. 391 (1976).

144. Id. at 397, 404-405.

145. In an ethics advisory opinion, the National Association of Criminal Defense Lawyers ruled that an attorney who knows that a criminal defendant intends to commit perjury should not reveal the client's intention to the court

pleted perjury in confidence, then the future crime exception does not apply and the defendant faces the risk of a perjury prosecution if the lawyer reveals the perjury to the court. It seems, therefore, that a lawyer's disclosure of the defendant's completed perjury would violate the defendant's privilege against self incrimination.

If the case is being tried before a judge rather than a jury, defense counsel's disclosure that the defendant plans to commit perjury poses an additional constitutional problem. The defendant's right to due process of law may be infringed because the trier of fact has been prejudiced. In such cases, defense counsel must take special care to avoid informing the court of the defendant's perjury. Use of the narrative solution is one possibility available to defense counsel. If defense counsel decides to move to withdraw or to inform the court, defense counsel must avoid prejudicing the judge as trier of fact. This could be done in either of two ways. The motion could be made to a judge not trying the case. The chief administrative judge for the court would be the natural choice. In the alternative, the lawyer could make the motion to the judge who has been assigned the case, but ask that the judge certify the case to another judge for trial.[146]

---

because the revelation would violate the client's privilege against self incrimination, and the privilege took priority over any rule of ethics that required disclosure. Adv. Op. 92-2, The Champion 23 (March, 1993). The opinion discussed the application of the crime/fraud exception as follows:

> It is important to consider, therefore, whether a lawyer's knowledge of a client's intention to commit perjury is within the future crime exception to the lawyer-client privilege.
>
> In fact, perjury has been construed as falling outside of the future crime exception. One reason is that it is "intrinsically and inextricably" related to the crime for which the defendant is being tried. In this respect, it is like the future crime of concealing the proceeds of a theft—that is, to reveal the future crime (ongoing concealment) is to implicate the client in the past crime (theft). This is not true, of course, of the future crime of bribing a juror. To reveal the client's intent to commit the bribery does not require revealing any confidences regarding his guilt of the past crime that is being tried.

Id. at 26.

146. For cases on the due process problems facing defense counsel when client perjury occurs in bench trials, see Lowery v. Cardwell, 575 F.2d 727 (9th Cir. 1978); Arizona v. Jefferson, 615 P.2d 638 (Ariz. 1980) (en banc); Butler v. United States, 414 A.2d 844 (D.C. 1980) (en banc).

K. CANDOR TO THE TRIBUNAL: DISCLOSURE OF PERJURY BY WITNESSES

Suppose a client wishes to call a witness that the attorney reasonably believes will be testifying falsely. What should the lawyer do? While criminal defendants have the right to decide whether to testify in their own behalf, lawyers have the authority to decide which witnesses to call. See Model Rule 1.2(a). Similarly, ABA Defense Function Standard 4-5.2(b) provides as follows:

> Strategic and tactical decisions should be made by defense counsel after consultation with the client where feasible and appropriate. Such decisions include what witnesses to call, whether and how to conduct cross-examination, what jurors to accept or strike, what trial motions should be made, and whatever evidence should be introduced.

Further, Model Rule 3.3(c) states "a lawyer may refuse to offer evidence that the lawyer reasonably believes is false."[147] Thus, if a lawyer reasonably believes that a witness will testify falsely, the lawyer has the authority and duty simply to refuse to call the witness.[148] As stated in Model Rule 1.2(a) and Defense Function Standard 4-5.2(b), the lawyer should take this step only after consultation with the client. If a lawyer learns that a witness has already testified falsely, the lawyer would have a duty to take reasonable remedial measures, including disclosure of the false testimony to the tribunal if necessary. See Model Rule 3.3(a)(4).[149]

The lawyer's refusal to call a witness could prompt a confrontation between lawyer and client that could in turn lead to the client's demanding that the lawyer withdraw. The matter would then be brought to the attention of the court, which could take such action as it thought appropriate, including granting counsel's permission to withdraw, directing counsel to call the witness, or allowing counsel to proceed without calling the witness.

147. See Restatement of the Law Governing Lawyers §180(3) (Tent. Draft #8, March 21, 1997).

148. See People v. Flores, 538 N.E.2d 481 (Ill. 1989), *cert. denied*, 497 U.S. 1031 (1990) (lawyer has discretion not to call nonclient witness in criminal case).

149. See also Restatement of the Law Governing Lawyers §180(2) (Tent. Draft #8, March 21, 1997).

L. DISCLOSURE OF MISCONDUCT BY ANOTHER LAWYER

Lawyers have disclosure obligations not only to the tribunals before which they practice but also to bodies established to administer professional standards. Model Rule 8.3(a) provides that a lawyer having knowledge of misconduct by another lawyer "that raises a substantial question as to that lawyer's honesty, trustworthiness or fitness as a lawyer in other respects, shall inform the appropriate professional authority."[150] Section (b) imposes a similar obligation on lawyers to report misconduct by judges.

An attorney's duty to report misconduct under Rule 8.3 is subject to the attorney's duty of confidentiality to the client: "This rule does not require disclosure of information otherwise protected by Rule 1.6 . . . ." Rule 1.6 states: "A lawyer shall not reveal information relating to representation of a client unless the client consents after consultation . . . [subject to certain exceptions]."

In In re Himmel,[151] the Illinois Supreme Court held that the attorney-client privilege did not excuse an attorney from the duty to report misappropriation of funds by the client's former lawyer. *Himmel* was decided under DR 1-103 of the Code of Professional Responsibility, and the same result probably does not follow under the Model Rules. DR 1-103, like Model Rule 8.3, states that the duty to report misconduct is qualified by the attorney's duty of confidentiality to the client. The scope of the confidentiality rule under the Code, however, was somewhat narrower than under the Model Rules. The Code referred to information subject to the attorney-client privilege. In *Himmel,* the attorney-client privilege did not prevent Himmel from reporting the former lawyer's misconduct because Himmel had received the information in a communication from his client that was not protected by the evidentiary attorney-client privilege. When the client told Himmel of the former lawyer's misconduct, a third party was present;

150. See Wieder v. Skala, 609 N.E.2d 105 (N.Y. 1992) (associate states cause of action against law firm for wrongful discharge when associate was fired because he insisted that firm report misconduct by another lawyer in firm). On disclosure obligations to bar admissions officials, see Model Rule 8.1.

151. 533 N.E.2d 790 (Ill. 1988).

Himmel also obtained information about the lawyer's misappropriation from an insurance company.[152]

By contrast, Model Rule 1.6 does not limit the duty of confidentiality to information subject to the attorney-client privilege; the duty applies to any information "relating to representation of a client." Indeed, one court has rejected the application of *Himmel* under the Model Rules and has held that a lawyer does not have a duty to report misconduct by another attorney when the lawyer received the information in a confidential communication.[153]

The duty to report misconduct by another lawyer only applies if the lawyer has "knowledge" of misconduct. The terminology section of the Model Rules draws a distinction between "know" and "reasonably should know." The former requires actual knowledge while the latter is an objective standard based on what a reasonably prudent and competent lawyer would know. It should be noted, however, that since it is impossible to penetrate into a person's mind, actual knowledge can be inferred from the circumstances.[154] Relevant also is a well-established body of criminal law involving lawyers and other professionals holding that a person has knowledge of a fact if the person's conduct shows conscious avoidance or deliberate ignorance of facts.[155]

In Attorney U v. Mississippi Bar,[156] an attorney was accused of failing to report that another lawyer had entered into an improper fee splitting agreement. The Mississippi Supreme Court held that an objective rather than a subjective standard applies in determining whether an attorney has knowledge of misconduct by another lawyer:

> The supporting evidence must be such that a reasonable lawyer under the circumstances would have formed a firm opinion that the conduct in question had more likely than not occurred and that the conduct, if it did occur, raises a substantial question as to the pur-

152. Id. at 794.

153. See In re Ethics Advisory Panel Opinion No. 92-1, 627 A.2d 317 (R.I. 1993) (distinguishing *Himmel* and holding that the duty to report under Rule 8.3 is subordinate to the duty of confidentiality under Rule 1.6).

154. See generally 1 Hazard & Hodes, The Law of Lawyering §402.

155. See generally John P. Freeman & Nathan M. Crystal, Scienter in Professional Liability Cases, 42 S.C. L. Rev. 783, 833-838 (1991).

156. 678 So. 2d 963 (Miss. 1996).

> ported offender's honesty, trustworthiness or fitness to practice law in other respects.[157]

On the facts, however, the court held that the attorney did not have sufficient reliable information of misconduct to trigger the duty to report. A dissenting justice criticized the majority's decision, noting that the attorney had sufficient knowledge of the fee splitting agreement to use the existence of the agreement on behalf of his client in what the justice considered to be tantamount to blackmail.

157. Id. at 972.

CHAPTER 5

Zealousness and Its Limits[1]

A. INTRODUCTION: A THEORY OF LIMITATIONS ON ZEALOUS REPRESENTATION: SUBSTANTIVE AND REMEDIAL PRINCIPLES

1. *Substantive Principles*

Lawyers are legally and ethically required to represent their clients loyally and with zeal. Lawyers serve as agents on behalf of their clients.[2] Section 387 of the Restatement (Second) of Agency imposes a duty of loyalty on agents. Canon 7 of the Code of Professional Responsibility states: "A lawyer should represent a client zealously within the bounds of the law." Comment 1 to Model Rule 1.3 provides: "A lawyer should act with commitment and dedication to the interests of the client and with zeal in advocacy upon the client's behalf." While the principle that lawyers must represent

1. Substantial portions of this chapter first appeared as Limitations on Zealous Representation in an Adversarial System, 32 Wake Forest L. Rev. 671 (1997).

2. See Wolfram, Modern Legal Ethics 145 (characterizing lawyers as "fiduciary agents").

their clients loyally and zealously is well established, what should be the limitations on that duty?

To begin to formulate an answer to this question, consider both the *purpose* of the American[3] judicial system and the *process* by which it functions. The fundamental purpose of our judicial system is the fair resolution of disputes. This objective serves an essential need of any society: maintenance of social stability. By providing parties who are involved in a dispute with a mechanism for resolving the controversy that the parties are likely to accept because of its fairness, a system of dispute resolution minimizes the possibility that individuals will take the law into their own hands.

The American legal system uses an adversarial method of presentation as its process for fair resolution of disputes. In the ideal model of the adversarial system, impartial decisionmakers (judge, jury, or some combination thereof) render a decision in the matter based on evidence presented by competent advocates each zealously representing their clients' interests in accordance with established rules.[4] This description is not meant to imply that only one model of the adversarial system exists or that the adversarial system has remained constant. In the United States, the adversarial system has undergone tremendous change. During the nineteenth century, David Dudley Field championed procedural reform. His efforts led to adoption in New York of the Field Code, which replaced the stylized writ system of pleading with fact pleading.[5] Many other states used the Field Code as a model to reform their procedural systems. Similarly, during the twentieth century, adoption of the Federal Rules of Civil Procedure dramatically modified

3. The discussion in this chapter is limited to the American judicial system. Methods of dispute resolution reflect deeply held cultural values of a society. While consideration of other systems can provide insight into the practices of one's own society and can also offer new ways of handling disputes that a society may not have previously employed, it is foolish to attempt to consider methods of dispute resolution outside of their cultural context.

4. See Charles W. Sorenson, Jr., Disclosure under Federal Rule of Civil Procedure 26(a) — "Much Ado About Nothing?," 46 Hastings L.J. 679, 762-766 (1995); Ellen E. Sward, Values, Ideology, and the Evolution of the Adversary System, 64 Ind. L.J. 301, 312-313 (1989). For a critique of the adversary system, see Carrie Menkel-Meadow, The Trouble with the Adversary System in a Postmodern, Multicultural World, 38 Wm. & Mary L. Rev. 5 (1996).

5. See generally Robert G. Bone, Mapping the Boundaries of a Dispute: Conceptions of Ideal Lawsuit Structure from the Field Code to the Federal Rules, 89 Colum. L. Rev. 1 (1989); Janice Toran, Essay, 'Tis a Gift to Be Simple: Aesthetics and Procedural Reform, 89 Mich. L. Rev. 352 (1990).

the adversarial system by providing much broader discovery of information prior to trial than had existed previously. As a result of these more liberal discovery provisions, the Supreme Court had to face the tension between access to information, which is central to the discovery process, and party control of information, which is fundamental to an adversarial presentation. In Hickman v. Taylor,[6] the Supreme Court resolved this tension by creating the work product doctrine. The doctrine balances the principles of access and control by limiting access to information that is prepared by the lawyer or the lawyer's client in anticipation of litigation unless the party seeking the information establishes good cause for its disclosure.[7] Despite such revolutionary changes in procedure during American legal history, however, certain aspects of our dispute resolution process have remained unchanged, including the requirement of impartial decisionmakers, adversarial presentation by lawyers, and rules of procedure and evidence to order the presentations.

Lawyers acting as representatives of clients who are engaged in a dispute are important components of our system of dispute resolution. To the extent that lawyers act consistently with the underlying purpose and process of the system, the rules of the system should encourage their conduct. By contrast, when lawyers undermine the purpose or process of the system, their conduct should be deterred.

When does a lawyer's conduct undermine either the purpose or process of the adversarial system of dispute resolution? Since the purpose of the judicial system is resolution of disputes, lawyers violate that purpose if they present claims that do not involve bona fide disputes. Call this the *bona fide dispute principle*. The adversarial system consists of dispute resolution by impartial decisionmakers. When lawyers interfere with the impartiality of decisionmakers, they undermine the adversarial process. This concept is referred to in this chapter as the *impartial decisionmaker principle*. Any system of dispute resolution must be structured by rules. When lawyers violate established rules of procedure, they undermine the functioning of the system. The concept of rule compliance requires

6. 329 U.S. 495 (1947).

7. See Fed. R. Civ. Proc. 26(b)(3). On the work product doctrine, see generally Restatement of the Law Governing Lawyers §§136-142 (Prop. Final Draft #1, March 29, 1996). See also Chapter 4.A supra.

further analysis, however, because adherence to rules alone does not provide a standard for formulation of the rules. The last section of this chapter argues that rules for adversarial presentations should be designed to be truth maximizing, i.e., a rule should exist if the presence of the rule makes it more likely that a dispute will be resolved truthfully than would be the case if the rule did not exist, subject to the qualification that any such rule must not violate fundamental rights, particularly constitutional provisions that embody individual rights. This concept is called the *principle of qualified truth-maximizing rules.*

2. *Remedial Principles*

A system of rules that imposes limitations on lawyers' zealous representation must face the question of what remedies are appropriate for violation of those restrictions. A number of mechanisms are available for enforcement of limitations on zealous representation: criminal prosecution, disciplinary enforcement, civil liability, and curative court order.[8]

Lawyers are subject to prosecution for conduct that exceeds the proper bounds of zealous representation and violates the criminal law, such as counseling clients to destroy evidence[9] or jury tampering.[10] Lawyers may also be punished by criminal contempt for extreme overzealousness.[11] Disciplinary proceedings, which are quasi-criminal in nature,[12] can be instituted against lawyers

8. These four mechanisms for enforcement are ordered generally from the most serious (criminal prosecution) to the least damaging to the lawyer (curative order), although there are exceptions. For example, in some instances professional discipline may be less damaging than a civil sanction. If a lawyer is disqualified in a major case and loses a substantial fee, the lawyer may find that to be a more serious penalty than a minor reprimand in a disciplinary case.

9. See United States v. Perlstein, 126 F.2d 789 (3rd Cir.), *cert. denied,* 316 U.S. 678 (1942) (lawyers convicted of conspiracy to obstruct justice when they advised clients to destroy documents if proceeding was initiated).

10. See 18 U.S.C. A. §1503 (Supp. 1997) (crime to attempt to influence juror in corrupt or threatening manner).

11. See Pounders v. Watson, 117 S. Ct. 2359 (1997) (upholding power of summary contempt without need to show pattern of repeated violations by counsel). Compare Restatement of the Law Governing Lawyers §165, comm. *e* (Tent. Draft #8, March 21, 1997) ("Advocacy ordinarily should not be punished as criminal contempt unless the lawyer's conduct constitutes an obstruction of justice.").

12. In re Ruffalo, 390 U.S. 544 (1968).

when their overzealousness results in violation of professional rules.[13]

Courts can impose a variety of civil sanctions on lawyers when their conduct exceeds the bounds of proper zealousness. One possible remedy is a civil action against a lawyer for violation of a duty to the person harmed by the lawyer's conduct. For example, lawyers can be held civilly liable for malicious prosecution or abuse of process.[14] Some jurisdictions recognize a cause of action for negligent destruction or spoilation of evidence.[15] Lawyers can also be subject to civil sanction for violation of the rules of civil procedure. The most common basis for sanctions against lawyers is Rule 11 of the Federal Rules of Civil Procedure.[16] Issuance of a curative court order is another remedy available for excessive zealousness. The nature of the order will, of course, vary depending on the circumstances, but may include disqualification of the lawyer, exclusion of evidence, instruction to the jury, or granting a new trial.[17]

Each of these sanctions has advantages and limitations. Discipline of a lawyer for misconduct can protect the public and the administration of justice from future misconduct by that lawyer, either by removing the lawyer from the practice of law or by at least giving the lawyer a substantial incentive not to engage in the misconduct in the future.[18] On the other hand, professional discipline has no effect on the particular proceeding in which the

13. See, e.g., Iowa Supreme Court Bd. of Professional Ethics & Conduct v. Hohnbaum, 554 N.W.2d 550 (Iowa 1996) (lawyer disciplined for making defendant unavailable at trial when defendant had informed lawyer of erroneous police report showing plaintiff's car striking defendant's vehicle); In re Barrow, 294 S.E.2d 785 (S.C. 1982) (public reprimand for removing warning label in products liability action).

14. See Chapter 5.B.4.

15. See, e.g., Velasco v. Commercial Bldg. Maintenance Co., 215 Cal. Rptr. 504 (Cal. Ct. App. 1985); Bondu v. Gurvich, 473 So. 2d 1307 (Fla. Ct. App. 1984); Federated Mut. Ins. Co. v. Litchfield Precision Components, Inc., 456 N.W.2d 434 (Minn. 1990).

16. See Chapter 5.B.3 for discussion of the standard of conduct required by Rule 11.

17. See Berger v. United States, 295 U.S. 78 (1935) (new trial granted because of improper witness examination and argument by prosecutor); Ferraro v. Koncal Assoc., 467 N.Y.S.2d 284 (App. Div. 1983) (party barred from offering evidence in support of defense due to destruction of evidence relevant to defense that had been requested during discovery).

18. See ABA Standards for Imposing Lawyer Sanctions §1.1, *reprinted in* Lawyers' Manual on Prof. Conduct (ABA/BNA) 1:807.

offense occurred. Discipline does not compensate the victim for any damage done by the lawyer and does not remedy any possible harm to the integrity of the proceedings. Similarly, civil sanctions have both advantages and disadvantages. A civil sanction can compensate the victim for harm and can deter the lawyer from engaging in similar misconduct in the future, but the threat of civil sanctions can produce excessive deterrence, making some lawyers too cautious about taking controversial cases or asserting new positions. Curative court orders can be tailored to respond to the harm done by the specific misconduct, but such orders may not produce sufficient deterrence, leading some lawyers to believe that the worst they face is loss of any benefit from their misconduct.

Since each of these remedies serves a different purpose, the same misconduct can be subject to more than one remedy. In choosing a remedy, two questions should be paramount. First, does use of this remedy serve the underlying purpose of the remedy? Second, recognizing that any remedy will have incentive effects on the participants to the proceeding, does the remedy on balance improve the incentives to preserve the purpose and process of the system? For example, in recent years it has become common for courts to order disqualification of lawyers because of a conflict of interest. Disqualification is appropriate when the lawyer's continued representation involves a threat to the integrity of the proceeding in which the disqualification is being sought, but disqualification is a poor remedy when no such threat is present.[19]

B. THE BONA FIDE DISPUTE PRINCIPLE

1. *Rationale for Prohibiting Frivolous Litigation*

The duty of lawyers not to engage in frivolous legal proceedings is an important limitation on zealous representation. ABA Model Rule 3.1 makes it unethical for lawyers to raise frivolous claims or defenses. The Federal Rules of Civil Procedure, particularly Rule

19. See Nathan M. Crystal, Disqualification of Counsel for Unrelated Matter Conflicts of Interest, 4 Geo. J. Legal Ethics 273 (1990).

11, also regulate frivolous conduct.[20] While Rule 11 only applies to actions in federal court, many states have rules of civil procedure modeled on federal Rule 11,[21] and state courts have usually relied on federal court decisions in interpreting their rules.[22] These rules apply not only to frivolous complaints, but also to answers, motions, and other documents filed in a legal proceeding. (The term *frivolous legal contentions* is used in this chapter to refer generally to any type of frivolous claim.)

Why should it be improper for a lawyer to present a frivolous legal contention to a tribunal? Suppose for the time being that we define a frivolous legal contention as one that has no chance of success. If a lawyer fully advises the client that a claim has no merit, but the client nonetheless decides to proceed, why should the

20. For comprehensive treatments of the rule, see Gregory P. Joseph, Sanctions: The Federal Law of Litigation Abuse (2d ed. 1994); Georgene M. Vairo, Rule 11 Sanctions: Case Law Perspectives & Preventive Measures (2d ed. 1992). Professor Vairo's treatise contains an extensive bibliography on the rule. See also A. Mitchell Polinsky & Daniel L. Rubinfeld, Sanctioning Frivolous Suits: An Economic Analysis, 82 Geo. L.J. 397 (1993).

Although Rule 11 is the best known provision regulating improper litigation tactics, in fact it is only one of an arsenal of weapons that federal courts (or state courts whose procedural systems are based on the federal rules) can use to punish litigation abuse, either through the award of attorney fees or other sanctions. See Fed R. Civ. P. 16(f)(failure to abide by pretrial order); 26(g)(improper discovery requests or objections); 30(g)(failure to attend a deposition or serve a subpoena on a party to be deposed); 37 (improper failure to respond to discovery); 41(b)(dismissal of action or claim when a party fails to comply with the federal rules or order of court); 45(e)(failure to obey subpoena); 56(g)(presentation of affidavit in summary judgment motion in bad faith or for the purpose of delay). See also Federal Rule of Appellate Procedure 38 (power to award damages and costs for a frivolous appeal). In addition, a federal statute, 28 U.S.C. §1927 (1994), provides as follows:

> Any attorney or other person admitted to conduct cases in any court of the United States or any Territory thereof who so multiplies the proceedings in any case unreasonably and vexatiously may be required by the court to satisfy personally the excess costs, expenses, and attorneys' fees reasonably incurred because of such conduct.

In Chambers v. Nasco, 501 U.S. 32 (1991), the Supreme Court in a 5-4 decision ruled that federal courts have inherent power to impose sanctions for bad faith conduct even when the conduct is not specifically covered by rules of procedure or statutory provisions, including fraud that occurs outside court.

21. See Restatement of the Law Governing Lawyers §170, Reporter's Note to comm. *c*, at 357-359 (Tent. Draft #8, March 21, 1997).

22. E.g., Gray v. Washington, 612 A.2d 839 (D.C. 1992); Bryson v. Sullivan, 412 S.E.2d 327 (N.C. 1992); Bryant v. Joseph Tree, Inc., 829 P.2d 1099 (Wash. 1992) (en banc).

lawyer be subject to sanctions? While the presentation of such a position might be a waste of the client's money, our society generally allows people to use their assets as they see fit, whether wisely or foolishly. Further, the client will at least have had his "day in court," which may have emotional or political benefit to the client even when the client's chance of success is nonexistent—consider, for example, a tax protester who wishes to use litigation as a political forum for expression of opposition to the government.

The "right to use assets argument" cannot justify lawyers' representation of clients in presenting frivolous legal contentions because legal proceedings are very different from purely private conduct. When people waste their resources on foolish endeavors, other people are generally not deprived of any legally protected right. By contrast, if a person brings a frivolous legal proceeding, societal resources (court personnel and facilities, judicial time, jury time) must be devoted to the proceeding. Further, a legal proceeding imposes costs on the other party, including time, legal fees, and in some cases unwanted publicity. An analogy to nuisance law is appropriate. If a person misuses his property to create public or private harm, the person is subject to liability. Similarly, if a person misuses the judicial system for purposes other than dispute resolution, he should be subject to sanctions.

Similarly, the "day in court" argument does not justify frivolous claims. Take the case of the tax protester who wishes to exercise a First Amendment right to protest against the government. The protester has that right, but the exercise of First Amendment rights is subject to reasonable time, place, and manner restrictions.[23] Prohibiting use of the court system to present frivolous claims, while allowing the tax protester other outlets for expression of grievances, is a reasonable time, place, and manner restriction on speech.

This analysis shows that the legal system may justifiably seek to control frivolous legal contentions. As noted above, both professional rules and the rules of civil procedure impose sanctions on lawyers who participate in the presentation of frivolous legal contentions on behalf of their clients. Why shouldn't the sanction be limited to the client, who is the principal in the relationship, rather than being imposed on the lawyer, who is a mere agent of the client? Several answers can be given. First, lawyers are officers of

23. See, e.g., Ward v. Rock Against Racism, 491 U.S. 781, 791 (1989).

the court who have duties not only to their clients but also to the legal system. Imposing sanctions on lawyers for participation in frivolous legal contentions reflects the principle that lawyers have obligations beyond their clients. Second, normally the lawyer is an active participant in the client's decisionmaking process. Imposing sanctions on both the lawyer and the client recognizes their joint responsibility. Indeed, with regard to certain tactical matters, the lawyer rather than the client has the authority to make the decision, so the lawyer rather than the client properly bears responsibility. Third, in some cases clients may not have sufficient assets to satisfy any award of sanctions, so sanctions directed only against the client will not be sufficient to deter frivolous legal contentions.

2. *The Meaning of Frivolousness*

Assuming that in principle it is appropriate to impose sanctions on parties or their attorneys who participate in presenting frivolous legal contentions, when should a legal contention be treated as "frivolous"? Defining the concept of a frivolous legal contention requires answers to two questions. First, will an objective or subjective standard be used? Second, what measurement of the probability of success of the contention is required for the contention not to be frivolous? The following chart summarizes several possible choices for defining frivolousness:

Standard (Subjective or Objective)	*Measurement of Probability of Success*
Good faith or reasonable	Any (greater than 0)
Good faith or reasonable	More than de minimis (greater than 5 percent)
Good faith or reasonable	Substantial (greater than 25 percent)
Good faith or reasonable	Probable (greater than 50 percent)

For example, one possible definition is that a lawyer makes a frivolous legal contention if the contention does not reasonably have a substantial chance of success, with substantial being defined as a probability of at least a 25 percent chance of success. While probability of success for a contention cannot be determined with mathematical precision, lawyers commonly make such probabilistic estimates of chances of success in evaluating their clients' legal positions.

Choice of the definition of a frivolous legal contention requires a balance between two competing values. On the one hand, the purpose behind having sanctions for frivolous contentions is to deter misuse of the judicial process. Thus, the "any chance of success" measurement should be rejected because it is too weak to deter misuse of the judicial process. Under this yardstick, almost no claim or defense would be frivolous. Some judges have, however, indicated that this is indeed the criteria to be used. For example, Judge Frank Easterbrook of the Seventh Circuit Court of Appeals has offered the following definition of frivolousness:

> [S]omething is frivolous only when (a) we've decided the very point, and recently, against the person reasserting it, or (b) 99 of 100 practicing lawyers would be 99 percent sure that the position is untenable, and the other 1 percent would be 60 percent sure it's untenable.[24]

On the other hand, if the criteria for measuring a frivolous contention is too broad, the standard may overdeter. Some clients and lawyers may be discouraged because of fear of sanctions from using the judicial system even if they have legitimate disputes. Thus, it seems appropriate to reject the criteria that the success of the claim must be "probable." Indeed, this measurement is essentially identical to the burden of proof in civil cases. The criteria for presenting a contention should obviously be less than the ultimate burden of proof for that contention.

Based on this analysis, it appears that the appropriate measurement for defining the chance or probability of success of a frivolous claim is either a de minimis chance of success or less than a substantial chance of success. In theory, the choice between these two measurements could be made by determining which one of them maximizes the differential between desirable deterrence (deterring lawyers from presenting frivolous contentions) and undesirable deterrence (deterring lawyers from presenting nonfrivolous contentions for fear of sanction), but we have no empirical studies on this issue. Historically, however, our society has strongly favored openness, particularly openness of the political and legal

24. Sanford Levinson, Frivolous Cases: Do Lawyers Really Know Anything at All?, 24 Osgoode Hall L.J. 353, 375 (1987) (quoting letter from Judge Easterbrook to Professor Levinson dated Jan. 29, 1986).

process. Based on this societal value, it seems appropriate to err on the side of a narrower criteria for determining frivolousness—the de minimis chance of success measure—at least until an empirical case is established that a broader standard is warranted.

When does a claim or defense have a de minimis chance of success? By way of analogy, IRS regulations regarding tax return positions asserted by tax practitioners draw a distinction between claims that have a "realistic possibility" of success and frivolous claims. A claim has a realistic possibility of success if it has at least a 1 in 3 likelihood of being sustained on the merits.[25] Thus, it seems that a claim having a de minimis possibility of success would be significantly less than 1 in 3. A 1 in 20 chance of success seems to be a reasonable level to set for a de minimis chance of success of a contention. This measurement of the probability of success seems to appropriately balance deterrence of misuse of the legal process with concern about over deterrence.

Should the definition of frivolousness use a subjective or an objective standard? The good faith standard is a plausible standard for frivolousness. Since the purpose of the judicial system is resolution of disputes, why shouldn't clients and lawyers be allowed to present claims and defenses that they honestly hold? On the other hand, a good faith standard is a very weak standard of frivolousness. Further, when people engage in activities that affect others, the law generally favors objective over subjective standards. For example, a person who drives an automobile on the public highways must comply with an objective rather than a subjective standard of due care. Moreover, the de minimis probability of success necessary to establish frivolousness is a fairly weak standard. It seems reasonable to balance this limited standard for measuring frivolousness by using an objective rather than a subjective standard. This analysis leads to the conclusion that the appropriate definition of a frivolous legal contention is one that objectively has less than a de minimis chance of success, with de minimis being defined as 5 percent.

A fundamental problem in constructing a definition of frivolous legal contentions involves change in the law. We recognize that the law does and must change to take into account evolving social circumstances and values. Thus, a definition of frivolous contentions must allow for the possibility of presenting contentions that

25. 31 C.F.R. ¶10.34(a)(4)(i) (1997).

are inconsistent with existing legal doctrine. On the other hand, too broad an exception for presenting contentions that seek to change existing law threatens to undermine the entire concept of frivolousness.[26] The objective de minimis definition of frivolousness reached above should meet this problem. Under this definition, an argument by a lawyer for change in the law is not frivolous if the argument objectively has more than a de minimis chance of success. For example, if the highest court of a jurisdiction adopted a particular legal doctrine many years ago, but courts in other jurisdictions have recently rejected or modified the doctrine, reasonable lawyers would almost certainly conclude that they have more than a de minimis chance of convincing the courts in the jurisdiction to change the law. By contrast, if the highest court in the jurisdiction had recently rejected a particular legal theory, it would probably be frivolous for a lawyer to bring a suit based on that rejected theory.[27]

The definition of frivolousness discussed so far has focused on the merits of legal contentions. In some cases, clients or lawyers may have an incentive to assert a meritorious contention for reasons other than dispute resolution. As noted above, legal proceedings impose costs on the other party. A person may wish to make a contention simply to inflict these costs on the opposing party because of animosity or other motivation. Further, some claimants may engage in strategic behavior, concluding that the other party may be willing to pay them something to avoid the cost of defending against a contention regardless of the merits of that contention. (The term *strike suit* is often used to refer to nonmeritorious claims brought for the purpose of extracting a payment to avoid the cost of defending the claim.)

Should the law ever impose sanctions on parties or their lawyers who assert meritorious contentions but for an improper purpose? Good arguments can be made both in favor of and against imposing such sanctions. On the one hand, it seems sound as a matter of principle to impose sanctions when a contention is asserted for a purpose other than resolution of a bona fide dispute. Such claims involve an attempt by parties to use the judicial system for their

26. Rob Atkinson, A Dissenter's Commentary on the Professionalism Crusade, 74 Tex. L. Rev. 259, 287-288 (1995).

27. Restatement of the Law Governing Lawyers §170, illus. 1 and 2 (Tent. Draft #8, March 21, 1997).

own ends rather than for the purpose for which it was intended. On the other hand, imposing sanctions on meritorious contentions that are brought for an improper purpose will discourage the assertion of some claims that have social benefits because by definition such contentions have legal merit.[28] In addition, even if in principle it makes sense to discourage contentions brought for an improper purpose, the costs of administering such a rule may well outweigh the benefits of the rule. Determination of a party's intentions is difficult and likely to be costly. Several questions must be answered in administering the rule. What constitutes an improper purpose? Is the claimant's purpose improper if the claimant has mixed motives, some of which are proper and some of which are not? On balance, therefore, it would probably be sounder as a matter of policy to focus only on the substantive merit of a legal contention rather than on the motivation for the contention.

3. *Analysis of Current Rules Regulating Frivolousness*

How do professional rules and legal standards regarding frivolous contentions compare with the analysis outlined above? Model Rule 3.1 provides as follows:

> A lawyer shall not bring or defend a proceeding, or assert or controvert an issue therein, unless there is a basis for doing so that is not frivolous, which includes a good faith argument for an extension, modification, or reversal of existing law. A lawyer for the defendant in a criminal proceeding, or the respondent in a proceeding that could result in incarceration, may nevertheless so defend the proceeding as to require that every element of the case be established.

Several points about the Model Rule are worth noting. First, the concept of frivolousness applies not only to complaints but also to answers, motions, and other steps in a legal proceeding. Thus, both counsel for plaintiffs and defendants are subject to the obligation

28. See Sussman v. Bank of Israel, 56 F.3d 450 (2d Cir.) *cert. denied,* 116 S. Ct. 305 (1995) (district court erred in awarding sanctions for improper purpose in filing complaint — threatening negative publicity to force settlement of related litigation — when complaint had legal merit).

not to engage in frivolous representation. Second, the rule contains an exception for defense of criminal proceedings. Presumably this exception reflects the criminal defendant's constitutional right to a presumption of innocence. Third, the rule does not contain a definition of frivolous, although the comments to the rule do provide some additional guidance. Comment 2 states that an action is not frivolous simply because the facts have not been fully developed or because the lawyer expects to develop facts in support of the contention during discovery. Further, an action is not frivolous "even though the lawyer believes that the client's position ultimately will not prevail." Fourth, a claim is not frivolous even if the claim is not warranted under existing law if the lawyer can make a "good faith argument for extension, modification or reversal of existing law." Finally, a claim may be frivolous if it is brought for an improper purpose, even if the claim has legal and factual merit. Comment 2 to Model Rule 3.1 states: "The action is frivolous, however, if the client desires to have the action taken primarily for the purpose of harassing or maliciously injuring a person . . . ."

The major difficulty with Rule 3.1 is that it fails to provide a clear definition of frivolousness. While the rule alludes to the concept of good faith, the Model Code comparison that accompanies the rule states: "[T]he test in Rule 3.1 is an objective test . . . ." The previous analysis suggests that the appropriate definition is whether a reasonable lawyer would conclude that the contention has more than a de minimis (5 percent) chance of success.

Unlike Model Rule 3.1, Rule 11 of the Federal Rules of Civil Procedure lists four specific obligations that lawyers have when they present pleadings, motions, or other papers in court:

- First, "after an inquiry reasonable under the circumstances," the lawyer believes that the document "is not being presented for any improper purpose, such as to harass or to cause unnecessary delay or needless increase in the cost of litigation."
- Second, "after an inquiry reasonable under the circumstances," the lawyer believes that the legal contentions "are warranted by existing law or by a nonfrivolous argument for the extension, modification, or reversal of existing law or the establishment of new law."
- Third, "after an inquiry reasonable under the circumstances," the lawyer believes "the allegations and other factual contentions have evidentiary support or, if specifically so identified,

are likely to have evidentiary support after a reasonable opportunity for further investigation or discovery."
- Fourth, "after an inquiry reasonable under the circumstances," the lawyer believes "the denials of factual contentions are warranted on the evidence or, if specifically so identified, are reasonably based on a lack of information or belief."

A lawyer's obligations under Rule 11 are governed by an objective rather than a subjective standard, but in determining compliance courts generally look to determine whether the pleading or paper is frivolous as a whole rather than whether any particular claim or argument is frivolous.[29] The Advisory Committee notes to the 1993 amendments to Rule 11 state that the purpose of the amendment was to eliminate the "empty-head pure-heart" justification for a frivolous argument. While Rule 11 improves on the Model Rule by clearly specifying an objective standard, it still falls short of providing an adequate definition of frivolousness because it fails to include any yardstick for measuring the probability of success of the contention.

Section 170 of the Restatement of the Law Governing Lawyers contains a definition of frivolous claims almost identical to Rule 3.1 of the Model Rules. Comment *d* to §170, however, provides a little more guidance: "A frivolous position is one that a lawyer of ordinary competence would recognize as so lacking in merit that there is no substantial possibility that the tribunal would accept it." This standard is very close to the standard of "objectively greater than a de minimis chance of success" argued for in this chapter, although the standard suggested in this chapter is more precise since it sets a 5 percent chance of success as the level for distinguishing frivolous from nonfrivolous claims.

4. *Sanctions and Tort Liability for Frivolous Contentions*

What form of sanction should be imposed on a party or lawyer who asserts a frivolous contention or one for an improper pur-

29. See, e.g., Golden Eagle Distrib. Corp. v. Burroughs Corp., 801 F.2d 1531 (9th Cir. 1986).

pose? The disciplinary process is designed to protect the public from lawyers who engage in conduct that falls below professional standards. If a lawyer engages in isolated instances of making frivolous claims or defenses, it does not appear that public protection warrants imposing disciplinary sanctions on the lawyer. A lawyer, however, who engages in a pattern or practice of presenting frivolous claims or defenses, or who commits a particularly egregious violation, should be subject to disciplinary action.

Improper use of the judicial process imposes costs both on the legal system and on the opposing party. Thus, a compensatory sanction seems appropriate for presenting frivolous claims. In principle, sanctions should be imposed in two amounts: one part to the court equal to the administrative cost of the frivolous legal contention and the other share to the opposing party equal to the costs incurred in responding to the frivolous legal contention. This measure of sanctions would not only compensate for injury done both to the judicial system and to the opposing party, but it should also create an appropriate level of deterrence against misuse of the legal process, without overdeterring use of the system for bringing legitimate claims. Determination of the actual administrative cost of a frivolous contention could be made in a variety of ways. One possibility would be to establish an hourly rate for judicial time that takes into account not only the judge's time but the other administrative costs associated with the judicial process. The cost of a frivolous claim would then be the judge's hourly rate multiplied by the amount of time that the judge devoted to the frivolous aspects of the case. The cost incurred by the opposing party will largely consist of attorney fees, but could involve other provable damages as well.

Should lawyers and their clients be subject to tort liability for bringing frivolous claims? A person is liable for the tort of malicious prosecution if the person brings a civil proceeding or initiates a criminal proceeding without probable cause, primarily for a purpose other than adjudication of the person's rights, and if the proceedings have been terminated in favor of the person against whom the proceedings were brought.[30] Note that the tort of malicious prosecution requires both frivolousness (lack of probable

30. Restatement (Second) of Torts §674 (1976). The tort in §674 is actually entitled "wrongful use of civil proceedings." The Restatement restricts the tort of "malicious prosecution" to improper initiation of criminal proceedings. Id. at 653. Many courts, however, refer to wrongful use of either the criminal or the civil

cause) and an improper purpose. Further, an element of the tort is termination of the proceeding in favor of the plaintiff.

Related to malicious prosecution is the tort of abuse of process. Section 682 of the Restatement (Second) of Torts defines abuse of process as use of criminal or civil process "primarily to accomplish a purpose for which it is not designed." Comparison of the elements of the two torts indicates that it should be easier to establish a claim for abuse of process than a claim for malicious prosecution. Both malicious prosecution and abuse of process call for an improper purpose. Malicious prosecution, however, requires termination of the proceeding in favor of the plaintiff, while abuse of process does not. In addition, malicious prosecution requires that the proceeding be brought without probable cause. Abuse of process does not have this requirement; the tort occurs when process is used for a purpose other than that for which it was intended.

With increasing frequency, disgruntled defendants have brought claims for malicious prosecution and abuse of process against attorneys for opposing parties.[31] Such claims involve a tension between two important public policies. On the one hand, the public has an interest in open access to courts. If courts hold attorneys liable for actions that they bring on behalf of clients, a "chilling effect" on the use of the judicial process may result. On the other hand, the judicial process should be used to resolve bona fide disputes rather than as a weapon to coerce defendants into paying money or for other improper purposes. Not surprisingly the courts have struck a balance between these two policies, recognizing the possibility of attorney liability for malicious prosecution or abuse of process, but indicating that liability will be imposed only in extreme cases.

The courts would do well to limit the torts of abuse of process and malicious prosecution to cases in which the person who instituted the proceedings is not subject to sanctions. Normally this will occur in criminal cases in which the complaining person is not a party. In cases in which the person who instituted the proceedings is a party, the injured party can seek compensation for the im-

---

process as malicious prosecution, and that terminology is adopted here. See 1 Mallen & Smith, Legal Malpractice §6.10, at 418.

31. On attorney liability for malicious prosecution and abuse of process, see Debra E. Wax, Annotation, Liability of Attorney, Acting for Client, for Malicious Prosecution, 46 A.L.R.4th 249 (1986); Debra T. Landis, Annotation, Civil Liability of Attorney for Abuse of Process, 97 A.L.R.3d 688 (1980). See also 1 Mallen & Smith, Legal Malpractice at 410-474.

proper proceeding by a motion for sanctions. Sanctions motions have efficiency advantages over tort claims because motions avoid duplicative legal proceedings. Moreover, the recognition of tort claims in addition to sanctions imposes the risk of overdeterring legitimate claims. An example of this approach is Detenbeck v. Koester,[32] where the Texas Court of Appeals held that the plaintiff doctor failed to state an abuse of process cause of action against the defendant and his attorneys for bringing a medical malpractice action against the plaintiff. The court ruled that bringing suit was not using process other than the purpose for which it was intended. The court also stated that if the suit were groundless the defendant could seek appropriate sanctions.[33] By contrast, the California Supreme Court's decision in Crowley v. Katleman[34] seems wrong. In *Crowley*, the court held that the plaintiff, an attorney, stated a cause of action for malicious prosecution against the defendant and her attorneys for challenging a will that left the defendant's husband's estate to the plaintiff attorney. The plaintiff and the decedent had been good friends; the plaintiff had not drafted the will; the decedent executed the will before he married the defendant; and the decedent did not revoke or revise the will during their marriage. The defendant wife had challenged the will on multiple grounds, including fraud, undue influence, and lack of mental capacity. The California Supreme Court found that a malicious prosecution claim could still be brought even though not all of the grounds were without probable cause. In addition, the court rejected the defendants' arguments that the appropriate remedy for frivolous claims was through court-imposed sanctions rather than by a tort action.

C. THE IMPARTIAL DECISIONMAKER PRINCIPLE

1. *The Meaning of Impartiality*

Our ideal of the adversarial system of justice envisions impartial decisionmakers. Indeed, the Sixth Amendment states that: "[i]n all

32. 886 S.W.2d 477 (Tex. Ct. App. 1994, no writ).
33. Id. at 482.
34. 881 P.2d 1083 (Cal. 1994) (en banc).

criminal prosecutions, the accused shall enjoy the right to a speedy and public trial, by an impartial jury." What does it mean for a decisionmaker to be impartial? The Supreme Court has said: "Impartiality is not a technical conception. It is a state of mind . . . of *appropriate indifference*."[35] Consider three ways in which a decisionmaker might not be impartial. (This chapter often refers to jurors rather than using the more general term decisionmaker, but the same analysis generally applies to judges.) First, a juror might have what could be called "factual bias," an inclination to favor one side based on knowledge of the particular facts involved in the dispute. Factual bias could result from personal knowledge or it could flow from exposure to media coverage of a case. Note that factual knowledge of a case is not the same as factual bias. A juror might have knowledge about a case, but might still have the ability to put that knowledge aside and decide the case impartially.

Second, a juror might have what could be called "relational bias," an inclination to favor one side in the case based on some specific relationship with the matter (e.g., stock ownership the value of which could be affected by the outcome of the matter), with one of the parties (e.g., relative of a party), or with one of the attorneys (e.g., prior representation of a juror by an attorney of record). As was true with factual knowledge, it is possible for a juror to have a relationship to the case without having relational bias. For example, a juror might have been represented by one of the lawyers in the case, but might also believe and be willing to state under oath that this relationship would not affect her ability to decide the case fairly.

Finally, the term "group bias" refers to attitudes that are more likely to be present in a member of a group than in the population as a whole and that tend to favor a party to a proceeding. For example, African Americans are more likely than the population as a whole to believe that racial discrimination is a major problem in our society. African American jurors may thus tend to favor African American defendants in cases in which discrimination may be a factor in the case.[36] Because Republicans generally are more likely to exhibit probusiness attitudes than the population as a whole, jurors with Republican affiliations may be more sympathetic to the claims of business interests. Perceptions of group

35. United States v. Wood, 299 U.S. 123, 145-146 (1936).

36. See Paul Shepard, Poll Finds Whites More Positive Than Blacks on Race Relations, Associated Press, June 10, 1997, 1997 WL 4870084.

bias, however, may be inaccurate. Individual members of a group may not hold a bias that some members of the group have (stereotyping), and membership in other groups may counteract group bias. For example, when selected for a jury, a juror becomes a member of a group that is bound by oath to uphold the law. This oath of office will counteract to some extent any group bias that members of the jury may have.

2. *Prohibitions on Direct Communication with Jurors and Judges*

Jurors or judges who have personal knowledge of the facts of a case are more likely to have an opinion about the outcome of the case than if they have not been exposed to these facts. An adversarial system of dispute resolution that is based on a principle of impartial decisionmakers must, therefore, adopt rules to control for factual bias.

In rare cases, a juror or judge may have been personally exposed to the facts of the case prior to being selected to serve as a juror or assigned the case as a judge. For example, a juror or the judge may have been a witness to an automobile accident. In these unusual cases, the juror or judge should be disqualified from participating in the case.[37] Disqualification should occur even if the judge or juror believes that she would be able to decide the case impartially. The risk that the decisionmaker's impartiality has been undermined from personal exposure to the facts of the case is too great to rely on the decisionmaker's assertion of impartiality.

Cases in which the juror or judge has some preexisting personal knowledge or involvement in the case are rare. A more substantial risk of factual bias comes from direct contact between jurors or judges and the lawyers in the case outside of official proceedings. Ex parte communications by the lawyers with jurors or judges pose several risks. The lawyers may relate facts that would be inadmissible under the rules of evidence. Moreover, ex parte communica-

37. See ABA Code of Judicial Conduct Canon 3(E)(1)(a), (b) (1990) (judge disqualified when he has personal knowledge of disputed evidentiary facts or when judge will be a material witness in the matter). But see State v. Thornton, 929 P.2d 676 (Ariz. 1996) (en banc), *cert. denied,* 117 S. Ct. 1706 (1997) (prospective juror who had listened to defendant's escape and capture on scanner set on police frequency was not "witness to the action" within meaning of statute).

tion does not provide an opportunity for cross-examination or rebuttal evidence. Thus, it is clearly inconsistent with the adversarial model for a lawyer to communicate about the facts of the case with a member of the jury or the judge except as part of the normal procedures for handling the case in court.

What about communications that do not involve the facts of the case? For example, may a lawyer engage in conversation with a juror that does not relate to the facts of the case? While social conversation does not have the danger that is associated with substantive conversation, strong reasons justify prohibition of advocates from having any communication with jurors. A conversation about social matters runs the danger that it will drift into discussion of the case itself. Even if the conversation were limited to nonsubstantive matters, the very existence of the conversation creates an appearance of impropriety that could undermine the perceived fairness of the process. Imagine the public reaction, for example, if one of the jurors in the O.J. Simpson case had been seen having lunch with a lawyer for either the prosecution or the defense. Moreover, if lawyers were allowed to have social conversations with jurors, lawyers would have an incentive to engage in such conversations either in the hope of obtaining some advantage over the other side or of counteracting an advantage that the other lawyer might have obtained. As a result, rules allowing social communication would promote contacts that neither jurors nor lawyers necessarily wanted and would deflect both lawyers and jurors from their primary roles.

The rules of professional conduct are consistent with this analysis. Model Rule 3.5(b) provides that a lawyer shall not "communicate ex parte with such a person [referring to a judge, juror, prospective juror or other official] except as permitted by law." The Restatement of the Law Governing Lawyers contains similar restrictions.[38] Similarly, Canon 3(B)(7) of the ABA's Code of Judicial Conduct generally prohibits judges from participating in ex parte communications. An ex parte communication is any communication between the judge and any other person regarding the case except a communication in the course of official proceedings. The

38. Restatement of the Law Governing Lawyers §§173(1) (prohibition on ex parte communication with judge or official before whom case is pending), 175(1), (2) (prohibition on communication with prospective and sitting jurors).

prohibition applies to parties, their lawyers, witnesses, and even third persons unconnected with the litigation.

The Code of Judicial Conduct provides several practical exceptions to the prohibition on ex parte communications to judges.[39] For example, the Code allows ex parte communications "for scheduling, administrative purposes or emergencies that do not deal with substantive matters or issues on the merits."[40] Even in these situations, however, the judge must reasonably believe that no party will gain a tactical advantage because of the ex parte communication, and the judge must promptly notify all parties of the ex parte communication and give them an opportunity to respond.[41]

What should be the remedy if a lawyer violates the prohibition on ex parte communications with either jurors or judges? Depending on the circumstances of the communication and the lawyer's intention, some form of disciplinary action seems appropriate.[42] Ex parte communications probably do not warrant reversal of a judgment absent a showing of prejudice.[43]

Should the anticommunication rule prohibit lawyers from gathering information about jurors prior to trial? Lawyers or their representatives can gather information about prospective jurors without personally contacting them. Further, lawyers need information about jurors in order to be able to exercise their peremptory challenges intelligently. Thus, information gathering about jurors, so long as it is done without contact with the prospective juror, seems consistent with the impartial decisionmaker principle. Under DR 7-108(E) of the Code of Professional Responsibility, lawyers were permitted to investigate jurors so long as the inquiry was not "vexatious or harassing." While the Model Rules do not specifically authorize investigation of jurors, that authorization should

39. See Canon 3(B)(7)(a)-(e).

40. Canon 3(B)(7)(a). See also Restatement of the Law Governing Lawyers §173, comm. *c* (Tent. Draft #8, March 21, 1997).

41. Canon 3(B)(7)(a)(i), (ii).

42. See In re Rivers, 331 S.E.2d 332 (S.C. 1984) (lawyer disciplined when investigator communicated with members of civil jury panel prior to trial).

43. Compare McElhanon v. Hing, 728 P.2d 273 (Ariz. 1986) (en banc), *cert. denied,* 481 U.S. 1030 (1987); Love v. State, 569 So. 2d 807 (Fla. Dist. Ct. App. 1990); Burgess v. Stern, 428 S.E.2d 880 (S.C. 1993), *cert. denied,* 510 U.S. 865 (1993) (reversal not warranted because no showing of prejudice), with Strothers v. Strothers, 567 N.E.2d 222 (Mass. Ct. App. 1991) (reversal warranted when ex parte communication had effect on judge's decision in divorce case).

be implicit from the fact that Rule 3.5(b) only prohibits communications.[44]

Should it be improper for lawyers to communicate with jurors after the conclusion of the case? The risk of undermining the impartiality of the jury does not exist with posttrial communications because the jury has already rendered its decision. In addition, legitimate reasons for posttrial communications exist. Lawyers may want to obtain jury impressions to improve their trial skills. Further, when the case is one of many similar cases (products liability cases, for example), lawyers can gather information that may help them improve their presentations in future cases. Posttrial communications do run the risk that jurors may be harassed or that their privacy may be invaded, but this risk can be controlled by directions of the trial judge at the end of the case that jurors once discharged are free to talk about the case but also have the right, if they wish, to refuse to discuss the case with anyone, including the lawyers. On balance, therefore, it seems proper for lawyers to be able to interview jurors after the case is over so long as they do not harass the jury.

Disciplinary Rule 7-108(D) of the Code of Professional Responsibility allowed lawyers to contact jurors after the conclusion of the case provided they did not harass the former jurors or attempt to influence their conduct in future jury service. Model Rule 3.5 does not address the issue. In State v. Furutani,[45] the Hawaii Supreme Court held that posttrial contacts with the jury could only take place in the presence of all parties or their representatives.[46] *Furutani* seems wrongly decided. Sound reasons for posttrial contact exist, while the risk to the adversarial process is small. A prohibition on harassing contacts, like that found in the Code, seems sufficient to protect the privacy of jurors, and this is the position adopted by the Restatement of the Law Governing Lawyers.[47]

While posttrial communication with jurors does not involve any

44. See also 1 Hazard & Hodes, The Law of Lawyering §3.5:201, at 655 n.1.

45. 873 P.2d 51 (Haw. 1994).

46. Id. at 56 n.8. In Rapp v. Disciplinary Bd., 916 F. Supp. 1525 (D. Haw. 1996), however, the Hawaii federal district court declared Rule 3.5, which prohibits communications with jurors "except as permitted by law," unconstitutionally vague.

47. See Restatement of the Law Governing Lawyers §175(3) (Tent. Draft #8, March 21, 1997). By contrast, the Supreme Judicial Court of Massachusetts has adopted rules of professional conduct that prohibit lawyers from contacting jurors after they have been discharged in the case. Mass. R. Prof. Cond. 3.5(d).

significant threat to the adversarial process, posttrial employment of former jurors to serve as trial consultants in future cases does create such a threat. The argument for permitting such employment is that members of a jury who have heard the evidence in a case that presents issues common to a group of other cases will have insights about the case that they can share with the lawyers to improve the quality of their presentation in those subsequent cases. The problem with hiring former jurors as consultants, however, is that once the practice becomes known, the possibility of future employment may then begin to sway jurors in their deliberations. The situation is analogous to that of the former government lawyer. A lawyer who moves from government to private practice may not undertake representation in a matter in which the lawyer had "participated personally and substantially" while a public officer or employee.[48] The rule applies even if the lawyer is not acting adversely to the government. The policy of the rule is to prevent the prospect of private employment from affecting decisionmaking by government employees.[49] The same should be true for jurors. The practice of hiring former jurors as consultants should be considered improper.

3. *Trial Publicity*

Media coverage of pending cases runs the risk that the impartiality of jurors or judges may be compromised or the testimony of witnesses influenced. Thus, if the integrity of the adversarial process were the only value involved in determining whether restrictions on media coverage of pending cases should be allowed, media coverage would be prohibited until the conclusion of the case. The integrity of the trial process, however, is not the only value at stake with regard to trial publicity. The risk to the adversarial process from trial publicity is in tension with constitutional rights of freedom of the press and free expression.

The Supreme Court has established several basic principles regarding the tension between the First Amendment rights of the press and the due process rights of parties to litigation. First, the press has a virtually unlimited right to publish what it considers

48. Model Rule 1.11(a).
49. See Model Rule 1.11, comm. 3.

important about legal proceedings. Courts will almost never grant prior restraints on publication.[50] After publication, the press may be subject to a damage action for libel, but in the case of public figures, the plaintiff must meet a higher standard than in an ordinary libel action. The plaintiff must prove that the publication was false and made with "actual malice" rather than mere negligence.[51]

Second, courts have broad power to control the conduct of anyone who appears in court, including members of the press, both to ensure order and to protect the rights of the parties. The leading case dealing with the constitutional obligation of courts to control their proceedings is Sheppard v. Maxwell.[52] Doctor Sam Sheppard was accused of bludgeoning his pregnant wife, Marilyn, to death. He claimed that he was innocent and that his wife had been killed by an unidentified intruder. The case appealed to the public's interest because of the wealth of the defendant, the mystery surrounding the case, and the fact that the defendant was having an affair. (The murder later became the basis of the highly popular television show, *The Fugitive*, and the 1993 movie by the same name.) In describing the extent of publicity in the case, the Supreme Court referred to five volumes of clippings from the Cleveland newspapers, almost all of which were incriminating; the Court also noted that the record did not reflect radio and television coverage, which it assumed to be at least as extensive as newspaper publicity. The Supreme Court reversed Dr. Sheppard's conviction. Referring to the "carnival atmosphere" at trial, the Court held the trial judge had failed to protect the defendant's right to due process of law. The Court outlined various measures that the trial judge should have taken, including stricter rules governing the use of the courtroom by the media; insulation of witnesses from press contacts; and some control over the "release of leads, information, and gossip to the press by police officers, witnesses, and the counsel for both sides."[53]

50. New York Times Co. v. United States, 403 U.S. 713 (1971) (refusing to enjoin publication of the "Pentagon Papers"); Vance v. Universal Amusement Co., 445 U.S. 308 (1980) (per curiam) (Texas public nuisance statute authorizing state judges to enjoin exhibition of films not yet found to be obscene was unconstitutional as authorizing an invalid prior restraint).

51. New York Times Co. v. Sullivan, 376 U.S. 254 (1964) (allowing criticism of public officials to be regulated by civil libel only if the plaintiff shows actual malice).

52. 384 U.S. 333 (1966).

53. Id. at 359.

Thus, Supreme Court decisions establish two poles for regulation of trial publicity. Judges have very broad authority to control the conduct of proceedings in court. Out of court, the press has virtually absolute freedom to publish what it determines to be newsworthy. Between these poles lies an important class of cases involving extrajudicial statements by officials, parties, witnesses, and their lawyers. In *Sheppard,* the Court's principal focus was on the trial judge's failure to control the conduct of the media in court. While the Court referred to the problem of extrajudicial statements, it did not explore the scope of this issue. Our focus is on the conduct of lawyers; extrajudicial statements by officials, parties, and witnesses pose somewhat different problems. To what extent should extrajudicial statements by lawyers about pending cases be subject to control?

Consider two models for regulating extrajudicial statements by lawyers about pending proceedings: the officer of the court model and the client representative model. The officer of the court model begins with the proposition that courts have the power to protect the integrity of their proceedings. This power includes control over all court officials and employees, including lawyers who are officers of the court. Since extrajudicial statements during the pendency of a proceeding pose a risk that the impartiality of decisionmakers will be compromised, courts may by rule or order prohibit lawyers from making such extrajudicial statements. Further, such control does not seriously affect the public interest in information about judicial proceedings because the press has practically unlimited freedom to gather and publish information about judicial proceedings.

Under the client representative model, lawyers' primary obligations are to their clients. In many instances, clients will have an interest in reducing trial publicity to protect their right to a fair trial. The *Sheppard* case is a clear example. In other cases, however, clients may have an interest in promoting publicity about their cases, particularly when they feel that existing public information or perceptions may be inaccurate, or when they feel that vindication in the public forum is essential to their defense. Under the client representative model, whether a lawyer participates in extrajudicial statement should largely be determined by the client after consultation with the lawyer.

When two fundamental values are in tension with each other, it is sensible to try to resolve the tension by searching for some accommodation or balance between the two. The drafters of the Model Rules attempted to construct a trial publicity rule that balanced fair trial and free expression rights.[54] Model Rule 3.6(a), as originally adopted in 1983 (the 1994 amendment is discussed below), stated that a lawyer may not make an extrajudicial statement if the statement has a "substantial likelihood of materially prejudicing an adjudicative proceeding." Section 3.6(b) listed a number of statements that "ordinarily" would have such an effect. The presumptively improper statements under §3.6(b) applied to civil jury cases, criminal cases, and any other proceeding that could result in incarceration. Rule 3.6(c) provided a "safe haven" for lawyers, a list of statements that lawyers were allowed to make, including statements referring to matters reflected in the public record.

The constitutionality of ABA Rule 3.6 and the tension between the officer of the court and the client representative models for regulating extrajudicial statements by lawyers came before the Supreme Court in Gentile v. State Bar of Nevada.[55] *Gentile* grew out of a prosecution of the owner of a Las Vegas vault company for theft of money and cocaine that had been used by the police in an undercover operation. The investigation originally focused on the owner of the vault company and the undercover officers as suspects, but the sheriff soon issued a statement stating that the officers had been cleared. The media continued to report evidence pointing to the owner's guilt, and he was ultimately indicted for the crime.

Gentile, the owner's attorney, was a well-known criminal defense lawyer in the Las Vegas area and the former Associate Dean of the National College for Criminal Defense Lawyers and Public Defenders. Hours after his client's indictment, Gentile called a press conference and delivered a statement in which he reviewed in detail the evidence that he would present at trial to show that his client was innocent. Gentile claimed that the evidence would show that one of the police officers rather than his client was the guilty party.[56] This was the first time in Gentile's professional career that he had called a formal press conference. He testified at his subsequent disciplinary hearing that he decided to call the

54. See comment 1 to Model Rule 3.6.
55. 501 U.S. 1030 (1991).
56. Id. at 1059-1060.

conference because of "concern that, unless some of the weaknesses in the State's case were made public, a potential jury venire would be poisoned by repetition in the press of information being released by the police and prosecutors, in particular the repeated press reports about polygraph tests and the fact that the two police officers were no longer suspects." Gentile gave as a second reason for calling the press conference the serious toll that the investigation had taken on his client.[57]

Before calling the press conference, Gentile researched the issue of whether the press conference would be likely to prejudice the trial. Considering the length of time before trial was scheduled to begin (six months), the size of the community, and prior First Amendment cases, he concluded that his statements would not be prejudicial.[58] The case went to trial on schedule six months later. All of the evidence referred to in Gentile's press conference was admitted into evidence, and his client was acquitted.[59]

The state bar subsequently instituted disciplinary proceedings against Gentile for violation of Nevada Supreme Court Rule 177, which was practically identical to the 1983 version of ABA Model Rule 3.6. The Nevada Disciplinary Board found that Gentile had violated the rule and the Nevada Supreme Court affirmed. The U.S. Supreme Court reversed in a 5-4 decision.

The opinions of Justice Kennedy and Chief Justice Rehnquist were largely in agreement that the standard set forth in Rule 3.6 of a "substantial likelihood of materially prejudicing an adjudicative proceeding" was constitutional.[60] The opinions differed on the constitutionality of the application of this standard, and on the significance of due process (fair notice), to the facts of the case. Four members of the Court (opinion of Justice Kennedy joined by Justices Blackmun, Marshall, and Stevens) would allow a state to impose discipline for pretrial statements by a lawyer only if the there was a clear showing of the likelihood of material prejudice. They found Rule 3.6 as applied to the facts of this case to be unconstitutional because the likelihood of prejudice was small.[61] These four justices also found an independent due process basis

57. Id. at 1042-1043.
58. Id. at 1044.
59. Id. at 1047.
60. Id. at 1036-1037 (opinion of Justice Kennedy) and 1075 (opinion of Justice Rehnquist).
61. Id. at 1037-1048.

for setting aside the decision of the Nevada Supreme Court. They found that Rule 3.6(c) "misled petitioner into thinking that he could give his press conference without fear of discipline . . . [because the rule] provides that a lawyer 'may state without elaboration . . . the general nature of the . . . defense.'"[62]

Four other members of the Court (opinion of Justice Rehnquist joined by Justices Scalia, Souter, and White) would give the states practically blanket authority to regulate pretrial speech by attorneys. Rather than requiring a clear showing of material prejudice, these justices focused on the special role of attorneys and the substantial state interest in protecting the integrity of criminal trials.[63] In light of the greater leeway that these justices would give to the states, they found no due process violation in the wording of Nevada rule.[64]

Justice O'Connor cast the deciding vote in the case. While agreeing with the Rehnquist opinion that states should be given substantial leeway in regulating pretrial speech by lawyers, she agreed with the Kennedy opinion that the wording of Rule 3.6 did not give Gentile fair notice that he would be subject to discipline.[65]

What conclusions can one draw from the *Gentile* case? First, it is clear that the standard of "substantial likelihood of materially prejudicing an adjudicative proceeding" is constitutional, having been accepted by all nine justices. Second, it also seems reasonably clear that a lawyer who gave a press conference like the one that Gentile gave could be subject to discipline if the applicable disciplinary rule did not have the due process infirmity that troubled Justice O'Connor. As a result, it appears that a majority of the Supreme Court in *Gentile* has adopted the officer of the court model, as least in criminal cases, providing that it is constitutional to prevent lawyers from engaging in extrajudicial statements even if the statements are made with the consent of their clients to respond to what the lawyer and client consider to be a highly damaging public atmosphere surrounding the case.

While the Supreme Court upheld the constitutionality of the officer of the court model for restricting public statements by lawyers about pending cases, the decision did not prohibit states

62. Id. at 1048.
63. Id. at 1065-1076.
64. Id. at 1078-1079.
65. Id. at 1081-1082.

from allowing lawyers greater leeway in making public comments about pending cases. In fact, amendments to Model Rule 3.6 show a movement in that direction.

In response to the Supreme Court's decision in *Gentile,* the ABA adopted a revised version of Model Rule 3.6. The new rule continues to use the "substantial likelihood of material prejudice standard" that was approved by the Supreme Court in *Gentile.* See Model Rule 3.6(a). Revised Rule 3.6(b) creates a "safe harbor" of statements that lawyers may make; these are substantially the same as under the former rule. Among the statements that are allowed are the following:

- 3.6(b)(1): "the claim, offense or defense involved and, except when prohibited by law, the identity of the persons involved"
- 3.6(b)(2): "information contained in a public record"

The most significant change made in the new rule, however, is the addition of Rule 3.6(c), which provides lawyers with a "right of reply":

> Notwithstanding paragraph (a), a lawyer may make a statement that a reasonable lawyer would believe is required to protect a client from the substantial undue prejudicial effect of recent publicity not initiated by the lawyer or the lawyer's client. A statement made pursuant to this paragraph shall be limited to such information as is necessary to mitigate the recent adverse publicity.

The right to reply found in revised Rule 3.6(c) goes a long way toward adopting the client representative model for extrajudicial statements, although not completely so since the rule does not permit lawyers to initiate the publicity. If Rule 3.6(c) had been in effect, it appears that Gentile would not have been subject to discipline for his press conference since he was responding to widespread reports that were adverse to his client's case.

Revised Model Rule 3.6 reflects an appropriate balance of the constitutional issues involved in trial publicity.[66] The rule does limit public commentary by lawyers participating in the proceed-

66. The proposed Restatement of the Law Governing Lawyers §169 (Tent. Draft #8, March 21, 1997) follows the approach of Model Rule 3.6.

ing, but the public interest in information about pending proceedings seems adequately protected by the press's virtually unlimited right to publish about pending proceedings. The rule allows lawyers involved in the case to provide basic information about the case. At the conclusion of the case, lawyers involved in the case can speak freely about nonprivileged matters. Moreover, even during the case, lawyers who are not involved in the proceeding may comment publicly on the issues raised by the case, and an abundance of such commentators appear regularly in the media. In most cases, the interest of parties to the proceeding in fair trials is served by restrictions on trial publicity. Recognition of the right to reply seems sufficient to address legitimate concerns that a party may have about unfair or prejudicial pretrial publicity.

It is unclear, however, whether most states will adopt the ABA's revised Model Rule 3.6 with its right to reply.[67] In states that have not adopted the ABA's amendment to Model Rule 3.6, a lawyer who makes an extrajudicial statement like the one that Gentile made is at disciplinary risk.

Some states are considering giving lawyers more protection than found in revised Model Rule 3.6. For example, the Professional Responsibility Committee of the Bar of the City of New York has recommended that the New York Code of Professional Responsibility be amended to adopt a "clear and present danger" standard for punishing lawyers for extrajudicial statements, rather than the "substantial likelihood" standard of Model Rule 3.6(a).[68] This approach seems unsound because it gives insufficient weight to the integrity of trial proceedings. The substantial likelihood of material prejudice standard coupled with a right to apply strikes a better balance.

Public comment by prosecutors poses a greater risk of danger to the impartiality of decisionmakers than statements by defense counsel because the public is more likely to give credence to statements by public officials than by defense counsel. The ABA has taken a step to impose greater restrictions on prosecutors by

67. In response to the extensive publicity surrounding the O. J. Simpson case, the California Supreme Court adopted a trial publicity rule based on ABA Model Rule 3.6 with its right to reply. Cal. R. Prof. Conduct 5-120.

68. See Committee on Prof. Resp., Assn. of Bar of City of New York, The Need for Fair Trials Does not Justify a Disciplinary Rule that Broadly Restricts an Attorney's Speech, 20 Fordham Urb. L.J. 881 (1993).

amending Model Rule 3.8, which deals with the ethical obligations of prosecutors, to include a new provision, Rule 3.8(g):

> The prosecutor in a criminal case shall: . . .
>
> (g) except for statements that are necessary to inform the public of the nature and extent of the prosecutor's action and that serve a legitimate law enforcement purpose, refrain from making extrajudicial comments that have a substantial likelihood of heightening public condemnation of the accused.

Comment 5 to the Rule, however, backs away from this approach by stating that prosecutors may ethically make statements allowed by revised Rule 3.6.

Gentile dealt with constitutionality of disciplinary action against an attorney for engaging in trial publicity. To prevent prejudicial pretrial publicity from occurring, many judges will consider imposing "gag" orders on all counsel involved in the proceeding. Because a gag order amounts to a prior restraint on free speech, the standard for imposition of a gag order is quite high. In United States v. Salameh,[69] the judge in the trial of defendants accused of the bombing of the World Trade Center Tower in New York issued an order prohibiting defense counsel from making statements in the press or media that "may have something to do with the case." The Second Circuit ruled that prior restraints on speech carry a "heavy presumption" against their constitutionality. The court stated that limitations on speech must be "no broader than necessary to protect the integrity of the judicial system and the defendant's right to a fair trial." In addition, the court must explore other available remedies.[70] The Second Circuit vacated the trial judge's order because it failed to meet these standards.[71]

Despite the stringent legal standard for upholding gag orders, many trial judges will consider issuing such orders to prevent publicity about significant pending cases. Increased use of gag orders is unfortunate for two reasons. First, if Rule 3.6 strikes an appropriate balance between the contending constitutional inter-

69. 992 F.2d 445 (2d Cir. 1993).

70. Id. at 447.

71. See also Monroe H. Freedman & Janet Starwood, Prior Restraints on Freedom of Expression by Defendants and Defense Attorneys: *Ratio Decidendi v. Obiter Dictum*, 29 Stan. L. Rev. 607 (1977).

ests, then use of a gag order should be presumptively inappropriate because it upsets the balance struck by Rule 3.6. Second, judges usually impose gag orders only after substantial publicity has taken place. Often this publicity will be adverse to the defendant. As a result, gag orders normally operate to the disadvantage of the defendant. Trial judges should refrain from imposing gag orders except in extreme cases. They should instead allow the lawyers to make public comments about pending cases so long as they comply with the standards of Rule 3.6.

4. *Disqualification and Reporting Misconduct of Jurors and Judges*

This section began by identifying three forms of bias that can undermine the impartiality of decisionmakers: factual, relational, and group bias. Factual bias can result when lawyers bring facts to the attention of the judge or a juror outside of normal procedures, either by ex parte communication or trial publicity. Relational bias occurs when the decisionmaker has a tendency to favor one side in the case because of some relationship between the decisionmaker and the subject matter of the case (such as a financial interest in the case), one of the parties to the case (family relationship, for example), or one of the attorneys appearing in the case (such as prior representation by a lawyer of one of the jurors).

Relational bias of jurors is controlled through the process of voir dire, during which jurors may be challenged for "cause or favor." A challenge for cause applies when the juror does not meet statutorily defined requirements for jury service. For example, federal law provides that a juror may be challenged for cause if the prospective juror

> (1) is not a citizen of the United States eighteen years old who has resided for a period of one year within the judicial district;
>
> (2) is unable to read, write, and understand the English language with a degree of proficiency sufficient to fill out satisfactorily the juror qualification form;
>
> (3) is unable to speak the English language;
>
> (4) is incapable, by reason of mental or physical infirmity, to render satisfactory jury service; or

> (5) has a charge pending against him for the commission of, or has been convicted in a State or Federal court of record of, a crime punishable by imprisonment for more than one year and his civil rights have not been restored.[72]

A challenge for favor applies if the juror is unable to decide the case fairly because of bias, prejudice, interest in the case, or other factors. While challenges for cause or favor refer to different concepts, it is common today to use the term *challenge for cause* to refer to both. Sometimes statutes will define circumstances when jurors are disqualified for favor, but typically the court determines whether a juror should be excused based on the juror's answers during voir dire to various questions posed by the court about the juror's background, relationship to the case, and relationship to the parties and their counsel. For example, federal law does not provide any specific grounds for disqualifying jurors for favor, leaving the matter for court determination: "All challenges for cause or favor, whether to the array or panel or to individual jurors, shall be determined by the court."[73] Similarly, judges are disqualified from hearing a case if the judge, the judge's spouse, or certain close relatives of the judge have an economic interest in the case or direct involvement in the proceeding (for example, as a material witness).[74] Chapter 7.C-D includes a detailed discussion of disqualification of judges.

Under the Code of Professional Responsibility, lawyers had an obligation to disclose juror misconduct to tribunals. DR 7-108(G) of the Code of Professional Responsibility stated: "A lawyer shall reveal promptly to the court improper conduct by a venireman or a juror, or by another toward a venireman or a juror or a member of his family, of which the lawyer has knowledge." For example, in In re R.,[75] the accused lawyer represented the plaintiff in a personal injury case. During the trial the plaintiff gave a ride to one of the jurors, who was hitchhiking to court. The plaintiff and the juror did not immediately recognize each other; when they did, they were both embarrassed. From the opinion it appears that the

72. 28 U.S.C. §1865(b) (1994).

73. 28 U.S.C. §1870 (1994).

74. See ABA Model Code of Judicial Conduct Canon 3(E)(1)(c), (d) (1990); 28 U.S.C. §455(b)(4), (5) (1994) (disqualification of federal judges).

75. 554 P.2d 522 (Or. 1976) (en banc).

plaintiff did not inform his lawyers of the contact until after a verdict was returned and then set aside on unrelated grounds. The plaintiff's lawyer, after consultation with his partners, decided not to inform the court because the verdict had been set aside and because no impropriety was involved in that the plaintiff and the juror had not discussed the case. The Oregon Supreme Court disagreed:

> We are of the opinion that it is immaterial when the accused learned of the juror contact because if an attorney learns of improper conduct at any time that any court can rectify the effect of that conduct, the attorney has an obligation to inform such court.
>
> Another reason the accused did not inform any court was his opinion, fortified by a like opinion of his partners, that there was no improper conduct because the client and juror had met inadvertently and had not discussed the case. This is a decision that the attorney makes at his peril; that is, despite a reasonable belief that the conduct of the juror was proper, and, therefore, the attorney does not inform the court, if it develops subsequently that the conduct was improper, the attorney is guilty of unethical conduct for not earlier informing the court. The reason for such a rule is that, otherwise, the attorney can make a unilateral decision that the conduct was proper and, therefore, not inform the court. Because of this lack of disclosure the conduct may never be known although it turns out to be highly improper and highly prejudicial to a party to the lawsuit. If there is the slightest bit of doubt in an attorney's mind whether he is obligated to inform the court of juror misconduct, that doubt should be resolved in favor of disclosure.[76]

The court dismissed the complaint, however, because it found no improper conduct by the plaintiff and the juror.

It is unclear whether the duty to disclose juror misconduct found in the Code survives the adoption of the Model Rules, which do not have an equivalent provision to DR 7-108(G). One court has, however, held that a prosecutor has a duty to disclose to the trial court information that the prosecutor had received regarding misconduct during the trial by a juror.[77]

While the Model Rules are unclear on the issue, for several reasons the rules should be changed to make it clear that lawyers

76. Id. at 524.
77. State v. Cady, 811 P.2d 1130 (Kan. 1991).

must disclose information regarding juror misconduct to the tribunal.[78] First, the client has no legitimate right to a result based on juror misconduct. Second, the client's confidentiality interest in such information is minimal or nonexistent, at least in cases in which the misconduct did not involve wrongdoing by the client. Third, juror misconduct is a serious violation of the adversarial process. Even when the client is involved in the misconduct (bribery of a juror, for example), the argument for requiring lawyers to disclose the client's bribery of a juror is strong. Lawyers are required to disclose perjury by a criminal defendant, and the case for requiring lawyers to disclose bribery of a juror is even more compelling. The system has built-in checks to prevent perjury from being successful, but the same is not true of bribery.

The Model Rules do not address the question of whether lawyers have a duty to inform the court of facts that may be grounds for disqualification of the judge. The disqualification rules are designed to protect the right of parties to an impartial judge and the public interest in having a dispute resolution process that commands public acceptance because of its fairness. In addition, both the Code of Judicial Conduct and the federal statute provide for waiver of disqualification, although they differ on when waiver is permissible.[79] Implicit in the procedure for waiver is the idea that disqualifying facts are brought to the attention of the court so that a waiver can be obtained where appropriate. Except in rare cases, the client will not have a confidentiality interest in the facts that would establish disqualification of the judge, and even in those

78. The lawyer codes in 15 jurisdictions currently require lawyers to disclose juror misconduct. See Restatement of the Law Governing Lawyers §175, Reporter's Note to comm. *a*, at 389 (Tent. Draft #8, March 21, 1997).

79. Under the Code, disqualification may be remitted (the Code uses the term *remittal*, while the federal statute uses the term *waiver*) in all cases except ones in which the judge is disqualified because of personal bias or prejudice concerning a party. Under the Code remittal of disqualification is allowed in situations in which the judge is disqualified because of economic interest. Canon 3(F). The procedure for remittal is as follows: The judge discloses the basis for disqualification on the record and asks the parties and their lawyers to consider, out of the presence of the judge, whether to waive disqualification. If all parties and the judge agree to waive disqualification, the judge may continue in the case. The agreement waiving disqualification should be made part of the record in the case. Canon 3(F).

Under the federal statute, waiver of disqualification is allowed only in cases involving the general standard of when the judge's impartiality might reasonably be questioned. Waiver is not allowed for any cases in which rules specifically provide for disqualification, including cases of disqualification because of financial interest. See 28 U.S.C. §455(e) (1994).

cases, the client's interest can be protected by making the motion under seal. The rules of professional conduct should be amended to require lawyers to disclose to the court facts known to the lawyer that raise a substantial question of whether the judge is disqualified from hearing the matter.

5. *Restrictions on Jury Selection*

Previous sections have examined rules for controlling factual and relational bias by jurors and judges. Should an adversarial system of dispute resolution attempt to control for group bias or prejudice (as opposed to factual or relational bias or prejudice)? If so, how?

Consider one possibility: Suppose the rules dealing with disqualification of jurors for cause were expanded to allow a juror to be removed for cause if the juror exhibited a general bias or prejudice, for example, certain attitudes toward women or minorities. Such a rule would be unworkable. Since everyone, to a greater or lesser degree, has a wide variety of biases and prejudices, an attempt to remove jurors who had these characteristics would leave us with few if any decisionmakers. Further, such a system would dramatically increase the administrative cost of choosing jurors because it would require extensive inquiry into a juror's background and psychological makeup.

Consider another alternative to the issue of general bias or prejudice. Rather than removing jurors for cause if they have a group bias or prejudice, we could strive to have a jury that is representative of the community. This approach, however, also suffers from major problems. Members of communities have a staggering range of characteristics and attitudes. Which ones will we choose to represent in the jury and how will selection be made? If we are concerned about ensuring representation based on race, what about gender, and what about economic background? The list of characteristics is great and the criteria for selection controversial. Further, the representational approach could not work with judges since at the trial level single judges, not panels, preside over cases.

Instead of dealing directly with the issue of group bias or prejudice, our system attempts to deal with this problem in two ways. First, methods of selection of the jury pool from which petit jurors are chosen should be as open and nondiscriminatory as possible.

For example, in 1968 Congress passed the Jury Selection and Service Act, which was designed to establish procedures to eliminate discrimination in jury service.[80] Second, parties to litigation are entitled to remove a certain number of jurors by peremptory challenge. Peremptory challenges may be exercised for any reason (except as discussed below) and are in addition to any challenges for cause. By exercising peremptory challenges, lawyers can remove jurors that they believe exhibit a group bias or prejudice against their clients for whatever reason.

The system of peremptory challenges suffers, however, from a fundamental problem. Since lawyers, rightly or wrongly, typically believe that bias or prejudice by jurors is associated with characteristics such as race or gender, the system of peremptory challenges promotes the use of challenges based on these characteristics. In other words, the system of peremptory challenges tends to promote the very stereotyping that it is designed to control.

In a series of cases beginning with *Batson v. Kentucky*,[81] the Supreme Court has attempted to address the problem of discriminatory exercise of peremptory challenges. The *Batson* Court held that the prosecution violates the defendant's right to equal protection when it exercises peremptory challenges to remove jurors solely on the ground of race. In subsequent cases, the Court has dramatically expanded its scrutiny of the use of peremptory challenges, although the rationale for the decisions has shifted. The Court held that exercise of peremptory challenges based on race by private litigants in civil cases is unconstitutional because this use of peremptory challenges violates *the equal protection rights of jurors*.[82] Similarly, the Court held that the defendant's exercise of peremptory challenges based on race in a criminal case was unconstitutional because it also infringed the jurors' right to equal protection. The Court rejected the argument that restriction of the defendant's right to use peremptory challenges amounted to a violation of the defendant's constitutional right to due process, reasoning that the defendant does not have a constitutional right to any particular system of peremptory challenges.[83] The Court has expanded the prohibition on the discriminatory use of peremptory

80. 28 U.S.C. §§1861 et seq. (1994).
81. 476 U.S. 79 (1986).
82. Edmonson v. Leesville Concrete Co., 500 U.S. 614 (1991).
83. Georgia v. McCollum, 505 U.S. 42 (1992).

challenges to include strikes based on gender as well as race,[84] but the Court has refused to extend the right to cover the use of peremptory challenges based on religion.[85]

The Court's approach to discriminatory exercise of peremptory challenges seems wrong. Attempting to draw a distinction between race and gender on the one hand and religion on the other seems arbitrary. Moreover, lawyers can often avoid the current restrictions by carefully developing nondiscriminatory reasons for the exercise of their peremptory challenges.[86] As some scholars have suggested, a better approach is the elimination of peremptory challenges.[87] Under such a system, the parties are more likely to have a jury that is representative of the community, the constitutional right of jurors to serve is protected, and the cost of administering the current system of peremptory challenges is eliminated.

D. COMPLIANCE WITH PROCEDURAL RULES

1. *Qualified Truth-Maximizing Rules*

The Rules of Professional Conduct require lawyers to comply with rules of procedure. Model Rule 3.4(c) provides that a lawyer shall not "knowingly disobey an obligation under the rules of a tribunal except for an open refusal based on an assertion that no valid obligation exists."[88] Section 165 of the Restatement of the Law

84. J.E.B. v. Alabama ex rel T. B., 511 U.S. 127 (1994).

85. Davis v. Minnesota, 511 U.S. 1115 (1994) (denial of certiorari in case involving exercise of peremptory challenge based on religion).

86. See Purkett v. Elem, 514 U.S. 765 (1995) (at second stage of *Batson* analysis, reason for preemptory challenge need not be plausible or persuasive as long as it is neutral; persuasiveness of reason considered when court weighs evidence).

87. Jeffrey Abramson, We, The Jury: The Jury System and the Ideal of Democracy 247 (1994); Raymond J. Broderick, Why the Peremptory Challenge Should be Abolished, 65 Temp. L. Rev. 369 (1992); Edward P. Schwartz & Warren F. Schwartz, The Challenge of Peremptory Challenges, 12 J.L. Econ. & Org. 325 (1996) (arguing for change to majority vote rather than unanimity with abolition of peremptory challenge). New York Federal Judge Constance Baker Motley has barred peremptory challenges in her courtroom on the ground that they are inherently unconstitutional. See Mark Hansen, Peremptory-Free Zone, 82 A.B.A. J. 26 (Aug. 1996).

88. See also ABA Model Code of Prof. Resp. DR 7-106(A).

Governing Lawyers sweeps more broadly to include not only procedural rules but law in general: "In representing a client in a matter before a tribunal, a lawyer must comply with applicable law, including rules of procedure and evidence and specific tribunal rulings." The statement of this general duty, however, begs a fundamental question: What should be the rules of procedure that lawyers are required to honor?

In 1975 federal Judge Marvin Frankel argued that the adversarial system did not give sufficient weight to the importance of truth:

> The advocate in the trial courtroom is not engaged much more than half the time — and then only coincidentally — in the search for truth. The advocate's prime loyalty is to his client, not to truth as such. All of us remember some stirring and defiant declarations by advocates of their heroic, selfless devotion to The Client. . . . Recall Lord Brougham's familiar words:
>
> > [A]n advocate, in the discharge of his duty, knows but one person in all the world, and that person is his client. To save that client by all means and expedients, and at all hazards and costs to other persons, and, among them, to himself, is his first and only duty; and in performing this duty he must not regard the alarm, the torments, the destruction which he may bring upon others. Separating the duty of a patriot from that of an advocate, he must go on reckless of consequences, though it should be his unhappy fate to involve his country in confusion.
>
> . . . There are, I think, no comparable lyrics by lawyers to The Truth. . . .
>
> The litigator's devices, let us be clear, have utility in testing dishonest witnesses, ferreting out falsehoods, and thus exposing the truth. But to a considerable degree these devices are like other potent weapons, equally lethal for heroes and villains. It is worth stressing, therefore, that the gladiator using the weapons in the courtroom is not primarily crusading after truth, but seeking to win.[89]

Judge Frankel contended that we should consider modifying our adversarial ideal to make truth a paramount objective. He offered a draft of a new rule of professional conduct that would incorporate this ideal:

89. Marvin E. Frankel, The Search for Truth: An Umpireal View, 123 U. Pa. L. Rev. 1031, 1035-1036, 1039 (1975). See also Marvin E. Frankel, Partisan Justice (1980).

> (1) In his representation of a client, unless prevented from doing so by a privilege reasonably believed to apply, a lawyer shall:
>
> (a) Report to the court and opposing counsel the existence of relevant evidence or witnesses where the lawyer does not intend to offer such evidence or witnesses.
>
> (b) Prevent, or when prevention has proved unsuccessful, report to the court and opposing counsel the making of any untrue statement by client or witness or any omission to state a material fact necessary in order to make statements made, in the light of the circumstances under which they were made, not misleading.
>
> (c) Question witnesses with a purpose and design to elicit the whole truth, including particularly supplementary and qualifying matters that render evidence already given more accurate, intelligible, or fair than it otherwise would be.
>
> (2) In the construction and application of the rules in subdivision (1), a lawyer will be held to possess knowledge he actually has or, in the exercise of reasonable diligence, should have.[90]

Professor Monroe Freedman responded critically to Judge Frankel's view that lawyers should have an obligation to foster the truth with a two-fold defense of the adversarial system. First, the adversarial system is a better mechanism for producing truth than the inquisitorial system. In particular, adversarial presentations tend to counteract the natural tendency of decisionmakers to reach conclusions on incomplete evidence.[91] Second, even if the adversarial system were not the best method of arriving at truth, it reflects values that are more important than truth:

> A trial is, in part, a search for truth . . . . We are concerned, however, with far more than a search for truth, and the constitutional rights that are provided by our system of justice serve independent values that may well outweigh the truth-seeking value, a fact made manifest when we realize that those rights, far from furthering the search

90. Frankel, The Search for Truth: An Umpireal View, 123 U. Pa. L. Rev. at 1057-1058. For a more recent argument in favor of the importance of truth as a value in criminal cases, see Akhil Reed Amar, The Constitution and Criminal Procedure: First Principles (1997).

91. Monroe H. Freedman, Judge Frankel's Search for Truth, 123 U. Pa. L. Rev. 1060, 1060-1061 (1975). See also Monroe H. Freedman, Understanding Lawyers' Ethics 26-33 (1990). See generally Stephen McG. Bundy & Einer R. Elhauge, Do Lawyers Improve the Adversary System? A General Theory of Litigation Advice and Its Regulation, 79 Cal. L. Rev. 313 (1991).

> for truth, may well impede it. What more effective way is there to expose a defendant's guilt than to require self-incrimination, at least to the extent of compelling the defendant to take the stand and respond to interrogation before the jury? The defendant, however, is presumed innocent, the burden is on the prosecution to prove guilt beyond a reasonable doubt, and even the guilty accused has an "absolute constitutional right to remain silent" and to put the government to its proof.[92]

While Freedman's argument applies most strongly in the criminal defense setting, he extends the analysis to civil litigation as well, because the civil system also has a constitutional foundation.[93]

Frankel and Freedman were both right. To show why, consider a distinction between two ways in which lawyers could have an obligation to promote truth in litigation: through direct responsibility and by rule compliance. A lawyer with direct responsibility to promote truth would conduct all aspects of the litigation with a view toward producing what the lawyer believes to be a truthful outcome. Section 1(c) of Frankel's proposed rule illustrates a direct obligation to promote truth; the section would require lawyers to question witnesses with "a purpose and design to elicit the whole truth." Questioning of witnesses is obviously not the only aspect of litigation in which lawyers could have an obligation to promote truth; the duty could be extended to other steps in the litigation process, including client interviewing, pleading, investigation, negotiation, and appeal. By contrast, a lawyer can have responsibility to promote the truth through compliance with rules rather than by direct responsibility. Whether compliance with rules promotes truth depends, of course, on the rules that lawyers are following. If the rules on the whole are designed to maximize the likelihood that truthful results will occur in litigation, then it is reasonable to characterize rule compliance as promoting truth.[94]

Frankel was correct to point out that advocates are concerned primarily with winning and only incidentally with the truth, and he was also correct to emphasize that truth should be given a greater value in our judicial system. On the other hand, Freedman

92. See Freedman, Judge Frankel's Search for Truth, 123 U. Pa. L. Rev. at 1063-1064. See also Freedman, Understanding Lawyers' Ethics, at 13.

93. Id. at 20.

94. This distinction between direct responsibility and rule compliance parallels a distinction in philosophy between act and rule utilitarianism. See David Lyons, Forms and Limits of Utilitarianism (Oxford 1965).

was right to emphasize that the adversarial system appears to be a better means of achieving truth than a system that places direct responsibility on an official or lawyer to determine the truth because the checks and balances of the adversarial system operate to control the deficiencies of factfinding and judgment by any one individual. Freedman was also right to emphasize that while truth may be an important value, in our society individual rights, particularly those that have been constitutionalized, are more important than truthful resolution of disputes.

The term *qualified truth-maximizing rules* represents a blend of Frankel's and Freedman's insights. A truth-maximizing rule is a rule that will increase the likelihood of a truthful outcome of a dispute over the situation that exists in the absence of a rule. In determining whether a rule will have a truth-maximizing result, the consequences of adoption of the rule, particularly the incentive effects on the parties and the lawyers, must be projected. By focusing on the truth-maximizing consequences of rules, the system of rules incorporates Frankel's concern that the legal system should give greater weight to truth.

At the same time, the concept of truth-maximizing rules incorporates Freedman's points about the importance of the adversarial system and of individual rights. Under a regime of qualified truth-maximizing rules, lawyers do not have direct responsibility to promote the truth. The lawyer's obligation is to follow the established rules of procedure, except in those cases in which a challenge is being made to the rules on nonfrivolous grounds.[95] Moreover, the term *qualified* is intended to recognize that truth is not the only value at stake and that truth-maximizing rules are sometimes limited because of our concern for individual rights.

The application of the concept of qualified truth-maximizing rules will not be straightforward or uncontroversial. Reasonable people can disagree over whether a rule is truth maximizing. Further, when individual rights should qualify truth-maximizing rules can also be a vigorously disputed subject. The concept of qualified truth-maximizing rules does provide, however, both a standard and a framework for analysis of existing or proposed rules for limiting zealous representation. The following sections critically consider the rules governing investigation, discovery, and trial conduct based on this principle.

95. See Chapter 5.B supra.

2. *Investigation*

Lawyers gather information in support of their positions in litigation through informal investigation and formal discovery. The next section considers limitations on lawyer conduct during formal discovery. What principles should govern lawyer conduct in connection with informal investigations?

a. Criminal Conduct and Misrepresentation

Criminal law contains some limitations on investigation by lawyers. For example, the federal wiretapping statute prohibits interception and disclosure of wire, oral, or electronic communications unless the recording is done with the consent of one of the parties to the communication.[96] A lawyer who directed an investigator to wiretap the opposing party's telephone conversations would be guilty of criminal conduct under this statute. Indeed, in some states it constitutes a crime to record a conversation without the consent of all of the parties.[97]

Beyond compliance with the criminal law, should there be any restrictions on lawyers' investigative conduct? Consider the following principle: A lawyer should not intentionally engage in misrepresentation of material fact in connection with investigation of a legal matter. Such a principle seems uncontroversial. No one is legally privileged to engage in fraud, so surely the same principle applies to lawyers. In response, it could be argued that a significant difference exists between fraud and misrepresentation to gather information. Actionable fraud involves intentional or reckless misrepresentation that deprives the other party of some legal entitlement, typically money or property. Misrepresentation in connection with investigation of a case could deprive the other party of a legal entitlement—for example, if the misrepresentation was used to obtain information that was subject to a protected privilege—but this would not always be the case. For example, a lawyer might employ an investigator who would misrepresent his identity when interviewing a potential party or witness to gain unprivileged factual information in support of the lawyer's case.

96. 18 U.S.C. §2511 (1994).
97. Ill. Ann. Stat. ch. 720, ¶5/14-2 (West 1993).

Despite this argument, the rules of professional conduct impose a higher standard on lawyers than not engaging in actionable fraud. Model Rule 8.4(c) defines misconduct to include "conduct involving dishonesty, fraud, deceit or misrepresentation." The position of the Model Rules seems generally sound for two reasons. First, using misrepresentation to gather information poses a risk that the lawyer or the lawyer's agent will invade a legally protected right. Second, the availability of formal discovery generally provides an alternative mechanism for gathering information. Nonetheless, exceptional circumstances might exist in which it should be proper for a lawyer to use misrepresentation to gather information: when the information was essential to advance the client's interest, no other reasonable alternative exists, and the means of gathering the information did not violate the legal rights of the person from whom the information was gathered.

b. Communication with People Who Are Represented by Counsel

An established rule of professional conduct is that a lawyer may not communicate with a person who is represented by counsel in a matter without the consent of that person's lawyer. Model Rule 4.2 provides as follows:

> In representing a client, a lawyer shall not communicate about the subject of the representation with a person the lawyer knows to be represented by another lawyer in the matter, unless the lawyer has the consent of the other lawyer or is authorized by law to do so.[98]

For example, in a divorce case, it is unprofessional for a lawyer representing one spouse to meet with the other spouse in an effort to negotiate a settlement, without the consent of the other spouse's attorney.[99]

Since opposing parties usually have significant information about a case, why do the rules of professional conduct prohibit investigating lawyers from contacting these parties to obtain information from them? An investigating attorney may have several

98. See also Restatement of the Law Governing Lawyers §158 (Tent. Draft #8, March 21, 1997).

99. E.g., In re Wehringer, 525 N.Y.S.2d 604 (App. Div. 1988).

reasons for using informal investigation rather than formal discovery to gather information from the opposing party. First, in the vast majority of jurisdictions, the tools of formal discovery are not generally available prior to filing suit. Second, even after suit is commenced, use of formal discovery, particularly depositions, is likely to be much more expensive that informal investigation. Third, in formal discovery the investigating attorney is likely to receive answers that are wholly or partially filtered through the litigation lens of opposing counsel. An investigating attorney would much prefer to receive the unadulterated answers of the opposing party.

Given these interests of the investigating attorney it is reasonable to turn the question to the other side and ask what interests justify any restrictions on informal investigation. The party opposing informal investigation could claim that it has an interest in not revealing without the advice of counsel information that may be damaging to its case. But this contention seems unpersuasive. No one wants to reveal information that is damaging to their legal position, but if the person has no right to keep the information confidential the argument against revelation is hollow. A party opposing informal investigation could, however, make a narrower argument against being subjected to informal investigation. The opposing party could claim that it has a legitimate interest in preventing the investigating attorney from obtaining privileged information (i.e, material protected under the attorney-client privilege, as work product, as a trade secret, or by statute). Informal contacts that occur without the presence of counsel for a party from whom information is sought run the risk of such disclosure. In addition, the opposing party may claim that informal contacts could lead to settlements and that it has a legitimate interest in not entering into any settlement without the advice of counsel.[100] Moreover, the opposing party could question the need of the investigating attorney to have such contacts. Formal discovery has some limitations but does provide for general inquiry into relevant facts.

The opposing party's legitimate concerns about preventing dis-

100. See John Leubsdorf, Essay, Communicating with Another Lawyer's Client: The Lawyer's Veto and the Client's Interests, 127 U. Pa. L. Rev. 683, 686 (1979); Stephen M. Sinaiko, Note, Ex Parte Communication and the Corporate Adversary: A New Approach, 66 N.Y.U. L. Rev. 1456, 1463-1476 (1991).

closure of privileged material and about uncounseled settlements could be protected by a narrower rule than one that prohibits the inquiring attorney from engaging in any type of informal investigation. One possibility is that the rules could allow an attorney to engage in informal investigation so long as the attorney did not seek or obtain privileged material and so long as the opposing party were warned that it should consider seeking the advice of counsel before concluding any settlement. Opposing parties might object, however, that this rule does not provide sufficient protection against intentional or inadvertent disclosure of privileged information, and that once the information has been released it may be too late to protect the opposing party's interests. Another possibility would be a rule that allowed an attorney to engage in informal investigation provided the attorney informed the individual (perhaps in writing) that the attorney represents a client with an adverse interest and that the person may want to seek the advice of counsel before discussing the matter further with the attorney. This "*Miranda* warning" approach, however, is likely to be functionally equivalent to a rule precluding the investigating attorney from obtaining information except through formal discovery.

Based on this analysis, the rule that prohibits oral communication with a represented person seems sound. The restriction on access to information imposed on the investigating attorney is relatively small and the risk to the opposing party substantial. The rule, however, prohibits communication in writing as well as orally. Thus, it is also improper for a lawyer to mail a settlement offer to the opposing lawyer's client.[101] It is difficult to justify this restriction since the risk of obtaining privileged information or coercion is nonexistent when the lawyer communicates in writing with copy to the opposing counsel.

The anticommunication rule is subject to some exceptions. Communication is permitted when authorized by law, for example, a communication pursuant to court rule or court order.[102] In our society, open access to government is a fundamental value, so the rule allows lawyers to communicate directly with governmental officials even when those officials are represented by counsel.[103]

101. Restatement of the Law Governing Lawyers §158, comm. *f* (Tent. Draft #8, March 21, 1997).

102. Id. §158, comms. *g*, *m*.

103. Model Rule 4.2, comm. 1; Restatement of the Law Governing Lawyers §161 (Tent. Draft #8, March 21, 1997).

The rule only applies to lawyers, not to their clients.[104] Thus, in a divorce case one spouse is free to negotiate directly with the other spouse. Lawyers may advise clients of their right to communicate directly with the opposing party but should not assist them in such a communication.[105] Communication in an emergency is also permissible.[106]

In 1995, the ABA broadened Rule 4.2 by substituting the word *person* for *party*. The amendment was intended to make it clear that the rule is not limited to formal parties to litigation, but also applies to persons represented by counsel prior to the institution of formal legal proceedings and also to persons represented by counsel in transactional rather than litigation matters. In jurisdictions that have not adopted this amendment, Model Rule 4.2 may be limited to parties to litigation.[107] The Restatement of the Law Governing Lawyers is in accord with the ABA's 1995 amendment to Model Rule 4.2.[108]

c. Communication with Current Employees of Represented Entities

The application of Rule 4.2 to represented individuals is relatively uncontroversial, but substantial dispute exists about the wisdom of applying the rule to employees of represented corporate parties (or other entities). It is important here to distinguish situations in which individual employees of a corporation are named as parties along with the corporation from cases in which only the corporation is named. If an individual employee is a named party

104. Restatement of the Law Governing Lawyers §158, comm. *k* (Tent. Draft #8, March 21, 1997).

105. Id.

106. Id. comm. *i*.

107. See Grievance Comm. for the S. Dist. of N.Y. v. Simels, 48 F.3d 640 (2d Cir. 1995) (no violation of DR 7-104(A)(1), the Code equivalent of Model Rule 4.2, to interview represented witness and potential co-defendant in drug case because rule uses term "party" and should be narrowly construed); Gaylard v. Homemakers of Montgomery, Inc., 675 So. 2d 363 (Ala. 1996) (not improper under Rule 4.2 to contact employee of defendant prior to filing suit because defendant not a "party" and lawyer did not know that employer was represented by counsel in matter).

108. Restatement of the Law Governing Lawyers §158, comm. *c* (Tent. Draft #8, March 21, 1997).

and is represented by counsel, Rule 4.2 clearly applies and prohibits a lawyer for the opposing party from communicating with the employee-party without the consent of the employee-party's counsel. Suppose, however, that only the corporation is a named party. Does Rule 4.2 prohibit an attorney for the opposing party from communicating with any of the employees of the corporation on the ground that they are "alter egos" of the corporation?

Since artificial entities like corporations can only act through agents, all courts agree that some corporate employees are subject to the no-communication rule. Courts and commentators differ, however, on how broadly to define the class of covered employees. The most favorable approach from the perspective of opposing counsel wishing to obtain information from corporate employees is the "control group" test.[109] Under this test, only upper-level management in position to make decisions on behalf of the corporation is subject to the no-communication rule. All lower-level employees are subject to informal interviews. Some commentators have criticized the "control group" test because it fails to provide sufficient protection to corporations.[110] At the opposite extreme, some authorities argue that the no-communication rule should apply to all corporate employees.[111]

Not surprisingly, neither of the extreme approaches has found much acceptance. Other authorities have searched for a middle ground. For example, in Wright v. Group Health Hospital,[112] the Washington Supreme Court adopted a "managing-speaking agent" test. Under this test, if the employee is a manager or is authorized to speak on behalf of the corporation in the matter in question, then the no-communication rule applies. This approach extends the no-communication rule beyond the control group to some

109. Fair Automotive Repair, Inc. v. Car-X Serv. Sys., Inc., 471 N.E.2d 554 (Ill. Ct. App. 1984).

110. See Jerome N. Krulewitch, Comment, *Ex Parte* Communications with Corporate Parties: The Scope of the Limitations on Attorney Communications with One of Adverse Interest, 82 Nw. U. L. Rev. 1274, 1286-1290 (1988); Sinaiko, Note, Ex Parte Communication and the Corporate Adversary: A New Approach, 66 N.Y.U. L. Rev. at 1481-1484.

111. See Sinaiko, Note, Ex Parte Communication and the Corporate Adversary: A New Approach, 66 N.Y.U. L. Rev. at 1490-1493; see also Samuel R. Miller & Angelo J. Calfo, Ex Parte Contact with Employees and Former Employees of a Corporate Adversary: Is It Ethical?, 42 Bus. Law. 1053, 1071 (1987) (arguing that while the case law is in conflict, lawyers should not contact current employees without consent of corporate counsel).

112. 691 P.2d 564 (Wash. 1984) (en banc).

management employees, but it would not cover lower-level employees who might have been involved in the matter or who were mere witnesses to the matter. Other authorities have argued for a "scope of employment" test or for a "balancing" test.[113]

Model Rule 4.2, comment 4 adopts a broad no-communication rule, one that applies to most, but not necessarily all, employees of a corporation. The comment refers to three classes of employees, all of whom are covered by the no-communication rule:

> In the case of an organization, this Rule prohibits communications by a lawyer for another person or entity concerning the matter in representation with persons having a managerial responsibility on behalf of the organization, and with any other person whose act or omission in connection with that matter may be imputed to the organization for purposes of civil or criminal liability or whose statement may constitute an admission on the part of the organization.

Thus, under comment 4, management-level employees and employees who were involved in the matter (i.e., ones whose act or omission may be imputed to the organization) are subject to the no-communication rule. Further, even employees who were not involved in the matter but who are mere witnesses are also covered by the rule if any statement by such an employee would "constitute an admission on the part of the organization."

When does a statement by an employee constitute an admission against the organization? The rule followed in many states is that a statement by an employee does not constitute an admission unless the employee was authorized to make the statement.[114] Under this rule, a statement by an ordinary employee would not be an admission against the organization. The Federal Rules of Evidence have broadened the category of employee statements that can constitute admissions against the organization. Federal

113. See Krulewitch, Comment, *Ex Parte* Communications with Corporate Parties: The Scope of the Limitations on Attorney Communications with One of Adverse Interest, 82 Nw. U. L. Rev. at 1285-1297; Ernest F. Lidge III, The Ethics of Communicating with an Organization's Employees: An Analysis of the Unworkable "Hybrid" or "Multifactor" Managing-Speaking Agent, ABA and Niesig Tests and a Proposal for a "Supervisor" Standard, 45 Ark. L. Rev. 801 (1993); Sinaiko, Note, Ex Parte Communication and the Corporate Adversary: A New Approach, 66 N.Y.U. L. Rev. at 1482-1495.

114. Sinaiko, Note, Ex Parte Communication and the Corporate Adversary: A New Approach, 66 N.Y.U. L. Rev. at 1459 n.16.

Rule of Evidence 801(d) provides as follows (with emphasis added):

> (d) Statements which are not hearsay.—A statement is not hearsay if—. . .
>
> (2) Admission by party-opponent.—The statement is offered against a party and is
>
> (A) the party's own statement in either an individual or a representative capacity, or
>
> (B) a statement of which the party has manifested an adoption or belief in its truth, or
>
> (C) *a statement by a person authorized by the party to make a statement concerning the subject*, or
>
> (D) *a statement by the party's agent or servant concerning a matter within the scope of the agency or employment, made during the existence of the relationship*, or
>
> (E) a statement by a coconspirator of a party during the course and in furtherance of the conspiracy.

Under Federal Rule 801, therefore, statements made by employees concerning matters within the scope of their employment made while the employment relationship continues constitute admissions against the organization. Even under this broader admission rule, however, not all employee statements constitute admissions. For example, in Wilkinson v. Carnival Cruise Lines, Inc.,[115] a passenger was injured when an electronically activated sliding glass door leading to a swimming pool closed on her foot. At trial the plaintiff offered the testimony of a cabin steward that the defendant had been having problems with the door. The Eleventh Circuit held that the statement was inadmissible under Rule 801(d) because the door was in an area in which the steward was not authorized to work; thus, the statement did not concern a matter that was within the scope of the steward's employment.

Depending on the scope of the rules of evidence dealing with admissions by employees of corporations, Rule 4.2 provides a broad prohibition against ex parte communication with employees of a corporate party. Moreover, comment 4 to Rule 4.2 refers to Rule 3.4(f). That rule states that it is improper for a lawyer to request that a person "refrain from voluntarily giving relevant

115. 920 F.2d 1560 (11th Cir. 1991).

information to another party," but it goes on to provide an exception if the person is "a relative or an employee or other agent of a client." Therefore, an attorney for a corporation could ask all of its employees, whether covered by Rule 4.2 or not, to voluntarily refrain from giving information to opposing counsel except through formal discovery.

The Restatement of the Law Governing Lawyers narrows the scope of the anticontact rule from that found in Model Rule 4.2. Section 159 provides:

> [A] represented non-client includes . . .
>
> (2) a representative of an organization represented by a lawyer:
>
> (a) who supervises, directs or regularly consults with the lawyer concerning the matter or who has power to compromise or settle the matter;
>
> (b) whose acts or omissions may be imputed to the organization for purposes of civil or criminal liability in the matter; or
>
> (c) whose statements, under applicable rules of evidence, would have the effect of binding the organization with respect to proof of the matter.

The Restatement rejects a broad anticontact rule because there is "no justification for permitting one party thus to control entirely the flow of information to opposing parties."[116] In two respects the Restatement narrows the categories of employees subject to the noncontact rule from Model Rule 4.2. First, under section (a) not all managers are subject to the rule.[117] Second, employees who make statements are covered by the Restatement rule only if the statement would be binding on the organization (in the sense that the organization could not introduce evidence to refute the statement) rather than simply being admissible against the entity. The Restatement explains that a "contrary rule would essentially mean that most employees with relevant information would be within the anti-contract rule, contrary to the policies described in Comment *b*."[118]

116. Restatement of the Law Governing Lawyers §159, comm. *b* (Tent. Draft #8, March 21, 1997).

117. Id. comm. *c*, and illus. 1, 2.

118. Id. comm. *e*.

Courts are, of course, free to craft the scope of their anticontact rule. In Niesig v. Team I,[119] the New York Court of Appeals adopted the following test:

> The test that best balances the competing interests, and incorporates the most desirable elements of the other approaches, is one that defines "party" to include corporate employees whose acts or omissions in the matter under inquiry are binding on the corporation (in effect, the corporation's "alter egos") or imputed to the corporation for purposes of its liability, or employees implementing the advice of counsel. All other employees may be interviewed informally.[120]

The *Niesig* test is closer to the Restatement approach than to Rule 4.2.[121] Unlike the comment to that rule, this test allows interviews with employees whose statements would constitute admissions, unless the employee is in one of the three categories listed by the court.[122]

During the course of an otherwise permissible communication with a current employee, a lawyer may not seek to obtain privileged information.[123] Further, even if an attorney may properly communicate with an employee, it may be improper for the attorney to seek documents from the employee because such a request circumvents the discovery process and prevents opposing counsel from raising objections to the discoverability of documents.[124]

The issue of the scope of permissible informal contacts that an investigating lawyer may make with employees of corporate parties involves a tension between competing policies. Lawyers representing clients against corporations need to be able to investigate the facts fully to properly represent their clients. Indeed, Rule 11 of the Federal Rules of Civil Procedure and ABA Model Rule 3.1 require adequate investigation. A rule that prohibits communication with employees of a corporate party who may have been

119. 558 N.E.2d 1030 (N.Y. 1990).

120. Id. at 1035.

121. Restatement of the Law Governing Lawyers §159, Reporter's Note (Tent. Draft #8, March 21, 1997).

122. See also Dent v. Kaufman, 406 S.E.2d 68 (W. Va. 1991) (following *Niesig* test, indicating that test was similar to but clearer than comment to Rule 4.2).

123. Restatement of the Law Governing Lawyers §162 (Tent. Draft #8, March 21, 1997).

124. See In re Shell Oil Refinery (Adams v. Shell Oil Co.), 143 F.R.D. 105 (E.D. La. 1992) (protective order entered requiring disclosure of documents obtained through ex parte contact with former employee and prohibiting their use in case).

witnesses to an accident or who may otherwise have relevant information interferes with the opposing counsel's ability to investigate the facts. While an attorney could always take the deposition of an employee after a suit has been filed, depositions are more expensive than interviews and may be impractical when large numbers of employees are involved. Also, in most jurisdictions an attorney cannot take a deposition or use other discovery devices prior to filing suit. In much modern litigation, the informational and resource balance favors the defense. Given this defense advantage, it seems reasonable to give plaintiffs greater investigative leeway so long as they do not encroach on privileged material. While corporations have a legitimate interest in not having privileged information revealed, the current rules seem overly broad in protecting that interest. A better balance would be struck by prohibiting informal contacts with control group members and with those who are carrying out the advice of counsel in the matter, but allowing informal communications with all other employees, provided copies of all statements are provided to opposing counsel.

d. Communication with Former Employees

Does Rule 4.2 apply to former rather than current employees? The argument against applying the rule to former employees is that they are no longer in a position to make a decision or admission on behalf of the corporation. On the other hand, if the former employee was involved in the matter in controversy, his conduct is still attributed to the corporation even though he has left employment. Further, an attorney communicating with a former employee could learn confidential information or could obtain privileged documents. A number of cases have considered the issue and the vast majority have ruled that an attorney may communicate with a former employee so long as the attorney does not try to obtain confidential or privileged information.[125]

125. Valassis v. Samelson, 143 F.R.D. 118 (E.D. Mich. 1992) (since Rule 4.2 only applies to parties, it does not apply to former employees who are no longer agents of entities); Dubois v. Gradco Systems, Inc., 136 F.R.D. 341 (D. Conn. 1991) (permissible to interview former employee so long as no privileged information sought); Polycast Technology Corp. v. Uniroyal, Inc., 129 F.R.D. 621 (S.D.N.Y. 1990) (DR 7-104 does not prohibit contacts with former corporate employees, at least when no showing that employee possessed privileged information); Conti-

In Formal Opinion 91-359, the ABA Committee on Ethics and Professional Responsibility adopted this majority view and ruled that lawyers were not prohibited from communicating with former employees under Model Rule 4.2, but the Committee cautioned attorneys about the possible application of other rules:

> With respect to *any* unrepresented former employee, of course, the potentially communicating adversary attorney must be careful not to seek to induce the former employee to violate the privilege attaching to attorney-client communications . . . . Such an attempt could violate Rule 4.4 (requiring respect for the rights of third persons).
>
> The lawyer should also punctiliously comply with the requirements of Rule 4.3, which addresses a lawyer's dealings with unrepresented persons. That rule, insofar as pertinent here, requires that the lawyer contacting a former employee of an opposing corporate party make clear the nature of the lawyer's role in the matter giving occasion for the contact, including the identity of the lawyer's client and the fact that the witness's former employer is an adverse party. . . .[126]

Similarly, the Restatement of the Law Governing Lawyers provides that communication with former employees is generally proper, except under limited circumstances, for example if the former employee continues to consult with counsel for the entity.[127] The Restatement also seems to adopt the view followed by some deci-

---

nental Ins. Co. v. Superior Court, 37 Cal. Rptr. 2d 843 (Cal. Ct. App. 1995) (California Rule 2-100 does not apply to former employees); H.B.A. Management, Inc. v. Estate of Schwartz, 693 So. 2d 541 (Fla. 1997) (no prohibition on communication with former employees because employee cannot bind entity; communication allowed even with employee whose conduct may be imputed to defendant in matter); Wright v. Group Health Hosp., 691 P.2d 564 (Wash. 1984) (en banc) (former employees could not possibly speak for or bind corporation). *Contra* Public Serv. Elec. & Gas Co. v. Associated Elec. & Gas Ins. Serv., Ltd., 745 F. Supp. 1037 (D.N.J. 1990) (Rule 4.2 covers all former employees); Porter v. Arco Metals Co., 642 F. Supp. 1116, 1118 (D. Mont. 1986) (rule bars communication with former employees who had "managerial responsibilities concerning the matter in litigation"). For an argument that contact with former employees should be regulated by amendment to the rules of civil procedure, see John E. Iole & John D. Goetz, Ethics or Procedure? A Discovery-Based Approach to Ex Parte Contacts with Former Employees of a Corporate Adversary, 68 Notre Dame L. Rev. 81 (1992).

126. ABA Comm. on Ethics and Prof. Resp., Formal Opinion 91-359, at 6.

127. Restatement of the Law Governing Lawyers §159, comm. *g* (Tent. Draft #8, March 21, 1997).

sions that a lawyer may not communicate with a former employee who has been "extensively exposed" to privileged information.[128]

e. Contacts with Represented Targets of Government Criminal Investigations

Model Rule 4.2 also has evoked controversy in the criminal context, particularly between the defense bar and federal prosecutors. The controversy began with the Second Circuit's decision in United States v. Hammad,[129] which held that an informant's contact with the suspect of a criminal investigation at the prosecutor's direction violated the no-communication rule. The Justice Department considered this to be a significant impediment to its law enforcement activities because major criminals were often represented by counsel while they were under investigation. In response, then Attorney General Richard Thornburgh issued an internal memorandum purporting to exempt all Justice Department lawyers from the ethics rule on the ground that, by virtue of federal law, their law enforcement activities were "authorized by law" within the meaning of the rule. The defense bar objected to this position, and the ABA adopted a resolution opposing the Thornburgh memorandum on the ground that it attempted to exempt Justice Department lawyers from the ethical obligations generally applicable to attorneys.[130]

The controversy continues to rage. The Second Circuit withdrew its earlier decision in the *Hammad* case. Its revised opinion provided that "legitimate investigative techniques" fell within the "au-

128. Id. §162, comm. *d.* See Camden v. Maryland, 910 F. Supp. 1115 (D. Md. 1996) (ex parte communication with university's former principal contact person in employment discrimination suit results in disqualification of plaintiff's counsel; court adopts Restatement rule prohibiting contacts with former employees who have been "extensively exposed" to confidential information).

129. 846 F.2d 854 (2d Cir.), *withdrawn*, 858 F.2d 834 (2d Cir. 1988), *cert. denied*, 498 U.S. 871 (1990).

130. For different perspectives on the issue, see Roger C. Cramton & Lisa K. Udell, State Ethics Rules and Federal Prosecutors: The Controversies over the Anti-Contact and Subpoena Rules, 53 U. Pitts. L. Rev. 291, 318-324 (1992); Nancy J. Moore, Intra-Professional Warfare Between Prosecutors and Defense Attorneys: A Plea for an End to the Current Hostilities, 53 U. Pitts. L. Rev. 515, 519-530 (1992); F. Dennis Saylor IV & J. Douglas Wilson, Putting a Square Peg in a Round Hole: The Application of Model Rule 4.2 to Federal Prosecutors, 53 U. Pitts. L. Rev. 459 (1992).

thorized by law" exception, although cases could arise in which prosecutors overstep their authority, leading to the suppression of evidence.[131] Other courts have rejected the position that the anti-contact rule applies at all until formal adversary proceedings have commenced against the defendant.[132] The Justice Department, under a new administration, has continued to assert its right to exempt government lawyers from the operation of state ethics rules under the Supremacy Clause of the United States Constitution, and it has issued a new regulation defining the scope of permissible contacts by government attorneys with individuals and organizations who are represented by counsel. The Department summarized the regulation as follows:

> In essence, this regulation permits federal prosecutors and agents to continue to conduct legitimate criminal and civil investigations against all individuals, whether or not those persons are represented by counsel. It allows government attorneys to continue to make or direct undercover or overt contacts with individuals and organizations represented by counsel for the purpose of developing factual information up until the point at which they are arrested or charged with a crime or named as defendants in a civil law enforcement action. However, the regulation generally does not permit federal prosecutors to attempt to negotiate plea agreements, settlements, or similar arrangements with individuals represented by counsel without the consent of their attorneys. This regulation also precludes, with certain narrow exceptions, any contacts with represented parties after an arrest, indictment, or the filing of a complaint on the subject matter of the representation.[133]

The ABA Committee on Ethics and Professional Responsibility, however, has issued a formal opinion questioning whether the Justice Department's regulation qualifies for the "authorized by law" exception to Model Rule 4.2. The Committee stated:

> The Committee believes that such directives will qualify as "law" for purposes of the Rule only when embodied in formal regulations

131. United States v. Hammad, 858 F.2d 834, 839 (2d Cir. 1988), *cert. denied*, 498 U.S. 871 (1990).

132. See United States v. Balter, 91 F.3d 427 (3d Cir. 1996); United States v. Heinz, 983 F.2d 609 (5th Cir. 1993); United States v. Ryans, 903 F.2d 731 (10th Cir.), *cert. denied*, 498 U.S. 855 (1990).

133. 59 Fed. Reg. 39,910 (Aug. 4, 1994) (codified at 28 C.F.R. pt. 77) (Summary).

> that have been properly promulgated pursuant to statutory authority that contemplates regulation of the character in question. Were any other regulation or fiat by an agency head to be considered an authorization by law, any government agency could "authorize" its lawyers to engage in conduct expressly prohibited by ethical codes simply by promulgating a regulation or policy.[134]

The Restatement does not take a position on this controversial issue other than to state that compliance by prosecutors with lawful regulations is permissible.[135]

f. Communication with Unrepresented People and Witnesses

The preceding sections examined the prohibition against any communication by lawyers with people who are represented by counsel in the matter. The prohibition on communication does not apply when lawyers deal with people who are not represented by counsel. For example, a lawyer may interview an unrepresented witness in litigation or negotiate a business matter on behalf of a client with an unrepresented person. Before communicating with people who may be represented by counsel in a matter, lawyers should inquire about representation and should cease any communication if the person is represented by counsel.

In dealing with unrepresented people, lawyers are, of course, prohibited from engaging in misrepresentation.[136] Because nonclients may misunderstand the lawyer's role, lawyers must exercise caution to clarify their role when dealing with nonclients. Model Rule 4.3 provides as follows:

> RULE 4.3 DEALING WITH UNREPRESENTED PERSON
>
> In dealing on behalf of a client with a person who is not represented by counsel, a lawyer shall not state or imply that the lawyer is disinterested. When the lawyer knows or reasonably should know that the unrepresented person misunderstands the lawyer's role in

134. ABA Comm. on Ethics and Prof. Resp., Formal Op. 95-396, at 22.

135. Restatement of the Law Governing Lawyers §158, comm. *h* (Tent. Draft #8, March 21, 1997).

136. Model Rule 4.1(a) and Restatement of the Law Governing Lawyers §157(1) (Tent. Draft #8, March 21, 1997).

> the matter, the lawyer shall make reasonable efforts to correct the misunderstanding.

The Restatement is similar.[137]

Giving legal advice constitutes the most difficult issue in dealing with nonclients. If lawyers purport to give advice to unrepresented people, they will either act inconsistently with their clients' interests or give incomplete and misleading advice to unrepresented people. On the other hand, a total prohibition on making any statements that relate to the law to an unrepresented person would be impractical and would amount to a rule prohibiting lawyers from dealing with anyone unless they were represented by counsel. The Model Rules provide little guidance on this issue. The comment to Model Rule 4.3 states: "During the course of a lawyer's representation of a client, the lawyer should not give advice to an unrepresented person other than the advice to obtain counsel." The Restatement rejects a blanket prohibition of giving legal advice. Under the Restatement, a lawyer may provide documents to an unrepresented person for that person's signature and may explain the general nature of the documents or of the transaction with the person. If the unrepresented person has specific legal questions, however, the lawyer should inform the person of the lawyer's role and suggest that the person obtain the advice of counsel.[138]

Another troublesome situation regarding dealings with unrepresented people arises when a lawyer for an entity is investigating a matter on behalf of the entity and is interviewing employees or other constituents who may have engaged in improper conduct. The interest of the entity client generally favors obtaining information about the matter in question, but revelation by the employee may be damaging to the employee's interest. The problem becomes particularly acute when the lawyer has dealt with the employee previously and the employee may look on the attorney as "my lawyer." Model Rule 1.13(d) requires entity lawyers to explain their role to constituents "when it is apparent that the organization's interests are adverse to those of the constituents with whom the lawyer is dealing." The Restatement is generally in accord. It provides that lawyers are not always required to provide a "*Miranda*

137. Restatement of the Law Governing Lawyers §163 (Tent. Draft #8, March 21, 1997).

138. Id. §163, comm. *d*.

warning" when investigating employees and other constituents. A warning may be necessary, however, when the lawyer does not reasonably believe that the employee understands that the lawyer represents the organization.[139] The Model Rules and the Restatement disagree, however, on the content of the warning to a constituent when a warning is required. Comment 8 to Model Rule 1.13 indicates that the lawyer should give an elaborate warning: The lawyer cannot advise the constituent, the constituent should consider retaining independent counsel, and any discussions between the lawyer and the constituent will not be privileged as to the lawyer's client. The Restatement favors a more limited warning in which the lawyer simply explains that the lawyer represents the entity, not the constituent.[140] On the content of the warning, the Restatement seems correct. Since the lawyer represents the entity, not the constituent, doubt about the scope of the warning should be resolved in favor of the entity. An elaborate warning would cause most employees to refuse to discuss the matter further and would therefore significantly interfere with the lawyer's ability to investigate the matter on behalf of the entity client.

3. *Discovery*

Informal fact investigation and formal discovery are designed to allow parties to gather information that can then be used in settlement negotiations or at trial. Quite clearly the rules structuring this process are designed to increase the likelihood of truthful results.

But the investigation and discovery process suffer from a fundamental problem. Because investigation and discovery, unlike trial, do not take place under the direct scrutiny of judges, lawyers have an incentive to engage in opportunistic behavior: to attempt to gain as much information while sharing as little information as possible. Discovery abuse has been defined as "(1) propounding unnecessarily broad discovery requests; and (2) withholding information from the propounding party to which that party is entitled."[141] How extensive is the problem of discovery abuse? Studies conducted in 1978 and 1980-1981 found discovery abuse to be a

139. Id. §163, comm. *e*.

140. Id. §163, Reporter's Note to comm. *e*.

141. Earl C. Dudley, Jr., Discovery Abuse Revisited: Some Specific Proposals to Amend the Federal Rules of Civil Procedure, 26 U.S.F. L. Rev. 189, 194 (1992).

significant problem, particularly in large cases.[142] A Harris poll conducted in 1989 of 200 federal judges and 800 state judges produced the following results:[143]

Q: Would you say that there are a lot, some, not many, or no problems with the discovery process in your jurisdiction?

	Federal Judges	*State Judges*
Base:	200	800
	%	%
Yes, A Lot of Problems	33	30
Yes, Some Problems	50	50
No, Not Many Problems	16	16
No, No Problems	3	4

Other writers, however, have argued that the view that the judicial system is infected by pervasive discovery abuse is unsupported.[144]

Assuming discovery abuse is a problem, what steps can be taken to deal with the issue? To the extent that part of the problem lies in lack of clarity in the rules governing discovery, the rules can be amended to provide lawyers with more specific guidance.[145] For example, until 1993 the Federal Rules of Civil Procedure failed to define improper conduct by lawyers during depositions. In 1993, the Federal Rules were amended to provide greater specificity regarding proper deposition conduct. Rule 30(d)(1) now provides as follows:

142. Paul R. Connolly et al., Judicial Controls and The Civil Litigative Process: Discovery (Federal Judicial Center 1978); Wayne D. Brazil, Views from the Front Lines: Observations by Chicago Lawyers About the System of Civil Discovery, 1980 Am. B. Found. Res. J. 217; Wayne D. Brazil, Civil Discovery: Lawyers' Views of Its Effectiveness, Its Principal Problems and Abuses, 1980 Am. B. Found. Res. J. 787; Wayne D. Brazil, Improving Judicial Controls over the Pretrial Development of Civil Actions: Model Rules for Case Management and Sanctions, 1981 Am. B. Found. Res. J. 875.

143. Louis Harris & Associates, Inc., Judges' Opinions on Procedural Issues: A Survey of State and Federal Trial Judges Who Spend at Least Half Their Time on General Civil Cases, 69 B.U. L. Rev. 731, 737 (1989) (Table 2.1).

144. See Linda S. Mullenix, Discovery in Disarray: The Pervasive Myth of Pervasive Discovery Abuse and the Consequences for Unfounded Rulemaking, 46 Stan. L. Rev. 1393 (1994); Jack B. Weinstein, What Discovery Abuse?, 69 B.U. L. Rev. 649 (1989).

145. Craig Enoch, Incivility in the Legal System? Maybe It's the Rules, 47 SMU L. Rev. 199 (1994) (arguing for change in rules to remove tools that enable lawyers to engage in abuse).

> Any objection to evidence during a deposition shall be stated concisely and in a non-argumentative and non-suggestive manner. A party may instruct a deponent not to answer only when necessary to preserve a privilege, to enforce a limitation on evidence directed by the court, or to present a motion under paragraph (3) [dealing with deposition conducted in bad faith].

A number of federal district courts have gone even further, adopting detailed guidelines for conducting depositions to deal with some of the problems that have arisen.[146]

Many cases of discovery abuse, however, do not flow from any lack of clarity in the rules. In Paramount Communications Inc. v. QVC Network Inc.,[147] the Delaware Supreme Court strongly condemned the conduct of well-known Texas attorney Joseph Jamail during a deposition taken in the case in which Jamail referred to opposing counsel as an "asshole" and told him that he could "gag a maggot off a meat wagon."[148] While the court was unable to impose sanctions on Mr. Jamail because he was not admitted to practice in Delaware either by regular or pro hac vice admission, the court expressed its strong opposition to such tactics and warned Delaware lawyers against participating in such misconduct.[149]

Another significant case of discovery abuse is Washington State Physicians Insurance Exchange & Assn. v. Fisons Corp.[150] *Fisons* was a products liability and medical malpractice case in which the plaintiffs claimed that a two-year-old girl suffered seizures and permanent brain damage caused by excessive amounts of the drug theophylline in her system. The defendant doctor cross-claimed against Fisons. Both the plaintiffs and the doctor served interrogatories and requests for production of documents on Fisons seeking correspondence between Fisons and other doctors about the hazards of the drug. Fisons failed to produce "dear doctor" letters that

146. See Standing Orders of the Court on Effective Discovery in Civil Cases, 102 F.R.D. 339 (E.D.N.Y. 1984); Hall v. Clifton Precision, Inc., 150 F.R.D. 525 (E.D. Pa. 1993).

147. 637 A.2d 34 (Del. 1994).

148. Id. at 54.

149. Id. at 53-56. For another example of misconduct by both plaintiff and defense counsel during depositions, see Eggleston v. Chicago Journeymen Plumbers' Local Union No. 130, U.A., 657 F.2d 890 (7th Cir. 1981), *cert. denied*, 455 U.S. 1017 (1982).

150. 858 P.2d 1054 (Wash. 1993) (en banc).

had been sent to other doctors warning about some of the dangers of the drug. The company simultaneously objected to the requests on spurious grounds while stating that, without waiving its objections, it would produce letters at times that were convenient to it. The Washington Supreme Court characterized Fisons conduct as follows:

> It appears clear that no conceivable discovery request could have been made by the doctor that would have uncovered the relevant documents, given the above and other responses of the drug company. The objections did not specify that certain documents were not being produced. Instead the general objections were followed by a promise to produce requested documents. These responses did not comply with either the spirit or letter of the discovery rules and thus were signed in violation of the certification requirement.[151]

In both *Paramount Communications* and *Fisons*, it appears that the lawyers were intentionally ignoring rules and standards of conduct because they believed that their actions served the interests of their clients. What can be done about flagrant disregard of rules of procedure? The professionalism movement represents one attempt to deal with what some lawyers and judges consider to be excessive zealousness. In broad terms, the professionalism movement refers to the promulgation by national, state, or local bar associations of a set of principles that the drafters believe embody the ideal of professional behavior for lawyers. Unlike the Model Rules, these standards are not binding but are instead intended to guide lawyers in the conduct of the practice of law. Professionalism standards focus on a wide range of problems that the drafters view as afflicting the legal profession, including commercialization, lack of competency, and excessive zeal.[152]

The ABA has not itself adopted standards of professionalism, but it did give approval to the Lawyer's Creed of Professionalism prepared by the Torts and Insurance Practice Section of the ABA. At its August 1988 meeting, the ABA House of Delegates adopted as ABA policy the recommendation of this section that state and local bar associations "encourage their members to accept as a guide for their individual conduct, and to comply with, a lawyers'

151. Id. at 1083.

152. See generally ABA Section of Legal Education and Admissions to the Bar, Teaching and Learning Professionalism (1996).

creed of professionalism." The House of Delegates made clear, however, that

> nothing in such a creed shall be deemed to supersede or in any way amend the Model Rules of Professional Conduct or other disciplinary codes, alter existing standards of conduct against which lawyer negligence might be judged or become a basis for the imposition of civil liability of any kind.

The ABA also authorized for dissemination to the profession the Lawyers' Pledge of Professionalism prepared by the ABA Young Lawyers Division.[153]

The professionalism movement seems to be based on three assumptions: First, professionalism has in fact declined. Second, the cause of the decline is a lack of knowledge by lawyers, particularly young lawyers, of basic standards of professional behavior. Third, development of a set of broad standards to supplement the Model Rules can improve professionalism. All three propositions are doubtful. First, the legal profession has undergone considerable change during the last 25 years, but much change has been for the better. The legal profession is more open to women and minorities and more competitive than it has been in the past. Openness and free markets are principles that our society values highly. Second, the drafters of professionalism creeds have offered no evidence to show that lack of knowledge of standards of behavior is the cause of any decline in professionalism. Many of the reported cases of professional abuse like *Paramount Communications* and *Fisons* involve established members of the bar, not novices who are unfamiliar with the rules. It is more plausible to believe that lawyers engage in marginal behavior because they decide that it serves their own interests and those of their clients, and because the risk of significant sanctions is small. Third, the remedy proposed by the professionalism movement is almost certain to be ineffective. Broad standards of behavior like those found in most professionalism standards provide little guidance in difficult cases. Moreover, these standards are expressly stated to be nonbinding.

The ultimate answer to discovery abuse lies in addressing the basic cause: Absence of judicial oversight has meant that lawyers

153. Lawyers' Man. Prof. Conduct (ABA/BNA) at 1:401.

have the incentive and opportunity to use the rules for their own interest rather than to live by the spirit of the rules.[154] *Paramount Communications* and *Fisons* may be examples of a changing judicial attitude toward overzealousness, but unfortunately many trial judges probably still remain reluctant to become involved in discovery disputes except in very extreme cases. Until this judicial attitude changes, discovery abuse will continue to plague litigation.

4. *Improper Trial Conduct*

Under an adversarial system of justice, attorneys are granted wide latitude in the presentation of cases on behalf of their clients, subject to general rules of law, court rules, and court orders.[155] Nonetheless, some specific restrictions apply to attorney conduct in dealing with documents and other real evidence, examination of witnesses, and advocacy.

Destruction or falsification of evidence directly undermines the truthfulness of legal proceedings and is both unethical[156] and illegal.[157] Many companies have document destruction programs and lawyers can face difficult questions of whether a client's compliance with such a program is improper. If the documents are subject to subpoena or court order, they clearly cannot be destroyed, but prudent lawyers would counsel clients against destruction of documents when the lawyer knows that legal proceedings in which the documents would have substantial evidentiary value are likely to occur within a reasonable period of time.[158] As discussed in Chapter 4 lawyers who obtain possession of stolen property or of physi-

154. See Charles Yablon, Stupid Lawyer Tricks: An Essay on Discovery Abuse, 96 Colum. L. Rev. 1618 (1996) (calling for more aggressive action by judges in responding to discovery abuse).

155. See Model Rule 3.4(c); Restatement of the Law Governing Lawyers §165 (Tent. Draft #8, March 21, 1997).

156. See Model Rule 3.4(a); In re Barrow, 294 S.E.2d 785 (S.C. 1982) (discipline for removing warning label in products liability case).

157. ALI, Model Penal Code §241.7 (1962) (offense of tampering with or fabricating evidence). See also Restatement of the Law Governing Lawyers §178 (Tent. Draft #8, March 21, 1997).

158. Restatement of the Law Governing Lawyers §178, comm. *c* (Tent. Draft #8, March 21, 1997).

cal evidence of a crime have a duty to turn this material over to the authorities within a reasonable period of time.[159]

A number of ethical and legal restrictions apply when lawyers deal with or examine witnesses.[160] Lawyers may not unlawfully interfere with the other side's access to a witness.[161] Further, lawyers may not request a witness to refrain from voluntarily giving information to the other side unless the witness is a client or the relative, employee, or agent of a client and the lawyer reasonably believes that the person will not be materially and adversely affected by a refusal to give information.[162]

Witnesses fall into two broad categories: fact witnesses and expert witnesses. The Model Rules provide that lawyers may not pay witnesses fees that are prohibited by law. Model Rule 3.4(b). As comment 3 indicates, the rule in most jurisdictions is that fact witnesses cannot be paid a fee for testifying, but they may be paid their expenses and any lost wages that they suffer because of time spent in testifying.[163] In Formal Opinion 96-402, the ABA Committee decided that lawyers could ethically pay fact witnesses a reasonable amount for their time in preparing for and in attending depositions. Expert witnesses may be paid reasonable fees for testifying, but the general rule is that expert witnesses may not be paid a fee contingent on their testimony or on the outcome of the case. Comment 3 to Rule 3.4(b).[164] The proposed Restatement of the Law Governing Lawyers follows the Model Rules.[165]

159. See Chapter 4.F supra; Restatement of the Law Governing Lawyers §§57, comm. *f* (Proposed Final Draft #1, March 29, 1996) (stolen property), 179 (Tent. Draft #8, March 21, 1997) (physical evidence of crime).

160. See Chapter 3.O supra on ethical and legal restrictions on a lawyer's acting as both advocate and witness at trial.

161. Restatement of the Law Governing Lawyers §176(2) (Tent. Draft #8, March 21, 1997).

162. Model Rule 3.4(f); Restatement of the Law Governing Lawyers §176(4) (Tent. Draft #8, March 21, 1997).

163. See Golden Door Jewelry Creations, Inc. v. Lloyds Underwriters Non-Marine Assn., 865 F. Supp. 1516 (S.D. Fla. 1994) *aff'd*, 117 F.3d 1328 (11th Cir. 1997) (defendant violated Rule 3.4(b) by paying fact witnesses for their testimony; court ordered all testimony tainted by improper payments to be stricken).

164. The District of Columbia Rules of Professional Conduct provide that an expert witness's fee may be contingent on the outcome of the case provided that the fee is not a percentage of the recovery. See D.C. R. Prof. Conduct 3.4, comm. 8.

165. Restatement of the Law Governing Lawyers §177 (Tent. Draft #8 March 21, 1997).

In preparing witnesses for trial, lawyers must distinguish the fine line between legitimate preparation and improper encouragement of false testimony. The proposed Restatement of the Law Governing Lawyers provides useful guidance on the difference:

> In preparing a witness to testify, a lawyer may invite the witness to provide truthful testimony favorable to the lawyer's client. Preparation consistent with the rule of this Section may include the following: discussing the role of the witness and effective courtroom demeanor; discussing the witness's recollection and probable testimony; revealing to the witness other testimony or evidence that will be presented and asking the witness to reconsider the witness's recollection or recounting of events in that light; discussing the applicability of law to the events in issue; reviewing the factual context into which the witness's observations or opinions will fit; reviewing documents or other physical evidence that may be introduced; and discussing probable lines of hostile cross-examination that the witness should be prepared to meet. Witness preparation may include rehearsal of testimony. A lawyer may suggest choice of words that might be employed to make the witness's meaning clear. However, a lawyer may not assist the witness to testify falsely as to a material fact.[166]

In examining witnesses, lawyers are bound to follow the rules of civil procedure and evidence in the applicable jurisdiction. Model Rule 3.4(c) provides that a lawyer shall not "knowingly disobey an obligation under the rules of a tribunal except for an open refusal based on an assertion that no valid obligation exists."[167] In addition, Rule 3.4(e) provides that a lawyer shall not

> in trial, allude to any matter that the lawyer does not reasonably believe is relevant or that will not be supported by admissible evidence, assert personal knowledge of facts in issue except when testifying as a witness, or state a personal opinion as to the justness of a cause, the credibility of a witness, the culpability of a civil litigant or the guilt or innocence of an accused.

166. Restatement of the Law Governing Lawyers §176, comm. *b* (Tent. Draft #8, March 21, 1997). See John S. Applegate, Witness Preparation, 68 Tex. L. Rev. 277 (1989); Richard C. Wydick, The Ethics of Witness Coaching, 17 Cardozo L. Rev. 1 (1995).

167. See generally William H. Fortune, et al., Modern Litigation and Professional Responsibility Handbook Chs. 9-13 (1996).

The Restatement expresses similar obligations.[168] If a lawyer anticipates that opposing counsel may attempt to engage in examination or offer evidence that is inadmissible, counsel should file a motion in limine seeking judicial determination of the issue in advance of trial.[169]

May a lawyer cross-examine a witness that the lawyer knows is telling the truth for the purpose of undermining the credibility of the witness? The basis for a lawyer's conclusion that a witness is telling the truth will often flow from confidential communications with the client. If lawyers are precluded from examining witnesses because of information gained from their clients, clients will become reluctant to share damaging information and the attorney-client relationship will be undermined.[170] The Model Rules support the view that lawyers may properly attempt to undermine the credibility of a witness that the lawyer knows is telling the truth. Model Rule 4.4 states:

> In representing a client, a lawyer shall not use means that have no substantial purpose other than to embarrass, delay, or burden a third person, or use methods of obtaining evidence that violate the legal rights of such a person.

Cross-examination of the truthful witness, however, has a substantial purpose other than harming the witness: calling into question the witness's credibility.[171] Similarly, the Restatement provides that lawyers may attempt to discredit a witness the lawyer knows is telling the truth, although the Restatement indicates that lawyers retain professional discretion whether to exercise this power.[172] The ABA Standards for the Prosecution and the Defense express different positions on the issue of cross-examination of the truthful witness. ABA Standard for the Prosecution Function 3-5.7(b) states:

168. Restatement of the Law Governing Lawyers §§165 (compliance with law, rules, and tribunal rulings), 167 (prohibition on reference to inadmissible evidence and expression of personal opinion) (Tent. Draft #8, March 21, 1997).

169. See William H. Fortune, et al., Modern Litigation and Professional Responsibility Handbook §11.6 at 370-371 (1996).

170. For a philosophical and moral justification for lawyers' cross-examination of truthful witnesses, see Monroe H. Freedman, Understanding Lawyers' Ethics 161-168 (1990).

171. See 2 Hazard & Hodes, The Law of Lawyering §4.4:102, at 756.

172. Restatement of the Law Governing Lawyers §166, comm. *c* (Tent. Draft #8, March 21, 1997).

> The prosecutor's belief that the witness is telling the truth does not preclude cross-examination, but may affect the method and scope of cross-examination. A prosecutor should not use the power of cross-examination to discredit or undermine a witness if the prosecutor knows the witness is testifying truthfully.

ABA Standard for the Defense Function 4-7.6(b), however, states: "Defense counsel's belief or knowledge that the witness is telling the truth does not preclude cross-examination."

While scores of books have been written on argumentative technique, the rules of ethics regarding argument are relatively sparse. Lawyers must, of course, comply with rules of procedure in connection with their arguments.[173] For example, this prohibition makes improper any argument based on inadmissible evidence or that appeals to bias or prejudice.[174] The rules prohibit lawyers from expressing personal belief or personal opinion regarding the merits of the case, although lawyers who are unable to convey (as opposed to say) genuine belief in their clients' cases are unlikely to be successful advocates.[175]

May a lawyer argue for inferences that he knows are false but that are reasonably supportable by the evidence? The question is similar to the question of whether it is proper for a lawyer to cross-examine a witness the lawyer knows is telling the truth. Case law seems to support the proposition that defense counsel may do so, but that it is improper for a prosecutor to adopt this tactic. An interesting example is United States v. Latimer,[176] a prosecution for bank robbery. At trial, two tellers testified that they had activated the bank's camera system during the robbery. The government failed to introduce any pictures because the camera malfunctioned, but it also failed to offer evidence of the malfunction. In closing argument, defense counsel contended that the jury should draw the inference from the government's failure to offer the film that the film did not identify the defendant, even though defense counsel knew that the camera was not working. In rebuttal, the United

173. See Model Rule 3.4(c); Restatement of the Law Governing Lawyers §165 (Tent. Draft #8, March 21, 1997). See generally William H. Fortune, et al., Modern Litigation and Professional Responsibility Handbook ch. 13 (1996).

174. Id. §§13.3.6., 13.6.4.

175. Model Rule 3.4(e) and Restatement of the Law Governing Lawyers §167(1) (Tent. Draft #8, March 21, 1997).

176. 511 F.2d 498 (10th Cir. 1975).

States attorney explained to the jury that the camera was inoperative.[177] The Tenth Circuit held that defense counsel properly argued for a favorable inference from the evidence. The court went on to find that the prosecutor had acted improperly. The court noted that even if defense counsel had made an improper argument, that does not open the door for an improper response by the prosecutor.[178] The court then discussed two ways in which the prosecutor's argument was improper:

> First, the argument went outside the record and made statements as to facts not proven . . . . Second, the statement put the personal knowledge and belief of the prosecuting attorney on the scales, which is also clearly improper.[179]

As a result the court remanded for a new trial.

E. NEGOTIATION

Negotiation spans all areas in which lawyers practice, both litigation and nonlitigation. In litigation practice, some settlements are subject to court approval, for example, settlements involving minors and class actions. On the whole, however, negotiated settlements, unlike litigation itself, are not subject to court rules. Given this lack of rules, what standards of conduct should govern lawyers in connection with negotiation of settlements?

The first section of this chapter argued that rules of professional conduct should prohibit lawyers from engaging in conduct that undermines the purpose or process of an adversarial system of dispute resolution. Since settlement agreements are a part of that system, it should also be improper for a lawyer to participate in a settlement agreement that undermines the purpose of the system of dispute resolution.

177. Id. at 502 nn.5-6.
178. Id. at 503. See also United States v. Young, 470 U.S. 1 (1985).
179. 511 F.2d at 503.

1. *Participation in Contractually Invalid Settlement Agreements*

When does a settlement agreement undermine the system of dispute resolution? A settlement agreement is a contract, but a particular type of contract — one formed to resolve a dispute. Contracts are voidable for a variety of reasons, including incapacity, misrepresentation, nondisclosure, mistake, duress, undue influence, and unconscionability.[180] It seems inconsistent with the purpose of the system of dispute resolution for a lawyer to participate in a settlement agreement when the lawyer knows that the agreement would not constitute a valid resolution of the dispute because the agreement is voidable under applicable contract law.

A short book such as this one cannot cover all of the contractual theories on which a settlement agreement could be voidable, but we will consider several doctrines that are particularly applicable to settlement negotiations, including misrepresentation, nondisclosure, mistake, and duress. Section 164(1) of the Restatement (Second) of Contracts provides that a contract is voidable if the agreement results from a either a fraudulent or a material misrepresentation on which the recipient is justified in relying. Section 162 goes on to define fraudulent and material misrepresentations as follows:

> (1) A misrepresentation is fraudulent if the maker intends his assertion to induce a party to manifest his assent and the maker
>
> (a) knows or believes that the assertion is not in accord with the facts, or
>
> (b) does not have the confidence that he states or implies in the truth of the assertion, or
>
> (c) knows that he does not have the basis that he states or implies for the assertion.
>
> (2) A misrepresentation is material if it would be likely to induce a reasonable person to manifest his assent, or if the maker knows that it would be likely to induce the recipient to do so.

Consider how these concepts would apply to four common representations made by lawyers during settlement negotiations: opin-

180. See Charles L. Knapp & Nathan M. Crystal, Problems in Contract Law chs. 8 and 9 (3d ed 1993).

ions about the relative merits of each side's case, facts of the case, settlement authority, and settlement demands.

During negotiations lawyers will normally make arguments to the opposing counsel about the relative merits of each side's case. Sometimes a lawyer will provide the other side with a candid assessment of the strengths and weaknesses of the lawyer's case, but more typically lawyers will misrepresent their actual opinions about the value of the case. This does not amount to improper behavior, however; under principles of contract law, a misrepresentation will invalidate a contract only when the recipient is justified in relying on the representation. In an adversarial process in which both parties are represented by counsel, neither party is justified in relying on representations by the other party about the merits of the case. Professor James White has used an analogy to poker to justify misrepresentations by lawyers of their opinions about the strength of their cases:

> Like the poker player, a negotiator hopes that his opponent will overestimate the value of his hand. Like the poker player, in a variety of ways he must facilitate his opponent's inaccurate assessment. The critical difference between those who are successful negotiators and those who are not lies in this capacity both to mislead and not to be misled.
>
> Some experienced negotiators will deny the accuracy of this assertion, but they will be wrong. I submit that a careful examination of the behavior of even the most forthright, honest, and trustworthy negotiators will show them actively engaged in misleading their opponents about their true positions. That is true of both the plaintiff and the defendant in a lawsuit. It is true of both labor and management in a collective bargaining agreement. It is true as well of both the buyer and the seller in a wide variety of sales transactions. To conceal one's true position, to mislead an opponent about one's true settling point, is the essence of negotiation.[181]

By contrast to misrepresentations of opinions about the merits of the case, it should be improper for a lawyer to make misrepresentations of material fact during negotiations because it is reason-

181. James J. White, Machiavelli and the Bar: Ethical Limitations on Lying in Negotiation, 1980 Am. B. Found. Res. J. 926, 927-928. See also Eleanor Holmes Norton, Bargaining and the Ethic of Process, 64 N.Y.U. L. Rev. 493 (1989) (necessities of bargaining process produce ethical functionalism with minimal truthfulness and fairness).

able for the opposing lawyer to rely on representations of material fact by counsel during negotiations. Misrepresentations regarding the contents of a document,[182] the testimony of a witness, the procedural posture of the case,[183] or the amount of insurance coverage are examples of improper misrepresentations of material fact.[184]

Representations regarding settlement authority could arise in two ways. First, a lawyer could make a representation regarding settlement authority for the purpose of inducing agreement by the opposing side. Second, the opposing party may ask a question about the lawyer's settlement authority. Should it be improper for a lawyer to make misrepresentations about settlement authority in either of these situations? While misrepresentations of opinions about the merits of the case are essential to the negotiation process, misrepresentation of settlement authority is not. Further, settlement authority is a matter of fact, not opinion. Thus, it seems that it should be improper for a lawyer to misrepresent settlement authority for the purpose of inducing settlement. If a lawyer chooses to speak about settlement authority, the lawyer should speak truthfully.

Responses to requests by the other side for information about settlement authority pose a more subtle problem. A lawyer's settlement authority will come from discussions with the client. These discussions will often involve confidential information—information received from the client that is subject to either the attorney-client privilege or the work product doctrine. Thus, a question about settlement authority inquires into privileged matters and seeks information that the other party is not entitled to know.[185] In addition, if lawyers and clients know that lawyers must respond truthfully to questions about authority, they can easily devise ways

182. Carlson v. Carlson, 832 P.2d 380 (Nev. 1992) (wife entitled to relief from property settlement agreement based on representations by husband and his attorney that division was essentially equal).

183. In re Broome, 615 So. 2d 1333 (La. 1993) (lawyer disciplined for obtaining personal injury settlement based on false representation by office personnel that suit had been timely filed).

184. Fire Ins. Exch. v. Bell, 643 N.E.2d 310 (Ind. 1994) (lawyer subject to liability for misrepresenting limits of insurance policy; as matter of law lawyers have right to rely on representations made by opposing counsel about amount of insurance).

185. Cf. ABA Comm. on Ethics and Prof. Resp., Formal Opinion 93-370 (judge does not have right to require lawyer to reveal settlement authority absent client's consent).

to avoid having to answer the question. Thus, good reasons exist why lawyers should not be required to answer truthfully questions about their settlement authority. On the other hand, it is probably unnecessary for the rules to permit lawyers to lie in response to inquiries about settlement authority because such questions can easily be deflected: "You know I can't discuss my authority," or "I'm not authorized to discuss my settlement authorization," or "Let's discuss the merits of the case, not my settlement authority."

Another misrepresentation that is problematic involves a "false demand," a contention injected into the negotiation process, not because it expresses a serious position by the side making the demand, but because a false demand can be used as a bargaining chip to improve the overall settlement. Should a false demand be improper? The answer depends somewhat on the way in which the demand is presented. Often a false demand is nothing more than an opinion about the merits of the case. Thus, in a wrongful discharge case it should be proper for a lawyer to make a claim for job reinstatement even if the client does not seriously want her job back because this demand is nothing more than a contention about the appropriate remedy in the case. On the other hand, some false demands either explicitly or implicitly are misrepresentations of material fact. For example, if a lawyer asks for damages to compensate the client for lost wages or for medical expenses, the demand either explicitly or implicitly states that the damages did in fact occur. It would clearly be fraudulent for a lawyer to request compensation for an injury that did not occur.

The Model Rules are largely consistent with this analysis. Model Rule 4.1(a) states that in representing a client a lawyer shall not knowingly "make a false statement of material fact or law to a third person."[186] Comment 2 to Rule 4.1, however, makes clear that some false statements are permissible because they do not amount to statements of material fact. The comment states that "[u]nder accepted conventions in negotiation, certain types of statements ordinarily are not taken as statements of material fact."

Some scholars have argued that it is simply wrong for lawyers to lie in negotiation, and to the extent that current practice or

186. See Restatement of the Law Governing Lawyers §157(1) (Tent. Draft #8, March 21, 1997). See also ABA Comm. on Ethics and Prof. Resp., Formal Opinion 94-387 (lawyer may negotiate regarding claim that is barred by statute of limitations and may file suit of time-barred claim so long as lawyer does not make any false representations; same rules apply to government lawyers).

rules allow misrepresentation and deceit, these rules should be changed.[187] Professor Gerald Wetlaufer has catalogued and systematically analyzed the various justifications and rationalizations that lawyers offer for lying. He concludes that lawyers need to acknowledge that many lies are morally impermissible "even though they effectively serve our interests and those of our clients—and even though they are not forbidden either by law or by our codes of professional self-regulation." He argues that lawyers may need to redefine winning:

> It might, for instance, be understood not as "getting as much as we can" but as "winning as much as possible without engaging in unacceptable behavior" and "unacceptable behavior" might then be understood to exclude not just those things that are stupid or illegal but also those other things that are unethical.[188]

So far the discussion has focused on the question of when misrepresentation by lawyers in negotiation should be improper. The issue of honesty in negotiation also raises a question of disclosure. When should lawyers be required to disclose information to the opposing party in connection with negotiation?

Discovery rules establish some situations in which a lawyer is required to disclose information. The 1993 amendments to the Federal Rules of Civil Procedure required disclosure of certain information after litigation is filed without the need for a request from the opposing party.[189] Because this change represented a substantial departure from prior discovery practice, the rule allowed the district courts to opt out of this provision by local rule, and many district courts have done so.[190] In addition, the rules require a party to supplement discovery if the party later learns that a prior discovery response is incorrect.[191]

Should lawyers be required to disclose information even if not required to do so by court rule? In certain situations, contracts are

187. The leading article expressing this view is Alvin B. Rubin, A Causerie on Lawyers' Ethics in Negotiation, 35 La. L. Rev. 577 (1975).

188. Gerald B. Wetlaufer, The Ethics of Lying in Negotiations, 75 Iowa L. Rev. 1219, 1272 (1990). See also Reed E. Loder, Moral Truthseeking and the Virtuous Negotiator, 8 Geo. J. Legal Ethics 45 (1994); Walter W. Steele, Jr., Essay, Deceptive Negotiating and High-Toned Morality, 39 Vand. L. Rev. 1387 (1986).

189. Fed. R. Civ. P. 26(a).

190. Id. 26(a)(1).

191. Id. 26(e).

voidable because of nondisclosure of material information. Just as it is improper for a lawyer to participate in a settlement agreement when the lawyer knows that the agreement is voidable because of misrepresentation, it should also be improper for a lawyer to participate in a settlement agreement when the lawyer knows that the agreement is voidable because of nondisclosure. Section 161 of the Restatement (Second) of Contracts outlines the following situations in which a nondisclosure is actionable:

> (a) disclosure of the fact is necessary to prevent some previous assertion from being a misrepresentation or from being fraudulent or material.
>
> (b) disclosure of the fact would correct a mistake of the other party as to a basic assumption on which that party is making the contract and if nondisclosure of the fact amounts to a failure to act in good faith and in accordance with reasonable standards of fair dealing.
>
> (c) disclosure of the fact would correct a mistake of the other party as to the contents or effect of a writing, evidencing or embodying an agreement in whole or in part.
>
> (d) where the other person is entitled to know the fact because of a relation of trust and confidence between them.[192]

Situation (b) establishes a general duty of disclosure when disclosure is necessary to correct a mistake by the other party about basic aspects of the transaction and the failure to disclose violates standards of good faith and fair dealing.[193] For example, in Virzi v. Grand Trunk Warehouse & Cold Storage Co.,[194] the court invalidated a settlement because the plaintiff's lawyer had failed to reveal the death of his client.[195] Similarly, in Spaulding v. Zimmerman,[196] the Minnesota Supreme Court held that a minor settlement in a personal injury case should be set aside because the lawyer for the defendant failed to disclose to the plaintiff a doctor's report received by the defendant that showed, unknown to the plaintiff, a life-threatening aneurysm.

192. See also Restatement (Second) of Torts §551 (1977).
193. See also id. §551(2)(e).
194. 571 F. Supp. 507 (E.D. Mich. 1983).
195. See Toledo Bar Assn. v. Fell, 364 N.E.2d 872 (Ohio 1977) (lawyer indefinitely suspended when he failed to reveal to worker's compensation board that his client had died).
196. 116 N.W.2d 704 (Minn. 1962).

Cases like *Virzi* and *Spaulding* involve fundamental facts dealing with the physical condition of the plaintiff, but some courts have gone even further in requiring disclosure. In Kath v. Western Media, Inc.,[197] the Wyoming Supreme Court invalidated a settlement because the defendant's attorney failed to disclose the existence of a letter in which the lawyer for all of the parties in a previous action contradicted testimony he had given in a deposition. In State ex rel. Nebraska State Bar Assn. v. Addison,[198] the court administered a six-month suspension to an attorney who failed to reveal to the administrator of a hospital, in connection with negotiation of a release of the hospital's lien, the existence of an insurance policy. By contrast, in Brown v. County of Genesee,[199] the Sixth Circuit held that a settlement agreement in an employment discrimination case should not be set aside because defense counsel and his client failed to reveal to the plaintiff and her attorney that they were mistaken about the highest pay level that plaintiff would have been entitled to had she been hired when she first applied. The court ruled that the plaintiff's counsel was at fault and this fault should not be attributed to the defendant and its counsel.[200]

From these cases, it seems clear that lawyers are required to disclose fundamental facts about the case when they know that the other side is mistaken about the fact. Physical condition and insurance coverage constitute fundamental facts. As to other facts, the duty is less clear but probably does not apply when the other side could easily determine the existence of the fact.

How do these principles compare with the approach of the Model Rules? Model Rule 4.1(b) states that a lawyer may not knowingly "fail to disclose a material fact to a third person when disclosure is necessary to avoid assisting a criminal or fraudulent act by a client, unless disclosure is prohibited by Rule 1.6." The "unless" clause was added to the rule during the floor debate before the House of Delegates on adoption of the Model Rules in 1983; the result is both confusing and contradictory. Professor Wolfram offers the following comment on the rule:

> Because MR 1.6 prohibits most if not all imaginable disclosures in the circumstance stated by the first part of MR 4.1(b), the "unless"

197. 684 P.2d 98 (Wyo. 1984).
198. 412 N.W.2d 855 (Neb. 1987).
199. 872 F.2d 169 (6th Cir. 1989).
200. Id. at 175-176.

> clause entirely stops the lawyer's mouth from uttering the disclosures that the rule otherwise requires.[201]

Both the Wolfram and the Hazard & Hodes treatises argue that the only way for Rule 4.1(b) to make sense is to construe the rule to require a lawyer to disclose information when required by "other law," which includes the law of civil procedure and common law dealing with actionable nondisclosure.[202] As discussed above, the analysis of Professors Wolfram, Hazard, and Hodes seems correct. Model 4.1 should be amended to provide that it is improper for a lawyer to "fail to disclose a material fact to a third person when disclosure is necessary to avoid assisting a criminal or fraudulent act by a client or when required by other law." The comments to the amended rule could then elaborate on when the rules of civil procedure and common law require disclosure of material information. The proposed Restatement of the Law Governing Lawyers adopts this approach. Section 157 states that a lawyer may not "fail to make a disclosure of information required by law," while §151(2) prohibits lawyers from counseling or assisting clients in criminal or fraudulent conduct.

Suppose during the course of negotiations a lawyer discovers that the other party has made a fundamental mistake about the settlement agreement. Should the lawyer inform the other side of this mistake? The Restatement of Contracts provides that nondisclosure is actionable when disclosure would correct a mistake by the other party about the contents or effect of a writing.[203] Informal Opinion 86-1518, the ABA Committee on Ethics and Professional Responsibility dealt with the issue of whether lawyers have a duty to disclose knowledge of inadvertent omissions of contract terms or other "scriveners' errors." The Committee ruled:

> Where the lawyer for A has received for signature from the Lawyer for B the final transcription of a contract from which an important

201. Wolfram, Modern Legal Ethics §13.5.8, at 724. See also 2 Hazard & Hodes, The Law of Lawyering §4.1:302, at 720.

202. Wolfram, Modern Legal Ethics §13.5.8, at 725-726. See also 2 Hazard & Hodes, The Law of Lawyering §4.1:303, at 721-722.

203. Restatement (Second) of Contracts §161(c) (1981). See also Restatement (Second) of Torts §551(2)(e) (1977) (duty to disclose facts basic to transaction if party knows that other party is about to enter into transaction based on mistake and because of customs of trade or other objective circumstances would reasonably expect disclosure).

> provision previously agreed upon has been inadvertently omitted by the lawyer for B, the lawyer for A, unintentionally advantaged, should contact the lawyer for B to correct the error and need not consult A about the error.

The Committee advised that client consent was unnecessary because, under Rule 1.4, a lawyer has an obligation to fulfill "reasonable client expectations," and an agreement based on a scrivener's error is not part of the client's reasonable expectations. The Committee also referred to the duty under Rule 1.2(d) not to counsel or assist a client in fraudulent conduct, the duty of disclosure under 4.1(b), and the duty not to engage in fraudulent conduct under Rule 8.4(c).

2. *Improper Threats During Negotiation*

To what extent should lawyers be limited in making threats during negotiations? Section 176 of the Restatement of Contracts contains a useful listing of improper threats:

> A threat is improper if:
> (a) what is threatened is a crime or a tort, or the threat itself would be a crime or a tort if it resulted in obtaining property,
> (b) what is threatened is a criminal prosecution,
> (c) what is threatened is the use of civil process and the threat is made in bad faith, or
> (d) the threat is a breach of the duty of good faith and fair dealing under a contract with the recipient.

Disciplinary Rule 7-105(A) of the Code of Professional Responsibility prohibited lawyers from threatening to use the criminal process solely to obtain an advantage in a civil matter: "A lawyer shall not present, participate in presenting, or threaten to present criminal charges solely to obtain an advantage in a civil matter." The drafters of the Model Rules intentionally omitted the ban on threats of criminal prosecution.[204] They believed that the prohibition found in the Code was unwise in two respects. First, the restriction was redundant because it was already covered by other rules, particularly by Model Rule 8.4(b), prohibiting lawyers from engaging in criminal conduct that reflects on their honesty, trust-

204. 2 Hazard & Hodes, The Law of Lawyering §4.4:103, at 759.

worthiness, or fitness to practice law, and by Model Rule 4.4, dealing with respect for the rights of third persons.[205] Second, the drafters concluded that the limitation was in some respects overbroad because some threats of criminal prosecution were proper tactics that lawyers should be allowed to use to protect clients' legitimate interests.[206]

In Formal Opinion 92-363, the ABA Committee on Ethics and Professional Responsibility discussed when a threat of criminal prosecution would be permissible under the Model Rules:

> Model Rule 8.4(b) provides that it is professional misconduct for a lawyer to "commit a criminal act that reflects adversely on the lawyer's honesty, trustworthiness or fitness as a lawyer in other respects." If a lawyer's conduct is extortionate or compounds a crime under the criminal law of a given jurisdiction, that conduct also violates Rule 8.4(b). It is beyond the scope of the Committee's jurisdiction to define extortionate conduct, but we note that the Model Penal Code does not criminalize threats of prosecution where the "property obtained by threat of accusation, exposure, lawsuit or other invocation of official action was *honestly claimed as restitution for harm done in the circumstances to which such accusation, exposure, lawsuit or other official action relates, or as compensation for property or lawful services.*" Model Penal Code, §223.4 (emphasis added). . . . [The Committee then went on to discuss other provisions of the Model Rules that a threat of criminal prosecution might violate, depending on the circumstances.]
>
> Rule 4.4 (Respect for Rights of Third Persons) prohibits a lawyer from using means that "have no substantial purpose other than to embarrass, delay, or burden a third person . . . ." A lawyer who uses even a well-founded threat of criminal charges merely to harass a third person violates Rule 4.4. See also Hazard & Hodes, supra, §4.4:104.
>
> Rule 4.1 (Truthfulness in Statements to Others) imposes a duty on lawyers to be truthful when dealing with others on a client's behalf. A lawyer who threatens criminal prosecution, without any actual intent to so proceed, violates Rule 4.1.
>
> Finally, Rule 3.1 (Meritorious Claims and Contentions) prohibits an advocate from asserting frivolous claims. A lawyer who threatens criminal prosecution that is not well founded in fact and in law, or threatens such prosecution in furtherance of a civil claim that is not well founded, violates Rule 3.1.[207]

205. See Wolfram, Modern Legal Ethics §13.5.5, at 718.
206. 2 Hazard & Hodes, The Law of Lawyering §4.4:103, at 760.
207. ABA Comm. on Ethics and Prof. Resp., Formal Opinion 92-363, at 4-5.

The Committee concluded that if a lawyer did not violate any of these rules, a threat of criminal prosecution to settle a civil matter was proper if the crime was *related* to the civil matter, for example if the crime was embezzlement and the settlement involved restitution of misappropriated funds. The Committee also decided that a lawyer could agree not to report a criminal offense provided such an agreement did not amount to compounding a crime.[208]

Under the definition of an improper threat set forth in the Restatement of Contracts, a lawyer may properly threaten the other side with actions that the client is legally entitled to take, such as exercising a right under a contract or bringing a lawsuit, so long as the lawyer is not acting in bad faith. On the other hand, threats to commit a tort or that involve bad faith are improper. For example, threats to publicize the opposing party's private activities have been held to be improper. In In re Dienes,[209] a lawyer received a public reprimand for making a veiled threat to inform the newspapers about his former employer's business unless the employer withdrew a motion seeking attorney fees from lawyer. Similarly, in State v. Harrington,[210] the Vermont Supreme Court held that a threat by the lawyer for the wife to publicize the husband's adultery, a crime, in order to coerce settlement of a divorce case amounted to criminal extortion.

3. *Fairness of Settlements*

Should the rules of ethics impose a general obligation on lawyers not to participate in unfair settlement agreements? For three reasons it seems unwise to require such a general duty of fairness in negotiation. First, there are no objective criteria of fairness that a lawyer or a disciplinary board could use to determine whether an

208. The West Virginia Supreme Court largely adopted the approach of ABA Formal Opinion 92-363 in Committee on Legal Ethics v. Printz, 416 S.E.2d 720 (W. Va. 1992) (attorney may ethically threaten criminal prosecution to obtain restitution of embezzled funds). See also Ruberton v. Gabage, 654 A.2d 1002 (N.J. Super. App. Div. 1995), *cert. denied*, 663 A.2d 1358 (N.J. 1995) (in wrongful discharge case threat by defense counsel to institute criminal charges unless plaintiff accepted settlement not actionable as abuse of process because process not used and because statements made in course of judicial proceeding are absolutely privileged). See generally Joseph M. Livermore, Lawyer Extortion, 20 Ariz. L. Rev. 403 (1978).

209. 571 A.2d 1303 (N.J. 1990).

210. 260 A.2d 692 (Vt. 1969).

agreement was fair. Thus, an ethical duty not to participate in an unfair outcome would be unworkable. Second, to the extent that rules of ethics prohibit lawyers from participating in settlement agreements that the lawyers know are invalid because of fraud, mistake, or other such cause, the rules already impose a substantial obligation of fairness. Third, a duty of fairness would be inconsistent with the adversarial system, under which the fairness of the outcome is judged by the fairness of the adjudication process. Rules of ethics do not prohibit lawyers from participating in adjudication that produces an outcome that some might consider to be substantively unfair as long as the process is a fair one. Similarly, the rules should not prohibit lawyers from engaging in negotiations that result in an agreement that some observers might consider to be unfair.

Some scholars, while agreeing that lawyers should not have an ethical duty to ensure the overall fairness of negotiations, have argued for a narrower proposition: Lawyers should have an obligation not to participate in an agreement that is unconscionable. Professor Lee Pizzimenti has proposed the adoption of the following rule of ethics:

> A lawyer shall not assist in the preparation of a written instrument containing terms which are unconscionable. A lawyer may assist in such preparation where there is a basis for concluding the terms are not unconscionable that is not frivolous, including a good faith argument for an extension, modification or reversal of existing law.[211]

Unconscionability is a ground for invalidating a conventional contract, so it is unobjectionable to recognize that lawyers should have an obligation not to participate in a settlement agreement that the lawyer knows is unconscionable. The difficulty is that it is hard to image a settlement agreement that would be unconscionable. The most widely accepted definition of unconscionability, adopted by the D.C. Circuit in Williams v. Walker-Thomas Furniture Co.,[212] requires a showing of an absence of meaningful choice coupled with terms that are unreasonably favorable to one of the parties.

211. Lee A. Pizzimenti, Prohibiting Lawyers from Assisting in Unconscionable Transactions: Using an Overt Tool, 72 Marq. L. Rev. 151, 174 (1989).

212. 350 F.2d 445 (D.C. Cir. 1965).

Rarely will a settlement agreement involve an absence of meaningful choice, especially when the party is represented by counsel.

The Model Rules reject a general duty of fairness in connection with negotiation. The original draft of the Model Rules stated: "In conducting negotiations a lawyer shall be fair in dealing with other participants."[213] Whether the drafters truly intended to include a general obligation of fairness is doubtful since the comment stated that fairness in negotiations implies that representations shall be truthful. In any event, the idea of an obligation of fairness was quickly abandoned in favor of narrower rules focusing on misrepresentation and nondisclosure.[214]

213. ABA, Model Rules of Professional Conduct, Rule 4.2(a). (Discussion Draft, Jan. 30, 1980).

214. See also Geoffrey C. Hazard, Jr., The Lawyer's Obligation to be Trustworthy When Dealing With Opposing Parties, 33 S.C. L. Rev. 181 (1981) (legal regulation of trustworthiness cannot go further than to proscribe fraud because of substantial difference in technical sophistication among lawyers).

CHAPTER 6

Delivery of Legal Services

Access to a lawyer is often necessary to the meaningful assertion of legal rights. Criminal prosecutions are an obvious example of cases in which the lack of a lawyer can seriously jeopardize the ability of individuals to protect their rights, but the need for legal representation sweeps across civil litigation and includes transactional matters. Issues of child custody in divorce cases or protective services proceedings present compelling claims for legal representation; lack of adequate legal advice can inhibit individuals from making appropriate arrangements for disposition of property on their death.

This chapter describes and analyzes the system for delivery of legal services in the United States. In broad terms the system can be divided into three components: indigents in criminal cases (Section A), indigents in civil cases (Section B), and clients able to afford legal representation at least to some significant extent (Section C). Each section examines the constitutional dimensions of delivery of legal services to that segment of society, the institutional mechanisms that have developed to provide legal services for that class of individuals, and alternative delivery mechanisms. The chapter concludes with an examination of certain other restrictions on the marketing of legal services, including ancillary business activities, sale of law practices, and covenants not to compete (Section D).

A. INDIGENTS IN CRIMINAL CASES

1. *Constitutional Right to Appointed Counsel*

The Sixth Amendment to the U.S. Constitution provides: "In all criminal prosecutions, the accused shall enjoy the right . . . to have the assistance of counsel for his defense." In Johnson v. Zerbst,[1] the Supreme Court interpreted the Sixth Amendment to require federal courts to appoint counsel for indigent defendants in criminal cases: "The Sixth Amendment withholds from federal courts, in all criminal proceedings, the power and authority to deprive an accused of his life or liberty unless he has or waives the assistance of counsel."[2]

The seminal case on right to appointed counsel in criminal cases in state court is Gideon v. Wainwright.[3] Charged with breaking and entering a poolroom with intent to commit a misdemeanor, a felony under Florida law, Gideon asked the trial court to appoint counsel to represent him. The trial judge denied the request, stating that under Florida law a right to appointed counsel existed only in capital cases; Gideon claimed that he had a constitutional right to appointed counsel even though he was not charged with a capital crime. Gideon represented himself at trial, where he was convicted and sentenced to five years in prison. He sought habeas corpus relief. His case reached the Supreme Court, which appointed Abe Fortas, a distinguished member of the Washington bar and later an associate justice of the Supreme Court, to represent Gideon. In an opinion by Justice Black, the Court held that the Fourteenth Amendment right to due process included the Sixth Amendment right to appointed counsel in any felony.[4]

In Argersinger v. Hamlin,[5] the Court addressed the issue of

1. 304 U.S. 458 (1938).
2. Id. at 463.
3. 372 U.S. 335 (1963). The case is chronicled in Anthony Lewis's book, *Gideon's Trumpet,* and is dramatized in the movie by the same name staring Henry Fonda as Gideon.
4. Id. at 344.
5. 407 U.S. 25 (1972).

whether the right to appointed counsel applied to misdemeanor as well as to felony cases. The defendant was charged with carrying a concealed weapon, an offense punishable under Florida law by imprisonment for up to six months, a $1,000 fine, or both. The defendant was convicted and sentenced to serve 90 days in jail. He brought a habeas corpus proceeding claiming that his conviction was unconstitutional because he was not represented by counsel. *Argersinger* was a difficult case because it involved a conflict between the principle of the importance of legal representation in criminal cases and the practical burden that would be imposed on the states from recognition of an overly broad right to counsel. The Court had before it five choices as to where to draw the line for appointment of counsel: (1) based on the classification of the crime as felony or misdemeanor, (2) based on whether the defendant was charged with a crime for which he was subject to imprisonment, (3) based on whether the defendant was subject to more than six month's imprisonment, which would make the right to counsel co-extensive with the right to jury trial,[6] (4) based on fundamental fairness as determined by the trial court, subject to appellate review, and (5) based on whether the defendant was in fact incarcerated (as opposed to being subject to incarceration).

The first option was clearly inappropriate. Classifications of crimes vary from state to state. Use of a felony test would mean that a defendant in one state might have a right to counsel for an offense while a defendant in another state would not have a right to counsel for an offense with greater potential penalties. On the other hand, the second alternative was also undesirable because it would require states to appoint counsel in almost all misdemeanor cases, an intolerable burden, especially for small communities. The Court seriously considered the third alternative, but it found that the right to a jury trial and the right to counsel were fundamentally different, and that counsel would often be needed even in petty offenses.[7] Two concurring justices, Powell and Rehnquist, argued for the fourth alternative.[8] The "fundamental fairness" standard suffered, however, from problems. Because the principle was vague, it would be likely to increase the number of appeals of cases involving the right to counsel. In addition, this standard would probably have led to varying treatment of defendants among the states.

6. Duncan v. Louisiana, 391 U.S. 145 (1968).
7. 407 U.S. at 33-37.
8. Id. at 47.

Thus, the Court adopted the last approach, imprisonment in fact, as the test for whether a right to counsel exists. The approach, which makes the determination of the existence to a right to counsel retrospectively rather than prospectively, at first seems odd, but in the end offers substantial benefits. Under this approach, a court cannot constitutionally sentence a defendant to imprisonment in a misdemeanor case unless the defendant has appointed counsel during the trial. As a result of this principle, the trial court is forced to make a decision at the beginning of the case. If the court wishes to reserve the possibility of sentencing the defendant to prison, the court constitutionally must appoint counsel. If the court decides to forgo the option of imprisonment, it may deny the motion for appointment of counsel.[9]

The *Argersinger* rule has two major advantages. It does not require appointment of counsel in all minor criminal cases, but instead leaves the decision to the trial judge. At the same time, the rule creates a bright-line standard for appointment of counsel — cases in which the court in fact orders imprisonment. The rule is not, however, without its difficulties. It requires trial courts to make determinations of the seriousness of the offense before hearing the evidence. Further, in small communities where few lawyers practice, courts may be forced to eliminate the possibility of imprisonment in many cases to avoid imposing an impossible burden of appointment on counsel.[10]

2. *Structure and Appraisal of the Present System for Delivery of Legal Services to Indigents in Criminal Cases*

States have adopted essentially three approaches to carrying out the constitutional mandate to provide legal services to indigents in criminal cases:

1. public defender programs, employing full-time staff attorneys

9. Id. at 40, 42.

10. Id. at 56-61. In Scott v. Illinois, 440 U.S. 367 (1979), the Court reaffirmed the *Argersinger* rule. More recently, the Court has limited the protections that flow from *Argersinger.* See Nichols v. United States, 511 U.S. 738 (1994) (uncounseled misdemeanor conviction may be taken into account under sentencing guidelines).

2. contract defense plans, in which private attorneys agreed to handle a certain volume of indigent cases for a specified fee
3. assigned counsel systems, where courts appoint members of the private bar on a case-by-case basis[11]

Courts must evaluate plans for providing counsel to determine whether they provide effective assistance as required by the Sixth Amendment. In Zarabia v. Bradshaw,[12] for example, the Arizona Supreme Court invalidated the district court's plan because it provided for random selection of counsel without considering expertise of appointed counsel and because it provided inadequate compensation in an amount less that the attorney's overhead.

In 1992, the American Bar Association released revised Standards for Providing Defense Services. The ABA concluded that full-time defender organizations were the most desirable method of providing defense services to indigents, but that participation by the organized bar through either assignment or contract system was also desirable.[13] Standard 5-1.2 provides as follows:

> (a) The legal representation plan for each jurisdiction should provide for the services of a full-time defender organization when population and caseload are sufficient to support such an organization. Multi-jurisdictional organizations may be appropriate in rural areas.
>
> (b) Every system should include the active and substantial participation of the private bar. That participation should be through a coordinated assigned-counsel system and may also include contracts for services. No program should be precluded from representing clients in any particular type or category of case.

11. For a description and critique of these delivery systems see Stephen J. Schulhofer & David D. Friedman, Rethinking Indigent Defense: Promoting Effective Representation Through Consumer Sovereignty and Freedom of Choice For All Criminal Defendants, 31 Am. Crim. L. Rev. 73, 83-96 (1993) (arguing for voucher system to provide indigent defendants with freedom of choice and to provide their attorneys with same incentives as retained counsel).

12. 912 P.2d 5 (Ariz. 1996) (en banc).

13. A 1992 study of indigent defense systems in nine state courts of general jurisdiction found that indigent defenders handled their cases more expeditiously and at least as competently as private counsel. National Center for State Courts, Indigent Defenders: Get the Job Done and Done Well 103-04 (1992).

The comments explain the justification for a mixed system as follows:

> When adequately funded and staffed, defender organizations employing full-time personnel are capable of providing excellent defense services. By devoting all of their efforts to legal representation, defender programs ordinarily are able to develop unusual expertise in handling various kinds of criminal cases. Moreover, defender offices frequently are in the best position to supply counsel soon after an accused is arrested. By virtue of their experience, full-time defenders also are able to work for changes in laws and procedures aimed at benefiting defendants and the criminal justice system.
>
> There are also definite purposes served by retaining the presence of substantial private bar participation in the system for criminal defense. Just as private attorneys often can learn from the full-time lawyers of defender organizations, there are many private attorneys, qualified by training and experience, who can contribute substantially to the knowledge of defenders. In addition, a "mixed" system of representation consisting of both private attorneys and full-time defenders offers a "safety valve," so that the caseload pressures on each group are less likely to be burdensome.
>
> In some cities, where a mixed system has been absent and public defenders have been required to handle all of the cases, the results have been unsatisfactory. Caseloads have increased faster than the size of staffs and necessary revenues, making quality legal representation exceedingly difficult. Furthermore, the involvement of private attorneys in defense services assures the continued interest of the bar in the welfare of the criminal justice system. Without the knowledgeable and active support of the bar as a whole, continued improvements in the nation's justice system are rendered less likely.
>
> Finally, private attorney representation in criminal cases is essential because of new and stricter policies within defense services programs regarding conflicts of interest, primarily in representation of codefendants. In some cases, these policies can result in the declaration of conflicts of interest in more than 25 percent of all cases assigned to a public defender program.[14]

The standards then go on to establish guidelines for various aspects of the system for providing defense services. Some of the more important standards include the following:

14. ABA, Standards for Criminal Justice, Providing Defense Services, Standard 5-1.2 (1992).

1. *Funding and Eligibility.* The standards call for funding the full cost of defense services sufficient to provide quality representation to all eligible persons. Standard 5-1.6. The standards go on to define eligible persons as those "who are financially unable to obtain adequate representation without substantial hardship." Standard 5-7.1. The commentary stresses the need for adoption of detailed written guidelines to implement the eligibility standard.

2. *Professional Independence.* Standard 5-1.3 provides that lawyers should be "free from political interference and should be subject to judicial supervision only in the same manner and to the same extent as are lawyers in private practice." Selection of lawyers for specific cases should be made by administrators of the state's plan for providing defense services rather than by the judiciary or elected officials. To support the independence of public defender organizations, the standard recommends that they be governed by independent boards of trustees that have the power to set general policy but not interfere in particular cases.

3. *Assigned Counsel.* The standards call for a plan for assignment of counsel implemented by administrators, rather than assignments made ad hoc by judges. Standard 5-2.1. Eligibility for assignments should be as widely distributed as possible among qualified members of the bar, but the standards reject the notion that cases should be assigned to all members of the bar regardless of qualifications. Standard 5-2.2. The standards state that cases should be assigned to lawyers "experienced and active in trial practice, and familiar with the practice and procedure of the criminal courts." Standard 5-2.2. The assignment plan should set forth specific qualification standards for particular types of cases. The standards state that a lawyer "should not seek to avoid appointment by a tribunal to represent a person except for good cause." Model Rule 6.2 is similar. Assigned counsel should receive prompt compensation at reasonable hourly rates and should be reimbursed for out-of-pocket expenses. Compensation should be paid for all hours necessary to provide quality representation. Standard 5-2.4.

4. *Defender Systems.* The standards call for the selection of the chief defender and staff on the basis of merit, and prohibit their selection by judges. Compensation for the chief defender and staff should be comparable to that for prosecutors. Standard 5-4.1.

5. *Workload.* Regardless of the type of system, whether defender, assigned counsel, or contract, the standards provide that lawyers should not accept workloads that because of excessive size inter-

fere with rendering quality representation. Standard 5-5.3. The comments refer to various methods for measuring caseloads and workloads. One standard mentioned as a rough measure of reasonable caseload was that of the National Advisory Commission on Criminal Justice:

- 150 felonies per attorney per year
- 400 misdemeanors per attorney per year
- 200 juvenile cases per attorney per year
- 200 mental commitment cases per attorney per year
- 25 appeals per attorney per year

The commentary goes on to discuss caseloads in capital cases, referring to a Florida study indicating that five capital cases per attorney per year when the defendant was not under a warrant of death and three cases per attorney per year when a warrant for execution had been issued.[15]

B. INDIGENTS IN CIVIL CASES

1. *Constitutional Right to Appointed Counsel*

While indigent criminal defendants have a broad constitutional right to appointed counsel under the Sixth and Fourteenth Amendments, the Supreme Court has refused to recognize a general right to appointed counsel in civil cases. The leading case is Lassiter v. Department of Social Services,[16] an action for termination of the defendant's parental rights. The defendant did not ask for appointed counsel, but on appeal she claimed that the hearing violated her constitutional rights because she was not represented by counsel.

The Supreme Court began its analysis with a presumption that appointed counsel was constitutionally required only in cases involving incarceration.[17] The Court went on to decide, however, that

15. For a criticism of inadequate funding of indigent defense and a call for systemic litigation to alleviate the problem, see Richard Klein, The Eleventh Commandment: Thou Shalt Not be Compelled to Render the Ineffective Assistance of Counsel, 68 Ind. L.J. 363 (1993).

16. 452 U.S. 18 (1981).

17. Id. at 26-27.

due process may require appointment of counsel in cases in which the defendant does not face a deprivation of physical liberty:

> The case of Mathews v. Eldridge, 424 U.S. 319, 335, propounds three elements to be evaluated in deciding what due process requires, viz., the private interests at stake, the government's interest, and the risk that the procedures used will lead to erroneous decisions. We must balance these elements against each other, and then set their net weight in the scales against the presumption that there is a right to appointed counsel only where the indigent, if he is unsuccessful, may lose his personal freedom.[18]

The Court found that the private and governmental interests involved in cases seeking termination of parental rights were great, and the risk of error in such cases was significant. Nonetheless, the Court held that the trial court did not commit error in failing to appoint counsel for Ms. Lassiter because on the facts of the case these factors did not outweigh the presumption against appointed counsel:

> [T]he petition to terminate Ms. Lassiter's parental rights contained no allegations of neglect or abuse upon which criminal charges could be based . . . . [N]o expert witnesses testified and the case presented no specially troublesome points of law, either procedural or substantive. . . . [T]he weight of the evidence . . . was sufficiently great that the presence of counsel for Ms. Lassiter could not have made a determinative difference. . . . Finally, a court deciding whether due process requires the appointment of counsel need not ignore a parent's plain demonstration that she is not interested in attending a hearing.[19]

Justices Blackmun, Brennan, Marshall, and Stevens dissented. Justice Blackmun's dissenting opinion concluded that the Court's analysis and his were "markedly similar." Both found "the private interest weighty, the procedure devised by the state fraught with risks of error, and the countervailing governmental interest insubstantial."[20] Blackmun criticized the Court's case-by-case approach to applying this balancing test, however. He noted that in the past the Court had always applied its due process analysis to arrive at rules for similarly situated cases, not in an effort to decide fairness

18. Id. at 27.
19. Id. at 32-33.
20. Id. at 48-49.

in individual cases. Blackmun found a case-by-case due process approach fundamentally flawed because it undermines the concept of general fairness on which due process is based, because it would be difficult for a reviewing court to determine from the record in a case whether the proceedings were fair since the absence of evidence in the record may be the source of unfairness, and because a case-by-case approach is cumbersome and costly.[21] In Justice Stevens's view, termination of parental rights cases were more serious than criminal cases and made a more compelling case for appointment of counsel as a matter of due process.[22]

The framework for analysis set by the Supreme Court in *Lassiter* continues to be the approach used by federal and state courts in deciding right to counsel issues in civil cases.[23]

2. *Legal Services Programs*

The Supreme Court in *Lassiter* noted that its decision was based on the minimal requirements of the Constitution: "A wise public policy, however, may require that higher standards be adopted than those minimally tolerable under the Constitution."[24] Both the federal and state governments have to varying degrees been willing to provide for appointed counsel in some civil cases as a matter of public policy; such programs are commonly referred to as *legal aid*.

The legal aid movement began in the latter part of the nineteenth and early twentieth centuries in New York, Chicago, and other large cities. Individuals and charities formed legal aid societies and other organizations to provide legal services to the poor, particularly to the large number of immigrants coming into the

21. Id. at 49-52.

22. Id. at 59-60.

23. See, e.g., Wilson v. State of New Hampshire, 18 F.3d 40 (1st Cir. 1994) (no constitutional right to counsel in civil contempt proceeding for nonpayment of child support); In re Emilye A., 12 Cal. Rptr. 2d 294 (Cal. Ct. App. 1992) (when due process requires appointment of counsel, right includes effective assistance of counsel); In re Interest of R.R., 475 N.W.2d 518 (Neb. 1991) (no right to counsel in proceeding to declare minor as juvenile in need of assistance); New York City Housing Auth. (NYCHA) v. Johnson, 565 N.Y.S.2d 362 (App. Div. 1990) (no right to counsel in proceeding to evict tenant from public housing project); Washington v. Washington, 419 S.E.2d 779 (S.C. 1992) (no right to counsel in domestic separation proceeding).

24. 452 U.S. at 33.

cities. The focus of legal aid at that time was charitable: to provide legal services to individuals who could not afford to hire lawyers.[25]

The legal aid movement showed little growth and change until the 1960s, when it underwent a fundamental transformation. One of the principal vehicles for change was the Ford Foundation, which began funding various experiments in providing legal services to the poor, including support for law reform efforts. The philosophy of law reform differs fundamentally from that of service. Under a law reform strategy, legal aid attorneys seek to use the legal system to make fundamental institutional and systemic changes that will remove discrimination against or provide benefits to the poor. Class actions and lobbying for legislative change became major tools of law reform efforts.[26]

In 1963, President Johnson called for a "War on Poverty." Among the programs passed by Congress in response to this initiative was the Office of Economic Opportunity (OEO), which included a Legal Services Program. Thus, for the first time, the federal government became involved in the funding of legal services for the poor.[27] During the next ten years, however, the Legal Services Program became embroiled in political controversy, particularly its funding of law reform activities. Federal funding for legal services still continued to enjoy substantial support in the bar, particularly in the ABA.

In 1974, with the support of the President and the ABA, Congress created the Legal Services Corporation (LSC). The LSC represented a political compromise between the proponents and opponents of government-funded legal services. Its creation showed a continued commitment by the federal government to fund legal services. Indeed, legal services were now "upgraded" from a program to the status of a separate federal corporation. In addition, by creating a separate federal corporation with its own board of directors, supporters of the LSC hoped to take legal services "out of politics." At the same time, however, the statute creating the LSC put strict limits on various types of law reform activities.[28]

25. Wolfram, Modern Legal Ethics §16.7.2, at 933.

26. Id. at 934-935.

27. Id. at 936.

28. On the history of the LSC, see id. §16.7.3, at 937-938. For articles tracing the history of legal services and discussing many of the problems confronting the effort to provide legal representation to the poor, see Marc Feldman, Political

The hope that the creation of the LSC would remove federal funding of legal services from politics has not been realized. When the Reagan Administration came to power in 1981, it targeted the LSC for abolition. Backers in Congress with the support of the ABA were able to save the LSC from extinction, but its appropriation lagged substantially behind inflation, and the number of attorneys funded by the LSC diminished.[29] In 1995, the Republican Congress again called for abolition of the LSC. In 1996, the Congress reauthorized funding for legal services but placed substantial new restrictions on the activities of legal services lawyers, including limitations on the use of funds received from nonfederal sources.[30]

Today most local legal services programs receive funding not only from the LSC but also from state and local sources as well. A major source of funding for legal services in many communities is IOLTA (Interest on Lawyer Trust Account) grants.[31] Various charities also provide support for legal services. Nonetheless, the bulk of financing for legal services programs still comes from the LSC.

Legal services programs, however, have woefully inadequate resources to meet the needs of low- and moderate-income individuals. The Legal Services Corporation funds approximately one legal services lawyer for every 10,000 individuals below the pov-

---

Lessons: Legal Services for the Poor, 83 Geo. L.J. 1529 (1995). For commentary on Professor Feldman's article see Gary Bellow & Jeanne Charn, Paths Not Yet Taken: Some Comments on Feldman's Critique of Legal Services Practice, 83 Geo. L.J. 1633 (1995); Alan W. Houseman, Political Lessons: Legal Services for the Poor—A Commentary, 83 Geo. L.J. 1669 (1995).

29. Wolfram, Modern Legal Ethics §16.7.3, at 938. For a description of the impact of cuts in federal funding on legal services programs, see David Barringer, Downsized Justice, 82 A.B.A. J. 60 (July 1996).

30. Omnibus Consolidated Rescissions and Appropriations Act of 1996, Pub. L. No. 104-134, §504, 110 Stat. 1321 (1996) (restricting the right to use federal funds to engage in activities such as class actions, to initiate rulemaking proceedings, or to claim attorney fees; the restrictions also prohibit recipients of federal funds from using private, state, or local donations for these purposes or from transferring nonfederal funds to anyone who does not follow the same restrictions).

31. The Fifth Circuit Court of Appeals has called into question the constitutionality of IOLTA programs by holding that clients have a constitutionally protected property interest in the interest on funds held in trust by their lawyers. Washington Legal Found. v. Texas Equal Access to Justice Found., 94 F.3d 996 (5th Cir. 1996), *cert. granted,* 117 S. Ct. 2535 (1997). Other appellate courts, however, have upheld the constitutionality of IOLTA programs. See, e.g., Washington Legal Found. v. Massachusetts Bar Found., 993 F.2d 962 (1st Cir. 1993); Cone v. State Bar of Florida, 819 F.2d 1002 (11th Cir.), *cert. denied,* 484 U.S. 917 (1987); Carroll v. State Bar of California, 213 Cal. Rptr. 305 (Cal. Ct. App.), *cert. denied,* 474 U.S. 848 (1985).

erty line.[32] Further, a number of studies have documented the existence of a vast unmet need for legal services. For example, a survey conducted for the ABA in 1992 showed that approximately 50 percent of both low- and moderate-income individuals had a new legal problem during 1992. Only 39 percent of moderate-income individuals and only 29 percent of low-income individuals took any action about their legal problems.[33] Because of these unmet needs, proposals for imposing an obligation on lawyers to assist in providing legal services have been made from a variety of quarters.

3. *Mandatory Pro Bono*

Since funded legal services programs do not have sufficient resources to come even close to satisfying the need for legal services by the poor, the bar has in recent years considered ways in which this need could be met, at least in part. One idea that has stirred considerable controversy within the profession is that lawyers should be required to devote a certain amount of time periodically to providing legal services to persons of limited means.

Mandatory pro bono proposals must deal with a number of issues. Probably the most detailed mandatory pro bono proposal to date is that offered in New York by the Marrero Committee;[34] the proposal had the following major elements:

1. *Quantity of Required Service:* 40 hours every two years.
2. *Coverage and Exemptions:* All attorneys admitted to practice law in New York and currently practicing. The Committee provided for exemptions for cause on a case-by-case basis. The Committee also recognized that some practical difficulties could arise in applying the proposal to government law-

32. Based on the poverty population as reported by the Bureau of the Census and funded attorneys as reported by the LSC.

33. Institute for Survey Research at Temple University, Findings of the Comprehensive Legal Needs Study (1994). A summary of the principal findings of the survey can be found in Mark Hansen, A Shunned Justice System, 80 A.B.A. J. 18 (April 1994).

34. Committee to Improve the Availability of Legal Services, Final Report to the Chief Judge of the State of New York (April 1990), *reprinted in* 19 Hofstra L. Rev. 755 (1991).

yers and other classes of attorneys, but it concluded that universal coverage was extremely important.

3. *Qualifying Services:* Services must be rendered to the poor or to organizations that serve the poor. The Committee rejected two broader definitions of pro bono services — uncompensated legal service and public interest legal service—because the underlying rationale for its proposal was the special needs of the poor to have access to the legal system.
4. *Compliance:* Generally compliance must be personal, however, the proposal recognized two exceptions: First, attorneys who are members of groups such as law firms can satisfy their pro bono obligation collectively. This means that partners in firms can assign associates to handle pro bono work and obtain credit for their services. It also means that firms could hire full-time pro bono lawyers and receive credit for their services. Second, the proposal provides for a financial contribution in lieu of service at the rate of $1,000 for 20 hours ($50 per hour). The buy-out option only applies, however, to lawyers practicing in firms of ten or fewer lawyers. The Committee felt that the group practice concept gave larger firms sufficient flexibility, but that smaller firms needed the additional buy-out option because the group alternative would not be as useful for smaller firms.
5. *Excess Time:* Excess time may be carried forward for no more than four years.
6. *Disbursements:* Reasonable expenses incurred in handling pro bono matters are reimbursable. The proposal does not specify the source or reimbursement but suggests two possibilities: funds generated by contributions in lieu of service and IOLTA funds.
7. *Professional Liability Insurance:* The Committee concluded that no special provision for insurance was necessary because most lawyers would already have insurance that would apply or such insurance could be obtained by sponsoring organizations.
8. *Incompetence:* The Committee concluded that the flexibility built-in to its proposal was adequate to deal with concerns about competency of representation.

What are the arguments in favor of and in opposition to mandatory pro bono? The Marrero Committee focused on several points to justify its proposal. First, numerous studies show a vast, unmet need for legal services by low-income households. Second, the failure to receive adequate legal services has inflicted an "intolerable toll" on both the poor and society as a whole. Lack of representation in eviction proceedings increases homelessness; absence of representation in domestic matters leads to violence; want of legal assistance in federal benefit cases increases the burden on the states. Further, lack of counsel undermines the legitimacy of the legal system itself.[35] The Committee considered the possibility that various alternatives other than mandatory pro bono could solve or reduce the problem, but it concluded that this was unrealistic. The Committee noted the decline in federal funding for legal services and the increased economic pressures on law firms making it less likely that voluntary efforts would be successful.[36]

Given the documented need and the likelihood that the need would not be met through either federal funding or voluntary efforts, the Committee turned to the role of the lawyer in providing legal services to the poor. While the Committee agreed with the proposition that society as a whole bore responsibility for redressing the problem, it concluded that "lawyers, independent of their ordinary duty as citizens, have a professional responsibility to mobilize their own resources in order to meet these needs."[37] The special duty of lawyers to provide legal services to the poor flows from the unique training and skills of lawyers, their exclusive license to practice law, and the lawyer's responsibility to promote the legitimacy and proper functioning of the legal system.[38]

The principal arguments against mandatory pro bono fall into four categories: quality of service, unfairness to lawyers, administrative and practical difficulties, and lack of benefit to the poor. Some critics have questioned whether lawyers who are forced to provide legal services would do so competently. In addition, many legal problems facing the poor (welfare, housing, employment, for example) involve complicated bodies of law in which private practitioners may have little knowledge or experience.[39] Quality of service issues could be addressed in several ways. While some legal problems facing the poor involve specialized bodies of law, many legal problems (divorce, wills, transfer of real estate) are

35. Id. at 774-775.
36. Id. at 776.
37. Id. at 780.
38. Id.
39. Roger C. Cramton, Mandatory Pro Bono, 19 Hofstra L. Rev. 1113, 1127 (1991).

fairly routine. In addition, for areas that require specialized knowledge, back-up facilities could assist lawyers in providing these services. In addition, the buy-out provision found in the Marrero proposal could generate funds sufficient to hire lawyers with expertise to provide specialized services.

Some opponents of mandatory pro bono argue that such proposals are unconstitutional because they involve violations of individual liberty and taking of lawyers' property without just compensation. Such constitutional arguments have generally been rejected by the courts, however, on the ground that the legal profession is a regulated industry and requiring lawyers to devote a limited amount of time or money to provide legal services for the poor falls within the scope of reasonable regulation.[40] Even if mandatory pro bono is not unconstitutional, some adversaries argue that it is unfair to impose this burden on lawyers when society as a whole should provide for legal services to the poor. As noted above, the Marrero report addressed this point; it concluded that lawyers have a special duty to provide legal services to the poor flowing from the unique training and skills of lawyers, their exclusive license to practice law, and the lawyer's responsibility to promote the legitimacy and proper functioning of the legal system. However, some critics, noting the increased competitiveness of the legal profession, question whether this justification is adequate.[41] Moreover, the program can generate other fairness issues. Mandatory pro bono tends to be regressive. The Marrero proposal suffers from this problem. Senior partners in large firms can satisfy their

40. Id. at 1131-1132.

41. Id. at 1134-1136. Professor Timothy Terrell and Mr. James Wildman also reject the monopoly argument for imposing a duty on lawyers to deliver legal services because they find that the existence of free entry, full competition, and lack of anticompetitive behavior in the legal profession means that lawyers no longer collect "monopoly rents." Timothy P. Terrell & James H. Wildman, Essay, Rethinking "Professionalism," 41 Emory L.J. 403, 421 (1992). Terrell and Wildman believe, however, that lawyers have a duty as professionals to enable those members of the profession who want to assist in delivering legal services to do so. Id. at 430. While rejecting any personal obligation to deliver legal services, Terrell and Wildman suggest that the bar could impose a tax on its members to assist other lawyers in their efforts. Id. at 431. For a contrary view, arguing that a duty to provide public service is justified because lawyers receive the benefits of a state monopoly, see Tigran W. Eldred & Thomas Schoenherr, The Lawyer's Duty of Public Service: More Than Charity?, 96 W. Va. L. Rev. 367 (1993-1994). See also Stephen Lubet, Professionalism Revisited, 42 Emory L.J. 197 (1993) (arguing that personal involvement of prestigious members of the profession can have a transformative impact on ways in which courts handle cases).

pro bono obligations by assigning associates to perform the work or by funding full-time poverty lawyers. These options are unavailable or less attractive for solo practitioners or lawyers in small firms. In addition, if the program has a fixed-dollar buy-out provision, this option also operates regressively, falling more heavily on lawyers with lower incomes.[42] To the extent that the obligation is imposed only on the lawyers of certain states (New York, for example), it places those lawyers at a competitive disadvantage with lawyers in other states who do not bear this "tax."[43]

Critics of mandatory pro bono refer to significant practical and administrative difficulties with any such program. The program must address whether the requirement applies to lawyers engaged in teaching, politics, business, or government practice.[44] The definition of qualifying services must be carefully considered. If charitable or bar work counts, then the goal of delivering legal services to the poor will be eroded, but if bar and charitable work does not qualify, the availability and willingness of lawyers to perform these services will diminish. A question exists as to whether reduced-fee work will qualify in part as pro bono work. In addition, the range of service options must be broad to avoid forcing lawyers into service that conflicts with their political or religious values.[45] Additional administrative personnel will be required to review reports to determine whether lawyers are in compliance with their pro bono obligations and to institute proceedings against lawyers who fail to do so. Finally, increasing the supply of legal services for the poor may harm rather than help the poor because more litigation may increase the cost of basic services provided to the poor, such as housing.[46]

The concept of mandatory pro bono has not been received with much enthusiasm by the bar. No state has adopted a mandatory

42. Roger C. Cramton, Mandatory Pro Bono, 19 Hofstra L. Rev. 1113, 1133-1134 (1991).

43. Id. at 1130-1131.

44. Id. at 1128.

45. Id. at 1129-1130.

46. Jonathan R. Macey, Mandatory *Pro Bono*: Comfort for the Poor or Welfare for the Rich?, 77 Cornell L. Rev. 1115 (1992). But see Ronald H. Silverman, Conceiving a Lawyer's Legal Duty to the Poor, 19 Hofstra L. Rev. 885 (1991). Professor Silverman's article is part of a symposium on mandatory pro bono, which includes the Marrero Report and the Cramton article cited earlier. See Symposium on Mandatory Pro Bono, 19 Hofstra L. Rev. No. 4 (1991). For other perspectives on the mandatory pro bono debate, see Symposium, Mandatory Pro Bono in Maryland, 49 Md. L. Rev. 1 (1990).

pro bono requirement, although there has been some movement to place greater emphasis on voluntary pro bono service. In 1993, the ABA amended Model Rule 6.1 to provide for a voluntary pro bono standard of 50 hours per year, a substantial majority of which should be directed to "persons of limited means." Prior to the amendment, the rule provided:

> A lawyer should render public interest legal service. A lawyer may discharge this responsibility by providing professional services at no fee or a reduced fee to persons of limited means or to public service or charitable groups or organizations, by service in activities for improving the law, the legal system or the legal profession, and by financial support for organizations that provide legal services to persons of limited means.

The older version of Rule 6.1 did not specify an hourly standard, nor did it direct lawyers to focus their pro bono efforts on the poor. Several states, including Arizona, Florida, and Kentucky, have changed their rules of professional conduct to include more substantial provisions on voluntary pro bono representation.[47] Nonetheless, the majority of states continue to adhere to the ABA's older version of Rule 6.1.

C. DELIVERY OF LEGAL SERVICES TO INDIVIDUALS ABLE TO AFFORD A LAWYER

1. *Constitutional Right of Lawyers to Engage in Marketing of Legal Services*

The traditional answer of the profession to the question of how legal services should be delivered to individuals who were able to afford a lawyer was by reputation. Commercial advertising or solicitation by lawyers was long considered to be unprofessional. Canon 27 of the original Canon of Ethics, adopted by the American Bar Association in 1908, provided as follows: "[S]olicitation of

47. Ariz. R. Prof. Conduct 6.1; Fla. R. Prof. Conduct 4-6.1; Kentucky Sup. Ct. R. 3.130 (6.1).

business by circulars or advertisements, or by personal communications, or interviews, not warranted by personal relations, is unprofessional." A line of Supreme Court cases beginning in 1977, however, has fundamentally altered these traditional restrictions on advertising and solicitation.

a. Basic Constitutional Principles Governing Regulation of Advertising and In-person Solicitation

During the last 25 years, the Supreme Court has established and expanded the constitutional right of lawyers to market their legal services. The genesis of this protection was the Court's decision in Virginia State Board of Pharmacy v. Virginia Consumer Council, Inc.[48] In *Virginia Pharmacy Board,* the Court rejected the commercial speech exception to the First Amendment and held that commercial speech was entitled to some measure of First Amendment protection. The Court in *Virginia Pharmacy* reserved judgment, however, on whether its decision applied to other professions.

One year later, in Bates v. State Bar of Arizona,[49] the Court applied its holding in *Virginia Pharmacy* to lawyer advertising. The question in *Bates* was whether the Arizona Supreme Court could constitutionally discipline lawyers for violating its Code of Professional Responsibility by making *truthful* newspaper advertisements about the *price* and *availability* of certain routine legal services, including uncontested divorce, adoption, nonbusiness bankruptcy, and change of name. The Court noted that the listener's interest in commercial speech is substantial and "often may be far keener than his concern for urgent political dialogue."[50] Further, commercial speech serves important societal interests by informing the public of the availability, nature, and price of products and services.[51] The Court held that such advertising was constitutionally protected under the First Amendment and could not be prohibited by the state.[52] In its opinion, the Court considered and rejected six justifications offered by the state of Arizona to support its ban on advertising of legal services: the adverse effect

48. 425 U.S. 748 (1976).
49. 433 U.S. at 350 (1977).
50. Id. at 364.
51. Id.
52. Id. at 384.

on professionalism, the inherently misleading nature of attorney advertising, the adverse effect on the administration of justice, the undesirable economic effects of advertising, the adverse effect of advertising on the quality of service, and the difficulties of enforcement.[53]

The Court in *Bates* was careful, however, to indicate the limitations of its opinion: First, the decision did not prevent state regulation of false, deceptive, or misleading advertising.[54] The Court reserved judgment on claims about the quality of legal services: "[A]dvertising claims as to the quality of services — a matter we do not address today — are not susceptible of measurement or verification; accordingly, such claims may be so likely to be misleading as to warrant restriction."[55] Second, in-person solicitation posed unique problems that might warrant restriction. Third, the Court left open the possibility that warning or supplementation might be required, even as to advertising like that involved in *Bates,* to prevent consumers from being misled. Fourth, like other forms of speech, a state may impose reasonable "time, place, and manner" restrictions. Fifth, advertising concerning illegal transactions could be prohibited. Finally, "the special problems of advertising on the electronic broadcast media will warrant special consideration."[56]

In In re R.M.J.,[57] the Court broadened its holding in *Bates,* setting

53. For articles discussing the policy issues involved in lawyer advertising, see Geoffrey C. Hazard, Jr., et al., Why Lawyers Should be Allowed to Advertise: A Market Analysis of Legal Services, 58 N.Y.U. L. Rev. 1084 (1983); Fred S. McChesney & Timothy J. Muris, The Effect of Advertising on the Quality of Legal Services, 65 A.B.A. J. 1503 (Oct. 1979). See generally Jay W. Stein, Advertising in the Legal Profession: A Descriptive Bibliography and Reference Guide (1993). In 1995, the ABA issued a comprehensive report on lawyer advertising, ABA Commission on Advertising, Lawyer Advertising at the Crossroads (1995). The report outlines 18 considerations and 40 strategies to guide policymakers in dealing with the complex array of issues involved in lawyer advertising and solicitation.

54. See, e.g., In re Zang, 741 P.2d 267 (Ariz. 1987) (en banc), *cert. denied,* 484 U.S. 1067 (1988) (lawyers disciplined for misrepresentation in advertisements regarding ability and willingness to take cases to trial). See also ABA Comm. on Ethics and Prof. Resp., Formal Opinion 94-388 (under Model Rule 7.1, which prohibits false and misleading communications regarding legal services, firm must provide full description of relationship with other firms to clients to whom information is reasonably believed to be relevant).

55. 433 U.S. at 383-384.

56. Id.

57. 455 U.S. 191 (1982).

forth general principles for determining the constitutionality of restrictions on lawyer advertising. After the Supreme Court's decision in *Bates,* the Missouri Supreme Court amended its Code of Professional Responsibility to allow some lawyer advertising, but the rules continued to limit advertising to a significant degree. The rules allowed lawyers to publish in the print media ten categories of information: name, address, and telephone number; areas of practice; date and place of birth; schools attended; foreign language ability; office hours; fee for an initial consultation; availability of a schedule of fees; credit arrangements; and the fixed fee to be charged for certain specified "routine" legal services. The state Supreme Court and the Advisory Committee charged with enforcing the rules interpreted them to mean that these ten categories were exclusive; lawyers could not advertise information beyond these categories. The Missouri rules also placed specific restrictions on the ways in which lawyers could advertise the areas in which they practiced.

Relying on its decision in Central Hudson Gas & Electric Corp. v. Public Service Commission,[58] the Court articulated three principles to be used in determining the constitutionality of restrictions on legal advertising:

- A state may constitutionally prohibit lawyers from engaging in false or inherently misleading advertising.
- A state may not prohibit advertising that is potentially misleading, but may regulate such advertising by a method "no broader than reasonably necessary to prevent the deception," such as by explanation or disclaimer.
- States retain the right to regulate truthful advertising in some limited circumstances if the state establishes "a substantial interest and the interference with speech must be in proportion to the interest served."[59]

The Court then considered three charges against R.M.J. in light of these principles: listing the areas of his practice in language or in terms other than those provided by the rule; listing the courts and states in which he had been admitted to practice; and mailing announcement cards to persons other than "lawyers, clients, for-

58. 447 U.S. 557 (1980).
59. 455 U.S. at 203.

mer clients, personal friends, and relatives." (R.M.J. conceded the constitutionality of the disclaimer requirement.) The Court found that none of the charges could be upheld constitutionally:

> [N]one of the three restrictions in the rule upon appellant's First Amendment rights can be sustained in the circumstances of this case. There is no finding that appellant's speech was misleading. Nor can we say that it was inherently misleading, or that restrictions short of an absolute prohibition would not have sufficed to cure any possible deception. We emphasize, as we have throughout the opinion, that the States retain the authority to regulate advertising that is inherently misleading or that has proved to be misleading in practice. There may be other substantial state interests as well that will support carefully drawn restrictions. But although the States may regulate commercial speech, the First and Fourteenth Amendments require that they do so with care and in a manner no more extensive than reasonably necessary to further substantial interests. The absolute prohibition on appellant's speech, in the absence of a finding that his speech was misleading, does not meet these requirements.[60]

Bates and *R.M.J.* dealt with the constitutionality of restrictions on lawyer advertising. In companion cases—Ohralik v. Ohio State Bar Assn.[61] and In re Primus[62] — the Court established constitutional principles governing in-person solicitation. *Ohralik* involved a classic case of "ambulance chasing." In casual conversation at a post office, attorney Ohralik heard about an automobile accident involving two young women. He telephoned the parents of the driver, learned that she was in the hospital, visited with the parents, and then met with their daughter in the hospital, where he offered to represent her on a contingency fee basis. Ohralik also contacted the passenger and volunteered to represent her as well. During these meetings, Ohralik secretly tape recorded the conversations. After both girls had signed contingency fee agreements, they decided that they did not want Ohralik to represent them, but he insisted that they were bound by their agreements with him.

The Supreme Court of Ohio indefinitely suspended Ohralik for solicitation of professional employment in violation of the Ohio

60. Id. at 206-207.
61. 436 U.S. 447 (1978).
62. 436 U.S. 412 (1978).

Code of Professional Responsibility. The Supreme Court affirmed. The Court rejected Ohralik's argument that, under the First Amendment, in-person solicitation was entitled to the same degree of protection as advertising. Instead, the Court found that in-person solicitation was distinguishable from advertising because it involved conduct as well as speech:

> In-person solicitation by a lawyer of remunerative employment is a business transaction in which speech is an essential but subordinate component. While this does not remove the speech from the protection of the First Amendment, as was held in *Bates* and *Virginia Pharmacy,* it lowers the level of appropriate judicial scrutiny.[63]

As a result, the state could constitutionally prevent solicitation in furtherance of important state interests. The Court found—indeed Ohralik conceded—that the state had an important interest in preventing those aspects of solicitation that involve fraud, undue influence, intimidation, overreaching, and other forms of "vexatious conduct."[64]

In re Primus[65] involved a radically different situation from *Ohralik.* Primus practiced with a public interest law firm that was affiliated with the American Civil Liberties Union (ACLU); she also served as the lawyer for the South Carolina Council on Human Relations, a nonprofit organization. During the summer of 1973, local and national newspapers had reported that pregnant women in Aiken, South Carolina were being sterilized as a condition for receiving continued medical benefits under the Medicaid program. Primus spoke at a meeting arranged by the Council on Human Relations to women who had been sterilized, including Mary Etta Williams. Ms. Primus informed the women attending the meeting of their legal rights, including the right to sue any doctor who had engaged in sterilization. Subsequently, the ACLU advised Ms. Primus that it was willing to provide representation to mothers in Aiken who had been sterilized. A representative of the Council on Human Relations told Ms. Primus that Ms. Williams wanted to bring suit. After Primus received this information, she wrote Williams a letter informing her of the ACLU's willingness to represent

63. 436 U.S. at 457.
64. Id. at 462.
65. 436 U.S. 412 (1978).

her in a suit against the doctor who had performed the sterilization.

The South Carolina Supreme Court publicly reprimanded Primus for solicitation in violation of the Code of Professional Responsibility. The Supreme Court reversed. The Court distinguished *Ohralik.* While *Ohralik* had involved solicitation for pecuniary gain, *Primus* involved solicitation for political purposes. In NAACP v. Button[66] and subsequent cases, the Court had held that under the associational freedom guaranteed by the First Amendment organizations such as the NAACP could solicit clients as part of "collective activity undertaken to obtain meaningful access to the courts." The Court found that there was not a "meaningful distinction" between the ACLU and the NAACP.[67] In particular, the Court rejected the argument that the ACLU should be treated differently than the NAACP under the First Amendment because the ACLU has as one of its primary purposes the rendering of legal services and because the ACLU has a policy of seeking the award of attorney fees.[68] Since Primus's solicitation came within the core of First Amendment protection, the Court ruled that she could be disciplined only if South Carolina could establish a compelling state interest and only if the means used are "closely drawn to avoid unnecessary abridgment of associational freedoms."[69] While the state could apply a prophylactic rule in commercial solicitation cases like *Ohralik,* in political solicitation cases like *Primus* the state must show actual injury.[70] The Court found that the state had failed to establish that any such injury occurred.[71]

b. Application and Development: Targeted Advertising, Direct Mail Advertising, and False or Misleading Communications

In subsequent cases, the Court has refined the application of the principles established in *Bates, R.M.J., Ohralik,* and *Primus.* The type of advertising that came before the Court in *Bates* and in *R.M.J.*

66. 371 U.S. 415 (1963). See discussion at Chapter 6.C.2.
67. 436 U.S. at 426-427.
68. Id. at 427-429.
69. Id. at 432.
70. Id. at 434-435.
71. Id.

was relatively bland. In a series of cases, however, a sharply divided Supreme Court has considered the issue of the constitutionality of restrictions on targeted advertising, i.e., advertising that deals with particular types of litigation, and direct mail advertising.

Zauderer v. Office of Disciplinary Counsel[72] involved the constitutionality of restrictions on targeted advertising. Zauderer ran advertisements in Ohio newspapers publicizing his availability to represent women who had been injured from using the Dalkon Shield contraceptive device. The advertisement included a drawing of the device with the question "DID YOU USE THIS IUD?"[73]

Before the Supreme Court, the state of Ohio conceded that Zauderer's Dalkon Shield advertisement was not false or misleading. Instead, it tried to justify discipline on three grounds. First, the state argued that Zauderer's advertisement should be treated the same as in-person solicitation in *Ohralik,* subject to a prophylactic rule. The Court rejected this argument. The Court found that the concerns that supported the Court's decision in *Ohralik*—the possibility of overreaching coupled with the potential for invasion of privacy—were not present when the lawyer used targeted advertising.[74] Second, the state argued that it could constitutionally prohibit the advertisement because it had a substantial interest in preventing lawyers from "stirring up litigation." In words that are sure to resonate with plaintiffs' lawyers, the Court stated: "[W]e cannot endorse the proposition that a lawsuit, as such, is an evil."[75] Finally, the Court found the state's claim of regulatory difficulties to be unpersuasive as a justification for prohibiting Zauderer's advertisement.[76]

The Court also held that illustrations were entitled to the same constitutional protection afforded verbal communications, rejecting the argument that the state had a substantial interest in prohibiting the use of illustrations in order to uphold the dignity of the profession. After noting that there was no suggestion that Zauderer's illustration was undignified, the Court's opinion swept more broadly:

72. 471 U.S. 626 (1985).
73. Id. at 630.
74. Id. at 641-642.
75. Id. at 643.
76. Id. at 645-646.

> [A]lthough the State undoubtedly has a substantial interest in ensuring that its attorneys behave with dignity and decorum in the courtroom, we are unsure that the State's desire that attorneys maintain their dignity in their communications with the public is an interest substantial enough to justify the abridgment of their First Amendment rights. Even if that were the case, we are unpersuaded that undignified behavior would tend to recur so often as to warrant a prophylactic rule.[77]

The Court also rejected Ohio's argument that the prohibition on illustrations was justified because illustrations were misleading due to the fact that they operate on an emotional or subconscious level:

> We are not convinced. The State's arguments amount to little more than unsupported assertions: nowhere does the State cite any evidence or authority of any kind for its contention that the potential abuses associated with the use of illustrations in attorneys' advertising cannot be combated by any means short of a blanket ban.[78]

In one respect, however, the Court found that Zauderer was subject to discipline. The Ohio Supreme Court had found that Zauderer violated its Code of Professional Responsibility by failing to disclose to potential clients that they would be liable for the expenses of litigation, even though they would not be liable for legal fees unless they obtained a recovery. The Court noted that "unjustified or unduly burdensome disclosure requirements might offend the First Amendment by chilling protected commercial speech." The Court ruled, however, that disclosure requirements, unlike prohibitions, were subject to less scrutiny and would be upheld "as long as [the] requirements are reasonably related to the State's interest in preventing deception of consumers."[79] The Court found that "the requirement that an attorney advertising his availability on a contingent-fee basis disclose that clients will have to pay costs even if their lawsuits are unsuccessful (assuming that to be the case) easily passes muster under this standard."[80]

In Shapero v. Kentucky Bar Assn.,[81] the Court considered the

77. Id. at 647-648.
78. Id. at 648.
79. Id. at 651.
80. Id. at 652.
81. 486 U.S. 466 (1988).

constitutionality of restrictions on "direct mail advertising" by lawyers. Shapero applied to the Kentucky Attorneys Advertising Commission for permission to send the following letter to individuals against whom foreclosure proceedings had been instituted:

> It has come to my attention that your home is being foreclosed on. If this is true, you may be about to lose your home. Federal law may allow you to keep your home by ORDERING your creditor [sic] to STOP and give you more time to pay them.
>
> You may call my office anytime from 8:30 A.M. to 5:00 P.M. for FREE information on how you can keep your home.
>
> Call NOW, don't wait. It may surprise you what I may be able to do for you. Just call and tell me that you got this letter. Remember it is FREE, there is NO charge for calling.[82]

The matter ultimately went to the Kentucky Supreme Court, which found that Shapero's letter violated Rule 7.3 of the Kentucky Rules of Professional Conduct, which prohibited lawyers from engaging in solicitation and defined solicitation to include a "letter . . . directed to a specific recipient."[83]

The Supreme Court granted certiorari and reversed. Characterizing the case as nothing more than "*Ohralik* in writing," the state of Kentucky contended that Shapero's letter could be prohibited without a showing of actual harm because of the serious potential for abuse involved in solicitation. Finding that this suggestion "misses the mark," the Court pointed out that the ban on solicitation approved in *Ohralik* rested on two fundamental differences between advertising and solicitation. First, the in-person character of solicitation creates a situation "rife with possibilities for overreaching, invasion of privacy, the exercise of undue influence, and outright fraud." Second, solicitation poses unique enforcement difficulties because it is "not visible or otherwise open to public scrutiny." The Court found that targeted direct-mail advertising was different from in-person solicitation in both respects.

The Court recognized that direct-mail advertising could be subject to abuse: Recipients might overestimate the lawyer's familiarity with their problem or believe that they have a legal problem (or a more serious legal problem) than is actually the case. The Court concluded, however, that these possibilities justified regula-

82. Id. at 469.
83. Id. at 471.

tion, but not prohibition, and suggested that states could require lawyers to file their direct-mail advertisement with a state agency to provide time and opportunity to review such mailings and that a state could force lawyers to identify direct mailings as "ADVERTISING MATERIAL."[84] The Court also pointed out that states could discipline lawyers for false or deceptive statements in direct mail advertising, the same as in media or print advertising, but it found nothing in the record to support the conclusion that Shapero's advertisement was overreaching or deceptive.

In a dissenting opinion in *Shapero*, Justice O'Connor criticized the line of decisions beginning with *Bates* because they failed to take into account fundamental differences between professional services and standardized consumer products. She also argued that the Court's decisions had failed to give sufficient weight to the substantial state interest in maintaining professional standards. She concluded: "In one way or another, time will uncover the folly of this approach. I can only hope that the Court will recognize the danger before it is too late to effect a worthwhile cure."[85]

Justice O'Connor's call in *Shapero* for a change in direction by the Supreme Court may have become a reality in the Court's decision in Florida Bar v. Went For It, Inc.[86] In 1989, the Florida Bar completed a two-year study of the effects of lawyer advertising on public opinion. Based on the study, the bar petitioned the Florida Supreme Court to adopt new restrictions on lawyer advertising.[87] As a result, the Florida Supreme Court issued new advertising rules, one of which provided as follows:

> (1) A lawyer shall not send, or knowingly permit to be sent, on the lawyer's behalf or on behalf of the lawyer's firm or partner, an associate, or any other lawyer affiliated with the lawyer or the lawyer's firm, a written communication to a prospective client for the purpose of obtaining professional employment if:
>
> (A) the written communication concerns an action for personal injury or wrongful death or otherwise relates to an accident or disaster involving the person to whom the communication is addressed or a relative of that person, unless the accident or

84. Id. at 477.
85. Id. at 491.
86. 515 U.S. 618 (1995).
87. The Florida Bar: Petition to Amend the Rules Regulating the Florida Bar—Advertising Issues, 571 So. 2d. 451 (Fla. 1991).

> disaster occurred more than 30 days prior to the mailing of the communication;[88]

Plaintiffs[89] brought suit challenging the constitutionality of the rule. The district court found the rule unconstitutional and entered summary judgment for the plaintiffs; the Eleventh Circuit affirmed.[90] In a 5-4 decision, the Supreme Court reversed.

Writing for the majority, Justice O'Connor stated that the Court's commercial speech cases had held that commercial speech was entitled to some constitutional protection, but that such protection was more limited than that afforded speech at the "core" of the First Amendment. Accordingly, the Court engaged in "intermediate" rather than "strict" scrutiny of the Florida Rule, using the framework established in *Central Hudson:*

> Under *Central Hudson,* the government may freely regulate commercial speech that concerns unlawful activity or is misleading. . . . Commercial speech that falls into neither of those categories, like the advertising at issue here, may be regulated if the government satisfies a test consisting of three related prongs: first, the government must assert a substantial interest in support of its regulation; second, the government must demonstrate that the restriction on commercial speech directly and materially advances that interest; and third, the regulation must be "narrowly drawn."[91]

The majority found that the Florida Bar had satisfied the first prong of the test because the rule was based on two substantial state interests: First, the rule protected the "privacy and tranquility of personal injury victims and their loved ones." Second, the rule represented an "effort to protect the flagging reputations of Florida lawyers by preventing them from engaging in conduct that, the Bar maintains, 'is universally regarded as deplorable and beneath

88. Fla. Sup. Ct. R. 4-7.4(b)(1).

89. Plaintiff Went For It, Inc. was a lawyer referral service. It was affected by Rule 4-7.4(b)(1) because Rule 4-7.8(a) prohibits lawyers from accepting referrals from a lawyer referral service if that service engages in communication that violates the Rules of Professional Conduct. Plaintiff Blakely was a Florida lawyer who was substituted as a plaintiff after the original individual plaintiff, McHenry, was disbarred in an unrelated matter. 515 U.S. at 621.

90. Id. at 621-622.

91. Id. at 623-624.

common decency because of its intrusion upon the special vulnerability and private grief of victims or their families.'"[92]

While stating that the second prong of the *Central Hudson* test could not be satisfied by "mere speculation and conjecture," the Court found, however, that the two-year study by the Florida Bar of the impact of lawyer advertising on public opinion supported the conclusion that the rule advanced the state interests in question "in a direct and material way."[93] The Court distinguished Edenfield v. Fane,[94] where the Court had invalidated a Florida rule prohibiting in-person solicitation by accountants on the ground that the State Board of Accountancy had presented no studies (or even any anecdotal evidence) to support its regulation.[95] The Court in *Went for It* also noted that the plaintiffs had failed to offer any evidence to refute the studies presented by the Florida Bar.[96]

Turning to the third prong of the *Central Hudson test,* the Court pointed out that the state was not required to meet a "least restrictive means" test to regulate commercial speech. Instead, the state was only required to show a reasonable "fit" between means and ends.[97] The plaintiffs argued that the rule was unconstitutionally overbroad because it did not distinguish between victims based on the severity of their injuries. The Court rejected this position, stating that it was hard to imagine a rule that would satisfy the plaintiffs on this point, and that the "Bar's rule is reasonably well-tailored to its stated objective of eliminating targeted mailings whose type and timing are a source of distress to Floridians, distress that has caused many of them to lose respect for the legal profession."[98] The plaintiffs also argued that the rule "may prevent citizens from learning about their legal options, particularly at a time when other actors — opposing counsel and insurance adjusters — may be clamoring for victims' attentions."[99] The Court rejected this argument as well because it found that there were numerous other ways in which lawyers could inform individuals of their rights during the 30-day period:

92. Id. at 624-625
93. Id. at 625.
94. 507 U.S. 761 (1993).
95. 515 U.S. at 626.
96. Id. at 628.
97. Id. at 632.
98. Id. at 633.
99. Id.

> Our lawyer advertising cases have afforded lawyers a great deal of leeway to devise innovative ways to attract new business. Florida permits lawyers to advertise on prime-time television and radio as well as in newspapers and other media. They may rent space on billboards. They may send untargeted letters to the general population, or to discrete segments thereof. There are, of course, pages upon pages devoted to lawyers in the Yellow Pages of Florida telephone directories.[100]

The majority opinion distinguished Shapero v. Kentucky Bar Assn.,[101] the case that had invalidated restrictions on direct-mail solicitation:

> . . . *Shapero* differs in several fundamental respects from the case before us. First and foremost, *Shapero's* treatment of privacy was casual. Contrary to the dissent's suggestions, . . . the State in *Shapero* did not seek to justify its regulation as a measure undertaken to prevent lawyers' invasions of privacy interests. . . . Rather, the State focused exclusively on the special dangers of overreaching inhering in targeted solicitations. . . . Second, in contrast to this case, *Shapero* dealt with a broad ban on all direct-mail solicitations, whatever the time frame and whoever the recipient. Finally, the State in *Shapero* assembled no evidence attempting to demonstrate any actual harm caused by targeted direct mail. The Court rejected the State's effort to justify a prophylactic ban on the basis of blanket, untested assertions of undue influence and overreaching. . . . Because the State did not make a privacy-based argument at all, its empirical showing on that issue was similarly infirm.[102]

Justice Kennedy's dissenting opinion agreed with the majority that the *Central Hudson* test should be used to evaluate the constitutionality of the Florida rule, but it disagreed with the majority on the application of every prong of the test. Regarding the state interests in question, Justice Kennedy found that protection of recipients from invasion of their privacy was not a substantial state interest: "[W]e do not allow restrictions on speech to be justified on the ground that the expression might offend the listener."[103] He

100. Id. at 633-634.
101. 486 U.S. 466 (1988), discussed supra.
102. 515 U.S. at 629.
103. Id. at 638.

also rejected the bar's argument that the rule was justified to protect the reputation and dignity of the profession:

> While disrespect will arise from an unethical or improper practice, the majority begs a most critical question by assuming that direct mail solicitations constitute such a practice. The fact is, however, that direct solicitation may serve vital purposes and promote the administration of justice, and to the extent the bar seeks to protect lawyers' reputations by preventing them from engaging in speech some deem offensive, the State is doing nothing more . . . than manipulating the public's opinion by suppressing speech that informs us how the legal system works.[104]

Justice Kennedy criticized the "studies" presented by the state for their poor methodology and general incompetence: "Our cases require something more than a few pages of self-serving and unsupported statements by the State to demonstrate that a regulation directly and materially advances the elimination of a real harm when the State seeks to suppress truthful and nondeceptive speech."[105] Finally, Justice Kennedy argued that prohibition of direct mail solicitation for 30 days was wildly disproportionate to any harm that might flow from such solicitation.[106] In conclusion, the dissenting Justices saw the Court's decision as a major retreat from First Amendment protection for commercial speech in general and lawyer advertising in particular.[107] After the Court upheld Florida's 30-day waiting period on direct mail solicitation, Congress enacted legislation prohibiting communications with victims or their families for 30 days after an airplane crash involving an interstate or foreign carrier.[108]

104. Id. at 639-640.
105. Id. at 641.
106. Id. at 642.
107. Id. at 644-645.
108. 49 U.S.C.A. §1136(g)(2) (Supp. 1997) provides as follows:

> In the event of an accident involving an air carrier providing interstate or foreign air transportation, no unsolicited communication concerning a potential action for personal injury or wrongful death may be made by an attorney or any potential party to the litigation to an individual injured in the accident, or to a relative of an individual involved in the accident, before the 30th day following the date of the accident.

The federal statute applies to any "potential party," so it would appear to prohibit efforts by defendants and their insurance carriers to settle cases during the 30-day period after an accident.

In *Bates* and *R.M.J.*, the Court had indicated that states remained free to prohibit lawyers from engaging in false or misleading advertising, but the Court did not address what types of advertisements fell within those categories. Peel v. Attorney Registration & Disciplinary Commn.,[109] examined the constitutionality of restrictions on advertising of certification of specialization. Recognizing the growing specialization in the legal profession, some states have adopted systems for certifying lawyers as specialists in various areas of practice. At the same time, a number of private organizations of lawyers also have adopted certification programs. Not surprising, some tension exists between state authorities and private certifying groups. This tension came to a head in *Peel.*

Peel was certified as a civil trial specialist by the National Board of Trial Advocacy (NBTA). NBTA standards, which were approved by judges, scholars, and practitioners, required "specified experience as lead counsel in both jury and nonjury trials, participation in approved programs of continuing legal education, a demonstration of writing skills, and the successful completion of a day-long examination." Certification expires after five years unless the lawyer continues to meet NBTA requirements. NBTA issued Peel a "Certificate in Civil Trial Advocacy" in 1981, and renewed the certification in 1986. Peel had tried to verdict more than 100 jury cases and more than 300 nonjury cases, and he had participated in hundreds of additional cases that had been settled. Peel listed his certification on his letterhead as follows:

> Gary E. Peel
> Certified Civil Trial Specialist
> By the National Board of Trial Advocacy
> Licensed: Illinois, Missouri, Arizona[110]

The Illinois Supreme Court held that Peel's letterhead constituted a false and misleading advertisement and that the letterhead violated Rule 2-105(a)(3) of the Illinois Code of Professional Responsibility, which provided as follows:

> A lawyer or law firm may specify or designate any area or field of law in which he or its partners concentrates or limits his or its

109. 496 U.S. 91 (1990).
110. Id. at 96.

> practice. Except as set forth in Rule 2-105(a), no lawyer may hold himself out as "certified" or a "specialist."[111]

The U.S. Supreme Court reversed in a plurality opinion authored by Justice Stevens and joined in by Justices Brennan, Blackmun, and Kennedy. The state of Illinois contended that the use of the term "certified specialist" was inherently misleading and could therefore be prohibited because it was a claim about the quality of legal services. The Court rejected this claim:

> This analysis confuses the distinction between statements of opinion or quality and statements of objective facts that may support an inference of quality. A lawyer's certification by NBTA is a verifiable fact, as are the predicate requirements for that certification. Measures of trial experience and hours of continuing education, like information about what schools the lawyer attended or his or her bar activities, are facts about a lawyer's training and practice. A claim of certification is not an unverifiable opinion of the ultimate quality of a lawyer's work or a promise of success . . . but is simply a fact, albeit one with multiple predicates, from which a consumer may or may not draw an inference of the likely quality of an attorney's work in a given area of practice.
>
> We must assume that some consumers will infer from petitioner's statement that his qualifications in the area of civil trial advocacy exceed the general qualifications for admission to a state bar. Thus if the certification had been issued by an organization that had made no inquiry into petitioner's fitness, or by one that issued certificates indiscriminately for a price, the statement, even if true, could be misleading. In this case, there is no evidence that a claim of NBTA certification suggests any greater degree of professional qualification than reasonably may be inferred from an evaluation of its rigorous requirements.[112]

The state also argued that the use of the term "certified specialist" by the National Board of Trial Advocacy when juxtaposed with the statement that petitioner was licensed in three states was actually misleading because consumers might believe that the state of Illinois had approved the system of certification. The Court rejected this argument also. It found no evidence that any person had

111. Id. at 97.
112. Id. at 101-102 (footnotes omitted).

been actually misled, and it trusted the consuming public to know the difference between state licenses and private certification.[113]

Finally, the Court considered the state's argument that the statement was, if not actually misleading, at least potentially misleading. The Court referred to its earlier decisions holding that when statements are potentially misleading, the remedy is not outright ban, but required disclaimer or disclosure.

Justice O'Connor in a dissenting opinion, joined by Justices Scalia and Rehnquist, argued that Peel's use of the term "certified specialist" could be banned by the state of Illinois because it was inherently misleading. Justice O'Connor rejected the plurality's argument that the statement was one of fact by noting that even statements of fact can be misleading. The test, according to Justice O'Connor, should be whether the statement is "readily understandable to the average consumer of legal services." She found that consumers are not in a position to either know certifying organizations or to assess their criteria.[114] Justice O'Connor also argued that the statement was equivalent to a claim about the quality of legal services, and that prior decisions of the Court had indicated that claims about quality are so likely to mislead as to justify their prohibition.[115]

c. Unanswered Questions

While the Supreme Court has developed the constitutional principles governing regulation of lawyer advertising and solicitation to a considerable extent, a number of important questions remain unanswered. First, is electronic media advertising subject to special restrictions? Second, to what extent are advertisements about the quality of legal services constitutionally protected? Third, to what extent is in-person solicitation constitutionally protected?

113. Id. at 103.

114. Id. at 122.

115. Id. at 123. In Ibanez v. Florida Dept. of Bus. & Prof. Reg., Bd. of Accountancy, 512 U.S. 136 (1994), the Supreme Court held that an attorney's use of CPA and CFP (Certified Financial Planner) designations qualified as commercial speech. Accordingly, the state could not prohibit truthful use of such identifications unless it established that it had a substantial interest in doing so and only if no less restrictive alternative was present. Florida had failed to make such a showing.

In *Bates,* the Court specifically reserved judgment on electronic advertising stating that "the special problems of advertising on the electronic broadcast media will warrant special consideration."[116] In 1991, the Florida Supreme Court adopted rules of professional conduct that impose special restrictions on electronic advertising.[117] Under the Florida rules, lawyers may provide only factual information and may not use slogans, jingles, or dramatizations. The Florida Rules also require the information to be presented "by a single voice, with no background sound other than instrumental music"; voices of celebrities are prohibited. Only lawyers or full-time employees may appear on screen.[118] The comments justify these special restrictions as follows:

> [T]he unique characteristics of electronic media, including the pervasiveness of television and radio, the ease with which these media are abused, and the passiveness of the viewer or listener, make the electronic media especially subject to regulation in the public interest. Therefore, greater restrictions on the manner of television and radio advertising are justified than might be appropriate for advertisements in the other media. To prevent abuses, including potential interferences with the fair and proper administration of justice and the creation of incorrect public perceptions or assumptions about the manner in which our legal system works, and to promote the public's confidence in the legal profession and this country's system of justice while not interfering with the free flow of useful information to prospective users of legal services, it is necessary also to restrict the techniques used in television and radio advertising.

Under the three-part test that the Court applied most recently in *Went for It,* truthful lawyer advertising can be regulated if the state shows a substantial interest in the regulation and if the regulation is in proportion to the interest served. Are the state interests set forth in the comment sufficient to uphold the Florida Rules? It is difficult to see why the pervasiveness of the media justifies greater restriction on media advertising unless some form of abuse is involved. Similarly, the "passiveness of the viewer or listener" does not seem to be a justification for regulation unless some abuse is involved. Indeed, in *Zauderer* the Court rejected the state's argu-

116. 433 U.S. at 384.

117. The Florida Bar: Petition to Amend the Rules Regulating the Florida Bar—Advertising Issues, 571 So. 2d. 451 (Fla. 1991).

118. Fla. R. Prof. Conduct 4-7.2.

ment that illustrations could be banned because they operated on an emotional or subconscious level.[119]

Thus, it seems that the central question regarding the constitutionality of the Florida Rules is whether use of media advertising involves some form of abuse by lawyers that the state has a substantial interest in regulating. The Florida Rules refer to the state interest in preventing "potential interferences with the fair and proper administration of justice." It is highly unlikely that such an interest is sufficient to allow restriction of electronic media advertising. The state's claimed interest is in preventing *potential* rather than actual abuses. Such a speculative interest is insufficient to justify restriction of First Amendment rights. As the Court indicated in *Went for It*, the state must show actual evidence of abuse to justify a regulation.[120] Further, any regulation must be in proportion to the state's interest. The comment fails to specify the abuses that the rule seeks to prevent, but it is likely that any abuses could be regulated as least as effectively by directly prohibiting the abuse rather than indirectly restricting advertising. For example, if one of the abuses the state has in mind is increased frivolous lawsuits, it can regulate frivolous filings by sanctions, like those found in Rule 11 of the Federal Rules of Civil Procedure.

The Florida Rule also refers to incorrect public perceptions or assumptions about the manner in which the legal system operates as a justification for restricting electronic advertising. If an advertisement contains false or misleading statements, it is already subject to prohibition. It is difficult to see how restriction of truthful advertising will alleviate incorrect public perceptions or assumptions about the legal system. If such perceptions or assumptions exist, a better remedy is more information to the public about how the legal system operates through bar-sponsored communications or similar means.

Finally, the Florida Rule refers to promoting public confidence in the legal profession and the system of justice. Whether protection of the public reputation of the legal profession is a sufficient state interest to justify regulation of speech is unclear. In *Zauderer*,

119. 471 U.S. at 648-649.

120. 515 U.S. at 626. See also Jacobs v. Florida Bar, 50 F.3d 901, 906 (11th Cir. 1995) (finding that lawyers who engaged in advertising prohibited by the rules had standing to bring suit and imposing the burden of proof on the Florida Bar to show that the "harms it recites are real and that its restriction will in fact alleviate them to a material degree").

which dealt with the constitutionality of targeted advertising (Dalkon Shield cases) coupled with illustrations, the Court expressed doubt about whether the state interest in the dignity of communications made by lawyers outside the courtroom was a substantial enough state interest to justify restriction of lawyers' First Amendment rights.[121] On the other hand, in *Went for It,* the Court indicated that the state does have a substantial interest in the reputation of lawyers.[122] *Went for It,* however, involved direct mail solicitation of accident victims or their survivors shortly after accidents, a practice that the Florida Bar characterized as "deplorable and beneath common decency."[123] Further, while the Court gave some weight to the state interest in the dignity of the profession, the principal interest involved in that case was the privacy interest of the recipients of direct mail solicitations. Thus, it still seems unlikely that a state has a substantial enough interest in the dignity of the profession to warrant the restrictions found in the Florida Rules.

Advertising about quality of legal service is another area in which the scope of constitutional protection is unclear. ABA Model Rule 7.1 prohibits a lawyer from making a "false or misleading" advertisement. 7.1(b) states that a communication is false or misleading if it "is likely to create an unjustified expectation about results the lawyer can achieve." The comment to that section states that this restriction "would ordinarily preclude advertisements about results obtained on behalf of a client, such as the amount of a damage award or the lawyer's record in obtaining favorable verdicts, and advertisements containing client endorsements. Such information may create the unjustified expectation that similar results can be obtained for others without reference to the specific factual and legal circumstances." It is questionable, however, whether this restriction is constitutional. The fact that such information is potentially misleading does not justify prohibition of such advertisements. The Court has held that the appropriate method for regulating potentially misleading advertising is by disclaimer or explanation rather than prohibition. Further, in *Peel* the Court held that advertising of certification when based on verifiable facts was not inherently misleading and was therefore

121. 471 U.S. at 647-648.
122. 515 U.S. at 625-626.
123. Id. at 625.

entitled to constitutional protection. The same seems to be true about other factual statements that may raise an inference about the quality of services that a lawyer can render.

Finally, important questions about the scope of constitutional protection for in-person solicitation remain unanswered by the Court. In *Ohralik,* the Court held that a state could adopt a per se rule prohibiting in-person commercial solicitation. By contrast, in *Primus* the Court held that solicitation by letter by a lawyer affiliated with a bona fide organization devoted to civil liberties (the ACLU) for the purpose of providing access to legal services rather than for commercial gain could not be prohibited unless the state showed actual harm resulting from the solicitation. It is unclear whether solicitation lacking some of the elements of *Primus* would be subject to the actual harm standard or to a per se rule. Suppose Primus had engaged in solicitation in person rather than by letter? Or suppose Primus had been a member of a public interest law firm that was not affiliated with an organization like the ACLU? It seems unlikely that the *Primus* factors are a litmus test for the application of the actual harm standard. Instead, it seems reasonable to believe that the actual harm standard will apply when the solicitation is aimed primarily at promoting civil or constitutional rights rather than commercial gain.

Another issue dealing with the scope of the constitutional protection afforded in-person solicitation deals with what Justice Marshall in *Ohralik* called "benign solicitation":

> By "benign" commercial solicitation, I mean solicitation by advice and information that is truthful and that is presented in a noncoercive, nondeceitful, and dignified manner to a potential client who is emotionally and physically capable of making a rational decision either to accept or reject the representation with respect to a legal claim or matter that is not frivolous.[124]

The Court in *Ohralik* was not required to address the constitutionality of benign solicitation because the case dealt with in-person solicitation under circumstances where actual overreaching was likely to occur and did in fact take place.

In Edenfield v. Fane,[125] the Court considered the constitutionality of a Florida Board of Accountancy Rule prohibiting in-person so-

124. 436 U.S. at 472 n.3.
125. 507 U.S. 761 (1993).

licitation by accountants. In holding the rule unconstitutional, the Court pointed out that *Ohralik* did not hold that a state may constitutionally prohibit all in-person solicitation, but only in-person solicitation in situations "inherently conducive to overreaching and other forms of misconduct."[126] The Court struck down the Accountancy Rule, but it distinguished accountants from lawyers on two grounds. First, "[u]nlike a lawyer, a CPA is not 'a professional trained in the art of persuasion.'" Second, the "typical client of a CPA is far less susceptible to manipulation than the young accident victim in *Ohralik*."[127] The Court, however, might apply the *Edenfield* approach if a lawyer solicited a sophisticated client rather than someone like the accident victim in *Ohralik*.[128]

2. *Group Legal Services*

The term *group legal services* refers to plans under which the sponsor of the plan contracts with a lawyer or law firm to provide designated legal services to members of the plan. Group legal services plans come in a wide variety of forms. Under most plans, the sponsor and the members have a preexisting relationship, such as employer and employee, labor union and member, or credit union and member. Methods of financing of plans vary considerably. In some plans, members may pay a premium for benefits (often referred to as "prepaid legal services" plans), while other plans offer their benefits to members without direct charge. Some plans may be insured to spread risk, while others are uninsured. Plans also differ in the range of choice offered to members to select counsel. "Closed panel" plans provide a list of attorneys from whom members must select. "Open panel" plans allow members to select counsel of their choice so long as counsel is willing to agree to the terms and reimbursement limitations of the plan.

126. Id. at 774.

127. Id. at 775. For a criticism of the Court's distinction between lawyers and accountants, see Jeffrey M. Brandt, Note, Attorney In-Person Solicitation: Hope for a New Direction and Supreme Court Protection after *Edenfield v. Fane*, 25 U. Tol. L. Rev. 783 (1994).

128. Rule 7.1(b) of the District of Columbia Rules of Professional Conduct allows lawyers to engage in benign solicitation. For an argument in support of this approach, see Kristina N. Bailey, Note, "Rainmaking" and D.C. Rule of Professional Conduct 7.1: The In-Person Solicitation of Clients, 9 Geo. J. Legal Ethics 1335 (1996).

Many plans will have a "gatekeeper" law firm that provides basic services under the plan. The gatekeeper firm will refer the member to a specialist when necessary.[129]

The essence of a group legal services plan is the tripartite relationship between sponsor, member, and lawyer. The injection of the sponsor into the attorney-client relationship, however, has made group legal services plans controversial within the profession. On the one hand, a sponsor can provide valuable services to its members: A sponsor can negotiate with lawyers to obtain better rates for legal services than individuals could obtain on their own. The sponsor can also provide oversight of the quality of legal services. On the other hand, because the sponsor pays the lawyers for the services that the lawyers render to their clients, this financial relationship may have an impact on the lawyers' independent professional judgment. Further, the presence of the third-party sponsor poses possible confidentiality and conflict of interest problems.[130]

The traditional attitude of the profession toward group legal services was one of hostility. Canon 35 of the ABA's Canons of Professional Ethics, entitled "Intermediaries," provided as follows:

> The professional services of a lawyer should not be controlled or exploited by any lay agency, personal or corporate, which intervenes between client and lawyer. A lawyer's responsibilities and qualifications are individual. He should avoid all relations which direct the performance of his duties by or in the interest of such intermediary.

In a series of decisions beginning in 1963, the Supreme Court considered the impact of the First Amendment on the bar's prohibition on cooperation with intermediaries.

In NAACP v. Button,[131] the Court examined the constitutionality of several Virginia statutes that made it unlawful for any person to solicit business on behalf of an attorney, or for an attorney to accept employment or compensation from any person who had engaged in solicitation on the attorney's behalf. The NAACP

129. For a description of the various types of group legal service plans, see Wolfram, Modern Legal Ethics §16.5.3, at 902-904.

130. For a discussion of the strengths and weaknesses of group legal services plans, see id. §16.5.4, at 904-910.

131. 371 U.S. 415 (1963).

sought to enjoin enforcement of the statutes on the ground that the statutes as applied to its litigation support activities violated the freedoms of expression and association guaranteed by the First and Fourteenth Amendments. The NAACP operated a Virginia Conference which for ten years had focused on financing litigation aimed at ending racial segregation in the public schools. The Conference maintained a staff of 15 attorneys who were elected at the annual convention of the Conference. Parents claiming that their children were victims of racial segregation could apply to the Conference for legal assistance. Typically, the parents learned of this option for legal assistance through meetings sponsored by the Conference at which staff attorneys appeared and spoke. If the Conference agreed to take the case, it assigned the case to one of its staff attorneys. The Conference paid staff attorneys a per diem fee for their services and all expenses of litigation. Conference attorneys agreed to abide by NAACP policies in the acceptance and conduct of litigation supported by the Conference.

Virginia contended that the activities of the NAACP were not protected by the First Amendment because they amounted to solicitation. The Supreme Court rejected this argument stating that labels cannot foreclose First Amendment analysis.[132] The Court went on to hold that First Amendment protections are not limited to "abstract discussion":

> In the context of the NAACP objectives, litigation is not a technique of resolving private differences; it is a means for achieving the lawful objectives of equality of treatment by all government, federal, state and local, for the members of the Negro community in this country. It is thus a form of political expression.[133]

The Court pointed out that the First and Fourteenth Amendments protect "certain forms of orderly group activity," and that "association for litigation may be the most effective form of political association."[134] The Court also rejected Virginia's claim that its interest in regulating the legal profession justified the statutes. Given the impact of the statutes on First Amendment rights, the Court held that the state must show a "substantial regulatory interest, in the form of substantive evils flowing from petitioner's

132. Id. at 429.
133. Id.
134. Id. at 430-431.

activities." The Court found that Virginia had failed to meet this burden.[135]

In Brotherhood of Railroad Trainmen v. Virginia ex rel. Virginia State Bar,[136] the Court expanded its holding in *Button*. The Brotherhood operated a plan to provide legal assistance to its members in asserting rights under federal statutes for damages as a result of personal injury. Unlike *Button*, the claims asserted by members were ordinary damage claims rather than claims involving violation of constitutional rights. The Brotherhood's plan divided the country into 16 regions. In each region, the Brotherhood selected a lawyer or firm "with a reputation for honesty and skill in representing plaintiffs in railroad personal injury litigation." When a worker was injured, the secretary of the local lodge would go to the worker or his family, would advise that the claim not be settled without the advice of counsel, and would recommend that in the union's judgment the designated lawyer for the area was the best lawyer to consult. The union admitted that the result of the plan was to channel legal business to certain lawyers. The state of Virginia sued to enjoin operation of the plan claiming that it amounted to improper solicitation.

The Supreme Court upheld the Brotherhood's claim that its plan was constitutionally protected under the First and Fourteenth Amendments:

> It cannot be seriously doubted that the First amendment's guarantees of free speech, petition and assembly give railroad workers the right to gather together for the lawful purpose of helping and advising one another in asserting the rights Congress gave them . . . , statutory rights which would be vain and futile if the workers could not talk together freely as to the best course to follow. The right of members to consult with each other in a fraternal organization necessarily includes the right to select a spokesman from their number who could be expected to give the wisest counsel. That is the role played by the members who carry out the legal aid program. And the right of the workers personally or through a special department of their Brotherhood to advise concerning the need for legal assistance — and, most importantly, what lawyer a member could confidently rely on — is an inseparable part of this constitutionally guaranteed right to assist and advise each other.[137]

135. Id. at 444.
136. 377 U.S. 1 (1964).
137. Id. at 5-6.

As in *Button*, the Court rejected the state's argument based on its power to regulate the legal profession because the state had failed to show any evil or harm to the public interest flowing from the plan.[138]

In United Mine Workers of America, District 12 v. Illinois State Bar Assn.,[139] the Illinois Bar Association sued to enjoin the union from employing an attorney on salary to handle workers' compensation claims on behalf of its members, claiming that the arrangement amounted to the unauthorized practice of law. Even though the attorney was employed on a salary basis rather than receiving referrals as in *Brotherhood of Railroad Trainmen*, the Court found the arrangement subject to the same constitutional protection. The Court also made clear that its holdings in *Button* and *Trainmen* were not limited to associational activities for the purpose of political expression but also encompassed ordinary forms of litigation.[140] Four years later, in United Transportation Union v. State Bar of Michigan,[141] the Court summarized its holdings in these cases as follows: "The common thread running through our decisions . . . is that collective activity undertaken to obtain meaningful access to the courts is a fundamental right within the protection of the First Amendment."[142]

In light of these decisions, the ABA was forced to change its rules of professional conduct, but the change represented only a grudging acceptance of group legal services plans. The Model Code of Professional Responsibility adopted by the ABA in 1969 allowed lawyers to participate with group legal services plans provided that the plans met certain requirements, one of which was that cooperation was permissible "only in those instances and to the extent that controlling constitutional interpretation at the time of the rendition of the services requires the allowance of such legal service activities." DR 2-103(D)(5).[143]

During the next few years, the ABA faced continued pressure both from some ranks of the profession and from the Antitrust Division of the Justice Department to change its restrictive stance on group legal services plans. In response to these pressures, the

138. Id. at 8.
139. 389 U.S. 217 (1967).
140. Id. at 223.
141. 401 U.S. 576 (1971).
142. Id. at 585.
143. See generally Wolfram, Modern Legal Ethics, §16.5.5, at 912.

Lawyer participation in group legal services plans will, of course, depend on the rules of ethics and other law applicable in each state.[147]

3. *Restrictions on the Unauthorized Practice of Law*

Nonlawyers have not always been prohibited from practicing law. From the colonial period through the nineteenth century, many states allowed nonlawyers to represent clients, even in court.[148] The modern concept of unauthorized practice did not develop until the early part of this century, particularly during the Depression. Beginning in the 1930s, the ABA and many state and local bar associations appointed unauthorized practice committees. These committees engaged in a variety of activities, including bringing lawsuits, to prevent the unauthorized practice of law. During this period, many states enacted or greatly expanded statutes prohibiting the unauthorized practice of law.[149] While bar officials claimed that their aggressive enforcement efforts originated because of public demand about improper activities by nonlawyers, evidence indicates that the bar was attempting to protect its economic position, which had deteriorated during the Depression.[150]

Rules prohibiting the unauthorized practice of law can be enforced in a variety of ways.[151] Traditionally, courts have held that they have the inherent power to determine who is admitted to practice law. Pursuant to this power courts have enjoined or held in contempt nonlawyers who practiced law.[152] Bar committees are typical plaintiffs in such proceedings. In the vast majority of states,

147. See Cal. R. Prof. Conduct 1-600; N.Y. Judiciary Law §496 (McKinney 1983).

148. Wolfram, Modern Legal Ethics §15.1.1, at 824-825.

149. See generally Barlow F. Christensen, The Unauthorized Practice of Law: Do Good Fences Really Make Good Neighbors—or Even Good Sense?, 1980 Am. Bar Found. Res. J. 159, 161-197; Deborah L. Rhode, Policing the Professional Monopoly: A Constitutional and Empirical Analysis of Unauthorized Practice Prohibitions, 34 Stan. L. Rev. 1, 6-10 (1981).

150. Id. at 8-9.

151. For a comprehensive study of enforcement efforts, see id.

152. See Florida Bar v. Brumbaugh, 355 So. 2d 1186 (Fla. 1978) (respondent, a nonlawyer operating as a secretarial service, was enjoined from preparing papers and giving advice to individuals in connection with divorce proceedings; court permitted respondent to publish divorce forms and to complete these forms using

ABA adopted amendments to the Model Code in 1974 and 19 but even with these changes lawyer participation in group leg services plans was severely restricted.[144]

The Model Rules of Professional Conduct represent a substantial shift in attitude toward group legal services plans from the bar's traditional hostility. The proposed final draft of Model Rule 5.4 included a provision allowing lawyers to participate with group legal services plans provided four relatively mild conditions were met. This section was deleted, however, from the final version of the Model Rules.[145] Given the historical controversy surrounding group legal services plans, it is surprising that such plans are barely mentioned in the Model Rules of Professional Conduct. (The one specific mention is in Rule 7.3(d).)

The absence of a Model Rule provision dealing with group legal services does not mean that lawyer participation in group legal services plans is without any restrictions. Lawyers' participating in group legal services plans must still comply with all rules of professional conduct, including those dealing with confidentiality and conflicts of interest. In Formal Opinion 87-355, the ABA's Committee on Ethics and Professional Responsibility dealt with the status of for-profit group legal services plans under the Model Rules of Professional Conduct and issued an opinion broadly endorsing such plans, provided certain ethical requirements were met:

> The plan must allow the participating lawyer to exercise independent professional judgment on behalf of the client, to maintain client confidences, to avoid conflicts of interest, and to practice competently. The operation of the plan must not involve improper advertising or solicitation or improper fee sharing and must be in compliance with other applicable law. It is incumbent upon the lawyer to investigate and ensure that the arrangement under the plan fully complies with the Rules before the lawyer participates in the plan. Where the plan or the plan sponsor is in violation of the Rules, the lawyer who participates in the plan may violate Rule 8.4(a) by assisting the plan sponsor or by violating the Rules through the acts of the plan sponsor.[146]

144. See id. at 912-915.
145. See id. at 915-916.
146. ABA Comm. on Ethics and Prof. Resp., Formal Opinion 87-355, at 2.

legislatures have enacted statutes making the unauthorized practice of law a crime.[153] Finally, the Model Rules of Professional Conduct indirectly prohibit the unauthorized practice of law because the rules forbid lawyers from assisting nonlawyers in the unauthorized practice of law. Model Rule 5.5(b).[154]

While the doctrine of the unauthorized practice of law and the judicial power to enforce the doctrine are well established, controversy regarding the unauthorized practice of law has intensified in recent years. The fundamental issue is whether broad restrictions on the unauthorized practice of law serve the public interest.[155] The basic argument in favor of prohibitions on the unauthorized practice of law rests on protection of the public. The argument runs as follows: Legal services are complicated. Because of this complexity, lay people are unable to evaluate the competency of nonlawyers who might offer to render such services. Therefore, the state is justified in prohibiting nonlawyers from engaging in the practice of law.

This argument in favor of prohibitions on the unauthorized practice of law is suspect. First, whereas some legal services are complex, many types of legal services are relatively uncomplicated and are routinely performed by paralegals, almost all of whom are nonlawyers. The usual response to this argument is that paralegals operate under the supervision of lawyers. But this response begs the question: It admits that nonlawyers can perform legal services, but argues that the proper form of regulation for such services is by direct lawyer supervision. Whether direct lawyer supervision should be the only means for regulating nonlawyer practice is

---

information supplied by clients); Florida Bar v. Furman, 451 So. 2d 808 (Fla. 1984) (respondent held in criminal contempt for violating injunction against engaging in unauthorized practice of law in divorce cases).

153. Deborah L. Rhode, Policing the Professional Monopoly: A Constitutional and Empirical Analysis of Unauthorized Practice Prohibitions, 34 Stan. L. Rev. 1, 11-12 (1981).

154. See People v. Laden, 893 P.2d 771 (Colo. 1995) (en banc) (lawyer guilty of aiding in unauthorized practice of law by cooperating with nonlawyer who counseled and sold living trust packages).

155. For an empirical study of the unauthorized practice rules in the area of pro se divorce, see Project, The Unauthorized Practice of Law and Pro Se Divorce: An Empirical Analysis, 86 Yale L.J. 104 (1976) (study casts substantial doubt on wisdom of restrictions on unauthorized practice for nonlitigation matters, especially for indigents or individuals of modest means; benefits to clients of unauthorized practice restrictions have been exaggerated and costs are substantial). For further analysis of the policy issues involved in the unauthorized practice rules, see Roger Hunter & Robert Klonoff, A Dialogue on the Unauthorized Practice of Law, 25 Vill. L. Rev. 6 (1979).

open to question. Moreover, experienced well-trained paralegals typically require little supervision, and at least some states authorize lawyers to employ independent paralegals whom they do not directly supervise.[156]

Second, the claim that lay people are unable to evaluate the competency of legal services that they might receive from nonlawyers is true, but does not justify the conclusion that such services should be prohibited. Lay people buy many products and services when they lack the ability to evaluate the quality of the product or service. Automobiles and insurance are two examples. A variety of solutions to lack of consumer information are possible. The market will often provide a response to lack of information. *Consumer Reports* and other publications provide information to consumers about quality of most consumer products. It is not difficult to imagine similar publications developing for legal services. Further, regulatory solutions short of prohibition, such as disclosure or limited licensing, can be considered.

Policy considerations and constitutional principles also raise questions about the wisdom of the prohibition on the unauthorized practice of law.[157] As noted previously, low- and moderate-income individuals have a vast unmet need for legal services. A national sample of low-income households found that 43 percent of respondents experienced legal difficulties during the last year, but legal services were unavailable for about 50 percent of those problems.[158] Other national and state studies have reached similar conclusions. Indeed, one consequence of the continued application of rules on the unauthorized practice of law is that individuals of modest means may increasingly turn to pro se representation.[159]

The prohibitions on the unauthorized practice of law also raise constitutional issues. In *Lassiter*,[160] the Supreme Court held that indigents do not have an absolute right to appointed counsel in

156. In re Opinion No. 24 of Committee on Unauthorized Practice of Law, 607 A.2d 962 (N.J. 1992). But see Carl M. Selinger, The Retention of Limitations on the Out-of-Court Practice of Law by Independent Paralegals, 9 Geo. J. Legal Ethics 879 (1996).

157. Deborah L. Rhode, The Delivery of Legal Services by Non-Lawyers, 4 Geo. J. Legal Ethics 209, 228-233 (1990).

158. The Spangenberg Group, National Survey of the Civil Legal Needs of the Poor 3, 18 (May 1989) (Report sponsored by ABA Consortium on Legal Services and the Public).

159. For a study of this issue, see Bruce D. Sales et al., Self-Representation in Divorce Cases (ABA 1993).

160. See Chapter 6.B.1 supra.

civil cases, but quite clearly access to counsel in civil cases has due process implications. Moreover, the Court has not yet addressed the question of the constitutionality under the First Amendment of prohibitions on advertising of legal services by nonlawyers. Under the *Central Hudson* test,[161] truthful advertising is subject to regulation if the state shows a substantial interest in the regulation and if the regulation is in proportion to the interest. States certainly have a substantial interest in regulation of legal services, but it is questionable whether prohibition of such services by nonlawyers is in proportion to that interest.

In 1983, Washington became the first state to provide for licensing of nonlawyers, but on an extremely limited basis. By rule the Supreme Court created a Limited Practice Board, which has the authority to certify "closing officers." Closing officers must pass an examination, demonstrate financial responsibility, and meet continuing education requirements. The rule allows closing officers to do the following:

> select, prepare and complete documents in a form previously approved by the Board for use in closing a loan, extension of credit, sale or other transfer of real or personal property. Such documents shall be limited to deeds, promissory notes, guaranties, deeds of trust, reconveyances, mortgages, satisfactions, security agreements, releases, Uniform Commercial Code documents, assignments, contracts, real estate excise tax affidavits, and bills of sale. Other documents may be from time to time approved by the Board.[162]

Closing officers cannot give legal advice and all parties to the transaction must consent to their participation.

New Jersey has adopted an even more open approach than Washington in real estate transactions. The New Jersey Supreme Court has held that activities of real estate brokers and title officers in preparing contracts and in closing real estate transactions constitute the practice of law, but that the public interest justifies allowing such practices provided the broker or title officer notifies the vendor and purchaser of their conflicting interest in such transactions and of the general risk involved in not being represented by an attorney.[163]

161. See Chapter 6.C.1.a supra.

162. Wash. Ct. Rules, Admission to Practice Rule 12(d).

163. In re Opinion No. 26 of the Committee on the Unauthorized Practice of Law, 654 A.2d 1344 (N.J. 1995).

Virginia has taken a quite different approach to the issue of the unauthorized practice of law. That state's Supreme Court has adopted a set of rules defining what constitutes the unauthorized practice of law in the following areas: practice before tribunals, lay adjusters, collection agencies, estate planning and settlement, tax practice, real estate practice, title insurance, trade associations, and administrative agency practice.[164] Rather than providing for licensing, the Virginia rules attempt to define fairly precisely the kinds of activities that nonlawyers may perform incident to their business activities. While the Virginia rules allow nonlawyers to perform certain legal services, they also operate as a restriction on nonlawyer practice by prohibiting those activities that they do not specifically allow.

The ABA initiated a study of the issue of the unauthorized practice of law by creating a special Commission on Nonlawyer Practice. In 1994, the Commission issued a discussion draft that contains a wealth of factual detail about the extent of nonlawyer practice in the United States.[165] The report describes practice by "legal technicians" (nonlawyers providing legal services without supervision by lawyers) in the following areas: federal and state administrative agency practice, immigration practice, federal and state taxation, specially authorized practice in certain courts, housing disputes, family law, real estate, independent claim adjusters, debt collection, debt counseling, and general practice.[166] The report also includes a summary of the current rules on nonlawyer practice in many jurisdictions.

In August 1995, the Commission issued a report, "Nonlawyer Activities in Law-Related Situations," finding that, with adequate protection for the public, nonlawyers had an important role to play in delivery of legal services to the public. The Commission recommended that the ABA reconsider its ethics rules and policies in a variety of areas, including those governing the unauthorized practice of law. The Commission proposed an analytical framework that could be used by states to determine whether a particular activity should be regulated, unregulated, or prohibited:

164. Va. Sup. Ct. Unauthorized Practice Rules and Considerations.

165. ABA Commn. on Nonlawyer Practice, Nonlawyer Practice in the United States: Summary of the Factual Record (1994).

166. Id. at 17-22.

- Does the activity if performed by nonlawyers present a serious risk to life, health, safety, or economic well-being of members of the public?
- Do potential consumers have sufficient knowledge to evaluate the qualifications of nonlawyers offering the services?
- Do the benefits to the public likely to accrue from regulation outweigh any likely negative consequences of regulation?

If the activity poses a serious risk of harm, the Commission indicated that the activity should be regulated; the form that the regulation takes would depend on a weighing of the costs and benefits of the regulation. The Commission outlined a wide range of regulatory options that states might consider, including registration, licensing, or disclosure. The Commission also summarized various areas in which states might consider regulation, including age, experience, education, training, recordkeeping, continuing education, and admission examinations.[167]

A central issue in connection with reevaluation of restrictions on the unauthorized practice of law is bar control. The bar obviously has a financial interest in limiting competition by nonlawyers. To the extent that the bar controls such restrictions, reform is unlikely to be great. The experience in California is illustrative. In July 1990, a Commission on Legal Technicians created by the California Bar issued a report recommending that the state Supreme Court adopt a rule allowing nonlawyers to practice law, initially in the areas of bankruptcy, family, and landlord-tenant, under a licensing and regulatory system.[168] Unsurprisingly, the report caused considerable controversy within the bar. In August 1991, the Board of Governors of the California Bar defeated a more limited proposal for a bar-controlled board that would license legal technicians only in the area of landlord-tenant.[169] Meaningful reform of the

167. The Commission's report is summarized in Lawyers' Manual Prof. Conduct (ABA/BNA), 11 Current Rep. 255 (1995). For criticism of the Commission's proposals, see Deborah L. Rhode, Essay, Professionalism in Perspective: Alternative Approaches to Nonlawyer Practice, 22 N.Y.U. Rev. L. & Soc. Change 701 (1996).

168. See Kathleen E. Justice, Note, There Goes the Monopoly: The California Proposal to Allow Nonlawyers to Practice Law, 44 Vand. L. Rev. 179 (1991). See also Ryan J. Talamante, Note, We Can't All Be Lawyers. . . . Or Can We? Regulating the Unauthorized Practice of Law in Arizona, 34 Ariz. L. Rev. 873 (1992).

169. Don J. DeBenedictis, California Bar Drops Technician Plan, 77 A.B.A. J. 36 (Nov. 1991).

rules on the unauthorized practice of law is likely to require reduction in bar control of the process.[170]

D. OTHER MARKET RESTRICTIONS

1. *Ancillary Businesses*

Rules of ethics have traditionally prevented lawyers from entering into partnerships (or corporations) with nonlawyers, including other professionals, when the activities of the entity will involve the practice of law. Canon 33 of ABA's 1908 Canons of Ethics provided as follows: "Partnerships between lawyers and members of other professions or nonprofessional persons should not be formed or permitted where any part of the partnership's employment consists of the practice of law." This prohibition was carried forward in DR 3-103(A) (partnerships) and DR 5-107(C) (corporations or associations) of the Code of Professional Responsibility and in Model Rules 5.4(b), (d). This restriction rested on two rationales: prevention of interference by nonlawyers with lawyers' independent professional judgment on behalf of their clients and concern about the unauthorized practice of law. See EC 3-8, EC 5-24, and comm. 5.4(b).[171]

In the 1980s, some prominent law firms began offering to their clients a variety of nonlegal services. A 1991 survey[172] identified the following "ancillary business" activities by law firms:

15 engaged in lobbying, legislative services, or government relations
13 tax, investment, and financial consulting
13 international trade
4 environmental consulting

170. See Deborah L. Rhode, The Delivery of Legal Services by Non-Lawyers, 4 Geo. J. Legal Ethics 209, 232-233 (1990). See also Alan Morrison, Defining the Unauthorized Practice of Law: Some New Ways of Looking at an Old Question, 4 Nova L.J. 363 (1980) (calling for creation of body consisting of lawyers, consumers, and competitors of lawyers to set standards for performance of legal services by nonlawyers).

171. See Wolfram, Modern Legal Ethics §16.4, at 898.

172. Stephanie B. Goldberg, More Than the Law: Ancillary Business Growth Continues, 78 A.B.A. J. 54 (March 1992) (citing a study done by Phyllis W. Haserot).

4 real estate brokerage and development
4 labor relations
3 economic research
3 public affairs
2 media relations

Some law firms provided these services directly by lawyers or nonlawyer employees of the firm. For example, many law firms have lawyers who engage in lobbying or other legislative activities. More typically, however, the firm created a corporate or partnership subsidiary to furnish ancillary services. The subsidiary form was particularly appealing when other professionals would be providing the ancillary services. Such professionals often demanded an ownership interest in any ventures in which they engaged. The rules of ethics, however, prohibited nonlawyers from owning an interest in a partnership or professional corporation that involved the practice of law. Thus, nonlawyer professionals could not own an interest in the law firm itself. The subsidiary form avoided this ethical problem because the subsidiary engaged only in nonlegal services.

Spurred by concerns expressed by Chief Justice Warren Burger about trends in the profession, in 1984 the ABA created a Commission on Professionalism (the Stanley Commission). The Commission issued a report in 1986 finding the development of ancillary businesses by law firms "disturbing" and calling for further study of the trend.[173] Two groups in the ABA then began to study the issue of ancillary businesses: the ABA Special Coordinating Committee on Professionalism (SCCOP), which was created to carry out the recommendations of the Stanley Commission, and the Task Force on Ancillary Business Activities of the Litigation Section of the ABA.[174]

The SCCOP report found that ancillary business activities by law firms did pose certain ethical problems, including client confusion, conflicts of interest, and confidentiality. The report recognized, however, the benefits to clients from ancillary services. As a result,

173. ABA Commission on Professionalism, ". . . In the Spirit of Public Service": A Blueprint for the Rekindling of Lawyer Professionalism, 112 F.R.D. 243, 281 (1986).

174. The discussion of the history of the ABA's ancillary business rule that follows is drawn from Ted Schneyer, Policymaking and the Perils of Professionalism: The ABA's Ancillary Business Debate as a Case Study, 35 Ariz. L. Rev. 363, 369-372 (1993).

it recommended regulation rather than prohibition of ancillary business activities.[175]

The ABA Committee on Ethics and Professional Responsibility, which has general responsibility for preparing amendments to the Rules of Professional Conduct, took up SCCOP's recommendation and offered to the ABA's House of Delegates proposed Model Rule 5.7. The Committee's proposed rule would have permitted law firms to engage in ancillary business activities, but would have regulated such businesses to deal with the problems that the SCCOP report had identified. The Committee's proposed rule first required a lawyer whose firm provided ancillary business services to disclose in writing to all customers of the ancillary business entity the nature of the relationship between the firm and the entity. The rule went on to provide that an ancillary business customer would be treated as a client of the law firm, entitled to the full protection of the rules of professional ethics, unless the ancillary services were unrelated to any matter in which the firm represented the customer and the customer had been notified that the relationship between the customer and the law firm was not one of lawyer and client. Finally, the ABA Committee's proposed rule outlined procedures that firms must have in place to ensure that nonlawyers providing ancillary services complied with the rules of professional conduct.

The Litigation Section's task force, however, took a quite different approach from the one offered by the ABA Committee. While the task force expressed concern about the ethical issues raised by SCCOP, its principal difficulty with ancillary business activities involved professionalism. The task force identified six professionalism concerns: (1) compromises to lawyers' independent professional judgment, (2) decline in the quality of legal work, (3) threats to the reputation of the profession, (4) nonlawyers obtaining interests in law firms, (5) nonlegal businesses being given the right to own law firms or to provide legal services, and (6) loss of the bar's right of self regulation. The task force recommended that law firms and lawyers be prohibited from engaging in all ancillary business activities, except under the following conditions: (1) the services are offered solely to clients of the firm and are "incidental to, in

175. See ABA, Special Coordinating Comm. on Professionalism, Special Report to the House of Delegates on Ancillary Business Activities of Lawyers and Law Firm 4-12 (Dec. 1990).

connection with and concurrent to, the provision of legal services by the law firm to such clients"; (2) such services are offered solely by the employees of the firm and not through an affiliated entity; (3) the law firm makes appropriate written disclosures to its clients; and (4) the law firm does not hold itself out as engaging in nonlegal activities except as specifically permitted by the rule. The Litigation Section's proposed rule would have eliminated many of the nonlegal service activities that law firms had developed during the 1980s.[176]

In 1991, the ABA's House of Delegates adopted the Litigation Section's proposed rule by a narrow vote of 197 to 186. The closeness of the vote and the drastic impact that adoption of the rule would have on the practice of some firms spurred an intense effort to have the rule rescinded. At its 1992 meeting, the House of Delegates reversed itself and deleted Rule 5.7 by a vote of 190 to 183. Finally, in 1994, the ABA's House of Delegates, again by a relatively close vote of 237 to 183, adopted a new version of Rule 5.7 to fill the gap left by its prior actions.[177] The new Rule 5.7 returns to the regulatory approach originally proposed by SCCOP:

> (a) A lawyer shall be subject to the Rules of Professional Conduct with respect to the provision of law-related services, as defined in paragraph (b), if the law-related services are provided:
>
> (1) by the lawyer in circumstances that are not distinct from the lawyer's provision of legal services to clients; or
>
> (2) by a separate entity controlled by the lawyer individually or with others if the lawyer fails to take reasonable measures to assure that a person obtaining the law-related services knows that the services of the separate entity are not legal services and that the protections of the client-lawyer relationship do not exist.
>
> (b) The term "law-related services" denotes services that might reasonably be performed in conjunction with and in substance are related to the provision of legal services, and that are not prohibited as unauthorized practice of law when provided by a nonlawyer.

Reviewing the history and arguments involved in the ABA's consideration of the ancillary business issue, Professor Ted Schneyer argues that the "lens of professionalism" distorted and marred the

176. See Dennis J. Block et al., Model Rule of Professional Conduct 5.7: Its Origin and Interpretation, 5 Geo. J. Legal Ethics 739, 764-777, 816 (1992) (Mr. Block was chair of the Litigation Section's Task Force on Ancillary Business Activities).

177. Lawyers' Manual Prof. Conduct (ABA/BNA), 10 Current Rprt. 13 (1994).

analysis of the underlying issues. To Schneyer, the lesson to be drawn from the episode is that the ABA should not debate the merits of rules of ethics in the "rhetoric or 'idiom' of professionalism" but should instead carefully analyze the costs and benefits of its rules.[178] Professor Gary Munneke offers a different perspective on the issue. He argues that rules of ethics prohibiting law firm diversification impede the ability of lawyers to compete in the market for professional services. Professor Munneke also claims that the rules may not withstand antitrust and First Amendment scrutiny.[179]

State supreme courts are, of course, free to adopt their own rules on the issue of ancillary businesses. (If a court does nothing, ancillary business activities would be largely unregulated when conducted through subsidiaries or affiliates. The Rules of Professional Conduct prohibit partnerships and fee splitting with nonlawyers, but these have little impact on ancillary business activities conducted through related entities.) The District of Columbia Court of Appeals has adopted the following provision as part of its Rules of Professional Conduct:

RULE 5.4 PROFESSIONAL INDEPENDENCE OF A LAWYER

(a) A lawyer or law firm shall not share legal fees with a nonlawyer, except that: . . .

(4) Sharing of fees is permitted in a partnership or other form of organization which meets the requirements of paragraph (b).

(b) A lawyer may practice law in a partnership or other form of organization in which a financial interest is held or managerial authority is exercised by an individual nonlawyer who performs professional services which assist the organization in providing legal services to clients, but only if:

(1) The partnership or organization has as its sole purpose providing legal services to clients;

178. Ted Schneyer, Policymaking and the Perils of Professionalism: The ABA's Ancillary Business Debate as a Case Study, 35 Ariz. L. Rev. 363, 365-366 (1993).

179. Gary A. Munneke, Dances With Nonlawyers: A New Perspective on Law Firm Diversification, 61 Fordham L. Rev. 559 (1992). For a contrary view on the constitutionality of restrictions on ancillary business activities, see Dennis J. Block et al., Model Rule of Professional Conduct 5.7: Its Origin and Interpretation, 5 Geo. J. Legal Ethics 739, 811-814 (1992).

> (2) All persons having such managerial authority or holding a financial interest undertake to abide by these Rules of Professional Conduct;
>
> (3) The lawyers who have a financial interest or managerial authority in the partnership or organization undertake to be responsible for the nonlawyer participants to the same extent as if nonlawyer participants were lawyers under Rule 5.1;
>
> (4) The foregoing conditions are set forth in writing.

The District of Columbia approach appears to take a middle position between the regulatory and prohibitory approaches debated by the ABA. Under current ABA Rule 5.7, ancillary businesses can opt out of the application of the Model Rules by written disclosure to the client. The District of Columbia rule subjects ancillary businesses to the rules of professional conduct and requires lawyers to supervise the activity of nonlawyers to ensure their compliance with these rules. It is questionable, however, whether it makes sense to apply all of the rules of professional conduct to ancillary business activities. For example, it is likely that the broad conflict of interest rules that apply to lawyers would be inappropriate when applied to ancillary business activities.

2. *Sale of a Law Practice*

Traditionally, the profession has viewed the sale of "good will" of a law practice as unethical. ("Good will" refers to the value of the list of clients as opposed to the tangible assets of the practice.) In Formal Opinion 266 (1945), the ABA Committee on Professional Ethics dealt with the issue as follows:

> A law firm has asked the opinion of the committee as to the ethical propriety of the purchase from the heirs or personal representatives of a deceased lawyer who had no partner, of his good will and practice, whether by payment of a lump sum or by an agreement to pay a stated percentage of the future receipts, gross or net, from his clients. . . .
>
> The good will of the practice of a lawyer is not, however, of itself an asset, which either he or his estate can sell. As said by the Committee on Professional Ethics of the New York County Lawyers' Association in its Opinion 109 (October 6, 1943):

> Clients are not merchandise. Lawyers are not tradesmen. They have nothing to sell but personal service. An attempt, therefore, to barter in clients, would appear to be inconsistent with the best concepts of our professional status.

Aside from professionalism concerns, sale of good will of a practice raises various ethical problems. Professor Leslie Minkus summarizes these as follows:

> (1) To turn over the selling lawyer's files to the purchasing lawyer would, in virtually all cases, constitute a violation of the selling lawyer's duty of confidentiality.
> (2) To the extent that the purchase price is a function of fees earned by the purchasing lawyer, the agreement violates the proscription of sharing fees without sharing the effort and/or responsibility.
> (3) To the extent that some or all of the purchase price is paid, not to the selling lawyer, but to his estate, the agreement violates the proscription against sharing of fees with laypersons.
> (4) The fact that the value of the lawyer's practice will depend largely on the number of clients who follow his recommendation and retain the purchasing lawyer puts the selling lawyer in a position of direct conflict with his clients.
> (5) The sale would almost inevitably involve the recommendation of employment of the purchaser in violation of the prohibition against the payment of money by a lawyer for the recommendation of him by another. Such recommendation might also be considered improper solicitation.
> (6) Because most sales include a covenant not to compete with the purchasing lawyer, the agreement arguably violates the prohibition against such covenants except as a condition to payment of retirement benefits by a lawyer's former firm.[180]

Some commentators argued, however, that the ethical concerns outlined above did not justify a total ban on the sale of the good will of law practices.[181] In addition, proponents of allowing sales of law practices made two arguments in favor of their position.

180. Leslie A. Minkus, The Sale of a Law Practice: Toward a Professionally Responsible Approach, 12 Golden Gate L. Rev. 353, 356-357 (1982).

181. See Stephen E. Kalish, The Sale of a Law Practice: The Model Rules of Professional Conduct Point in a New Direction, 39 U. Miami L. Rev. 471 (1985); Leslie A. Minkus, The Sale of a Law Practice: Toward a Professionally Responsible Approach, 12 Golden Gate L. Rev. 353, 357-377 (1982).

First, they made a "consumer protection" case for permitting sales of practices. By allowing such sales, sole practitioners would have a financial incentive to provide for the orderly transition of their cases in the event of their illness, retirement, or death. The present prohibition on sales removes that incentive. Second, proponents made a fairness case for allowing sales. They argued that the rules of ethics discriminated in favor of partners over sole practitioners.[182] Under the Code of Professional Responsibility and the original Model Rules of Professional Conduct, partners and their beneficiaries could receive retirement payments that included compensation for the good will value of their partnerships interests. See DR 2-107(B), 3-102(A), and Model Rule 5.4(a). Sole practitioners, however, could not capitalize on their good will by selling their interests.[183]

It should be noted, however, that the traditional prohibition on sale of a law practice did not actually prevent many sole practitioners from receiving compensation for their goodwill. Sole practitioners could ethically provide for the orderly transition of their practices after their retirement or death by entering into a partnership agreement in which the new partner could continue the practice while paying death or retirement benefits to the former partner.

In 1989, the California Supreme Court amended its Rules of Professional Conduct to allow lawyers to sell their practices, including good will, provided certain conditions for the protection of clients were met.[184] Following the lead of the California Supreme Court, the ABA amended the Model Rules of Professional Conduct at its February 1990 meeting to include Model Rule 1.17, permitting the sale of law practices.[185]

182. But see James K. Sterrett II, The Sale of a Law Practice, 121 U. Pa. L. Rev. 306 (1972) (arguing that different treatment for sole practitioners, who were prohibited from selling their practices, and partners, who were permitted to receive retirement payments based on their partnership interests, was justified because the quality of legal service that clients may expect to receive from partners is higher than the quality that they can expect to receive from purchasers of practices). See also ABA Comm. on Prof. Ethics and Grievances, Formal Opinion 266 (1945) (permissible to make arrangements for handling cases in event of emergency).

183. See generally Laurel S. Terry, Law Firms for Sale . . . The Rules are Changing, 12 Pa. Law. 7 (June 1990) (on Westlaw).

184. Cal. R. Prof. Conduct 2-300.

185. For a criticism of various aspects of Model Rule 1.17, see Scott M. Schoenwald, *Model Rule* 1.17 and the Ethical Sale of Law Practices: A Critical Analysis, 7 Geo. J. Legal Ethics 395 (1993).

Only a few states, however, have adopted the ABA Model Rule. In states operating under the Code of Professional Responsibility or the Model Rules without Rule 1.17, sale of the good will of a law practice is still unethical.[186] Further, any resulting contract may be unenforceable because it violates public policy. For example, in O'Hara v. Ahlgren, Blumenfeld & Kempster,[187] the Illinois Supreme Court held that the widow of a deceased attorney could not enforce a contract for the sale of her husband's law practice because the agreement violated the ethical prohibition on fee splitting.

3. *Covenants Not to Compete and Other Restrictions on Departures from Firms*

In recent years, the legal profession has witnessed a growth in lawyer turnover. Lawyers leave their old firms, join new firms, and open their own practices.[188] Departures of lawyers from their firms raise some difficult legal and ethical issues. Two issues have commonly arisen in connection with separation of lawyers from their firms. First, what are the financial implications of a lawyer's departure? In particular, who is entitled to the fees from cases that the lawyer was handling prior to the lawyer's departure? Second, what restrictions, if any, may the former firm impose on the new practice of a departing lawyer?

The issue of the respective rights and obligations of the departing lawyer and the lawyer's former firm regarding fees from cases that the lawyer was handling prior to the lawyer's departure can produce considerable tension between the parties because of the potential financial impact on both the lawyer and the firm. This tension can be exacerbated by different expectations and perceptions of the departing lawyer and the remaining partners. In addition, relations between the parties can be complicated because of misunderstanding of the governing legal and ethical principles.

What are the legal and ethical principles that govern departures

186. See, e.g., In re Kaiser, 489 N.Y.S.2d 735 (App. Div.), *appeal dismissed*, 483 N.E.2d 135 (N.Y. 1985); Lake County Bar Assn. v. Patterson, 413 N.E.2d 840 (Ohio 1980); In re Laubenheimer, 335 N.W.2d 624 (Wis. 1983).

187. 537 N.E.2d 730 (Ill. 1989).

188. See Robert W. Hillman, Law Firms and Their Partners: The Law and Ethics of Grabbing and Leaving, 67 Tex. L. Rev. 1, 2-4 (1988).

of lawyers from their firms?[189] First, both the departing lawyer and the firm must recognize that clients do not "belong" to either of them. Clients have the right to choose to have either the departing lawyer or the firm represent their interests.[190] Client choice does not, however, resolve the issue of the relationship between the departing lawyer and the firm or of the disposition of fees from clients' cases.

Second, departing partners owe fiduciary duties to their partners. The fiduciary duty of departing lawyers means that during the continuation of the partnership, including any period in which partnership affairs are being wound up because of the withdrawal of the partner,[191] departing partners may not use their position for their personal benefit and to the detriment of the partnership.[192]

Departing lawyers who violate their fiduciary obligations can be subject to disciplinary action. For example, in In re Smith,[193] during the two and one-half months prior to his departure from his firm Smith met secretly with 31 clients and had them sign individual retainer agreements. He did not open firm files for these cases while he was planning his departure. When he left the firm, he took with him the information relating to these cases as well as the files in other cases that he was handling. The attorney immediately wrote to these clients informing them that they should contact his

189. The discussion that follows focuses on partners withdrawing from partnerships, but similar rules should apply to withdrawals by associates, see In re Smith, 843 P.2d 449 (Or. 1992) (en banc) (associate disciplined for breach of fiduciary duty in connection with departure from firm), and to withdrawals from professional corporations, see Fox v. Abrams, 210 Cal. Rptr. 260 (Cal. Ct. App. 1985) (partnership principles apply to dissolution of professional corporation).

190. 2 Hazard & Hodes, The Law of Lawyering §5.6:202; Robert W. Hillman, Law Firms and Their Partners: The Law and Ethics of Grabbing and Leaving, 67 Tex. L. Rev. 1, 16-17 (1988).

191. Under the Uniform Partnership Act, the withdrawal of a partner amounts to a dissolution of the partnership. Unif. Partnership Act §29, 6 U.L.A. 752 (1995). The partnership continues, however, during the period necessary to wind up partnership business. Id. §30. The Revised Uniform Partnership Act makes some fundamental changes in partnership law, one of which is that the "dissociation" of a partner does not necessarily result in the dissolution of a partnership. Unif. Partnership Act §801 and comm. 1 (1994), 6 U.L.A. 92 (1995). The Revised Act was adopted by both the National Conference of Commissioners on Uniform State Laws and the ABA in 1994. See 6 U.L.A. 3 (1995).

192. See generally Unif. Partnership Act §21 (partner as fiduciary), 6 U.L.A. 608 (1995). The Revised Uniform Partnership Act continues to recognize partners as fiduciaries but limits the fiduciary obligations to those of loyalty and care. Unif. Partnership Act §404 (1994), 6 U.L.A. 58 (1995).

new office regarding their cases. The Oregon Supreme Court imposed a four-month suspension on the attorney for misconduct. The Court pointed out that his conduct involved potential harm to clients because of his failure to open files. In addition, the Court found that the attorney's conduct violated his fiduciary duties to his firm:

> Although there is no explicit rule requiring lawyers to be candid and fair with their partners or employers, such an obligation is implicit in the prohibition of DR 1-102(A)(3) [See Model Rule 8.4(c)] against dishonesty, fraud, deceit, or misrepresentation. Moreover, such conduct is a violation of the duty of loyalty owed by a lawyer to his or her firm based on their contractual or agency relationship.[194]

Departing lawyers who violate fiduciary obligations to their former firms can also be subject to civil liability to their firms. In the leading case of Meehan v. Shaughnessy,[195] the Supreme Judicial Court of Massachusetts held that departing partners owed fiduciary obligations to their remaining partners and that they could be held civilly liable for breach of those obligations. The court decided that the withdrawing partners did not breach their fiduciary obligations by making "logistical arrangements" (executing a lease, preparing a list of clients they expected to retain after their departure, and arranging for financing based on their expected clientele) for their new firm because fiduciaries may "plan to compete with the entity to which they owe allegiance," provided that they do not otherwise breach their fiduciary obligations.[196] The court found, however, that the withdrawing partners did breach their fiduciary duties by seeking and obtaining prior to their departure secret consents from clients to retain their services after they left the firm.[197] The court remanded for a determination of whether there was a causal connection between the departing lawyers' breach of fiduciary duty and damage to the partnership.

193. 843 P.2d 449 (Or. 1992).

194. Id. at 452.

195. 535 N.E.2d 1255 (Mass. 1989).

196. Id. at 1264. See also Graubard Mollen Dannett & Horowitz v. Moskovitz, 653 N.E.2d 1179 (N.Y. 1995) (summary judgment denied in breach of fiduciary duty claim against departing lawyer who sought and received assurances from long-term client that client would continue to retain lawyer after lawyer left firm; court outlines poles of permitted and improper conduct).

It imposed the burden of proving lack of causation on the departing lawyers because of their breach of duty.[198]

The third principle governing departures of lawyers from their firms is often called the "no additional compensation" rule regarding winding up of partnership matters. This traditional rule of partnership law means that withdrawing partners are not entitled to additional compensation for services rendered in winding up partnership business.[199] Thus, under the no additional compensation rule, if a lawyer leaves a firm and a client that the lawyer was representing while a member of the firm elects to have the lawyer complete the client's case, the lawyer is *not* entitled to the full fee from that matter. Under partnership law, the fee would be paid to the firm, and the lawyer would receive the lawyer's share pursuant to the partnership agreement or pro rata based on the lawyer's interest in the partnership in the absence of an agreement.[200] It should be noted that departing partners also receive benefits from the no additional compensation rule because they receive their percentage in any cases that remain with the firm, even though they will not be performing any services on those cases. Partners are free to modify the no additional compensation rule in their agreement.[201]

197. 535 N.E.2d at 1264.

198. Id. at 1267. See also Rosenfeld, Meyer & Susman v. Cohen, 194 Cal. Rptr. 180 (Cal. Ct. App. 1983).

199. Unif. Partnership Act §18(f), 6 U.L.A. 526 (1995). Jewel v. Boxer, 203 Cal. Rptr. 13 (Cal. Ct. App. 1984) (postdissolution fees should be allocated to partners based on their respective partnership interests without any additional compensation for work done to complete cases); Fox v. Abrams, 210 Cal. Rptr. 260 (Cal. Ct. App. 1985) (rule of Jewel v. Boxer applies to professional corporations). The Revised Uniform Partnership Act reverses this rule, §401(h), 6 U.L.A. 52 (1995).

200. For a case that follows a different approach, awarding the firm from which the lawyers departed compensation on a quantum meruit basis, see In re L-Tryptophan Cases, 518 N.W.2d 616 (Minn. Ct. App. 1994).

201. Unif. Partnership Act §18, 6 U.L.A. 526 (1995) (rules are subject to any agreement between the parties); Unif. Partnership Act §103 (1994), 6 U.L.A. 16 (1995). See Kelly v. Smith, 611 N.E.2d 118 (Ind. 1993) (recognizing "no additional compensation rule" but interpreting partnership agreement to provide that firm would be paid on quantum meruit basis for work done on cases where clients elected to retain departing lawyer). Comprehensive treatment of issues involved in departures from law firms is available in several books and articles. See Robert W. Hillman, Hillman on Lawyer Mobility: The Law and Ethics of Partner Withdrawals and Law Firm Breakups (1994), and his article, Law Firms and Their Partners: The Law and Ethics of Grabbing and Leaving, 67 Tex. L. Rev. 1 (1988). See also Vincent R. Johnson, Solicitation of Law Firm Clients by Departing

Another issue that arises in connection with departures by lawyers from their firms involves covenants not to compete. In the business world, covenants not to compete are quite common and are legally enforceable provided the covenant protects a legitimate interest of the covenantee and provided the covenant is reasonable in its restrictions. Thus, a reasonable covenant by a seller of a business not to compete with the purchaser, or by an employee not to compete with his employer, is valid.[202]

By contrast to this "rule of reason" that governs covenants in general, covenants by lawyers not to compete are per se invalid. See Model Rule 5.6(a) and DR 2-108(A). The rationale for this prohibition rests on the interests of clients. The client-attorney relationship is personal and fiduciary in character. It is against public policy to deprive a client of the right to employ the lawyer of the client's choosing.[203] The rule also protects young lawyers from bargaining away their future.[204]

The rule applies not only to direct restrictions on a lawyer's right to practice law, but also to indirect restrictions as well. Partnership agreements typically provide for payments to a departing partner of that partner's share of the capital of the partnership and of any earned but uncollected fees. If a partnership agreement provides that a departing lawyer forfeits that partner's share of termination payments when the partner continues practice in competition with the partner's former firm, courts are likely to find such a provision invalid as an indirect restriction on the departing lawyer's right to practice law. In Cohen v. Lord, Day & Lord,[205] the New York Court of Appeals ruled that a partnership agreement that conditioned payment of a departing partner's share of earned but uncollected revenues on noncompetition by the former partner was unenforceable because of the ethical prohibition on restriction

---

Partners and Associates: Tort, Fiduciary, and Disciplinary Liability, 50 U. Pitt. L. Rev. 1 (1989); Laurel S. Terry, Ethical Pitfalls and Malpractice Consequences of Law Firm Breakups, 61 Temp. L. Rev. 1055 (1988).

202. See Restatement (Second) of Contracts §188 (1979).

203. See Dwyer v. Jung, 336 A.2d 498, *aff'd*, 348 A.2d 208 (N.J. Super. Ct. App. Div. 1975). It is interesting to note that in contrast to covenants not to compete between lawyers, covenants not to compete by other professionals are enforceable provided that they satisfy the general reasonableness requirements. See, e.g., Karlin v. Weinberg, 390 A.2d 1161 (N.J. 1978).

204. See 2 Hazard & Hodes, The Law of Lawyering §5.6:201, at 824.

of practice by lawyers.[206] Other courts have agreed with this approach.[207]

Cases like *Cohen* are fairly extreme because in all of them the lawyers who continued to practice law forfeited all compensation from their former firms for their partnership interests. Less restrictive provisions may be valid. For example, provisions may be valid if they reasonably reduce the amount that a departing lawyer receives to reflect the financial impact on the firm of the lawyer's departure, or if they attempt to measure compensation due the firm for its quantum meruit contribution to cases in which clients elect to retain the departing lawyer rather than continue to have the firm represent them.[208]

In Howard v. Babcock,[209] the California Supreme Court rejected decisions from other states and held that a contractual provision imposing a reasonable cost on departing partners to compensate their former firm for their loss was enforceable. The court noted the change in economic climate in which law firms now operate. It expressed the view that such provisions could benefit clients by reducing the "culture of mistrust" among partners that can damage law firm stability.[210]

Model Rule 5.6 does contain an exception to the general prohibition against covenants not to compete among lawyers: Covenants not to compete are permissible when the lawyer is receiving

205. 550 N.E.2d 410 (N.Y. 1989).

206. See also Denburg v. Parker Chapin Flattau & Klimpl, 624 N.E.2d 995 (N.Y. 1993) (financial disincentives objectionable on public policy grounds because they interfere with client's choice of counsel). But see Hackett v. Milbank, Tweed, Hadley & McCloy, 654 N.E.2d 95 (N.Y. 1995) (arbitrator's determination that clause requiring reduction of departing partner's payments to extent compensation from other sources exceeds $100,000 does not violate public policy because clause was "competition neutral").

207. See Jacob v. Norris, McLaughlin & Marcus, Inc., 607 A.2d 142 (N.J. 1992) (service termination agreement providing that departing partners could receive compensation only if they did not render services to clients of firm during one year following termination was unenforceable); Spiegel v. Thomas, Mann & Smith, P.C., 811 S.W.2d 528 (Tenn. 1991) (agreement that denied deferred compensation to withdrawing stockholder who continued to practice law was void as against public policy set forth in rules governing attorney ethics).

208. See Barna, Guzy & Steffen, Ltd. v. Beens, 541 N.W.2d 354 (Minn. Ct. App. 1995) (shareholder agreement that required departing lawyer to turn over 50 percent of contingent fees received upheld; since lawyer would have received less than 50 percent of fee if lawyer remained with firm, agreement does not operate as financial restriction on practice), *rev. denied* (1996). See generally Lawyers' Manual Prof. Conduct (ABA/BNA), 10 Current Rep. 392-399 (1994).

209. 863 P.2d 150 (Cal. 1993).

"benefits upon retirement." In that case, the public interest in unfettered selection of counsel is not involved since the lawyer is retiring from the practice of law.[211] Comment 3 to Rule 5.6 states that the prohibition against covenants not to compete does not apply to the sale of a practice under Rule 1.17. One of the conditions of Rule 1.17 is that the selling lawyer must cease to engage in the practice of law (either in the geographical area or in the jurisdiction, as elected by the jurisdiction). See Model Rule 1.17(a).

210. Id. at 159.

211. See Miller v. Foulston, Siefkin, Powers & Eberhardt, 790 P.2d 404 (Kan. 1990) (provision that prevented departing partner who practiced law from receiv-

CHAPTER 7

Lawyers in Public Positions: Judges and Government Lawyers

The Statistical Abstract of the United States reports 805,872 lawyers practiced in the United States in 1991. Of this number, 87,763 or approximately 10.9 percent were engaged in some form of public legal service rather than private practice. This number consisted of the following:

Federal government	27,985
State government	38,242
Federal judicial	3,119
State and county judicial	18,417[1]

Lawyers engaged in public rather than private practice face special ethical problems because their roles and the governing standards differ from those of private counsel. Federal and state judges perform their duties subject to codes of judicial conduct and to various special statutory provisions. Federal and state prosecutors act pursuant to a wide range of statutory provisions, and they are required to adhere to ethical standards that differ from those applicable to private counsel.

1. United States Bureau of the Census, Statistical Abstract of the United States 210 (chart no. 327) (1994).

This chapter examines ethical issues facing lawyers in public service. Part I considers questions of judicial conduct, focusing on three topics: judicial selection, disqualification of judges, and restrictions on the activities of judges off the bench. Part II examines ethical issues facing government lawyers: identification of the government lawyer's client, the government lawyer's duty of confidentiality, and conflicts of interest arising from movement of lawyers into and out of government practice.

Part I
Judicial Conduct

A. SELECTION OF JUDGES

The choice of method of judicial selection involves a tension between the goals of independence and accountability. On the one hand, the rule of law, one of the core principles of our society, requires an independent judiciary in which judges render decisions based on the law rather than on political considerations or favoritism to one of the litigants. Yet, at the same time, the rule of law demands that judges, like other public officials, must be accountable for their conduct. Our society has traditionally been fearful of the prospect of a tyranny of the judiciary in which unaccountable judges render decisions on issues that should properly be made through the political process.

The Constitution adopts a system of judicial selection that emphasizes independence over accountability. Federal judges are nominated by the President, subject to confirmation by the Senate.[2] Once appointed, federal judges serve for life tenure and may be removed from office only through the impeachment process.[3]

During the last 60 years, the federal judiciary has come to exercise significant power over important social issues both through

2. U.S. Const. art. II, §2, cl. 2 ("[The President] shall nominate, and by and with the Advice and Consent of the Senate, shall appoint Ambassadors, other public Ministers and Consuls, Judges of the Supreme Court, and all other Officers of the United States, whose Appointments are not herein otherwise provided for, and which shall be established by Law. . . .").

3. U.S. Const. art. II, §4.

constitutional decisions and cases involving statutory interpretation. As a result of this expansion of judicial power, the accountability of federal judges has become an increasingly important issue. One effort to achieve greater judicial accountability has involved creation of a system for discipline of federal judges short of impeachment. In 1980, Congress passed the Judicial Councils Reform and Judicial Conduct and Disability Act.[4] The law authorizes creation of judicial councils in each federal circuit to take disciplinary action against federal judges, short of removal from office.[5] The judicial council of each circuit consists of the chief judge of the circuit, who presides over the council, and an equal number of circuit and district judges elected by majority vote of such judges in the circuit.[6] Federal judges may obtain review of decisions of the judicial council of their circuit by the Judicial Conference of the United States,[7] which consists of the Chief Justice of the Supreme Court, the chief judges of each of the circuit courts of appeal, the chief judge of the Court of International Trade, and a district judge from each judicial circuit.[8] If a judge has committed misconduct that could amount to grounds for impeachment, the judicial council for the circuit must certify the matter to the Judicial Conference of the United States for its consideration and possible referral to the House of Representatives for commencement of impeachment proceedings.[9]

Some studies of the process of judicial discipline for federal judges established by the 1980 Act have questioned the constitutionality of the legislation.[10] Because of these and numerous other questions about the federal system for disciplining and impeaching judges, in 1990 Congress passed the National Commission on Judi-

4. Pub. L. No. 96-458, 94 Stat. 2035 (*codified in various sections* in 28 U.S.C.).
5. 28 U.S.C. §372(c) (1994).
6. Id. §332(a) (1994).
7. Id. §372(c)(10) (1994).
8. Id. §331 (1994).
9. Id. §372(c)(7), (8) (1994).
10. See Paula Abrams, Spare the Rod and Spoil the Judge? Discipline of Federal Judges and the Separation of Powers, 41 DePaul L. Rev. 59 (1991) (arguing that Act is unconstitutional because it authorizes judicial discipline for impeachable offenses); Drew E. Edwards, Comment, Judicial Misconduct and Politics in the Federal System: A Proposal for Revising the Judicial Councils Act, 75 Cal. L. Rev. 1071 (1987) (contending that Act is unconstitutional for several reasons, including its authorization of de facto removal of judges by providing for sanction of temporary nonassignment of cases). See generally Symposium, Disciplining the Federal Judiciary, 142 U. Pa. L. Rev. 1 (1993).

cial Discipline and Removal Act.[11] The legislation created a National Commission on Judicial Discipline and Removal, which was charged with the responsibility of studying the problems involved in discipline and removal of Article III judges, evaluating possible alternatives to the present system, and preparing a report of its work. The Commission issued its report in August 1993. The Commission's exhaustive study examines a number of constitutional issues and makes recommendations to the legislative, executive, and judicial branches. While the Commission's report includes numerous thoughtful recommendations, it does not propose a fundamental overhaul of the present system.[12]

The Senate has been active in seeking to increase the accountability of federal judges. Beginning with the confirmation hearings of Robert Bork in 1987, the Senate Judiciary Committee has conducted searching inquiries into the constitutional and judicial philosophies of nominees.[13] The Senate has also moved to streamline the impeachment process by passing a rule that allows a Senate committee rather than the full Senate to take testimony and gather evidence. Prior to 1980, impeachment of federal judges was rare. During the 1980s, under the new Senate procedure, three federal judges were impeached and convicted.[14] In Nixon v. United States,[15] the Supreme Court rejected a constitutional attack on the Senate rule, holding that the issue was nonjusticiable.

Most states originally struck the balance between independence and accountability more toward the accountability side than was the case at the federal level, but the general trend among the states has been toward greater judicial independence. During the colonial era, judges were appointed by the king. After the Revolution, distaste with the arbitrary exercise of royal power led many states to place the authority to appoint judges with one or both houses

11. Pub. L. No. 101-650 §408, 104 Stat. 5122 (1990).

12. Report of the National Commn. on Judicial Discipline and Removal, 152 F.R.D. 265 (1993). For criticism of the report, see generally Victor Williams, Third Branch Independence and Integrity Threatened by Political Branch Irresponsibility: Reviewing the Report of the National Commission on Judicial Discipline and Removal, 5 Seton Hall Const. L.J. 851 (1995).

13. Stephen J. Wermiel, Confirming the Constitution: The Role of the Senate Judiciary Committee, 56 Law & Contemp. Probs. 121 (Autumn 1993) (part of Symposium: Elected Branch Influences in Constitutional Decisionmaking).

14. See Victor Williams, Third Branch Independence and Integrity Threatened by Political Branch Irresponsibility: Reviewing the Report of the National Commission on Judicial Discipline and Removal, 5 Seton Hall Const. L.J. 851 (1995).

15. 506 U.S. 224 (1993).

of the legislature. In the "democratic period" in American history, the vast majority of states moved to popular elections to select judges. Later dissatisfaction with some of the political excesses resulting from popular elections (particularly control of judges by political machines) produced a late nineteenth-century movement for reform of judicial selection. Some states changed to "nonpartisan" elections, but this system also had its critics because it failed to take politics out of the election process and because it deprived voters of information about the party affiliation of candidates.[16] During the early twentieth century, reformers presented various proposals for judicial nominating commissions. In 1940, Missouri became the first state to adopt a nominating commission. (Today, a plan to use a judicial nominating commission, regardless of form, to select judges is often referred to as a "Missouri Plan.")[17]

A study of methods of judicial selection currently used throughout the country comments on the lack of uniformity among the states:

> One of the first things to strike one who looks at judicial selection in the states is the amazing variability not only between states, but within the individual states. Almost no two states choose all their judges the same way. Very few states use the same selection method for all levels of court.[18]

States generally follow, however, one of four models of judicial selection,[19] although a state may choose to use different methods for different courts:

> Appointive systems — the governor or the legislature appoints and/or reappoints judges;
>
> Partisan elective systems—voters select and/or retain judges from among competing candidates identified by political party label;
>
> Nonpartisan elective systems—voters select and/or retain judges

16. For a criticism of the legitimacy of an elective judiciary, see Steven P. Croley, The Majoritarian Difficulty: Elective Judiciaries and the Rule of Law, 62 U. Chi. L. Rev. 689 (1995).

17. On the history of judicial selection, see American Judicature Socy., Judicial Selection in the United States: A Compendium of Provisions 3-6 (Lyle Warrick ed., 2d ed. 1993).

18. Id. at v.

19. For a detailed discussion of the various methods of selection and retention of judges in each state, see id.

through elections where competing candidates are not identified by party label; and

"Merit selection" systems — the governor initially appoints judges from a short list of candidates evaluated and recommended by a nominating committee and voters decide periodically whether to keep judges in office by voting "yes" or "no" on their retention.[20]

More than 30 states now use some form of nominating commission for selection of judges. The details of nominating commissions vary from state to state, but some features are common to commission plans. Typically, the legislature creates a permanent nominating commission consisting of both lawyers and nonlawyers. Various public and private officials (as set forth in the enabling legislation) appoint members of the commission. The commission has the task of identifying, investigating, and evaluating candidates for judicial office. Typically, it will hold public hearings on candidates. When a judicial vacancy occurs, the commission, after investigation and deliberation, forwards to the governor a list of nominees (three to five is a common number). The governor appoints judges from the list for a probationary period of one to three years. At the end of the probationary period, the judge runs unopposed on the question of whether the judge should be retained in office for a full term. Periodically, the judge must stand for unopposed reelection in which the public votes whether to retain or to remove the judge from office.

Developments during the last decade indicate that the public may believe that the movement toward greater independence of state judges has gone too far. Until 1986, retention elections for judges were low-profile. In that year a coalition of groups was successful in obtaining a negative vote to reelect Chief Justice Rose Bird and two associate justices of the California Supreme Court.[21] In Texas, a coalition of medical, business, and insurance interests was successful in ousting a number of state supreme court justices who were viewed as pro-plaintiff.[22] In the 1996 election, grass roots political campaigns removed a number of judges from state appellate courts.[23]

20. Sara Mathias, Electing Justice: A Handbook of Judicial Election Reforms 5 (1990).

21. Stephen B. Bright, Casualties of the War on Crime: Fairness, Reliability and the Credibility of Criminal Justice Systems, 51 U. Miami L. Rev. 413, 416 (1997).

22. See Rogers v. Bradley, 909 S.W.2d 872 (Tex. 1995) (with appendix containing "Court Wars" report from the television show *60 Minutes*).

23. West Legal News 1996 WL 652140, 652141 (11-12-96).

The appropriate balance between judicial independence and accountability is controversial, and opinions will vary on where the line should be drawn. Nonetheless, indications exist that the movement toward increased accountability may now have gone too far. During the 1996 presidential election, Republican candidate Robert Dole criticized federal district judge Harold Baer for issuing a ruling suppressing evidence of seizure of cocaine and heroin by New York City police officers. Dole called for Judge Baer's impeachment. In response to Dole's charge, the White House suggested that President Clinton would ask for Judge Baer's resignation unless he changed his decision. Judge Baer did in fact reverse his ruling.[24] When partisan politics intrudes into decisions by judges in particular cases, the process of seeking judicial accountability has become a threat to the rule of law. Because of these developments, the ABA appointed a special committee to conduct hearings and to make recommendations on the issue of judicial independence.[25]

B. STANDARDS OF CONDUCT AND PROCEDURES FOR DISCIPLINE OF JUDGES

Regulation of the behavior of judges both in their official and in their unofficial capacities rests on important policies. First, the adversarial system is founded on a principle of judicial impartiality. As a matter of fairness, litigants are entitled to have judges who are not swayed by bias, prejudice, or favoritism. Second, the primary function of our judicial system is to provide a mechanism for resolving disputes nonviolently. Public use of and acceptance of the results of the judicial system depends in part on the public's respect for judicial integrity.

The ABA has been active in establishing standards of conduct for judges, just as it has been for lawyers. The ABA first adopted Canons of Judicial Ethics in 1924. In 1972, the ABA approved the

24. Stephen B. Bright, Casualties of the War on Crime: Fairness, Reliability and the Credibility of Criminal Justice Systems, 51 U. Miami L. Rev. 413, 415-416 (1997).

25. See Henry J. Reske, Where to Draw the Line, 82 A.B.A. J. 99 (Dec. 1996); John Gibeaut, Mending Judicial Fences, 83 A.B.A. J. 92 (Aug. 1997) (recommendations of ABA Comm. on Separation of Powers and Judicial Independence).

Code of Judicial Conduct to replace the Canons of Ethics. Almost every state adopted the Code or used it as the model for standards of judicial conduct.[26]

In 1990, the ABA issued a major revision of the Code of Judicial Conduct. The 1990 Code is divided into five articles. Canons 1 and 2 are relatively short. Canon 1 provides that judges "shall uphold the integrity and independence of the judiciary." Canon 2 directs judges to "avoid impropriety and the appearance of impropriety in all of the judge's activities." An important addition to the 1990 Code, not found in the 1972 Code, is Canon 2(C), which prohibits judges from holding membership in any organization that practices invidious discrimination on the basis of race, sex, religion, or national origin. Canons 3, 4, and 5 contain the bulk of the substantive provisions of the Code. Canon 3 deals with a judge's adjudicative responsibilities, while Canon 4 regulates nonjudicial conduct. Canon 5 controls a judge's political activities.

All states and the District of Columbia have judicial conduct commissions or organizations that have the power to investigate, prosecute, and adjudicate allegations of judicial misconduct. The structure and method of appointment of these organizations vary from state to state.[27] In August 1994, the American Bar Association adopted Model Rules for Judicial Disciplinary Enforcement.[28] The ABA rules call for the creation of a 12-member Commission on Judicial Conduct, consisting of four judges of the intermediate or appellate courts of the state, appointed by the highest court in the state; four lawyers appointed by the bar association; and four members of the public appointed by the governor. Rule 2(C). The Commission has responsibility for investigation charges of misconduct against judges, conducting hearings into such charges, and making recommendations to the highest court of the state. The ABA rules provide that the highest court of the state has the power to discipline judges found guilty of misconduct, including the power to remove a judge from office. Rule 6(B)(1).

The Judicial Conference of the United States adopted the Code of Judicial Conduct to apply to federal judges in 1973.[29] The Code

26. Jeffrey M. Shaman et al., Judicial Conduct and Ethics §1.02 (2d ed. 1995).
27. See Irene A. Tesitor & Dwight B. Sinks, Judicial Conduct Organizations (2d ed. 1980).
28. See Lawyers' Manual Prof. Conduct (ABA/BNA) §§1:3101 et seq.
29. Judicial Conf. of United States, Rep. of Proc. at 9-11 (1973).

of Conduct for federal judges has been amended to include some of the provisions from the ABA's 1990 Code, but it is still based largely on the 1972 Code.[30] As discussed previously, under the federal system, judges may be removed from office only through impeachment, although the Judicial Councils Reform and Judicial Conduct and Disability Act of 1980 provides for discipline of judges short of removal from office.

C. DISQUALIFICATION OF STATE JUDGES

Canon 3 of the 1990 Code of Judicial Conduct requires judges to handle their judicial duties impartially and diligently. Canon 3(B) imposes a number of specific adjudicative responsibilities. The 1990 Code, unlike the 1972 Code, requires judges not to manifest bias or prejudice in the performance of judicial duties, to prevent such conduct by court personnel, and to require lawyers appearing before them to refrain from such conduct. Canon 3(B)(5)(b). The 1990 Code also makes changes dealing with ex parte communications between judges and lawyers. Canon 3(B)(7).

One of the most important aspects of judicial conduct involves disqualification of judges from hearing cases.[31] Canon 3(E) of the Code of Judicial Conduct deals with disqualification of judges. The Code begins with a general principle of disqualification: whenever the judge's "impartiality might reasonably be questioned." The Code contains, however, a number of specific rules of disqualification, and because of the vagueness of the general standard, it is useful to begin with the specific rules first. The disqualification rules draw a distinction between circumstances affecting the judge personally and situations in which a judge is disqualified because of a relationship with another person who has an interest in the matter.

30. For the current text of the Code of Judicial Conduct applicable to United States judges, see 150 F.R.D. 307 (1992).

31. See Richard E. Flamm, Judicial Disqualification (1996).

1. *Disqualification Because of the Judge's Personal Involvement or Interest in the Matter*

Four situations requiring disqualification of judges based on personal involvement in the matter are fairly straightforward. A judge is disqualified when the judge

(1) has personal knowledge of disputed evidentiary facts (Canon 3(E)(1)(a))
(2) served as a lawyer in the matter in controversy before assuming the bench (Canon 3(E)(1)(b))
(3) has been a material witness to the matter in controversy (Canon 3(E)(1)(b))
(4) is a party to the proceeding, or an officer, director, or trustee of a party (Canon 3(E)(1)(d)(i))

While these disqualification rules are relatively easy to apply, two further disqualification provisions are more difficult. The Code of Judicial Conduct requires disqualification when a judge has "personal bias or prejudice concerning a party." Canon 3(E)(1)(a). The meaning of this provision and its interrelationship with the general standard that requires disqualification when a judge's "impartiality might reasonably be questioned" has been the subject of several Supreme Court decisions. These cases are discussed in the section below that examines disqualification of federal judges.

Under the 1990 Code, judges are subject to disqualification when the judge either personally or as a fiduciary has an economic interest in the subject matter in controversy or in a party to the proceeding. Canon 3(E)(1)(c). The 1990 Code of Judicial Conduct made a substantial change from the 1972 Code regarding disqualification because of economic interest. (The 1972 Code used the term "financial interest.") Under the 1972 Code, a judge's financial interest in a party or in the subject matter of a proceeding, *no matter how small,* required disqualification. Thus, under the 1972 Code, if a judge held one share of stock in a party, the judge was disqualified. By contrast to the 1972 Code, the 1990 Code provides that "economic interest" means "ownership of a more than de minimis legal or equitable interest, or a relationship as officer, director, advisor or other active participant in the affairs of a party," subject to certain exceptions. (See Terminology section of

1990 Code, definition of "economic interest.") The Code goes on to define a de minimis interest as "an insignificant interest that could not raise reasonable question as to a judge's impartiality." (See Terminology section of 1990 Code, definition of "De minimis.")

The Code of Judicial Conduct lists certain exceptions to what constitutes an economic interest:

> (a) Ownership of a mutual fund does not amount to ownership of securities owned by the fund unless the judge participates in the management of the fund or unless the case could substantially affect the value of the fund shares;
> (b) Service by the judge or a member of the judge's family in an active role in a charitable or similar organization does not create an economic interest in securities owned by the organization;
> (c) Deposits in financial institutions, ownership of insurance policies, and similar propriety interests do not constitute economic interests in those institutions unless the proceeding could substantially affect the value of the judge's interest; and
> (d) Ownership of government securities is not an economic interest in the issuer unless the proceeding could substantially affect the value of the judge's interest.

(See Terminology section, definition of "Economic interest.") These exceptions are sensibly designed to allow judges to continue to have routine financial interests without forcing their disqualification.

2. *Disqualification of Judges Based on Relationship with Persons Who Have an Interest in the Matter*

Judges are subject to disqualification not only because of personal involvement or interest in a matter, but also because of certain relationships with persons interested in a matter. Canon 3(E)(1)(b) provides that a judge is disqualified if "a lawyer with whom the judge previously practiced law served during such association as a lawyer concerning the matter." Note that the mere fact that the judge's former law partner appears in a case is not disqualifying under this rule; the case must be one that was "in the office" when the judge was practicing. Should judges recuse themselves from cases involving their former firms on the ground that the judge's "impartiality might reasonably be questioned"? In Informal Opinion 87-1524, the ABA Committee on Ethics and Professional Responsibility ruled that a judge was not required to disqualify himself simply because the judge had been associated with counsel for one of the parties two years earlier. The Committee indicated that a period of one or two years after termination of professional association was appropriate, depending on factors such as the closeness of the relationship and the amount of continued contact.[32]

As noted above, a judge is disqualified if the judge personally has an economic interest in the subject matter in controversy or in a party to the proceeding. The judge is also disqualified if close family members — the judge's spouse, the judge's parent or child wherever residing, or any other member of the judge's family residing in the judge's household — have an economic interest in the subject matter or a party to the proceeding. Canon 3(E)(1)(c). Thus, if the judge's grandchild residing in the judge's house has more than a de minimis financial interest in a party to a proceeding, the judge is disqualified.

Finally, the Code of Judicial Conduct requires disqualification when the judge's spouse or a person within the third degree of relationship to either of them, or the spouse of such a person,

> (i) is a party to the proceeding, or an officer, director or trustee of a party;
> (ii) is acting as a lawyer in the proceeding;
> (iii) is known by the judge to have a more than de minimis interest that could be substantially affected by the proceeding;
> (iv) is to the judge's knowledge likely to be a material witness in the proceeding.

The following relatives are included within the third degree of relationship: great-grandparent, grandparent, parent, uncle, aunt, brother, sister, child, grandchild, great-grandchild, nephew, or niece. (See Terminology section of 1990 Code, definition of "third degree of relationship.") Cousins are not included. Under this rule, a judge is disqualified if one of the listed relatives is a lawyer

32. See generally Anne M. Payne, Annot., Judge's Previous Legal Association with Attorney Connected to Current Case as Warranting Disqualification, 85 A.L.R.4th 700 (1991).

in the proceeding, but would not be disqualified simply because the relative is a member of a firm that is handling a case, unless the relative has an interest that could be substantially affected by the case. (See the commentary to Canon 3(E)(1)(c).) This could occur, for example, if the firm was handling a major class action and the relative's potential compensation from the case was substantial.

D. DISQUALIFICATION OF FEDERAL JUDGES

Two statutes, 28 U.S.C. §§144, 455, govern disqualification of federal judges. Section 455 is the broader of the two statutes. It applies to all federal judges, whether trial or appellate, and specifies numerous grounds for disqualification. Section 144, which was enacted much earlier, deals only with disqualification of district court judges because of bias or prejudice. Most cases will be governed by §455 because of its broader scope. The only aspect of §144 that is not covered by §455 is the requirement of filing a timely affidavit of disqualification.

Section 455 was based on the ABA's 1972 Code of Judicial Conduct. Because the ABA's 1990 Code incorporates many principles from the 1972 Code, the 1990 Code and §455 remain very similar in many respects. Section 455, like the Code of Judicial Conduct, has two broad disqualification provisions. Section 455(a) provides that a judge is disqualified if the judge's "impartiality might reasonably be questioned." See also Canon 3(E)(1). Section 455(b)(1) provides that a judge is disqualified if the judge "has a personal bias or prejudice concerning a party." See also Canon 3(E)(1)(a) (which adds "or a party's lawyer").

1. *Disqualification Based on Personal Bias or Prejudice*

Disqualification based on "personal bias or prejudice" is the older of the provisions. In United States v. Grinnell Corp.,[33] the Court considered a motion by the defendants to disqualify the district

33. 384 U.S. 563 (1966).

judge in an antitrust case under 28 U.S.C. §144 on the ground that the judge had expressed views regarding the merits of the government's case. Ironically, it was the defendants who had sought the judge's expression of his position on the government's case. In affirming the denial of the disqualification motion, the Court stated: "The alleged bias and prejudice to be disqualifying must stem from an *extrajudicial source* and result in an opinion on the merits on some basis other than what the judge learned from his participation in the case."[34] Over the years, *Grinnell* came to stand for an "extrajudicial source doctrine." Under this doctrine, disqualification was not appropriate unless the basis for disqualification arose from an extrajudicial source. Thus, anger or irritation expressed by a judge during a case,[35] consistent rulings by the judge against a party,[36] and participation in previous proceedings involving a party[37] were all insufficient to warrant disqualification.

In Liteky v. United States,[38] the Court largely discarded the extrajudicial source doctrine, although not the results of the cases that had used the doctrine. *Liteky* was a criminal prosecution for a political protest at a military installation. The judge hearing the case had presided over a prior case involving one of the defendants. During the case, the judge admonished and limited defense counsel's representation in several respects. The Court in *Liteky* decided that the extrajudicial source doctrine should not be used as a litmus test to decide disqualification based on bias or prejudice. Instead, extrajudicial source was only a factor to be used in deciding whether bias or prejudice existed. Nonetheless, the Court reaffirmed the results of decisions that had used the extrajudicial source doctrine:

> As we have described it, however, there is not much doctrine to the doctrine. The fact that an opinion held by a judge derives from a source outside judicial proceedings is not a *necessary* condition for

34. Id. at 583 (emphasis added).

35. E.g., Souder v. Owens-Corning Fiberglas Corp., 939 F.2d 647 (8th Cir. 1991).

36. E.g., Nilsson, Robbins, Dalgarn, Berliner, Carson & Wurst v. Louisiana Hydrolec, 854 F.2d 1538 (9th Cir. 1988).

37. E.g., United States v. Bond, 847 F.2d 1233 (7th Cir. 1988).

38. 510 U.S. 540 (1994). *Liteky* actually involved the scope and meaning of §455(a), which deals with disqualification because a judge's impartiality might reasonably be questioned. The Court considered the meaning of §455(b)(1), which deals with disqualification due to bias or prejudice, because it was examining the interrelationship between §455(a) and 455(b)(1).

"bias or prejudice" recusal, since predispositions developed during the course of a trial will sometimes (albeit rarely) suffice. Nor is it a *sufficient* condition for "bias or prejudice" recusal, since *some* opinions acquired outside the context of judicial proceedings (for example, the judge's view of the law acquired in scholarly reading) will *not* suffice. Since neither the presence of an extrajudicial source necessarily establishes bias, nor the absence of an extrajudicial source necessarily precludes bias, it would be better to speak of the existence of a significant (and often determinative) "extrajudicial source" *factor,* than of an "extrajudicial source" *doctrine,* in recusal jurisprudence.

The facts of the present case do not require us to describe the consequences of that factor in complete detail. It is enough for present purposes to say the following: First, judicial rulings alone almost never constitute a valid basis for a bias or partiality motion. See United States v. Grinnell Corp., 384 U.S. at 583. In and of themselves (i.e., apart from surrounding comments or accompanying opinion), they cannot possibly show reliance upon an extrajudicial source; and can only in the rarest circumstances evidence the degree of favoritism or antagonism required (as discussed below) when no extrajudicial source is involved. Almost invariably, they are proper grounds for appeal, not for recusal. Second, opinions formed by the judge on the basis of facts introduced or events occurring in the course of the current proceedings, or of prior proceedings, do not constitute a basis for a bias or partiality motion unless they display a deep-seated favoritism or antagonism that would make fair judgment impossible. Thus, judicial remarks during the course of a trial that are critical or disapproving of, or even hostile to, counsel, the parties, or their cases, ordinarily do not support a bias or partiality challenge. They *may* do so if they reveal an opinion that derives from an extrajudicial source; and they *will* do so if they reveal such a high degree of favoritism or antagonism as to make fair judgment impossible. An example of the latter (and perhaps of the former as well) is the statement that was alleged to have been made by the District Judge in Berger v. United States, 255 U.S. 22 (1921), a World War I espionage case against German-American defendants:

> One must have a very judicial mind, indeed, not [to be] prejudiced against the German Americans" because their "hearts are reeking with disloyalty. Id., at 28.

Not establishing bias or partiality, however, are expressions of impatience, dissatisfaction, annoyance, and even anger, that are within the bounds of what imperfect men and women, even after having been confirmed as federal judges, sometimes display. A judge's ordinary efforts at courtroom administration — even a stern and short-tempered judge's ordinary efforts at courtroom administration — remain immune.[39]

2. *Disqualification Because the Judge's Impartiality Might Reasonably be Questioned*

Disqualification because a judge's impartiality might reasonably be questioned under §455(a) was added to the statute in 1974. The Court first addressed the meaning of this provision in Liljeberg v. Health Services Acquisition Corp.,[40] an action by Health Services seeking a declaration of ownership of a hospital corporation. The district court found for Liljeberg. Ten months after the decision, Health Services learned that at the time the district judge rendered his decision he was a member of the board of trustees of Loyola University and that Liljeberg had been negotiating with Loyola to purchase a parcel of land on which to construct a hospital. The success and benefit of these negotiations turned in part on Liljeberg's prevailing in the litigation with Health Services.

Health Services moved to vacate the judgment under Federal Rule of Civil Procedure 60(b)(6) on the ground that the judge was disqualified under 28 U.S.C. §455. Section 455(b)(4) provides that a judge shall disqualify himself when he "knows that he, individually or as a fiduciary, . . . has . . . any other interest that could be substantially affected by the outcome of the proceeding." The Supreme Court found that the judge was not disqualified under that section because the evidence showed that the judge did not "know" of Loyola's interest when he decided the case. Nonetheless, the Court held that the judge was disqualified under §455(a) because a reasonable person would conclude that the judge's impartiality might reasonably be questioned. The Court reasoned that knowledge was irrelevant to determining whether a violation of §455(a) had occurred because the purpose of the section was "to promote public confidence in the integrity of the judicial process."[41] The Court recognized that it was absurd to require judges

39. 510 U.S. at 554-556.
40. 486 U.S. 847 (1988).
41. Id. at 860.

to disqualify themselves based on facts of which they are unaware, but when the matter was brought to the judge's attention, the judge could then decide whether his impartiality might reasonably be questioned.[42]

The Court also discussed the interrelationship between the specific disqualification provisions of §455(b) and §455(a). Liljeberg contended that §455(a) was limited by §455(b)(4), and accordingly the judge was not disqualified absent actual knowledge of the disqualifying circumstances. The Court rejected this argument. Noting several differences between §455(b) and §455(a), the Court found that the sections were independent, i.e., a judge is disqualified if any of the provisions of §455(b) apply, but in addition the judge's participation in the case is also subject to the general standard of whether the judge's impartiality might reasonably be questioned.[43] Three dissenting Justices argued that an actual rather than a constructive knowledge standard should apply under §455(a) as well as under §455(b). Given the trial judge's lack of knowledge, they also questioned the propriety of the remedy of vacating the judgment.

The Court also addressed the remedy appropriate for violation of §455(a). The statute itself does not specify a remedy, and the Court declined to adopt a per se rule that required vacating the judgment simply because the judge was disqualified from hearing the case. Instead, the Court stated:

> We conclude that in determining whether a judgment should be vacated for a violation of §455(a), it is appropriate to consider the risk of injustice to the parties in the particular case, the risk that the denial of relief will produce injustice in other cases, and the risk of undermining the public's confidence in the judicial process.[44]

On the facts of the case, the Court found the "violation is neither insubstantial nor excusable," and agreed with the Court of Appeals that the judgment should be vacated and a new trial ordered.[45]

The Court's opinion in *Liteky*, however, decided six years after *Liljeberg*, raises questions about the standard that applies in cases governed by §455(a). In *Liljeberg*, the Court held that a judge was

42. Id. at 861.
43. Id. at 860 n.8.
44. Id. at 864.
45. Id. at 867.

disqualified under §455(a) if a reasonable person would conclude that the judge should be disqualified. The Court also reasoned that §455(a) established a standard for disqualification that was separate from and not limited by §455(b). By contrast, in *Liteky*, the Court held that under §455(a) the standard for disqualification was whether "fair judgment was impossible" and that §455(a) was limited by the specific standards of §455(b).

On both the standard for §455(a) and the interrelationship between §455(a) and §455(b), *Liljeberg* rather than *Liteky* seems correct. The language of the statute indicates that the two sections are independent. Section 455(b) states: "He shall *also* disqualify himself in the following circumstances." Further, the legislative history of §455(a) indicates that Congress intended to adopt a reasonable person standard for disqualification under §455(a) to avoid public perception of partiality:

> This general standard is designed to promote public confidence in the impartiality of the judicial process by saying, in effect, if there is a reasonable factual basis for doubting the judge's impartiality, he should disqualify himself and let another judge preside over the case.[46]

3. *Disqualification Because of Financial Interest*

One important difference between the ABA's 1990 Code and the federal disqualification statute deals with disqualification because of financial interest. Compare Canon 3(E)(1)(c) with 28 U.S.C. §455(b)(4). The federal statute is based on the 1972 Code of Judicial Conduct, which provides that a judge is disqualified from hearing a matter if the judge has a financial interest in the subject matter of a proceeding or in a party to the proceeding. Unlike the 1990 Code of Judicial Conduct, however, the statute goes on to define "financial interest" to mean "ownership of a legal or equitable interest, however small. . . . "[47] Thus, if a federal judge owns one share of stock in a party to the proceeding, the judge is disqualified from hearing the matter. Note that federal judges are also dis-

46. 1974 U.S. Cong. Code & Admin. News at 6355.
47. 28 U.S.C. §455(d)(4) (1994).

qualified if their spouses or minor children residing in their household have even a small financial interest in a party.[48] In In re Cement Antitrust Litig.,[49] a federal judge who had been handling a class action antitrust case for more than five years was required to disqualify himself because his wife owned stock in seven of the 210,235 members of the plaintiff class. The Court of Appeals for the Ninth Circuit bemoaned the strictness of the statute and called for legislative evaluation of the reasonableness and consequences of the per se rule.[50]

In 1988, Congress took action to ameliorate the harshness of the "however small" rule, adding 28 U.S.C. §455(f), which allows judges to avoid disqualification by divestiture of financial interests in a party when the disqualifying interest appears or is discovered after substantial judicial time has been devoted to the matter. The divestiture rule also applies to financial interests held by a judge's spouse and minor children. The section does not apply, however, if the interest could be substantially affected by the outcome of the case. The Code of Judicial Conduct does not have a rule on divestiture equivalent to the federal statute.

If the judge has an interest other than a financial interest, the impact on the judge must be substantial to warrant disqualification. For example, in In re New Mexico Natural Gas Antitrust Litig.,[51] the Tenth Circuit held that the district judge's status as natural gas consumer did not warrant disqualification because the judge would not be substantially affected by the outcome of the proceeding.

E. WAIVER OR REMITTAL OF DISQUALIFICATION

Both the Code of Judicial Conduct and the federal statute provide for remittal (the term used by the Code) or waiver (the term used by the federal statute) of disqualification, but they differ dramati-

48. 28 U.S.C. §455(b)(4) (1994).

49. 688 F.2d 1297 (9th Cir. 1982), *aff'd by absence of a quorum,* Arizona v. United States Dist. Court, 459 U.S. 1191 (1983).

50. Id. at 1315.

51. 620 F.2d 794 (10th Cir. 1980).

cally in the situations in which waiver is allowed. Under the Code, disqualification may be remitted in all cases except ones in which the judge is disqualified because of personal bias or prejudice concerning a party. The Code allows remittal in situations in which the judge was disqualified because of economic interest. Canon 3(F). The procedure for remittal is as follows: The judge discloses the basis for disqualification on the record and asks the parties and their lawyers to consider, out of the presence of the judge, whether to waive disqualification. If all parties and the judge agree to waive disqualification, the judge may continue in the case. The agreement waiving disqualification should be made part of the record in the case. Canon 3(F).

Under the federal statute, waiver of disqualification is allowed only in cases involving the general standard of when the judge's impartiality might reasonably be questioned. Waiver is not allowed for any cases in which rules specifically provide for disqualification, including cases of disqualification because of financial interest.[52]

F. LIMITATIONS ON JUDGES' EXTRAJUDICIAL CONDUCT AND ACTIVITIES

1. *In General*

Canon 4 of the Code of Judicial Conduct deals with limitations on judges' nonjudicial activities. The Canon reflects a balance between contending policies. On the one hand, judges should avoid any conduct that casts doubt on their impartiality, demeans their office, or interferes with their judicial duties. Canon 4(A). On the other hand, judges should not be isolated from the people and activities of the communities in which they live. See commentary to Canon 4(A).

The Code prohibits extrajudicial activities that clearly violate one or more of the policies expressed in Canon 4(A). Thus, judges may not practice law (except that they may act pro se, and they

52. 28 U.S.C. §455(e) (1994).

may draft or review legal documents and give legal advice to family members without compensation). Canon 4(G). Similarly, judges may not appear as private arbitrators or mediators unless authorized by law. Canon 4(F). The Code also prohibits judges from serving in a fiduciary capacity (for example, as a personal representative, a trustee, or a guardian), except for family members, and even then the judge cannot appear if it is likely that the judge as fiduciary would handle a matter that would come before the judge. Canon 4(E). Note that some provisions of the Code (including the prohibitions against practicing law, serving as arbitrators or mediators, and acting as fiduciaries) do not apply to part-time judges. See Application of the Code of Judicial Conduct §E.

By contrast to these prohibited activities, the Code broadly authorizes judge to "speak, write, lecture, teach and participate in other extra-judicial activities concerning the law, the legal system, the administration of justice and non-legal subjects, subject to the requirements of this Code." Canon 4(B). Under this section, a judge may speak or write on controversial topics of policy as well as ones that involve technical improvements of the legal system, and may advocate change in the law. The limitation expressed in Canon 4(B)—"subject to the requirements of this Code"—is intended to remind judges that even in connection with educational activities, judges are still subject to other Canons of the Code. For example, a judge should not engage in public comment about a proceeding that "might reasonably be expected to affect its outcome or impair its fairness." Canon 3(B)(9). Judges are always subject to the dictates of Canon 1, which requires them to maintain high standards of integrity and independence.

The Code allows judges to receive compensation and expense reimbursement for speaking and writing, subject to the financial reporting requirements of Canon 4(H). Thus, within the guidelines of Canon 4(H)(1), a judge could receive a salary for teaching part-time at a law school, and could accept an honorarium and expense reimbursement for delivering a speech. Canon 4(H)(1) provides that compensation and expense reimbursement must be reasonable and the source of payments must not "give the appearance of influencing the judge's performance of judicial duties or otherwise give the appearance of impropriety."

2. *Governmental, Civic, and Charitable Activities*

The difficulty of striking a balance between social involvement and regulation of nonjudicial conduct appears quite clearly in connection with governmental, civic, and charitable activities. Canon 4(C). The Canon provides that judges may not appear at public hearings or consult with legislative or executive bodies or officials except on matters concerning "the law, the legal system or the administration of justice," or except when the judge appears pro se in a matter affecting the judge's own interest. Although the Canon is written as a prohibition, it can be construed as a rather broad authorization for judicial participation in governmental and civic activities, because such participation will often involve issues of law. Indeed, even some of the most controversial political topics of our day—abortion, health care reform, deficit reduction—arguably involve "the law, the legal system or the administration of justice." On the other hand, perhaps a fair reading of the intent of the Canon is that judges should not become involved with other branches of government in issues of public policy or politics. Viewed in that light, an appearance by a judge at a legislative hearing on health care reform would probably be improper. This distinction finds support in the wording of Canon 4(C)(2), which states that a "judge shall not accept appointment to a governmental committee or commission or other governmental position that is concerned with issues of fact or policy on matters others than the improvement of the law, the legal system or the administration of justice [subject to exceptions for ceremonial occasions]." It should be noted that this provision prohibiting judges from serving on governmental committees and commissions constitutes a departure from the historical practice of many respected judges. Probably the most famous example of judicial service that would now be a violation of this Canon was Chief Justice Earl Warren's acceptance of an appointment to serve as chair of the commission investigating the assassination of President Kennedy.

Canon 4 allows a judge to serve as an official (officer, director, trustee) or nonlegal advisor of an organization or governmental agency devoted to the improvement of law, the legal system, and the administration of justice and of "an educational, religious, charitable, fraternal or civic organization not conducted for profit," subject to "other requirements of this Code." Canon 4(C)(3). A judge may not engage in such service if the organization is likely to be involved in proceedings before the judge or in any court subject to the appellate jurisdiction of the court of which the judge is a member. Canon 4(C)(3)(a).

The Code limits judges' involvement in fund-raising activities and membership solicitation on behalf of such organizations. A judge may help in planning fund raising and may give advice regarding fund raising and investments, but may not participate personally in fund raising (except that a judge may solicit contributions from other judges over whom the judge does not have appellate jurisdiction or supervisory authority), nor may a judge lend the prestige of the judge's office to fund raising or membership solicitation (for example, by including a quotation or statement that the judge endorses the activities of the organization). Canon 4(C)(3)(b). The commentary to Canon 4(C) draws some precise distinctions. For example, a judge may attend but may not speak at a fund-raising dinner. A judge may be listed on the letterhead of an organization's fund-raising letter, provided comparable listings are made for other persons. Note also that under the 1990 Code, a judge may also not hold membership in (much less serve in a leadership capacity) any organization that practices "invidious discrimination" on the basis of race, sex, religion, or national origin. Canon 2(C).

3. *Business and Financial Activities, Including Gifts*

Business and financial activities by judges pose two potential problems. First, judges can exploit their public position for private gain. Second, judges can be placed in a position where they must disqualify themselves because of financial interest in a party or proceeding. See Canon 4(D)(1). The Code generally allows judges to hold and manage their own investments and those of their family members and to engage in remunerative activity, but this authorization is subject to other provisions of the Code. Canon 4(D)(2). The Code requires judges to manage their investments "to minimize the number of cases in which the judge is disqualified," and judges are directed to divest themselves of financial interests that might require frequent disqualification. Canon 4(D)(4). Judges may not serve in a managerial capacity in a business, with two exceptions: a business closely held by the judge or members of the judge's family and a business entity operated primarily to manage the investments of the judge or members of the judge's family. Participation in even these entities would still be improper if the entity would regularly appear before the judge. Commentary to Canon 4(D)(3).

Acceptance by judges of gifts, bequests, loans, and favors poses obvious problems of improper influence. Canon 4(D)(5) states a broad general rule prohibiting judges from accepting any gift, bequest, favor, or loan from anyone, subject to certain exceptions. The Canon requires judges to urge family members residing in the judge's household to comply with the rule. The broadest exception is found in Canon 4(D)(5)(h), which allows the judge to accept a gift, bequest, favor, or loan from any person so long as the transaction does not involve a person or interest that has appeared or is likely to appear before the judge and provided the judge reports any such transaction that exceeds $150.

A number of the other exceptions to the general prohibition on gifts, loans, bequests, and favors recognize that judges should not be required to act as hermits and are allowed to engage in many activities in which other citizens can engage. Thus, Canon 4(D)(5)(f) permits judges to receive loans from lending institutions in the regular course of business of the institution on the same general terms available to others. Similarly, Canon 4(D)(5)(g) permits the receipt of scholarships or fellowships awarded on the same general terms and criteria applied to other applicants. Canon 4(D)(5)(d) permits gifts from relatives or friends on special occasions (weddings and birthdays), provided the gift is commensurate with the occasion and the relationship. Canon 4(D)(5)(e) allows judges to receive gifts, bequests, and loans from a relative or close friend "whose appearance or interest in a case would in any event require disqualification under Section 3E." Canon 4(D)(5)(b) allows the spouse of a judge or a family member residing in the judge's household to accept gifts, awards, or other benefits "incident to the business, profession or other separate activity" of such person, even if the judge receives an incidental benefit, provided the transaction "could not reasonably be perceived as intended to influence the judge in the performance of judicial duties."

One potentially troublesome exception is Canon 4(D)(5)(c), which permits judges to accept "ordinary social hospitality." The section allows judges to have social contacts with anyone, including lawyers who regularly appear before them. The Reporter's Notes to the 1972 Code of Judicial Conduct, which also included a "social hospitality" exception to the prohibition on gifts, stated that a "judge should not be excluded from all social relationships with lawyers or persons who are likely to be litigants in his court."[53] The Code does not, however, define what is meant by "ordinary social hospitality." De minimis matters such as infrequent lunch or dinner engagements with lawyers or others should clearly be proper under the exception. Suppose, however, the judge has regular and substantial contacts with either a lawyer or another person who may appear regularly before the judge. The Reporter's Notes give the following example of conduct that exceeds the ordinary social hospitality exception:

> The Committee felt that there are common sense limits and that the standard is understandable and defensible; for example, the offer to a judge of a month at the mountain cabin of a lawyer friend who practices in the judge's court is clearly not ordinary social hospitality, and acceptance is prohibited.[54]

Canon 4(D)(5)(a) allows judges to accepts gifts incident to public testimonials and to accept materials from publishers on a complimentary basis for official use. That Canon also allows judges to accept gifts (expense payments, for example) incident to bar-related functions or to activities devoted to the improvement of the law, the legal system, or the administration of justice. The comment to that section states, however, that the Canon does not allow such gifts from individual lawyers or groups of lawyers. Such gifts would be subject to Canon 4(D)(5)(h), which prohibits judges from accepting gifts from any person whose interests have or are likely to come before the judge. Thus, it appears to be improper for a judge to receive an expense-paid weekend at a convention sponsored by a specialized bar group, for example, one representing either the plaintiffs' bar or the defense bar, but it would be proper for a judge to receive an expense-paid weekend at a convention sponsored by the bar association representing the entire bar membership of the state. Could a judge make a speech before a specialized bar group and receive as compensation for the speech (rather

53. E. Wayne Thode, Reporter's Notes to Code of Judicial Conduct 84 (1973).
54. Id. at 84-85.

than a gift) an honorarium plus expenses? As discussed above, Canon 4(H) allows judges to receive compensation and expense reimbursement for activities permitted by the Code (note that Canon 4(B) authorizes judges to speak, write, or lecture on legal topics), provided the compensation and expense reimbursement are reasonable and provided that the source of payments "does not give the appearance of influencing the judge's performance of judicial duties or otherwise give the appearance of impropriety." Canon 4(H)(1). Expense reimbursement may include that of the judge's spouse or guest, "where appropriate to the occasion." Canon 4(H)(1)(b).

G. RESTRICTIONS ON JUDGES' POLITICAL ACTIVITIES

The relationship between judging and political activity poses both interesting questions about legal theory as well as practical questions regarding permissible nonjudicial activities. A widely accepted ideal for judges is one of political neutrality. Under this view, law and politics are separate activities. Judges should decide cases in accordance with the law; issues of politics should be left to the legislative and executive branches. A substantial body of scholarly literature challenges the view that judges can be politically neutral. Under this view, all law is to a greater or lesser extent vague or "open textured." Because law has this characteristic, judges must develop approaches or theories to a wide range of legal questions, many of which involve controversial questions of morals, values, and politics.[55]

Even if one accepts the view that the judicial process inherently involves questions of politics or values, it does not follow that judges should participate in other political activities, particularly the work of political parties and organizations. Such participation undermines public confidence in the independence of judges and exposes them to situations in which they may be forced to disqualify themselves. The Code of Judicial Conduct establishes some restrictions on political activity by judges. Canon 5(A)(1) imposes

55. See generally Ronald M. Dworkin, Taking Rights Seriously (1977).

broad restrictions on participation in political activities by all judges and candidates for judicial office, including prohibitions on participation in political gatherings and fund-raising activities. Canon 5(A)(3) directs candidates for judicial office to "maintain the dignity appropriate to judicial office." The Code then defines this limitation more specifically to include, among other restrictions, prohibitions on campaign pledges and public statements on pending controversies. Canon 5(A)(3)(d). Canon 5(B) sets forth restrictions on political activity applicable to judges seeking judicial appointments; Canon 5(C) limits political activity by judges subject to public election. These canons reflect obvious differences between these selection methods. For example, when the state uses an appointive method of selection, candidates can engage in only very limited political activity. On the other hand, when judges are selected or retained by public election, the Code permits greater political activity. Thus, a candidate for an appointive position may not solicit campaign funds, Canon 5(B)(1), while a candidate for an elected position may solicit funds through a campaign committee, Canon 5(C)(2). Model Rule 8.2(b) requires lawyers who are candidates for judicial office to comply with the Code of Judicial Conduct. In addition, Model Rule 8.2(a) prohibits lawyers from making statements that the lawyer knows to be false or with reckless disregard of the truth about the qualifications or integrity of judges, candidates for judicial office, or other public legal officers. Section 174 of the proposed Restatement of the Law Governing Lawyers adopts similar standards.

Part II
Government Lawyers

H. THE ROLE OF THE GOVERNMENT LAWYER AND THE DUTY TO SEEK JUSTICE

The prevailing ethic of the profession is that lawyers representing private clients do not have a professional obligation to strive for a fair outcome or to seek justice in cases that they handle. Thus, a private lawyer may assert a defense such as the statute of limitations even if the defense would bar a claim that the lawyer knows to be otherwise valid. This position flows from the role of lawyers in an adversarial system. The adversarial system is process oriented rather than substantively based. The system assumes that as long as the process is fair, the outcome that occurs is fair. Indeed, for lawyers to undertake obligations to produce substantively fair outcomes would itself be procedurally unfair since it would undermine the adversarial process.[56]

To say that lawyers in private practice do not have a professional obligation to seek a fair outcome in cases they handle is not the same, however, as claiming that lawyers should be indifferent to fairness. Under the current model of lawyers' professional obligations, lawyers should counsel their clients regarding both legal and nonlegal aspects of their cases, including the fairness of any action that the client intends to take. Code of Professional Responsibility EC 7-8; Model Rule 2.1.[57] The crucial point, however, is that under the standard model of lawyers' professional obligations, the client retains the right to reject the advice of the lawyer, and the lawyer does not bear any responsibility if the client chooses to act in a way that is unfair. Model Rule 1.2(b). Some commentators have questioned this view of lawyers' ethical obligations and have argued that lawyers should, at least in some circumstances, have obligations regarding the fairness of the outcomes of matters in which they are involved.[58]

Do government lawyers have different obligations from lawyers in private practice regarding the fairness of the outcomes of cases they handle?

> The conventional wisdom . . . suggests that zealous representation of clients is inappropriate for government lawyers. Most lawyers and judges who have considered the ethical responsibilities of the government lawyer have assumed that government counsel should temper their advocacy in the interests of "justice." This notion has been expressed by judges both on and off the bench, by

56. See, e.g., Catherine J. Lanctot, The Duty of Zealous Advocacy and the Ethics of the Federal Government Lawyer: The Three Hardest Questions, 64 S. Cal. L. Rev. 951, 958-964 (1991).

57. See also Restatement of the Law Governing Lawyers §151(3) (Tent. Draft #8, March 21, 1997).

58. See articles cited and discussed in Chapter 1.B.3.

> the American Bar Association, by former government attorneys, by scholars, and by other commentators generally. . . .[59]

Various justifications have been offered for the view that the government lawyer has an ethical obligation to seek justice. It has been argued that government lawyers represent the public interest rather than particular individuals or agencies. Since the public interest favors just resolution of cases, imposing an obligation on government lawyers to seek just outcomes does nothing more than require government lawyers to carry out the goals of their "clients." Further, since the government usually has substantially greater resources than private litigants, imposing an obligation of fairness on government lawyers helps prevent governmental oppression of private citizens.[60]

As noted above, one of the principal arguments in support of imposing a duty to seek fairness or justice on government lawyers is that the government lawyer's client is the public interest rather than an agency or official of the government. Professor Geoffrey Miller has vigorously attacked this view:

> Despite its surface plausibility, the notion that government attorneys represent some transcendental "public interest" is, I believe, incoherent. It is commonplace that there are as many ideas of the "public interest" as there are people who think about the subject. . . . If attorneys could freely sabotage the actions of their agencies out of a subjective sense of the public interest, the result would be a disorganized, inefficient bureaucracy, and a public distrustful of its own government. More fundamentally, the idea that government attorneys serve some higher purpose fails to place the attorney within a structure of democratic government. Although the public interest as a reified concept may not be ascertainable, the Constitution establishes procedures for approximating that ideal through election, appointment, confirmation, and legislation. Nothing systemic empowers government lawyers to substitute their individual conceptions of the good for the priorities and objectives established through these governmental processes. Accordingly, the initial intui-

59. Catherine J. Lanctot, The Duty of Zealous Advocacy and the Ethics of the Federal Government Lawyer: The Three Hardest Questions, 64 S. Cal. L. Rev. 951, 955-957 (1991) (footnotes omitted).

60. See generally id. at 981-982; Jack B. Weinstein & Gay A. Crosthwait, Some Reflections on Conflicts Between Government Attorneys and Clients, 1 Touro L. Rev. 1, 11-12 (1985).

> tion, which suggested that sabotage might be justified as a means of combating a bad policy, seems seriously misguided.[61]

Professor Miller goes on to argue that because an agency lawyer operates within a constitutional system, the agency lawyer's client is the executive branch. This means that the attorney's duties run to the official who has legal authority to decide a matter. Normally, that will be an official within the agency, although circumstances may exist in which the President has delegated authority to decide a matter to a person outside the agency.[62]

What is the position of the Code of Professional Responsibility and the Model Rules on the issue? EC 7-14 of the Code of Professional Responsibility seems to accept the position that government lawyers have special responsibilities to justice:

> A government lawyer who has discretionary power relative to litigation should refrain from instituting or continuing litigation that is obviously unfair. A government lawyer not having such discretionary power who believes there is lack of merit in a controversy submitted to him should so advise his superiors and recommend the avoidance of unfair litigation. A government lawyer in a civil action or administrative proceeding has the responsibility to seek justice and to develop a full and fair record, and he should not use his position or the economic power of the government to harass parties or to bring about unjust settlements or results.

The Model Rules do not include a provision similar to EC 7-14. In Formal Opinion 94-387, the ABA Committee on Ethics and Professional Responsibility concluded that the Model Rules impose no greater obligation on government attorneys than on private lawyers to achieve just outcomes. On the other hand, comment 4 of the Scope section of the Model Rules recognizes the possibility that "other law" may grant government lawyers greater authority than private counsel over the outcome of litigation:

61. Geoffrey P. Miller, Essay, Government Lawyers' Ethics in a System of Checks and Balances, 54 U. Chi. L. Rev. 1293, 1294-1295 (1987).

62. Id. at 1298. See also Catherine J. Lanctot, The Duty of Zealous Advocacy and the Ethics of the Federal Government Lawyer: The Three Hardest Questions, 64 S. Cal. L. Rev. 951, 1012-1015 (1991) (also rejecting the view that government lawyers have an obligation to do justice or to produce fair outcomes, resting the conclusion on the benefits of the adversarial system in addition to constitutional principles).

> Under various legal provisions, including constitutional, statutory and common law, *the responsibilities of government lawyers may include authority concerning legal matters that ordinarily reposes in the client in private client-lawyer relationships.* For example, a lawyer for a government agency may have authority on behalf of the government to decide upon settlement or whether to appeal from an adverse judgment. Such authority in various respects is generally vested in the attorney general and the state's attorney in state government, and their federal counterparts, and the same may be true of other government law officers. Also, lawyers under the supervision of these officers may be authorized to represent several government agencies in intragovernmental legal controversies in circumstances where a private lawyer could not represent multiple private clients. They also may have authority to represent the "public interest" in circumstances where a private lawyer would not be authorized to do so. These Rules do not abrogate any such authority. (Emphasis added.)

A government lawyer possessing authority that "ordinarily reposes in the client" presumably could exercise this power in the interests of justice or fairness. As the Model Rules indicate, when this authority exists, it is based on constitutional, statutory, and common law principles.

The Restatement of the Law Governing Lawyers agrees with the approach of the Model Rules.[63] Under the Restatement, government lawyers, like private attorneys, do not have a general obligation to represent the public interest or to promote justice. Instead, government lawyers are required to follow the directions of their clients, which are normally the agencies by which they are employed.[64] The Restatement, like the Model Rules, recognizes that applicable law sometimes grants governmental lawyers (prosecutors, for example) discretionary authority, which they should exercise to advance the governmental and public objectives of the lawyer's client.[65]

When do constitutional, statutory, or common law principles provide a government attorney with "client authority" over a matter? Suppose, for example, that the Justice Department is repre-

63. Restatement of the Law Governing Lawyers §156 (Tent. Draft #8, March 21, 1997).

64. Id. comms. *c*, *f*.

65. Id. comm. *g*.

senting a federal agency in litigation. Who has the authority to decide what the government's position will be if the Justice Department and the agency have different views on the issue? The highest legal official in the federal government is the Attorney General. Federal law provides that the Attorney General has the power to control litigation in which the United States is involved:

> Except as otherwise authorized by law, the conduct of litigation in which the United States, an agency, or officer thereof is a party, or is interested, and securing evidence therefor, is reserved to the officers of the Department of Justice, under the direction of the Attorney General.[66]

This authority is exclusive and plenary, so long as the Attorney General acts within the law.[67] Thus, the Attorney General has the authority to determine the legal position of the United States and to authorize settlement, subject to legal restrictions.[68] If an agency disagrees with the position the Justice Department plans to take in litigation, the agency can attempt to convince the Justice Department to change its position. If this is unsuccessful, the agency's only resort would be to the President, who has authority over the executive branch, including the Attorney General. If the President agrees with the position of the agency rather than the Attorney General, the President can order the Attorney General to adopt the agency's view as the official position of the United States in litigation. Since the Attorney General serves at the pleasure of the President, the President could discharge an Attorney General who refused to follow the President's policy.[69] In summary, in the federal system, Justice Department lawyers, acting pursuant to the authority of the Attorney General, rather than agency officials, have the right to control litigation, unless authority is specifically given by statute to the agency rather than to the Attorney General.[70]

66. 28 U.S.C. §516 (1994). See also 28 U.S.C. §§518, 519 (1994) (argument of cases and supervision of litigation).

67. See, e.g., Executive Business Media, Inc. v. United States Dept. of Defense, 3 F.3d 759 (4th Cir. 1993).

68. Id. at 762.

69. See 28 U.S.C. §503 (1994).

70. See, e.g., FDIC v. Irwin, 727 F. Supp. 1073 (N.D. Tex. 1989), *aff'd*, 916 F.2d 1051 (5th Cir. 1990) (FDIC has statutory authority to litigate without approval of Attorney General).

The authority of the attorneys general in the states depends on the particular constitutional, statutory, and common law framework of each state. Some states are much like the federal system with the attorney general having the power to control litigation involving the state, subject to the authority of the governor. For example, in People ex rel. Deukmejian v. Brown,[71] the California Supreme Court held that the attorney general of California did not have authority to seek a writ of mandamus to stop the governor from enforcing an allegedly unconstitutional statute because the authority of the attorney general was subject to that of governor, who was entrusted with executive power of state. In other states, the attorney general may be the final legal authority for the state. In Feeney v. Commonwealth,[72] the Supreme Judicial Court of Massachusetts decided that the attorney general had authority to seek judicial review of a lower court decision holding that a civil service preference for veterans unconstitutionally discriminated against women, despite objections of the agency and the governor.

Suppose an attorney in the Justice Department or in the office of the attorney general in a state disagrees with the policy position taken by that attorney's superiors. The attorney can, and should, argue for the position that the attorney believes is correct. If the attorney's superiors reject those arguments, however, the attorney is bound to follow the decision of the superiors since they have the legal authority to make the decision. If the attorney in good conscience cannot accept the decision, the attorney should ask to be relieved from participation in the matter or resign. To the extent that the decision of the superior involves ethical rather than policy issues, the subordinate lawyer may still follow the senior attorney's decision if it is a "reasonable resolution of an arguable question of professional duty." See Model Rule 5.2(b).

Attorneys who are employed by agencies rather than by the Justice Department or the office of a state attorney general do not have "client authority." That authority is vested in the officials of the agency. Thus, agency attorneys normally should follow the decision of the official of the agency authorized to make decisions in the matter. In some cases, agency attorneys may be justified in taking a matter higher in the government. See Model Rule 1.13 and

71. 624 P.2d 1206 (Cal. 1981 en banc).
72. 366 N.E.2d 1262 (Mass. 1977).

comment 7. In situations that involve illegal conduct by officials, agency attorneys may be justified in revealing the matter beyond the agency. The next section discusses the scope of the government attorney's duty of confidentiality.

I. CONFIDENTIALITY OF INFORMATION: GOVERNMENT LAWYERS AND WRONGDOING BY GOVERNMENT OFFICIALS

Unlike private lawyers, government lawyers are subject to extensive statutory and regulatory provisions that control the confidentiality of information:

> [P]ervasive regulations govern much of the information with which a government lawyer must necessarily deal. A large portion of the information in the hands of the federal government consists of public records or information available upon request to the public. Recent legislation, in particular the Freedom of Information Act, provides citizens with access to a wide range of government documents. An obvious corollary to such legislation is that a government lawyer's duty of confidentiality does not extend to information that the government has made available upon request to the public. In terms of the professional ethics rules, the government in effect has consented to disclosure. Government lawyers also deal with more sensitive and more protected information than lawyers in the private sector. For example, government lawyers have access to military secrets, sensitive negotiations with foreign governments, grand jury minutes dealing with investigation of federal crimes and millions of records dealing with the most private matters of individuals and corporations. Information in the last category includes income tax records, medical records, and trade secrets. Not surprisingly, a detailed regulatory scheme limits the government lawyer's use of this information and prohibits its improper dissemination. Protection of information of this character is not dependent solely on the attorney-client privilege or the lawyer's professional duty of confidentiality.[73]

73. Roger C. Cramton, The Lawyer as Whistleblower: Confidentiality and the Government Lawyer, 5 Geo. J. Legal Ethics 291, 294-295 (1991).

The ethical obligations of government lawyers are, of course, subject to these legal requirements.

Sections D, E and F of Chapter 4 considered the issue of the scope of a private lawyer's duty of confidentiality when a client has engaged or intends to engage in wrongdoing. As discussed in that chapter, lawyers in private practice may not counsel or assist their clients in conduct that is illegal or fraudulent. Lawyers must generally maintain the confidentiality of information that they received regarding client wrongdoing, but they have a limited area of discretion to reveal confidential information to prevent clients from committing future crimes. Lawyers employed by organizations have a duty to protect the organization from harm caused to the organization by its constituents. In fulfilling this duty, lawyers have discretion to reveal information about wrongdoing by constituents to higher authority in the organization.

Do government lawyers have any special legal or ethical obligations when they learn of wrongdoing by employees of an agency that they represent? The Code of Professional Responsibility and the Model Rules of Professional Conduct do not contain any specific provisions regarding the scope of the duty of confidentiality as applied to government lawyers. Comment 7 to Model Rule 1.13, which deals with an organization as client, states that the rule also applies to governmental organizations.[74] The comment goes on to refer to the complexity of the matter when the client is a governmental entity and to the possible applicability of statutes and regulations. The Restatement takes the position that a government lawyer should follow the principles applicable to entity clients when dealing with wrongdoing by a constituent, unless applicable law provides otherwise.[75]

Statutory provisions at the federal, state, or local level, however, affect the scope of the duty of confidentiality of the government lawyer. Federal law provides that the head of an agency or department shall report violations of federal criminal law to the Attorney General.[76] A federal government lawyer may report "corrupt conduct and other illegal conduct of a criminal character, that is, the

74. On a lawyer's duties to an organization when the lawyer learns that constituents of the organization are engaging in wrongful conduct, see Chapter 4.D.

75. Restatement of the Law Governing Lawyers §156(2) and comm. *j* (Tent. Draft #8, March 21, 1997).

76. 28 U.S.C. §535(b) (1994).

willful or knowing disregard of or breach of law, in either the legislative or executive branch" to the head of the department or agency. If the head officer is involved, the attorney may report directly to the Attorney General or other appropriate Justice Department official.[77] Such disclosure does not involve a breach of confidentiality if the client of the government attorney is considered to be the executive branch of the government since the agency head and the Attorney General are both part of that branch.[78]

In addition, Congress has enacted "whistleblower" legislation to protect government employees who disclose information against retaliation for their disclosures, particularly loss of their jobs.[79] The Act makes its unlawful for the government to take a personnel action against a governmental employee who discloses information that the employee "reasonably believes evidences" either (1) "a violation of any law, rule, or regulation" or (2) "gross mismanagement, a gross waste of funds, an abuse of authority, or a substantial and specific danger to public health or safety." The Act allows an employee to make disclosure within the government either to a designated official in the agency or to the Office of Special Counsel of the Merit Systems Protection Board.[80] Further, the Act authorizes employees to disclose information outside the government provided "such disclosure is not specifically prohibited by law and if such information is not specifically required by Executive order to be kept secret in the interest of national defense or the conduct of foreign affairs."[81] Disclosure outside the government could be made to a reporter, congressional staffer, or interest-group representative.[82]

The whistleblower provision does not expressly apply to government attorneys, nor does it expressly exclude government attorneys from its application. While it is possible that courts would construe the Act not to override an attorney's duty of confidentiality, given the strong public policies behind the Act and the absence of any specific exclusion for attorneys, it is unlikely that they will do so. In an analysis of the Act, Professor Roger Cramton argues

77. See Fed. Bar Assn. Op. 73-1, 32 Fed. B.J. 71, 73-74 (1973).

78. Roger C. Cramton, The Lawyer as Whistleblower: Confidentiality and the Government Lawyer, 5 Geo. J. Legal Ethics 291, 303 (1991).

79. Civil Service Reform Act of 1978 as amended by the Whistleblower Protection Act of 1989, 5 U.S.C. §2302(b)(8) (1994).

80. Id. §2302(b)(8)(B).

81. Id. §2302(b)(8)(A).

82. Roger C. Cramton, The Lawyer as Whistleblower: Confidentiality and the Government Lawyer, 5 Geo. J. Legal Ethics 291, 308 (1991).

that the general professional obligation of confidentiality is "overridden by the more specific permission of disclosure afforded by the whistleblower enactments."[83] Professor Cramton finds this to be a desirable result to the extent that a lawyer is reporting government corruption, but he questions the wisdom of the Act to the extent it would give protection to lawyers for reporting what are in essence policy disagreements:

> In other situations, however, not involving a high level cover-up of corrupt conduct, but only reasonable differences of opinion concerning the legality or wisdom of a proposed agency action (e.g., does the agency's rule sufficiently protect health or safety?), there is a serious concern that the whistleblower protection goes too far in eroding the loyalty and confidentiality that government lawyers owe to the government client.[84]

It should be noted, however, that the Whistleblower Act does not require government attorneys to disclose confidential information. Assuming the legislation applies to attorneys, the Act would simply protect them against various personnel actions, including discharge, if they did blow the whistle. As of 1991, there was no reported instance of a government lawyer invoking the protection of the Act, even though whistleblower protection had been in existence since 1978. A variety of factors, including especially the socialization of lawyers to protect their clients, make it unlikely that attorneys will use the Act.[85]

J. THE "REVOLVING DOOR": MOVEMENT OF LAWYERS INTO AND OUT OF GOVERNMENT PRACTICE

The "revolving door" refers to "the phenomenon of individuals who move between government and the private sector and who are often regulators one day, regulated the next, and regulators

83. Id. at 313.

84. Id.

85. On the issue of the government lawyer's duty of confidentiality, see also Robert P. Lawry, Confidences and the Government Lawyer, 57 N.C. L. Rev. 625 (1979).

again the day after."[86] While the term is often used derogatorily, the revolving door offers both public benefits as well as problems. A Harvard Developments Note identifies the following benefits and problems:

> BENEFITS OF THE REVOLVING DOOR
>
> The first and most fundamental benefit of the revolving door is avoidance of the likely alternative: a permanent legal bureaucracy .... [The] professionalism of government service is in direct conflict with the model of citizen participation in government ....
>
> The revolving door also enhances the quality of official decision-making. Policymakers must always strike a careful balance between independence and accountability, and an official will be better able to maintain his independence if he is relatively free to leave the government. . . .
>
> Finally, the revolving door is an important aid to government recruitment of attorneys with talent and imagination. The main advantages that government agencies have to offer young attorneys are training and experience, both of which can be turned into financial gain when and if the attorney chooses to leave the government. . . .
>
> PROBLEMS OF THE REVOLVING DOOR
>
> Perhaps the most frequently voiced fear concerning the revolving door is that the government attorney might abuse his position to benefit his future career in the private sector. . . .
>
> A second danger of the revolving door involves one of the principal bases for conflict of interest regulation in all types of legal practice: protection of client confidences. . . . This danger is real, but its significance should not be exaggerated [because of the presence of various statutes that make a wide variety of government information public].
>
> A third problem with the revolving door is the unfair advantage that it might give private parties who are able to hire former agency attorneys having special contacts and expertise. . . .
>
> A fourth abuse attributed to the revolving door is that it encourages favoritism to former government attorneys by their former colleagues in the agency or department in which they worked. . . .
>
> Finally, there is a basic objection to the fact that the revolving

86. Developments in the Law — Conflicts of Interest in the Legal Profession, 94 Harv. L. Rev. 1244, 1428 (1981).

door continually permits the fundamental impropriety of "switching sides."[87]

Regulation of the revolving door occurs through a complex array of rules of ethics, statutes, and regulations. Model Rule 1.11 deals with ethical limitations on successive governmental and private employment. (See also Model Rules 1.12 dealing with former judges and arbitrators.) Rules 1.11(a), (b), and (c)(2) apply to movement from government service into private practice, while Rule 1.11(c)(1) applies to movement from private practice to government service.

Rule 1.11(a) prohibits a lawyer who leaves government service from representing a "private client" in a "matter in which the lawyer participated personally and substantially as a public officer or employee, unless the appropriate government agency consents after consultation." The term "private client" as used in the rule is broadly construed. See Rule 1.11, comm. 4.[88] Several aspects of the scope and limitations of Rule 1.11 are particularly significant.

First, the rule bars representation of all private clients as to matters in which the attorney was personally and substantially involved while in government employment. It is not necessary that the former government client be involved in the matter or have an adverse interest to the lawyer's private client.[89] While the rule protects the government from disloyalty and misuse of confidential information, it has a broader goal. The rule prevents the prospect of private employment from tainting the lawyer's judgment while in public service.[90] See also Model Rule 1.11, comm. 3.

Second, Rule 1.11(a) only restricts the activities of a former government lawyer as to a "matter" in which the lawyer participated personally and substantially. Under Rule 1.11(d), a matter generally is limited to a proceeding involving specific parties, as distinguished from rulemaking and issues of general policy, although conflict of interest rules of an agency may define a matter

87. Id. at 1428-1433.

88. See also General Motors Corp. v. City of New York, 501 F.2d 639 (2d Cir. 1974) (attorney disqualified from representing city in antitrust action when attorney had participated in same matter while Justice Department attorney; attorney was engaged in private employment because of contingent fee agreement with city).

89. 1 Hazard & Hodes, The Law of Lawyering §1.11:201, at 353.

90. Id.

more broadly. Thus, a lawyer who was directly involved in drafting regulations for a governmental agency would not be precluded from advising a private client about those regulations after leaving government service, unless the agency's conflict of interest rules provide otherwise.[91]

Third, Rule 1.11(a) provides that, with the consent of the agency, a lawyer may handle a matter in which the lawyer was personally and substantially involved. If the agency refuses to consent, the lawyer is personally disqualified from handling the matter, but other members of the firm are not disqualified from handling the matter if the disqualified lawyer is screened from any participation in the matter, receives no part of the fee from the matter, and the agency receives notice so that it can monitor compliance with the rule.[92] It is interesting to note that the Model Rules have different provisions on screening of former government lawyers and screening when private lawyers switch firms. See Model Rule 1.10, comm. 5. Section 214 of the proposed Restatement follows Model Rule 1.11 in most material respects.

Professor Monroe Freedman has criticized the screening and waiver provisions of Rule 1.11(a) on three grounds. First, "no workable standards for the screening have ever been suggested." Second, "it is virtually impossible to police violations of screening once a waiver has been given." Third, "waiver by a government agency compounds the initial conflict of interest. Agency lawyers who are called upon to grant or deny a waiver on behalf of a former colleague's law firm have a substantial personal incentive to be generous in granting the waiver, because they will themselves be making similar requests within a short time when they leave government service." Freedman also argues that the rationale for the provision — the government's need to be able to attract competent lawyers — is totally speculative.[93]

It is important to understand, however, the limits of screening under Model Rule 1.11(a). The screening provisions only apply if

91. See 50 F.R. 39622-01 (1985) (the term "matter" includes participation in drafting, providing advice, or making recommendations in development of EPA regulations).

92. See Armstrong v. McAlpin, 625 F.2d 433 (2d Cir. 1980) (en banc), *vacated for lack of jurisdiction*, 449 U.S. 1106 (1981) (denying motion to disqualify firm when former government lawyer who joined firm had been screened from participation in matter).

93. Monroe H. Freedman, Understanding Lawyers' Ethics 208-209 (1990).

the government is not an adverse party in the matter in which the former government lawyer's firm is involved. "Sideswitching" is controlled by Rule 1.9(b). Under Rule 1.9(b) and 1.10, the former governmental lawyer who engages in sideswitching is personally disqualified *and the lawyer's entire firm is disqualified.*[94]

Rule 1.11 applies to all government lawyers, whether federal, state, or local. The rule must be read, however, in conjunction with federal and state statutory and regulatory provisions. This body of law imposes restrictions on former government lawyers in addition to those found in Rule 1.11. The statutory provisions are not limited to lawyers, as in Rule 1.11, but apply to other government officials and employees. Moreover, violation of these statutory provisions may subject government officials to criminal penalties. State statutes and regulations dealing with former governmental employees vary considerably, so attorneys leaving state governmental employment must consult these provisions. For federal governmental employees, the most important provision is 18 U.S.C. §207 (1994). That statute contains two provisions somewhat similar to Rule 1.11, although these provisions are narrower in scope than the rule. Section (a)(1) provides as follows:

> (a) Restrictions on all officers and employees of the executive branch and certain other agencies.—
>
> (1) Permanent restrictions on representation on particular matters.—Any person who is an officer or employee (including any special Government employee) of the executive branch of the United States (including any independent agency of the United States), or of the District of Columbia, and who, after the termination of his or her service or employment with the United States or the District of Columbia, knowingly makes, with the intent to influence, any communication to or appearance before any officer or employee of any department, agency, court, or court-martial of the United States or the District of Columbia, on behalf of any other person (except the United States or the District of Columbia) in connection with a particular matter—
>
> (A) in which the United States or the District of Columbia is a party or has a direct and substantial interest,
>
> (B) in which the person participated personally and substantially as such officer or employee, and

94. 1 Hazard & Hodes, The Law of Lawyering §1.11:102, at 351-352.

(C) which involved a specific party or specific parties at the time of such participation,

shall be punished as provided in section 216 of this title.

The section is narrower than Rule 1.11(a) in at least two respects. First, it only applies to communications or appearances before the federal government or the District of Columbia, while Rule 1.11 applies to any private representation. Second, the statute only applies if the United States is a party or has a direct or substantial interest; Rule 1.11 applies even if the United States is not directly involved.

Federal statute 18 U.S.C. §207(a)(2) is similar to section (a)(1) except that it only applies to matters that the former employee reasonably should know were "under his or her official responsibility." In this case, the restriction is for two years, rather than permanently.

Remaining subsections of 18 U.S.C. §207 are quite different in scope than Rule 1.11. These sections establish one-year "cooling off" periods for certain executive and legislative officials and employees, prohibiting various appearances or contacts. For example, certain former employees of federal agencies are prohibited for a period of one year from making any appearances or communications with employees of their former agencies with an intention to influence a decision.[95] Similarly, any employee of a senator or member of Congress is prohibited for one year after termination of employment from communicating with the senator or member for whom the former employee worked or with any employee of that senator or member with the intention to influence an official decision.[96]

In 1993, President Clinton issued an Executive Order requiring high-level executive branch appointees to agree to an Ethics Pledge as a condition of employment. The pledge prohibits various activities, including lobbying any officer or employee of an agency in which the appointee served for a period of five years.[97] The Executive Order applies in addition to other legal restrictions.[98]

The Model Rules contain one provision dealing with lawyers joining government service. Rule 1.11(c)(1) prohibits a government

95. 18 U.S.C. §207(c) (1994).
96. 18 U.S.C. §207(e)(2) (1994).
97. Exec. Order No. 12,834, 58 Fed. Reg. 5911 (1993).
98. Id. §1(a)(5).

lawyer from participating in a matter in which the lawyer participated "personally and substantially" while in private practice, unless no one else is legally authorized to act in the matter. The rule is the converse of Rule 1.11(a).

Much more important for lawyers who join federal government service is the vast array of statutory and regulatory provisions governing their conduct, which have been codified by the government.[99] Each state will have its own statutory and regulatory scheme for government attorneys.[100]

The preceding material has focused on the ethical problems facing lawyers employed by the government. A related area involves ethical issues facing lawyers who are elected to serve in state legislatures. In most states, service in the state legislature is a part-time job. As a result lawyer/legislators must deal with a variety of conflicts of interest between their official duties and their private interests.[101]

99. See generally 5 C.F.R. pt. 2600, subch. B et seq. (1997) (Government Ethics). See Crandon v. United States, 494 U.S. 152 (1990) (separation payment by company to official leaving company to accept government position did not violate statutory provision prohibiting dual compensation for government employees).

100. For a critical evaluation of such restrictions, see W.J. Michael Cody & Richardson R. Lynn, Honest Government: An Ethics Guide for Public Service (1992).

101. See George F. Carpinello, Should Practicing Lawyers be Legislators?, 41 Hastings L.J. 87 (1989); Dennis M. Henry, Commentary, Lawyer-Legislator Conflicts of Interest, 17 J. Legal Prof. 261 (1992); Thomas M. Kellenberg, When Lawyers Become Legislators: An Essay and a Proposal, 76 Marq. L. Rev. 343 (1993).

CONCLUSION

Problems and Prospects Facing the Legal Profession

In this concluding section, it seems appropriate to step back from the specific professional obligations that have been the subject of the previous seven chapters to consider some of the broader issues facing the legal profession as a whole, particularly the organized legal profession.

The history of professions has been a subject of considerable interest to sociologists. As part of this inquiry, scholars have focused on the meaning and attributes of a profession.[1] In defining the meaning of a profession and in distinguishing professions from other occupations, four criteria stand out in importance:

1. Competent practice of a profession requires *specialized knowledge,* normally gained through graduate education.
2. Professional behavior is subject to *self-regulation,* i.e., regulation by the organized profession rather than by other institutions, typically through codes of professional conduct.
3. Licensing and other restrictions exist to prevent *unauthorized practice* by nonprofessionals.

1. See Geoffrey C. Hazard, Jr. & Deborah L. Rhode, The Legal Profession: Responsibility and Regulation 2-5 (3d ed. 1994).

4. While professionals earn a livelihood through their practices, professional practice involves *public service.*

The four criteria are mutually reinforcing rather than independent. Thus, the criterion of specialized knowledge supports the principles of self-regulation and unauthorized practice. Because the practice of law requires specialized knowledge, nonlawyers are not in a position to understand or to regulate professional behavior. Since nonlawyers cannot evaluate the competency of professional services, restrictions on unauthorized practice must exist to prevent nonprofessionals from harming members of the public. Similarly, the criterion of public service bolsters the concepts of self-regulation and unauthorized practice. The profession must regulate the behavior of its members to ensure the proper balance between practice and public service. Further, professional commitment to public service helps justify substantial benefits that professional membership entails.

Affiliation with a profession that has these four characteristics offers significant benefits to its members. Professional association provides status and prestige. For many lawyers, their self image is intimately connected with their membership in a profession. Professionals enjoy far greater independence in their work than is available to nonprofessionals. Moreover, professional membership has valuable economic benefits. Prohibitions on the unauthorized practice of law exclude competition from nonlawyers. Indeed, professional self-regulation can limit competition even among members of the profession. For example, the bar prohibited competition among lawyers by commercial advertising until the Supreme Court found that such restrictions were unconstitutional.[2]

The special attributes and status available to professionals ultimately must be justified, however, not by whether they benefit members of the profession but by whether they serve the public interest. In evaluating the public benefits of professional status, it is important to recognize that the foundations of contemporary professional structure are neither preordained nor necessarily desirable. For example, it is not difficult to image a legal profession in which lawyers gain the specialized knowledge they need to practice law through experience, rather than formal education. Indeed, during the nineteenth century, most lawyers in the United

2. See Chapter 6.C.1.

States were trained through an apprenticeship system rather than by attendance at law school. Only during the twentieth century have law schools come to dominate legal education.[3] Similarly, it is perfectly possible to restructure the regulatory system so that lawyers are supervised by institutions not under their control. Bankers, for example, are subject to both administrative and judicial regulation rather than self-regulation. Lawyers could be governed by a similar system.

During the last quarter century, trends both within the legal profession and more broadly in society have been eroding each of the four criteria central to the concept of a profession. First, the concept that the practice of law requires specialized knowledge obtained through graduate education has come under attack. In almost all areas of practice, lawyers make extensive use of paraprofessionals. Schools for paralegals have opened around the country, and the number of paralegals has grown to the point where they have formed their own professional organizations, the National Federation of Paralegal Associations (NFPA) and the National Association of Legal Assistants (NALA).[4] While paralegals formally practice under the supervision and control of lawyers, experienced paralegals often enjoy significant independence. Indeed, some states now permit paralegals to offer their services to lawyers as independent contractors.[5] The growth of paralegals demonstrates that many aspects of law practice can be handled by individuals who have less than the full three years of graduate training required of lawyers. As paralegals have been growing in importance, the value of legal education for the practice of law has come under scrutiny. A number of lawyers and judges have criticized legal education for becoming overly theoretical and divorced from the practical concerns of lawyers,[6] and an ABA task force, chaired by former ABA President Robert MacCrate, has recom-

3. On the history of legal education in the United States, see Lawrence M. Friedman, A History of American Law 606-620 (2d ed. 1985); Kermit L. Hall, The Magic Mirror: Law in American History 218-221 (1989).

4. See James Podgers, Crumbling Fortress, 79 A.B.A. J. 50 (Dec. 1993). The NFPA issues ethics advisory opinions for its members. See www.paralegal.org.

5. See Carl M. Selinger, The Retention of Limitations on the Out-of-Court Practice of Law by Independent Paralegals, 9 Geo. J. Legal Ethics 879 (1996).

6. Harry T. Edwards, The Growing Disjunction Between Legal Education and the Legal Profession, 91 Mich. L. Rev. 34 (1992); Harry T. Edwards, The Growing Disjunction Between Legal Education and the Legal Profession: A Postscript, 91 Mich. L. Rev. 2191 (1993).

mended changes in legal education to better prepare students for the practice of law.[7]

Several trends are undermining the principle of self-regulation: criticism of the lawyer disciplinary process, legalization of lawyers' obligations, subjection of lawyers to market discipline, and diversity in the profession. In 1970, the first major study of the lawyer disciplinary process in the United States, conducted by the ABA's Clark Committee, found the "existence of a scandalous situation that requires the immediate attention of the profession."[8] Since the issuance of the Clark Committee report, the disciplinary process has increasingly become subject to public scrutiny. In most states, the control of the disciplinary process has been removed from the bar and centralized in the highest court in the state.[9] While judges are, of course, lawyers, judges are selected through a process that makes them politically accountable for their conduct. Nonlawyers now participate in the disciplinary process, and rules dealing with confidentiality of disciplinary proceedings have been relaxed.[10] Despite these changes, criticisms of lawyer control of the disciplinary process continues to be voiced by citizens groups, such as Help Against Legal Tyranny, known as "Halt."[11]

The principle of self-regulation has been eroded by legalization of professional responsibility. As discussed throughout this book, issues of lawyer ethics are now litigated not only in the disciplinary process, but through disqualification motions, tort actions against lawyers, administrative proceedings, and criminal prosecutions. The American Law Institute is nearing completion of its Restatement of the Law Governing Lawyers. The need for the Restatement shows a fundamental fact about lawyer obligations—the subject has become legalized. Legalization of lawyer ethics has shifted the locus of control of lawyer conduct from the bar to other lawmaking institutions.

7. ABA Task Force on Law Schools and the Profession, Narrowing the Gap, Legal Education and Professional Development (1992) (the MacCrate Report).

8. ABA Special Comm. on Evaluation of Disciplinary Enforcement, Problems and Recommendations in Disciplinary Enforcement 1 (1970).

9. See ABA Model Rules for Lawyer Disciplinary Enforcement, Rules 1, 2 (comprehensive system under control of state supreme court).

10. Id. Rules 2(B) (disciplinary board composed one-third of nonlawyers), 16 (proceedings public after finding of probable cause).

11. See Kay A. Ostberg, Attorney Discipline National Survey (1990) (report prepared for HALT).

The growing importance of market forces on the legal profession is also undermining the principle of self-regulation. Beginning with Bates v. State Bar of Arizona, the Supreme Court has issued a line of decisions gradually expanding the area of constitutionally protected commercial speech by lawyers. As a result of these decisions, lawyers face growing competition within the profession, particularly for lucrative personal-injury cases. At the same time, larger firms have become much more aggressive and innovative in marketing their services to corporate clients. Taken together, these factors mean that market forces rather than bar-made rules are playing a growing role in determining lawyer conduct.

The last quarter century has also seen a remarkable growth in the number of lawyers and in the diversity of the profession.[12] The legal profession is now much more open to women and minorities than in the past, although an affirmative action backlash may restrain and perhaps even reverse this trend.[13] But a diverse profession has its costs, one of which is that diversity makes it much more difficult for the profession to formulate a position on a contentious issue. For example, the profession has debated without resolution for a number of years what stand, if any, to take on the problem of discrimination within the profession.[14] In February 1994, the ABA's Standing Committee on Ethics and Professional Responsibility offered but then withdrew a proposal to the House

12. See Robert L. Nelson, The Futures of American Lawyers: A Demographic Profile of a Changing Profession in a Changing Society, 44 Case W. Res. L. Rev. 345 (1994).

13. See Hopwood v. State of Texas, 78 F.3d 932 (5th Cir. 1996), *cert. denied*, 116 S. Ct. 2580 (1996) (state law school's admissions policies that discriminated in favor of minority applicants violated equal protection).

14. For discussions of the issue of discrimination in the profession, see Susan D. Gilbert & Michael P. Allen, Commentary, Overcoming Discrimination in the Legal Profession: Should the *Model Rules* Be Changed?, 6 Geo. J. Legal Ethics 933 (1993) (proposing rule that would prohibit discrimination by lawyers in employment practices and in course of representation); Ronald D. Rotunda, Racist Speech and Lawyer Discipline, 6 Prof. Law. 1 (Feb. 1995) (arguing against disciplinary rules prohibiting racist speech on First Amendment grounds); Andrew E. Taslitz & Sharon Styles-Anderson, Still Officers of the Court: Why the First Amendment Is No Bar to Challenging Racism, Sexism and Ethnic Bias in the Legal Profession, 9 Geo. J. Legal Ethics 781 (1996). A significant case on the issue is United States v. Wunsch (In re Swan), 84 F.3d 1110 (9th Cir. 1996) (reversing sanction imposed on male lawyer under California statute prohibiting lawyers from exhibiting an "offensive personality" for sending sexist letter to female lawyer accusing female lawyers in general of not playing by the rules on ground that statute was unconstitutionally vague).

of Delegates to amend Model Rule 8.4 to make it improper for a lawyer to "knowingly manifest by words or conduct, in the course of representing a client, bias or prejudice based upon race, sex, religion, national origin, disability, age, sexual orientation or socio-economic status." The rule would not have applied to a "lawyer's confidential communications to a client" or preclude "legitimate advocacy with respect to the foregoing factors."[15]

Bar-supported restrictions on the unauthorized practice of law have also come under increasing scrutiny. Scholars of the legal profession, led by Professor Deborah Rhode, have argued that restrictions on the unauthorized practice are overly broad, protective of lawyer interests, and insufficiently sympathetic to the needs of the public for delivery of legal services.[16] In August 1995, the ABA Commission on Nonlawyer Practice issued a report, "Nonlawyer Activities in Law-Related Situations." The Commission found that, with adequate protection for the public, nonlawyers had an important role to play in delivery of legal services. The Commission recommended that the ABA reconsider its ethics rules and policies in a variety of areas, including those governing the unauthorized practice of law. Professor Rhode has criticized the Commission for not going far enough,[17] but the Commission's existence and report is indicative of the trend toward relaxation of restrictions on the unauthorized practice of law.

Finally, the image of the lawyer as a public servant, as a minister of justice, is on the verge of collapsing. In a diverse, secular society such as ours, it is difficult if not impossible to reach consensus on principles of substantive justice, so the legal profession has traditionally articulated an ideal of procedural justice. Under this ideal, neutral decisionmakers resolve disputes based on adversarial presentations made by lawyers who zealously represent each side of the case. But the profession is having difficulty maintaining even this vision of procedural justice. Many members of the public see lawyers as concerned principally with advancing their own finan-

15. See Lawyers' Manual Prof. Conduct (ABA/BNA), 10 Current Rep. 13 (1994).

16. Policing the Professional Monopoly: A Constitutional and Empirical Analysis of Unauthorized Practice Prohibitions, 34 Stan. L. Rev. 1 (1981); The Delivery of Legal Services by Nonlawyers, 4 Geo. J. Legal Ethics 209 (1990).

17. See Essay, Professionalism in Perspective: Alternative Approaches to Nonlawyer Practice, 22 N.Y.U. Rev. L. & Soc. Change 701 (1996).

cial interest.[18] Lawyers are accused of perverting the legal system through frivolous lawsuits, dilatory tactics, excessive fees, and other abuses. Highly publicized criminal cases, particularly the O.J. Simpson case, have also contributed to the image that lawyers will use the rules of procedure to produce outcomes that are unjust.[19]

Taken as a whole, these trends have resulted in a profession that is diminished in prestige, less secure, more competitive, and more diverse. Young lawyers entering the profession will find significant challenges and pressures, but enormous opportunities as well. In such an environment, sensitivity to a lawyer's obligations, whether based on professional rules, legal standards, or moral values, is likely to be even more important than it has been in the past.

18. See Mary Ann Glendon, A Nation Under Lawyers (1994); Anthony T. Kronman, The Lost Lawyer (1993); Kenneth Lasson, Lawyering Askew: Excesses in the Pursuit of Fees and Justice, 74 B.U. L. Rev. 723 (1994).

19. For a vigorous justification of the conduct of defense counsel in the case, see Alan M. Dershowitz, Reasonable Doubts: The O.J. Simpson Case and the Criminal Justice System (1996).

APPENDIX *A*

Multiple Choice Questions with Analysis

The multiple choice questions that follow can be used to review doctrinal issues taught in most professional responsibility or legal ethics courses and to prepare for the Multistate Professional Responsibility examination administered by the National Conference of Bar Examiners. Answers with analysis follow all of the questions, beginning at page 456.

In answering the questions, choose the answer that seems best even if you do not completely agree with any of the alternatives. Comments to the Model Rules should be consulted for guidance in interpreting the rules. The questions use terminology that is similar to the terminology used in the multistate examination. The following terms apply:

- **Subject to discipline** asks whether the conduct referred to or described in the question subjects the attorney to discipline under the ABA Model Rules or the judge to discipline under the ABA Code of Judicial Conduct (1990).
- **Proper** asks whether the conduct referred to or described in the question is professionally appropriate in that it (a) would not subject an attorney to discipline or (b) would not subject a judge to discipline.

- **Subject to liability** asks whether the conduct referred to or described in the question subjects the attorney to civil liability for damages, whether for negligence, breach of fiduciary duty, violation of the rules of civil procedure, or other theory of recovery.

Chapter 2 The Client-Lawyer Relationship

2.1. C retains L to handle a personal injury case. L has a well-run office with procedures for docketing of cases. By mistake, however, L's secretary loses the file. As a result, L fails to file the complaint and the statute of limitations expires.

(1) L is subject to discipline, and L is also subject to malpractice liability.
(2) L is subject to discipline, but L is not subject to malpractice liability.
(3) L is not subject to discipline, but L is subject to malpractice liability.
(4) L is not subject to either discipline or malpractice liability.

2.2. A and B agree to form a limited liability company (LLC) for the purpose of real estate development. L handles the formation of the LLC and prepares an agreement defining the relative rights and duties of A and B regarding ownership of the LLC. Subsequently, a dispute develops between A and B. A asks L to represent her in the dispute with B. B objects, claiming that L has a client-attorney relationship with B.

I. L has a client-attorney relationship with B because a lawyer who represents an entity is treated as representing the principal owners of the entity.
II. L has a client-attorney relationship with B unless L made it clear that he was representing only the LLC and not its owners.
III. L does not have a client-attorney relationship with B if the LLC rather than B paid L's fees.

(1) I only.
(2) II only.
(3) III only.
(4) II and III, but not I.

2.3. P is involved in a serious automobile accident in which P's car is destroyed and P suffers personal injuries. L agrees to represent P in a personal injury action on a contingency fee basis. L and P enter into a written contingency fee agreement that states that the fee will be one-third of the total recovery in the case before deduction of expenses regardless of whether the case is settled or goes to trial. P wishes to purchase a new car to replace the vehicle that has been destroyed. The dealer is willing to sell P a car if L signs an agreement to pay the dealer out of the proceeds of any settlement in the case. L signs the agreement.

(1) L is subject to discipline because the contingency fee is the same regardless of whether the case is settled or goes to trial. L is also subject to discipline for signing the agreement with the car dealer.
(2) L is subject to discipline because the contingency fee is the same regardless of whether the case is settled or goes to trial, but L is not subject to discipline for signing the agreement with the car dealer.
(3) L is not subject to discipline because the contingency fee is the same regardless of whether the case is settled or goes to trial, but L is subject to discipline for signing the agreement with the car dealer.
(4) L is not subject to discipline because the contingency fee is the same regardless of whether the case is settled or goes to trial, and L is also not subject to discipline for signing the agreement with the car dealer.

2.4. C has asked L to represent her in a divorce action against her husband. L informs C that he charges for his time in the case on an hourly basis. L also tells C that he requires a nonrefundable retainer of $10,000 for taking the case, and that he will be entitled to a bonus of $10,000 if he is successful in obtaining custody of C's minor children for her in the divorce.

(1) L is subject to discipline for charging a nonrefundable retainer. L is also subject to discipline for charging C a bonus for obtaining custody of C's minor children.
(2) L is subject to discipline for charging a nonrefundable retainer, but L is not subject to discipline for charging C a bonus for obtaining custody of C's minor children.

(3) L is not subject to discipline for charging a nonrefundable retainer, but L is subject to discipline for charging C a bonus for obtaining custody of C's minor children.
(4) L is not subject to discipline for charging a nonrefundable retainer, and L is also not subject to discipline for charging C a bonus for obtaining custody of C's minor children.

2.5. L has agreed to represent the plaintiff, C, in a wrongful death action involving an airplane crash. Because L is not experienced in aircraft litigation, L wishes to associate out-of-state co-counsel, O, who is an expert in such matters. L and O agree to divide the fee in the matter. L also informs C of the need to present expert witness testimony to support C's case. C agrees to allow L to retain an expert provided C will not be responsible for the expert's fee if there is no recovery. L retains E as an expert witness and pays E $5,000 for E's evaluation of the matter. L and E agree that if the case goes to trial E will receive a fee of an additional $5,000.

I. L is subject to discipline for the fee splitting agreement with O because such agreements are unethical.
II. L is subject to discipline for agreeing that C will not be responsible for E's fee if there is no recovery in the case.
III. L is subject to discipline for agreeing to pay E a fee of $5,000 contingent on the case going to trial.

(1) I only.
(2) II only.
(3) III only.
(4) Neither I, II, or III.

2.6. L agrees to represent D in a highly publicized criminal case. L informs D that his fee will be $25,000 payable in advance plus 25 percent of any payments that D receives as a result of the publicity involving the case. D agrees to this fee arrangement and pays L $25,000 in cash.

(1) L is subject to discipline for receiving a cash payment. L is also subject to discipline for agreeing to a fee of 25 percent of any payments that D receives resulting from the publicity involving his case.
(2) L is subject to discipline for receiving a cash payment, but L

is not subject to discipline for agreeing to a fee of 25 percent of any payments that D receives resulting from the publicity involving his case.

(3) L is not subject to discipline for receiving a cash payment, but L is subject to discipline for agreeing to a fee of 25 percent of any payments that D receives resulting from the publicity involving his case.
(4) L is not subject to discipline for receiving a cash payment. L is also not subject to discipline for agreeing to a fee of 25 percent of any payments that D receives resulting from the publicity involving his case.

2.7. L is the closing attorney for a residential real estate transaction. The buyer, B, appears at closing with a certified check drawn on a local bank. L informs the parties that she cannot disburse funds until she receives actual funds in her trust account from the certified check. Both the seller and broker protest that they are entitled to receive their payments immediately, and they subsequently file grievances against L.

I. L is subject to discipline for refusing to disburse funds immediately based on the buyer's certified check.
II. L is subject to discipline for failing to have the buyer present a check in advance of closing so that funds would be available for disbursement at closing.
III. L is not subject to discipline.

(1) I only.
(2) II only.
(3) III only.
(4) I and II, but not III.

2.8. L represents D in a prosecution for murder. D informs L that he committed the crime and that he wishes to enter a guilty plea. D also informs L that he does not want L to offer any evidence in mitigation of punishment. L is concerned about D's mental capacity to make informed decisions, but D refuses to undergo a psychiatric examination.

I. It would be proper for L to consult a psychiatrist despite D's objections.
II. L is subject to discipline if L moves to have the court

determine D's competency to stand trial over D's objections.

III. It would be proper for L to refuse to submit the guilty plea if L does not believe that a guilty plea is in D's best interests.

(1) I only.
(2) II only.
(3) III only.
(4) None of the above.

2.9. C hires L in a breach of contract action. After L has done extensive work on the matter, C fires L without cause. C owes L a substantial amount for legal services rendered. C asks L to turn over all documents in the case to C. L refuses to do so until C pays L's fees and until C signs a release that relieves L from all liability in connection with L's representation of C.

(1) L is subject to discipline both for refusing to turn over the files to C and for demanding that C sign the release.
(2) L is subject to discipline for refusing to turn over the files to C unless C pays L's fees, but not for demanding the release.
(3) L is not subject to discipline for refusing to turn over the files to C unless C pays L's fees, but L is subject to discipline for demanding that C sign the release.
(4) L's actions were a proper response to C's nonpayment of fees.

Chapter 3 Loyalty

3.1. L represents Corporation (C) in a number of small debt collection actions. X has asked L to represent her against C in a breach of contract action. Is L subject to discipline if he represents X against C in the contract action while also representing C in the debt collection matters?

I. No, so long as the breach of contract action and the debt collection matters are not substantially related.

II. No, if L reasonably believes that he can adequately represent X and X consents after full disclosure of the conflict.

III. Yes, because of the appearance of impropriety.

(1) I only.
(2) II only.
(3) III only.
(4) None of the above.

3.2. Law Firm has represented ABC corporation in various labor matters for a number of years. XYZ corporation asks L, a partner in Law Firm, to represent it in a major patent infringement action against C corporation, a wholly owned subsidiary of ABC.

I. It would be proper for L to undertake representation of XYZ against C if Law Firm is not currently handling any matters for ABC provided the patent infringement matter and the labor matters are not substantially related.
II. It would be proper for L to undertake representation of XYZ against C because Law Firm has represented only the parent corporation, ABC, not the subsidiary, C corporation.
III. L is subject to discipline if L undertakes representation of XYZ without advising it of his firm's representation of ABC corporation.

(1) I only.
(2) II only.
(3) III only.
(4) I and II, but not III.

3.3. Several years ago, L represented C corporation in an application to the Patent and Trademark Office to obtain a patent for a product developed by C. L, a member of Law Firm, successfully obtained the patent for C. X corporation now wishes to retain Law Firm to bring suit against C claiming that C's patent infringes a preexisting patent that X has.

I. It would be proper for Law Firm to represent X if L has left the firm taking C's file with her.
II. If L is still a member of Law Firm, it would be proper for L to represent X in the patent infringement action so long as the legal issues in the patent application and the infringement action are different.

III. If L is still a member of Law Firm, it would be proper for Law Firm to handle X's case so long as L is screened from any participation in the matter.

(1) I only.
(2) II only.
(3) III only.
(4) None of the above.

3.4. Several years ago, L handled the title work for the purchase of a home by husband and wife. The wife has now asked L's firm to represent her in a divorce action against her husband. Is it ethically proper for the firm to do so?

(1) Yes, because the prior representation is not substantially related to the divorce action.
(2) Yes, but only if another lawyer in L's firm handles the matter.
(3) No, because division of the home will be an issue in the divorce case.
(4) No, because a lawyer is subject to discipline for bringing suit against a former client.

3.5. A represented C1 and C2 in the formation of a corporation in which C1 provided capital and C2 provided services. A drafted a buy/sell agreement providing for the sale of stock of either party to the other if certain events took place. A dispute has now developed between C1 and C2 about the interpretation of the agreement, and C1 and C2 have been unable to resolve the dispute amicably.

I. A is subject to discipline because the Model Rules prohibit a lawyer from representing multiple parties in the formation of a corporation.
II. A is subject to discipline if he represents either C1 or C2 in connection with the dispute.
III. In a subsequent dispute between C1 and C2, communications made by either C1 or C2 during the formation of the corporation would not be subject to the attorney-client privilege.

(1) II only.
(2) I and II, but not III.
(3) II and III, but not I.
(4) I, II, and III.

3.6. L works for Law Firm which is well-known nationally for its practice in the area of environmental law. L has been asked to testify before a Senate Committee on revision of federal environmental protection statutes. L plans to give testimony calling for changes in the law that would be beneficial to the interests of some of L's clients, but could be harmful to other clients. L's firm engages in litigation around the country. On occasion, the firm has been called on to take conflicting positions on legal questions before federal appellate courts in different circuits.

(1) L is subject to discipline if he testifies before the Senate Committee because of the conflict of interest between his clients, and members of L's firm who take inconsistent legal positions are subject to discipline because they are engaged in a conflict of interest.
(2) L is subject to discipline if he testifies before the Senate Committee because of the conflict of interest between his clients, but members of L's firm who take inconsistent legal positions are not subject to discipline for engaging in a conflict of interest.
(3) L is not subject to discipline if he testifies before the Senate Committee, but members of L's firm who take inconsistent legal positions are subject to discipline because they are engaged in a conflict of interest.
(4) L is not subject to discipline if he testifies before the Senate Committee, and members of L's firm who take inconsistent legal positions are not subject to discipline for engaging in a conflict of interest.

3.7. The Lawson Law Firm is deciding whether to hire a new associate A, who currently works for the Anderson Law Firm. The Lawson Law Firm is handling a products liability action against one of the clients of the Anderson Law Firm. A has had no involvement and no knowledge whatsoever about the products liability case.

(1) The Lawson firm will be disqualified from handling the products liability case if A works on the matter when she joins the Lawson firm.
(2) The Lawson firm will be disqualified from handling the products liability case unless it promptly establishes appropriate procedures to screen A from any participation in the matter.
(3) The Lawson firm will be disqualified from handling the products liability case if A joins the firm, regardless of the steps the firm takes.
(4) The Lawson firm will not be disqualified from handling the products liability case if A joins the firm.

3.8. A fire at a local hotel has killed and injured a number of guests. Several of the injured guests and several families of deceased guests have asked L to represent them in actions against the hotel.

I. L is subject to discipline if she undertakes representation of all of the plaintiffs because of the potential for conflicts of interest.
II. It would be proper for L to undertake representation if she obtains a written waiver of conflicts of interest from the plaintiffs.
III. It would be proper for L to negotiate an aggregate settlement of the claims of all of her clients, with settlement funds distributed to the clients in proportion to the extent of their injuries.

(1) I only.
(2) II only.
(3) II and III, but not I.
(4) Neither I, II, or III.

3.9. L has been retained by Insurance Company to defend a legal malpractice action brought against attorney A. Under the terms of the policy, claims based on fraud are excluded while claims based on negligence are covered. The plaintiff's complaint contains allegations of both fraud and negligence.

I. During discovery, it would be proper for L to attempt to establish that A acted fraudulently.

II. L is subject to discipline if L represents the Insurance Company in a subsequent declaratory judgment action against A to determine whether the plaintiff's claims are covered by the policy.

III. L is subject to discipline unless she withdraws from representation because of the potential for a conflict of interest.

(1) I only.
(2) II only.
(3) III only.
(4) II and III, but not I.

3.10. L has just concluded representation of C in a personal injury case in which C has obtained a settlement of $200,000. C informs L that C would like to invest the money and obtain a good rate of return. L informs C that L would be interested in borrowing the money from C. L gives C an unsecured promissory note for $200,000, payable in installments with interest at 10 percent, a rate that is higher than the current market rate of interest that C could obtain.

I. L is subject to discipline because a lawyer may not borrow money from a client.

II. L is subject to discipline because the note is unsecured.

III. L is subject to discipline because C did not have a reasonable opportunity to seek advice of independent counsel.

(1) II only.
(2) III only.
(3) II and III, but not I.
(4) I, II, and III.

3.11. C, a long-time friend and client of A, asks A to draft C's will, naming A as personal representative and providing for a bequest of $10,000 to A.

I. A is subject to discipline for drafting a will in which A is named as personal representative.
II. A is subject to discipline for drafting a will in which A receives a substantial bequest.
III. It would be proper for A's partner, P, to draft the will naming A as personal representative and beneficiary of the bequest.

(1) I only.
(2) II only.
(3) I and II, but not III.
(4) I, II, and III.

3.12. L represented T in planning T's estate. L drafted T's will, supervised its execution, and acted as one of the subscribing witnesses. On T's death, the executor asked L to represent the estate in probate and tax matters. Unfortunately, a dispute has developed because T has disinherited one of T's children. The child has challenged the will on the ground that T was incompetent. It appears that L will need to be a witness on behalf of the estate to establish T's competency.

I. L is subject to discipline if L testifies on behalf of the estate.
II. It would be proper for L to avoid the possibility of a conflict of interest by not testifying on behalf of the estate.
III. If L testifies, it would be proper for L's partner, P, to represent the estate in the will contest, so long as L's testimony would not be adverse to the estate.

(1) I only.
(2) II only.
(3) III only.
(4) I and II, but not III.

Chapter 4 Confidentiality

4.1. A represents H in a divorce action brought by W. One afternoon, A receives a telephone call from H, who is emotionally distraught. H says that he has learned that W is involved with another man. H sounds out of control emotionally and says that he is going to kill W's lover.

I. A is subject to discipline if he informs the police of H's threat.
II. It would be proper for A not to inform the police if A does not believe that H's threat is serious.
III. If A does not inform the police and H carries out his threat, A is not subject to liability because A's sole duty is to his client, H, not to the lover.

(1) I only.
(2) II only.
(3) II and III, but not I.
(4) I and III, but not II.

4.2. L is general counsel for C corporation. V, vice president of C corporation, asks for an appointment with L. At the meeting, V informs L that V has embezzled money from the corporation. V tells L that V plans to make restitution of the embezzled funds to the corporation. V asks for L's advice as to how to proceed.

I. L is subject to discipline unless L withdraws from handling the matter because L faces a conflict of interest in representing C corporation and V.
II. L is subject to discipline if L informs the president or the board of directors of V's embezzlement.
III. L is subject to discipline if L fails to inform V that L represents C corporation.

(1) I only.
(2) II only.
(3) III only.
(4) II and III, but not I.

4.3. L is defending D in a prosecution for murder. D informs L that D has committed several other murders that have not yet been solved by the police, and asks for L's advice about these crimes.

(1) L is subject to discipline if L voluntarily informs the authorities that D committed these crimes. L can be compelled by

subpoena, however, to testify about D's admissions because the attorney-client privilege does not apply.

(2) L is subject to discipline if L voluntarily informs the authorities that D committed these crimes, and L cannot be compelled by subpoena to testify about D's admissions because the attorney-client privilege applies.

(3) L is not subject to discipline if L voluntarily informs the authorities that D committed these crimes. L can also be compelled by subpoena to testify about D's admissions because the attorney-client privilege does not apply.

(4) L is not subject to discipline if L voluntarily informs the authorities that D committed these crimes, but L cannot be compelled by subpoena to testify about D's admissions because the attorney-client privilege applies.

4.4. L is representing H in a divorce action. During the representation, H admits to L that he has sexually abused his 12-year-old daughter. Is L subject to discipline if L does not inform the authorities that H has engaged in child abuse?

(1) Yes, because the welfare of children is always the primary value in family court matters.

(2) Yes, because H has committed the crime of sexual abuse.

(3) Yes, because L's continued representation would be a fraud on the court.

(4) No, because the information is confidential.

4.5. C retains L to prepare an insurance trust to hold a large life insurance policy for which C has applied. During the course of representation, L learns that C has failed to disclose serious health problems on C's insurance application.

I. L is subject to discipline if L prepares the insurance trust and assists C in transferring ownership of the policy to the trust.

II. L is subject to discipline if L fails to inform the insurance company of C's failure to disclose C's health problems.

III. It would be proper for L to continue to represent C in completing the insurance trust so long as L does not make any misrepresentations to the insurance company.

(1) I only.
(2) II only.
(3) III only.
(4) I and II, but not III.

4.6. L represents D in a prosecution for criminal sexual conduct. D's mother comes to L's office with D's diary that she found in D's room. The mother tells L that the diary contains a number of incriminating statements.

I. If L reviews the diary, L is subject to discipline unless she turns the diary over to the authorities.
II. It would be proper for L to advise D's mother that she should keep the diary in a safe place.
III. It would be proper for L to retain the diary in L's office for safekeeping.

(1) I only.
(2) II only.
(3) III only.
(4) I and II, but not III.

4.7. L represents a corporation that is about to file a registration statement with the Securities and Exchange Commission (SEC) in connection with a new offering of stock. L learns that the president of the corporation has made illegal payoffs in order to obtain lucrative contracts for the corporation. The president refuses to include the information in the registration statement or to delay the registration. Failure to include material information in a registration statement is both fraudulent and criminal.

I. L is subject to liability under the federal securities laws as an "aider and abettor" if L participates in the registration.
II. It is proper for L immediately to withdraw from the matter.
III. If the SEC subsequently names L in a suit against the corporation for securities fraud, it would be proper for L to cooperate with the SEC by providing information about the president's conduct.

(1) I and II.
(2) I and III.
(3) II only.
(4) III only.

4.8. L has made a motion for summary judgment against the plaintiff in an employment discrimination action pending in federal district court in South Carolina. After oral argument in the case, the Seventh Circuit Court of Appeals renders a decision that is directly against L's position. Is L subject to discipline if L fails to inform the district court of the decision of the Seventh Circuit?

(1) No, because the Seventh Circuit decided the case after oral argument of the district court case.
(2) No, because South Carolina is in the Fourth Circuit.
(3) Yes, because L has an obligation to inform the judge of all relevant authority.
(4) Yes, because the decision was handed down by a higher court.

4.9. A, B, and C were eyewitnesses to a murder and robbery. A and B have identified the defendant, D, as the perpetrator of the crime, but C has been unable to do so.

I. It would be proper for the solicitor not to call C as a witness.
II. The solicitor is subject to discipline if she fails to inform the defense that C has been unable to identify D.
III. It would be proper for the solicitor to agree to drop criminal charges against C in an unrelated matter if C agrees to testify that he saw D commit the crime.

(1) I only.
(2) II only.
(3) I and II, but not III.
(4) I and III, but not II.

4.10. L represents the defendant, D, in an armed robbery case. D has admitted involvement in the crime to L, but insists on taking the stand and presenting an alibi defense that he was at his girl friend's house when the robbery occurred.

I. If L threatens D that L will move to withdraw if D testifies falsely, D's Sixth Amendment right to effective assistance of counsel has been infringed.

II. L is subject to discipline if L calls the girl friend as an alibi witness.

III. If L informs the court that D has testified falsely, L is subject to discipline for breaching the duty of confidentiality.

(1) I only.
(2) II only.
(3) III only.
(4) I and III, but not II.

Chapter 5 Zealousness and Its Limits

5.1. D, a doctor, asks L to represent him in a malicious prosecution action against a lawyer who brought an unsuccessful medical malpractice action against D. After filing the suit, L learns that the state supreme court had ruled two years earlier that a lawyer is absolutely immune from liability for malicious prosecution brought by an adverse party in litigation.

I. L is not subject to discipline for filing the suit on D's behalf if L acted in good faith but simply overlooked the supreme court decision.

II. L's conduct is proper so long as L promptly reveals the decision to the court.

III. L is subject to liability for filing the suit on D's behalf because of the recent decision.

(1) I only.
(2) II only.
(3) III only.
(4) I and II, but not III.

5.2. During a lunch break of a trial, the lawyer for the plaintiff happens to run into one of the jurors in a cafeteria near the courthouse. Because the cafeteria is crowded, the juror and the lawyer have lunch at the same table. They engage in casual conversation that has nothing to do with the case. At the same time, the lawyer for the defendant stops by the judge's office to discuss with the judge the possibility of recessing the case for two days because of a scheduling conflict.

(1) Both plaintiff's counsel and defense counsel are subject to discipline.
(2) Plaintiff's counsel is subject to discipline, but defense counsel is not subject to discipline.
(3) Plaintiff's counsel is not subject to discipline, but defense counsel is subject to discipline.
(4) Neither plaintiff's counsel not defense counsel are subject to discipline.

5.3. After a lengthy investigation of a brutal bombing, the government arrested and indicted three individuals. At a press conference called after the indictments, P, the prosecutor in charge of the case, stated that the government was confident that the three defendants were guilty of the crime, that the defendants have a lengthy record of involvement in terrorist activities, and that the government would seek the death penalty. The next day, defense counsel, DC, called a press conference in which they criticized the prosecution for trying the case in the media, stated that the prosecution had falsely portrayed their clients, and proclaimed that their clients were innocent of all charges.

(1) Both P and DC are subject to discipline for their press conferences.
(2) P is subject to discipline for P's press conference, but DC are not subject to discipline for their press conference.
(3) P is not subject to discipline for P's press conference, but DC are subject to discipline for their press conference.
(4) Neither P nor DC are subject to discipline for their press conferences.

5.4. L represents the plaintiff in a products liability action against C corporation. C corporation is represented by A. E is the chief engineer in charge of product design for C corporation. Without informing A, L contacts E and asks to interview E about the company's product design procedures. E refuses because A has previously asked E not to voluntarily give any information to L.

(1) L is subject to discipline for contacting E, and A is also subject to discipline for asking E not to voluntarily give information to L.
(2) L is subject to discipline for contacting E, but A acted properly in asking E not to voluntarily give information to L.
(3) L acted properly in contacting E, but A is subject to discipline for asking E not to voluntarily give information to L.
(4) Both L and A acted properly.

5.5. Law firm represents the defendant in a hotly contested antitrust action. P, a partner in the firm, and A, an associate, are handling the case for the defendant. In reviewing a box of documents to prepare a response to a discovery request, A discovers a very damaging memorandum. A informs P of the memorandum. P tells A not to deliver the memorandum in response to the discovery request, even though the discovery request covers the memorandum. A follows P's instructions and does not deliver the memorandum in response to the discovery request.

I. P is subject to discipline for not delivering the memorandum.
II. All other partners in the firm are subject to discipline because they are vicariously responsible for P's misconduct.
III. A's conduct is proper because he worked under P's direction and control and followed P's orders.

(1) I only.
(2) I and II, but not III.
(3) I and III, but not II.
(4) I, II, and III.

5.6. L represents the plaintiff in a personal injury action. Defendant, D, makes an offer to settle the case for $25,000. L rejects the offer stating: "My client won't accept anything less than $50,000." In fact, L's client has authorized him to settle the case for $30,000. D asks L to convey the offer to his client but L refuses.

(1) L is subject to discipline for making a false statement about plaintiff's settlement intentions, and L is also subject to discipline for refusing to convey the offer to L's client.
(2) L is subject to discipline for making a false statement about plaintiff's settlement intentions, but L is not subject to discipline for refusing to convey the offer to L's client.
(3) L is not subject to discipline for making a false statement about plaintiff's settlement intentions, but L is subject to discipline for refusing to convey the offer to L's client.
(4) L is not subject to discipline for making a false statement about plaintiff's settlement intentions, and L is not subject to discipline for refusing to convey the offer to L's client.

5.7. L, who represents the plaintiff, has been involved in heated settlement negotiations on the eve of trial with C, counsel for the defendant. About an hour before trial, the parties reach a settlement. C drafts the settlement agreement, which is signed by both parties. As L is about to close the file in the case, L notices that the agreement omits a significant provision that had been orally agreed to. The omitted provision would have been favorable to the defendant if included in the agreement.

(1) It would be proper for L to do nothing about the mistake because C drafted the agreement.
(2) It would be proper for L to urge L's client to disclose the mistake to C.
(3) L is subject to discipline for failing to disclose the mistake because lawyers have a duty of candor to opposing counsel in negotiations.
(4) L is subject to discipline if L fails to disclose the mistake because L would be assisting L's client in fraud.

Chapter 6 Delivery of Legal Services

6.1. The Family Court appoints L to defend C pro bono in a case in which the Department of Social Services is seeking to terminate C's parental rights on the ground that C abused C's children. Which of the following would be proper grounds for L to request court permission to be relieved of the appointment:

I. L does not believe that L can defend C because L was a victim of abuse when a child.

II. L's practice does not include Family Court matters.
III. L is currently handling another case pro bono.

(1) I only.
(2) II only.
(3) III only.
(4) I and II, but not III.

6.2. L runs a television advertisement in which L states that L's firm is "one of the most outstanding products liability firms in the country" and that the firm has obtained "numerous multimillion dollar settlements and judgments."

(1) L is subject to discipline for advertising that the firm is "one of the most outstanding products liability firms in the country." L is also subject to discipline for advertising that the firm has obtained "numerous multimillion dollar settlements and judgments."
(2) L is subject to discipline for advertising that the firm is "one of the most outstanding products liability firms in the country." L is not subject to discipline for advertising that the firm has obtained "numerous multimillion dollar settlements and judgments."
(3) L is not subject to discipline for advertising that the firm is "one of the most outstanding products liability firms in the country." L is subject to discipline for advertising that the firm has obtained "numerous multimillion dollar settlements and judgments."
(4) L is not subject to discipline for advertising that the firm is "one of the most outstanding products liability firms in the country." L is also not subject to discipline for advertising that the firm has obtained "numerous multimillion dollar settlements and judgments."

6.3. After an airplane crash, L writes a letter to the relatives of each of the victims. The letter is very brief and simply informs the relatives that L is available to handle their cases if they wish to call for an appointment. The envelope containing the letter states: "Important legal information. Please open immediately."

I. L is subject to discipline for writing the letter.
II. Writing the letter is proper because the letter is constitu-

tionally protected under Florida Bar v. Went for It, Inc., 515 U.S. 618 (1995).

III. L is subject to discipline if L follows up the letter with a personal telephone call.

(1) I only.
(2) II only.
(3) III only.
(4) I and III, but not II.

6.4. A law firm plans to send out its firm brochure to all of its existing clients. The brochure describes the types of work that the firm has done in the past, gives biographical information on members of the firm, and states the names of clients that the firm has represented.

I. Members of the firm are subject to discipline because sending the brochure constitutes improper solicitation.

II. Members of the firm are subject to discipline because it is improper to include the names of the firm's clients.

III. Members of the firm are subject to discipline unless they label the brochure as "Advertising Material."

(1) I only.
(2) II only.
(3) III only.
(4) Neither I, II, or III.

6.5. The local federally funded legal services program has decided to target landlord/tenant cases for use of its limited resources. The program plans to use several paralegals who will go door-to-door through housing projects contacting residents to determine if they are the victims of housing code violations. Paralegals will conduct a full interview with any resident who has a complaint. Paralegals will work under the direct supervision and control of L, an attorney, who is designated the Coordinator of the Landlord/Tenant Project. At one of the meetings of the board of directors of the program, a member of the board questions the ethical propriety of the proposal. She claims that it constitutes improper solicitation and the unauthorized practice of law.

(1) L is subject to discipline for using paralegals for improper solicitation, and L is also subject to discipline for assisting in the unauthorized practice of law.
(2) L is subject to discipline for using paralegals for improper solicitation but not for assisting in the unauthorized practice of law.
(3) L is not subject to discipline for using paralegals for improper solicitation, but L is subject to discipline for assisting in the unauthorized practice of law.
(4) L's conduct is proper.

6.6. A local bank has a staff of attorneys that it employs on salaried basis. Management of the bank has decided to offer its customers a "will preparation service." For a fee paid to the bank, lawyers on the bank's staff will prepare wills for the bank's customers. Is it proper for these lawyers to participate in this service?

(1) Yes, so long as it is clear that the lawyers are representing the customers, not the bank.
(2) Yes, because the lawyers are salaried employees of the bank.
(3) No, because the bank is involved in the unauthorized practice of law.
(4) No, because the plan involves improper solicitation.

6.7. Law Firm (LF) has a substantial environmental law practice. The firm has entered into discussions with a group of environmental engineers (EE) regarding some form of affiliation.

I. Members of LF are subject to discipline if the firm enters into partnership with EE.
II. Members of LF are subject to discipline if it forms a subsidiary corporation, owned by members of LF and EE, to provide engineering services.
III. It would be proper for LF and EE to enter into an association agreement in which LF agrees to refer engineering business to EE and EE agrees to refer legal work to LF.

(1) I only.
(2) I and II, but not III.

(3) II and III, but not I.
(4) I, II, and III.

6.8. L, a sole practitioner, has decided to retire. L enters into an agreement to sell L's practice to C. As part of the agreement, L promises not to practice law in the city in which L formerly practiced.

I. L and C are subject to discipline for entering into an agreement to sell L's practice.
II. L and C are subject to discipline for entering into an agreement that restricts L's right to practice law.
III. L and C are subject to discipline unless all of C's clients consent in writing to the sale.

(1) I only.
(2) II only.
(3) III only.
(4) Neither I, II, or III.

Chapter 7 Lawyers in Public Positions: Judges and Government Lawyers

7.1. In which of the following situations is a state court judge subject to discipline for failure to recuse herself from hearing the case?

I. The judge's first cousin is a party to the case.
II. The judge's former law partner represents one of the parties in the case.
III. The judge knows that her husband owns ten shares of stock in a corporation that is a party to the case. The stock is worth less than $250.

(1) I only.
(2) II only.
(3) III only.
(4) Neither I, II, or III.

7.2. The husband of a federal judge inherits from his mother stock in a company that is the defendant in a major case that has been pending before the judge for a number of years.

(1) The judge must disqualify herself in the matter only if the value of the stock is a significant part of her family's assets.
(2) The judge does not have to disqualify herself if she informs counsel for the plaintiff and defendant in chambers about her husband's stock ownership and both consent to the judge continuing in the case.
(3) The judge must disqualify herself unless her husband promptly sells the stock.
(4) The judge does not have to disqualify herself if her husband places the stock in blind trust.

7.3. Ms. J has been appointed to the state supreme court.

I. Ms. J is subject to discipline for leading the United Way's annual fund-raising drive.
II. Ms. J is subject to discipline for acting as the personal representative of the estate of a client when the judge represented the client before appointment to the bench.
III. Ms. J is subject to discipline for teaching as adjunct professor for the local law school for compensation in addition to her judicial salary.

(1) I and II, but not III.
(2) I and III, but not II.
(3) II and III, but not I.
(4) I, II, and III.

7.4. L was previously employed by the office of the Attorney General in the Consumer Affairs Division. While working there, L was responsible for the office's investigation of charges of alleged deceptive practices by certain used car dealers. L has now left the Attorney General's office to enter private practice. Would it be proper for L to represent the plaintiffs in a class action against the same used car dealers, seeking damages for the conduct that was the subject of L's investigation while in the AG's office?

(1) Yes, if the Attorney General's office has concluded the matter involving the investigation of the used car dealers.
(2) Yes, if L does not use any confidential information gained while working for the Attorney General's office.

(3) Yes, if L advises L's clients in the class action of L's prior representation and obtains their consent.
(4) No, because L is personally involved in the class action.

ANSWERS WITH ANALYSIS

Chapter 2 The Client-Lawyer Relationship

2.1. (3).

L is not subject to discipline. Model Rule 5.3 deals with lawyers' responsibilities for their subordinates. The rule has three levels of obligation. Under Rule 5.3(a), partners have an obligation to make sure that their offices have in place measures designed to give reasonable assurance that employees will act in accordance with the professional obligations of lawyers. L seems to have complied with this requirement. Model Rule 5.3(b) requires lawyers with direct supervisory authority over nonlawyers to "make reasonable efforts to ensure that the person's conduct is compatible with the professional obligations of the lawyer." L appears to have acted reasonably; L's secretary simply made a mistake. Model Rule 5.3(c) provides that a lawyer is subject to discipline for the conduct of a nonlawyer if the lawyer directs the conduct, ratifies, or fails to take reasonable remedial measures. L does not seem to have violated any of these provisions. L did not direct or ratify the secretary's mistake. When L did learn about the mistake, it was too late to take remedial action because the statute of limitations had run.

L is subject to malpractice liability. The secretary was negligent in losing the file. As an employer, L is vicariously liable for the negligence of L's employees.

2.2. (2).

I is *incorrect.* Under Model Rule 1.13(a), a lawyer who represents an organization has a client-lawyer relationship with the entity and not any of its constituents. A lawyer can form a client-attorney relationship with an owner of an entity either expressly or by implication, but such a relationship does not follow automatically from the representation of the entity.

II is *correct.* A lawyer representing a closely-held entity must exercise care to make sure that the owners of the entity do not have an expectation that the attorney is representing them.

III is *incorrect.* Payment of legal fees is a factor in deciding whether a client-attorney relationship exists, but payment of fees is not conclusive on the issue.

2.3. (4).

L is not subject to discipline for entering into a contingency fee agreement in which the contingency percentage does not vary with the stage at which the case is concluded. Model Rule 1.5(c) requires a contingent fee agreement to state the percentage to be applied if the case is concluded at various stages, but so long as the percentage is disclosed, nothing in the rule precludes the fee agreement from having the same percentage at different stages of the case. It should be noted that some states have statutes or court rules that limit the amount of contingent fees, and these would control over Rule 1.5(c).

L is also not subject to discipline for signing the agreement with the dealer. Model Rule 1.8(e) states that a lawyer "shall not provide financial assistance to a client in connection with pending or contemplated litigation," except that a lawyer may advance court costs and expenses of litigation. The automobile is obviously not a litigation expense, but the lawyer is not providing financial assistance to the client by agreeing to pay the dealer out of the proceeds of any personal injury settlement. The lawyer would have acted improperly if the lawyer had advanced funds to the client to buy a car or for other personal expenses. A guarantee by the lawyer of such payments would also probably be improper.

2.4. (3).

Some jurisdictions have declared nonrefundable retainers to be improper in some cases because they amount to excessive fees. See, e.g., In re Cooperman, 633 N.E.2d 1069 (N.Y. 1994). Absent such a decision, however, nonrefundable retainers are ethically permissible.

L is subject to discipline for agreeing to a fee arrangement in which L will receive a bonus if the client obtains custody of the children on divorce. A fee that is contingent on divorce is unethical. See Model Rule 1.5(d)(1).

2.5. (4).

I is *incorrect*. L is not subject to discipline for entering into a fee splitting agreement with O because such agreements are not per se unethical. See Model Rule 1.5(e).

II is *incorrect*. L acted properly in agreeing with C that C would not be responsible for E's fees if there is no recovery in the case. Model Rule 1.8(e) states that a lawyer may advance expenses of litigation "repayment of which may be contingent on the outcome of the matter." This represents a change from the Code of Professional Responsibility, which provided that the client must remain ultimately liable for repayment. See DR 5-103(B).

III is *incorrect*. L also acted properly in agreeing to pay E a fee of $5,000 contingent on the case going to trial. Model Rule 3.4(b) states that a lawyer shall not "offer an inducement to a witness that is prohibited by law." Comment 3 states that "it is improper to pay an expert witness a contingent fee." While the comment does not state what kind of contingency is improper, clearly payment contingent on the case going to trial is not an improper contingency since it simply means that the expert will not be paid if the expert does not have to testify. To be an improper contingent fee, the fee must be contingent on the content of the expert's testimony or the outcome of the case. See DR 7-109(C).

2.6. (3).

L is not subject to discipline for receiving his fee payment in cash. The Model Rules do not prohibit cash payment of fees, and there is nothing per se illegal about receiving a cash payment, although the IRS does require lawyers to report cash payment of fees in excess of $10,000. 26 I.R.C. §6050I. In some circumstances, fee payments to lawyers can be subject to forfeiture to the federal government when they are derived from certain illegal activity, such as money derived from violation of the drug felony statutes. 21 U.S.C. §853(c).

L is subject to discipline for entering into a fee agreement that gives him an interest in literary or media rights prior to the conclusion of the matter, since such an interest may affect the lawyer's independent professional judgment on behalf of the client. See Model Rule 1.8(d).

2.7. (3).

I is *incorrect*. In most jurisdictions, lawyers are allowed to disburse based on certified or bank checks, but such disbursement does pose a risk to the lawyer and to other clients who have funds in the lawyer's trust account if the check should be dishonored for some reason. Cautious lawyers may refuse to disburse except against collected funds, and this is entirely proper under Model Rule 1.15.

II is *incorrect.* A lawyer may, of course, inform the parties of what will be necessary in order for disbursement to be made at closing, but the lawyer does not have an ethical duty to require the buyer to present funds in advance of closing. Indeed, it would be ethically improper for the lawyer to do so unless the contract required the buyer to deposit funds in advance of closing because the lawyer would be demanding that the buyer assume an obligation not set forth in the contract that would cost the buyer additional interest.

III is *correct.* As the text indicates, however, competitive pressures may force real estate lawyers to seek a solution that allows them to make disbursements at closing consistent with their ethical obligations.

2.8. (1).

I is *correct.* L is impliedly authorized under Model Rule 1.6 to reveal confidential information to determine whether a client is competent under Model Rule 1.14. See ABA Informal Opinion 89-1530.

II is *incorrect.* Model Rule 1.14 states that lawyers should attempt to maintain normal attorney-client relationships with clients who suffer from disabilities, but §(b) provides that a lawyer "may seek the appointment of a guardian or take other protective action with respect to a client, only when the lawyer reasonably believes that the client cannot adequately act in the client's own interest." If L has reasonable doubts about D's capacity, L would not be subject to discipline for taking action under Rule 1.14(b).

III is *incorrect.* A client has the right to decide whether to enter a guilty plea. A lawyer may not refuse to allow a client to submit a plea simply because the lawyer believes that such a plea is not in the client's best interest. See Model Rule 1.2(a).

2.9. (3).

L acted properly in refusing to turn over the files to C until C paid L's fees. In most jurisdictions, lawyers have a retaining lien on the client's file as security for unpaid legal fees. Lawyers should use caution and judgment in exercising such liens to avoid substantial prejudice to the client, but there is no evidence of prejudice given from the facts. See ABA Informal Opinion 1461.

L is subject to discipline for demanding the release. Model Rule 1.8(h) prohibits lawyers from entering into agreements prospectively limiting liability for malpractice except when permitted by law and the client is independently represented in the matter.

Chapter 3 Loyalty

3.1. (4).

I is *incorrect.* The "substantial relationship" test applies to representation against a former client. Representation directly adverse to a current client without that client's consent is improper, regardless of whether the matters are related or not; such representation violates the lawyer's duty of loyalty. Model Rule 1.7(a) and comm. 3.

II is *incorrect.* While disclosure and consent by X is necessary, L has a duty of loyalty to C that requires disclosure and consent by C as well.

III is *incorrect.* The appearance of impropriety is found in Canon 9 of the Code of Professional Responsibility, but the concept is not found in the Model Rules. In fact, the drafters of the Model Rules deleted the concept because of its vagueness. Model Rule 1.9, comm. 5.

3.2. (3).

I is *incorrect.* This answer assumes that ABC is a former rather than a current client simply because the firm is not currently handling any matter for ABC. The mere fact that the firm is not currently handling a matter for ABC does not, however, make ABC a former client. Several courts have held that a pattern of continuous representation can result in a current client-attorney relationship, even when the firm is not currently handling a matter for the client. The leading case is International Business Machines Corp. v. Levin, 579 F.2d 271 (3d Cir. 1978) (law firm disqualified from handling antitrust action against IBM when firm had done labor work for IBM for a number of years, even though firm was not doing any work for IBM when it filed antitrust action).

II is *incorrect.* Most courts have held that subsidiaries are treated as the alter egos of their parents. See, e.g., McCourt Co. v. FPC Properties, Inc., 434 N.E.2d 1234 (Mass. 1982).

III is *correct* or at least the best available choice. XYZ is entitled to know that Law Firm has represented C's parent, ABC corporation, because Law Firm's representation of XYZ "may be materially limited" by Law Firm's responsibilities to ABC. See Model Rule 1.7(b). It should be noted that while disclosure and consent by XYZ are necessary, they are not sufficient. ABC must also consent to the representation. See Model Rule 1.7(a).

3.3. (1).

I is *correct.* If a lawyer departs a firm, the former firm is not precluded from undertaking representation against a client of the departing lawyer unless the firm actually has confidential information that it could use against the former client. Model Rule 1.10(b). In this case, since L has taken C's file, it appears unlikely that Law Firm would have confidential information that could be used against C.

II is *incorrect.* If L is still a member of Law Firm, both L and the entire firm are disqualified if X's patent infringement action is substantially related to C's patent application. While overlap of legal issues is a factor in deciding whether the matters are substantially related, that aspect is not conclusive. The fundamental question is whether L would be in a position to use confidential information against C. Since both matters involve C's patent, use of confidential information appears likely. In addition, L's representation of X would probably violate L's duty of loyalty to C because L is attacking her own work product.

III is *incorrect.* The Model Rules reject the possibility of screening of a disqualified lawyer except in cases involving movement of government lawyers to private practice. Compare Model Rule 1.10 and 1.11(a). Further, even those courts that have allowed screening have only done so in cases involving movement of a lawyer to a firm, not in a case such as this when the lawyer has continued to practice with the firm.

3.4. (1).

(1) is *correct.* Under Model Rule 1.9(a), a lawyer may undertake representation against a former client so long as the current and former representation are not "substantially related." It should be noted that while a lawyer may undertake such representation, a lawyer is not required to do so, and may as a matter of judgment, prudence, or personal discretion refuse to do so.

(2) is *incorrect.* If L is disqualified, that disqualification would be

imputed to L's firm and would not be relieved by the fact that L was not personally involved in the representation. See Model Rule 1.10(a).

(3) is *incorrect.* While division of the home may be an issue in the divorce case, that does not mean that the divorce case and the real estate transaction are substantially related. To be substantially related, there must be a realistic risk that the lawyer could use confidential information against the former client. Such a risk seems remote in this case.

(4) is *incorrect.* Under Model Rule 1.9(a), a lawyer may undertake representation against a former client so long as the current and former representation are not "substantially related."

3.5. (3).

I is *incorrect.* Under Model Rule 2.2, a lawyer may represent multiple parties in transactional matters, such as formation of corporations, provided certain requirements are met.

II is *correct.* Under Model Rule 2.2(c), a lawyer must withdraw as an intermediary if the conditions for multiple representation are no longer satisfied. On withdrawal, both clients would be former clients, and A would be precluded from representing either former client against the other under Model Rule 1.9(a). See also comment 10 to Model Rule 2.2.

III is *correct.* When a lawyer engages in multiple representation, any communications made by the clients to the lawyer are not privileged in a subsequent dispute between the clients. Model Rule 2.2, comm. 6. This aspect of multiple representation is one of the factors that the lawyer should discuss with the clients before they agree for the lawyer to act as an intermediary. See Model Rule 2.2, comm. 1.

3.6. (3).

Under Model Rule 6.4, a lawyer may take a public position on a legal issue even though the lawyer's public position may be detrimental to the interests of the lawyer's clients so long as the lawyer is not acting adversely to the client's legal position in a particular matter. The public is served if lawyers can take public positions on controversial legal issues without being limited by their clients' general interests. Since L is calling for a change in the law, it seems unlikely that the lawyer's testimony would affect clients in particular legal matters. Under Model Rule 6.4, L should disclose, however, that his testimony will be of benefit to some of his clients, without disclosing the identity of the client.

Positional conflicts are not per se improper, but may be improper when there is a substantial risk that the lawyer's position in one case will have an adverse impact on the client's position in a second case. Adverse positions before federal appellate courts in environmental cases appear to have this risk because federal appellate courts would give significant weight to decisions by their fellow courts and because of the national aspects of environmental practice.

3.7. (4).

(1) is *incorrect.* This answer flows from Model Rules 1.9(a), (b) and Model Rule 1.10(a). Under Model Rule 1.10(a), to determine whether a firm is disqualified, it is necessary to determine if any member of the firm is disqualified. Thus, the issue is whether A would be disqualified if A joined the firm. Model Rule 1.9(a) provides that a lawyer is disqualified if the lawyer formerly represented the client in a substantially related matter. That rule does not apply to A because A did not represent the client while a member of the Anderson firm. Model Rule 1.9(b) provides that, when a lawyer leaves a firm, the lawyer may not undertake representation against a client of the lawyer's former firm if the lawyer acquired confidential information. This rule also does not apply because A does not have any knowledge about the case. Since A would not be disqualified under either Model Rules 1.9(a) or (b), then the Lawson Firm would not be disqualified if A joined the firm.

(2) is *incorrect.* For the reasons set forth in (1) above, A is not personally disqualified, so screening procedures are unnecessary. Further, the Model Rules do not authorize screening as a solution to conflict of interest problems except in the case of the former government lawyer. See 1 Hazard & Hodes, The Law of Lawyering §1.10:207; see also Model Rule 1.11(a).

(3) is *incorrect.* For the reasons set forth in (1) above, A is not personally disqualified, so the firm is not disqualified.

(4) is *correct.*

3.8. (4).

I is *incorrect.* While the potential for conflicts of interest exists, that potential does not preclude the lawyer from undertaking multiple representation of clients in a matter. See Model Rule 1.7(b) and comm. 7.

II is *incorrect.* The Model Rules require consent after consultation with the clients of the implications, advantages, and disadvantages of multiple representation. Model Rule 1.7(b). Written waiver of conflicts of interest by the clients is neither necessary nor sufficient.

III is *incorrect.* Model Rule 1.8(g) precludes aggregate settlements without full disclosure and consent by each of the clients.

3.9. (2).

I is *incorrect.* The prevailing view of the lawyer's role in insurance defense practice is that the lawyer has undertaken multiple representation of both the insured and the insurance company. ABA Formal Opinion 282. As a result, the lawyer owes a duty of loyalty to both clients. For the lawyer to attempt to establish that A acted fraudulently violates that duty of loyalty that L owes to A because it would undermine A's claim of coverage.

II is *correct.* Under Model Rule 1.9(a) a lawyer may not represent a client against a former client in a substantially related matter. Here the issue of coverage and the original malpractice action are obviously substantially related.

III is *incorrect.* Normally, the insurance company and the insured have a harmony of interests such that multiple representation is proper. If an actual conflict of interest develops, the lawyer would be required to withdraw, but the potential for a conflict does not require withdrawal. See Model Rule 1.7 and comm. 10.

3.10. (3).

I is *incorrect.* Many courts have said that business transactions between lawyers and clients will be strictly scrutinized, and that lawyers enter into such dealings at their own peril. The Model Rules, however, do not prohibit loans from clients to lawyers, provided certain requirements are met. See Model Rule 1.8(a).

II is *correct.* Model Rule 1.8(a)(1) requires business transactions between lawyer and client to be "fair." Security for commercial loans is the standard practice. A loan without security is at least presumptively unfair to the client.

III is *correct.* See Model Rule 1.8(a)(2). If a lawyer has decided to enter into a business transaction with a client, a prudent lawyer would insist that the client obtain independent legal advice about the matter.

3.11. (2).

I is *incorrect.* As discussed below, subject to certain exceptions, lawyers may not ethically draft instruments in which they will receive gifts from their clients. Model Rule 1.8(c). When a will names a lawyer as personal representative of an estate, the lawyer will receive compensation from the estate, but that compensation is for services rendered and does not amount to a gift. The fact that a lawyer may ethically draft a will in which the lawyer is named as personal representative does not mean that lawyers should attempt to convince their clients to name them as personal representatives. Lawyers have an obligation to render independent and candid advice to assist their clients in choosing a personal representative that best meets their clients' needs. See Model Rule 2.1.

II is *correct.* Model Rule 1.8(c) precludes a lawyer from drafting an instrument in which the lawyer will receive a substantial gift from the client, unless the lawyer and client are related. Here A and C are long-time friends, but they are not related. A should insist that another lawyer draft the will for A. See comm. 2.

III is *incorrect.* If A is precluded from drafting the will because A will be the beneficiary of a substantial bequest, that disqualification is imputed to all members of A's firm. See Model Rule 1.10(a), which refers specifically to Rule 1.8(c).

3.12. (3).

I is *incorrect.* A lawyer is never precluded from testifying on behalf of a client. As discussed below, if a lawyer's testimony is necessary, the lawyer and the lawyer's firm may be precluded from representing the client, but the possibility of a conflict of interest does not prevent the lawyer from testifying on behalf of the client.

II is *incorrect.* Model Rule 3.7(a) states that a lawyer may not act as an advocate if the lawyer is "likely to be a necessary witness," subject to certain exceptions. Lawyers cannot avoid advocate/witness conflicts simply by refusing to testify. Moreover, if a lawyer's testimony is necessary to the client's case, the lawyer would be violating duties of loyalty and care to the client by not testifying. It should be noted that it is possible that L's testimony would not be necessary because other subscribing witnesses could testify. It is likely, however, that an experienced estate planner's testimony would be better evidence of competency than that of lay subscribing witnesses.

III is *correct.* Under the Code of Professional Responsibility, if a lawyer was disqualified from representing a client in a matter because the lawyer would be a witness, that disqualification was imputed to the entire firm. DR 5-102(A). The Model Rules reduce the application of the rule of imputed disqualification for lawyer/witness conflicts of interest. See Model Rule 3.7(b) and comm. 4. Note that this is an exception to the normal rule of imputed disqualification. See Model Rule 1.10. Disqualification is only imputed to the firm if lawyer's testimony would create a conflict of interest under Rule 1.7 or involve the use of confidential information under Rule 1.9. Neither situation applies here.

Chapter 4 Confidentiality

4.1. (2).

I is *incorrect* because, under Model Rule 1.6(b)(1), A "may reveal" confidential information "to prevent the client from committing a criminal act that the lawyer believes is likely to result in imminent death or substantial bodily harm."

II is *correct* because Model Rule 1.6 provides lawyers with professional discretion (see comms. 12, 13) and because the lawyer must "reasonably believe" that harm will result before making disclosure.

III is *incorrect.* A professional may be liable to a third party for negligent failure to warn. See Tarasoff v. Regents of the University of California, 551 P.2d 334 (Cal. 1976) (en banc) (psychotherapist subject to liability); Hawkins v. King County, 602 P.2d 361 (Wash. Ct. App. 1979) (lawyer not subject to liability on facts of case, but court indicates that on appropriate facts lawyers could be held liable to third parties for failure to warn of dangerous clients).

4.2. (3).

I is *incorrect.* L does not face a conflict of interest because L represents C, not V. Model Rule 1.13(a) states that a "lawyer employed or retained by an organization represents the organization acting through its duly authorized constituents." See also comm. 3, which states that constituents of the organization are not clients.

II is *incorrect.* Since L represents C, not V, L's duty is to C. Informing the president or the board of V's actions may be necessary. See Model Rule 1.13(b).

III is *correct.* V appears to believe that L represents V. L has a duty to correct this misunderstanding and to inform V that L represents C. See Model Rule 1.13(d). See also Model Rule 4.3 (dealing with unrepresented party).

4.3. (2).

L is subject to discipline if he informs the authorities of D's crimes. Model Rule 1.6 does not have an exception for past criminal conduct; thus, the general duty of confidentiality applies. L would violate the duty of confidentiality by revealing the information to the authorities.

L cannot be compelled to testify about D's statements to him because D's communications seem to fall squarely within the attorney-client privilege. D made communications to L in confidence for the purpose of seeking legal advice. The crime/fraud exception to the privilege only applies when the advice is sought to carry out a criminal or fraudulent scheme, not when advice is sought about past conduct.

4.4. (4).

(1) is *incorrect.* While the welfare of the children is certainly an important if not the primary value in family court matters, that is not the same as saying that lawyers in a family court matter have a duty to protect the welfare of the children. The welfare of the children is for the court to decide based on adversarial presentations by the lawyers.

(2) is *incorrect.* Although H may have committed a crime, a lawyer has a duty of confidentiality regarding past criminal acts. If the lawyer reasonably believed that the sexual abuse was ongoing, however, the lawyer would have discretion to reveal the information under Model Rule 1.6(b)(1).

(3) is *incorrect.* A lawyer does not commit a fraud on the court because the lawyer continues to represent a client even though the lawyer knows facts that are damaging to the client's position. It is possible that this situation could result in fraud being perpetrated on the court, for example, if H sought custody of the daughter and wanted to take the stand to testify as to his fitness as a parent. The mere fact of continued representation, however, is not a fraud on the court.

(4) is *correct.* The information received from the client in confidence about past wrongful acts is subject to the ethical duty

of confidentiality. Model Rule 1.6 does not have an exception for past criminal conduct.

Many lawyers would be morally outraged by the suggestion that they should continue to represent a client who has committed child abuse. At least three possible approaches are available that are consistent with a lawyer's ethical obligations. First, the lawyer could urge H to seek counseling or take other steps to deal with his problem. See Model Rule 2.1 (lawyer as advisor). Second, the lawyer could move to withdraw. See Model Rule 1.16(b)(3) (withdrawal because client pursues objective that lawyer considers "repugnant or imprudent"). Third, if the lawyer believed that the abuse was ongoing, rather than a past act, the lawyer would have discretion to reveal the information under Model Rule 1.6(b)(1).

4.5. (1).

I is *correct*. Lawyers may not "counsel or assist" clients in conduct that they know is criminal or fraudulent. Model Rule 1.2(d). By preparing the trust that will receive the policy and by participating in the transfer, the lawyer is assisting in conduct that the lawyer knows is fraudulent.

II is *incorrect*. The information relates to L's representation, so it is subject to the duty of confidentiality. Model Rule 1.6(a). Neither of the exceptions in Model Rule 1.6(b) applies. Note that even if C's conduct is considered to be a continuing crime, L could still not disclose the information under Model Rule 1.6(b)(1) because C is committing a financial fraud rather than an act involving death or substantial bodily harm. Under the Code of Professional Responsibility and under the rules of ethics adopted in some states, the exception for future wrongful acts is broader than that found in Model Rule 1.6(b)(1). DR 4-101(C)(3), for example, provided that a lawyer may reveal confidential information to prevent the client from committing a crime. Under these broader rules, L would have discretion to reveal C's conduct.

III is *incorrect*. It would be improper for L to make misrepresentations to the insurance company. See Model Rules 4.1(a), 8.4(c). However, even if L does not engage in active misrepresentation, L is still required not to counsel or assist a client in fraudulent or criminal conduct. See the discussion above. In other words, the duty not to counsel or assist in fraud is independent of and in addition to the duty not to engage in misrepresentation.

4.6. (1).

I is *correct.* A number of cases have held that lawyers who take possession of fruits, instrumentalities, or tangible evidence of a crime have a duty to turn the material over to the authorities after a reasonable period of time to inspect the material. See, e.g., Morrell v. State, 575 P.2d 1200 (Alaska 1978) (legal pad with kidnapping plan); State v. Carlin, 640 P.2d 324 (Kan. Ct. App. 1982) (tape recordings); State ex rel. Sowers v. Olwell, 394 P.2d 681 (Wash. 1964) (knife). Note that this obligation flows from common law and from obstruction of justice statutes, rather than from a specific Model Rule.

II is *incorrect.* Under Model Rule 4.3, when a lawyer deals with a person who is not represented by counsel, the lawyer should not imply that the lawyer is disinterested. The comment to that rule states that a lawyer should not give legal advice to an unrepresented person, other than the advice to consult counsel.

III is *incorrect* because L would be assisting in hiding evidence of a crime. See In re Ryder, 263 F. Supp. 360 (E.D. Va. 1967), *aff'd,* 381 F.2d 713 (4th Cir. 1967) (lawyer disciplined for moving proceeds of bank robbery from client's safety deposit box to lawyer's).

4.7. (4).

I is *incorrect.* The Supreme Court has held that the federal securities laws do not provide for "aider and abettor" liability. Central Bank of Denver, N.A. v. First Interstate Bank of Denver, N.A., 511 U.S. 164 (1994). Note that lawyers may still be liable as aiders and abettors under state law and that a lawyer may still be subject to discipline for aiding and abetting illegal or fraudulent conduct.

II is *incorrect.* When a lawyer for a corporation learns that an officer of the corporation intends to engage in conduct that is a "violation of law which reasonably might be imputed to the organization," the lawyer must proceed "as is reasonably necessary in the best interest of the organization." Typically, this will involve taking the matter to a higher level in the organization. See Model Rule 1.13(b). Withdrawal may be the ultimate response that the lawyer is forced to take, but it is not the first step. See Model Rule 1.13(c).

III is *correct.* A lawyer may reveal confidential information to "respond to allegations in any proceeding concerning the lawyer's representation of the client." Model Rule 1.6(b)(2). See Meyerhofer v. Empire Fire & Marine Ins. Co., 497 F.2d 1190 (2d Cir.), *cert. denied,*

419 U.S. 998 (1974) (proper for lawyer to provide affidavit regarding securities matter when lawyer named as defendant in civil action).

4.8. (2).

(1) is *incorrect.* Model Rule 3.3(a)(3) imposes an obligation on lawyers to disclose "legal authority in the controlling jurisdiction known to the lawyer to be directly adverse to the position of the client and not disclosed by opposing counsel." Rule 3.3(b) states that obligations under the rule "continue to the conclusion of the proceeding." While oral argument is over, the proceeding has not been concluded until the district court renders its decision and the time for appeal has expired.

(2) is *correct.* As noted above, the duty to disclose adverse legal authority only applies if the authority is in the controlling jurisdiction and is directly adverse. Here the authority is in another federal circuit, which is not the controlling jurisdiction.

(3) is *incorrect.* The duty to disclose is not that broad. Indeed, the ABA rejected a broader disclosure standard when it adopted the Model Rules. Proposed Model Rule 3.1(c) provided as follows:

> If a lawyer discovers that the tribunal has not been apprised of legal authority known to the lawyer that would probably have a substantial effect on the determination of a material issue, the lawyer shall advise the tribunal of that authority.

ABA Commission on Evaluation of Prof. Standards, Rule 3.1(c) (Discussion Draft Jan. 30, 1980).

(4) is *incorrect.* Once again the duty to disclose is not that broad. The duty does not apply to all higher court decisions, but only to decisions in the controlling jurisdiction.

4.9. (3).

I is *correct.* All lawyers have an obligation not to offer false evidence. Model Rule 3.3(a)(4). Lawyers do not, however, have an obligation to present the testimony of a witness. Further, C has only been unable to identify D as the perpetrator of the crime. That is not the same as C stating that D was not the person who committed the crime.

II is *correct.* Model Rule 3.8(d) states that a prosecutor must "make timely disclosure to the defense of all evidence or information known to the prosecutor that tends to negate the guilt of the accused or mitigates the offense." The fact that one of three eyewitnesses cannot identify the defendant tends to negate the defendant's guilt.

III is *incorrect.* The prosecutor would in essence be paying C to testify falsely, in violation of Model Rule 3.3(a)(4).

4.10. (2).

I is *incorrect.* Nix v. Whiteside, 475 U.S. 157 (1986), held that a defendant's Sixth Amendment right to effective assistance of counsel was not infringed when a lawyer threatened to take various steps after the defendant stated that he planned to take the stand and to testify falsely.

II is *correct.* A lawyer may not offer evidence that the lawyer knows is false. Model Rule 3.3(a)(4).

III is *incorrect.* Model Rule 3.3(a)(4) states that a lawyer who has offered false, material evidence shall take "reasonable remedial measures." Comments 10 and 11 state that revealing the perjury to the court is the proper step for a lawyer to take when withdrawal will not rectify the situation. In other words, the Model Rules take the position that the lawyer's duty as an officer of the court overrides the duty of confidentiality when the client commits perjury.

Chapter 5 Zealousness and Its Limits

5.1. (3).

I is *incorrect.* Model Rule 3.1 provides that a lawyer shall not bring a frivolous action. Lawyers have a duty to research the law to determine if an action is well grounded in the law. Model Rule 3.1 provides an exception if the lawyer has a good faith argument for an extension, modification, or reversal of the law, but that does not seem to be the case here since the supreme court decided the adverse case only two years ago. Good faith conduct that is negligent is still subject to discipline under Model Rule 3.1.

II is *incorrect.* Under Model Rule 3.3(a)(3), a lawyer shall not knowingly "fail to disclose to the tribunal legal authority in the controlling jurisdiction known to the lawyer to be directly adverse to the position of the client and not disclosed by opposing counsel." Thus, if opposing counsel failed to disclose the supreme court decision, L would have a duty to do so. Disclosure does not, however, exhaust L's obligations. L is also subject to the independent duty not to bring a frivolous action under Model Rule 3.1.

III is *correct.* Most states have procedural rules similar to the Federal Rules. Under Federal Rule 11, L could be subject to financial sanction for failing to make reasonable inquiry into the legal basis for D's suit.

5.2. (2).

Plaintiff's counsel is probably subject to discipline. Model Rule 3.5(b) provides that a lawyer shall not "communicate ex parte with [a judge, juror, prospective juror, or other official] except as permitted by law." Under the rules applicable in most jurisdictions, any form of communication with jurors during the pendency of a case is improper. See also Code of Professional Responsibility, DR 7-108(B).

Defense counsel is not subject to discipline. Comment 1 to Model Rule 3.5 refers to the Code of Judicial Conduct for standards regarding ex parte communications with judges. Canon 3(B)(7), dealing with ex parte communications, provides that such communications for scheduling purposes are permissible provided certain requirements are met.

5.3. (2).

P is subject to discipline. Comment 5 to Model Rule 3.6 provides guidelines as to types of extrajudicial statements that are more likely than not to be prejudicial in criminal cases. P's statement violates two of these guidelines. First, P has spoken about the "character, credibility, reputation or criminal record" of the defendants. Second, P has given an opinion as to the guilt of the defendants.

DC are not subject to discipline. Under Rule 3.6(c), DC have a right to reply to the prosecution to counterbalance the effect of prejudicial pretrial publicity by the prosecution. Given the extreme nature of the prosecution's press conference, DC's remarks seem to fall within the right to reply.

5.4. (2).

L is subject to discipline. Model Rule 4.2 states that a lawyer "shall not communicate about the subject of the representation with a person the lawyer knows to be represented by another lawyer in the matter, unless the lawyer has the consent of the other lawyer or is authorized by law to do so." Comment 4 states that "[i]n the case of an organization, this Rule prohibits communications by a lawyer for another person or entity concerning the matter in representation with persons having managerial responsibility on behalf of the organization, and with any other person whose act or omission in connection with that matter may be imputed to the organization for purposes of civil or criminal liability or whose statement may constitute an admission on the part of the organization." Since E is the chief engineer for product design, E almost certainly qualifies as a person with managerial responsibility. In addition, E's acts with regard to product design could be imputed to the organization.

A is not subject to discipline. Model Rule 3.4(f)(1) states that a lawyer shall not request a person to refrain from voluntarily giving relevant information unless "the person is a relative or an employee or other agent of a client." Since E is an employee of A's client, A's request is proper under Rule 3.4(f)(1). Some critics of the Model Rules have pointed to the disparity between these rules as evidence of a pro-defense slant in the Model Rules.

5.5. (1).

I is *correct.* Model Rule 3.4(d) states that a lawyer shall not "fail to make reasonably diligent effort to comply with a legally proper discovery request by an opposing party." Model Rule 3.4(c) states that a lawyer shall not "knowingly disobey an obligation under the rules of a tribunal except for an open refusal based on an assertion that no valid obligation exists."

II is *incorrect.* Model Rule 5.1 deals with the responsibilities of partners and supervisory lawyers. Section (c) states:

> A lawyer shall be responsible for another lawyer's violation of the Rules of Professional Conduct if:
>
> (1) the lawyer orders or, with knowledge of the specific conduct, ratifies the conduct involved; or
>
> (2) the lawyer is a partner in the law firm in which the other lawyer practices, or has direct supervisory authority over the other lawyer, and knows of the conduct at a time when its consequences can be avoided or mitigated but fails to take reasonable remedial action.

To be responsible for the conduct of another lawyer, a partner must either order the conduct, ratify the conduct, or fail to take remedial action when the consequences of the conduct could be mitigated. The rule is not simply one of vicarious responsibility.

III is *incorrect.* Model Rule 5.2 deals with the responsibilities of subordinate lawyers. Section (a) makes it clear that subordinate lawyers are still personally responsible for compliance with the Rules of Professional Conduct. Section (b) provides that a subordinate lawyer may follow the decision of a supervisory lawyer if the supervisor's decision is a "reasonable resolution of an arguable question of professional duty." Here the duty to produce the memorandum does not appear to be arguable, nor has P given any reasonable basis for P's decision not to comply with the discovery request.

5.6. (3).

L is not subject to discipline for making a false statement about plaintiff's settlement intentions. Model Rule 4.1 states that lawyers shall not knowingly make false statements of material fact or law to a third person. Comment 2 provides that whether a statement is one of fact depends on the circumstances. The comment goes on to state that under generally accepted conventions in negotiation, certain statements are not treated as statements of fact, including "a party's intentions as to an acceptable settlement of a claim."

L is subject to discipline for not conveying the settlement offer to L's client. See Model Rule 1.2(a). Comment 1 to Rule 1.4 states: "A lawyer who receives from opposing counsel an offer of settlement in a civil controversy or a proffered plea bargain in a criminal case should promptly inform the client of its substance unless prior discussions with the client have left it clear that the proposal will be unacceptable."

5.7. (2).

(1) is *incorrect.* L at least has a duty to advise L's client about the mistake and to discuss whether the client wishes to disclose the mistake. The client may well decide that disclosure is the right thing to do or that it is desirable to disclose in order to protect an advantageous agreement.

(2) is *correct.* Model Rule 2.1 states that lawyers should render candid advice and that such advice may include moral, economic, social, and political factors in addition to purely legal considerations.

(3) is *incorrect.* Lawyers have an obligation not to counsel or assist clients in fraud, but they do not have an obligation of candor in negotiations. See Model Rule 4.1(b).

(4) is *incorrect.* Lawyers have an obligation not to counsel or assist clients in fraud, Model Rule 4.1(b), but this situation seems to involve a unilateral mistake rather than fraud.

Chapter 6 Delivery of Legal Services

6.1. (1).

I is *correct.* Under Model Rule 6.2(c), a lawyer may seek to avoid appointment in a matter when "the client or the cause is so repugnant to the lawyer as to be likely to impair the client-lawyer relationship or the lawyer's ability to represent the client." See also Model Rule 1.7(b) (lawyer should not represent client when representation may be materially limited by lawyer's own interests).

II is *incorrect.* Model Rule 6.2(a) states that a lawyer may seek to avoid appointment if the appointment would result in a violation of the rules of professional conduct. If L could not handle the matter competently, L would have good cause to seek to avoid appointment. See Model Rule 6.2, comm. 2. The mere fact that L is not experienced in Family Court matters, however, should not be sufficient to decline appointment because L can become competent or associate competent counsel. See Rule 1.1, comm. 2. If scope of practice were a basis for avoiding pro bono appointments, many lawyers practicing with the most prestigious firms in the most sophisticated areas of practice could avoid pro bono appointments in ordinary legal matters.

III is *incorrect.* Model Rule 6.2(b) states that a lawyer may seek to avoid appointment if the appointment "is likely to result in an unreasonable financial burden on the lawyer." The fact that the lawyer is already handling another case pro bono should not alone be sufficient to establish financial hardship.

6.2. (1).

L is subject to discipline for both aspects of the advertisement. Model Rule 7.1 states that a lawyer shall not make a false or misleading advertisement. Rule 7.1(c) states that an advertisement is false or misleading if it "compares the lawyer's services with other lawyers' services, unless the comparison can be factually substantiated." How can the firm substantiate factually that it is one of the most outstanding firms in the country?

Model Rule 7.1(b) states that a lawyer shall not make an advertisement that is "likely to create an unjustified expectation about results the lawyer can achieve." See comm. to Rule 7.1.

6.3. (4).

I is *correct.* Model Rule 7.3 imposes certain restrictions on direct mail advertising, including a requirement that the advertising be identified as "Advertising Material" on the outside envelope. Model Rule 7.3(c). The Supreme Court stated in Shapero v. Kentucky Bar Assn., 486 U.S. 466, 477 (1988), that an advertising-disclosure requirement was constitutionally permissible. L has failed to meet this requirement.

II is *incorrect.* The Supreme Court in *Went for It* held that a prohibition on direct-mail advertising of accident victims and their relatives during the 30-day period after the accident was constitutionally permissible because it protected the privacy interests of victims and their relatives and because it promoted the state interest in the dignity of the profession.

III is *correct.* Model Rule 7.3(a) prohibits in-person or live telephone solicitation when a significant motive is pecuniary gain. See Ohralik v. Ohio State Bar Assn., 436 U.S. 447 (1978) (upholding the constitutionality of prohibitions on in-person commercial solicitation).

6.4. (4).

I is *incorrect.* Solicitation is proper when the lawyer has a "prior professional relationship" with the client. Model Rule 7.3(a). Since the firm is sending the brochure to existing clients, this exception to the prohibition on solicitation applies.

II is *incorrect.* Comment 2 to Rule 7.2 states that a lawyer may advertise names of clients regularly represented with consent of the clients.

III is *incorrect.* Rule 7.3(c) requires targeted mailings to include the words "Advertising Material," but that requirement only applies if the communication is to a person "known to be in need of legal services in a particular matter." Here the firm is making a general mailing not targeted to clients with particular legal problems.

6.5. (4).

L is not subject to discipline for assisting in the unauthorized practice of law. Model Rule 5.5(b) states that a lawyer should not assist a nonlawyer in conduct that "constitutes the unauthorized practice of law." However, the comment to that rule states that the rule "does not prohibit a lawyer from employing the services of paraprofessionals and delegating functions to them, so long as the lawyer supervises the delegated work and retains responsibility for their work." Here L supervises the work of the paralegals and remains responsible for their activities.

L is not subject to discipline for improper solicitation. Model Rule 7.3(a) prohibits in-person solicitation (and solicitation by live telephone contact) when "pecuniary gain" is a significant motive. Since the solicitation is by a legal services program, pecuniary gain is not a motive here. L and the paralegals must not, of course, solicit individuals who make it known that they do not wish to be solicited, and they must not engage in any form of coercion, duress, or harassment. See Model Rule 7.3(b).

6.6. (3).

(1) is *incorrect*, or at least not the best answer. While the lawyers would have a obligation to make sure that it was clear that they represented the bank's customers and not the bank, see Model Rule 1.8(f), that action does not solve the unauthorized practice problem discussed below.

(2) is *incorrect*. Just because the lawyers are salaried employees of the bank does not eliminate the requirement that they comply with the rules of professional conduct, including the prohibition against assisting a nonlawyer in the unauthorized practice of law. Model Rule 5.5.

(3) is *correct*. The bank would be performing legal services for others through its lawyer-employees for a fee. The lawyer-employees would be assisting in this conduct, in violation of Model Rule 5.5(b). Note that Model Rule 5.4(b) states that it is improper for a lawyer to form a partnership with a nonlawyer if the activities of the partnership involve the practice of law. Since it is unethical to form a partnership with a nonlawyer, it is even more clearly unethical for the lawyer to be in the position of an employee of an entity performing legal services for a third party. Note also that the rules do not prohibit commercial entities from hiring lawyers to perform legal services for the entity itself. The prohibition only

applies when the entity attempts to perform legal services for others. Also relevant is Model Rule 5.4(a), which prohibits fee spitting with nonlawyers.

(4) is *incorrect.* No evidence of improper solicitation exists. The plan could be offered through advertisement rather than personal contact. Further, if it were offered through personal contact with bank customers, arguably the "prior professional relationship" exception to the prohibition on solicitation would apply. Model Rule 7.3(a).

6.7. (1).

I is *correct.* Lawyers may not enter into partnerships with nonlawyers if any of the activities of the partnership would constitute the practice of law. Model Rule 5.4(b). The purpose of the rule is to protect the professional independence of lawyers from control by nonlawyers.

II is *incorrect.* Since none of the activities of the subsidiary involve the practice of law, it would not violate Model Rule 5.4(b) for nonlawyers to have ownership interests with lawyers. Model Rule 5.7, adopted by the ABA in 1994, recognizes that lawyers can have ownership interests in separate entities that provide law-related services. The rule states that if lawyers provide law-related services through a separate entity, those services shall be treated as legal services subject to the requirements of the Rules of Professional Conduct unless the lawyer takes reasonable measures to make sure that the person receiving law-related services knows that they are not legal services and are not subject to the protections of the client-lawyer relationship. Note also that if the law-related services are provided through the law firm rather than through a separate entity (for example, if the firm employed engineers), then those services are subject to all of the requirements of the Rules of Professional Conduct. See Model Rule 5.7(a)(1).

III is *incorrect.* Model Rule 7.2(c) states that a lawyer "shall not give anything of value to a person for recommending the lawyer's services," subject to three exceptions. Here LF is paying EE for referrals by giving its own referrals. Moreover, the agreement improperly restricts LF's ability to give candid advice. See Model Rule 2.1.

6.8. (4).

I is *incorrect.* Model Rule 1.17 allows lawyers to enter into agreements to sell their practices, including good will. The rule, which was adopted in 1990 by the ABA based on California Rule 2-300, changes the long-standing professional prohibition against sale of professional good will. A significant rationale for the rule was to eliminate disparity between law firms, which had built-in mechanisms for dealing with lawyer retirement, and sole practitioners, who did not have this advantage. Only a few states have adopted the rule; in other states, the prohibition on sale of a practice remains in effect. In such states, lawyers can accomplish the same result as a direct sale through proper retirement planning. The successor lawyer can form a partnership before the retiring lawyer leaves practice. See Model Rule 5.4, which allows payments to nonlawyers through retirement plans.

II is *incorrect.* While agreements that restrict the right of lawyers to practice law are generally unethical, such agreements are not improper when part of the sale of a law practice under Model Rule 1.17. See Model Rule 5.6, comm. 3.

III is *incorrect.* Under Model Rule 1.17(c)(4), clients are entitled to receive notice of the sale, but they do not have to consent in writing. Their consent is presumed unless they object within 90 days after receiving notice.

Chapter 7 Lawyers in Public Positions: Judges and Government Lawyers

7.1. (4).

I is *incorrect.* Canon 3(E)(1) deals with judicial disqualification. Section (d) states that a judge shall disqualify herself when a "person within the third degree of relationship" to the judge is a party to the proceeding. The Terminology section defines third degree of relationship and does not include first cousins. The judge must still determine whether the relationship with the cousin is sufficiently close that the judge's "impartiality might reasonably be questioned." Canon 3(E)(1).

II is *incorrect.* Canon 3(E)(1)(b) deals with situations in which relationships with former partners require disqualification. That section only requires disqualification if the matter before the judge was one being handled by the former partner while the judge was associated with the lawyer. The mere fact that a former partner appears before the judge does not require disqualification. The judge must still determine whether the relationship with the former partner is sufficiently close that the judge's "impartiality might reasonably be questioned." Canon 3(E)(1). In Informal Opinion 87-1524, the ABA Committee on Ethics and Professional Responsibility ruled that a judge was not required to disqualify himself simply because the judge had been associated with counsel for one of the parties two years earlier. The Committee indicated that a period of one or two years after termination of professional association was appropriate, depending on factors such as the closeness of the relationship and the amount of continued contact.

III is *incorrect.* Canon 3(E)(1)(c) deals with financial disqualification. The canon requires disqualification if the judge or the judge's spouse has an "economic interest" in a party. The Terminology section defines "economic interest" to mean more than a "de minimis legal or equitable interest." Here the interest of the judge's spouse seems de minimis. Note that this represents a change made by the 1990 Code of Judicial Code over the 1972 Code. Under the 1972 Code, a financial interest "however small" required disqualification. Note also that the "however small" standard still applies to federal judges. See 28 U.S.C. §455(b)(4).

7.2. (3).

(1) is *incorrect.* Under 28 U.S.C. §455(b)(4), a federal judge must disqualify herself whenever she or a spouse or minor child residing in the judge's household has a "financial interest" in the subject matter or in a party to litigation. Unlike the Code of Judicial Conduct, the federal statute defines financial interest to include ownership of a legal or equitable interest "however small." Id. §455(d)(4).

(2) is *incorrect.* The federal statute only allows waiver of disqualification when disqualification is based on the general standard of whether the judge's impartiality might reasonably be questioned. 28 U.S.C.§455(a). Disqualification based on financial interest is not waivable. 28 U.S.C. §455(e). Note that this is another way in which the federal statute differs from the Code of Judicial Conduct, because the Code allows remittal of disqualification based on financial interest. See Canon 3(F).

(3) is *correct.* See 28 U.S.C. §455(f).

(4) is *incorrect.* A judge is disqualified if the judge or the judge's spouse has a legal or equitable interest. See 28 U.S.C. §455(d)(4) (definition of financial interest). Placing the stock in a blind trust would simply transform the interest from legal into equitable ownership.

7.3. (1).

I is *correct.* Canon 4(C)(3)(b)(i) states that a judge "shall not personally participate in the solicitation of funds." Note that the Code allows judges to participate in a wide range of civic and charitable activities, but it imposes certain restrictions on that participation.

II is *correct.* Canon 4(E) states that a judge "shall not serve as executor, administrator or other personal representative, trustee, guardian, attorney in fact or other fiduciary, except for the estate, trust or person of a member of the judge's family," and then only if service will not interfere with the judge's official duties. See also Canon 4(G), which prohibits judges from practicing law. Neither canon has exceptions for former clients.

III is *incorrect.* Canon 4(B) allows judges to teach on subjects concerning the law, the legal system, the administration of justice, and on nonlegal subjects. Canon 4(H)(1) allows judges to receive compensation and expense reimbursement for their extrajudicial activities permitted by the Code "if the source of such payments does not give the appearance of influencing the judge's performance of judicial duties or otherwise give the appearance of impropriety." Compensation from the local law school does not seem to violate these restrictions.

7.4 (4).

(1) is *incorrect.* Model Rule 1.11(a) states that a government lawyer "shall not represent a private client in connection with a matter in which the lawyer participated personally and substantially as a public officer or employee," unless certain requirements are met. The fact that the government proceeding has ended is irrelevant. The rationale for the rule is to prevent government lawyers from having their official decisions affected by the prospect of private employment.

(2) is *incorrect.* Model Rule 1.11(b) prevents a former government lawyer from using confidential information, but that restriction is in addition to Model Rule 1.11(a).

(3) is *incorrect.* Consent by L's clients does not address the governmental interest at stake as reflected in Model Rule 1.11(a).

(4) is *correct.* Under Model Rule 1.11(a)(1), a disqualified former government lawyer must be screened from participation in the matter. L's personal involvement is disqualifying.

APPENDIX B
Essay Questions with Model Answers

Each of the following questions poses issues of professional responsibility drawn from topics covered in several chapters in this book and in most books on professional responsibility. The questions can be used in a variety of ways. After completing a course on professional responsibility, students can use these questions as a pretest before in-depth study to determine areas of weakness. Students can also use the questions for individual or group review after they have largely completed study for the examination. The questions can also be used together with the multiple choice questions to prepare for the Multistate Professional Responsibility Examination.

Essay Question I

Several months ago, Helene Sanders, the wife of well-known television star, J.O. Sanders, was brutally stabbed to death. There were no eyewitnesses to the murder. The police had few leads, but they centered their investigation on Helene's estranged husband. After months of intensive work, the authorities developed sufficient circumstantial evidence to indict Sanders for murder. Immediately after the indictment, the prosecutor, Martha Pearson, called a press conference to inform the media of the indictment. At the press conference, Pearson summarized the history of the investigation. She stated that the police had been hampered by the fact that there were no eyewitnesses, but that DNA testing of blood found at the scene of the crime had finally enabled the police to "break the case."

After the indictment was issued, Sanders's attorney, Nathan Deniro, received a visit from Sanders's best friend, Herb Friendly. Friendly produced a package that he said contained a knife that Sanders left at his house on the night that Helene was killed. Friendly asked Deniro what he should do with the knife. Ironically, on the same day that Deniro was meeting with Friendly, Pearson had a meeting with one of the police officers involved in the case; the officer showed Pearson Helene's diary, which the police had found in her home. Several entries in the diary referred to someone named "John" and showed that Helene was having an affair.

Discuss the issues of professional responsibility.

Essay Question II

Herbert Lawson is interviewing a new client, Joan Crane. Crane tells Lawson that she has several legal problems to discuss with him. One problem relates to an automobile accident in which Crane was involved. According to Crane, a driver ran a stop sign and hit her from the side. As a result of the accident, Crane missed two weeks of work and incurred significant medical bills.

Crane also tells Lawson that she and her husband, Jim, recently separated after Jim told her that he wanted a divorce because he was in love with another woman. Crane wants Lawson to represent her in divorce proceedings against her husband. She also wants Lawson to represent her in an action against Jim's girlfriend for alienation of affections. Crane says she doesn't care whether she wins that suit or not: "I just want to get her any way I can."

Because Crane's husband left her with two small children, her financial situation is tenuous. Crane says that she understands that most lawyers charge a one-third contingency fee for accident cases. She asks if Lawson would be willing to handle her divorce case for no charge, but increase the fee in the accident case to 50 percent. Crane also tells Lawson that because of her various problems she is undergoing psychological counseling. She asks whether Lawson would advance her $2,500 to continue her counseling. She promises to repay the advance from the proceeds of her tort action or property settlement.

Before agreeing to take Crane's cases, Lawson does a conflict of interest check. He finds that two years ago another lawyer in his firm, Norm McDonald, represented the driver of the car that struck Crane's vehicle in a matter relating to the formation of a business for the driver.

Discuss the issues of professional responsibility.

Essay Question III

Georgia Palmer was employed as an assistant vice president for sales of the National Insurance Company until she was discharged last year. Palmer claims that her discharge resulted from her refusal to give in to sexual advances made by her immediate supervisor, Alan Sindel. Palmer has brought an employment discrimination and wrongful discharge action against Sindel and National. Dena Landers represents Palmer. Henry McSwaine represents Sindel and National.

McSwaine took Palmer's deposition during discovery. At the deposition, McSwaine asked a variety of questions about Palmer's sex life, including whether she had ever had an affair with a married man or woman. Palmer answered "No" to this question. A few days after the deposition, Palmer called Landers and told her that she needed to tell her something about the deposition. She said that when she was in graduate school she had had an affair with the professor who supervised her master's thesis. When she broke off the affair, the professor persisted in continuing the affair. She finally contacted the dean and was assigned another professor as her advisor. She says that she didn't mention the matter during the deposition because she never brought formal charges, because it was embarrassing, and because she didn't want to harm the professor, who is married.

After discovery was completed in the case, the parties engaged in substantial settlement negotiations. Defendants made a cash settlement offer that Landers considered to be very favorable. Palmer, however, found the offer unacceptable. Palmer insisted that she would not accept a settlement offer that did not include reinstatement in her job and that did not provide for Sindel's discharge. Landers told Palmer that National was unlikely to offer Palmer her job back. She said that Palmer might be able to obtain reinstatement to her job if she was successful at trial, but that she would not be able to obtain relief that involved Sindel's discharge. Palmer, however, insisted on pursuing these issues. The case has been scheduled for trial, but Landers has just learned that the judge who has been assigned the case was a member of the law firm that represented National Insurance until the judge was appointed to the bench 18 months ago.

Discuss the issues of professional responsibility.

Essay Question IV

Ellen Pearson represents the plaintiff in a products liability action against Demon Corporation. Demon is represented by Herbert Dart. Melanie Edwards is the chief engineer in charge of product design for Demon. After filing suit, Pearson telephones Edwards and asks for an appointment to discuss Demon's procedures for product design. Edwards refuses to meet with Pearson because Dart has instructed her not to give any information about the case to Pearson.

Pearson has filed various discovery requests including a request for production of all documents relating to the design of the product. In reviewing documents to prepare a response to this discovery request, an associate in Dart's firm, Brenda Anderson, discovers a report by a product engineer that questions the safety of the product. Anderson informs Dart of this document and asks whether it needs to be produced. Dart directs Anderson not to produce the document. Dart tells Anderson in his opinion the document does not "relate" to the design of the product because the product was redesigned based on the concerns of this engineer and others.

Discuss the issues of professional responsibility.

Essay Question V

Margaret Counsel of the firm of Counsel, Counsel & Lawyer is outside counsel representing Henderson Automotive Associates. Henderson owns and manages more than 50 automobile distributorships in several states. Six months ago, Henderson's treasurer,

Edward Tomar, came to Counsel and told her that he had learned that Richard Henderson, the company's CEO and a major shareholder, had been paying bribes to officials of several automobile manufacturers to obtain favorable treatment in distribution of vehicles. Tomar asked Counsel's advice. Counsel told Tomar that he must not become involved in any bribery and must not engage in any misreporting of Henderson's finances.

Henderson's bribery has now been exposed, and the automobile manufacturers have brought suit against Henderson Automotive and against Henderson personally. Henderson has retained his own attorney. Counsel represents Henderson Automotive Associates. Plaintiffs have taken Tomar's deposition and learned that he had informed Counsel that Tomar knew of Henderson's bribery. The manufacturers have informed Counsel that they are considering adding her as a party to the case, claiming that she should have disclosed to the manufacturers her knowledge of Henderson's fraud.

Discuss the issues of professional responsibility.

Essay Question VI

John Anderson has recently moved into the state and has been admitted to practice. Prior to moving to this state, Anderson was a plaintiff's personal injury attorney for 15 years in California. Anderson has opened his own office and has run the following advertisement in the yellow pages:

> John L. Anderson
> Attorney at Law
> 1412 Main Street
> New Town, State
> 266-5747
> 15 years experience specializing in personal injury practice

Lawson also plans to have the advertisement printed and distributed by teenagers at shopping centers.

A few days ago, Anderson learned about a train derailment in which a number of passengers were injured. Anderson was able to obtain the names of several of the victims through public records. He has written each of the victims a letter. The letter is very brief and simply informs the victims that Anderson is available to handle their cases if they wish to call for an appointment. The envelope containing the letter states: "Important legal information. Please open immediately."

Discuss the issues of professional responsibility.

MODEL ANSWERS TO ESSAY QUESTIONS

Model Answer I

The first issue deals with the prosecutor's press conference. Model Rule 3.6 (as amended by the ABA in 1994) provides as follows:

> A lawyer who is participating or has participated in the investigation or litigation of a matter shall not make an extrajudicial statement that a reasonable person would expect to be disseminated by means of public communication if the lawyer knows or reasonably should know that it will have a substantial likelihood of materially prejudicing an adjudicative proceeding in the matter.

The prosecutor, Martha Pearson, did not violate Rule 3.6 by calling the press conference to announce Sanders' indictment. As comment 1 to Rule 3.6 indicates, the public has a "legitimate interest in the conduct of judicial proceedings, particularly in matters of general public concern." However, Pearson probably went too far when she referred to the results of DNA testing. Comment 5 outlines certain subjects that are likely to have a material effect on a proceeding, particularly civil jury trials, criminal prosecutions, or other matters that could result in incarceration. Section (3) of the comment refers to statements about "the performance or results of any examination or test." In addition, the results of such a test may well be inadmissible, which would be a violation of Section (5) of the comment. Pearson should also have stated in her press conference that, while Sanders had been charged with a crime, the charge was merely an accusation, and Sanders was presumed to be innocent until and unless proven guilty. See Section (6) of the comment. Because of Pearson's improper public comments, Deniro may reply publicly to prevent prejudice to his client. Model Rule 3.6(c).

The fact situation is obviously drawn from the O.J. Simpson case. Both prosecution and defense counsel in the Simpson case engaged in extensive trial publicity, but California at that time did not have a rule limiting extrajudicial statements by lawyers, although the California Supreme Court has now adopted a rule based on Model Rule 3.6. Cal. R. Prof. Conduct 5-120.

The second issue raised by the problem deals with the knife that Friendly has brought to Deniro. Of course, Deniro does not know whether the knife is incriminating, but that is a reasonable possibility given the situation. If the knife were exculpatory, presumably Sanders would have already told Deniro about it. Courts around the country have generally held that an attorney who takes possession of evidence of a crime has a duty to turn the evidence over to the authorities, after a reasonable period of time to inspect the evidence. See Chapter 4.F. Thus, if Deniro takes possession of the knife from Friendly, it may seriously damage Sanders's case: Deniro would be required to turn the knife over to the authorities and in some jurisdictions the fact that the knife came from Deniro would not be privileged.

While the courts impose a duty on a lawyer who takes possession of incriminating evidence to turn the evidence over to the authorities, the courts have not gone so far as to require a lawyer to take possession of incriminating evidence, nor is a lawyer required to disclose mere knowledge of incriminating evidence to the authorities. Thus, the strategically sound and ethically proper course of action for Deniro is to refuse to take possession of the knife from Friendly.

If Deniro refuses to take the knife, Friendly may ask for Deniro's advice about how to handle the knife. Deniro cannot advise Friendly to hide the knife since that would be counseling or assisting in a crime. See Model Rule 8.4(b). Deniro could suggest that Friendly simply return the knife to the location where he found it, without making any effort to hide the knife. The problem with this approach is that Friendly apparently took the knife from Sanders and kept it in his home. This advice could expose Friendly to criminal liability. Further, it may be improper for Deniro to give Friendly any advice since Friendly is not represented by counsel and his interests may conflict with Sanders. Probably, the best course of action for Deniro is to inform Friendly to seek advice of independent counsel regarding how to handle the knife. See Model Rule 4.3. This approach may mean, however, that Friendly receives advice to turn the knife over to the authorities, although perhaps Friendly and his counsel can turn the knife over to the authorities anonymously.

The third issue raised by the problem deals with the fact that the prosecutor, Martha Pearson, has learned that Helene Sanders kept a diary that referred to an affair with "John." Prosecutors, unlike defense counsel, have an ethical duty to disclose knowledge of exculpatory evidence to the defense. See Model Rule 3.8(d). This special duty is imposed on prosecutors because their role is different from that of defense counsel; prosecutors represent the state and have a duty to seek justice. See Model Rule 3.8, comm. 1. In addition, failure of a prosecutor to disclosure exculpatory material violates the defendant's right to due process of law. See Brady v. Maryland, 373 U.S. 83 (1963). It is questionable on these facts, however, whether Pearson has a duty of disclosure. The diary simply refers to an affair with John. There is no indication that John was a danger to Helene or had anything to do with her murder. These facts alone may not be admissible in evidence and probably would not tend to negate Sanders' guilt. A more subtle question is whether the authorities have a duty to investigate potentially exculpatory evidence. As citizens we would certainly expect the authorities to do so, but there does not appear to be a specific ethical duty to investigate possible exculpatory evidence.

Model Answer II

Crane has told Lawson that she wishes to bring a lawsuit against her husband's girlfriend for alienation of affections. As a general rule, a lawyer has an obligation to represent his client zealously and advance his client's interests in any way possible. There are, however, certain limitations on this general duty, one of which is that a lawyer may not bring a frivolous claim. Model Rule 3.1; Rule 11 of the Federal Rules of Civil Procedure. By statute or court decision, many jurisdictions no longer recognize alienation of affection claims. In such jurisdictions, Crane's suit would be frivolous because it is not well-grounded in law. Even if the jurisdiction continues to recognize alienation of affection claims, a lawyer may not bring a claim for an improper purpose. Comment 2 to Model Rule 3.1 states that an action is frivolous "if the client desires to have the action taken primarily for the purpose of harassing or maliciously injuring a person." Here, Crane has said that she does not care about the amount of recovery but simply wants to inflict harm on her husband's lover.

Crane has also asked Lawson to handle her legal matters on a contingent fee basis. Contingent fee agreements are generally proper, especially when the client is unable to afford to pay a fixed fee. This appears to be the case here. There are, however, certain limitations on the use of contingent fees. In divorce cases, an agreement for a contingent fee is improper because of the public policy in favor of promoting reconciliation rather than divorce. Model Rule 1.5(d)(1). Thus, it would be proper for Lawson to enter into a contingent fee agreement with Crane as to her tort litigation, but not her domestic case. Query whether the fee arrangement between Lawson and Crane amounts to a disguised contingency fee in a divorce case. On the one hand, the entire fee is contingent, but on other hand, the fee is contingent on the outcome of the tort case, not on "securing of a divorce." A prudent lawyer would avoid such a questionable fee agreement.

Crane's request for a loan poses another ethical problem. Model Rule 1.8(e) provides that "a lawyer shall not provide financial assistance to a client in connection with pending or contemplated litigation," except that a lawyer may advance "court costs and expenses of litigation." Unless the counseling expenses are directly related to litigation, for example, if the counselor will be an expert witness, this advance is improper. Lawson should reduce any fee agreement to writing so as to avoid any misunderstandings with Crane. The agreement should specify Crane's liability for expenses. See Model Rule 1.5(c) on the requirements of contingent fee agreements.

Crane's request that Lawson represent her in the automobile accident case poses a conflict of interest issue. Lawson's partner, McDonald, represented the driver of the other vehicle two years ago in the formation of the driver's business. The rules of professional conduct allow a lawyer to undertake representation against a former client provided the current matter is not "substantially related" to the former matter. Model Rule 1.9(a). In addition, the rules prohibit a lawyer from using confidential information against a former client. Model Rule 1.9(c). The automobile accident and the formation of a business appear to have nothing in common, but it is possible that McDonald acquired information about the driver's assets during the formation of the business that could be useful in the automobile case. So long as the firm does not use confidential information against the driver, the representation seems proper.

If the automobile case is substantially related to the business formation, or if the firm has confidential information that could be used against the driver, then the entire firm is disqualified because McDonald's disqualification is imputed to Lawson. Model Rule 1.10(a). If the firm is not disqualified, Lawson should still inform Crane of the firm's previous representation of the driver and obtain her consent before proceeding in the matter. Model Rule 1.7(b). Crane might conclude that the Lawson firm would be less vigorous in representing her against a former client of the firm than a conflict-free firm.

Model Answer III

McSwaine is representing both Sindel and National against Palmer's claim of sexual harassment. A lawyer may represent multiple defendants who do not have an actual conflict provided the lawyer reasonably believes that he can undertake the representation and both clients consent after the lawyer consults with them about the "implications of the common representation and the advantages and risks involved." Model Rule 1.7(b). See also Model Rule 1.13(e). McSwaine should inform Sindel and National that he will be required to withdraw should an actual conflict develop between them and that any communications that they make to him will not be privileged should a dispute subsequently arise between them. Prudent lawyers will obtain written consent to multiple representation.

McSwaine's inquiry into Palmer's prior sexual history raises an ethical issue. Model Rule 3.4(c) provides that a lawyer shall not "knowingly disobey an obligation under the rules of a tribunal except for an open refusal based on an assertion that no valid obligation exists." This rule requires lawyers to adhere to obligations under rules of evidence and procedure, except when openly challenging those rules. Thus, the ethical propriety of defense counsel's inquiry into Palmer's sexual history and practices turns on whether such an inquiry is permitted under the rules of procedure and evidence. In most jurisdictions, prior sexual history can be admissible if relevant and the value of the evidence is not outweighed by its prejudicial nature. For example, under the Federal Rules of Evidence, evidence of sexual behavior is admissible in civil cases if its "probative value substantially outweighs the danger of harm to any victim and of unfair prejudice to any party." Fed. R. Evid. 412(b)(2). Since prior sexual history may be admissible, defense counsel's inquiry is ethically permitted under Model Rule 3.4.

Also relevant to the analysis is Model Rule 4.4, dealing with respect for rights of third persons, which provides as follows:

> In representing a client, a lawyer shall not use means that have no substantial purpose other than to embarrass, delay, or burden a third person, or use methods of obtaining evidence that violate the legal rights of such a person.

If defense counsel were using the tactic of inquiring into sexual practice for the purpose of embarrassing Palmer so as to force her into a disadvantageous settlement, defense counsel would be in violation of Model Rule 4.4. On the other hand, if defense counsel has a plausible legal justification for the inquiry, the conduct probably does not violate Model Rule 4.4. This turns on defense counsel's intent and on the legal justification for the inquiry.

Palmer's revelation of her affair with the professor poses another ethical problem. A lawyer has an obligation to take reasonable remedial measures when the lawyer has offered false evidence. Model Rule 3.3(a)(4). This rule has most often been applied to perjury by criminal defendants, but it also applies to testimony under oath at a deposition. See ABA Formal Opinion 93-376. Further, the duty to take remedial actions is not limited to perjury but also applies to innocent but mistaken testimony that is materially false. In addition, counsel has an obligation to comply with rules of procedure. Model Rule 3.4(c). These rules include a duty to supplement answers to discovery that are later found to be incorrect. See, e.g., Fed. R. Civ. P. 26(e) (supplementation of responses). Landers could take a narrow view of these rules and conclude that she has not offered the evidence because McSwaine was taking the deposition. This approach, however, seems inconsistent with the clear intent of the rules. Moreover, from a strategic perspective, disclosure now is likely to do little harm, while keeping the information secret could be devastating if it came out at trial.

The defense has made a settlement offer that Landers has strongly recommended to Palmer, but which she has refused to accept. Landers has an obligation to counsel Palmer regarding any settlement. Model Rule 2.1. Palmer retains, however, the ultimate authority to decide whether to accept or reject any settlement offer.

Model Rule 1.2(a). Landers must abide by this decision unless she feels so strongly about the matter that she decides to move to withdraw. Withdrawal in this situation would be permissive rather than mandatory. Model Rule 1.16(b)(3) (withdrawal because client follows course of conduct that lawyer considers imprudent). Any withdrawal would require court permission and would be likely to affect Landers' fee in the case.

Palmer's insistence that Landers raise a claim to have Sindel fired poses an additional problem, however. Depending on applicable law, the claim may be frivolous. In addition, Palmer may be making this claim to retaliate against Sindel. In either case, Landers would be acting improperly by making the claim. See Model Rules 3.1, 4.4. If Palmer insisted on Landers' pursuing a claim that was clearly improper under either Rule 3.1 or 4.4, Landers would be required to withdraw. Model Rule 1.16(a)(1).

Canon 3(E) of the Code of Judicial Conduct deals with disqualification of judges. Under Canon 3(E)(1)(b), a judge is disqualified if a lawyer with whom the judge practiced served as a lawyer in the matter during the period of their association. It is unclear from the facts whether this case was in McSwaine's office while the judge was a member of the firm. Since the case is coming to trial and the judge was appointed 18 months ago, it is certainly possible that the case was in the office while the judge was in private practice. If so, the judge is disqualified. Even if the judge left the firm before the firm undertook representation in the case, the judge still must decide whether he is disqualified under Canon 3(E)(1) on the ground that his impartiality might reasonably be questioned. Given the relatively short time since the judge's separation from the firm, disqualification seems appropriate. See ABA Informal Opinion 87-1524 (period of one to two years of separation appropriate depending on factors such as closeness of relationship).

Model Answer IV

The first issue deals with the propriety of Pearson's contacting Edwards, Demon Corporation's chief engineer. Model Rule 4.2 states:

> In representing a client, a lawyer shall not communicate about the subject of the representation with a person the lawyer knows to

> be represented by another lawyer in the matter, unless the lawyer has the consent of the other lawyer or is authorized by law to do so.

The text of the rule is unclear about its application to employees of corporate defendants, but comment 4 deals with this issue:

> In the case of an organization, this Rule prohibits communications by a lawyer for another person or entity concerning the matter in representation with persons having managerial responsibility on behalf of the organization, and with any other person whose act or omission in connection with that matter may be imputed to the organization for purposes of civil or criminal liability or whose statement may constitute an admission on the part of the organization.

Under this comment, it appears likely that Person acted improperly in contacting Edwards. As a chief engineer, Edwards has managerial responsibility. In addition, since this is a products liability case, it is possible that Edwards's "act of omission" in the matter may be imputed to the organization.

Edwards has refused to meet with Pearson because Dart, Demon's lawyer, has instructed her not to give any information about the case to Pearson. Model Rule 3.4(f)(1) states that it is improper for a lawyer to request a person not to give relevant information to a party, but provides an exception if the person is an employee. Perhaps Dart went too far, however, in instructing Edwards not to give information rather than simply requesting that she not do so.

The next issue deals with Dart's decision not to produce the engineer's report questioning the safety of the product on the ground that it does not "relate" to the design of the product since the product has been redesigned. Dart's justification is the purest sophistry, inconsistent with both the letter and spirit of the discovery rules. Model Rule 3.4(d) states that it is improper for a lawyer to fail to comply with a legally proper discovery request. Rule 3.4(c) states that a lawyer may not knowingly refuse to disobey an obligation under the rules of procedure "except for an open refusal based on an assertion that no valid obligation exists." For a case in which defense counsel acted improperly in failing to produce documents based on a similar justification, see Washington State Physicians Ins. Exch. & Assn. v. Fisons Corp., 858 P.2d 1054 (Wash. 1993) (en banc).

The final issue deals with Anderson's obligations as an associate.

Model Rule 5.2 deals with the obligations of subordinate lawyers. The rule makes two fundamental points. First, associates and other subordinate lawyers are personally bound by the rules of professional conduct even though they act at the direction of another person. In other words, "I was just following orders," is not a defense to a charge of misconduct. Second, the rule recognizes that subordinate lawyers typically do not have the knowledge or experience of their superiors and that they may rely on a superior's "reasonable resolution of an arguable question of professional duty." Here, however, Dart's decision does not involve an arguable question of professional duty. Under Rule 5.2, Anderson must take some action, rather than simply following Dart's orders. Anderson should first explain to Dart why his refusal to produce the report is wrong. If this fails, Anderson should consider taking the matter to other attorneys in the office, such as the head of the section in which Anderson works, the managing attorney, or the firm's ethics committee if it has one.

Model Answer V

While Counsel was correct to inform Tomar against becoming involved in any illegal activity or misreporting of finances, she did not go far enough in her advice. Counsel represents the corporation, not Tomar. Model Rule 1.13(a). A lawyer who learns that an officer of a company is engaged in illegal conduct that may cause substantial injury to the corporation has a duty to act in the best interest of the corporation. Model Rule 1.13(b). The Model Rules give lawyers discretion about what steps to take. For example, Counsel could advise Tomar that Tomar has a fiduciary duty to the corporation to take action regarding Henderson's actions. If Tomar fails to act, Counsel must consider reporting the matter to the highest authority in the company, which is probably its board of directors. Model Rule 1.13(b)(3). Counsel should also have informed Tomar that Counsel represents the corporation, not Tomar, and that if Tomar is concerned about his exposure in this matter, Tomar should consider retaining his own attorney. Model Rules 1.13(d), 4.3.

Plaintiffs have alleged that Counsel had a duty to disclose Henderson's fraud to them. Model Rule 1.6(b) provides that a lawyer may reveal confidential information to prevent the client from committing a criminal act that involves "imminent death or substantial bodily harm." Under this rule, however, a lawyer may not reveal a client's past or future intention to commit a financial fraud. The lawyer's duty to a corporation under Model Rule 1.13 is consistent with Model Rule 1.6. Under Rule 1.13(b), a lawyer may report misconduct by a corporate official to the highest authority in the organization. If the highest authority refuses to act on the matter, however, the lawyer may withdraw from representation. Model Rule 1.13(c). Some jurisdictions have adopted a broader exception to the duty of confidentiality than is found in ABA Model Rule 1.6. The most common variation of Rule 1.6 allows a lawyer to reveal confidential information to prevent a client from committing a crime. Under this rule, Counsel would have discretion, but not a duty, to reveal Henderson's fraud to the manufacturers.

Counsel's continued representation of the company in the matter appears doubtful. Model Rule 3.7(a) provides that a lawyer shall not continue to serve as an advocate on behalf of a client if it is likely that the lawyer will be called as a necessary witness. It is unclear whether Counsel will be a necessary witness in this case. Counsel's testimony could show that Tomar, another corporate official, knew of Henderson's fraud, and therefore the fraud should be imputed to the corporation. Tomar has admitted this, however, so Counsel's testimony may be cumulative. Counsel could solve this problem if another lawyer in her firm handles the trial of the case. Model Rule 3.7(b). If the plaintiffs add Counsel as a party defendant, however, she and her firm will be required to withdraw because they will have a conflict of interest with the company. Model Rule 3.7(b).

Model Answer VI

Model Rule 7.1 prohibits lawyers from making "false or misleading" communications about their legal services. One issue raised by this advertisement is whether the statement "15 years experience" is misleading. While Lawson has been in practice for 15 years, that practice occurred while he was in California; only recently has he begun practicing in New Town. Under these circumstances, it could be argued that the advertisement is misleading and should be rewritten to state "15 years practice in California."

Lawson's advertisement states that he specializes in personal injury. The Model Rules allow a lawyer to communicate fields of practice, but impose limitations on advertising of "specialization," which vary depending on the jurisdiction. Model Rule 7.4.

Analysis of the propriety of the distributorship of flyers by teenagers depends on what the teenagers do. If the teenagers have personal contact with recipients of the advertisements, the conduct is likely to be viewed as in-person solicitation. Solicitation is improper under Model Rule 7.3(a). Further, the Supreme Court has held that a state may constitutionally prohibit in-person solicitation. Ohralik v. Ohio State Bar Assn., 436 U.S. 447 (1978). If the teenagers simply place the advertisements on car windows without having any personal contact, however, their actions probably amount to permissible advertising.

Anderson's letter to the victims of the train derailment is direct mail advertising. In Shapero v. Kentucky Bar Assn., 486 U.S. 466 (1988), the Supreme Court held that direct mail advertising was constitutionally protected, but the Court also decided that states could impose restrictions on direct mail advertising, including a requirement that the advertising be identified as advertising material. Anderson's letter violates Model Rule 7.3(c) because it does not include the words "Advertising Material" on the outside of the envelope. In Florida Bar v. Went For It, Inc., 515 U.S. 618 (1995), the Supreme Court upheld a Florida rule prohibiting direct mail advertising of accident victims for 30 days following the accident. Anderson's letter would be improper in a state that had adopted such a rule.

Table of Articles, Books, and Reports

Table of Cases

Table of Model Rules and Other Standards

ABA Model Rules of Professional Conduct

ABA Model Code of Professional Responsibility

ABA Model Code of Judicial Conduct (1990)

ABA Formal and Informal Opinions

ABA Standards for Criminal Justice

ALI Proposed Restatement of the Law Governing Lawyers

Index